SAGE was founded in 1965 by Sara Miller McCune to support the dissemination of usable knowledge by publishing innovative and high-quality research and teaching content. Today, we publish over 900 journals, including those of more than 400 learned societies, more than 800 new books per year, and a growing range of library products including archives, data, case studies, reports, and video. SAGE remains majority-owned by our founder, and after Sara's lifetime will become owned by a charitable trust that secures our continued independence.

Los Angeles | London | New Delhi | Singapore | Washington DC | Melbourne

Advance Praise

Globalization is more than economic interdependence or connectivity. It is now a multidimensional phenomenon that cuts across traditional disciplines. This edited volume is a commendable compendium that dissects this complex issue for clearer understanding. A must-read for students, scholars and the policy community.

Chintamani Mahapatra, Rector & Professor, Jawaharlal Nehru University, New Delhi, India

This edited volume provides a comprehensive account of the most recent debate on globalization. It addresses some of the most controversial issues, such as trade and finance, environment, and terrorism, as well as cultural and technological issues. What is most important is the discussion of the politics of globalization, which is well represented in the examination of the global networks, resistance movements and the shift to the South. The book will be an excellent tool for those who want to understand a crucial phenomenon of our time.

Raffaele Marchetti, Professor of International Relations, Faculty of Political Science and the School of Government, LUISS Guido Carli, Roma, Italy

Of late, global politics is assuming greater relevance, obtaining urgency to introduce textbooks in Indian context. This book, as essential reading, will cater to not only college- and university-going students but also general readers who desire to comprehend different dimensions and complexities of global politics.

Narender Kumar, Professor of Political Studies, Jawaharlal Nehru University, New Delhi, India

Global Politics

Thank you for choosing a SAGE product!
If you have any comment, observation or feedback,
I would like to personally hear from you.

Please write to me at **contactceo@sagepub.in**

Vivek Mehra, Managing Director and CEO, SAGE India.

Bulk Sales

SAGE India offers special discounts
for bulk institutional purchases.

For queries/orders/inspection copy requests,
write to **textbooksales@sagepub.in**

Publishing

Would you like to publish a textbook with SAGE?
Please send your proposal to **publishingtextbooks@sagepub.in**

Get to know more about SAGE

Be invited to SAGE events, get on our mailing list.
Write today to **marketing@sagepub.in**

Global Politics

Issues and Perspectives

Edited by

Nirmal Jindal

*Senior Associate Professor, Department of Political Science,
Satyawati College, University of Delhi*

Kamal Kumar

*Assistant Professor, Department of Political Science, Shivaji College,
University of Delhi*

⑤SAGE | TEXTS

Los Angeles | London | New Delhi
Singapore | Washington DC | Melbourne

First published in 2018 by

⑤SAGE | TEXTS

SAGE Publications India Pvt Ltd
B1/I-1 Mohan Cooperative Industrial Area
Mathura Road, New Delhi 110 044, India
www.sagepub.in

SAGE Publications Inc
2455 Teller Road
Thousand Oaks, California 91320, USA

SAGE Publications Ltd
1 Oliver's Yard, 55 City Road
London EC1Y 1SP, United Kingdom

SAGE Publications Asia-Pacific Pte Ltd
3 Church Street
#10-04 Samsung Hub
Singapore 049483

Published by Vivek Mehra for SAGE Publications India Pvt Ltd, typeset in 10/12.5 pts Minion Pro by Zaza Eunice, Hosur, Tamil Nadu, India.

Library of Congress Cataloging-in-Publication Data

Names: Jindal, Nirmal, editor. | Kumar, Kamal, editor.
Title: Global politics: issues and perspectives/edited by Nirmal Jindal
    and Kamal Kumar.
Description: New Delhi, India; Thousand Oaks, California: SAGE
    Publications, [2018] | Includes bibliographical references and index.
Identifiers: LCCN 2018009642 | ISBN 9789352806836 (pbk.)
Subjects: LCSH: Globalization. | World politics. | International relations.
Classification: LCC JZ1318 .G516 2018 | DDC 327—dc23 LC record available at
https://lccn.loc.gov/2018009642

ISBN: 978-93-528-0683-6 (PB)

SAGE Team: Amit Kumar, Anveshi Gupta, Alekha Chandra Jena and Ritu Chopra

Brief Contents

Detailed Contents

CHAPTER 9
Nuclear Proliferation   174
Nirmal Jindal

CHAPTER 10
International Terrorism: Non-state Actors and State Terrorism—Developments Post-9/11   198
Shivali Aggarwal

List of Tables

List of Figures

List of Boxes

List of Abbreviations

AAAS	American Association for the Advancement of Science
ABM	Anti-Ballistic Missiles
ADB	Asian Development Bank
AIIB	Asian Infrastructure Investment Bank
APEC	Asia-Pacific Economic Cooperation
AQC	Al Qaeda Central
ASEAN	Association of Southeast Asian Nations
ATTAC	Association for the Taxation of Financial Transactions and for Citizens' Action
ATR	African traditional religions
AU	African Union
B2B	business-to-business
B2P	business-to-people
BCBS	Basel Committee on Banking Supervision
BPO	business process outsourcing
BRICS	Brazil, Russia, India, China and South Africa
CAR	Central African Republic
CARE	Cooperative for Assistance and Relief Everywhere
CBCS	Choice Based Credit System
CBD	Convention on Biological Diversity
CBDR	common but differentiated responsibilities
CBRN	chemical, biological, radiological and nuclear
CCP	Chinese Communist Party
CDDRL	Center on Democracy, Development, and the Rule of Law
CDM	Clean Development Mechanism
CEDAW	Convention on the Elimination of All Forms of Discrimination against Women
CERI	Centre for International Studies and Research
CFC	chlorofluorocarbon
CFR	Council on Foreign Relations
CGAP	Consultative Group to Assist the Poor

CGIAR	Consultative Group for International Agricultural Research
CH_4	Methane
CHS	Commission on Human Security
CIA	Central Intelligence Agency
CIPOD	Centre for International Politics, Organization and Disarmament
CISAC	Center for International Security and Cooperation (Stanford)
CLAIM	Citizen's Network for Peace, Reconciliation and Human Security
CND	Campaign for Nuclear Disarmament
CNPC	Chinese National Petroleum Corporation
CO_2	carbon dioxide
COE	centre of excellence
COE	committee of experts
COP	Conference of the Parties
CR groups	consciousness-raising groups
CRISPR	clustered regularly interspaced short palindromic repeats
CRPD	Convention on the Rights of Persons with Disabilities
CRY	Child Rights and You
CSDE	Centre for the Study of Discrimination and Exclusion
CSI	Container Security Initiative
CSIR	Council of Scientific and Industrial Research
CSIS	Centre for Strategic and International Studies
CSW	Commission on the Status of Women
CTBT	Comprehensive Test Ban Treaty
CU	Customs Union
DAWN	Development Alternatives with Women for a New Era
DDT	Dichlorodiphenyltrichloroethane
DOE	Department of Energy
DPRK	Democratic People's Republic of Korea
DSA	Defence and Security Alert
ECOSOC	Economic and Social Council
EDF	Environmental Defense Fund
EFA	Education for All
EFSF	European Financial Stability Facility
EME	emerging market economy
EPI	Environmental Policy Institute
ERA	Equal Rights Amendment (US)
EU	European Union
Exim Bank	Export-Import Bank of India
FAO	Food and Agriculture Organization
FBI	Federal Bureau of Investigation
FCRA	Foreign Contribution Regulation Act

FDI	foreign direct investment
FIRST	Financial Sector Reform and Strengthening Initiative
FMCT	Fissile Material Cut-off Treaty
FMWG	Fissile Materials Working Group
FSB	Financial Stability Board
FSF	Financial Stability Forum
FSI	Freeman Spogli Institute for International Studies
FTAA	Free Trade Area of the Americas
FTA	free trade area
G20	Group of Twenty
G2B	government-to-business
G2P	government-to-people
G-8	Group of Eight
G-33	Group of 33
G-77	Group of 77
GA	General Assembly
GAD	gender and development
GATS	General Agreement on Trade in Services
GATT	General Agreement on Tariffs and Trade
GAVI	Global Alliance for Vaccines and Immunization
GCNEP	Global Centre for Nuclear Energy Partnership
GDLN	Global Development Learning Network
GDP	gross domestic product
GDRC	Global Development Research Center
GEF	Global Environment Facility
GEFI	Global Education First Initiative
GFN	Global Footprint Network
GHG	greenhouse gas
GICNT	Global Initiative to Combat Nuclear Terrorism
GPE	global political economy
GSM	global social movement
GUI	graphical user interface
GWP	Global Water Partnership
HELI	Health and Environment Linkages Initiative
HFC	hydrofluorocarbons
HHA	Harmonization for Health in Africa
HRF	Haiti Reconstruction Fund
HSN	Human Security Network
IADA	International Atomic Development Authority
IAEA	International Atomic Energy Agency
IBRD	International Bank for Reconstruction and Development

ICANN	Internet Corporation for Assigned Names and Numbers
ICAO	International Civil Aviation Organization
ICC	International Criminal Court
ICD	International Classification of Diseases
ICISS	International Commission on Intervention and State Sovereignty
ICJ	International Court of Justice
ICPD	International Conference on Population and Development
ICRC	International Committee of the Red Cross
ICT	information and communication technology
IDA	International Development Association
IDP	internally displaced person
IDSA	Institute for Defence Studies and Analyses
IET	International Emissions Trading
IFAD	International Fund for Agricultural Development
IISS	International Institute for Strategic Studies
ILO	International Labour Organization
IMF	International Monetary Fund
INF	Intermediate-Range Nuclear Forces Treaty
INGO	international non-governmental organization
IO	international organization
IPCC	Intergovernmental Panel on Climate Change
IPE	international political economy
IR	international relations
ISA	International Studies Association
ISCN	Integrated Support Center for Nuclear Non-proliferation and Nuclear Security
ISIL	Islamic State in Iraq and the Levant
ISIS	Islamic State in Iraq and Syria
IT	information technology
ITA	Information Technology Agreement ITA-II second Information Technology Agreement
ITU	International Communication Union
IUCN	International Union for Conservation of Nature
JI	Joint Implementation
LGBT	lesbian, gay, bisexual and transgender
LTTE	Liberation Tigers of Tamil Eelam
M&A	mergers and acquisitions
MAD	mutual assured destruction
MDGs	Millennium Development Goals
MENA	Middle East and North Africa
MESIS	Middle East Scientific Institute for Security
MFN	most-favoured-nation

MNLF	Moro National Liberation Front
MNC	multinational corporation
MOP28	28th Meeting of the Parties to the Montreal Protocol
MTCR	Missile Technology Control Regime
N_2O	Nitrous Oxide
NAFTA	North American Free Trade Agreement
NATO	North Atlantic Treaty Organization
NDB	New Development Bank
NDCs	nationally determined contribution
NET	National Eligibility Test
NGO	non-governmental organization
NIEO	New International Economic Order
NNSA	National Nuclear Security Administration
NOW	National Organization for Women (US)
NOW	National Organization for Working Communities
NPT	Treaty on the Non-proliferation of Nuclear Weapons
NSG	Nuclear Suppliers Group
NSM	new social movement
NWFZ	Nuclear-Weapon-Free Zone
OAS	Organization of American States
OCP	Onchocerciasis Control Programme
ODS	ozone-depleting substances
OECD	Organisation for Economic Co-operation and Development
OIOS	Office of Internal Oversight Services
OPAD	Organization for Poverty Alleviation and Development
Oxfam	Oxford Committee for Famine Relief
PCENS	Pakistan Centre of Excellence for Nuclear Security
PFC	perfluorocarbon
PLO	Palestine Liberation Organization
PRC	People's Republic of China
PRIO	Peace Research Institute Oslo
PSC	Peace and Security Council
PSI	Proliferation Security Initiative
PTA	preferential trade agreement
PTBT	Partial Test Ban Treaty
R2P	Responsibility to Protect
RDD	radiological dispersal device
SAARC	South Asian Association for Regional Cooperation
SALT	Strategic Arms Limitation Talks

SARS	severe acute respiratory syndrome
SC	Security Council
SCBD	Secretariat of the Convention on Biological Diversity
SDGs	Sustainable Development Goals
SDR	special drawing right
SEWA	Self-Employed Women's Association
SEZ	special economic zones
SF_6	Sulphur Hexafluoride
SIPRI	Stockholm International Peace Research Institute
SORT	Strategic Offensive Reductions Treaty
START	Strategic Arms Reduction Talks/Treaty
TKDL	Traditional Knowledge Digital Library
TNC	transnational corporation
TPP	Trans-Pacific Partnership
TRIPS	Trade-related Aspects of Intellectual Property Rights
TTIP	Transatlantic Trade Investment Partnership
UAE	United Arab Emirates
UDHR	Universal Declaration of Human Right
UGC	University Grants Commission
UKIP	United Kingdom Independence Party
UN	United Nations
UNAIDS	Joint United Nations Programme on HIV/AIDS
UNCED	United Nations Conference on Environment and Development
UNCHE	United Nations Conference on the Human Environment
UNCLOS	United Nations Convention on the Law of the Sea
UNCTAD	United Nations Conference on Trade and Development
UNDESA	United Nations Department of Economic and Social Affairs
UNDP	United Nations Development Programme
UNEP	United Nations Environment Programme
UNESCO	United Nations Educational, Scientific and Cultural Organization
UNFCCC	United Nations Framework Convention on Climate Change
UNHCR	United Nations High Commissioner for Refugees
UNICEF	United Nations Children's Fund
UNIFEM	United Nations Development Fund for Women
UNIFTPA	United Nations Interagency Framework Team for Preventive Action
UNPD	United Nations Population Division
UNSCOM	United Nations Special Commission
UNTC	United Nations Treaty Series
UNTFHS	United Nations Trust Fund for Human Security
US	United States (of America)
USAID	United States Agency for International Development

USGCRP	US Global Change Research Program
USSR	Union of Soviet Socialist Republics
USTR	United States Trade Representative
VDPA	Vienna Declaration and Programme of Action
WAE	Women and the Environment
WANO	World Association of Nuclear Operators
WB	World Bank
WCED	World Commission on Environment and Development
WEAP	World Ecological Areas Programme
WFP	World Food Programme
WHO	World Health Organization
WMD	weapon of mass destruction
WMO	World Meteorological Organization
WNO	World Nature Organization
WSF	World Social Forum
WSP	Water and Sanitation Program
WTI	Wildlife Trust of India
WTO	World Trade Organization
WWF	World Wildlife Fund

Preface

The idea of producing this textbook was generated in the gardens of Satyawati College in December 2016, when some of our colleagues talked about the scarcity of reading material to support the global politics syllabus introduced for undergraduate honours students under the University Grants Commission's Choice Based Credit System (UGC CBCS), and various similar courses offered in most Indian universities. Some of the texts from the Western world used for teaching global politics do not touch upon the realities or implications of globalization in the developing world. For a nuanced understanding of globalization and what it means to the developing countries, it is important to assess globalization from the developing countries' perspective as well. This edited volume seeks to provide diverse perspectives on the critical issues related to globalization, so that readers can understand the complex issues and develop an analytical perspective.

We are indebted to many people who have helped us in the preparation of the book. First and foremost, we thank all the contributors who agreed to be a part of the project and patiently revised the chapters to incorporate all the suggestions put forward from time to time to improve the quality of the finished work. We are also extremely grateful to the Department of Political Science, Computer Centre, library and office staff and senior colleagues of Satyawati College, for their generous support in preparation of the book.

We are highly honoured to be associated with the SAGE Text Book Project. Our special thanks to the SAGE team for responding so promptly and positively to our proposal. The constant feedback from their editorial team kept us on our toes and allowed our understanding and vision to be transformed into this volume. We extend our thanks and acknowledge the anonymous reviewers at SAGE for accelerating the progress of this project, and enabling its journey from conception to completed volume. We also express our indebtedness to our students, whose choices in seeking out education generated a pressure to produce a quality Indian work on globalization.

Finally, we must acknowledge the contribution of our families, who have always been wonderful, ever trusting and supportive during the process of writing this book. They are daily reminders that what was once unthinkable is in fact thinkable and possible. This project would not have been possible without their constant support, love and encouragement. The book is dedicated to our respective family members—B. C. Gupta, Jashua Gupta and Ankita Gupta, and Surajmal, Om Wati, Heera, Devki and Nisha.

Nirmal Jindal
Kamal Kumar

About the Editors and Contributors

Editors

Nirmal Jindal is an Associate Professor of Political Science at Satyawati College, University of Delhi. She has been a recipient of Fulbright (predoctoral) fellowship at the Center for Science and International Affairs, John F. Kennedy School of Government, Harvard University in 1984–1985. She was also awarded a Diploma in Advanced International Studies on Peace and Conflict Resolution from the Department of Peace and Conflict Research, Uppsala University, Sweden, in 1991. She is a recipient of the 'Best College Lecturer Award' for the year 2017–2018, awarded by Directorate of Higher Education, Delhi Government. She has authored two books, titled *War as a Political Weapon in the Nuclear Age* and *US Foreign Policy: Issues and Perspectives*. She has contributed numerous articles and research papers on issues of security, foreign policy, the Indo–Pakistan conflict in Kashmir, strategic deterrence and globalization in various journals and edited volumes of national and international repute. She has been a visiting faculty to various reputed universities and organizations, including the Department of Political Science, University of Delhi; the Internal Security Academy, Central Reserve Police Force (CRPF) Camp, Mount Abu; and the Centre for Professional Development in Higher Education (CPDHE), University of Delhi. She has participated in various national and international conferences and presented about 50 research papers, including at the International Studies Association (ISA), Portland, USA, and St Gallen University, Switzerland. At present, she is working on the issue of environmental security. She has also participated in panel discussions on foreign policy and security issues on Zee News, NDTV, and other channels several times. She is also interested in and associated with aviation security training for civilians, which has been covered by electronic and print media including the *Fox History Channel*, *NDTV*, *Zee News*, the *Times Magazine,* and *Harmony* magazine, and various newspapers, including *India Today*.

Kamal Kumar is an Assistant Professor at Shivaji College, University of Delhi. He has also taught at Hindu College, Lakshmibai College and Satyawati College. He has received the Academic Excellence Award while graduating from Hindu College and secured a University Position at the University of Delhi. He was awarded an MPhil in 2013 from the Department of Political Science, University of Delhi, and presently, he is pursuing a PhD from the same institution. He was awarded an All India Postgraduate

Scholarship in 2011 and the UGC Junior Research Fellowship in 2013. He has also been awarded the ICSSR INTERNATIONAL TRAVEL GRANT in 2018 for participating in the 76th Annual Midwest Political Science Association Conference held in Chicago, US. He has attended the U21 Masters Intensive Module 2012 organized in collaboration by the University of Birmingham, University of Delhi and University of Melbourne. He has published five research articles in UGC-approved journals like *Mainstream, Social Change* and *Intellectual Resonance*, and contributed two articles in national newspapers. He has authored over ten articles for different textbooks and reference books published by reputed publishers like Orient BlackSwan and Tripura University. He has also presented around eleven research papers in various national and international conferences. His research interests include comparative politics, environmental politics in South Asia and social movements.

Contributors

Shivali Aggarwal teaches political science at Daulat Ram College, University of Delhi. She was the topper of her batch and secured a university position on graduation. She was awarded *Shri Tilak Raj Memorial Award* in Daulat Ram College for securing highest marks in Political Science. She was awarded an MPhil and a PhD by the Department of Political Science, University of Delhi. She was selected for the prestigious University Teaching Assistantship at the University of Delhi and had four years of teaching experience in the Department of Political Science. She had the credit of writing chapters for reputed publishing houses. She has published three books on topics as varied as Indo-Canadian relations, development issues in India and poverty in India. She has presented research papers in various international and national conferences. Her research interests include comparative politics, the Indian political economy, political theory and political thought.

Manisha Chaurasiya is an Assistant Professor in the Department of Political Science, Lady Shri Ram College, University of Delhi. At present, she is also pursuing a PhD from the Centre for International Politics, Organization and Disarmament (CIPOD), Jawaharlal Nehru University. She completed her MPhil dissertation on 'Understanding the "Grand Bargain" between the Nuclear Weapon States and the Non-nuclear Weapons States: Evolution, Strategies and Motivations' in 2016. She has contributed five articles in reputed national journals like *Air Power, World Focus* and *Defence and Diplomacy*, and magazines like *Defence and Security Alert*. She has also presented research papers in several national and international seminars at different Central and State Universities.

Alisha Dhingra is an Assistant Professor at the Department of Political Science, University of Delhi. She has twice received the Academic Excellence Award at Hindu College, at the undergraduate level. She has obtained an MPhil from the Department of Political Science, University of Delhi. She has been awarded the Central Sector scholarship by the Ministry of Human Resource and Development (July 2008–June 2013) and a Junior Research Fellowship from the UGC (August 2013–July 2015), and at present is availing UGC Senior Research Fellowship since February 2016. Her research interests include gender studies, constitutionalism and rule of law. She has authored six articles and co-authored one more. She has presented papers in national and international seminars and workshops. She has been associated with the *Leverhulme* international research network project titled 'Continuity and Change in Indian Federalism'.

Shruti Joshi is as an Assistant Professor in the Department of Political Science, Satyawati College, University of Delhi. She has earlier taught in the Department of Political Science at the University of Allahabad, and completed her PhD from the same university. She has recently authored a book titled *E Governance: Theory and Practice*. She has several articles to her credit in various national and international journals, on issues such as electronic governance (e-governance), the Gandhian perspective of governance, B. R. Ambedkar's views on development, farmers' suicides and energy security in India.

Arvind Kumar is a Doctoral Scholar at the Centre for Political Studies, Jawaharlal Nehru University, New Delhi, and a guest faculty at the Department of Political Science, Satyawati College, University of Delhi. His primary research interests include rising economic inequality and the politics of liberalization. He has submitted his MPhil dissertation on 'Inequality and Democracy—Exploring Possibilities of Equity the 21st Century'. In addition to teaching and research, he regularly writes columns in newspapers, magazines and academic journals.

Ketan Kumar is an Assistant Professor in the Department of Political Science, Ramjas College, University of Delhi. He holds the distinction of being the gold medallist in BA (Hon.), Political Science at the University of Delhi (2013). Presently, he is pursuing his PhD at the Centre for Political Studies, Jawaharlal Nehru University. His research interest lies in international politics, India's Foreign Policy and Indian government and politics.

Virendra Kumar is a Senior Assistant Professor of Political Science at Satyawati College, University of Delhi. His research areas include development studies, international political economy and public policy. He has published articles in two edited books and presented papers at national and international seminars.

Aditaya Narayan Mishra is an Assistant Professor in the Department of Political Science at Satyawati College, University of Delhi. He has obtained a PhD from the Centre for South Asian Studies, School of International Studies, Jawaharlal Nehru University. His areas of interest include Bangladesh, India's foreign policy, water disputes, and South Asian politics. He has published a number of articles in journals of national and international repute.

Rounak Kumar Pathak is an Assistant Professor at Kalindi College, University of Delhi. He is also pursuing his PhD from the Department of Political Science, University of Delhi. His areas of interest include Indian politics, the party system, electoral politics and voting behaviour. He has published six research articles in journals, in the areas of party politics and economic federalism. He has been awarded an Academic Excellence Award as the college topper in his batch in the year 2011. He is also the winner of the 2011 Indian Political Science Conference Prize as the university topper from the University of Delhi. He has been awarded a Central Sector scholarship by the Ministry of Human Resource and Development (2008–2013) and a Junior Research Fellowship by the UGC in 2016. He has also presented conference papers at a Leverhulme international workshop titled 'Continuity and Change in Indian Federalism', held jointly at the University Delhi and Panjab University.

Bhavna Sharma is presently serving as Assistant Professor at the University of Delhi. She was awarded the University gold medal while graduating with a BA (Hon.) degree in political science from the University of Delhi. She obtained her MPhil from the Department of Political Science, University of

Delhi. Presently, she is enrolled as a doctoral student at the Centre for the Study of Discrimination and Exclusion (CSDE), Jawaharlal Nehru University. Her work focuses on the influence of student politics on governmental policies.

Parmeet Singh is currently an Assistant Professor in the Department of Political Science, Pannalal Girdharlal Dayanand Anglo Vedic (PGDAV) College (Evening), University of Delhi. He has also taught political science at Sri Guru Nanak Dev (SGND) Khalsa College, University of Delhi. He holds an MPhil from the Department of Political Science, University of Delhi. His areas of interest include political theory, Indian democracy and communal violence. His articles and chapters have been published in journals, newspapers and books. Apart from academics, Indian semi-classical music is also one of his areas of contribution.

Neelu Anita Tigga teaches political science at the Department of Political Science, Satyawati College (Day), University of Delhi. She has a bachelor's degree from University of Delhi (Jesus and Mary College), and a master's and an MPhil from Jawaharlal Nehru University. She specializes in gender studies.

Ashutosh Trivedi is an Assistant Professor in the Department of Political Science, Satyawati College, University of Delhi. His PhD was on 'Women Empowerment and Sociopolitical Development in Ghana'. His areas of interest include international relations, African studies, gender, public administration and the environment. He has authored a book titled *Understanding the Neglected Pillars (Women) in GHANA* in 2014. Another book jointly edited by him is *Contemporary Africa: Issues and Concerns* published in 2011. He has also written a few reference articles for edited volumes based on the University of Delhi syllabus.

Introduction

Globalization has become the most commonly used concept both in academic and mainstream political discourse. The term 'globalization' denotes a complex phenomenon, which is difficult to comprehend. It refers to integration, interdependence and multilateralism leading to peace and stability in the international system, which appears to be a departure from the traditional, realist approach to international politics. The revolution in information technology and means of communication and transportation have acted as the critical facilitator in turning the world into a 'global village' by shrinking it in time and space. The neo-liberals projected globalization as an enlargement of modernity from society to the world. The term 'globalization' is inextricably linked with liberalization, privatization and democratization. Most of the countries in the post-cold war world adopted economic liberalization and political democratization in order to assimilate in the process of development and were quite optimistic about the implications of globalization. In addition, the champions of globalization are projecting globalization as a means to achieve peace, security and development globally. In this context, the divergent perspectives of globalization are critically examined in this book. An empirical study of the impact of globalization is also given attention for a basic understanding of the intricacies of the process.

A number of theorists present globalization primarily as an economic activity of deepening economic integration, increasing economic openness and growing economic interdependence among all the countries of the world, in which the state should play a minimal role. More than two decades' experience of globalization indicates that the process of global integration has inherent contradictions. The burgeoning optimism about modernization due to the availability of computers, cars, electronic devices, laptops, mobiles, foreign airlines, fashion and design must be tempered with cynicism, as only a section of society benefits by this kind of change and it is not a sign of development, but superficial modernization of only the upper section of the society in developing countries. The rules of international economic agencies like the United Nations (UN), the World Trade Organization (WTO), the International Monetary Fund (IMF) and the World Bank are set by the major global powers, who are the capital exporters, technology leaders and service providers in the world economy. These are the agencies of global governance that set the rules of the game for the whole world. Three regional blocs appeared to have dominated the emerging economic order: the United States (US), the European Union (EU) and the Asia–Pacific Rim. The WTO policies imposed on the developing countries have been reassessed in view of the major power policies. In this context, the opportunities and challenges posed by globalization have been highlighted. The implications of the policies of the WTO, World Bank and IMF for the developing countries are also discussed in order to understand the constraints faced by the developing countries.

The poverty-stricken developing countries are unable to assimilate themselves in the process of development as the majority of their population lacks literacy and skills. These countries have also been facing the problems of technology denial and technology dumping that negatively impacting their indigenous industrial capabilities. Due to globalization, the states in the Global South are also unable to generate funds from customs and excise. It further reduces the states' capacity to perform the role of social welfare. It is likely to have an impact on social relations and endanger the internal security situation in the developing countries.

Globalization has caused an uneven and asymmetrical development in the world as it has not been able to remove the gap between rich and poor. The developing countries with low income and output levels cannot participate in the world market. These countries with economic underdevelopment, lack of technology and production, and poor human resource development are unlikely to use the opportunities put forward by the economic globalization. In the free-market system, there is no attempt on the part of developed nations to develop the developing countries. No doubt, some of the Asian countries are recipients of foreign direct investment (FDI) and it has increased to a great extent, but about 80% of it is used in the industrialized countries and only 20% in the developing countries. The major foreign investments in the developing countries are not coming into the primary or manufacturing sectors, but merely in service sectors. The major powers are also obsessed with intellectual property rights (IPR) as they want to preserve the benefits of scientific research for their own countries rather than sharing with the whole world, particularly with developing countries. Teaching and research are commodities for export and not for the benefit of all. Due to intellectual property rights and patenting norms, most of the basic commodities and services are available at international prices, thereby placing them simply beyond the reach of people in poor countries. In the absence of states able to perform the social welfare role (particularly in health and education), the socio-economic instability is likely to increase in poor countries. Moreover, only state can have political and economic interaction with the outside world to improve distribution gains from cross-border and economic interactions, practise prudence in macro management of economic affairs to reduce asymmetries and economic inequalities.

Another important aspect of globalization is the globalization of Western culture, leading to rapid social change and increased inequalities and challenges to cultural identities of different nations, predominantly in the developing countries. Globalization has led to the pluralization of societies and many proto-ethnic and proto-national groups have emerged, claiming their right to self-determination and impairing the security matrix of many states. However, the development of a global culture does not mean unification or homogenization of cultures, though cultures are becoming revitalized upon contact with each other.

The issue of migration and human security has also become quite intense in the age of globalization. There are multiple reasons for human migrations, such as a search for better economic opportunities, fear of violence, avoiding persecution or environment and climatic conditions. It is estimated that there will be mass migration of humans from West Asia in the future due to environmental reasons or climatic change. In the contemporary world, developed countries use stringent migration policies, as they fear demographic change and are moving towards automation and robotics to prevent migration of workers to their own countries. Moreover, the emergence of global terrorism is also one of the factors that forces countries to adopt more stringent immigration policies. The issue of human security is also discussed in detail, as it is assuming greater significance in the contemporary world, unlike traditional international politics, which focused primarily on the militaristic aspect of security.

It is interesting to note that despite overemphasis on economic factors and nuclear non-proliferation and arms control, major powers are not only maintaining their own nuclear systems but are trying to improve their quality to deal with the newly emerging threats in the new nuclear age. This accelerates the process of nuclear proliferation among smaller countries, as they perceive it an effective tool to protect their interest. In the post-cold war world, the developed countries defence expenditure is reducing whereas the poor countries' expenditure is showing an upward trend. The control of nuclear technology and nuclear material by non-state actors or terrorist groups is the most serious challenge the world is confronting in the age of globalization. Global terrorism, though conceptually recognized after the 9/11 attack, has been prevalent in some form in different countries of the world earlier as well. Global terrorism is a hidden and secret warfare, a weapon of the weak and based on jihad and Islamic fundamentalism. Different Islamic groups are carrying out terrorism in different countries on different issues, but the basis is jihad. Such non-state actors and terrorist groups are posing a serious threat to world peace and security, which again re-establishes and reinforces the state's role of dealing with such threats. Terrorist attacks on democratic countries have compelled the state to introduce more stringent methods to curb such activities, thereby hurting the democratic values of these countries. Moreover, the state has to spend exorbitant amounts for its homeland security, which is against the essence of globalization.

Globalization exhibits the characteristics of competition and fragmentation among major powers as well. The declining US hegemony and emergence of new centres of power are indicative of global shifts in power and governance. It is imminent that the state system in the new global order continues where states failed to share the responsibility for freedom and justice. In this context, the role of the UN in the post-cold war scenario requires serious attention and analysis, and various reform options need to be explored for effective and democratic functioning of the UN. The impact of globalization on women and women's role in international politics for peaceful and democratized international politics is also a significant area of research that needs to be evaluated from the postcolonial perspective.

The new global order has, no doubt, led to globalization in terms of information delivery, economic resources, human rights, global social movements and international non-governmental organizations. This is a significant contribution of globalization. Technology has facilitated the global social movements and the transnational and non-governmental organizations functioning at the international level. States share responsibilities with these transnational and non-governmental organizations on issues of global significance, such as environmental protection and human security, and social issues such as women's upliftment, to name a few. The roles of social movements, transnational actors and NGO networks are discussed in detail in this book to study the changing nature of relationships between the state and transnational actors. To summarize, these non-state actors are playing a significant role in dealing with most of the challenges posed by globalization. As long as the state persists as an important source of political agency, they will construct the state system with its own rules and norms.

Outline of the Book

This textbook consists of 15 chapters, primarily written for this volume. In the opening chapter of the book, 'Understanding Globalization and its Alternative Perspective', the author, Shruti Joshi, has tried to explore the varied nuances of the concept of globalization and has attempted to provide a broad understanding of this multilayered phenomenon. The chapter not only dwells on the historical trajectory and the prevailing theorizations of this complex phenomenon, but also exhaustively explores the varied types of globalization. The author also tries to decode the process of globalization by exploring its alternative perspectives. Joshi, in this regard, explores the three schools of thought relating to globalization and tries to identify its effect on broader aspects of statehood and sovereignty, thus providing a holistic view of this much-debated phenomenon.

In Chapter 2, 'Political Globalization: Debates on Sovereignty and Territoriality', Ashutosh Trivedi makes an attempt to explore the political aspect of the process of globalization. The author theorizes about the concepts of sovereignty and territoriality and attempts to explore the effect of globalization on them, in terms of expanding or narrowing down sovereignty and deterritorialization. Amid the growing interconnectedness across political cultures, the chapter tries to highlight the need to revisit the discourse on territoriality and sovereignty of nation states. In this regard, while discussing the three main schools of thought, namely, hyperglobalists, sceptics and transformationalists, the author highlights the need to redefine the traditional notion of sovereignty in order to enable nation states to survive in this globalized world.

In Chapter 3, 'Global Political Economy: Evolution and Significance of the World Economic Order', Arvind Kumar provides deep insight into this newly emerging approach as well as discipline, whose objective is to provide solutions to the problems that have arisen due to the blurring of old binaries such as domestic–international, political–economic, social–economic, and so on, in the era of globalization. The conventional disciplines of the social sciences are unable to explain the problems associated with globalization. The route of historicity, which this chapter adopts for explaining the current avatar of political economy, also provides theoretical underpinnings for the macro theme of this book. The chapter not only traces the origin of global political economy (GPE) in classical political economy, but also makes readers aware of how the modern disciplines of social science—such as economics, political science and sociology—have evolved from classical political economy, as a result of which, classical political economy is referred to as the mother of the social sciences. After discussing the root of GPE in classical political economy, this chapter takes a step back and provides a detailed analysis of physiocracy and mercantilism, two intellectual traditions from Europe that made a pioneering contribution in the evolution of classical political economy. The chapter concludes with the discussion of the role of anchors in GPE, which includes the state and non-state actors, including individuals.

In Chapter 4, 'Economic Globalization: Global Trade and Finance', the author, Virendra Kumar, aims to examine global trade and global finance from the vantage point of the Global South. Keeping in view empirical developments, especially the deadlock over the Doha Development Agenda and repeated financial instability as also theoretical debates on globalization, the author argues that the nation states of the Global South, barring few, need to carve out policy space to address their specific needs instead of succumbing to financial institutions, conditions and prescriptions dominated by the West. A close look at global trade flow, the author notes, reveals that the major advanced regions trade among themselves, while developing and low-income countries' primary products do not get access to the former market on various grounds. This skewed nature of global trade, along with the volatility of the financial system, owing to capital market liberalization around the world, makes it imperative for the Global South to seek more maneuver to manage the market and free trade so as to have economic stability and to address increasing inequality and informalization, despite a high growth rate.

In Chapter 5, 'Global Governance: The IMF, the World Bank, the WTO and TNCs', Ketan Kumar looks into the process of global governance, which has become an inevitable reality of the present world order. The post-cold war era has triggered a number of issues and phenomenons, which were previously unidentified. The growing idea of globalization as a significant theme and the subsequent weakening of the nation states points to a prospect of transferring to a global level of regulatory instruments. Not only is global life marked by a density of populations, it is also dense with organized activities, thereby extending the process of global governance. Global life in the twenty-first century is more complicated than ever before. It is partly because the world is host to ever greater numbers of organizations in all walks of life and every corner of every continent. In this chapter, the author has looked into the roles and influences of various international actors, especially the International Monetary Fund (IMF), the World Bank, the World Trade Organization (WTO) and transnational corporations (TNCs), with respect to global governance. Besides, he has also highlighted global trade and finance and global environmental politics, the issue of the global commons and the North–South divide. The chapter also deals with the rise in the strategic dominance of the United States (US) as a consequence of the capitalist orientation and Northward bias of global politics. The chapter concludes by looking into the growing influence of India as a significant strategic actor in world politics.

In Chapter 6, 'Technological and Cultural Dimensions of Globalization', Bhavna Sharma and Virendra Kumar focus on the cultural and technological dimensions of globalization. With the increasing interconnectedness of global cultures and intensification of social relations, globalization through its forces has made a deep impact on the cultural fabric of nation states. The free movement of goods, capital, services, people and values has resulted in a homogenization of cultures across the globe. This has created a great possibility of developing a more inclusive and enriched understanding of culture. On the other hand, it has also situated the question of cultural identity at the centre of contemporary debates. However, the scope of globalization has widened chiefly due to technological developments, which emerge as a key enabler and facilitator of this all pervasive process. The technological dimension of globalization is associated with the rise of the 'global network' which has emerged as the gateway of information, technology and knowledge worldwide. The chapter highlights the basic tenets of culture and how it has undergone a metamorphosis in the wake of the globalization spree and what have been its implications for the world as a whole. Culture works in close proximity with the technological advancements which are available for society, and they both are directly related to each other. Changing technology has widened the network base, which has also had a tremendous impact on the developmental levels of societies.

In Chapter 7, 'Global Resistance: Global Social Movements and NGOs', the authors Kamal Kumar and Bhavna Sharma analyse the challenges posed by global social movements and non-governmental organizations (NGOs) to the global power structure and the functioning of international organizations. The chapter begins with explaining the meaning of social movements and how the aggregation which was once confined to a particular country has assumed global dimensions. There are some common issues and problems which can be resolved by the collective efforts of such countries. Such issues that implicate the global community have given rise to global social movements. The chapter also studies the role of NGOS that act free from governmental control, but nonetheless work in close cooperation with them. The global social movements play a significant role in democratizing global governance and power structures by mobilizing the marginalized and strengthening the concerns and interests of developing countries. In contemporary international politics, the non-state actors such as NGOs have become an indispensable tool for effective governance, and their partnership with the governmental bodies has been proving beneficial in dealing with emerging international and national issues.

Various issues like ecological, international terrorism and nuclear threats pose a serious threat to both national and human security. Such issues started gaining prominence in the discourse of international politics by the late 1970s and have become a major global concern today. Since the Stockholm Conference of 1972, all countries (both developed and developing) had shown considerable enthusiasm towards the need for environmental protection. However, this enthusiasm was confined to only announcements of environmental agreements and laws. Despite introducing various laws and agreements, there has been no effective change in the situation. One of the reasons is that the agenda of capitalist development is still dominating governmental discourses at both the domestic and global levels. Due to a lack of genuine political will, the structural procedures and mechanisms evolved by different governments for maintaining environmental health have proved to be insufficient. Over time, the limitless and incessant exploitation of natural resources has further deteriorated the state of the global environment. In Chapter 8, 'Ecological Issues: A Historical Overview of International Environmental Agreements, Climate Change, and the Global Commons Debate', Kamal Kumar presents an overview of major international environmental agreements and scholarly debates on climate change and the global commons. This chapter is primarily divided into three sections. The first section analyses the key international environmental agreements aiming at improving and protecting the health of the environment. This is followed by a discussion of climate change and its implications on the security of global community. In this context the global efforts to mitigate the issue of environmental protection and human health are also taken into consideration. The chapter concludes with the debates on the global commons.

In Chapter 9, 'Nuclear Proliferation', Nirmal Jindal has critically examined the complexity of the issue of nuclear non-proliferation and arms control. The reasons for nuclear proliferation and the divergent perspectives on nuclear non-proliferation are critically examined in detail. The chapter highlights that nuclear proliferation is one of the most critical security issues in the age of globalization. Despite serious efforts undertaken to check nuclear proliferation, it is showing an upward trend. In this context, the theoretical framework of the implications of the development of nuclear weapons on the concept of war is discussed. In order to make students understand the difference between conventional weapons and nuclear weapons and their usability, the destructive capability of nuclear weapons is discussed to show how the development of nuclear weapons has revolutionized the character of war and rendered war as a political weapon obsolete. It is shown that though nuclear weapons have no military utility, they have political and diplomatic utility, which legitimizes the use of nuclear weapons and motivates nations to acquire nuclear weapons. In this regard, the inherent contradictions in the nuclear non-proliferation measures and initiatives are critically examined. The complexity of the issue of nuclear proliferation in the new nuclear age is also addressed. Nuclear proliferation by weak civilian governments, rogue states and terrorist groups is posing the most serious threat to global peace and security. Throughout the nuclear age, deterrence replaced war among nuclear countries. In the age of globalization, access to nuclear technology and nuclear material among terrorist groups poses a serious challenge to the effectiveness of the very concept of deterrence that maintained peace throughout the nuclear age. Terrorism is a hidden and secret warfare, where the enemy is invisible, and therefore, impossible to deter. In conclusion, the necessity for new mechanisms to deal with newly emerging threats is emphasized.

In Chapter 10, 'International Terrorism: Non-state Actors and State Terrorism—Developments post 9/11, Shivali Aggarwal attempts to understand, unlock and unravel many dimensions of global terrorism. The world is facing major security issues, and terrorism is the first among them. The world has witnessed two major world wars, and terrorism can be understood as the third and the most strenuous of all. Terrorism is a global problem and, with expansion of globalization, global terrorism has also engulfed the world, and the result is mass killings and death. Many countries, including peaceful India since its independence, have been facing this problem, but now terrorism has assumed a new dimension and no country in the world can claim itself free from its perils. Global terrorism brings up many inter-linked issues, such as illegal activities, corrupt practices, black money, the defence business, international relations and political issues in some countries. Over the decades, from the cold war to the 9/11 attack, the Iraq War, and the present scenario, terrorism has frequently changed its objectives and forms. This chapter is an attempt to reach the root cause of global terrorism, its forms, funding, objectives, measures to eliminate it and its effect on international relations, and also to understand the humane implications of its prevention.

In Chapter 11, 'Migration', the author Manisha Chaurasiya discusses the emerging global challenge of population migration in an increasingly globalized world. Although the very concept and context of globalization favours a borderless world, the Herculean volumes of migration of human populations from their places of origin has led to a daunting contemporary challenge. The chapter theoretically evaluates the various forms of immigrants: refugees, migrants, illegal immigrants, and so on. It traces the origin of human migration historically, while discussing the enhanced intensity, scope and volume of the same. It discusses the legal mechanisms available to refugees and migrants and the role of the UN's specialized agencies in this regard. The chapter also discusses various international case studies on the issue. It also analyses contemporary developments such as the stringent anti-immigration policies of the US under President Donald Trump, the plight of the Rohingya refugees and the implications and causes of Brexit. The chapter discusses a range of issues from the illegal immigration of Bangladeshi migrants into Indian territory to the migrant workers' strike in Dubai.

In Chapter 12, 'Human Security', Aditaya Narayan Mishra has made an attempt to understand the concept of human security, its various definitions, approaches, dimensions and the role of the international community in its promotion. The chapter is divided into four parts. The introductory part of the chapter has tried to discuss the background and context of human security. It highlights that the traditional meaning of security revolved around the protection of the state from external military threats. After the end of the cold war, there was euphoria that the militaristic aspect of security that dominated international politics throughout the cold war would take a back seat. In the age of globalization, it was hoped that states would focus on the non-militaristic aspect, or the human aspect of internal security. The concept of human security contrasts with the traditional meaning of 'security' and emphasizes the individual as the referent object. The second part of the chapter covers the various theoretical aspects of human security while examining the various definitions given by different policymakers, organizations and scholars. In addition, it has also dealt with the evolution of human security as a discourse, approaches to human security, its criticisms and underlined characteristics. It also provides a comparison of various approaches and debates related to the concept, such as the broad versus the narrow view. As defined, human security refers to the comprehensive aspects of security which includes the various dimensions of security such as economic security, food security, health security, environmental security, personal security, community security and political security. The third section of the chapter deals with these different dimensions of human security. The fourth and last part of the chapter evaluates the role of international organizations in dealing with human security problems.

In Chapter 13, 'Global Shifts: Power and Governance', Parmeet Singh analyses the major global shifts in the field of political, economic and military power. The chapter examines the conceptual relationship between power and global governance, which are intertwined, and how power influences the process of global shifts. In the era of globalization, the changing and shifting roles of power and governance are significant to understand the role of states and international institutions in managing international relations and politics. The centres of power and governance have always been dynamic in nature. The chapter deals with the historical evolution and development of different stages of shifts in global power and governance. The post-cold war era saw a recurrence US hegemonization in political, economic, military as well as cultural fields, but this is not free from challenges. The twenty-first century has brought global politics to a new juncture in a multipolar world, where the hegemony of the US declined in proportion to the increasing importance of new economic powers such as China, the European Union, Japan and India.

Feminist international relations identifies malestream international relations theory as one of the discourses that helps perpetuate a distorted and partial world view that reflects on the disproportionate power of control and influence that men hold, resulting in characteristics associated with 'manliness', such as toughness, courage, power, independence and even physical strength, being the most valued in the conduct of politics, particularly international politics, making the study of international politics gender-blind. It was only in the 1980s that the feminist perspective on world affairs gained prominence by reflecting on a growing acceptance that people's understanding of the world is shaped by the social and historical context in which they live and work. In Chapter 14, 'The Feminist Perspective on International Relations', Neelu Anita Tigga provides an overview of the various theories of feminism, particularly as the contemporary post-cold war world is distinctly different from previous periods because of the effects of globalization, for there appears a paradox of the triumph of Western, market-led values as well as the emergence of values different from Western notions, depending on the social, cultural, economic and political spaces one occupies in a globalized world. The chapter thus examines the ways in which gender helps to structure world politics. It begins with an explanation of the concepts of feminism and proceeds to give an overview of feminist theories more generally, and offers a feminist definition of gender, defining gender as an unequal structural relationship of power. The chapter concludes by outlining some policy practices that are helping to lessen gender inequalities.

In the final chapter, 'The United Nations: Organizational Structure, Role and Imperative for Reforms', the authors Alisha Dhingra and Rounak Kumar Pathak attempt to comprehend the operative essence of the United Nations. As an international organization, the UN has been playing a major role in promoting a collective security system; maintaining peace, economic and social development; advancing disarmament; protecting both human rights and environment; and serving as a roadblock to terrorism. This has been made possible through the syncretism of its organizational structure. It is in this context that the chapter will give readers an understanding of UN's organizational system and an analysis of its evolution in history. Further, readers would also come across a scrutiny of the UN's role in the acquirement of its assorted objectives and a silhouette for quintessential reforms.

This work is a collective effort by scholars and teachers from the University of Delhi to provide a detailed and comprehensive study of significant issues and divergent perspectives around globalization and global politics. The book will be a handbook for any general readers interested in contemporary world issues, such as terrorism, global governance, environmental security, power shifts, migration, global social movements, human security and nuclear threats, among others. In particular, it will be useful to undergraduate and postgraduate students of political science and global politics. This book is also useful for aspirants taking the Civil Services and State Service examinations or the UGC's National Eligibility Test (NET).

1

CHAPTER

Understanding Globalization and Its Alternative Perspectives

Shruti Joshi

LEARNING OBJECTIVES

- To understand the basic concept of globalization
- To discuss the history of globalization
- To analyse the types of globalization
- To discuss the theoretical underpinnings of globalization
- To examine the alternate perspectives of globalization

Globalization, as a macrosystemic change in the global market space, political realm and world sociocultural fabric, has attracted much attention from theorists and academicians. With the shrinkage of time and space, with national economies integrating with global economies, with perforated borders and a redefined notion of sovereignty, globalization has reconfigured and reconceptualized the prevailing theorizations. Within the broader discourse, on one hand, there are the hyperglobalists, trumpeting the world of a new global dynamics under the forces of globalization, and on the other hand are the sceptics, who uphold the centrality and importance of the state. Between these two, a third view emerges in the form of the transformationalists, who try to take a middle path between the two opposing views and argue for reconceptualizing the notion of the nation state and not its demise. The present chapter is an attempt to understand the varied nuances of the concept of globalization and to explore its alternative perspectives.

Understanding Globalization

Globalization has emerged as a catch phrase in recent decade, attracting attention of academicians worldwide. It is understood as a multi-role, multi-layered phenomenon which has manifested itself into political, economic, cultural, military and ideological sphere of human existence. Owing to the progress in information and communication technology, the forces of globalization have helped in transforming the world into a global village where conditions of common consumptions of benefit occur.

Meaning and Definition

The meaning and definition of globalization, its historical trajectory and its influence on statehood have been a subject of discourse and have drawn an open-ended debate. Ramesh B. Karky could not have stated the position better when he said succinctly, that it is hard to get a single definition of globalization (Karky 2009, 75). The term has been defined and explained within the academic circle in diverse ways. A brief explanation could be as follows:

Globalization as the Narrowing of Time and Space

With the advent of information and communication technologies and of the modern transport system, distances are getting shorter and events in one part of the world reach other parts instantaneously. In this way, globalization has helped in transforming the world into one global society. This theory regarding globalization as the 'compression of time and space' is upheld by many thinkers, such as James Mittelman, Tomas Larsson, Walters, Roland Robertson, and so on.

BOX 1.1:   Globalization: Key Definitions

According to Mittelman (2006, 64), globalization can be defined as 'a compression of time and space in a way that events in one part of the world have instantaneous effects on distant locations'.

Sharma and Bareth (2004, 10) hold, 'In the era of globalization, geographical distances are waning away and territorial boundaries are no longer impediments'.

In the same way, Walters (1995, 3) conceives of globalization as 'a social process in which geographic obstacles to social and cultural arrangements lose importance and where people are becoming increasingly aware that they lose importance'.

Swedish journalist Tomas Larsson, in his book *The Race to the Top: The Real Story of Globalization* (2001, 9) states that 'globalization is the process of world shrinkage, of distances getting shorter, things moving closer. It pertains to the increasing ease with which somebody on one side of the world can interact, to mutual benefit, with somebody on the other side of the world'.

In the words of Robertson (1992, 8), globalization is also defined as a 'compression of the world and intensification of consciousness of the world as a whole'.

Globalization as Global Flow of Goods, Products, Services, Technology, Ideas, etc.

Globalization could also be defined as an intensification of the global flows of goods, products, services, technology, ideas, and so on, owing to the development of modern transportation and means of communication (Mittelman 2006, 64). In this regard, in 2000, the International Monetary Fund (IMF) identified four basic aspects of globalization (IMF 2000). These aspects are: flow of trade and transactions, increasing capital and investment movements, rapid migration and movement of people, and dissemination of knowledge.

Globalization as Intensification of World Social Relations

Globalization is also defined as the intensification of social relations across the globe. According to Jan Aart Scholte, it refers to processes whereby many social relations become relatively delinked from territorial geography (Onoja et al. 2004, 6). Anthony Giddens argues in this regard that, due to intensification of worldwide social relations, local happenings get shaped by events occurring many miles away and vice versa (Giddens 1990, 64). Steve Smith and John Baylis also consider globalization as the process of increasing interconnectedness between societies such that events in one part of the world exhibit effects on peoples and societies far away (Onaja et al. 2004, 6).

Thus, one way of understanding globalization is by referring to it as a process where intense interdependence occurs between people all around this planet. People get linked together, economically and socially, by trade, investments and governance. These links are spurred by market liberalization and information, communication and transportation technologies (ILO n.d.).

Globalization as Internationalization

Globalization can also be understood in terms of trans-boundary relations between nations, marked by intensive transactions and interdependence among them. This leads to the creation of a global world in which a cross-border flow of messages, ideas, merchandise, money, investments, pollutants and people occurs between nation states. On this premise, certain authors, like Hirst and Thompson, consider the global as a subset of the international, and thus globalization is considered as an intense form of internationalization (Scholte 2005, 55). However, to equate both the terms sometimes seems objectionable, since internationalization considers world social relations only in terms of political units. As such, it ignores other modes of organization, governance, identity, etc., which stand important in understanding the process of globalization.

Globalization as Universalization

Globalization is a phenomenon which facilitates spreading of various objects and experiences to people at all corners of the earth, thus making them 'worldwide' (Scholte 2005, 57). Or, in other words, understanding globalization as universalization includes a process wherein there occurs a convergence of cultural, economic, legal and political spheres worldwide. This creates conditions for standardization and homogenization. However, cultural protectionism opposes globalization in this regard.

Having glanced at these various aspects of globalization, we can converge on one operational definition and understanding of this concept, which is all-encompassing and inclusive.

Globalization not only signifies a cross-border flow of goods, products, services, technology, ideas, etc., but also exhibits intensification of world social relations. With the advancement of information and communication technologies and a modern transport system, and a subsequent narrowing of time and distance, this process manifests the transformation of the world into one global society. The emergence of one global society indicates the abolition of state-imposed regulatory and authoritative mechanisms. Thus, in the neo-liberalist perspective, the phenomenon of globalization entails all the three processes of liberalization, privatization and deregulation.

History of Globalization

Historicizing the process of globalization is a challenge since it involves a complex interaction among the economic, political, sociocultural and biological factors at different time scales of human history. Thus, the debate centres around the chronology or the timeline of the origin of this composite phenomenon. Scholars differ on such concerns as: 'Is the spread of global relations new or contemporary? Or did the trend start several generations, centuries or even millennia ago? Or is globalization a cyclical phenomenon that comes and goes from time to time?' (Scholte 2005, 19). However, the chronology of the phenomenon varies with the varied definitions that scholars adopt.

For those who define globalization in terms of internationalization or liberalization, it is a recurrent phenomenon which might have occurred previously in different points of human history. In this regard, Ian Clark has distinguished 'alternating phases of "globalization" and "fragmentation" in international history' (Scholte 2005, 19). Studies have further highlighted that the transport of merchandise, investment, migration among different parts of the world, in proportionate terms, was relatively the same in the late nineteenth century as in 2000. On this ground, some scholars argue that contemporary globalization is nothing new.

While agreeing that globalization has a long history, some other scholars view its trajectory as linear rather than cyclical. This set of scholars traces back the history of globalization to ancient civilizations. Scholars such as Andre Gunder Frank and Barry Gills argue that 'the existence of the same world system in which we live stretches back at least 5,000 years' (Frank and Gills 1993, 3). They trace the earliest forms of globalization to the trade link between the Sumerian civilization and the Indus valley civilization. In the later ages, evidences suggest that there were not only strong trading ties between countries such as India, Egypt, Greece and the Roman Empire, but that regular business links were also established between the Parthian empire, the Roman Empire and the Han dynasty. Trade routes such as the Silk Road facilitated the trade links tremendously. The Islamic period in the medieval age, when the Jewish and Muslim trades started venturing out for trade purposes, emerged as yet important epoch in the history of globalization. The introduction of the postal service in China and the invention of paper gave a further fillip to this process. Expeditions carried out by scholars such as Columbus and Vasco da Gama led to the discovery of new countries, which facilitated further trade links and interconnectedness around the globe. In fact, some view the period after 1500 as inaugurating 'a genuinely global epoch of world history'. They see globalization in relation to the 'big bang' significance of 1492, when Christopher Columbus stumbled on the Americas in search of spices, and 1498, when Vasco da Gama made an end run around Africa and snatched monopoly rents away from the Arab and Venetian spice traders (Bentley 1996, 768–769). In fact, these were two important and historical events. But still, scholars such as James Tracy of the early modern world expressed their scepticism about the 1490s big bang theory (Bentley 1996, 749–770).

According to Bentley, 'even before 1500, trade networks reached almost all regions of Eurasia and sub-Saharan Africa and large volumes of commerce encouraged specialisation of agricultural and industrial production' (Bentley 1999, 7). Frank also believes that 'there was a single global world economy with a worldwide division of labour and multilateral trade from 1500 onward' (Frank 1998, 52).

Another view which seems relevant here is the role of African countries such as Ghana in facilitating the early development of Western European capitalism through providing gold, slaves and raw materials in the early sixteenth century. The gold provided by West African countries such as Ghana was necessary and even helped Europe's long-distance trade with Arab and Asian countries (Howard 1978, 17). According to J. D. Fage, 'by the beginning of 16th century about 100,000 pounds worth of gold was travelling annually from Ghana to Portugal, whereas, Sylvia Harrop believes it was around 350,000 pounds per annum' (Howard 1978, 28). Therefore, it seems that around the sixteenth century, the world witnessed the emergence of a European world economy based upon the capitalist mode of production. However, critics of this theory do believe that long-distance trade has been overemphasized by students of the early modern period and that the international economy was poorly integrated before 1800.

The exchange of merchandise and trade relations within the world were further accelerated with the advent of the Industrial Revolution in the nineteenth century. 'In this fashion, Roland Robertson has spoken of a "germination phase" of globalization between the early fifteenth and the mid-eighteenth centuries and a "take off" period from the middle of the nineteenth century' (Scholte 2005, 19). Within this phase, the processes of industrialization and colonization made countries around the world into consumers of the European market.

Tracing globalization to recent decades, scholars such as Michael Porter and the world systems theorist Christopher Chase-Dunn have situated the commencement of globalization in the late nineteenth century. For them, globalization in its true sense emerged after the Second World War, when Afro-Asian countries became independent and started framing their own economic system and trade relations with rest of the world. The establishment of the United Nations (UN) and World Trade Organization (WTO) emerged as milestones in the history of globalization. Thus, free trade was facilitated and organizations such as the WTO provided a unique platform to settle trade and commercial disputes.

Some others have linked the dawn of globalization with the advent of jet aeroplanes and the mushrooming of computer networks. In this light, they have linked this process to the present times. 'From such a perspective, current history is experiencing a "first global revolution" and a sudden leap to new realities' (Scholte 2005, 20).

As far as the future course of globalization is concerned, scholars again have offered divergent views. The first perspective in this regard is that the twenty-first century will witness the continuation of this overarching process. It is not necessary that the rate of this process should accelerate, but it will go along. A second perspective in this regard suggests that the process will get arrested or decelerated once it reaches a particular tableland. The third prediction considers globalization as a cyclical process which will witness rising global interconnectedness succeeded by another phase of descent. Consequently, the last perspective anticipates the process of 'de-globalization', under the forces of nationalist and regional forces.

Thus, the history and future course of globalization are mired in deep-seated controversies and remain open to debate.

Dimensions of Globalization

Economic Globalization

Economic globalization involves four distinct factors (Figure 1.1): production, distribution, management, and trade and finance (Sørensen 1998, 83–100). The key features of economic globalization are:

First, there is integration of the national economies due to the mushrooming of multinational corporations (MNCs) and transnational corporations (TNCs). Actually, this took place in the 1960s and 1970s,

FIGURE 1.1   Dimensions of Globalization

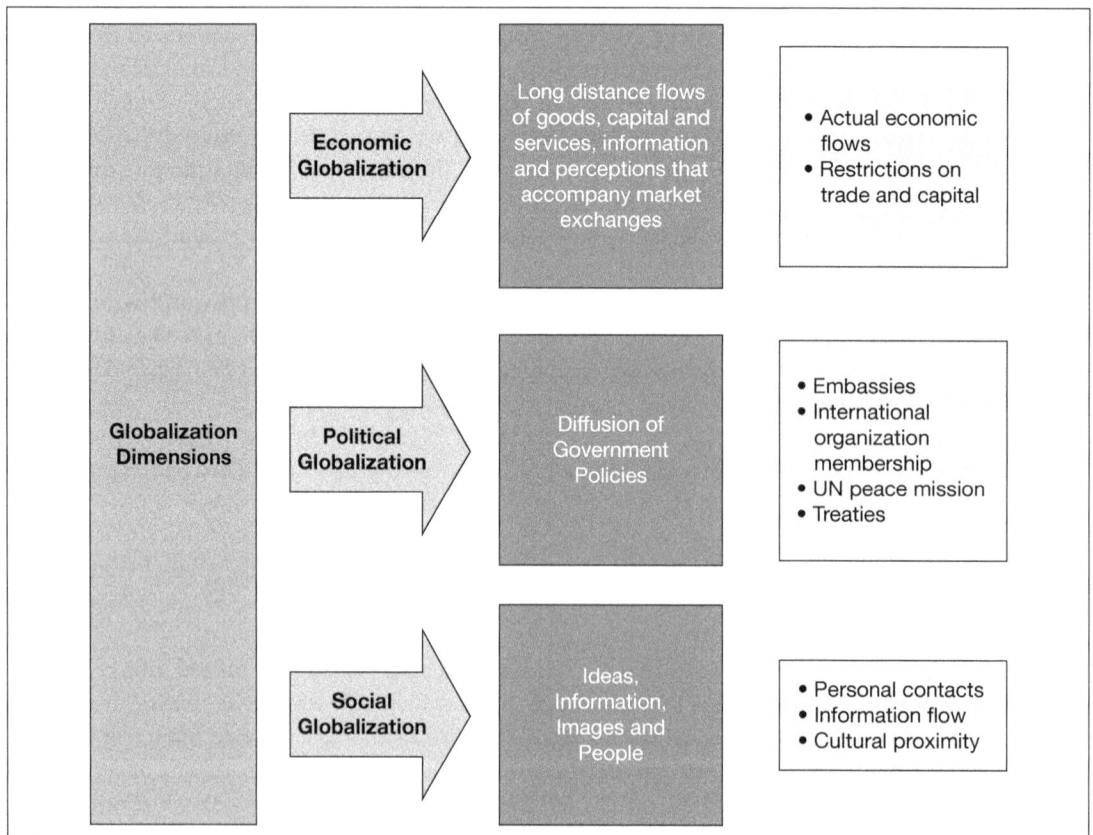

Source: www.slideshare.net (modified).

when American MNCs started progressing immensely. The pace of the world economy further accelerated with the growth of Japanese and West European MNCs, and foreign direct investments (FDIs) arising from them. In a relatively short span, newly industrialized countries such as Taiwan and South Korea also emerged as key players in the global economy. Thus, with the rise of MNCs, TNCs and FDIs, national economies got integrated with global economy. However, one important implication of economic globalization is the increasing power of MNCs in such a way that power gets shifted from the states to these MNCs (Strange 1996, 365–369).

Second, there is an important transformation in financial markets and systems, which is often termed as financial globalization. Under massive economic integration, financial flows have increased, including portfolio-type transactions. As an effect of this, national capital becomes integrated with international financial capital and gets affected by it. For instance, stock-market trading in the New York Stock Exchange affects financial hubs such as Tokyo and Hong Kong. Another caveat of financial globalization is the growing interconnectivity of world cities, not nations. This process further gets accelerated with the development of information and communication technology. An ill effect of this could be that national economies become vulnerable to global economic turbulence. For instance, the financial crisis in East Asia (1997–1998) and US sub-prime crisis not only affected the economy of that region, but many countries worldwide as well. This clearly illustrates the fact that under the aegis of globalization, it becomes difficult for the states to control trans-boundary financial movement and keep economic sovereignty intact.

Third, economic derivatives such as markets, commodities, production and business organization have all attained a global perspective. This results in the process of economic liberalization, which is marked by liberalization of trade, facilitated by internationalization of production and markets, swift global movement of people and material, and global competition.

However, it has often been argued that economic globalization and its related processes have kept the economic sovereignty of the states at crossroads. The mushrooming of MNCs, business process outsourcing (BPOs) and multilateral economic pacts urging free trade under the WTO regime has no longer kept economic sovereignty an exclusive phenomenon of nation states. Elaborating, we can say that in the era of globalization, with the flooding of global products, national economies have become part of global economies. As a result, national governments are losing control of national economic policies and their own economic future.

The growing hegemony of the Global North over the Global South through multilateral institutions such as the IMF and the World Bank further endangers the economic sovereignty of the developing world. The economic policymaking of the developing South gets influenced by these global bodies.

In extreme arguments, economic globalization is considered to put an end to the system of independent sovereign states and thus leads to the erosion, loss and diminution of nation states. This argument is explicitly presented in publications such as *The End of the Nation State* (Ohmae 1995) and *The Retreat of the State* (Strange 1996). A possible reason for this could be that growing economic globalization signals the supremacy or triumph of the market over the nation state and of economics over politics (Haas and Litan 1998, 2–6).

Political Globalization

Political globalization is interpreted as 'the shifting reach of political power, authority and forms of rule' (Held and McGrew 1998, 219–243). Political globalization could be understood in the following ways:

First, it represents a process wherein the political relations between countries become closely and deeply linked (Held and McGrew 1998, 219–243). Due to this, domestic policies get affected by international policies. Under the process of globalization, the distinction between domestic and international policies has become insignificant.

Second, political globalization also means the emergence of international organizations and regimes, transnational bodies and non-state actors whose activities spill on to the international sphere. This in turn affects the authority of the nation states (Held and McGrew 1998, 219–243). In other words, political globalization indicates institutionalization of international political structures (Chase-Dunn 1999, 187–215). In the era of complex interdependence, the non-state actors—or as Rosenau (1990, 327) calls them, 'sovereignty-free' actors—such as MNCs, international governmental and non-governmental organizations and ethnic groups influence the state's authority (Keohane and Nye 1989).

Third, political globalization demonstrates the existence of global governance at the international level, which includes the emergence of both specialized and general international organizations. This phenomenon has been termed 'global governance' by Craig Murphy (1994) and others. The general organizations that have emerged at a global level include the Concert of Europe, the League of Nations and the United Nations (Chase-Dunn 1999, 187–215). Thus, political globalization indicates the emergence of global institutions for addressing global issues. It also refers to the development of 'global civil societies' which work on global issues, sometimes in isolation, sometimes through collaboration with each other and sometimes through international organizations such as the UN (Bretherton 1996, 8–9).

Fourth, under the rising tide of political globalization, now issues in global politics are no longer confined to geopolitical concerns only, that is, security and territorial issues. Rather, its study has expanded to include non-security issues (which are sometimes referred as low politics), namely, economic, social and environmental questions.

Fifth, with the integration of national and global politics, the present era of political globalization involves the emergence of regional and global law, which in turn poses a challenge to state sovereignty (Held and McGrew 1998, 219–243).

Thus, we can argue that national boundaries are no longer intact and are perforated in this era of globalization, thereby placing political sovereignty in peril. In such a situation, the economic and political policies also get influenced by supranational factors and no longer remain the exclusive domain of democratic nation states.

At the same time, in this era of globalization, the centralized nation state is giving way to both supranational and subnational institutions. This signifies a major change in the traditional notion of the nation state. Also, the role of the nation state in a global world has become largely a regulatory one. While the domestic role of the nation state remains largely unchanged, states that were previously isolated are now forced to engage with one another to set international commerce policies.

Cultural Globalization

Cultural globalization means the intensification and expansion of cultural flows across the globe (Steger 2009, 11). This includes a free flow of cultural norms, values, ideas, lifestyle, food habits and so on, across national borders.

This process is marked by the common consumption of cultures that have been diffused by the Internet, popular culture, media and international travel. Cultural globalization thus involves the formation of shared norms and knowledge with which people associate their individual and collective cultural identities (Rothlauf and de Gruyter 2014, 3). This free flow of cultural norms, values and ideas across the globe makes it clear that globalization can affect the cultural sphere of human existence in multiple ways.

First, it can have a heterogenizing effect at the cultural level, wherein due to the expansion of information and communication technology, the cultural uniqueness of diverse regions of the world might be recognized and accepted by other societies and regions. This process also enriches and enhances cultural diversity around the globe.

Second, the same information and communication technology revolution can also posit a homogenizing effect at the cultural level. Within this process, the mighty culture affects the local culture and even becomes the dominant culture of that particular region. This may be seen in terms of the overwhelming expansion of the cultural norms and ideas of the Global North over the Global South. This results in the loss of individual or local cultures.

Apart from these two, another phenomenon of cultural hybridization has also evolved. This means that at times, diverse cultures get fused or hybridized and assume altogether a new shape.

Thus, in the era of globalization, cultural sovereignty is being transformed under the rising tide of an uninterrupted inflow of ideas and products from across the territorial border and their subsequent amalgamation into local and regional taste.

Cultural globalization can be best understood by analysing the new phenomenon of 'McDonaldization'. It is a process of the growing dominance of the principles of fast-food restaurants all around the world. On one hand, the growing chains of McDonald's across the world reflect the homogenizing effect of cultural globalization. On the other hand, McDonald's is probably one of the best examples of how TNCs adapt their global brand and products to the local marketplace and customize their menus to suit local tastes in various countries. This phenomenon is referred to as 'glocalization' (global + local). Despite having nearly 70 million customers daily in over 30,000 restaurants in nearly 120 countries worldwide, McDonald's is constantly trying to expand and increase its market share. The following is a list of some ways that McDonald's has adapted its brand and products to increase its market share:

- In Muslim countries, pork has been removed from the menu.
- In Hindu countries, beef has been removed from the menu.
- In Muslim countries, halal food is used and in Jewish countries, kosher food is used.
- Certain local festivals or customs may be celebrated, that is, during Ramadan in Muslim countries, McDonald's will offer iftar buffets at the breaking of fast.
- The types of burgers/products are changed to local tastes, that is, there is McRice in Indonesia and McAloo Tikki in India.

This phenomenon of TNCs adapting themselves to local culture and taste is the relative inverse of Americanization, which aims at suppressing the local preferences in favour of goods dictated by foreign entities.

The effect of globalization on cultural sovereignty can therefore be understood on two planes: it could lead to a narrowing of sovereignty in the sense that expansion of a dominant culture in different regions of the world could be a threat to the authenticity of local goods and taste.

On the other hand, cultural globalization has also led to the expanding of sovereignty, in the sense that a local culture, lifestyle or taste has tried to influence global products and brands. For example, food brands such as KFC or McDonald's have tried to modify or introduce new food forms, like 'paneertika' or 'allotika', suiting the Indian palate or tastes. This amalgamation of global food forms with regional taste has not only changed the global predominant taste and form but has also modified the authentic local or desi taste so as to meet consumer demands and appetite.

An attack on cultural sovereignty in this era of globalization can also be understood by analysing the new phenomenon of 'fusions', which has become an interesting field of analysis. Cultural practices including traditional music, dance, recipes, lifestyles and styles of dressing can be lost or turned into a fusion of traditions under the forces of globalization. Globalization is now expanding its scope such that the term often includes hybrid subgenres such as 'world fusion', 'global fusion', 'ethnic fusion', 'fusion music', 'fusion dance', etc.

Globalization of Ideas

The globalization of ideas is another important dimension of the process of globalization. It signifies the free flow of social, economic, political and cultural ideas all across the globe due to compression of time and space. The globalization of ideas posits two interesting effects. First, the free flow of ideas within diverse regions could help in generating a cosmopolitan culture (Bretherton 1996, 9–10). Second, with the globalization of ideas, new notions have emerged in the international scenario, namely, global warming, global citizenship, world citizenship, world peace, international security and international trade, which appeal at a global level.

Military/Security Globalization

Military globalization was defined by David Held as the process which embodies:

a. an expanding network of worldwide military ties and relations among the political units of the world,
b. key military technological innovations (from steamships to satellites), which over time, have reconstituted the world into a single geostrategic space (Held et al. 1999, 88),
c. globalization of the war system,
d. and the global system of arms production and transfers, which means that arms get produced and transferred globally within different nations (Held et al. 1999, 89).

For Robert Keohane and Joseph Nye, in this era of complex interdependence, military globalization also implies firmer integration of the armed forces around the world into the global military system (Keohane and Nye 1989, 196). All these processes are linked to technological development, which further creates a condition of interdependence and complexity at the global level (Krishnan 2008, 158).

Another dimension of military globalization is that states are becoming more sensitive to and conscious of security and military developments in other regions of the world, due to increasing financial, trade and economic relations (Chan 2000, 391–403; Held and McGrew 1998, 230).

Actually, globalization has widened the scope of security and, in this regard, has redefined the traditional agenda of national security. Traditionally, national security is understood as 'the acquisition, deployment and use of military force to achieve national goals' (Held and McGrew 1998, 226). But now, globalization has changed the entire notion of 'security'. International security, in this regard, now also includes the entire gamut of environmental issues such as global warming, ozone depletion and acid rain.

BOX 1.2: David Held

David Held (born 1951) is Master of University College, Durham, and Professor of Politics and International Relations at Durham University. He is a prominent British political theorist, active in the field of political science and international relations.

Professor Held has been pursuing a multilevel inquiry into the nature and changing form of national and international politics. The empirical dimensions of his work have included books such as *Global Transformations: Politics, Economics and Culture* (1999), *Globalization/Anti-globalization: Beyond the Great Divide* (2007), *Global Inequality: Patterns and Explanations* (2007) and *Gridlock: Why Global Cooperation is Failing When We Need it Most* (2013). These books map the changing global context of politics, how the world has become increasingly interconnected, and how failures of leadership and negotiation at the global level are creating a breakdown of multilateralism and global governance.

He has also essayed a critical evaluation of the concepts of democracy, sovereignty, governance and cosmopolitanism, among other concepts. Books that have explored these themes include: *Democracy and the Global Order: From the Modern State to Cosmopolitan Governance* (1999), *Models of Democracy* (2006), *Cosmopolitanism: Ideals and Realities* (2010).

Professor Held, in his works like *Global Covenant: The Social Democratic Alternative to the Washington Consensus* (2004) and *Debating Globalization* (2005) has tried to explore how and in what ways one can move beyond the crises and dilemmas of politics and governance in the contemporary world.

His main research interests include the study of globalization, the changing forms of democracy and the prospects of regional and global governance.

Source: Profiles, David Held, https://www.dur.ac.uk/sgia/profiles/?id=10282; also see http://newspaperslibrary. org/articles/eng/David_Held.

Theoretical Underpinning of Globalization

Theories of globalization have been categorized under five heads: liberalism, political realism, Marxism, postmodernism, feminism and postcolonialism. Each one of them carries several variations.

Theory of Liberalism

Globalization may be understood, in terms of liberalism, in the following way:

The liberal theory of globalization believes that the 'process of globalization', is a result of 'natural' human desires for economic welfare and political liberty. In other words, human activities to acquire and enhance material well-being and to exercise basic freedoms have resulted in trans-planetary connectivity. They have also given rise to the interlinking and spread of humanity across the planet. All this has resulted in the process of globalization.

For liberals, the process of globalization fructifies in the form of technological advancement, including transportation, communication and information processing, which also results in other types of advancement.

One of the primary focuses of liberals is the spreading of liberal democracy, democratic values and norms worldwide. This results in the globalization of dominant ideas and values around the globe. While fulfilling this objective, they even demonstrate a mechanism of suitable legal and institutional arrangement to enable markets to promote and establish liberal democracy further. Therefore liberalists, in a way, stress upon the necessity of constructing institutional infrastructure to support globalization. Liberals believe that all this results in technical standardization, administrative harmonization, laws of contract and guarantees of property rights.

In a nutshell, liberals explain globalization as a result of technological advances and the construction of suitable institutional infrastructure.

However, there are several critiques of the liberal theory of globalization:

First, since liberalism is a market-driven philosophy and the market is a profit-based institution, liberal theory lacks a sense of social responsibility. There is also very little space for welfare activities, including sectors such as health and education. It therefore seems that the liberalist neglects the social aspect of globalization.

Second, it is difficult to assume that all people think equally materialistically. It is also not possible that all people are equally desirous of increasing globality in their lives.

Third, liberals also overlook the phenomenon of power structure. There are structural and institutional power inequalities which are clearly visible in different types of societies. These inequalities contribute to power hierarchies between different states, classes, cultures, races and sexes. In fact, these inequalities even influence resource distribution and are visible in promoting globalization and shaping its course.

Theory of Political Realism

Within this theory, globalization is understood in terms of power, power struggle and national interest. This may be understood in the following way:

Political realists are more interested in the question of 'power'. Their thoughts move around the issues of power in international politics and inter-state relations. For them, the issues of state power, the pursuit of national interest and conflict between states are of key concern. According to them, states are self-serving, with objectives based upon their own national interests. These national interests are different for different countries, which places them in a power struggle. These power struggles are persistent in nature and can be traced throughout history.

At this point, there emerge two theories of political realism which help in understanding the process of globalization. One is the theory of 'balance of power' and the other is the theory of the 'hegemonic state'.

Some of the scholars stand for the concept of balance of power, which was prudent not just during the cold war phase of international politics, but also in the phase of globalization. After the disintegration of the former Union of Soviet Socialist Republics (the USSR), the world seemed unipolar, with the United States of America (the US) leading the world. But slowly the hegemony of the US was challenged by other powers and the world drifted into a multipolar world. The reason for such a power-block dispersal and a multipolar world was globalization, and related phenomena, such as technological developments, better communication systems and the spread of sophisticated weapons, including nuclear technology. Realist theorists, in this regard, concentrate on the activities of Great Britain, China, France, Japan, the US and some other large states. Thus, within the thesis of 'balance of power', the political realists highlight the issues of power and power struggles and the role of states in generating global relations and furthering the process of globalization.

Another group within the political realists supports the theory of the 'hegemonic state' in understanding the process of globalization. It suggests that a dominant state can bring stability to the world order. At the same time, the 'hegemonic state' maintains and defines international rules and institutions in a way that fulfils its own national interests. This becomes possible because of a free flow of dominant products, services, markets, ideas and so on, from the 'hegemonic state' due to the forces of globalization. The role of the US as a 'Big Brother' in international affairs and its dominance at the global institutional and policymaking level reflects the same view.

Thus, for political realists, globalization may be understood as a strategy for the contest for power between several major states in contemporary world politics.

There are several criticisms regarding this theory:

Critics argue that political realists focus exclusively upon power and neglect other dimensions of globalization, namely, cultural, ecological, economic and psychological, which are not reducible to power politics.

The power theorists also neglect the importance and role of other actors in contributing to globalization. These actors are substantial authorities, macro-regional institutions, global agencies and private-sector bodies. Additionally, power relations along the lines of class, ethnicity, culture and gender, which affect the course of globalization, are also neglected under this theory.

Theory of Marxism

This theory of globalization may be understood in the following way:

Marxism is principally concerned with modes of production, class exploitation through unjust distribution, and social emancipation through the abolition of capitalism. Marxists believes that the process of globalization is enhanced by trans-boundary capital movement, marked by profit-making on one hand and surplus accumulation on the other. In other words, for Marxists, globalization is an outgrowth of the process of capitalism. In this way, Marxists reject the hypothesis of both liberalists and political realists regarding globalization.

The neo-Marxists in dependency and world-system theories examine the capitalist system and its accumulation, its working mechanism and its disadvantages on a global scale. They also examine the growth of capitalism and its influence in core capitalist and peripheral or semi-capitalist countries.

Some major criticisms regarding this theory are:

Some critics argue that considering globalization as a result of profit-making and surplus accumulation cannot be justified, as there are other factors as well which contributed to the commencement of globalization.

Critics further argue that Marxists have offered a narrow analysis of the process of globalization. While it exclusively deals with class division and exploitation, there are other divisions as well, based on cultures, genders, etc. For example, issues like West-centric cultural domination and racism cannot be explained by the class dynamics within capitalism. Though class is an important element of power in globalization, it is not the sole contributing element.

Theory of Postmodernism

The postmodernist theory of globalization may be understood in the following way:

It highlights the significance of structural power in the construction of identities, norms and knowledge. It understands society in terms of the power of knowledge, which is shaped by power structures. According to this, specific knowledge structures support particular power hierarchies. In this sense, the dominant framework of knowledge in modern society is 'rationality'. This means the ability to question and to find out 'why'. This leads to a kind of cultural imperialism and subordination. It is this aspect of cultural domination and subordination which becomes an important feature of cultural globalization.

Critics point out that, instead of focusing upon the problem of globalization, postmodernist theory focuses more upon injecting its own superiority. In this way, Western rationalism controls indigenous cultures and other non-modern lifestyles. A significant example in this regard could be the subordination of the African traditional religions (ATR) in Africa by Europeans.

Theory of Feminism

This theory emphasizes the social construction of masculinity and femininity. It differentiates between sex and gender, and further talks about the subjection of women in societies around the world. For feminists, globalization is a product of patriarchal domination and unequal gender relations.

Feminists argue that though women folk have contributed tremendously in the development of their respective families and societies, still they are among the most marginalized sections of society throughout the history. As far as global communication, finance and governance are concerned, women are still marginalized and silenced, and their rights are still violated.

The status of women all around the globe is based upon their structural subordination in comparison to men. Therefore, the main concern of feminists is to improve conditions and raising the status of women in comparison to their male counterparts.

Feminist theorists try to identify the role of women in the process of globalization. They also attempt to explore mechanisms and support systems to increase women's participation in the process of globalization, to make their presence felt. With the help of all this, feminists believe that women will be visible and will get their share in resource distribution.

Theory of Postcolonialism

The postcolonial view emerged in the last decade of the twentieth century. It was a corollary to globalization, especially in the developing countries.

This view believes that though colonialism has ended, its effects are still visible in the political, economic, cultural and social (mainly through media) lives of colonial territories of the world. Postcolonialists, therefore, aim at countering these impacts of colonialism upon the people and societies of these erstwhile colonies. At the same time, they believe that the colonial empires were established on the false myth of 'supremacy of whites over the blacks'. They argue that even after the end of colonialism and the independence of these Afro-Asian colonies, the natives of colonial empires still consider the inhabitants of colonial territories, or 'non-whites', as inferior and less civilized.

Postcolonialists opine that the impact of colonial powers over the Afro-Asian world is still evident in areas such as sports, language and culture. For example, English, which at one point of human history originated in Britain, has expanded its scope through the entire length and breadth of the globe, thereby marginalizing the mother tongues of many developing countries. Similarly, many former colonial territories such as India, Pakistan, South Africa and the West Indies excel in sports such as cricket, which were once exported by the colonial power of Britain to these colonies. While doing so, these sports are surpassing the traditional sports of these former colonies. What's more, these former colonial territories still remain under Western domination, especially in the cultural sphere. All this has led to the origin of a new form of colonialism, called 'neocolonialism'.

As far as the postcolonialist view on globalization is concerned, it does not consider globalization as a benign or beneficial process for the developing world or the former colonial territories. The reason is that it considers globalization as an offshoot of colonialism itself. For postcolonialists, globalization is an exploitative mechanism to fulfil the ambitions of powerful countries which were once colonial powers. These powerful countries are influencing the developing world in political, social and economic spheres. This influence is perpetuated by institutions such as the IMF, the World Bank and other supranational institutions which influence the policymaking of the developing countries. For postcolonialists, globalization is an unequal process which leads to unequal resource sharing and distribution.

Postcolonialists even argue that through the process of globalization, as distances are getting shorter and interconnectedness is increasing across the globe, the dominant culture of Western world might spread across the globe and erode the local and indigenous cultures of the developing world. This phenomenon is called cultural imperialism. Postcolonialists also believe that this could lead to the replacement of local cultures by one single standard culture, also called 'cultural homogenization'.

A severe criticism of postcolonialists could be that they conceive the differences between the East and the West or the developing and the developed world as unbridgeable and their interests as irreconcilable. In doing so, they ignore all possibilities of 'universal aspirations' and 'universal interests'.

Alternative Perspectives on Globalization

There is a massive discourse within the academic circle regarding any single definition of globalization, its characteristics, classifications, impact, causes, and so on. At this juncture, there are three schools of thought, or alternative perspectives, for decoding the process of globalization.

These are: the hyperglobalists, the transformationalists and the sceptics. Each school of thought assesses the distinctive features of globalization from different perspectives.

Hyperglobalists

Hyperglobalists such as Ohmae and R. Reich are very enthusiastic about the overwhelming effect of the process of globalization. For them, globalization, and the subsequent global economy, has a profound impact on politics, markets, ideas and the world at large. Ohmae argues, 'Today's world economy is genuinely borderless. Information, capital and innovation flow all over the world at top speed, enabled by technology and fuelled by consumers' desire for access to the best and the least expensive products' (Ohmae 1995, inside front cover). In the words of Reich, 'We are living through the transformation that will rearrange the politics and economics of the coming century. There will be no national products or technologies, no national corporations, no national industries. There will no longer be national economies' (Reich 1992, 3). For them, globalization is a progressive and socially desirable process, without any precedent in the history of human civilization. Also, its effect is legitimate and irrepressible in terms of creating a world social and economic order, which surpasses national borders.

According to them, with the rising global market and technological progress, the significance of the nation state is declining. They argue that the phenomenon of globalization creates conditions of global civilization. This means, markets get integrated at the apex global level, MNCs become carriers of economic growth, ideas gets globalized and prevailing hierarchical structures get deconstructed. Hyperglobalists argue that under these conditions, the role of the state as the supreme decision-making authority in both domestic and international spheres gets taken over by international institutions.

Hyberglobalists view the future course of human civilization under the forces of globalization. They predict that the world will transform into a fully integrated global society, with a common set of values, ideas, culture, economy, and so on. In other words, the heterogeneous cultures will get diluted under the liberal cultural forces and get homogenized. In this sense, a well-known assumption about the 'end of history' is generated, which implies that the modern global capitalism along with liberal democracy will represent the last stage of socio-economic evolution (Fukuyama 1992).

The aforementioned approach thus provides a deterministic character to globalization. 'Globalization is seen as a kind of final stage in the spontaneous and self-enforcing process of creating a global society, as the most efficient model of society, which stops the further process of selection of types of socio-economic order' (Stefanović 2008, 265). This conception of globalization as an all-pervasive phenomenon with overwhelming influence is even reflected in the works of liberalism-oriented authors such as Theodore Levitt and Thomas Friedman as well as proponents of neoclassical economic theory such as J. D. Sachs, Friedman and others.

Sceptics

As opposed to the hyperglobalists, the sceptics, such as P. Hirst and G. Thompson consider globalization as largely a myth. For them, the arguments of the hyperglobalists regarding the furore of globalization are merely an exaggeration, and the spread of global trade has been uneven, being concentrated in the major developed economies of Europe, the Asia-Pacific and North America.

BOX 1.3: Yoshihiro Francis Fukuyama

Yoshihiro Francis Fukuyama (born 27 October 1952), an American political scientist and political economist, is the Olivier Nomellini Senior Fellow at the Freeman Spogli Institute for International Studies (FSI) and the Mosbacher Director of FSI's Center on Democracy, Development, and the Rule of Law (CDDRL).

Dr Fukuyama has written widely on issues relating to democratization and the international political economy. His book *The End of History and the Last Man,* was published by Free Press in 1992 and has appeared in over 20 foreign editions. Fukuyama is known for this book, which argued that the worldwide spread of liberal democracy and the free-market capitalism of the West and its lifestyle may signal the end point of humanity's sociocultural evolution and become the final form of human government. Dr Fukuyama predicted the eventual global triumph of political and economic liberalism. However, his subsequent book *Trust: The Social Virtues and the Creation of Prosperity* (1995) modified his earlier position to acknowledge that culture cannot be cleanly separated from economics.

Source: https://cddrl.fsi.stanford.edu/people/fukuyama.

This group of theoreticians, who express scepticism with regard to the ubiquity of the process of globalization, poses a strong critique of globalization. For them, the level of liberalization, openness and integration of the world economy is not unprecedented, as argued by hyperglobalists.

Sceptics believe that nation states and national economies still hold significance and play a seminal role in promoting liberalization and cross-border activity. Many economic and political policies which are crucial for the existence and nurturing of citizens are still performed by nation states.

As opposed to the hyperglobalist argument that national economies are losing their significance within global economies, sceptics argue that the international economy is an aggregate of nationally located economies. In fact, according to them, the international economy is still determined by national economies (Hirst and Thompson 1999, 10).

At the same time, they strongly oppose the view of the hyperglobalists that globalization is giving birth to a world society or a world economy. According to them, along with the rise of overarching global institutions, the world is witnessing the emergence of regional bodies which are shaping world politics in their own unique way. 'The creation of regional blocks as the essential characteristic of the world economy offers argumentation that the world economy is less integrated than it was in the late nineteenth century' (Held and McGrew 2007, 5).

Sceptics also raise doubts on the homogenizing capability of globalization and its forces as far as social relations, culture and ideas are concerned. According to them, the possibility of heterogeneity and, at times, hybridization also exists. In fact, globalization has provided new space for the assertion of identity and resistance within civil society. Huntington, in this regard, opines that the possibility of a single unified world is being reduced. A possible reason could be the rise of radical resistance within individual cultures, which in the end can lead to a conflict of civilizations (Huntington 1997).

Thus, scepticism is expressed not only in terms of the presence and impact of globalization, but also in terms of sustainability of the unification which it produces at the global level (Stefanović 2008, 267).

Transformationalists

In between these two extreme positions is the third school of thought, represented by scholars such as James N. Rosenau, Giddens, Scholte, Manuel Castells and Gregorio Walerstein.

They assume that globalization plays a tremendous role in restructuring the world order and in creating rapid economic, political and social changes. In the words of Held and McGrew, 'Globalization denotes the intensification of worldwide social relations and interactions such that distant events acquire very localised impacts and vice versa' (Held and McGrew 2007, 2). Through globalization, individuals' day-to-day activities are increasingly influenced by events happening on the other side of the world. Conversely, local lifestyle habits also tend to get global attention (Holmes 2009, 134).

Transformationalists thus are more moderate and assume a centrist position as far as the presence and effect of globalization process are concerned. For these scholars, though globalization has been a distinctive and significant development in the contemporary world, its effect, scale and consequences need to be evaluated in a qualified and controlled way. For them, it is not the only process which has transformed human history. Scholte argues that the process of globalization unfolds alongside and is closely interlinked with other major social trends, such as shifts in the structures of production, governance, identity and knowledge (Scholte 2005, 19).

The argument of the transformationalists is that through globalization, the world not only witnesses the emergence of a new 'sovereignty regime' but also experiences the emergence of powerful new non-territorial forms of economic and political organizations in the global domain, such as MNCs, transnational social movements, international regulatory agencies, and so on. In this sense, the world order can no longer be conceived as purely state-centric or even primarily state-governed, as authority has become increasingly diffused among public and private agencies at the local, national, regional and global levels (Held et al. 2000, 9).

Globalization, according to this school, may create new networks and dissolve old ones. As Held argues in this regard, under the forces of globalization, relationships among nations and people will be reconfigured and power relationships will get restructured (Parker 2005, 21). They thus take a middle course and argue that the process of globalization will not lead to the end of nation states, but rather a reconstruction of nation states.

Out of all three, the views of the transformationalists seems most balanced and poised.

Concluding Observations

Globalization may be understood as a worldwide movement, characterized by intense interdependence and interaction among nations, which constitutes a phenomenal effect on the economy, cultures, political systems and also physical well-being of people at large. Economically, it is an act or process of creating a global world, marked by an increasingly integrated economy, facilitated by free trade, free flow of capital and availability of a cheap labour market, aided by the intense development of information technology. In other words, it enables the development of a globally integrated economic system. Culturally, it facilitates the interaction and interpenetration of ideas, norms, values and ways of life among nations. Politically, it creates conditions for governance at the supranational level, above national and regional levels. Within this multidimensional aspect of globalization, the role of the state and its position in global politics gets manifested by alternative perspective holders, namely, hyperglobalists, sceptics and transformationalists. Amidst the two extreme perspectives—one arguing the demise of the nation state within the aegis of globalization, and the other upholding the existence and significance of the state system—the moderate view of the transformationalists appears most accurate. In fact, the process of globalization has not ended the existence of nation states; rather, it has created conditions wherein new patterns have evolved, state functions have been restructured and power relations reconfigured.

Summary

- The phenomenon of globalization may be understood in diverse ways. It may be interpreted as an intensification of world social relations or the narrowing of time and space or as a global flow of goods, products, services, technology and ideas. Some scholars explain this process in terms of internationalization, liberalization and universalization.
- Deciphering the historical trajectory of globalization is a challenge, since scholars remain divergent on this question. For some, globalization is a recurrent phenomenon, while for some it exhibits a linear trajectory. Some sets of scholars trace back the history of globalization to ancient civilizations, while some considers it a new phenomenon.

- The process of globalization has multiple dimensions. Various types of globalization might be: economic globalization, political globalization, military/security globalization, cultural globalization and globalization of ideas.
- The concept of globalization has been theorized by liberalists, realists, Marxists, postmodernists and feminists in their own peculiar ways. The vantage point of explaining globalization is different for each. While liberalists explain the process of globalization as an expansion of modernization based on and influenced by the market, realists understand globalization in terms of power relations between states. Marxists consider globalization as an outgrowth of capitalism, while for postmodernists, globalization is explained as an outcome of imperialism of rationalism. Feminist scholars, however, explain globalization on the basis of gender relations.
- As far as the nature and role of the state in the era of globalization is concerned, three alternative perspectives appear, namely, hyperglobalists, sceptics and transformationalists. Out of the two extreme views, transformationalists pose the most balanced arguments.

Suggested Questions

1. Explain the concept of globalization with suitable definitions.
2. Discuss the historical trajectory of globalization. Is it a new phenomenon or an old, recurrent process?
3. Globalization is a multidimensional phenomenon. Explain its various dimensions with suitable examples.
4. Discuss the theoretical underpinning of the concept of globalization. Illustrate the arguments of liberalists, realists, Marxists, postmodernists and feminists.
5. Discuss the alternative perspectives of understanding globalization. Which perspective explains globalization in the most appropriate way?

References

Bentley, J. H. 1996. 'Cross-cultural Interaction and Periodization in World History.' *American Historical Review* 101 (3) (June 1996): 749–770.

———. 1999. 'Asia in World History'. *Education About Asia* 4, no. 1 (Spring 1999): 5–9.

Bretherton, Charlotte. 1996. 'Introduction: Global Politics in the 1990s.' In *Global Politics: An Introduction*, edited by Charlotte Bretherton and Geoffrey Ponton. Oxford: Blackwell Publishers.

Chan, Victor D. 2000. 'Globalization and the Study of International Security.' *Journal of Peace Research* 37 (3): 391–403.

Chase-Dunn, Christopher. 1999. 'Globalization: A World-Systems Perspective.' *Journal of World-System Research* 5 (2): 187–215.

Frank, A. G. 1998. *ReOrient: Global Economy in the Asian Age*. Berkeley, CA: University of California Press.

Frank, A. G., and B. Gills, eds. 1993. *The World System: Five Hundred Years or Five Thousand?* London: Routledge.

Fukuyama, F. 1992. *The End of History and the Last Man*. New York, NY: Oxford University Press.

Giddens, A. 1990. *The Consequences of Modernity*. Stanford, CA: Stanford University Press.

Haas, R. N., and R. E. Litan. 1998. 'Globalization and Its Discontents: Navigating the Dangers of a Tangled World.' *Foreign Affairs* 77 (3): 2–6.

Held, David, and Anthony McGrew. 1998. 'The End of the Old Order? Globalization and the Prospects for World Order.' *Review of International Studies* 24 (5): 219–245.

———. 2007. *Globalization Theory: Approaches and Controversies*. Cambridge: Polity Press.

Held, David, Anthony McGrew, David Goldblatt and Jonathan Perraton. 1999. *Global Transformations: Politics, Economics and Culture*. Cambridge: Polity Press.

———. 2000. 'Global Transformations: Politics, Economics and Culture'. In *Politics at the Edge*, edited by C. Pierson et al. Political Studies Association.

Hirst, P. Q., G. F. Thompson and S. Bromley. 1999. *Globalization in Question: The International Economy and the Possibilities of Governance*, 2nd ed. Cambridge: Polity Press.

Holmes, Alison. 2009. *The Third Way: Globalisation's Legacy*. UK: Troubador Publishing Ltd.

Howard, Rhoda. 1978. *Colonialism and Underdevelopment in Ghana*. London: Croom Helm.

Huntington, Samuel P. 1997. *The Clash of Civilization? The Debate*. New York: Simon & Schuster.

ILO. n.d. *Globalization and Workers' Rights*. International Labour Office. http://www.ilo.org/actrab (accessed 10 October 2017).

IMF. 2000. 'Globalization: Threat or Opportunity?' Washington, DC: IMF Publications.

Karky, Ramesh B. 2009. 'Globalization and Least Developed Countries'. In *Contemporary Issues on Public International and Comparative Law: Essays in Honour of Professor Christian Nwachukwu Okeke*, edited by C. C. Nweze. Florida, USA: Vandeplas Publishing.

Keohane, Robert O., and Joseph S. Nye, Jr. 1989. *Power and Interdependence*. New York, NY: Harper Collins.

Krishnan, Armin. 2008. *War as Business: Technological Change and Military Service Contracting*. London & New York, NY: Routledge.

Larsson, Tomas. 2001. *The Race to the Top: The Real Story of Globalization*. Washington, DC: Cato Institute.

Mittelman, James. 2006. 'Globalization and its Critics'. In *Political Economy and the Changing Global Order*, edited by Richard Stubs and Geoffrey Underhill. Oxford: Oxford University Press.

Murphy, Craig N. 1994. *International Organization and Industrial Change: Global Governance Since 1850*. Cambridge: Polity Press.

Ohmae, Kenichi. 1995. *The End of the Nation State: The Rise of Regional Economies*. New York, NY: Free Press.

Onoja, E., V. Tarhulw, E. Kennen, and M. Dura. 2004. 'Fostering International Peace and Security in a Globalised World: The Different Facets of the Peace Process and the Continuing Challenges of the United Nations'. In *Globalization, National Development and the Law*, edited by D. A. Guobadia and Epiphany Azinge, 314–331. Proceedings of the 40th Annual Conference of the Nigerian Association of the Law Teachers, Lagos, Nigeria: Nigerian Institute of Advanced Legal Studies.

Parker, Barbara. 2005. *Introduction to Globalization and Business: Relationships and Responsibilities*. London: SAGE Publications.

Reich, Robert B. 1992. *The Work of Nations: Preparing Ourselves for 21st Century Capitalism*. New York, NY: Vintage Books.

Robertson, Roland. 1992. *Globalization: Social Theory and Global Culture*. London: SAGE Publications.

Rosenau, James N. 1988. 'Patterned Chaos in Global Life: Structure and Process in the Two Worlds of World Politics'. *International Political Science Review* 9 (4): 327–364.

Rothlauf, J. 2014. *A Global View on Intercultural Management: Challenges in a Globalized World*. Berlin: Walter de Gruyter GmBH.

Scholte, Jan Aart. 2005. *Globalization: A Critical Introduction*, 2nd ed. New York, NY: Palgrave Macmillan.

Sharma, B. M., and Roop Singh Bareth, eds. 2004. *Good Governance, Globalization and Civil Society*. Jaipur: Rawat Publications.

Sørensen, George. 1998. 'IR Theory after the Cold War'. *Review of International Studies* 24 (5): 83–100.

Stefanović, Zoran. 2008. 'Globalization: Theoretical Perspectives, Impacts and Institutional Response of the Economy'. *Facta Universitatis: Economics and Organization* 5 (3): 263–272.

Steger, Manfred. 2009. *Globalization: A Very Short Introduction*. New York, NY: Oxford University Press.

Strange, Susan. 1996. *The Retreat of the State: The Diffusion of Power in the World Economy*. Cambridge, NY: Cambridge University Press.
Waters, Malcolm. 1995. *Globalization*. London and New York, NY: Routledge.

Further Reading

Bhagwati, Jagdish. 2007. *In Defence of Globalization*. USA: Oxford University Press.
Eriksen, Thomas H. 2007. *Globalization: The Key Concepts*. Oxford: Berg Publisher.
Friedman, Thomas L. 2005. *The World Is Flat: A Brief History of the 21st Century*. New York, NY: Farrar, Straus and Giroux.
Rodrik, Dani. 2011. *The Globalization Paradox: Democracy and the Future of the World Economy*. New York, NY: W. W. Nortan.
Wolf, Martin. 2005. *Why Globalization Works*. New Haven, CT: Yale University Press.

Political Globalization: Debating Sovereignty and Territoriality

Ashutosh Trivedi

LEARNING OBJECTIVES

- To provide a basic understanding of political globalization
- To examine the concept of state sovereignty and territoriality
- To analyse the impact of globalization on the sovereignty and territoriality of nation states
- To revisit the sovereignty and territoriality debate in the era of globalization

In the era of globalization, the world is witnessing free movement of goods, services, capital, ideas and technology, surpassing national boundaries and territories. Through this process, geographical distances are waning away and territorial boundaries are no longer an impediment (Sharma and Barreth 2004, 10). With the emergence of a borderless world, it has often been argued that the state is not able to perform its gatekeeping role as effectively as it has been doing traditionally and that the role of the state as an intermediary agent is declining fast. Such is the pervasive effect of this phenomenon that no country could keep itself immune from its effect. However, under this rising tide of globalization, the traditional notion of sovereignty and territoriality has undergone a transformational shift. In other words, globalization has played a crucial role and has acted as a driving force in shaping the discourse regarding state sovereignty and territoriality. The present chapter is an attempt to explore the discourse on territoriality and the sustainability of the sovereignty of nation states.

Understanding Globalization in Terms of Sovereignty and Territoriality

The process of globalization and the increase in global connectedness have resulted in the diminution of territorial boundaries and structures (Bretherton 1996, 3). According to Martin Albrow (1990, 8), this

has led to the creation of a single world society. This indicates that the territorial boundaries are opening up and the world is increasingly becoming borderless. Ohmae (1992) also supports this notion of 'borderless world', whereas Jan Aart Scholte (2000, 14) even talks about social relations acquiring relatively distanceless and borderless qualities.

The growing interconnectedness between the nation states on one hand encourages the process of democratization, and on the other hand, it leads to the domination of the weak by the rich and powerful states. At the same time, governance is becoming multilayered, with the emergence of not only supranational organizations but regional groups as well. Territorial distinctions are getting deconstructed and the world is becoming borderless. Considering these factors and the antiglobalization protest movements around the world, we ask what has globalization done to the sovereignty and territoriality of nation states'.

Concept of Sovereignty and Territoriality

The concept of sovereignty and territoriality is intrinsically linked with the idea of the state. In fact, there is a deep connection between the origin and development of sovereignty and that of the state. The term 'sovereignty' can be defined as a 'final and absolute authority in the political community' (Held 1993,

---

BOX 2.2:   Concept of Political Globalization

The concept of political globalization may be decoded in diverse ways:

David Harvey views globalization as, '… the compression of time and space' (Holton 1998, 8).

Scholte views globalization as an intensification of social relations. In his view, globalization 'refers to processes whereby many social relations become relatively delinked from territorial geography, so that human lives are increasingly being played out in the world as a single place' (Scholte 2001, 14–15).

Anthony G. McGrew also considers globalization as 'a process which generates flows and connections, not simply across nation-states and national territorial boundaries, but between global regions, continents and civilizations'. This invites a definition of globalization as 'an historical process which engenders a significant shift in the spatial reach of networks and systems of social relations to transcontinental or inter-regional patterns of human organization, activity and the exercise of power' (McGrew 1998, 327).

---

215). It means that there is a political authority in a community which has the undisputed right to determine the framework of rules and regulations in a given territory.

A glimpse into the historical backdrop of sovereignty helps us understand that this concept was systematically developed in the modern era. The reason was that in the classical Greek world, the idea of sovereignty was not linked with the classical Greek city state or polis. In the city state, or polis, there was no differentiation between state and society. 'In ancient Athens citizens were at one and the same time subjects of state authority and the creators of public rules and regulations' (Held 1993, 216). The Athenian concept of 'citizenship' entails that the people, or 'demos', engage in the legislative and judicial functions, thereby participating directly in the affairs of the state. That is, the public and personal spheres were closely intertwined with each other in the polis.

However, with the rise of the Roman Empire, an entirely new conception of sovereignty emerged. The Romans witnessed the crystallization of the rule of a single central authority. This notion emerged with the doctrine of the *lex regia*, conceived by Justinian, the sixth-century Byzantine emperor, in his work, the *Corpus Juris Civils* (a compilation of Roman law). *Leges regia* meant the 'royal laws', which were introduced by the kings of Rome. According to this doctrine, the emperor became the ultimate authority, in the sense that people surrendered all their power and rights into his hands (Held 1993, 217).

However, this idea of sovereignty as a distinct form of lawmaking power of the state declined with the fall of the Roman Empire and the rise of the Christian faith and theology. This dominant influence of church in the political sphere did not last long, either, and the end of the sixteenth century saw a decline in the authority of the church and the rise of secular absolutism in Europe. The seventeenth-century political developments in Europe, the most important being the Treaty of Westphalia in 1648, which ended the Thirty Years War in Europe, laid the genesis of the modern nation-state system. 'Based on the newly formulated principles of sovereignty and territoriality, the ensuing model of self-contained, impersonal states challenged the medieval mosaic of small polities in which political power tended to be local and personal in focus but still subordinated to a larger imperial authority' (Steger 2009, 75).

The Treaty of Westphalia opened up a new chapter in the history of international politics by introducing the concept of state sovereignty. Earlier, all the states used to fight among themselves, which caused lots of wars. The Treaty of Westphalia led to the end of the Thirty Years War and gave rise to the hope of peace by ending all wars, due to the establishment and recognition of the sovereignty of each state.

According to political scientist David Held, the Westphalian model contained the following essential points (Steger 2009, 75–76):

a. The world consists of, and is divided by, sovereign states that recognise no superior authority.
b. The processes of law-making, the settlement of disputes, and law enforcement are largely in the hands of individuals states.
c. International law is oriented towards the establishment of minimal rules of coexistence; the creation of enduring relationships is an aim, but only to the extent that it allows state objectives to be met.
d. Responsibility for wrongful acts across the borders is a 'private matter' concerning only those affected.
e. All states are regarded as equal before the law, but legal rules do not take account of asymmetries of power.
f. Differences among states are often settled by force; the principle of effective power holds sway. Virtually, no legal fetters exist to curb resorting to force; international legal standards afford only minimal protection.
g. The collective priority of all states should be to minimise the impediments to state freedom.

Thus, the Peace of Westphalia (1648) formalized the modern notion of statehood in a more concrete way. By establishing states as sovereign entities, it made states the principal actors on the world stage. 'International politics was thus thought of, as a state system' (Heywood 2011, 112). In this light, with the seventeenth century, a new conception of international law emerged, with all states exercising equal rights of self-determination. Bestowed with the element of sovereignty, each state thus became the sole authority of decision-making within its definite territory.

The eighteenth century witnessed the rise of imperialism and colonialism in several parts of the world. During this period, sovereignty remained confined to the colonial powers of Europe. In fact, these colonial powers increased their territorial boundaries and their sovereign authority by subjugating the colonial territories. At the same time, the colonized countries were denied political sovereignty and their natives were enslaved. The concept of sovereignty therefore remained Eurocentric even after the Treaty of Westphalia.

However, with the dawn of the twentieth century, especially during the cold war era, many Afro-Asian countries obtained independence. The colonizers left the colonies with weak economic and political institutions. The territorial boundaries of these colonies were also not well defined or demarcated. This resulted in political strife and conflicts over territorial boundaries among these newly independent countries. All this kept their political sovereignty at a crossroads. At the same time, it is interesting to point out that though they were endowed with political independence, they came under a new form of domination. This was the emergence of 'neocolonialism', wherein, though these countries were not colonized physically, yet their policymaking, both internal and external, was influenced by the developed world. Actually, the phase of the cold war saw the emergence of many supranational institutions, such as the International Monetary Fund (IMF) and the World Bank (WB), which remained dominated by the developed world comprising America and Europe. The developed world, through these institutions and other forms (loans, aids), influences the policymaking of the developing countries. Their influence is witnessed in the political, economic and cultural spheres of the developing world. Thus, it could be argued that even after independence, the political, cultural and economic sovereignty of these countries still remains under jeopardy or at grave risk.

If we try to understand the theoretical aspects of the term 'sovereignty', we can argue that with the Italian Renaissance historian Niccolò Machiavelli, the modern doctrine of sovereignty emerged in Europe. For Machiavelli, the security of the prince and the stability of the state constituted an end which justified all means for its attainment. For him, the sovereignty of the state rested in the prince, who was not bound by ethics or morality. As far as territory was concerned, he believed that the prince should continuously make efforts to extent his territories.

Jean Bodin, the French jurist, discussed elaborately the characteristics of sovereignty and considered it as an essential attribute of the state and the body politic. However, with the social contract theory, the concept of sovereignty became even more systematic and refined. While for Thomas Hobbes, sovereignty was bestowed on the 'Leviathan', a metaphor for the state, which was absolute, inalienable and indivisible, for John Locke and Jean-Jacques Rousseau, the sovereignty was not centred, but rather people as a whole constituted the sovereign.

G. W. F. Hegel further strengthened the power of the state by stating, 'The state is the march of God through the world. The existence of the state is a presence of god upon earth, or the march of god in the world, that is what the state is' (Avineri 1974, 176). In *The Philosophy of Right*, Hegel further elaborates the concept of sovereignty by making a distinction between the internal and external aspects of sovereignty. The external or juridical sense of sovereignty refers to the non-accountability of a state to any higher authority. On the contrary, the internal sense of sovereignty implies a normative content, specifying who rules over what and with what justification, extension and limits (Moggach 1999, 175).

This concept of sovereignty was further elaborated by Austin, who propounded the monistic theory of sovereignty. Austin's sovereign had no external superior or internal rival. According to him, if a determinate human superior, who was not in the habit of according obedience to a like superior, received habitual obedience from the bulk of a given society, that determinate superior was the sovereign in the society.

Thus the discourse of sovereignty underwent a vast journey. It would indeed be interesting to explore how and to what extent the notion of sovereignty and territoriality has transformed under the forces of globalization.

BOX 2.3:   Peace of Westphalia or Treaty of Westphalia (1648)

The Treaty of Westphalia was an international covenant among European states that was agreed upon after the end of the Thirty Years War over religious issues. This peace settlement is widely known to have provided the foundational principles of the modern state system in international politics. The treaty recognized the principle of a 'sovereign state' with fixed geographical boundaries and equal respect for other sovereign states. The underlying idea is that all states are equal and have an equal right to exist and that the authority of a government that personifies the state is supreme and accepted as legitimate and lawful. These sovereign states are to conduct their inter-state relations through diplomacy and international law in the form of treaties and agreements. This international peace covenant is also said to have made possible the separation of the public domain of the state from the private domain of religion, thus laying down the principles of 'secularism' and 'religious tolerance'.

This Treaty of Westphalia thus constitutes a seminal framework or paradigm to make sense of international politics and history. Various mainstream theories, such as realism, the English school and constructivism, among others, draw their initial premises from the Westphalian narrative. Critics, however, have rejected a significant part of this narrative. Osiander (2001) has called the 'Peace of Westphalia' a myth, as many institutions and norms attributed to the treaty emerged later in the eighteenth and nineteenth century. Osiander holds that the French Revolution, together with the process of industrialization and nationalism, played an important role in the transition from multiple heteronomous political authorities to neatly divided sovereign territorial units. This sovereignty, based on military capability rather than mutual empowerment, in his view, has tended to produce a narrow perception of international political phenomena as being driven by powerful actors. European powers often deviated from the norms of equal sovereignty and territorial jurisdiction and claimed extraterritorial jurisdiction in non-Western societies, which is known as colonialism and imperialism. They invoked principles grounded in the Westphalian treaty to justify the acts of subjugation in the name of the privileged position of states that were deemed 'civilized' and purported to be spreading the rule of law, tolerance and civilization.

Kayaoglu (2010) contends that the Westphalian narrative in part substantiates a European exceptionalism, which idealises the European or Western order and elevates its ideas and ideals in international relations scholarship. In this narrative, Western states are seen as 'producing' the norms, principles and institutions of international society and non-Western societies 'lack' these until they are socialized into the norms and principles of international society. Thus a kind of perpetual normative hierarchy exists, wherein non-Western societies, being at a lower level, attempt to catch up with a fast-evolving Western society but will never actually be able to catch up. Moreover, the commitment to the Westphalian narrative prevents international scholars from adequately theorizing about cross-regional and cross-civilizational interdependencies and accommodating global diversity through pluralism. Scholarship around the world has been contesting the universalist claims of international institutions and concepts rooted in the Westphalian system. It is argued that increasing interdependence and globalization have presented a formidable challenge to sovereignty-based theories of international relations.

Impact of Globalization on the Sovereignty and Territoriality of Nation States

It is within the upsurge of the global world and, subsequently, the rise of both transnational and national tendencies that there emerges a need to revisit the sovereignty debate. Since globalization implies the flow of goods, services and ideas both inwards and outwards, the debate on its impact on sovereignty and territoriality becomes even more complex.

The effect of globalization on sovereignty and territoriality can be analysed on two broad bases—in terms of a narrowing or restricting of sovereignty, and in terms of a broadening or expanding of sovereignty.

In terms of the narrowing of sovereignty, it could be argued that under the forces of globalization, first, the phenomenon of deterritorialization has emerged. This means that the traditional territorial divisions between states are losing significance. In other words, the national boundaries are no longer sacrosanct and are perforated in this era of globalization, thereby keeping political sovereignty at the crossroads. Since territory remains a key attribute of the concept of sovereignty, deterritorialization and seamless transborder movement of people, goods, services, capital, technologies and ideas has narrowed political sovereignty.

Secondly, the role of the state as an intermediary agent is declining fast. In other words, it is often believed that the state is not able to perform its gatekeeping role as effectively as it had been doing traditionally. This becomes even more evident when local or subnational bodies try to rally themselves across boundaries and engage with extraterritorial entities. It is for this reason that the debate on the sustainability of sovereignty and its varied facets—namely, political, economic and cultural sovereignty—has arisen, especially in the era of emerging globalization.

On the contrary, in terms of the broadening or expanding of sovereignty, it could be argued that when national governments initiate policies, rules and regulations to regulate transborder movement of goods and services, they basically use their sovereign national power in permitting or restricting such movement. In this sense, national sovereignty gets broadened. Also in the era of neocolonialism, the sovereignty of big powers is expanding and, in some instances, even transgressing upon that of the smaller states. In this sense, the sovereignty of powerful states is expanding.

It becomes quite interesting to see that the same forces of globalization are on one hand narrowing the sovereignty of smaller or weaker states and on the other hand, with the opening up of territorial boundaries and the flooding of products and services from the big powers into the small states, expanding the sovereign horizons of bigger, more powerful states.

The general impact of globalization on political sovereignty and territoriality can be analysed in the following way:

Trans-boundary Spillage of Issues and Declining Decision-making Power of the State

Globalization has led to deterritorialization and has resulted in trans-boundary trade. Along with this, technological innovation, especially in the fields of information and communication technology, telecommunication and transportation, has also accelerated. All this has accelerated the trans-boundary movement of goods, services, people, capital, ideas, and so on. This has integrated the world together and has led to a 'borderless world'.

An important fallout of these developments is the spillage of issues across the borders of nation states, which now requires regulations and norms spelled out at the transnational level. This shift in terms of setting norms, under the forces of globalization, has transformed the traditional notion of state sovereignty, wherein the state remained the key decision maker.

In other words, the ability of the state to monitor and control global flows and activities within its territory has decreased and this has put conventional state sovereignty at risk (Clark 1999, 70). In such a situation, the economic and political policies also get influenced by supranational factors and they no longer remain under the exclusive domain of democratic nation states. In this regard, Isin and Wood argue that with the increasing globalization of production and consumption of industrial products and services, the capacity of modern nation states to regulate economic and social matters has been significantly curtailed (Isin and Wood 1999, 157).

In fact, globalization has drastically affected the sovereignty of nation states by influencing the state will or outcome of decision-making in internal as well as external matters (Clark 1999, 81). However, for certain traditional domains, the state still remains the key decision-making authority.

Rise of International Political Structures

Under the aegis of globalization and subsequent interconnectedness, the world has been witnessing the emergence of international political structures. This phenomenon has been termed 'global governance' by Craig Murphy (Chase-Dunn 1999, 193). These emerging international political structures include both specialized and general international organizations. The prominent general international organizations include the erstwhile League of Nations and its successor, the United Nations (UN). At the regional levels, there are organizations such as the European Union (EU), the African Union, the Organization of American States (OAS), the Arab League, Brazil, Russia, India, China and South Africa (the BRICS) and the Association of Southeast Asian Nations (ASEAN).

The process of institution building within these organizations signifies an important attribute of political globalization. All these international and specialized institutions attempt to influence the decision-making of the member states through their norms and legislations. It is often been argued that increasing concentration of power in these international institutions eventually leads to a situation in which the political sovereignty of the nation state is subjugated to the dictates of these institutions (Chase-Dunn 1999, 193).

With the growth of international and regional organizations and their increasing membership base, it may be ascertained that more and more countries are trying to conform to the norms propounded by these multilateral organizations, thereby narrowing the decision-making powers of the states and putting their political sovereignty at peril.

Multilayered Systems of Governance

In this era of growing interconnectedness and interpenetration, the world is witnessing problems which cannot be addressed solely at the national level. Issues such as terrorism, cross-border crimes, environmental degradation and poverty (discussed in the subsequent chapters of this book) affect not only a single nation or region, but the entire world. These issues, thus, have a global significance and therefore need an international insight along with national efforts. Let's take the example of the North–South dialogue in terms of global warming or pollution, where the developed and developing worlds both have their own reservations regarding the issues concerned. The issue of global warming or pollution is not associated with one or a few states and thus cannot be solved or raised in isolation by nations.

In fact, the impact of such issues are global, therefore, such issues are raised at a global platform. Against this backdrop, national decision-making is influenced in two ways:

- First, decision-making and norm setting on the aforementioned transnational issues get transferred from the exclusive domain of the state to international institutions.
- Secondly, the increased demands of democratization and participation require consultation at the local level within nations, as well.

Thus decision-making gets trifurcated between international, national and local levels, in order to make it more universal and inclusive. This implies that public policies are attempted at multiple levels.

Internationalization of Human Rights Issues

In an era when human rights are being internationalized, nation states can no longer treat citizens and aliens according to their own national settings. Nation states have to conform to the international standards, which are laid down in various international human rights treaties and declarations to which they are signatories.

Thus, state sovereignty is not absolute today and remains restricted. The state cannot act in isolation from international norms, neither may it violate the human rights of people, as both internal and external forces are monitoring and (directly or indirectly) continuously influencing and restricting state action. Such forces include people, international organizations such as the UN, regional organizations, civil societies, and so on. Thus, as a checking and support mechanism, such forces are working beyond territories and restricting state sovereignty to some extent.

At the same time, globalization has provided viable platforms for human rights assertions. This is evident from the rise of human rights groups or civil society organizations. Isin and Wood, in this regard, argues that globalization has a dual impact. On one hand, it may be weakening the nation states; on the other hand, it is also opening up new spaces for groups to enact new type of policies (Isin and Wood 1999, 157).

New Notions of Citizenship

Citizenship and statehood have a long and intrinsic relationship. Since the French Revolution, the concept of citizenship has historically been associated with national identity and the nation state (Kadioglu 2007, 284). However, under the wave of globalization and the rising importance of supranational and subnational entities, the idea of citizenship has undergone tremendous changes. In fact, the growing importance of global processes has created conditions in which many notions like citizenship, which were previously uniquely bound with the nation states, are moving to other private, supranational and subnational institutions and spheres (Sassen 2000, 579).

Under the aegis of globalization, new notions of citizenship have emerged, such as modernization and cultural citizenship; consumer rights and consumer citizenship; new ethics of care and ecological citizenship; new social movements and sexual citizenship; computer, new technology and technological citizenship; and global cities and urban citizenship (Isin and Wood 1999, 156–160).

However, keeping in mind the political dimension of globalization, the present study will focus mainly upon 'denationalized citizenship' and 'global citizenship'.

Denationalized Citizenship

Denationalized citizenship is a concept which has emerged due to complex processes associated with globalization. It is due to the changes in the role of the nation state, due to privatization, deregulation and increased prominence of the international human rights regime (Sassen 2002, 277). Under the influence of globalization, with the blurring of boundaries and rising integration of regional and local authorities with supranational bodies, a stronger assertion of regional identity is made, apart from national identity. In this sense, a concept of denationalized citizenship has emerged wherein communities have a stronger sense of belonging and identification with smaller cultural and social groups than with their nation state (Sassen 2002, 281).

Global Citizenship

Under the influence of globalization, the world is facing common issues which need to be addressed globally. The core social, political, economic and environmental realities of the world need to be addressed at multiple levels: by individuals, by civil society organizations and by nation states, and that too through a global perspective. With political and geographic borders no longer intact and concerns being universal, the solutions lie somewhere beyond the narrow national interests. Thus the role and identity of the individual does not remain confined within the national territory, but rather expands beyond it. Against this backdrop emerges the concept of 'global citizenship'.

It relates to the rights, responsibilities and duties that pertain to each individual as a member of the global entity, apart from being a member of a particular nation or territory. The idea is that responsibility and rights are not limited within the geography of political borders; rather, they can even be derived from being a member of a much wider class, that is, 'humanity'. 'This does not mean that such a person denounces or waives their nationality or other, more local identities, but such identities are given "second place" to their membership in a global community' (Israel 2012).

With the rise of the notion of a global society, terms such as 'world citizen' and 'cosmopolitan citizen' have arisen. A synonymous expression could be that of *vasudhaiva kutumbakam*, a Sanskrit phrase found in Hindu texts such as the *Maha Upanishad*, meaning 'the world is one family'. In general, global citizenship is a phenomenon which places global identity over and above any nationalistic or local identities.

Thus, we can argue that within the process of globalization, the traditional conception of citizenship based upon national territoriality has undergone a drastic change. Not only has an entirely new understanding of citizenship and nation state emerged, but a new way of interacting with it and beyond it has also come forth.

State Security and Non-state Actors

Security has been the prime agenda for all states, especially in the era of globalization and rising interconnectedness. Apart from other challenges which the state security faces, one of the most important challenges under the aegis of globalization is the threat which the non-state actor poses to state sovereignty and territoriality (Figure 2.1).

Before further discussing this debate, it seems necessary to understand non-state actors.

FIGURE 2.1 Security and Non-state Actors

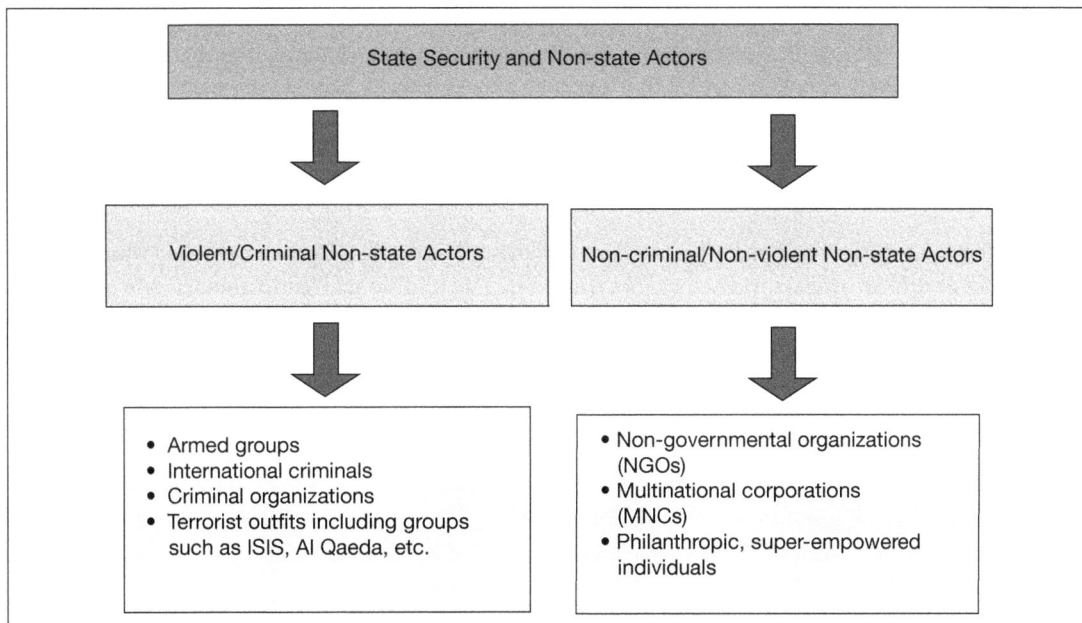

Non-state actors are non-sovereign entities and therefore not allied to any particular country or state. They exhibit their presence beyond the national territorial boundaries and therefore emerge as extraterritorial actors. In fact, they are individuals or organizations with significant economic, political or social power and influence to cause and even change national politics and international relations.

These non-state actors can be divided into two types:

Non-criminal/Non-violent Non-state Actors

These actors include non-governmental organizations (NGOs), multinational corporations (MNCs) and philanthropic super-empowered individuals.

NGOs: The first type of non-criminal/non-violent non-state actor comprises NGOs. Globalization has also influenced and changed the notion of traditional NGOs and their functioning. Today NGOs are converted into big business houses having multiple head or branch offices. This huge sector is based upon international funding and has initiated global campaigns with the help of an advanced information technology (IT) sector.

Since the beginning of globalization, NGOs and philanthrocapitalists such as Bill Gates' and Richard Branson's charities have started focusing and working more on transnational issues such as poverty, environment, refugees, social and economic justice, and peace. While doing so, they have garnered the power to influence policies and decision-making processes worldwide, thereby influencing the policies of national and international actors. While functioning as information providers and lobbying groups and demonstrating themselves as setters of agendas or generators of norms, NGOs influence the foreign policymaking of national actors both directly and indirectly.

A significant example in this regard could be that of the Bill and Melinda Gates Foundation, one of the largest NGOs based in the US, which has strongly urged the US government to provide more foreign aid to promote economic growth in the world's poorest nations at a time when the US itself was facing a huge economic crisis. Similarly, Amnesty International, which is working as a symbolic protector of human rights, has through its interventions and directives helped in changing the shared perception of human rights in many countries. In another instance, Greenpeace, a non-governmental environmental organization, was able to exert pressure at an international level against whale hunting and consequently the government of Japan was compelled to officially cancel plans to hunt whales in the Southern Ocean under the direction of the UN's International Court of Justice in 2014.

MNCs: The second type of actor in this category comprises MNCs. MNCs are enterprises which manage production or deliver services in two or more countries. The traditional multinationals were similar to a private company headquartered in one country. Globalization has drastically changed this notion of multinationals and their functioning. These MNCs are now globalized and they execute global strategies to achieve cost efficiencies and compete in broader and interconnected markets to win their market share.

Under the forces of globalization, a relatively recent trend of 'multinationalization' of state-owned enterprises has also come into force. For example, the Chinese National Petroleum Corporation (CNPC) and Russia's arms-export monopoly Rosonboronexport are now no longer restricted within their territorial boundaries, but rather have started establishing their footholds worldwide.

It could be argued that MNCs are not only endowed with the political power to influence political and territorial sovereignty of nation states but even manifest significant economic clout to adversely affect the state economy if it tries to oppose them. Also, since the majority of these MNCs are controlled by developed countries, they emerge as agents for 'eroding the sovereignty of smaller state system' by influencing the policies and decisions of developing countries with the help of their lucrative offers and opportunities.

Philanthropic Super-empowered Individuals: The third set of actors in this category are the philanthropic super-empowered individuals. It includes industrialists, media moguls, celebrities, religious leaders and other people having unique political, economic, intellectual or cultural influence over human beings. Such non-state actors are highly motivational and acceptable not only to national governments but even to governments of other states and international organizations. One such example of positive intervention in the international system by philanthropic super-empowered individuals could be that of Daisaku Ikeda, who is a world-renowned leader of the Buddhist faith and works towards international peace. Since many years, he has been annually presenting peace proposals to the UN, targeting specific international issues, and many of his suggestions have been acknowledged by the UN itself. He is also working tirelessly at constructing a bridge of friendship between China and Japan.

Violent/Criminal Non-state Actors

This includes armed groups, international criminals, criminal organizations and terrorist outfits, including groups such as the Islamic State in Iraq and Syria (ISIS) and the Al Qaeda.

With globalization, and especially after the disintegration of the former Union of Soviet Socialist Republics (USSR), world politics has witnessed so many changes having a major influence on international relations. One such major change was a power shift which witnessed the transformation of a bipolar world into a unipolar one with an established US hegemony. Further, the interconnectedness of the world and the role of sovereign states and non-state actors have opened the way to a 'multipolar world', where power was disseminated into different blocks of state and non-state actors.

The disintegration of the former USSR also fuelled an environment which created conditions for the easier availability and transfer of weapons of mass destruction, including nuclear weapons. Not only states, but some non-state terrorist actors also started claiming possession of these nuclear weapons or their blueprints.

Terrorist outfits such as the Al Qaeda, ISIS and others started challenging not only the political sovereignty and the decision-making powers of modern nation states in general but also the hegemony of the superpowers, the US in particular. The 9/11 attack, allegedly by the Osama bin Laden-led Al Qaeda outfit, shattered the legendary invincibility of the US supremacy.

These violent non-state actors are also using the same modern technology, including satellite phones, the Internet, and sophisticated weapons, which the state actors are using. The economic aspect of their functioning—in terms of international funding for terror activities, training camps and weapons—is also influenced by the forces of globalization. Whether we talk about the terrorist outfits of the Al Qaeda and ISIS or criminal outfits such as the D-Company, all have equally benefitted from globalization and related forces. In fact, globalization has also globalized the activities and presence of these violent non-state actors. The 26/11 Mumbai attack in India, the Boko Haram-led incidents in Nigeria in 2016, the London attack of 2017, the Stockholm attack of April 2017, the Manchester terror attack of May 2017, the Paris shooting of a police officer in April 2017 (later claimed by the ISIS) are some of the recent examples to prove the spread of terrorism and violent non-state actors across the globe.

Revisiting the Sovereignty and Territoriality Debate

Sovereignty and territoriality, thus, are no longer exclusive functions of statehood. Within the discourse on the changing nature of sovereignty and territoriality in this era of globalization, there emerge three main schools of thoughts.

The first school of thought is represented by the hyperglobalists, including thinkers such as Kenichi Ohmae and Robert B Reich. They argue that the world is now more borderless, especially in the economic field. National economies are now part of a global economy where international financial markets and transnational transactions dominate. They argue that there is an emerging trend wherein national governments are just transmission belts for global capital. For them, the power of the nation state has been supplanted by business activities. Today, it is more global finance, rather than the state, that has influence over the organization, location and distribution of economic power and wealth. According to them, under the influence of globalization, the world is moving towards a borderless economy, where

BOX 2.4: Kenichi Ohmae

Kenichi Ohmae (born 1943) is the only internationally renowned Japanese guru who is known for his thinking about strategy rather than about operations. Indeed, he is often referred to as 'Mr Strategy'. Ohmae translated Japanese business culture and strategy into English. His books are full of Japanese examples and they helped familiarize Western audiences with Japan's management breakthroughs. He was first trained as a nuclear scientist at the Tokyo Institute of Technology and then at the Massachusetts Institute of Technology (MIT) in Cambridge, Ohmae became head of McKinsey & Company's Tokyo office in the early 1970s. From there, he was an early observer of and commentator on the phenomenon of globalization.

As an author, he has published over 100 books and has also contributed numerous articles to major publications. *The Mind of the Strategist: The Art of Japanese Business* (McGraw-Hill), *Triad Power: The Coming Shape of Global Competition* (Free Press), *Beyond National Borders: Reflections on Japan and the World* (Dow Jones-Irwin), *The Borderless World: Power and Strategy in the Interlinked Economy* (Harper Business), *The End of the Nation State: The Rise of Regional Economies* (Free Press) and *The Evolving Global Economy: Making Sense of the New World Order* (Harvard Business School Press) are among the most popular of his books printed in English. In his books *Triad Power* and *The Borderless World*, he expounded the view that companies which did not have a full presence in the world's three main trading blocs (Europe, North America and the Pacific Rim) were dangerously vulnerable to competition from those that did.

Source: Kenichi Ohmae, The Economist, 17 July 2009, http://www.economist.com/node/14031208 (accessed 14 October 2017); 'Biography of Kenichi Ohmae', http://www.ohmae-report.com/pro/bioe.html (accessed 14 October 2017).

states become territorially limited and global markets escape national political regulations. They thus predict the demise of the nation state in the sense that its role as the final decision-making authority in both internal and external spheres is getting taken over by international organizations.

In contrast, the sceptics, notably P. Hirst and G. Thompson, disagree with this thesis. They believe that the world has not evolved much and that instead of being in a globalized world, we are now in a more international world. For the sceptics, the international economy is an aggregate of nationally located functions (Hirst and Thompson 1999, 10). This means that the state remains central to national and international business activities and is a key actor in influencing domestic economy. In fact, they believe that national economies still remain a significant factor in determining the processes of international economy. In other words, international phenomena are outcomes that emerge from the distinct and differential performance of the national economies. For instance, MNCs having headquarters in different countries can be described as national companies operating internationally and thus subject to national regulation. Moreover, the state still exercises a crucial role in the scheme of governance and regulation and, through elections, it remains the critical agency of popular representation.

The third school of thought is that of the transformationalists, which includes thinkers such as Anthony Giddens, Jan Aart Scholte, James N. Rosenau, Manuel Castells and I. Wallerstein. These

---

BOX 2.5: Anthony Giddens

Anthony Giddens was born (18 January 1938) in London and grew up in a lower middle-class family. He obtained his bachelor's degree in sociology and psychology from the University of Hull in 1959, his master's degree from the London School of Economics and his PhD from the University of Cambridge.

Three notable stages can be identified in his academic life. In the first stage, Held presented a theoretical and methodological understanding of sociology. In this regard, his major publications included *Capitalism and Modern Social Theory: An Analysis of the Writings of Marx, Durkheim and Max Weber* (1971) and *New Rules of Sociological Method: A Positive Critique of Interpretive Sociologies* (1976). In the second stage, Giddens developed the theory of structuration, an analysis of agency and structure, in which primacy is granted to neither. His works from that period, such as *Central Problems in Social Theory: Action, Structure and Contradiction in Social Analysis* (1979) and *The Constitution of Society: Outline of the Theory of Structuration* (1984), brought him international fame on the sociological arena.

The most recent stage concerns modernity, globalization and politics, especially the impact of modernity on social and personal life. This stage is distinguished by his critique of postmodernity and discussions of a new 'utopian-realist' third way in politics, visible in *The Consequences of Modernity* (1990), *Modernity and Self-Identity: Self and Society in the Late Modern Age* (1991), *The Transformation of Intimacy: Sexuality, Love and Eroticism in Modern Societies* (1992) and *Beyond Left and Right: The Future of Radical Politics* (1994).

He has brought many ideas and concepts to the field of sociology. Of particular importance are his concepts of reflexivity, globalization, structuration theory and the third way (a political philosophy which seeks to redefine social democracy for a post-cold war and globalized era). Some of his other publications include: *The Class Structure of the Advanced Societies* (1973), *Studies in Social and Political Theory* (1977) and *The Third Way: The Renewal of Social Democracy* (1998).

Source: https://www.goodreads.com/author/show/25998.Anthony_Giddens (accessed 14 October 2017).

thinkers take a middle-ground approach between the previous two extreme views of globalization. They argue that globalization is a multi-scaled process and do not believe in a single global society. In their view, globalization is creating new economic and political circumstances that, however, are transforming state powers and the context in which states operate (Held et al. 2000, 15).

Globalization, according to this school, may create new networks and dissolve old ones. David Held argues that under the forces of globalization, relationships among nations and people will be reconfigured and power relationships will get restructured (Parker 2005, 21). Thinkers of this school believe that globalization will not lead to the demise of the state, but rather will reconstruct the notion of the state in a peculiar way. Power relations will be reconfigured and the world will witness the emergence of a new 'sovereignty regime'. Thus, the existence of the state will not end; rather, it would be redefined to cater to the complexities offered up by the forces of globalization.

Summing up, we can say that these three schools of thought have tried to interpret globalization and its effects on sovereignty and territoriality of nation states in their own peculiar ways. However, among these different theories, the transformationalists' one seems to be the more accurate.

Concluding Observations

Thus it may be concluded that, in this era of globalization, the traditional notion of statehood and sovereignty has undergone a change. Deterritorialization has led to the growth of MNCs, business process outsourcing (BPOs) and multilateral economic pacts across borders. The transnational inward and outward movement of goods, services, ideas and values has not only resulted in homogenization of cultures across the globe but has even resulted in hybridization of existing cultures. This has, on one hand, created conditions for common consumption of cultures; on the other hand, it has opened a Pandora's box regarding the question of political and cultural identity. National boundaries are open, thereby putting the political sovereignty of nation states at risk. The blurring of the distinction between domestic and international politics, trans-boundary spillage of issues and emergence of global and regional laws has posed a serious challenge to the traditional notions of sovereignty and territoriality. In such a situation, the economic and political policies also get influenced by supranational factors and no longer remain the exclusive domain of nation states. Sovereignty, thus, is no longer a sanctuary. In fact, it has often been argued that it would be prudent on the part of the states to redefine the hitherto traditional notion of sovereignty. This will enable them to sustain themselves and thrive more effectively in this interconnected, globalized world.

Summary

- Globalization is a worldwide, multidimensional phenomenon, marked by the intensification of social relations, compression of time and space and interconnectedness between people and societies around the globe.
- It also involves cross-boundary movement of goods, services, ideas, technology and culture, thus making the world borderless. Herein comes the discourse regarding the existence of the nation state and the sanctity of territorial borders under the aegis of globalization.

- In this era of complex interdependence, when the world is witnessing greater interconnectedness across political cultures and intensification of political relations, globalization through its forces has aroused the need to revisit the debate on sovereignty and territoriality of nation states.

- The concept of sovereignty and territoriality is intrinsically linked with the idea of the nation state. The rise of secular absolutism in Europe and political developments such as the Treaty of Westphalia in 1648 laid the basis of the modern state system. Based on the newly formulated principles of sovereignty and territoriality, this treaty recognized states as sovereign units with no superior authority. However, it is interesting to understand how this notion of state sovereignty and territoriality got transformed under the forces of globalization.

- The aforesaid transformation takes place on two planes: one in terms of narrowing of sovereignty and the other in terms of broadening of sovereignty. With rising deterritorialization and seamless trans-boundary movement of goods and services, national boundaries are no longer sacrosanct. Thus the political sovereignty of the state gets narrowed and the state is not able to perform its gatekeeping role as effectively as it had been doing traditionally. At the same time, when the nation state exercises sovereign rights to regulate trans-boundary movement and when neo-imperialist big states curtail the power of small state systems, it signifies the broadening of the big states' sovereignty.

- The impact of globalization on state sovereignty and territoriality can be understood as:

  ❖ Trans-boundary spillage of issues and declining decision-making power of the state
  ❖ Rise of international political structures
  ❖ Multilayered system of governance
  ❖ Internationalization of the issues of human rights
  ❖ Rise of new notions of citizenship, namely, 'denationalized citizenship' and 'global citizenship'

- It therefore becomes imperative to revisit the debate on state sovereignty and territoriality. In this regard, three schools of thought emerge: hyperglobalists, sceptics and transformationalists. While hyperglobalists are too optimistic about the influence of globalization and predict the demise of the nation state, sceptics believe that the state still remains central to the national and international business activities and is a key actor in influencing domestic economy. Between the two extreme views, transformationalists present the most balanced view. For them, the world is not witnessing the end of the nation state, but rather the reconstruction and reconfiguration of the nation state.

Suggested Questions

1. Discuss the political dimension of globalization in regard to state sovereignty and territoriality.
2. Analyse the theoretical underpinning of the evolution of state sovereignty and territoriality.
3. Critically analyse the impact of globalization on the sovereignty and territoriality of nation states.
4. Is there a need to revisit the sovereignty debate in the era of globalization? Elaborate while mentioning the three alternative perspectives in this regard.

References

Albrow, Martin. 1990. 'Introduction.' In *Globalization, Knowledge and Society: Readings from International Sociology*, edited by Martin Albrow and Elizabeth King, 8. London: SAGE Publications.

Avineri, Shlomo. 1974. *Hegel's Theory of the Modern State*. Cambridge: Cambridge University Press.

Bretherton, Charlotte. 1996. 'Introduction: Global Politics in the 1990s.' In *Global Politics: An Introduction*, edited by Charlotte Bretherton and Geoffrey Ponton, 3. Oxford: Blackwell Publishers.

Chase-Dunn, Christopher. 1999. 'Globalization: A World-Systems Perspective.' *Journal of World-Systems Research* 5 (2): 187–215.

Clark, Ian. 1999. *Globalization and International Relations Theory*. Oxford: Oxford University Press.

Giddens, Anthony. 1990. *The Consequences of Modernity*. Stanford, CA: Stanford University Press.

Held, David. 1993. *Political Theory and the Modern State*. Oxford, UK: Blackwell Publishers.

Held, David, Anthony McGrew, David Goldblatt and Jonathan Perraton. 2000. 'Global Transformations: Politics, Economics and Culture'. In *Politics at the Edge*, edited by Chris Pierson and Simon Tormey, 14–28. London: Palgrave Macmillan.

Heywood, Andrew. 2011. *Global Politics*. New York, NY: Palgrave Macmillan.

Hirst, Paul Q., and Grahame F. Thompson, eds. 1999. *Globalization in Question: The International Economy and the Possibilities of Governance*, 2nd ed. Cambridge: Polity Press.

Holton, Robert J. 1998. *Globalization and the Nation-State*. London: Macmillan Press.

Isin, Engin F., and Patricia K. Wood. 1999. *Citizenship and Identity*. Thousand Oaks, CA: SAGE Publications.

Israel, Ronald C. 2012. 'What Does It Mean to be a Global Citizen?' *Kosmos*, Spring–Summer. Accessed 2 December 2017. http://www.kosmosjournal.org/article/what-does-it-mean-to-be-a-global-citizen/.

Kadioglu, Ayse. 2007. 'Denationalization of Citizenship? The Turkish Experience.' *Citizenship Studies* 11 (3): 283–299.

Kayaoglu, Turan. 2010. 'Westphalian Euro-centrism in International Relation Theory.' *International Studies Review* 12 (2): 193–207.

McGrew, Anthony G. 1998. 'Global Legal Interaction and Present-Day Patterns of Globalization'. In *Emerging Legal Certainty: Empirical Studies on the Globalization of Law*, edited by Volkmar Gessner and Ali Cem Budak, 327. Ashgate: Dartmouth Publishing Company.

Moggach, Douglas. 1999. 'Concepts of Sovereignty: Historical Reflections on State, Economy and Culture'. *Studies in Political Economy: A Socialist Review* 59 (1): 173–193.

Ohmae, Kenichi. 1992. *The Borderless World: Power and Strategy in the Global Marketplace*. London: HarperCollins.

Osiander, Andreas. 2001. 'Sovereignty, International Relations, and Westphalian Myth'. *International Organization* 55 (2): 251–287.

Parker, Barbara. 2005. *Introduction to Globalization and Business: Relationships and Responsibilities*. London: SAGE Publications.

Sassen, Saskia. 2000. 'The Need to Distinguish Denationalized and Postnational'. *Indiana Journal of Global Legal Studies* 7 (2): 575–584.

———. 2002. 'Towards Post-National and Denationalized Citizenship'. In *Handbook of Citizenship Studies*, edited by Engin F. Isin and Bryan S. Turner. London: SAGE Publications.

Scholte, Jan Aart. 2001. 'The Globalization of World Politics'. In *The Globalization of World Politics: An Introduction to International Relations*, edited by John Baylis and Steve Smith. New York, NY: Oxford University Press.

Sharma, B. M., and Roop Singh Bareth, eds. 2004. *Good Governance, Globalization and Civil Society*. Jaipur: Rawat Publications.

Steger, Manfred B. 2009. *Globalization: A Brief Insight*. New York, NY: Sterling Publishing.

Further Reading

Albrow, Martin, and Elizabeth King, eds. 1990. *Globalization, Knowledge and Society: Readings from International Sociology*. London: SAGE Publications.

Baylis, John, Steve Smith, and Patricia Owens, eds. 2014. *The Globalization of World Politics: An Introduction to International Relations*. Oxford: Oxford University Press.

Bretherton, Charlotte, and Ponton Geoffrey, eds. *Global Politics: An Introduction*. Oxford: Blackwell Publishers.

Giddens, Anthony. 2011. *Runaway World: How Globalization is Reshaping Our Lives*. London: Profile Books.

Holton, Robert J. 2005. *Making Globalization*. New York, NY: Palgrave Macmillan.

Hoogvelt, Ankie. 2001. *Globalization and the Postcolonial World: The New Political Economy of Development*, 2nd ed. New York, NY: Palgrave Macmillan.

Larsson, Tomas. 2001. *The Race to the Top: The Real Story of Globalization*. Washington, DC: Cato Institute.

Leslie, Sklair. 1999. 'Competing Conceptions of Globalization'. *Journal of World-Systems Research* 5 (2). Accessed 30 November 2017. https://doi.org/10.5195/jwsr.1999.140.

Robertson, Roland. 1992. *Globalization: Social Theory and Global Culture*. London: SAGE Publications.

Scholte, Jan Aart. 2000. *Globalization: A Critical Introduction*. Basingstoke: Palgrave.

———. 2005. *Globalization: A Critical Introduction*, 2nd ed. New York, NY: Palgrave Macmillan.

Stiglitz, Joseph E. 2003. *Globalization and its Discontents*. New York, NY and London: W. W. Norton & Company.

Sugden, R., and J. R. Wilson 2001. 'Globalisation, the New Economy and Regionalisation'. In *Globalization and World Cities (GaWC) Research Bulletin*. Accessed 28 November 2017. http://www.lboro.ac.uk/gawc/rb/rb70.html.

3

CHAPTER

Global Political Economy: Evolution and Significance of World Economic Order

Arvind Kumar

LEARNING OBJECTIVES

- To understand the economic dimension of global politics
- To understand the causes and history of the evolution of political economy
- To understand the evolution and convergence of social-science disciplines
- To understand the methodological complexity which globalization has introduced
- To understand the importance of interdisciplinarity in political analysis

Global political economy (hereafter GPE), traditionally known as 'international political economy' (hereafter IPE), is an emerging discipline of the social sciences in general and of international relations in particular, which primarily deals with the interaction between political and economic factors at the global level. In this interaction, each factor shapes the other by placing enabling and disabling conditions on the other. For example, the 'political' constrains the economic choices of a government, such as policymaking, and the policy choices of individuals as well as social groups; likewise, economic factors determine individual's political choices, such as voting behaviour, unions' power of political lobbying and the government's internal and external policies. In addition to the interaction between the political and the economic, GPE also deals with the interaction between the international and the domestic and, to some extent, between the material and the ideal.

The preliminary observation of the subject matter of GPE poses a set of curious interrelated questions. What is the contemporary significance of GPE? How is GPE different from IPE? Is GPE merely a discipline of the social sciences or a method? Is GPE simply a sub-branch of international relations? What are the objectives of GPE? And how does GPE envisage to achieve those objectives?

The answers of these questions are embedded in the objectives of this chapter, and will gradually unfold as our discussion proceeds with analysing the historical trajectory of GPE. The principal objective of this chapter is to introduce readers about the importance of this incubating discipline of the social sciences, called GPE. This chapter tries to achieve this objective by providing a descriptive analysis of the significance, evolution, and anchors of this newly emerging discipline. In the section on its significance, a description has been given of how international treaties, negotiations and accords affect domestic policies and how internal policies of countries affect international politics. The next section focuses on the evolutionary aspects of GPE. In this section, an attempt has been made to provide an in-depth analysis of the evolution of GPE as a discipline of the social sciences. Subsequently, this section not only traces the origin of GPE in classical political economy but also makes readers aware of how the modern disciplines of the social sciences—economics, political science and sociology—have evolved from classical political economy, as a result of which classical political economy is referred to as the mother of the social sciences. After discussing the root of GPE in classical political economy, this chapter takes two steps backwards and provides a detailed analysis of physiocracy and mercantilism—two intellectual traditions of Europe that made a pioneering contribution to the evolution of classical political economy. Towards the second half of this chapter, readers will become aware of how certain principles of physiocracy and mercantilism are still prevalent across the globe, and hence, are shaping the trajectory of GPE. In addition to this, this section will enable readers to distinguish between the foundational principles of classical political economy and GPE. The last section of this chapter discusses the role of anchors in GPE, which comprise state and non-state actors, including individuals. The discussion on the anchors of GPE unfolds the role of individuals as statesmen (statespersons), policymakers and public intellectuals in shaping the contours of international politics through their association with multinational corporations (MNCs), international institutions and non-governmental organizations (NGOs).

Understanding Contemporary Significance of Global Political Economy

We are living in the era of globalization where, due to compression of time and space, interdependence between nations and individuals has been increasing rapidly. The ultimate outcome of this is that the 'political' and the 'economic' are not only interacting with each other but also framing each other. In addition to this, to some extent, globalization has also opened up vistas for individuals to directly participate in and formulate policies in international politics—a domain which was earlier exclusively reserved for the nation state—as a member of MNCs, NGOs, and international organizations. Historically, IPE has positioned the state as the central actor in international politics, as a result of which international trade, international finance, North–South relations and hegemony acquired pre-eminent positions in the arena of international politics, leaving the individual to be considered as an insignificant actor. But with the onset of globalization, the individual regained their position in the arena of international politics in the capacity of statesman, policymaker, and member of civil society, as a result of which the individual has been framing the contours of international politics. GPE is an attempt to rectify this erstwhile error of IPE by incorporating the individual along with the state at the central stage of the analysis of international politics.

Globalization, on the one hand, has been providing an opportunity for individuals to interact with the larger world, but on the other hand, has been simultaneously taking away the role of policy framing from the nation states on the pretext of the universality of certain problems, such as poverty, hunger, malnour-ishment, rising inequalities, pollution and technological transformation. The public policies of our times—domestic or external—are framed in order to provide solutions to these problems, but these problems cut artificial boundaries across the nation states; therefore, they require a coordinated effort from the nation states. The attempts at coordinating efforts are further increasing the interdependence between nation states. The increased interdependence between nation states is making the territorial boundaries of nation states porous, which were formulated according to the Treaty of Westphalia (1648). In addition to making the territorial boundaries of nation states porous, globalization has blurred the boundaries between the political and the economic, the international and the domestic, and to some extent, the material and the ideal. The consequence of the blurring of these boundaries is the emergence of a new world order that has a different economic order as well. This new economic world order has raised a demand for searching out economic principles on the basis of which this economy can be man-aged. One concern of this chapter is also to provide descriptive analysis of this new world economic while investigating the economic principles through which the new economic world order is supposed to be governed. In nutshell, the core concern of GPE is how world economy can be governed in the era of globalization?

Though the principle objective of GPE is very clear, there exists a religious divide between scholars whether GPE is the objective application of economic principles to international issues or whether it is a more interpretative, historical and structural way of thinking about the global economic order (Higgott 2007). I argue that GPE is more than merely the objective application of economic principles to interna-tional issues. It is a method as well as a discipline which has twin functions—as a method, it explains the causes and implications of globalization; and as a discipline, it tries to unite the disciplines of the social sciences—economics, political science and sociology—that were historically separated out from classical political economy. Nowadays, these major disciplines of the social sciences separately are unable to explain the phenomenon of globalization, since its implications can be seen in the social, economic and political spheres of life. Therefore, there is demand for the deployment of interdisciplinary tools and methods for studying globalization. GPE has been evolving due to such interdisciplinary efforts. The offspring of this interdisciplinary effort is named 'global political economy' because classical political economy was the mother of the major social-science disciplines. However, GPE should not be seen as an attempt at merely reviving ideas from classical political economy, but as a strategy for entering the future while learning from the past. But this also does not mean that GPE discards all the teachings of classical political economy. How and in what respect the subject matter of GPE is inspired by and differs from classical political economy is answered by the discussion on the evolution of classical political economy. This discussion will also provide a detailed analysis of how the cardinal principles of political economy have evolved while passing through different sociopolitical contexts.

Explaining Evolution of Political Economy

The evolution of political economy is dated at not earlier than the latter half of the eighteenth century. With the advent of the modern nation state after the Treaty of Westphalia, the questions related to the source (population or land) of the prosperity of a nation and efficient management of those sources became dominant in eighteenth-century Europe. The stability of the newly emerging nation was to be based on maintaining a large army, and for maintaining the large army, huge money and man power were required. It was envisaged that a large population would provide both money through taxation and men as soldiers; therefore, the population was supposed to be the greatest source of the prosperity of the nation. Accepting the population as the greatest source of prosperity of the nation implies that a rise or decline in the population of the nation would mean increasing or decreasing power for the nation state. The issue of the rise or decline of the population raised a huge debate in eighteenth-century Europe.

The idea of the population as the best source of prosperity for the nation was contested by the idea that land was the best source of the prosperity of a nation, because land is required for agriculture and mining. Agriculture gives food grains for sustaining the population whereas land also provides precious metals required for transactions. The question of whether population or land was the best source of the prosperity of a nation led to investigation of the most efficient method for managing the economy of the nation. The attempt to provide a scientific answer through systematic investigation of these questions led the emergence of two schools of thought—physiocracy and mercantilism—in eighteenth-century Europe. The extraordinary works of the thinkers associated with these schools became the stepping stones in the emergence of classical political economy, which later became the mother of the major social-science disciplines.

Physiocracy

Physiocracy was an intellectual movement that developed in the latter half of the eighteenth century in France. Founded by François Quesnay (1694–1774) in 1760, this school flourished in the court of Louis XV, where a group of intellectuals, mainly disciples of Quesnay, made an attempt to construct the first systematic and comprehensive theoretical 'model' of economic processes and management. Initially, those intellectuals called themselves 'the economists', but later they used 'physiocracy' to describe their doctrine of the economic model. Quesnay published his celebrated manuscript the *Tableau Économique* in 1758, in which he presented his model of the economic system in a geometrical diagram. Next to Quesnay, Victor Riqueti, marquis de Mirabeau (1715–89) was another important person, whose work on population became a stepping stone to physiocracy. Mirabeau, a disciple of Quesnay, had achieved great popularity before meeting Quesnay for his celebrated manuscript on population, *The Friend of Mankind, or a Treatise on Population* (1756), in which he had argued that population growth was the main factor behind the economic progress of a nation; therefore, the main object of state policy should be to encourage reproduction. Two years after the publication of his manuscript on population, Mirabeau met Quesnay and became persuaded that land, not labour, was the main source of economic wealth. After that meeting, Mirabeau not only became an ardent disciple of Quesnay but also a tireless promoter of the latter's ideas. This is the reason why some historians date the origin of the physiocratic school from the first meeting of Quesnay and Mirabeau in the summer of 1758.

In English, the term 'physiocracy' sounds like 'physiology' since Quesnay was a physician, but in French, its actual meaning is the 'law of nature'. The physiocratic model was built on the assumption that social phenomena, just like physical phenomena, are governed by the 'laws of nature'. Such laws can be discovered by applying human reason but their functioning is independent of human will and intention. The title of Mercier de la Rivière's book, one of the major physiocratic writings, *The Natural and Essential Order of Political Societies* (1767) captures this idea successfully. This underlying principle of physiocracy was based on the analogical argument drawn from the natural sciences, where the task of the physicists was to discover the natural laws of physical phenomena so that the engineer could design machines in

---

BOX 3.1:   François Quesnay—Father of Physiocracy

Born on 4 June 1694 in Paris, France, François Quesnay was the founder of physiocracy, the first systematic school of political economy. He began his intellectual journey as consulting physician to King Louis XV at Versailles, but later developed a keen interest in economics.

Quesnay's system of political economy depicts the relationship between the different economic classes and sectors of society and the flow of payments between them. In his Tableau, Quesnay developed the notion of economic equilibrium, a concept frequently used as a point of departure for subsequent economic analysis. Quesnay was also the originator of the term 'laissez-faire', which later became one of the cardinal doctrines of liberalism.

The methodology of Quesnay's physiocratic system and his principles of policy sprang from the doctrine of natural law, which he believed represented the divinely appointed economic order. He was, indeed, one of the originators of the nineteenth-century doctrine of the harmony of class interests and of the related doctrine that maximum social satisfaction occurs under free competition.

Quesnay died on 16 December 1774 in Versailles, France.

Source: https://www.britannica.com/biography/Francois-Quesnay.
Image Source: Wikimedia Foundation.

---

accordance with that. The task of the economists, correspondingly, became to discover the natural law[1] governing economic phenomena so that governmental policies could be designed accordingly. The economic policies were supposed to be successful those regard the laws of matter and motion (Gordon 1991). This analogy was drawn from the natural sciences of Descartes, Newton and Kepler, which were based on two premises: that natural phenomena are governed by the laws of nature and that those laws can be discovered by applying reason. The conclusion of these premises is that every rational person has the ability to discover the laws of nature by applying mental reason. On the basis of this analogy, Quesnay and his disciples made an attempt to discover the laws of economy and formed Quesnay's *Tableau* accordingly. Quesnay's *Tableau* is regarded as the central pillar of physiocratic theory.

The basic ideas underlying the physiocratic model is summarized under following categories:

Class

The basic assumption of the physiocrats' model was that the producers produce goods and services not only for direct use, but also for selling to others. In the selling of produced goods and services, the market

---

[1] The idea of the market having a natural law implies that such laws would be universally applicable because they would hold beyond time and space. The extrapolation of this would mean that the economy cannot be controlled within the territorial boundary of nation states, since such an act would be interference in the law of nature. This idea led to the first wave of globalization, whose offshoots were colonialism and imperialism.

works as a system of transaction of goods and services. Physiocrats see economy from the standpoint of the market, where the economy consists of three sectors—agriculture (fishing and mining), landowner-ship and manufacturing. The people involved in these sectors correspondingly make three classes—farmers, landlords and workers.

Single Taxation

The physiocrats discovered that the agricultural sector was the only productive sector since it produced a surplus. On the basis of their discovery, they argued for the imposition of a single tax on the agricul-tural sector. Physiocrats argued that production in the agricultural sector requires the intermixing of labour and natural resources such as sunlight and water, which falls on agriculture free of cost. The people involved in the agricultural sector receive wages for mixing their labour but the landowner gets a share of the natural resources such as sunlight and water. In contrast to the agricultural sector, the manu-facturing sector was supposed to be producing equal to what it consumed in terms of raw materials and food and other materials required for workers and work. This made the manufacturing sector a sterile sector, but that did not mean it was a worthless sector for the physiocrats. Calling agricultural sector the only productive sector was based on its capacity to produce a surplus. On the basis of this, the physiocrats argued for the abolition of the multilayered taxation system and the imposition of a single taxation system on the sector that produced the surplus.

Force of Production

The physiocrats contended that there were only two forces of production—land and labour. They refuted the long-held belief that labour was the main force of production. They argued that labour cannot pro-duce anything without cost, whereas land can render without cost since sunlight and water fall on land free of cost. The share of the natural resources—sunlight and water—were the surpluses produced by the agriculture sector, going to the landowner. The surplus was the reason why physiocrats argued for the imposition of a single tax on the agricultural sector, since it was ethical to impose a tax on the sector which produced the surplus. On the basis of their findings, physiocrats resolved the puzzle of whether land or population (labour) was the main source of the wealth and progress of the nation. They argued that land, instead of the population, was the main source of wealth and progress.

Laissez-faire

The central premise of physiocracy was that, just like in the natural sciences, the economy too had laws of nature; and from those laws, economic principles could be derived that would assist in formulating public policies. The laws of nature have the characteristics of being universal in nature and functioning impartially without the will or intention of human beings. These characteristics gave birth to the idea of a single world economy governed by the economic principles derived from the laws of nature. This idea further gave birth to the idea of laissez-faire ('leave us alone') because the restrictive laws of the govern-ment were seen as damaging the economy by interfering in the laws of nature. This idea finally culmi-nated in the genesis of the idea of a free-market economy. The state refraining from intervening in the market led to the emergence of the ideas of the 'limited state', 'minimal state' and 'laissez-fair state'. These concepts further resulted in the evolution of the conception of 'liberty'.

Mercantilism

Mercantilism, also known as economic nationalism is the second school of thought which is associated with the genesis of classical political economy. This school of thought dominated the Western European economic thoughts from the sixteenth to the late eighteenth centuries, and built up a system with the purpose of developing a wealthy and powerful nation state. The policies of this school sought to enrich the nation state by restraining imports and encouraging exports. The primary goal of mercantilist policies was to achieve a 'favourable' trade balance that could bring gold and silver into the country for maintaining domestic employment. In contrast to the physiocrats, who promoted the idea of a *laissez-faire* state, the mercantile system supported the idea of state-directed economic activity for achieving a favourable trade balance.

Though it is very difficult to club mercantilist ideas in a common rubric since it contains wider nationalist ideas and practices, what we know as mercantilism today was popularized by Adam Smith, who coined the term 'mercantile system' for describing the system of political economy that he attacked in his theory of political economy. With the advent of capitalism, mercantilism emerged in the sixteenth-century Europe, and by the seventeenth century, mercantilist thoughts started unfolding. Maintaining the domination of national interest in economic policies through the central role of the state in directing economic activity and creating a favourable trade balance emerged as the central concern of this school of thought. Conventional wisdom suggests that the mercantilists asserted the primacy of the nation state over the economy and the subordination of wealth creation to power maximization. The nation state was assumed to maximize wealth in the pursuit of security (aggressive or defensive), which shows the necessity of wealth in power of the nation state. Mercantilists see the international economy as a zero-sum game where different countries compete at capturing precious metals such as gold and silver.

Mercantilist thinkers such as Jean-Baptiste Colbert, Thomas Mun, Friedrich List and Alexander Hamilton describe different aspects of mercantilism, but they agree on some common grounds—national security, state-building and wealth creation. A strong nation state, according to mercantilists, was to have a large population, since the large population was supposed to provide a supply of labour, consumers for market goods, and soldiers. The human desire for imported luxury goods were to be minimized since they drained off precious foreign exchange. Thrift, saving and parsimony were regarded as virtues in the mercantilist school, because these were to be helpful in the creation of capital. These ideas of mercantilism provided a favourable climate for the early development of capitalism and expeditions into new territories for extracting precious metals and exporting goods, which ultimately ended in the emergence of colonialism and imperialism.

Rise of Political Economy

The term 'political economy' came into European use in the seventeenth century and became common in the eighteenth century. The widespread use of this term across Europe (in France, the term was *Économie politique*; in Italy, *economia politica*; and in German, *Nationalökonomie*) reflects the rise of national consciousness and the centralization of political power in the nation state (Gordon 1991, 169). This rising consciousness shifted the orientation of students of economic matters towards advocating political policy aimed at promoting the prosperity of nations.

BOX 3.2:   Adam Smith: Father of Classical Economics

Baptized on 5 June 1723 in Kirkcaldy, Fife, Scotland, Adam Smith was a Scottish social philosopher and political economist. Smith is considered the father of classical economics since his pioneering work *An Inquiry into the Nature and Causes of the Wealth of Nations* (1776) gained the status of a classic in the history of economic thought and provided the first comprehensive system of political economy.

Inspired by the doctrine of natural laws of the physiocrats, Smith is known for advocating the idea of the 'invisible hand' of the market in his *Wealth of Nations*. The said idea was nothing but a belief in the natural law of the market. In addition to the physiocrats, the principles of the *Wealth of Nations* were also derived from his earlier treatise The Theory of Moral Sentiments (1759), which interrogated 'the general principles of laws and government and of the different revolutions they have undergone in the different ages and periods of society'. Smith tried to find the 'universal solution' to the 'perennial question' about the source of the ability to form moral judgements, including judgements on one's own behaviour, in the face of the seemingly overriding passions for self-preservation and self-interest.

Smith died on 17 July 1790 in Edinburgh, Scotland.

Source: Encyclopaedia Britannica. Accessed 17 April 2018. https://www.britannica.com/biography/Adam-Smith.

This term was first used in an English book, Sir James Steuart's *An Inquiry into the Principles of Political Economy* (1767). However, Adam Smith, the father of economics, also used the term 'political economy' in the text of his *An Inquiry into the Nature and Causes of the Wealth of Nations* (1776), though not in the title. The popularity of this book by default increased the popularity of the term 'political economy' both inside as well as outside of Europe. Smith on the one hand heavily borrowed from physiocracy; on the other hand, he criticized the body of literature called mercantilism. It is argued that before publishing his seminal manuscript, Smith had already met the physiocrats in France and had a long discussion with Quesnay. Therefore, the impact of physiocracy is very much evident in Smith's formulation of the market having an 'invisible hand'[2], which is nothing but a modified version of the physiocrats' idea that the market has natural laws. In addition to incorporating the ideas of the physiocrats, Smith severely criticized the trade policy of mercantilism. At the core of Smith's critique was the rejection of state intervention in the economy as propounded by the mercantilists. He argued for a free market promoting individual enterprise. Smith saw the role of the state as supporting, not hindering market transactions. Smith rejected the mercantilist idea of trade as a zero-sum game in which one

---

[2] In addition to Adam Smith's 'invisible hand', David Ricardo's theory of rent, Karl Marx's theory of exploitation as well as his theory of infinite accumulation, Alfred Marshall's theory of maximum welfare (the law of diminishing utility plus the law of diminishing returns) and John Stuart Mill's laws of production can be included in the laws of the market.

> **BOX 3.3:** David Ricardo: Father of Political Economy
>
> Born on 18/19 April 1772 in London, England, David Ricardo was the English economist who gave a systematized, classical form to the rising science of economics in the nineteenth century. What we know of political economy nowadays has a lot to do with the ideas of David Ricardo; therefore, he is referred to as the father of political economy. However, Adam Smith is considered the father of classical economics.
>
> Inspired by a galaxy of friends from his time that included James Mill, Jeremy Bentham and Thomas Robert Malthus, Ricardo proposed theories such as the Iron Law of Wages, labour theory of value, theory of comparative advantage and theory of rents. His important publications include *The High Price of Bullion, a Proof of the Depreciation of Bank Notes* (1810), *An Essay on the Influence of a Low Price of Corn on the Profits of Stock* (1815) and *On the Principles of Political Economy and Taxation* (1817). He had also published letters in the *Morning Chronicle*.
>
> Ricardo died on 11 September 1823 in Gatcombe Park, Gloucestershire, England.
>
> **Source:** Encyclopaedia Britannica. Accessed 17 April 2018. https://www.britannica.com/biography/David-Ricardo.

nation's gain is the loss of another nation. Instead of a zero-sum game, Smith proposed the absolute advantage of trade, where each partner in the trade gains a benefit.

Besides Smith, David Ricardo (1776–1834) was another signature figure in classical political economy, whose critique of mercantilism made a significant contribution to the development of the classical political economy. Ricardo laid down the foundation of the comparative advantage theory, which still provides powerful support for free-trade policies. Smith's and Ricardo's ideas on the economy were further contested up to the next two generations, which produced a large body of texts that historians call classical liberal political economy. Apart from Smith and Ricardo, Thomas Robert Malthus (1766–1834), John Stuart Mill (1806–1873) and Karl Marx (1818–1883) are other important economic thinkers whose names are associated with classical political economy.

Decline of Political Economy

The term 'political economy' was replaced with the term 'economics' in the second half of the nineteenth century. The primary reason for this replacement was the awkwardness in the use of this two-word term as an adjective. To remove this awkwardness, William Stanley Jevons (1835–1882), one of the originators of neoclassical economics and the author of *The Theory of Political Economy* (1871), suggested using the term 'economics' so that it could become analogous with modern subject names such as mathematics, physics, ethics, and so on. Alfred Marshall, the chief theorist of neoclassical economics, felt that the adjective 'political', referring to a policy or nation, had come to denote a particular sectional interest within the nation; therefore, he not only abandoned using the adjective 'political' with 'economics' but also popularized the new term 'economics' through his lectures and writings. He titled his text *Principles of Economics* (1890), which became the seminal treatise of the neoclassical economy.

Though the initial objective of Alfred Marshall and others was only removing the awkwardness of the two-word term 'political economy', the exercise gradually resulted in the evolution of a new discipline. The new discipline which emerged due to the efforts of Alfred Marshall and others had something more than just a name change. The basic analytical model of neoclassical economics was different in fundamental respects from the older classical political economy. This shift was in terms of the emphasis of study: classical political economics pushed for studying economic growth and historical developments, whereas the neoclassical economic pushed towards studying the functioning of the market and efficient use of limited productive resources. The change of the subject matter of analysis in neoclassical economics led to the emergence of a new discipline called 'microeconomics'. The subject matter of the new discipline was paradigmatically different from the old one. Therefore, historians retained the term 'political economy' for studying the set of ideas, concepts and theories which are often associated with the thoughts of David Ricardo. This does not mean that political economy derecognized the works of Adam Smith but for avoiding confusion since the name of Smith is associated with the modern economics.

The moving of neoclassical economy towards the natural sciences in general and mathematics in particular resulted in the carving out of the 'economic' from political economy and leaving the 'political' far behind. Therefore, for studying the political, another discipline called 'political science' emerged. Similarly, sociology emerged for studying the social. This is how the major disciplines of the social sciences—economics, political science and sociology—came out of political economy, as a result of which classical political economy is called the 'mother of the social sciences'.

A series of incidents in the first half of the twentieth century—the First World War, the communist revolution in Russia and the Great Depression—contributed to the emergence of another discipline of economics, called 'macroeconomics'. Macroeconomics, associated with J.M. Keynes, further acted as a big blow to classical political economy, since it questioned the basic premise that the market has a natural law with which economy can be managed efficiently, provided that the state refrained from intervening in the market's function. The success of the Union of Soviet Socialist Republics (USSR) with state intervention in the economy and the failure of the United States of America (US) and Europe without state intervention in the economy during the Great Depression brought the nation state back to the helm of affairs in the market. But this does not mean that another premise of classical liberalism, that the market was the best mechanism to manage the economy, was also abandoned. The belief in this premise remained intact.

The changing belief regarding the role of the state in the economy demanded the development of a new consensus for managing the economy, which was developed during the Second World War. Inspired by J. M. Keynes's work *The General Theory of Employment, Interest and Money* (1936), the new consensus brought a 'paradigm shift' in the idea of the market's functioning, leading to the further decline of classical political economy. Under the new consensus, the responsibility for managing the economy was distributed between both the market and the state. At the production level, the state was supposed to produce public goods whereas the market was supposed to produce consumer goods, and on the policy front, the state was given the task of managing fiscal policy whereas monetary policy was to be managed by an autonomous central bank.

By bringing the state back into managing the economy, the new consensus almost refuted the idea of the market having a natural law, because under the schema of the new consensus, the market was to be regulated by the central banks and the financial institutions, and the laws of these institutions were made by humans. For implementing the mandates of the new consensus, not only did central banks come into existence at the domestic level across countries, but also the Bretton Woods Institutions—the World Bank and the International Monetary Fund (IMF)—were established at the international level. These regulatory institutions were given the task of framing the law for the market at an international level.

Rearrival of Political Economy as Global Political Economy

The end of the Second World War led to the emergence of a new world order based on the ideological division between the US and the USSR. This division caused a polarization of the new world order around these two superpowers and resulted in the beginning of the cold war. Though the two superpowers were engaged in the cold war, they agreed on the principle of managing the economy of the new world order via the newly established Bretton Woods Institutions, that is, the IMF and World Bank. The structure of these institutions was such that they began tilting towards the US within two decades of their establishment. These institutions expanded their mandate from merely managing the world economy to forcing countries to open up their economy through structural adjustment programmes. In this task, the US actively assisted the Bretton Woods Institutions, by placing its currency at the centre of transactions in the world economy. But in the decades of the 1960s, the US realized that it might get caught up in the Triffin Dilemma[3] in the near future, which would be a big blow to its economy, and the ultimate result of which would be losing the status of a superpower. To solve this dilemma, the US withdrew its currency from the central stage of the world economy in in the second half of the decades of the 1960s. This act of the US resulted in the beginning of the second wave of globalization, since the currencies of other countries now once again started gaining worth in the transactions of goods and services in the world market.

The onset of the second wave of globalization started increasing the interdependency between nations, as a result of which the competition between nation states increased. This increased competition has transformed the nation state from 'state security' to 'state competition'. When the state was seen merely as a 'security state', the study of diplomacy and security was seen as high politics, whereas the study of international economic relations—trade and licences—was seen as low politics. But globalization broke down this hierarchy by giving primacy to policy matters. The deregulation promoted by globalization has transformed the state authority in policymaking as well as market power. And by doing this, globalization has posed new sets of problems about governing the world economy. The problem is, how would the world economy be managed in the era of globalization? This problem is nothing but the derivative of the problem of classical political economy that asked how the economy should be managed efficiently.

---

[3] The Triffin Dilemma is named on Robert Triffin who was a profound critic of the Bretton Woods System in the 1960s. Triffin had suggested turning of the IMF into a 'deposit bank' for central banks and creating a new 'reserve asset' under the control of the IMF. Following his advice, in 1967, Special Drawing Rights (SDR), also known as Paper Gold, was created and gold was replaced.

The search for the solution to the problem—how the economy should be managed efficiently in the era of globalization—has raised very serious methodological concerns, since the impact of globalization on the economy, polity and society is very complex in nature and hence cannot be studied without adopting the righteous methodology. To solve methodological concerns, a consensus has been emerging across the 'methodological churches' that there should be an interdisciplinary study of globalization and its implications. Another agreement has been emerging that the analytical separation between the economic and the political, the domestic and the international which led to the evolution of the major social-science disciplines in the later nineteenth and early twentieth century is no longer sustainable because of its incapability in explaining globalization and its implications. This consensus has further translated into a convergence of the social-science disciplines on a single point, and that is the economy. The major disciplines of the social sciences—economics, political science and sociology—historically emerged from (classical) political economy; therefore, the newly emerging discipline is referred to as 'global political economy' (GPE).

The mandate of GPE is primarily to study the domains of international activities in which the behaviour of markets—as a provider of finance, services and public goods—is the major form of global activity. It sees the post-Second World War economy as nothing but the domestication of the international economy which prioritized issues of security and diplomacy while taking economic decisions; but globalization has freed the international economy from domestication by pushing issues of security and diplomacy to the back seat and placing decision-making in the driver's seat in world politics. In globalization, the state is still a central actor of policymaking, but its *a priori* concern has changed and now it is only competing to secure economic profit. This is the reason why the state is nowadays termed a 'competitive state' rather than a 'security state'.

It is interesting to note that with the onward march of globalization, there emerged strong concerns for environment and ecology which gradually took the driver's seat in world politics. The environmental and ecological concerns impelled the states to move towards cooperation, since we have our common future. In this movement towards a common future, non-state and intergovernmental actors play a very significant role. Therefore, the focus of GPE is not only studying the changing relationship between the state authority and the market players but also the non-state actors and intergovernmental actors. It should be noted that the publication of the books *The Limits to Growth* (Meadows et al. 1972) and *Small Is Beautiful: A Study of Economics as if People Mattered* (Schumacher 1973) in the early decades of the 1970s brought about a paradigm shift in world politics by creating such intense debate across the world that it forced nation states to sit down together and think about solutions to the environmental and ecological problems.

The seminal book *Limits to Growth,* in addition to creating global awareness about ecological and environmental concerns, also provided effective tools for understanding GPE. The importance of this book for scholars of political economy is that it offered the first scientific model which provided evidence for Malthus's theory of population. Robert Malthus, one of the classical political economists, had argued that the population would grow exponentially if food availability would be abundant. Taking world population, industrialization, pollution, food production and resource depletion as the five variables of analysis, this book provided a computer simulation of the exponential relation between population and economic growth, keeping resource supply finite. This computer simulation not only regenerated a classical theory but also proved that conceptual categories such as land, labour, capital and population are still relevant for economic analysis.

Global Political Economy in the Twenty-first Century: New Issues and Anchors

The consequential analysis of the policies of the post–Second World War economic institutions—World Bank and IMF—has been proven to be structurally biased in favour of the developed countries. Those policies acted as soft coercion on other countries for opening up of their market. Such acts by these institutions have produced uneven impacts vis-à-vis developed, developing and underdeveloped countries. The imposition of those policies has resulted into the erosion of state's sovereignty, resulting into ignoring domestic issues in the policy framing. But up to some extent, the onward march of globalization has turned the table upside down by providing voice to state, civil society and individual in the decision-making structure and procedures. The re-arrival of state in the domain of decision-making has brought back the domestic issues once again at the forefront of public policymaking.

The return of the domestic to the domain of public policy has resulted in making global certain local practices, cultures, foods and garments of developing countries. Although the charge of domestication of economic policies used to be levelled during the heydays of the Bretton Woods Institutions, that was true only for developed countries. In reality, it was the developing countries which were the real victims of domestication of economic policies in the hands of the developed countries, since the former had to accept the policies propagated by the developed countries on the pretext of universalism. The second wave of globalization, to some extent, has de-domesticated economic policies, as a result of which, local practices and cultures from developing countries have started acquiring some significance in the global market. The global significance of these practices and cultures is nowadays explained with new terminologies like 'glocal', 'rurban', and so on.

On the one hand, local practices and cultures have been getting pre-eminence position in decision-making in the onward march of the second wave of globalization, but on the other hand, the establishment of the World Trade Organization (WTO) for designing trade policies after the disintegration of the USSR has once again brought back the question of the design of a market being structurally biased in favour of developed countries in general and the elites in particular. The outcome of these structural biases has been resulting in the rise of regional disparity. The spread of regional disparity has further resulted in increasing economic inequality globally, which further has multiple implications in the social, political and economic spheres of human life. Globalization has accelerated the increasing economic inequality, as a result of which the global financial crisis of 2008 happened. The GPE primarily studies the consequences of globalization; inequality and financial crisis are interlinked with globalization. Therefore, the study of these issues has been gradually becoming the central concern of this new discipline in the twenty-first century.

The process of globalization has been subordinating labour, and making capital more free. Therefore, the nature of capital as well as ownership has been changing. Capital has been becoming global in nature. Global capital has been leading to the evolution of MNCs and regional trade blocks across the world, which are the new anchors of GPE in the twenty-first century. These new anchors of GPE have been further accelerating economic inequality.

The study of inequality transcends disciplinary boundaries and covers new concerns such as the 'digital divide'. It should be noted that the inventions in the field of information and communication technology in the last decades of the twentieth century have brought about a technological revolution across the world. The dawn of the twenty-first century bore witness to the information technology (IT) revolution, the seeds of which were sown in the last two decades of the twentieth century. This revolution on the one hand empowered people, but on the other hand, it has also disempowered people. It is disempowering people by producing new categories of haves and have-nots. The IT revolution has been dividing the whole population into two sets of people, those who know technology and those who do not know technology. In the language of Marx, the former are the haves and the latter are the have-nots. This new forms of inequality have been promoting a sense of powerlessness and helplessness in the have-nots, among those who are from marginalized and vulnerable sections of society. The globalization which has shrunk time and space has been once again at the forefront in bringing about the IT revolution and transforming society into a network society, in which different components are merely nodes.

The study of the financial crisis and the increasing economic inequality, which is leading to the escalation of other kinds of inequalities, have once again brought back the old conceptual categories such as land, labour, capital and population for analysing the contemporary world economy and understanding new trends and patterns. The return of these conceptual categories in the analysis of global economy can be best seen in Thomas Piketty's recent work *Capital in the Twenty-first Century* (2014) which is nothing but the reproduction of the (classical) political economy in the twenty-first century.

Concluding Observations

In summing up, it can be concluded that GPE is a discipline as well as an approach which has emerged for solving the problems which globalization has posed since its beginning in 1970. Globalization has carved out a global market. As a new discipline, GPE analyses the principles that are supposed to be used for managing and regulating the global market. While discussing the concerns about the managing principles of the global market, GPE departs from its previous avatar of classical political economy, from discovering the natural law through which the global market can be regulated, and moves on to arguing that such an assumption relies on a myth. The global market is functioning on laws made by humans, as a result of which the problems in the world economy need to be solved through human laws, and that is possible only through the democratization of the structures of the lawmaking economic institutions.

The compression of time and space in the onward march of globalization has. on the one hand, pushed states and individuals towards greater interdependency and interconnectedness; on the other hand, it has blurred the old binaries between the political and the economic, the domestic and the international, as well as the ideal and the material, the categories which used to act as effective mechanisms for studying social, economic, political, domestic and international phenomena. This blurring has posed a serious challenge to studying the complex implications of globalization, such as increasing economic inequality and the threat of its further escalation. Here, GPE has come to the rescue and acts as an approach to solve the problems which globalization has posed. It has helped by appealing for a greater interdisciplinary approach, where the division between disciplines of the social sciences get erased. The economy is the point where they converge; therefore, the new approach has taken the economy as the prime subject of analysis. The modern social-science disciplines have emerged from classical political economy; therefore, this newly emerged discipline is named 'global political economy' (GPE). The heavy borrowing of conceptual categories from classical political economy has forced us to trace the evolution of GPE from classical political economy.

Summary

- The global political economy is a product of the globalization which began in 1970. Globalization has compressed time and space, as a result of which interconnectedness and interdependency between states and individuals have increased. This phenomenon has further led to the emergence of a global market. GPE evaluates the principles through which the global market is supposed to be regulated.
- Globalization has also blurred the boundaries between old binaries such as the political and the economic, the domestic and the international, and to some extent, the material and the ideal. This blurring has created a crisis for modern disciplines of the social sciences in studying the complex implications of globalization. GPE, while incorporating a multidisciplinary approach, provides an approach to study the complex phenomenon of globalization.
- GPE traces the idea of the world having a single market through which the economy can be managed efficiently from classical political economy. Classical political economy evolved while drawing on principles from physiocracy and mercantilism. The physiocrats, borrowing the idea of natural laws from the natural sciences, argued that the market too has such natural laws, through which the economy could be best managed, provided the state refrained from interfering.
- Classical political economy was also concerned with questions about what decides the value of any goods. Why did a good having high utility have low value, whereas the other good of low utility had higher value? What is the source of wealth—population or land? Was the population on earth declining or increasing?
- Classical political economy is the mother of the major disciplines of the social sciences—economics, political science and sociology. The separating out of these disciplines led to the decline of classical political economy.
- Globalization has brought back the question of the best way of managing the global economy. Classical political economy was dealing with similar sets of questions. This is why the evolution of GPE is also seen as the rearrival of classical political economy.
- GPE unites all the major disciplines of the social sciences while adopting a multidisciplinary approach. In this way, GPE is an approach for studying the implications of globalization.
- GPE has to face the challenges of escalating inequalities, technological transformation, a network society, the knowledge economy, and environmental and ecological problems in the twenty-first century.

Suggested Questions

1. Critically examine the contemporary significance of global political economy (GPE).
2. Discuss the process of the evolution of classical political economy.
3. Examine the causes which might be attributed to the decline of classical political economy.
4. What role has globalization played in the emergence of GPE?
5. Discuss the contemporary challenges which GPE would be facing in the twenty-first century.
6. How did globalization transform the role of the state and the individual in the world economy?
7. Evaluate the contemporary relevance of the ideas which were propounded by the physiocrats and the mercantilists.

References

Gordon, Scott. 1991. *The History and Philosophy of Social Science.* London: Routledge.

Higgott, Richard. 2007. 'International Political Economy'. In *A Companion to Contemporary Political Philosophy,* vol. 1, edited by Robert E. Goodin, Philip Pettit and Thomas W. Pogge, 153–182. Victoria: Blackwell Publishing House.

Further Reading

Backhaus, J. G. ed. 2012. *Handbook of the History of Economic Thought: Insights on the Founders of Modern Economics.* New York: Springer.

Cohn, Theodore H. 2009. *Global Political Economy: Theory and Practice.* New Delhi: Routledge.

Falkner, R. 2005. *International Political Economy.* London: University of London.

Gilpin, Robert. 2001. *Global Political Economy: Understanding the International Economic Order.* New Jersey: Princeton University Press.

Palan, Ronen, ed. 2013. *Global Political Economy: Contemporary Theories.* London and New York: Routledge.

Piketty, Thomas. 2014. *Capital in the Twenty-first Century.* Translated by Arthur Goldhammer. London: Harvard University Press.

Ravenhill, John. ed. 2014. *Global Political Economy.* London: Oxford University Press.

Underhill, Geoffrey R. D. 2004. 'State, Market, and Global Political Economy: Genealogy of an (Inter-?) Discipline'. In *International Affairs* 76 (4): 805–824. Accessed 17 August 2017. http://www.jstor.org/stable/2626461.

Veseth, Michael. 'What Is International Political Economy?' Accessed 17 April 2018. http://www2.ups.edu/ipe/whatis.pdf.

Walter, Andrew, and Gautam Sen. 2009. *Analyzing the Global Political Economy.* Princeton: Princeton University Press.

Economic Globalization: Global Trade and Finance

Virendra Kumar

LEARNING OBJECTIVES

- To understand the competing theoretical perspectives on economic globalization
- To examine the nature and pattern of global trade with special reference to the Global South
- To critically analyse financial globalization with a focus on economic crises both in developed and developing economies
- To evaluate the pattern of inequality and informalization in the Global South

At the outset, it must be acknowledged that the idea of globalization is highly contested, and any explanation of this phenomenon reflects a particular point of view. Globalization is conceived of as a process of increasing integration and interdependence across multiple spheres of social relations. It refers to a new pattern of social interaction and new modes of transnational social organization which transcend regions and national frontiers and thus challenge the territorial principle of modern political organization. The process of globalization tends to disrupt the correspondence between society, economy and polity within an exclusive and bounded national territory. Territory and space are relevant, but under the condition of contemporary globalization, they are reinvented and reconfigured in a global context. Moreover, globalization also involves the reordering of power relations between and across the world's major regions such that key sites of power and those who are subject to them are oceans apart (Held and McGrew 2000, 8). This characterization represents the economic liberal's perspective, which considers contemporary globalization a real and significant historical development. Those who see globalization as an irreversible process of increasing integration at multiple levels, which cannot as such be explained with reference to capitalist modernity or technological determinism, are referred to as 'globalists'.

The Marxist perspective tends to dismiss the descriptive or explanatory value of the concept of globalization. They believe that a more valid conceptualization of the current trend is captured by the terms 'internationalization' (i.e., growing links between essentially discrete national economies or societies) and 'regionalization' (the geographical clustering of cross-border economic and social exchanges). This perspective lays emphasis on the continuing primacy of territory, place and national government to the distribution of power, production and wealth in the contemporary world order. In the literature on globalization, those who see globalization as primarily an ideological construct which has marginal explanatory value are called 'sceptics'.

Having delineated these two contending perspectives, this chapter on global trade and finance intends to present a balanced view in light of empirical evidence gained over the past thirty years. The chapter analyses the pattern of global trade and finance from the vantage point of the Global South, which houses millions of poor and vulnerable people. Since after the Second World War, Bretton Woods Institutions such as the General Agreement on Tariffs and Trade (GATT) and the International Monetary Fund (IMF) have been driving the developing economies in matters of trade and finance. These institutions, in their rule-making structure, favour the interests of the advanced economies of the North Atlantic. They prescribe deregulation, privatization and liberalization of trade as a panacea for all economic ills gripping the developing and traditional economies. While the Global South has witnessed the emergence of new Asian Tigers, such as China, India, and Malaysia, inequality and wage gap still remain realities. Also, these economies have been vulnerable to many financial shocks. Outside Asia, very few countries have made advances. I will begin by presenting the contending theoretical perspectives on globalization, followed by a discussion on the World Trade Organization (WTO) and how it promotes global trade. While discussing the limitations of the WTO and the skewed nature of global trade, I will highlight the parallel process of regionalization. While analysing global finance, I will focus on the increasing vulnerability of developing economies and the need for regulation of global finance. In the last section, I have tried to show that the Global South is not globalized except for the dominance of a handful of Asian countries in South–South trade and North–South trade.

Economic Globalization: Theoretical Underpinnings

Globalization entails the integration of national economies into more open economies so as to derive material prosperity for all. The free flow of goods and capital without restrictions tends to create a large competitive market, offering wider consumer choices at relatively less cost. The advocates of globalization draw theoretical insights from classical liberals such as Adam Smith and David Ricardo as also from such modern economists as Bertil Ohlin, Paul Samuelson and Milton Friedman.

Classical Economic Liberalism: Free Trade

Economic liberalism emerged against the practice of monopoly capitalism and protectionism from the sixteenth to the eighteenth century in Europe. Adam Smith (1723–1790) advocated the idea of free trade and its impact on maximizing the national wealth, as against protectionism. According to Smith, individual preferences and choices must guide the organization of economic activity, that is, resource allocation process. The interaction of self-interested individuals results in a collective good (wealth generation). A competitive environment, however, is essential for restraining the few individuals or firms who are tempted to form monopolies in order to increase their profits at the expense of both consumers and workers. In this perspective, government intervention in the form of tariffs or quotas distorts resource allocation and creates inefficiency and wasteful monopolies in the market. The state is only to play a minimal role in the economy, such as by enforcement of property rights, administration of security, and so on (Macheda 2012).

David Ricardo introduced the concept of specialization and comparative advantage in international trade in the early nineteenth century, and argued that trade between two countries could benefit both the countries and raise the living standard of their people if each country exported the goods in which it had a comparative advantage. The comparative advantage is said to exist when the opportunity cost of producing those goods (compared to other goods) is lower in that country than it is in the other country. The underlying idea is that a country can specialise in the production of a few goods and trade based on this would increase the world output with relatively less unit labour (Krugman et al. 2010, 25–34). Subsequent research establishes that economies of scale allow countries to specialize and trade even in the absence of differences in resource or technology. The economy of scale implies the tendency of the unit cost to be lower with larger output. The creation of an integrated and larger market than the domestic market supports a large number of firms, each producing at a large scale, and this lowers the average cost. Consumers have a greater variety of goods and lower prices. Because of competitive pressure only the more productive (lower cost) firms thrive and expand while less productive (higher cost) ones are forced to exit (Krugman et al. 2010, 187).

Economic liberalism has evolved a lot since Smith and Ricardo. Neo-liberal economists still favour the elimination of trade barriers and minimal interference in markets, but they see a greater role for international economic institutions. They argue that market efficiency produces greater wealth for the whole world and leaves every one better off, though there may be economic inequality (Mansbach and Taylor 2012, 463).

Neo-Marxist Perspective

Neo-Marxist scholars see globalization as form of capitalism engulfing the whole world in a way that perpetuates capitalist class domination and exploitation of poor people around the world. Robert Cox believes that the process of economic globalization has created a situation where nation states have lost substantial power over the economy and yet the nation state is very much required to provide a political and legal framework for the continued process of economic globalization (Cox 1994). The advanced industrial economies of the US, Europe and Japan are reaping the benefits of globalization by taking advantage of asymmetrical and unfair rules that characterize the global financial institutions (Nayyar 2007, 91–116).

Despite internationalization of financial markets and the increasing importance of international trade in key areas, nation states remain a pivotal institution. The open international economy is characterized by competition between predominantly national companies, trading from their national bases in distinctive national regulatory systems. Business firms are likely to make better investment decisions and develop better production and marketing strategies if there is stability in the exchange rate and there exist common property rights and trade rules internationally. Companies cannot create these conditions for themselves even if they are transnational. A common regime of trade standards and stability to carry out free trade is possible only if states work together to achieve a common international regulation (Hirst and Thompson 2010, 308). Moreover, states are the main source of legitimacy for international agreements between states and subnational authority structures at various levels. Though populations are becoming mobile, they still need citizenship of a nation state and get recognition in other states only if they have a passport, visa and other nationally determined qualifications (Hirst and Thompson 2010, 311).

Globalization: Origin

The origins of economic globalization can be traced to industrialization and the beginning of capitalism in Britain in the eighteenth century. The phenomenal advancement in transport and communications, such as the steamship, the railway and the telegraph, along with machine-based mass production of goods, created huge wealth in Europe. After achieving its own industrialization, Britain, as the pioneer of industrial power, through political and military coercion, made peripheral territories around the world to open their door to economic penetration. The process of economic penetration across the globe was not accomplished all at once, but took place in a succession of expanding concentric circles (Nayyar 2007, 3). The predominance of European military powers underpins the first extensive phase of economic globalization, which can be said to have lasted from 1870 to 1913 (prior to the First World War), when internal peace prevailed among the North Atlantic powers, even as these powers were engaged in extending their economic and political sway over the entire world. The First World War and subsequent great depression of the 1930s saw protectionist policies adopted by major states. As the Second World War ended with the defeat of fascist forces, the process of globalization resumed under US auspices, though it was confined to mainly to the world outside the Soviet bloc. Economic globalization was sought to be achieved through multilateral institutions under US patronage. The breakdown of a fixed exchange rate under the Bretton Woods system and the rising oil prices of the early 1970s provided the required foundation for the contemporary intensive phase of globalization.

Contemporary Globalization: From Shallow to Deep Integration

The contemporary globalization process can be taken to have started with the establishment of the Bretton Woods Institutions meant to provide a stable economic order after the Great Depression (1930s) and the economic chaos following the Second World War. Scholars of Marxist persuasion see this as the beginning of a shallow globalization, with the state dictating the foreign capital, whereas globalization since the late 1970s is called 'deep globalization', wherein foreign capital and the market dictate to the state. Major powers including the US took the initiative to establish a liberal trade regime by establishing multilateral institutions such as GATT, the World Bank and the IMF. These institutions, especially GATT and the IMF, sought to steer and guide the new economic order based on a free market, free trade and entrepreneurial freedom. Free trade in goods was encouraged under a system of fixed exchange rate, but states still possessed enough policy space and room to manoeuvre to respond to their social and economic needs (Rodrik 2011, 69). The state was to focus on full employment, economic growth and welfare of citizens and might devise a suitable policy strategy in the market process to achieve these ends.

The economic crisis of the 1970s involving high oil prices, high inflation and unemployment across the developed world, however, paved the way for contemporary globalization, seen as a process towards integrating domestic economies with larger international economies without restrictions and barriers of any sort. The free flow of goods and capital across national borders without state restrictions, argue globalists, will lead to higher economic growth, and this in turn will help reduce poverty and help undertake other social welfare measures (Bhagwati 2004, 55–61). The role of the state is to create and preserve an institutional framework so as to facilitate the proper functioning of the market and secure private-property rights. Beyond this, state intervention in the market (once created) must be kept to a minimum because the state cannot possibly possess enough information to second-guess market signals (prices) and also because powerful interest groups will inevitably distort state intervention in their own favour (Harvey 2005).

This neo-liberal perspective advocating the supremacy of market wisdom in efficient allocation of scarce resources and achieving higher economic growth, as against the Keynesian philosophy of state intervention to achieve full employment and welfare of citizens, found expression in the economic policies of Margaret Thatcher and Ronald Reagan in the early 1980s in UK and the US respectively. These two leaders represented this ideological shift, and sought to cut down public expenditure meant for social welfare and lowered the corporate taxes to encourage private capital. They also sought to liberalize their regulatory framework, giving more free space to their capital market, the movement of portfolios (equities and bond) and direct investment. The same policy prescriptions were given to countries of Asia, Africa and Latin America, who were reeling under economic crises of varying natures in the 1980s and early 1990s. The fall of the Berlin Wall (1989) and subsequent dissolution of the USSR further paved the way for deep and intensive economic integration and globalization. The phenomenal advancement in satellite technology and information communication technology further helped economic globalization for developing and least developed economies. The developed world, led by the US, enjoyed greater leverage in framing and devising the rules and principles of the multilateral financial Institutions which steered the economic and financial globalization.

Global Trade and WTO

GATT had been devised in 1944 to promote international trade by the gradual removal of trade barriers through mutual consultation and negotiation. Though it did not have a formal structure and mass membership, various rounds of negotiations till 1990 led to substantial reduction of tariff across products.[1] The WTO, which replaced GATT, was established to expand global trade in agriculture and services, apart from manufactures. Besides, intellectual property rights and health and safety standards were also

---

[1] The General Agreement on Tariffs and Trade (GATT) was a legal agreement, signed on 30 October 1947, between many countries to promote international trade by reducing tariffs and other trade barriers on a reciprocal and mutually advantageous basis. Beginning in Geneva in 1947, GATT had eight rounds of negotiations till 1994, when the World Trade Organization (WTO) came into being: in Annency (1949), Torquay (1951), Geneva (1955–1956), Dillon (1960–1962), Kennedy (1962–1967), Tokyo (1973–1979) and Uruguay (1986–1994). The Uruguay round saw the participation of developing countries and sought to include new areas, such as agriculture, intellectual property rights, services, and so on. Medium-sized agricultural exporters such as Brazil, Australia, Indonesia and New Zealand formed the Cairns Group and pressed for trade liberalization in agricultural products.

incorporated in the WTO negotiations. The principles of most-favoured-nation (MFN) and non-discrimination are to be followed by member countries in granting market access to each other's goods. This implies that tariff concessions given by country A to country B would be applicable to other countries as well. The removal of agricultural quotas, tariffs and subsidies was advocated with differentiated obligation for developed and developing countries. Countries were required to open up their service sectors, such as banking, telecom and insurance, for foreign multinationals. The quota regime of the multi-fibre agreement dealing with restricted trade in textiles among developed countries was to be phased out. Besides, health and safety regulations became subject to WTO scrutiny if they were not in sync with international standards. Rules relating to patent and copyright required developing countries to bring their domestic patent laws into conformity with those in advanced countries. These new rules explicitly helped multinationals having their origin in the US and Western Europe to enter the markets of developing economies without much strict regulation relating to labour laws, wages, taxes and environment. Russia, China and many erstwhile communist economies joined the WTO and opened up their economies in agriculture, manufactures and services.

Global Trade Pattern and Success Stories

Various studies show that globalization and the free-trade system under the WTO have had great success over the last two decades. Tariff barriers and non-tariff barriers have been significantly reduced, with tariff protection against industrial products at the historically lowest level in almost all countries (Bhagwati et al. 2014). The bound tariff indicates that concerned countries will not raise the tariff rate in future. Developed countries have bound virtually all their tariff while developing countries have bound a substantial portion of their tariff lines. Moreover, in the developed world, a simple average applied tariff uniformly stands at 5%. In Latin America, applied tariff averages below 15%. India has applied tariffs averaging around 10% while China has maintained tariffs at 8.7% (Bhagwati et al. 2014, 5).

There has emerged a transnationalization of production, trade and finance. Multinational corporations (MNCS) and transnational corporations (TNC) have spread their production network to different parts of the world in order to avail locational advantages such as cheap labour, flexible labour laws, less taxes, and so on. This has created global value chains (GVC) and helped magnify transactions in goods and services in world trade. Linkages between national economies are influenced by cross-border value-adding activities within TNCs and within networks established by TNCs (Dicken 2000, 253). The increasing expansion of value-added production activities has created a process of 'competitive flattening', in which developing and emerging economies compete to see who can give companies the best tax break and subsidies on top of their cheap labour to attract MNCS to their shores (Friedman 2005, 138–146). The decreasing transportation and telecommunication costs have helped global movement of goods and services too.

The flow of foreign direct investment (FDI) in East Asian and South-East Asian countries has transformed the region into a major source of manufactures export. Taiwan, Hong Kong, Singapore, Malaysia and South Korea account for the largest number of transnational corporations and have become major sources as well as recipients of FDI. These countries initially began with manufacture of low-skill, labour-intensive goods, but gained momentum with the emergence of the semiconductor industry, which increasingly set up offshore assembly plants (Ferguson and Mansbach 2012, 197).

China has emerged as the most potent economic and political competitor of the US, attracting billions in FDI and possessing a huge foreign reserve. Though successive Chinese rulers since Deng Xiaoping's economic reform (begun in 1979) have emphasized deregulation, export and free movement of foreign investment, it still relies heavily on state-owned enterprises. China's trade surplus with the rest of the world peaked in 2008 at nearly $300 billion, but narrowed down in 2010 at $183 billion.

With a vast but shrinking pool of cheap labour, China has become a leading destination for US and Japanese transnational corporations wishing to reduce production costs and increase global competitiveness. Besides, the US trade deficit with China has persisted for a long time, with a trade deficit of over $140 billion between 2000 and 2009. This has meant a loss of jobs in US and elsewhere. Economists argue that this happens because of China's unfair trading practices, including refusing to allow its currency to appreciate in value relative to the US dollar, thereby making US exports to China less expensive (Mansbach and Taylor 2012, 168). China's enormous dollar reserve has enabled it to finance US trade and budgetary deficits by purchasing US securities.

Parallel to China, India has also made advances in merchandise and service trade after introducing economic reforms in 1991 as part of the loan conditionality put forth by the IMF. Telecommunications and banking sectors have attracted huge FDI and witnessed growth in productivity. India emerged as a major software exporter, apart from Indian business firms such as Tata Motors and the Mittal Steel Company increasing their involvement in global business mergers and acquisitions (M&A), especially after 2000. Riding on the success of the information technology (IT) sector after liberalization, India has experienced double-digit growth in its exports, averaging around 15% annually between 1990 and 2010. Middle-income economies such as Brazil, Turkey, South Korea, Indonesia and Thailand have experienced nearly 10% export growth (Bhagwati et al. 2014, 8).

The share of North–South trade has remained at around 37% since 2000. This indicates that a large share of trade in the countries of the developed world occurs among themselves (about 63%), whereas South–South trade has increased from 8% to 24% between 1990 and 2011 (World Trade Organization 2013, 62). The rising share of South–South trade in world export is underpinned by an increasing number of preferential trade agreements (PTAs) negotiated between developing economies. Such agreements account for the majority of the new PTAs concluded since 1990.

The share of manufactured goods in world merchandise trade has increased relentlessly. It rose from 40% of total trade in 1990 to 70% in 2000, before falling back to 65% in 2011. In contrast, the share of agricultural products saw a declining trend, from 12% in 1990 to 9% in 2011. The advance of manufactured goods was slowed by rising primary-commodity prices, of especially fuel and mining products (World Trade Organization 2013, 66). Resource-rich developing economies (e.g., Nigeria, Algeria and Venezuela) and least developing countries (the Central African Republic, Niger and Madagascar) tend to have relatively little intra-industry trade, whereas developed economies (the US and the EU) engage in more intra-industry trade with other developed economies, and rapidly industrializing developing economies such as Hong Kong, Malaysia and Thailand have more industry trade (World Trade Organization 2013, 69).

Agricultural trade has also witnessed expansion in the 1990s and 2000s, but its share remained less than 10% of merchandise trade. All the gain in agriculture during the 1990s came from expansion of export to other developing countries. More than 48% of world agricultural trade is still accounted for by trade between industrial countries, within EU and North American Free Trade Agreement (NAFTA) members. Despite comparative advantages in various traditional and non-traditional agricultural commodities (seafood, fruits, dairy products, and so on), low-income developing economies export more to middle-income countries. Their products have been denied market access in Organisation for Economic Co-operation and Development (OECD) countries on account of not meeting food safety and health standards (Aksoy and Beghin 2005, 5). Globalists argue that agricultural trade liberalization leads to higher world prices, which will benefit poor farmers in developing economies, provided they are net sellers of food and the price changes reach them. The fact, however, is that millions of farmers in low-income and middle-income countries practise subsistence farming and do not produce a surplus for the market. There also exist infrastructure deficits which inhibit value additions and export diversification. The least-developed African countries' reliance on a small number of agricultural commodities leaves them vulnerable to world price fluctuations and downward turns. World agricultural prices also fluctuate and go down on account of huge subsidies (over $100 billion) provided by the US and European countries to their rich farmers (Aksoy and Beghin 2005, 3). The huge subsidy to their cotton growers has badly hurt poor cotton farmers in West and Central Africa, as also Indian farmers, many of whom are forced to commit suicide out of frustration with lower remuneration for their produce in the market. But they vociferously oppose the moderate levels of subsidy provided by developing countries, including India, to ensure food security and to support poor farmers' income as per the WTO provisions over subsidy. Since agriculture constitutes a source of livelihood and food security for millions in Asia, Africa and Latin America, the WTO's Doha round of negotiation has almost died over this issue. India, China and Brazil have also gained the support of other developing nations in advancing the cause of poor farmers by not succumbing to pressure from the developed world to give up public stockholding of agricultural produce. Developing nations, having formed the Group of 33 (G-33) at the WTO ministerial meet in Bali (2013), were able to get a peace clause passed, an interim provision allowing public stockholding in return for supporting trade facilitation.

Globalization and Regionalism: Preferential Trade Agreements (PTAs)

The WTO, through Article 5 of the General Agreement on Trade in Services (GATS), does allow countries to enter into preferential trade agreements in the form of free trade areas (FTAs) and customs unions (CU) with one another. Since the 1980s, there has been a substantial increase in regional trading blocs, which are essentially economic in character. These trade blocs operate as regional spaces through which states can interact, rather than being drawn into EU-style supranational experiments (Heywood 2014, 495). The Asia-Pacific Economic Cooperation was created in 1989 and, having 21 members as of now, encompasses countries that account for 40% of the world population and over 50% of the global gross domestic product (GDP). The signing of the treaty of Asunción (1991) led to the formation of Mercosur, which links Argentina, Brazil, Paraguay, Uruguay and Venezuela, with Chile, Colombia, Ecuador, Peru and Bolivia as associate members, and constitutes Latin America's largest trading bloc. NAFTA was constituted in 1994, with the US roping in Canada and Mexico. It was further extended to the Free Trade Area of the Americas (FTAA) to encompass North America, the Caribbean and South America. Besides, the ASEAN (Association of Southeast Asian Nations) free-trade area also came into being.

This new economic regionalism tends to engage more effectively with global market forces. Bhagwati (2008; as cited in Heywood 2014, 495) believes that although states have wished to consolidate into trading blocs in the hope of gaining access to a wider market, they have not turned their back on a wider global market. The growth of cross-regional interaction and attempts to influence the WTO and other bodies testifies to this fact. He argues, however, that the steady growth of regional trade has meant that, instead of a common global free-trade system, there is a bewildering array of complex and overlapping bilateral and regional arrangements. Each of these trading arrangements has conflicting and contradictory provisions (Ibid.).

Between 1990 and 2010, the number of PTAs has tripled from 70 at the beginning of the period to nearly 300 at the end (World Trade Report 2013). A large proportion of trade takes place within the same region (being intra-regional). The share of intra-regional trade in the total exports of North America (including Mexico) rose from 41% in 1990 to 56% in 2000, and declined to 48% in 2011. The reduced percentage is due to the US concluding trade agreements with South and Central America (Chile, Colombia and Panama). The share of Asia's regional trade has grown from 42% in 1990 to 52% in 2011. The share of intra-EU trade of total merchandise exports is over 70% between 1990 and 2011 (World Trade Organization 2013, 76). Merchandise trade between selected pairs of regions has witnessed an upward swing in the said period too. Recently, the US has signed the Trans-Pacific Partnership (TPP) with the Asia–Pacific countries to promote trade and growth through slashing tariffs. But US president Donald Trump pulled out from the TPP deal on the pretext that it will cause loss of American jobs while both the US and EU countries are in the process of finalizing the another big regional bloc, named the Transatlantic Trade Investment Partnership (TTIP), though differences of perspectives exist in crucial areas.[2]

Reforming WTO: Accommodating Voices from the Global South

Though the WTO decision-making rules are based on the sovereign equality of states, powerful states (the transatlantic nations) dominate the agenda setting and bargaining outcomes. Countries like the US receive deeper concessions than they offer, while developing economies such as India, South Korea and Thailand offer much deeper concessions than they receive (Steinberg 2010, 185). Powerful states find the sovereign equality rules to lend greater legitimacy to outcomes of WTO negotiations than weighted voting would. Moreover, the equality rules also give powerful states the opportunity to collect the information necessary for a successful agenda-setting process favourable to them. Weaker states tend to offer detailed information about their preferences and risk tolerances on issues at stake, as negotiators for the major powers offer them assurances of including their interests on the agenda. Major states use this

---

[2] The Trans-Pacific Partnership (TPP) is a trade agreement between Asia–Pacific countries (Australia, Brunei Darussalam, Canada, Japan, Malaysia, Mexico, New Zealand, Peru and Singapore) and the US. The deal was signed on 14 February 2016 by President Barrack Obama in order to reduce the signatories' dependence on Chinese trade and bring them closer to the US. Concerns had been raised regarding the protection of intellectual property rights of drug MNCs and the exclusion of labour rights in the TTP deal. The newly elected US president Donald Trump signed a presidential memorandum to withdraw US participation on 23 January 2017. The other 11 TPP countries agreed, however, to revive the deal without US participation. The Transatlantic Trade Investment Partnership (TTIP) is a proposed agreement between the US and the EU to promote trade and multilateral economic growth. It is considered a companion agreement to TPP and sets an example for future partnerships and agreements because of its global reach. The negotiations were planned to be finalized by the end of 2014, but due to differences in perspectives and priorities on issues such as agricultural subsidies, service regulation and competition policy and the economic slowdown in some EU countries, the final agreement has been delayed. The withdrawal of the US from the Paris climate deal has further aggravated uncertainty in major European countries.

information in the invisible weighting process during informal negotiations and produce an asymmetric distribution of outcomes for trade negotiations.

Most of the rules and principles governing trade and related issues are, therefore, skewed in favour of the major industrialized countries. While binding tariff reductions are sought in international trade, non-tariff barriers are not a binding system and this provides industrialized countries a pretext to bend the rules of trade liberalization whenever necessary (Nayyar 2007, 109). Western countries have denied India and other developing countries exports many times in recent years under the pretext of labour standards (child labour), technical standards and sanitary standards. Non-tariff barriers were raised in Europe and the US against pharmaceutical items, marine products and processed food items such as milk and dairy (Vivekanandan 2007, 318). This is a clear example of protectionism while telling developing economies to be open. The European market is shrinking for non-EU members. Similarly, in GATS,

---

BOX 4.1: Doha Development Agenda and Present Status

The Doha round of WTO negotiations, formerly the Doha Development Agenda, was launched in November 2001. The work programme covered about 20 areas of trade, including agricultural services, trade, market access for non-agricultural products, and certain intellectual property issues. Except a few initial successes, disagreements repeatedly arose between major trading countries in the developed and the developing world over a host of issues, including market access, agricultural subsidy and tariff reduction. While the negotiations at times showed signs of life, for the most part expectations remained low. The WTO's most recent ministerial conference took place in Nairobi, Kenya, in December 2015. The most contentious topic has been agricultural trade, where protections for developed countries have caused trade conflicts. Developing countries have used a combination of strategies such as export subsidies, domestic support and stockpiling for food security to ensure livelihood security for its resource-poor farmers.

In Nairobi, a formal decision was taken to phase out export subsidies, but the issue of domestic agricultural subsidies was not resolved. These subsidies remain high and are proliferating. India has strongly clarified its position to continue with some of its subsidies, particularly those meant to ensure food security for poor people. This issue was not resolved and will remain on the agenda as rich countries also continue with their domestic subsidies. Beyond agriculture, some progress was made on trade facilitation. Additional countries ratified the new trade facilitation agreement, although not enough yet for it to take effect. A second Information Technology Agreement (ITA-II) was signed among 53 WTO members to lower duties on a MFN basis on a wide range of technology products.

Future of the Doha Agenda

Should the WTO continue working on the Doha Agenda, trying to resolve the outstanding issues, or should it move on to other issues? Both the US and the EU have emphasized the end of Doha and suggested moving on to new issues and approaches. The EU has noted that the new issues could include investment, digital trade, e-commerce and regulatory issues affecting goods and services beyond the borders, better discipline for subsidies and local content obligations.

Source: http://www.cato.org/publication/free trade bulletin.

developing countries have not been given any favourable rules on labour mobility so that they can exploit their comparative advantage in services. In contrast, it caters to the interests of the industrialized countries, which have a comparative advantage in capital-intensive or technology-intensive services. Thus developing countries are to provide market access to the developed world without corresponding access to technology and are expected to accept capital mobility without a corresponding provision for labour mobility (Nayyar 2007, 110).

The deadlock over agricultural subsidies and public stockholding during the Doha round of trade negotiations (launched in 2001) points to a limitation of open trade and the need for a policy space for national governments to address the pressing issues of food security and rural development. While the US and European countries give huge subsidies (worth billions of dollars) to their farmers, but they resist developing countries' effort to maintain their agricultural subsidies including price support for resource-poor farmers at WTO negotiations. India was able to get support from many developing economies (G-33), including China and Brazil, for continuing price support to public stockholding for poor farmers. The repeated failures to resolve outstanding issues of agricultural trade at the Doha negotiation reveal the futility of multilateral negotiations and vindicate sceptics' observations that nation states are important and that they manoeuvre and seek a policy space. The continued impasse may force the governments to resort to unilateral protectionism outside the existing rules, inviting retaliation from others.

Reforming the international trade regime needs to be directed towards giving more policy space to national governments to pursue locally tailored growth policies and protect social programmes and regulation. Expanding the policy space to accommodate domestic objectives is a precondition for an open multilateral regime (Rodrik 2011, 253).

Global Finance

There has been unprecedented growth in international finance over the last two-and-a-half decades. The free capital movement, it is argued, should increase investment and economic growth by enabling global savings to be put to their most productive uses. After the Great Depression, the US financial system was highly regulated, with restrictions on investment, provisions for loans and purchase of government securities. Since the 1980s, the regulatory framework has undergone a change: interest rates have been deregulated, banks been allowed to structure their assets into pools and securitize those pools, and able to sell these securities for a fee to institutional investors and portfolio managers. This has meant that those who created the credit assets tend to understate the risks associated with them. Further, financial liberalization increased the number of layers in an universalized financial system with the extent of regulation varying across sectors. The regulation was light in the case of investment banks, hedge funds and private equity firms, and this implied that financial companies could borrow a huge amount based on a small amount of their own capital and undertake leverage investments to create complex products, which were often traded over the counter rather than through exchanges. This made the financial system vulnerable to crises as profit was made through proliferating risks (Chandrasekhar 2012: 266). UK and other countries followed the USA in liberalising their financial sector to different degree.

Developing countries too, facing balance-of-payment crises and liquidity crunches in the 1980s and early 1990s sought to liberalize their capital accounts and financial markets to attract foreign capital. The IMF prescribed that these countries open up their economy to foreign capital, as availability of capital would not only solve the liquidity crisis but also lead to higher growth. Joseph Stiglitz, eminent critic of free-market globalization, opines that the IMF's prescriptions of liberalization of financial markets in developing countries have only resulted in a major economic crisis later on, which were beyond their own capacity to manage (Stiglitz 2002, 2004). We will return to this below while analysing the East Asian crisis of 1997 and the US financial recession of 2007–2009. With the easing of controls and regulations, there occurred a huge explosion of FDI inflow and portfolio flow (short-term capital investment in equity, bond and derivatives called 'hot money'). FDI by increasing numbers of multinationals is growing more rapidly than either production or international trade, though this growth has been volatile, with dramatic rises and falls (World Trade Organization 2013, 54). By 2009, it was estimated that more than 82,000 MNCs in operation were controlling more than 810,000 subsidiaries worldwide and controlling more than two-thirds of world trade (World Trade Organization 2013, 54).

The expansion of international banking and the consequent jump in bank credits have played a very important role in the huge surge of FDI by multinationals in developing and transitional economies since the 1980s (Gilpin 2001, 5–9). As a proportion of the world's gross fixed domestic investment, net international bank loans rose from 51.1% in 1980 to 131.4% in 1991 (UNCTAD 2016). The gross size of the international banking market was roughly twice that of net international bank lending. Cross-border interbank liabilities rose from a modest $455 billion in 1970 to $5,560 billion in 1990 (Nayyar 2007, 96). US dollar-denominated international credit (bank loans and debt securities) to non-bank borrowers in emerging market economies (EMEs hereafter) and Euro cross-border credits to borrowers outside the euro area have witnessed continuous growth since 2009, though there has been a contraction in 2016 (BIS 2016). Of late, borrowing through the international debt securities market has been seen to be more robust than borrowing through banks, both in advanced economies and EMEs.

Worldwide trade in the foreign-exchange market has seen unprecedented growth since the 1990s. The daily turnover in the foreign exchange market has risen to $1.5 trillion, almost 60 times the level of world trade, apart from expanding trade in government bonds and private equity. For globalists, these developments represent the emergence of a perfect global market—in particular, through continuous trading in currencies—and the financial market dictates the macroeconomic policy of national governments (Held and McGrew 2000, 292). The international market for financial assets has also experienced massive growth since liberalization on the part of developing economies. Portfolio investment in developing countries in the form of investment in bonds and equities rose from $1.3 billion during 1983–1990 to $19.1 billion during 1991–1992, $80.9 billion in 1993 and $91.8 billion in 1996 (Nayyar 2007). This massive volume of transactions is underpinned by phenomenal advancement in computer and Internet technology and satellite technology. With the swipe of a finger, billions of dollars are moved from one stock market to another in order to avail higher returns on account of interest rate differentiation on similar assets in the world capital market. With the mushrooming digital economy and with thin regulation of the different layers of financial markets, there has emerged speculative trading at a massive scale, with all the uncertainty and vulnerability in developing economies.

Boom and Bust Cycle

East Asian economies such as South Korea, Malaysia, Singapore and Thailand had witnessed high economic growth during the 1980s and early 1990s. Globalists argue that this East Asian economic miracle was possible due to the replacement of an inward-looking, import-substitution development strategy with export-led growth (Krugman et al. 2010, 636). These high-growth economies exhibit high rates of savings and investment, improving the educational level of the workforce and openness to and integration with the world market. Marxist scholars, however, hold the view that behind the high growth rate lies the government's active role in allocation of capital among industries and the easy availability of business credit to domestic entrepreneurs. As growth requires the diversification of both production and domestic demand, import substitution policies may well be required to enable a country to achieve production capabilities that allow it eventually to export. All the successful exporting economies employed some combination of both strategies, which amounts to managed trade rather than free trade policies (Ghosh 2012, 172). Before the 1990s, these growing Asian economies financed the bulk of their high investment rates out of domestic savings. But as they liberalized, their financial policies to attract foreign investors, especially from advanced countries, they became prone to economic crises (Chandrasekhar 2012: 267). Since the 1990s, financial crises have become a recurring feature of developing economies that were seen as promising destinations for international financial capital. Mexico experienced a major economic crisis in 1994–1995 and the impact was felt in the entirety of Latin America. The East Asian crisis of 1997 is believed to have started with the devaluation of Thai currency (baht). With the real-estate market and stock market already in decline, devaluation sparked massive speculation not only in Thailand but also in its immediate neighbours, Malaysia, Indonesia and South Korea. In each case, domestic banks had large debts denominated in dollars and the economies were dependent on trade (Krugman et al. 2010, 641). Furthermore, crises gripped Russia (1998), Brazil (1998–1999), Turkey (2000) and Argentina (2001).

The global financial crisis of 2007–2009 had its origin in the US mortgage market. During the mid-2000s, the mortgage lender extended loans to the borrower at low, temporary teaser rates of interest even if they lacked the financial means to make payments if the interest rates were to rise. When the US Federal Reserve tightened monetary policy to ward off inflation, US housing prices started to decline in 2006. These sub-prime loans were securitized and sold off by the original lenders, often bundled with other assets. It became extremely difficult to know which investor was exposed to sub-prime default risk. Also, banks in the US and Europe bought these securitized sub-prime related assets in some cases, staying out of reach of regulators through huge opaque transactions of off-balance sheet items (Ibid., 603). As defaults on sub-prime mortgages began to grow in 2007, lenders pulled back from the market. Borrowing costs rose and many participants in the financial market, including hedge funds, were forced to sell assets to get cash. A number of derivative assets could not find potential buyers. Investment banks such as Lehman Brothers and Bear Stearns suffered losses and became bankrupt. The US Congress stepped in and allocated $700 billion to buy troubled assets. The crisis also spread to Europe, where a number of financial institutions failed (leading to the eurozone sovereign debt crisis in Greece, Portugal, Italy and Spain) and the EU government issued a blanket guarantee to save banks from failure.[3]

---

[3] The eurozone debt crisis started in 2009 when Greece found itself in a situation of not being able to pay its debts in bonds and securities to international lenders. By 2011, other European economies such as Portugal, Italy, Ireland and Spain also found themselves in almost same situation of being defaulters on debt. A sovereign debt crisis is when a country is unable to pay its bills and cannot get a low interest rate from lenders, as lenders—having seen the country's inability to pay the bonds—require higher yields to offset their risk. It creates a vicious circle. The higher the yields, the more it costs the country to refinance the sovereign debt. Over a period of time, the spiraling borrowing cost becomes huge and countries cannot afford to keep rolling over the debt and they default. This kind of situation gripped the aforementioned countries. Major European economies such as Germany and France initiated bailouts from European central banks and the IMF. They disbursed 110 billion ($163 billion) to Greece in the spring of 2010. Ireland and Portugal also received bailouts. The eurozone members created the European Financial Stability Facility (EFSF) to provide emergency lending to countries in financial difficulty. The European central banks also announced

---

BOX 4.2: Financial Globalization: Recent Trends

There has been growing concern about unmanageable and high debts in emerging economies due to the heavy financial flow and cheap credit since 2009 on account of the extensive quantitative easing programme in the developed world. According to the Bank of International Settlements (BIS), the debts of non-financial corporations in these economies increased from $9 trillion at the end of 2008 to just over $25 trillion by the end of 2015, and doubled as a percentage of the gross domestic product (GDP) from 57% to 104% over the same period. Past experiences show that, if much of the non-performing private-sector debt is large and denominated in a foreign currency—as in Latin America, for example—it tends to end up on the public balance sheet, thus risking a sovereign debt crisis. The exception is China, where corporate debt is about 170% of GDP, up from 100% in 2008, but it mainly consists of domestic bonds and claims by domestic bans. While there is no danger of an external debt crisis, the high debt level is exerting considerable pressure on domestic banks and the financial sector in general. There was a 40% increase in the dollar-denominated debt of non-financial corporations in 13 selected developing countries between 2010 and 2014, during which the debt-to-service ratio also soared—a solid warning, indicative of a systematic banking crisis in the making.

Source: UNCTAD (2016).

Limitation of Self-regulating Markets: Need for State Regulation

These crises are characterized by massive capital flight (portfolio investment) by financial investors, collapse of asset prices because of shaken credibility regarding meeting commitments to creditors, and slowing of the flow of credit, which adversely affects the real economy and business cycles. The combination of factors related to financial globalization and the free-market economy underpins these crises and therefore underlines the need for strict regulation on the part of the state. Jagdish Bhagwati, a free-market globalist, advocates that free capital flow is associated with various kinds of risks. These include short-term speculation, costly adjustments caused by reversal in short-term capital flow and a propensity to panics. Keeping in view these risks, he argues that countries need to regulate and control capital flow. It is argued that 'asymmetric information', in interaction with other market distortions, tends to create the wrong price signals and leads to market failure. The boom and bust cycles and the panics in financial markets are results of such information asymmetries, and therefore free capital and financial flow has to be regulated (Stiglitz 2004, 202–203). The IMF, which aims to promote free financial flow, has not devised suitable strategies to discipline investment firms' and banks' propensity to keep expanding leverage and risks.

In the context of the East Asian financial crisis, the IMF had advised closures of insolvent financial banks, enforcement of a capital adequacy ratio and adoption of Western accounting practices. Bank

---

that they would purchase government bonds if necessary, in order to keep yields from spiraling to a level that countries could no longer afford. In December 2011, European central banks made $639 billion in credit available to the region's troubled banks at ultra-low rates.

closures in the midst of a financial panic invited even greater panic, while harsh enforcement of a capital adequacy standard in conjunction with the general credit squeeze contributed to a recession, by making it impossible for many companies to obtain even working capital (Bowles 2010, 456). Further, the IMF encouraged the dismantling of national monopolies, the opening up of the financial and insurance sectors to foreign investors and the elimination of tariff and non-tariff barriers to trade. Bhagwati, as a neo-liberal economist, argued that the 'Wall Street—Treasury complex' had got it wrong for speedy capital-account liberalization in Asia (Bowles 2010, 457). Many other critics saw the IMF strategy as nothing but an attempt to implant Anglo-American style capitalism on Asian countries. Needless to say, despite IMF's tried-and-trusted stabilization and structural adjustment programme, the crisis-hit countries suffered downturn. While other countries continued to take IMF's prescribed medicine, Malaysia broke ranks and imposed extensive controls on capital movement and ensured space for sufficient monetary and fiscal policy manoeuvring. China and Taiwan, which maintained capital control and had current account surpluses over the pre-crisis periods, were largely untouched by the crisis (Krugman 2011, 642). Russia also did not follow IMF's stabilization programme after being hit by a crisis (1998), and yet it recovered.

The underlying set of factors causing the US financial crisis of 2007–2009 tends to contradict the conventional wisdom that financial markets are rational and equilibrating. Risks to banks' creditworthiness had fallen steadily between 2002 and 2007, reaching a historic low in the early summer of 2007, just before the worst crisis; and yet neither credit default swap spreads nor equity prices for banks provided any forewarning of impending disaster. Instead, they strongly reinforced a surge of over-exuberant and under-priced credit extensions to the real economy, a bubble which finally burst, causing instability and panic (Turner 2010, 12). It is also argued that excessive liquidity in the financial market is beneficial up to a point and this benefit tends to decline after a certain point because of the negative effect arising from speculative activity. Besides, the point of optimal benefit varies by market and, over time, there exists no perfect instrument through which to gain the benefits without disadvantages (Turner 2010, 17). National governments always come up with capital injections along with a central bank liquidity provision to save big banks which claim 'too big to fail'. But a more stable financial system requires the nation state to put in place a robust regulatory framework that could discipline market participants and their functioning before any major crisis erupts: limitations on the allowable loan-to-value ratio, regulations to influence borrower as well as lender behaviour, discretionary variation of capital requirements and regulating incentive structures (Turner 2010, 13–16).

The Financial Stability Forum (FSF), the direct precursor of the Financial Stability Board (FSB), proved ineffective to ensure better surveillance and identification of policy responses to avoid a future crisis. The Basel Committee on Banking Supervision (BCBS) finds it hard to discipline financial activities on account of the divergent approaches of nation states. The varying national circumstances and associated national interests make international coordination less effective. When such coordination is successful, it produces either weak agreement based on the lowest common denominator or tougher standards that may not be appropriate to all (Rodrik 2011, 261–262). Nation states are required to devise particular kinds of regulations keeping in mind their domestic institutional resilience, even if this means imposing restrictions on cross-border finance. More regulatory powers in the national government and legislature would reduce the influence of technocrats and would cater to wide, democratic legislature groups. The IMF needs to accommodate voices from developing nations and increase financial transparency and information sharing and to place limits on financial 'safe havens' that export financial instability. Brazil, Russia, India, China and South Africa (BRICS), which account for 40% of global GDP, have

BOX 4.3: Emergence of Alternative Financial Institutions: BRICS Bank and AIIB

BRICS—representing Brazil, Russia, India, China and South Africa—is an independent international organization encouraging commercial, political and cultural cooperation between these nation, and was formed in 2011. BRICS operates a bank named the New Development Bank (NDB) formerly referred to as the BRICS Development Bank. The goal of the bank is to mobilize resources for infrastructure and sustainable development projects in BRICS and other emerging economies and developing countries. The Asian Infrastructure Investment Bank (AIIB) is an international financial institution which is focused on supporting infrastructure in the Asia–Pacific region. AIIB is regarded by some to be a rival economic and political influence to compete with the likes of the IMF, the World Bank and the Asian Development Bank (ADB), which is dominated by both Japan and the US. Both banks aim to provide an alternative to the existing US- and European-dominated World Bank and IMF. The main difference between them is that AIIB operates in the Asia–Pacific region but NDB's operations concentrate on the BRICS nations.

They were set up out of a shared frustration with the existing multilateral lending forum, whose voting structures are stacked against emerging markets. Despite accounting for a quarter of the global economic output between them, the BRICS nations are given a mere 10.3% of the votes at the IMF. Meanwhile, Japan, Germany, France and UK each hold a greater voting share than China, despite the latter being the world's second largest economy. Furthermore, the presidency of the IMF is confined to Europeans, whereas the US has sole discretion over the top role at the World Bank and Japan has led the ADB since its founding in 1966. The BRICS Development Bank also seeks to avoid the strict conditionality of market and structural reforms with which loans from the World Bank and the IMF have been administered. Over the years, various host countries have seen condescending and brusque attempts to transplant the model of the democratic market, while failing to account for their specific development needs. Indeed, the World Bank's insistence on austerity measures and forced financial liberalization in Thailand and Indonesia are held to have led to disastrous outcomes following the Asian financial crisis in 1997.

Source: https://the diplomat.com (Jonathan Dove, posted on 26 April 2016).

set up the New Development Bank (NDB) to provide financial assistance to developing and emerging economies for their infrastructure development and promote growth without being dependent on the Western-dominated IMF and World Bank for loans. This major international grouping of emerging economies has sought to challenge the dominance of the OECD (Organisation for Economic Co-operation and Development) countries in the voting shares in the IMF and to undertake a coordinated approach to challenge the dollar as the only international currency for global trade and as lender of last resort to provide financial stability.

Skewed Globalization and Inequality

The pattern of global trade and finance over the last 30 years has produced only a handful of countries from the Global South with a substantial share in world trade. Developing economies' export share rose from 34% in 1980 to 47% in 2011. China's share in world exports has risen from 1% in 1980 to 11% by

2011, making it the largest developing exporter in the world when compared to individual EU members. The Republic of Korea, India and Thailand accounted for 3%, 2% and 1%, respectively, by 2011 (World Trade Organization 2013, 58). The increased share of developing economies in world imports tends to offset the gains from rising exports. The share of developing and emerging economies in world imports rose from 29% in 1980 to 42% in 2011. China's share in world imports was slightly less than its share in world exports (10% rather than 11%), but India's share in imports was larger than exports, at 3% compared with 2% (World Trade Organization 2013, 59).

Most of the African countries, except the island nation of Mauritius and South Africa, remain untouched by the globalization process. With less than a 2% share of world trade, modest investment flow and widespread poverty, sub-Saharan Africa is confined to the peripheries of globalization. The rare foreign capital that has flowed into the region has been contingent on investors being granted monopoly rights and protection from competition (Ferguson and Mansbach 2012, 235). Despite efforts towards regional cooperation under the African Union (AU), poverty and malnutrition have been rampant in most of the sub-Saharan countries, including Nigeria, Chad, Sudan and Congo.

The Arab states of MENA (Middle East and North Africa) are almost excluded from the flow of private capital that has driven global finance. The entire region receives less FDI than Sweden. Exceptions are Jordan, Israel and Turkey, which are well integrated with the global economy. The region as a whole has witnessed large-scale labour migration and an informal hawala system of moving funds. They see globalization as a threat to their indigenous Islamic culture (Ferguson and Mansbach 2012, 232).

Except Brazil, Chile and Mexico, the Latin American countries (South America) are poorly linked with global trade and finance too. The region presents a contradictory picture in that, on the one hand, populist movements led by the left parties blame global capitalism for financial setbacks and income inequality, and on the other, Peru and Colombia have signed free-trade agreements with the US while Chile has remained committed to neo-liberal globalization and joined the OECD (Ferguson and Mansbach 2012, 229). Brazil is the biggest economy which accounts for roughly 40% of the region's GDP, and it is likely to become an alternative to China as a site for industrial outsourcing. Countries such as Venezuela, Ecuador and Bolivia remained less attractive sites for FDI inflows. Much of Central America, excepting Panama and Costa Rica, remain poor and many states, such as Guatemala and El Salvador, have become violent societies.

The regional breakdown of the global integration process does point towards a hierarchy of global capital and a financial system with a few bright spots presenting themselves to be emulated by others. Though the developing countries' share in world merchandise trade has increased from 23% during 1960–1990 to almost 50% over 1990–2015, East, South East and South Asia accounted for two thirds of developing countries' total merchandise trade (UNCTAD 2016, 102). The other regions, such as transition economies in West Asia, Africa and South America, also increased their share in both export and import of merchandise, on account of rising commodity prices (agriculture, fuel and mining). In manufactures, the developed countries continue to trade with other developed countries despite an increase in the developing countries' participation. For developed countries, intra-group trade constituted about 62% of their total merchandise trade in 2013 (UNCTAD 2016, 102).

Economists differ on whether increasing economic integration leads to a reduction in inequality. Globalists argue that more open trade leads to higher growth, which in turn reduces poverty and inequality. Countries that have become more globalized, in the sense of becoming more open to trade and FDI, have grown faster, and higher growth makes everyone better off (Dollar and Kraay 2001, 44). China, India and other East Asian economies have reduced their poverty levels by a substantial percentage after adopting market reform. Marxist scholars, however, contend that the issue of inequality does not need to be confused with poverty reduction. It is indisputable that poverty has declined dramatically in countries such as China and Vietnam following market reform. Nevertheless, relative inequality has risen just as dramatically, creating a host of problems (Galbraith and Wells 2002, 41). The net worth of the world's 200 richest individuals exceeds that of the world's poorest 2.5 billion people. Moreover, rising inequality in industrial pay after 1980, with exceptions in Scandinavia and in South East Asia before 1997, has been a constant feature of globalization (Galbraith 2001, 39). The per capita income gap between the developed world and developing societies has been substantial since the 1980s. Huge gaps in per capita income and rural–urban divide characterize the countries of the Global South.

The high growth rate in a handful of developing economies has not been accompanied by commensurate remunerative employment generation. The increasing expansion of informal and less remunerative employment during the high growth process has been visible for two of the global economy's recent success stories: China and India. In China, formal employment in manufacture fell between 1997 and 2007 and informal contract undertaken by migrant labour, with few rights, increased (Ghosh 2012, 176). There is huge inequality between coastal China and interior China in terms of per capita income. Besides, an ageing population has led to an upward swing in wages and consequent shift of outsourcing sites to less expensive countries such as Vietnam (Ferguson and Mansbach 2012, 202). India has also witnessed an increase in low-paid casual work in unorganized industries and precarious self-employment in the period 1993–1994, though the number of people living below a dollar a day (2005 prices) has come down from 42% to 24% over the period 1981–2005. These estimates of poverty figures have been controversial, as the Tendulkar Committee appointed by the Planning Commission had put the poverty figure at around 36% in 2010 by using a methodology which includes non-food items as well (Datt and Sundharam 2010). India's emergence as an information technology (IT) and software exporter and as an attractive site for business processing outsourcing (BPO) has absorbed only a small percentage of the English-speaking and skilled workforce, while the agrarian sector, which provides over 50% of the employment, was left behind. In Africa and Latin America, a vast percentage of the workforce is employed in low-productivity jobs which are less remunerative.

Concluding Observations

The mainstream, neo-liberal globalization process has produced winners and losers over the past 30 years. The global multilateral financial institutions, through subtle clauses and rules, tend to further the economic and business interests of industrially advanced economies, which also house thousands of big transnational corporations, International banks and investment firms. Global institutions such as the WTO and the IMF, which drive global trade and finance, need to be democratized and reformed so as to bring about fair rules and a larger policy space for national governments. As the above discussion shows, developing countries' export products are denied access to the developed world's markets on account of various non-tariff barriers (labour standards, health and environmental concerns, and so on) despite advocacy for free trade on various multinational fora. The continuation of huge subsidies (in billions) on the part of the developed world under the guise of WTO-permitted subsidies also blocks developing countries' agricultural products from gaining access to their market and renders millions of farmers across the globe vulnerable. Likewise, financial globalization has caused huge speculative trading and financial instability both in the developed and the developing world, affecting business cycles, growth and employment generation. Many believe that the US financial crisis of 2007–2008 is similar to the 1930s' economic crisis in its adverse impact and with wider ramifications for the global economy as a whole. Various studies point out that a crisis of such magnitude has slowed down growth patterns and global demand has still not picked up. Meanwhile, the United Kingdom's exit from the EU and the withdrawal of the US from various global pacts such as the Paris climate deal and TPP of late have made other national governments look inwards and undertake protectionist policies in order to further national interest. The ascendency of Donald Trump and Theresa May in the US and the UK heralds the new era of de-globalization, where national governments will have greater leverage and a larger policy space to tailor their development strategies to suit their national needs. In the context of developing and transitional societies, this is more than imperative as they need various coordinating institutional arrangements reflecting the complementary role of the state and the market. This will enable them to focus on expanding the domestic market, as also benefiting from global trade and finance but managing their downturn. BRICS' expanding economic and strategic clout, along with the newly set up New Development Bank and currency reserve fund represent an alternative institutional arrangement to the Western-dominated multilateral institutions in driving global trade and finance.

Summary

- Globalization is a highly contested idea. The competing theoretical perspectives look at the assumptions and principles underpinning the concept and how it furthers economic prosperity or otherwise.
- Economic liberals such as Adam Smith provided the pioneering idea of free trade as benefiting all concerned against the backdrop of monopoly capitalism continued between sixteenth and eighteenth century in England. To his thinking, the state ought to play a minimal role and should not interfere in the form of tariffs or quotas that distort resource allocation and create inefficiency. David Ricardo provided detailed justification of how trade between two countries based on comparative advantage benefited both. Subsequent economic liberals enriched the idea of how expanding markets and economies of scale bring about lower costs, along with a wider choice of goods and services, and thus make every one better off.
- The Marxist school lays emphasis on the centrality of the nation state in an increasingly integrated world. Hirst and Thompson (2010) argue that nation states play an important role in creating a congenial atmosphere in the form of compliance with rules, common property rights and exchange rate stability, which enable business firms to operate without uncertainty. The state provides legitimacy to both international agreements and subnational authority structures within domestic jurisdiction.
- The origin of economic globalization may be traced to eighteenth-century industrialization and the beginning of capitalism in Europe. It did spread to other parts of the world but not without the military coercion of the European powers. The first extensive phase of economic integration can be said to have lasted from 1870 to 1913. The interwar period and the Great Depression of the 1930s witnessed the adoption of inward protectionist policies.
- After the Second World War, multilateral institutions such as the GATT, the IMF and the World Bank were established to promote international trade through the reduction of barriers, but the nation states did enjoy space to manoeuvre and manage market and capital. These institutions are called the Bretton Woods Institutions. A combination of factors, including rising oil prices, increasing inflation

and unemployment, led to abandonment of the fixed exchange rate and the adoption of a floating exchange rate. Since the 1980s, the national financial systems had been opened up for international finance and capital flow as the OECD countries eliminated all capital control. The trading of new financial instruments meant to raise funds was allowed.

- The countries of Asia, Africa and Latin America, which were reeling under economic crises of varying natures in the 1980s and early 1990s, had to adopt these policies of financial and trade liberalization, coupled with deregulation and privatization as a part of loan conditionality.

- The WTO, replacing GATT in the 1990s, sought to broaden international trade by bringing in trade in agriculture and services, apart from manufactured products. Besides intellectual property rights, health and safety regulations were incorporated along with safeguard mechanisms to check import surges.

- Tariff rates have been significantly reduced across products both in developed and developing countries. Transportation and telecommunication costs have fallen continuously since the 1950s. This has reduced the cost of trade and made a range of goods and services tradable and subject to international competition. Middle-income developing economies have registered high export growth in the last 30 years. The intensity of trade has increased, as trade has risen faster than income. This has led to a huge jump in the world exports to GDP ratio from 10% in the 1950s to 15–20% in the 1990s.

- A large number of MNC and TNCS are able to break the production chain around the globe in response to differences in local conditions in terms of low wages, less taxes, and so on. Governments are forced into competition in offering increasing incentives for MNCS to base production in their country. Their turnover has grown faster than the world income. The US, EU and East Asian MNCs invested heavily to reach other regions in the 1980s.

- The number of preferential trading agreements (PTAs) and regional trading blocs has multiplied in the period between 1990 and 2010. Recently, the US has signed the Trans-Pacific Partnership (TPP) and the Transatlantic Trade Investment Partnership (TTIP), while China has joined the BRICS and has established the Asian Investment Infrastructure Fund (AIIF).

- The Doha Development Agenda has been stuck over the issue of agricultural subsidy despite various ministerial meetings with major groups not willing to give up domestic subsidies. The transatlantic nations use non-tariff barriers such as labour and health standards to deny market access to products from developing nations.

- In WTO decision-making, powerful states (the US, the EU and Japan) dominate the agenda setting and bargaining outcomes even when there are sovereign equality rules and each has an equal vote. Most of the rules and principles are skewed in favour of the major industrialized countries.

- There is a need to reform the WTO regime to give equal voice to developing nations in framing rules. Then the international trade regime needs to give more policy space to national governments to pursue locally tailored growth policies and protect social programmes and regulations.

- Since the 1980s, regulatory frameworks guiding the financial and capital market underwent a change in the developed world: a floating exchange rate was introduced, interest rates were deregulated, restrictions on securitization of assets were removed, and there was light regulation for investment banks, hedge funds and private equity firms.

- Developing countries facing a liquidity crisis sought to liberalize their capital account and financial market to attract foreign capital.

- With the easing of controls and regulations, there occurred a huge explosion of FDI and portfolio investment (short-term capital flow in bond and equities) in developing countries. Trade in foreign currency magnified manifold, along with expansion of bank credits by international banks. Borrowing, through the international debt securities market, increased in advanced and emerging market economies.

- Since the 1990s, financial crises have become a recurring feature of developing economies, with major crises in Mexico (1994), the East Asian countries (1997), Brazil (1998) and Argentina (2001).
- The US financial crisis (2007–2009) shook the world and exposed the limitations of financial globalization, which relied on proliferating and transferring risk among various stakeholders in the system.
- The persistence of crises calls for the regulation of global finance. The BCBS has not been very effective. The IMF has not been able to devise suitable strategies to discipline investment firms or the banks' propensity to keep expanding leverage and risk. The varying national circumstances and capabilities to cope with financial shocks underline the need for giving more policy space and room to manoeuver to nation states. For example, Malaysia adopted capital control after the 1997 crisis.
- The intensive economic globalization, with increasing trade and financial flow, has produced only a handful of nation from the Global South with a substantial share in world trade. These include China, Korea, Thailand, Brazil, South Africa, India, Singapore and Malaysia. There exists a hierarchy in the global capital and financial system.
- Developed countries' trade with developing countries is dominated by Asia, with most international production networks being highly concentrated in Asia. High inequality within and between the countries has been a constant feature of economic globalization, though the number of people below the poverty line has come down significantly.

Suggested Questions

1. Do you think globalization is creating a situation where the share of labour is decreasing? How do global value chains and technological innovations impact real wages in developing countries?
2. The BRICS group has emerged as a major alternative to the US hegemony. To what extent does BRICS pose a challenge to the dollar as the international currency for global trade?
3. How can central banks and governments keep a check on growing securitization and proliferating risks in the financial system?
4. How can African economies move on to a sustainable growth path? Do you think they need a mix of strategies instead of the 'free trade' recipe?
5. With the US retreat from playing a major global role, do you think China will steer the globalization process?
6. More South–South trade is happening since the mid-1990s and still inequality is rising within and between developing countries. Why?
7. What is the impact of economic globalization on the Global South?

References

Aksoy, M. Ataman, and John C. Beghin, eds. 2005. *Global Agricultural Trade and Developing Countries*. Accessed 2 October 2017. http://siteresources.worldbank.org/INTGAT/Resources/GATfulltext.pdf.

Bank of International Settlement (BIS). 2016. *Quarterly Review*. Accessed 25 September 2017. www.bis.org.

Bhagwati, Jagdish. 2004. *In Defence of Globalization*. New York, NY: Oxford University Press.

Bhagwati, Jagdish, Pravin Krishna and Arvind Panagariya. 2014. 'The World Trade System: Trends and Challenges'. Accessed 5 September 2017. http://indianeconomy.columbia.edu/sites/default/files/paper1-the_world_trading_system.pdf.

Bowles, Paul. 2010. 'Asia's Post-Crisis Regionalism: Bringing the State Back In, Keeping the (United) States Out'. In *International Political Economy: A Reader*, edited by Axel Hülsemeyer, 456–457. Oxford: Oxford University Press.

Chandrasekhar, C. P. 2012. 'Global Finance'. In *International Relation*, edited by B. S. Chimni and Siddharth Mallavarapu, 260–269. New Delhi: Pearson.

Cox, Robert. 1994. As cited in Robert Jackson and George Sørensen. 2015. *Introduction to International Relations*. New York: Oxford University Press.

Datt, Ruddar, and K. P. M. Sundharam, eds. 2010. *Indian Economy*. New Delhi: S. Chand Publication.

Dicken, Peter. 2000. 'A New Geo Economy'. In *The Global Transformations Reader: An Introduction to the Globalization Debate*, edited by David Held and Anthony McGrew, 253–254. London, UK: Polity Press.

Dollar, David, and Aart Kraay. 2001. 'Spreading the Wealth'. In *Globalization: Challenges and Opportunity*, 31–44. New York, NY: Foreign Affair.

Ferguson, Yale H., and Richard W. Mansbach, eds. 2012. *Globalization: The Return of Borders to a Borderless World?* London and New York, NY: Routledge and Oxford University Press.

Friedman, Thomas L. 2005. *The World Is Flat: A Brief History of the Twenty-first Century*. New York: Farrar Straus and Giroux.

Galbraith, P. J., and Dang Wells. 2002. 'Is Inequality Decreasing in Globalization: Challenges and Opportunity'. *Foreign Affair*: 38–44.

Gilpin, Robert. 2001. *Global Political Economy: Understanding the International Economic Order*. Princeton, NJ: Princeton University Press.

Ghosh, J. 2012. 'Development'. In *International Relation*, edited by B. S. Chimni and S. Mallavarapu, 172–178. New Delhi: Pearson.

Harvey, David. 2005. *A Brief History of Neoliberalism*. New York: Oxford University Press.

Held, David, and Anthony McGrew. 2000. *The Global Transformations Reader*, pp. 1–15, 292. London: Polity Press.

Heywood, Andrew. 2014. *Global Politics*. New York, NY: Palgrave Macmillan.

Hirst, Paul, and Grahame Thompson. 2010. 'Globalization and the Future of the Nation-State'. In *International Political Economy: A Reader*, edited by Axel Hülsemeyer, 298–314. Oxford: Oxford University Press.

Krugman, Paul R., Maurice Obstfeld and Marc Melitz. 2010. *International Economics: Theory and Policy*, 9th ed. US: Pearson.

Macheda, Francesco. 2012. 'The Roots of "Globalization": Adam Smith and the Virtues of Free Trade'. Accessed 10 September 2017. http://www.academia.edu/11290012/The_Roots_of_Globalization_Adam_Smith_and_the_Virtues_of_Free_Trade.

Mansbach, Richard W., and Kirsten L. Taylor. 2012. *Introduction to Global Politics*. London: Routledge.

Nayyar, Deepak. 2007. 'Globalization: The Game, the Players and the Rules'. In *Globalization and Politics in India*, edited by Baldev Raj Nayyar, 3, 91–116. New Delhi: Oxford University Press.

Rodrik, Dani. 2011. *The Globalization Paradox: Why Global Markets, States and Democracy Can't Coexist*. UK: Oxford University Press.

Steinberg, Richard H. 2010. 'In the Shadow of Law or Power? Consensus-Based Bargaining and Outcomes in the GATT/WTO'. In *International Political Economy: A Reader*, edited by Axel Hülsemeyer, 173–185. Oxford: Oxford University Press.

Stiglitz, Joseph E. 2002. *Globalization and Its Discontents*. New York, NY: Oxford University Press.

———. 2004. 'Globalism's Discontents'. In *The Globalization Reader*, edited by Frank J. Lechner and John Boli, 201–205. UK: Blackwell Publishing.

Turner, Adair. 2010. 'After the Crises: Assessing the Costs and Benefits of Financial Liberalisation'. Accessed 10 September 2017. https://rbi.org.in/scripts/BS_SpeechesView.aspx?Id=475.

United Nations Conference on Trade and Development (UNCTAD). 2016. *Trade and Development Report, 2016.* Accessed 30 September 2017. http://unctad.org/en/pages/PublicationWebflyer.aspx?publicationid=1610.

Vivekanandan, B. 2007. 'Globalization and India'. In *Globalization and Politics in India*, edited by Baldev Raj Nayyar, 317–321. New Delhi: Oxford University Press.

World Trade Organization (WTO). 2013. *Factors Shaping the Future of the World*. Part II of *World Trade Report 2013*. Accessed 2 October 2017. https://www.wto.org/english/res_e/publications_e/wtr13_e.htm.

Further Reading

Chomsky, Noam. 1999. *Profit Over People: Neoliberalism and Global Order*. New York: Seven Stories Press.

Dove, Jonathan. 2016. 'The AIIB and the NDB: The End of Multilateralism or a New Beginning'. *The Diplomat*, 26 April 2016. Accessed 5 October 2017. https://thediplomat.com/2016/04/the-aiib-and-the-ndb-the-end-of-multilateralism-or-a-new-beginning.

Frieden, Jeffry A. 2006. *Global Capitalism: Its Fall and Rise in the Twentieth Century*. New York, NY: W. W. Norton.

Kose, M. Ayhan, and Marco E. Terrones. 2017. *Collapse and Revival: Understanding Global Recessions and Recoveries*. Washington, DC: International Monetary Fund.

Milanovic, Branco. 2017. *Global Inequality: A New Approach for the Age of Globalization*. Cambridge: Harvard University Press.

Perraton, Jonathan David Goldblatt, David Held and Anthony McGrew. 2000. 'Economic Activity in Globalizing World'. In *The Global Transformations Reader*, edited by David Held and Anthony McGrew, 288–293. London: Polity Press.

Scholte, Jan Aart. 2005. *Globalization: A Critical Introduction*, 2nd edn. London: Palgrave Macmillan.

Trebilcock, Michael, Robert Howse and Antonia Eliason. 2012. *The Regulation of International Trade*, 4th edn. London: Routledge.

Global Governance: IMF, World Bank, WTO and TNCs

Ketan Kumar

LEARNING OBJECTIVES

- To understand the concept of global governance
- To examine the impact of international institutions on political and economic governance
- To describe the role of transnational actors as agents of change
- To explain the issues of the North–South divide with respect to the global environment
- To evaluate the strategic impact of global governance

The post-cold war era witnessed the re-emergence of various issues and phenomenon on the international podium that were previously overshadowed by the cold-war politics. A new paradigm emerged, based on certain issues: the growing idea of globalization was a significant theme and the subsequent weakening of the nation states opened up the prospect of transitioning to a global level of regulatory instruments. An intensification of the environmental concerns symbolized a new approach that has conceptually evolved the term 'global commons'. Not only is global life marked by a density of populations; it is also dense with organized activities, thereby complicating and extending the processes of global governance. Global life in the twenty-first century is more complicated than ever before in history; it is partly because the world is host to ever greater numbers of organizations in all walks of life and every corner of every continent. As globalization occurs, the states lose control over their destinies and problems become bigger than the capacities of the individual governments to solve them. Therefore, the states are bound to delegate the political authority to supranational entities with powers that more nearly coincide with the scope of the issues and actors to be managed. As a result of all these developments, 'global governance' turns out to be a prominent alternative.

Global governance can be understood as the process of cooperative leadership that brings together the state and non-state actors, such as transnational companies and civil society, to achieve commonly accepted goals. The contours of global governance include and are not confined only to the international political economy, the environment, human rights and health to bring about the overall development of humankind across all states. It is a multilevel and multi-actor system characterized by a global governance pattern. Therefore, to analyse the dynamics of governance, it is important to understand the interaction between global, regional, local and domestic politics. However, before dwelling further into the details and complexities around global governance, it is essential to understand what is global governance, its features and evolution.

Global Governance: Definition and Meaning

The definitions of global governance have been various, and there are as many definitions of global governance as there are thinkers on international politics. However, some of the extended definitions of global governance that would help us in developing our understanding of it are worth mentioning. J. N. Rosenau has defined global governance in a comprehensive way as a 'system of rules at all levels of human activity—from the family to an international organization in which the pursuit of goals through the exercise of control has transnational repercussion' (Rosenau 1995, 13). In other words, the term is used, according to M. Albert and T. Kopp-Malek, to designate all regulations intended for organization and centralization of human societies on a global scale (Albert and Kopp-Malek 2002). On the other side, Rosenau explains that it stipulates no hierarchy between actors; the mode of steering is predominantly non-hierarchical and often based on arguing rather than traditional bargaining (Rosenau 1995, 13–43).

Global governance or world governance is a movement towards political cooperation among transnational actors, aimed at negotiating responses to problems that affect more than one state or religion. The modern question of world governance exists in the context of globalization and globalizing regimes of power: geographic, social, cultural, economic or political; it reflects upon the process of designating laws, rules or regulations intended for organization and centralization of human societies on a global scale.

In simpler terms, it refers to the management of global processes in the absence of a global government. Thus global governance is not global government; it is not a single world order; it is not a top-down, hierarchical structure of authority. It is the collection of governance-related activities, rules and mechanisms, formal and informal, existing at a variety of levels in the world today. It can be referred to as 'pieces of global governance' (Mingst 2015).

Lawrence S. Finkelstein has described,

> Governance should be considered to cover the overlapping categories of functions performed internationally; among them: information creation and exchange; formulation and promulgation of principles and promotion of consensual knowledge affecting the general international order, regional orders, particular issues on the international agenda. Moreover, efforts to influence the domestic rules and behavior of states; good offices, conciliation, mediation, and compulsory resolution of disputes; regime formation, tending and execution; adoption of rules, codes, and regulations; allocation of material and program resources; provision of technical assistance and development programs; relief, humanitarian, emergency, and disaster activities; and maintenance of peace and order. (Finkelstein 1995, 371–372)

Andrew Heywood in his book *Global Politics* has also dwelled on the issue of global governance. He argues that the term

> global governance has often been understood and used synonymously to terms like international anarchy, global hegemony and world government. However, the concept of the global governance is different from this phenomenon and structure of global politics.… He has described global governance as a broad, dynamic and complicated process of interactive decision making at the global level that involves formal and informal mechanism as well as governmental and non-governmental bodies. State and government remain the primary institution for articulating public interests and those of the global community as a whole. (Heywood 2011, 456–460)

However, global governance also involves intergovernmental and sometimes supranational bodies (Figure 5.1). Global policy is made by a system of horizontal and vertical interactions in which officials in different branches of government work with a counterpart in other countries as well as with non-state actors. Sometimes it is used more narrowly to indicate the institutions through which these interactions take place.

It is also essential to understand how the international bodies conceived the concept of global governance, as they are instrumental to the operation of global governance. The United Nations (UN), in its research report *Global Governance and Rules for the Post-2015 Era*, has demonstrated that global governance encompasses the institutions, policies, norms, procedures and initiatives through which states and their citizens try to bring more predictability, stability, and order to their responses to transnational challenges (Alonso and Ocampo 2015).

The term 'global governance' is often confused with terms such as 'regime', 'world government' and 'global government'. Global government is the idea of all humankind united under one political authority. It is based on the assumption of centralization of authority in a supranational body which would

FIGURE 5.1   Components of Global Governance

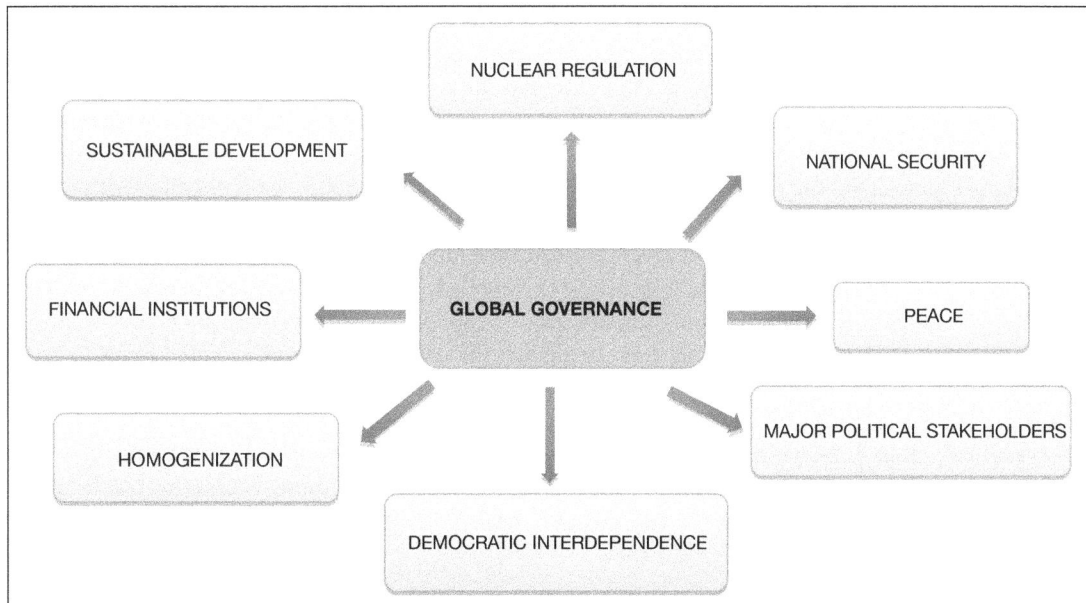

possess legislative and executive powers. It is based on the social contract theory. Global governance, on the other hand, is the management of global policies without the presence of any central government. Polycentrism characterizes the process of global governance, intergovernmentalism, mixed actor involvement, multilevel processes and deformatization (Heywood 2011, 458–459). Some of the key features of global governance are:

- Global governance is multiple rather than singular, with a different institutional framework and decision-making mechanism.
- States have considerable voice in the process of global governance.
- There is no distinction between state and non-state actors—transnational companies (TNCs), non-governmental organizations (NGOs) and civil society—in global decision-making.
- It operates through interaction between groups and institutions at various levels.
- It does not emphasize operation through formal and informal legally constituted bodies (Heywood 2011, 458–459).

From the discussion above, it becomes clear that global governance operates at various levels—on environmental, health, rights, educational and various other socio-economic platforms. However, these complex issues have been more prominent in the fields of the economic sphere.

Evolution of Global Governance

The complicated process of global governance can be traced back to the interwar period. During the interwar period, the effects of the poor mechanisms of collective governance were visible. After the First World War ended, the leaders of the victorious Allies gathered in Paris in 1919 for around six months of talks aimed at redrawing many of the world's national borders and establishing a permanent forum—the League of Nations—to deal with future issues and problems. More than 30 countries sent delegations to the Paris peace conference, but the four great powers of the winning side—France, Italy, the United Kingdom (UK) and the US—dominated and controlled the proceedings.

The collapse of the gold standard and the reluctance on the part of the US to fill the gaps that were earlier occupied by Great Britain and other European powers resulted in economic problems that were beyond the states' abilities to cope up. During the Great Depression in 1929, states did away with policies of free trade and emphasized policies of trade protectionism.

The lessons of the interwar period created turbulence among the leaders, policymakers as well as academics, who opined that economic aggressions eventually lead to wars. International peace and security can prevail and be maintained only in conditions of sound economic governance. A quarter of a century later, as the Second World War drew to a close, the Allied delegations gathered again to set up new institutions to replace the failed League and to prevent the economic disasters that had characterized much of the interwar period.

From those storied discussions, most of which were held under the overwhelmingly influence of the US—at Bretton Woods, New Hampshire; at the Dumbarton Oaks mansion in Washington, D.C.; and in San Francisco, California—resulted the emergence of multilateral agencies that would mould economic and political relations for the next six decades.

The United Nations (UN), with its Security Council (SC) and its specialized agencies; the Bretton Woods Institutions—the World Bank and the IMF; and the General Agreement on Tariffs and Trade (GATT) came into the international arena. This model of global governance, in which the few countries that sat at the pinnacle of the world economic structure persuaded others to participate in this complex process without rolling off much control, became the prevailing paradigm for the postwar era. The establishment of the Bretton Woods system was the outcome of such a paradigm shift in global politics and economy.

The Bretton Woods Agreement was signed in 1942, when the leaders of the US, Great Britain and 42 other states met at the UN Monetary and Financial Conference at Bretton Woods to decide the contours of the new international financial system. Consequently, three brainchildren of this conference emerged in the forms of the IMF, the International Bank for Reconstruction and Development (IBRD, which later came to be known as the World Bank) and the General Agreement on Tariffs and Trade (GATT, which later became the WTO). Since their inception, the three (collectively called the Bretton Woods system) have been playing a pivotal role in the international economy.

The Bretton Woods system, along with the other multilateral organizations, has regulated the international economy. It has led to the expansion of trade, economic growth and economy across the world. However, the growing integration of the world economy and the process of globalization has opened up new challenges for the Bretton Woods system, and the critics of global governance have pointed out to what many of us call a crisis in the global economic governance. However, before dwelling further on the debates on this crisis, it is important to analyse these institutions.

International Monetary Fund

The IMF is an international organization created in 1945, with an objective of fostering global monetary cooperation. It is headquartered in Washington D.C., comprising 189 countries. It aims to maintain global monetary cooperation, secure financial stability, facilitate international trade, promote high employment and sustainable economic growth, and reduce poverty around the world (IMF 2017). According to the IMF itself, it works to foster global growth and economic stability by providing policy support, by providing advice and finance to members and by working with developing nations to help them achieve macroeconomic stability and to reduce poverty. The rationale for this is that international capital markets function imperfectly and many countries have limited access to financial markets. Such market imperfections, together with balance-of-payments financing, justify official financing, without which many countries could only correct large external payment imbalances through measures with adverse economic consequences.

The IMF is mandated to oversee the international monetary and financial system and monitor the economic and financial policies of its member countries. This activity is known as surveillance, and facilitates international cooperation. Since the demise of the Bretton Woods system of fixed exchange rates in the early 1970s, surveillance has evolved mostly by way of changes in procedures rather than through the adoption of new obligations. The responsibilities changed from those of guardian to those of overseer of members' policies (Bossone 2008).

Decision-making at the IMF was designed to reflect the relative positions of its member countries in the global economy. Since its inception, the IMF has been primarily involved in ensuring the stability of the international monetary system. The IMF also aims at the following:

- promoting international monetary cooperation
- facilitating the expansion and balanced growth of international trade

- promoting exchange stability
- assisting in the establishment of a multilateral system of payments
- making resources available (with adequate safeguards) to members experiencing balance-of-payments difficulties

The financial assistance provided by the IMF enables countries to rebuild their international reserves, stabilize their currencies, continue paying for imports and restore conditions for strong economic growth while undertaking policies to correct the underlying problems. Unlike development banks, the IMF does not lend for specific projects but provide practical assistance to members. The IMF highlights possible risks to stability and advises on needed policy adjustments (IMF 2017). The IMF seeks to build on synergies between technical assistance and training to maximize their effectiveness.

The member countries of the IMF provide most of the resources for IMF loans, primarily through their payments of quotas. Quota subscriptions are a central component of the IMF's financial resources. Each member country of the IMF is assigned a quota, based broadly on its relative position in the world economy. Apart from that, the IMF has the provision of a special drawing right (SDR) that was created in 1969 as an international reserve asset, which acts as the supplement to member states' official reserves. While the quota subscriptions of member countries are the IMF's primary source of financing, the Fund can supplement its quota resources through borrowing if it believes that they might fall short of members' needs. Portugal, Greece, Ukraine and Pakistan are the most significant borrowers (IMF 2017).

The IMF has played a significant role in shaping the global economy since the end of the Second World War. During the post-war period, the warring states had to rebuild their national economies. The IMF is charged with overseeing the international monetary system to ensure exchange rate stability and with encouraging members to eliminate exchange restrictions that hinder trade. The IMF assisted the states to deal with the aftermath of the collapse of the fixed exchange rate system and the subsequent oil shock in 1973–1974 and 1979. With the collapse of the Union of Soviet Socialist Republics (USSR) in 1990, the IMF also played a pivotal role in assisting the countries of the Eastern bloc in transforming their economy, based on market-driven principles (Figure 5.2).

World Bank

The World Bank is an international financial institution that provides loans to the countries of the world for capital programmes. It comprises two institutions: the IBRD and the International Development Association (IDA). The World Bank is a component of the World Bank Group, which is part of the UN system. The World Bank's stated official goal is the reduction of poverty (Michie and Smith 2005).

The World Bank was created at the 1944 Bretton Woods Conference, along with three other institutions, including the IMF. The president of the World Bank is, traditionally, an American. The World Bank and the IMF are both based in Washington, D. C., and work closely with each other. Although many countries were represented at the Bretton Woods Conference, the US and the UK were the most powerful in attendance and dominated the negotiations (Goldman 2005).

The World Bank Group is a vital source of financial and technical assistance to developing countries around the world. It aims to provide a unique partnership to reduce poverty and support development. Initially, the bank provided loans to the states devastated by the Second World War to rebuild and

FIGURE 5.2 IMF and World Bank: Spring Meetings, 2017

Source: IMF (2017).

reconstruct their economy. Over time, the focus of the Bank shifted to development processes, with a heavy emphasis on developing infrastructure such as dams, electrical grids, irrigation systems and roads.

By the mid-1950s, the World Bank had expanded its contours and started lending to private companies and financial institutions in developing countries. Since then, the bank has been involved in providing loans, low-interest credits and grants to developing countries and in promoting investments in areas such as education, health, public administration, infrastructure, financial and private-sector development, agriculture, and environmental and natural resource management.

Apart from this, the bank also provides support to developing countries through policy advice, research and analysis, and technical assistance. The World Bank Group works with country governments, the private sector, civil-society organizations, regional development banks, think tanks and other international institutions on issues ranging from climate change, conflict and food security to education, agriculture, finance and trade.

Some of the global partnerships in which the World Bank works closely with other state and non-state actors include the Onchocerciasis Control Program (OCP), the Global Alliance for Vaccines and Immunization (GAVI), the Global Environment Facility (GEF), Roll Back Malaria, the Consultative Group to Assist the Poor (CGAP), the Joint United Nations Programme on HIV/AIDS (UNAIDS), the Financial Sector Reform and Strengthening Initiative (FIRST), Education for All (EFA), the Global Water Partnership (GWP), the Global Development Learning Network (GDLN), the Haiti Reconstruction Fund (HRF), Harmonization for Health in Africa (HHA) and the Water and Sanitation Program (WSP).

GATT and World Trade Organization

The GATT is yet another agreement established under the Bretton Woods system. The WTO replaced it in 1995. The World Trade Organization (WTO) is an inter-governmental organization that regulates international trade. The WTO was officially formed on 1 January 1995 under the Marrakesh Agreement, signed by 123 nations on 15 April 1994, replacing the GATT, which was signed in 1948. It is the largest international economic organization in the world.

Currently having 164 members, mostly from the developing states, with its secretariat located in Geneva, the WTO provides a platform for negotiating agreements that may help in reducing impediments and obstacles to international trade, thus contributing to economic growth and development of countries throughout the Continent. The World Bank has also been involved in providing a legal and institutional framework for the implementation and monitoring of trade-related agreements, and in enabling the settling of trade- and tariffs-related disputes arising among the concerned states. Presently the trade-related agreements enacted by the WTO have comprised different multilateral agreements (to which all WTO members are parties) and two different plurilateral agreements (to which only some WTO members are parties). The WTO emphasizes open borders, the guarantee of the most-favoured-nation principle and non-discriminatory treatment by and among members.

The WTO deals with regulation of trade between participating countries by providing a framework for negotiating trade agreements and a dispute resolution process aimed at enforcing participants' adherence to WTO agreements, which are signed by representatives of member governments and ratified by their parliaments.

Many developing countries voiced their dissatisfaction with their lack of involvement in the decision-making processes in Seattle, but this is a long-standing criticism. The WTO describes itself as 'a rules-based, member-driven organization—all decisions are made by the member governments and the rules are the outcome of negotiations among members'. The WTO agreement foresees votes where consensus cannot be reached, but the practice of consensus dominates the process of decision-making (Sampson 2001).

Decisions in the WTO are taken by consensus of the entire membership. The Ministerial Conference is the highest institutional body, which meets roughly every two years. A General Council is responsible for conducting the organization's business in the intervals between Ministerial Conferences (Sampson 2001). Both of these bodies comprise all WTO members. Some of the other vital activities of the WTO include:

- negotiating the reduction or elimination of obstacles to trade (import tariffs, other barriers to trade) and agreeing on rules governing the conduct of international trade (e.g., anti-dumping policies, subsidies, product standards, and so on)
- administering and monitoring the application of the WTO's agreed rules for trade in goods, trade in services and trade-related intellectual property rights
- monitoring and reviewing the trade policies of members as well as ensuring transparency of regional and bilateral trade agreements
- building the capacity of developing countries' government officials in international trade matters
- assisting the process of accession of some 30 countries who are not yet members of the organization
- conducting economic research and collecting and disseminating trade data in support of the WTO's other main activities
- explaining to and educating the public about the WTO, its mission and its activities

Transnational Corporations (TNCs)

Global governance is a broad, dynamic and complicated process of interactive decision-making at the global level that involves formal and informal mechanisms as well as governmental and non-governmental bodies. Besides the institutional structures mentioned above, there are other significant actors as well who catalyse the process of global governance. The state and institutional structures are not sufficient to shape the process of global governance. There always exists a gap, which is filled by the transnational actors.

Transnational actors refer not only to the formal state institutions and organizations, but also all organizations and pressure groups—from multinational corporations (MNCs) and transnational social movements to non-governmental organizations (NGOs), which pursue goals and objectives for transnational rule and authority. These non-state actors do not possess sovereignty in the real sense of the term. Unlike the states, they do not possess the magnitude of resources, but are likely to be influential in substantive measures.

A transnational corporation (TNC) is any company that is registered and which operates in many different countries, regardless of trade boundaries. It manages production and delivers services in more than one country. The International Labour Organization (ILO) has defined it as

> a corporation that has its management headquarters in one country known as the home country, and operates in several other countries, known as the host country. This is of increasing interest to governments as well as to employers and workers and their respective organisations. Through international direct investment and other means such enterprises can bring substantial benefits to home and host countries by contributing to the more efficient utilisation of capital, technology and labour. (ILO 2017)

The United Nations Conference on Trade and Development (UNCTAD) defines transnational corporations as

> incorporated or unincorporated enterprises comprising parent and their foreign affiliate. A parent enterprise is defined as an enterprise that controls assets of other entities in countries other than like home country, usually by owning a certain equity capital stake.

TNCs play a key role in the process of economic growth across the globe. They are the 'embodiment par excellence of the liberal ideal of an interdependent world economy. They have integrated the national economies beyond trade and money to the internationalisation of production. The production of goods and their marketing rises above the national economies' (Mingst and Arreguín-Toft 2014, 312).

The TNCs are against the norms of trade barriers and tarrifs. At times, they move abroad to circumvent the tough governmental regulations at home, such as banking rules, currency restrictions or environmental regulations. In the process, they turn into political organization versus economic ones, and influence the policies of both home and host governments (Mingst and Arreguín-Toft 2014, 312).

The transnational actors aim at negotiating responses to problems that affect more than one state or religion. These corporations are not bound by the boundaries of any particular state. They engage themselves in various countries through foreign direct investments (FDIs). As a result, the distinction related to specific country's finance and governance inside its territorial boundaries and dichotomy inside the international order get blurred. Moreover, their impact is not confined to any single domain. Their influence in world politics is characterized by their presence in almost all walks of life.

The role of TNCs and their influence can be seen from various vantage points. The liberal school of thought considers them as a positive instrument of development. It opines that the TNCs help in the improvement of the world economy and its dependents worldwide. They argue in favour of free-market trade as propagated by the laissez-faire doctrine. The influence of the government in regulating these TNCs is not justified in their views. 'The liberal economists argue that the role of government should be limited and confined merely to protecting property rights and providing a functioning legal system. They consider international system as healthy and desirable' (Mingst and Arreguín-Toft 2014, 313).

It has been often claimed by the liberals that the involvement of TNCs brings about democratic credentials in the international institutions. However, for them, the traditional source of legitimacy for international institutions—problem-solving effectiveness—is no longer sufficient in itself. It must be supplemented with more democratic procedures of decision-making.

The TNCs do improve the infrastructure, economy and employment status of the host countries. People in these less-developed countries are often attracted by the new job arena. Besides, the government with the help of TNCs generates new wealth in the form of revenue. It is also benefitted by the new technologies that the TNCs bring with them. Moreover, the customers gain the privilege to access a large range of products of their choice at a competitive rate. A fluidity of the economy of the host country is bound to happen with the advent of TNCs.

The role of the TNCs seems to be very attractive. But the flipside of it doesn't portray a rosy picture. There are various criticisms as well associated with the role of the TNCs. By investing in a developing country, the TNCs are exempted from the idea of providing a national minimum wage. As a result, their cost of manufacturing remains low and it leads to high profits, which ultimately are invested in the production and innovation of new technology. Their main aim is to crush all local or lesser companies in order to become the dominant corporation.

Besides, they instil a modern culture, which can be afforded only by a limited population inside the developing countries. This creates a divide and an instability among the masses. Moreover, very slowly and gradually, they aim to take over the local resources, so as to enjoy a monopoly position. The local traders finds it very difficult to compete with the TNCs, given their limited access to capital and technology. At times, the TNCs play crucial roles in determining the course of politics inside the host country.

In various instances, TNCs have generated clashes of sovereignty between different governments. Domestic deregulation and globalization of economic activity mean that regulation is now occurring at a global level rather than within individual countries (Baylis et al. 2014).

Thus it seems very obvious that the TNCs help the home country (i.e., the capitalist one) to substantiate their power and influence across the globe. It helps them to control the less developed and developing countries of the world in various measures, sometimes even determining their internal politics through lobbying with various stakeholders.

Global Trade and Finance

Global trade and finance is a portion of the global economy, constructed on the international exchange of goods and services. It is an interchange among several countries entangled, and its consequences may be positive or negative.

Therefore, this entire process of global trade and finance is related to the global economy, which shifts the exchange between the various countries from one way to another through integrated trade and finance, and subsequently, this whole course can be comprehended as globalization. In the era of globalization, global trade and finance inflates its boundaries from individual economies to the interconnected economies of different countries, and it affects the other economies of the world.

During the past two decades, the influence and scope of globalization have been mounting a lot by thwarting the barriers and restrictions on trade, finance and business; the boundaries of different countries have condensed. This process opens the gateway for the companies to sell commodities to the global market through trade. Similarly, people can buy the goods according to their choice and get services in various parts of the world.

After the 1990s, with the end of the cold war era, new contests were in progress regarding the integration of Eastern European countries with the global economy, trade and finance. Actors such as the World Bank and the IMF became acutely encompassed in the management of integration. These institutions broaden and hold finance for good global governance between member countries (Kumar et al. 2017, 48). The WTO enriched the scope of trade through trade-related investments. These actors such as TNCs create the space for trade and exchange in the international field, and provide the podium for finance. Cases such as the Asian financial crises in 1997 and the crises in the world economy in 2008 transported new angles for the international financial construction (Kumar et al. 2017, 48).

With the passage of time, the world is turning out to be more interdependent regarding trade, finance, global economics and global governance. Eventually, this process will be insisting on sustainable development. As the escalation of trade, finance and capital flows has been intensifying, the vulnerability of other countries in copying policies is clearly visible. World trade has been increasing for the last three decades; there are some assured changes taking place in the living standards of people; and in the area of imports and exports, it produces pressure on each nation. For instance, the US fixed the price of Japanese steel and, on the other hand, Europe blames the US for destabilizing its papermakers. Even the occurrence of a new protectionism in the Western world signposts the success of interventionists and welfarists over the market economy. Trade and finance in the international system are not as easy as we might conjecture; there are assuredly fetters as well on trade. These can be in the form of domestic safeguards or voluntary export restraints (Ruggie 1982, 411).

International trade entails international finance, and vice versa. Trade takes time to establish and it needs finance to flourish. Finance and international trade have been continuously intertwined. Trade generates the prospects for building up financial security and ties for the trading markets. Moreover, the IMF scrutinizes the connections among the member nation states regarding finances and international trade, and it typically includes a yearly Article IV consultation. Asymmetries in trade and finance at the

---

BOX 5.1: North–South Divide

The North–South division is mostly deliberated in the fields of socio-economics and politics. The most developed part of the world is the northern part, which is in fact rich, compared to the southern part of the world, which is poor and underdeveloped. Moreover, the greater part of the world resources is being held by the North, and 95% of the North has enough food and shelter. The North is frequently portrayed as the guardian of the environment and the South as the guardian of the poor. The North continually seeks to establish that economic growth is the solitary solution to both environment and economic problems.

global level can be absorbed. 'Asymmetrical dependency' can be the best twig and encapsulates the subtleties of the economic affairs of the US, European countries and the other members of the UN (Bird et al. 2009, 407).

It is noted that 'in broad-spectrum, trade and finance comprises of borrowing and expanding trade credit as security and obtaining the insurance contrary to the probability of trade credits defaulting' (JaeBin et al. 2011, 298). The commencement of development in the global partnership arena, especially after 2015, provides the space and an opportunity to reposition the subjects concerning trade, finance and the global economy and build up the collaboration and coordination among nations. Through collaboration and coordination among the nations, the global partnership endorses the culpability on the global regimes, and it helps to endorse the coherence and better global governance. Global partnerships assist in the execution of an equitable and inclusive system of global governance through the development of trade and finance between the member countries. Global partnerships intend to augment multilateral trade with the developing countries, which can open the space for equitable global governance. However, the flip side of this post-2015 development agenda is the 'asymmetrical dependency' of the developing nations. The US clenches the major institutions at the global level, and most of the developing countries endure enslavement to the developed countries rather than equitable rights.

Another compelling reason for the asymmetrical dependency of the developing countries is groups such as the Group of Twenty (G20), which influences multilateral issues by informal decision-making. One of the ways to confirm this dependency is through the integration of core dimensions such as economy, environment and peace and security issues in the global governance that is, the inclusion of the post-2015 development agenda, meaning development in the spheres of the social, the economic, the environment, and peace and security.

Ultimately, in the more interconnected and interdependent world, there is a prerequisite for transparency and equity among nations, for sustainable economic growth and trade. The concept of a global partnership for equitable development can subsidize the objective of integrated global governance in the post-2015 agenda of sustainable and equitable development.

BOX 5.2:   Thomas Piketty: Capital in the Twenty-first Century

When the rate of return on capital exceeds the rate of growth of output and income, as it did in the nineteenth century and seems quite likely to do again in the twenty-first, capitalism automatically generates arbitrary and unsustainable inequalities that radically undermine the meritocratic values on which democratic societies are based.

—**Thomas Piketty**

Global Environmental Politics

Global environmental politics entails a very long history. It spans at least the epoch of European colonization, when the colonizers arrogated land to themselves, excavated large mines and twisted the operation of ecosystems into agricultural plantations. In a different sense, however, global environmental politics is a very specific phenomenon, extending back less than 40 years, ingrained in modern environmentalism with its emphasis on the 'global environment' as an object of concern. This idea ascended in the public consciousness, predominantly in the US, as a consequence of several factors, together with fears about 'global' (implying really underdeveloped or developing countries) population growth, apprehension about the consequences of industrialization and images of Earth seen from the space which can cause severe strategic crisis.

Governance is a fundamental subject in global environmental politics today. In adding to general calls for global replies to address global environmental problems, mainly climate change, there is also the propagation of new actors such as non-governmental organizations and there is a discourse on the relationship between trade and the environment, and new environmental management that incorporates both explicit international laws and intergovernmental organizations.

The scenario of globalization is a complex and complicated process of relationships between the overuse of resources and environment degradation. This process of disproportionate use of resources and environmental degradation spawns difficult circumstances for sustainable development (Baylis, Smith and Owens 2014, 331). The divide between North and South—and moreover, their informal and formal politics—complicate the environmental issues, which are associated with environmental degradation, environmental conflict and marginalization.

Within the parameter of this politics, the North is frequently considered as the guardian of the environment and the South as the defender of the poor, and it is presumed that economic growth is presented as the principal solution to both environmental and economic problems. One noteworthy result is the sharp rise in international environmental regimes since the 1970s.

The first UN Conference on the Human Environment was held in Stockholm in 1972. It was the first international meeting of its kind which focused on global environmental problems, and it was initially intended to deal with the issues raised by environmentalists (mostly from the Northern region) about the undesirable effects of both industrialization and population growth, together with pollution and scarce resources. Countries of the South apprehended that their foremost problem was not too much of industrialization, but too little. The South found that poverty and global inequity meant massive discrepancies in wealth between the North and the South.

The establishment of environmental development was consequently entrenched in 'sustainable development', a term that first appeared in the late 1970s; however, it was endorsed and transported resolutely on to the international agenda in the 1987 UN-commissioned report for *Our Common Future*. It is also called the 'Brundtland Report'. The report introduced the concept 'sustainable development', which leads to development that can manage contemporary needs without compromising the ability of future generations to meet their own needs. Implementation of sustainable development was the primary subject matter of the UN Conference on Environment and Development which was held in Rio de Janeiro in 1992.

Bretton Woods System: US Strategic Dominance

The objectives and the functions of the institutions of the Bretton Woods system give a rosy picture of the inclinations of the Global North and more specifically the US to build a more humane world. However, the underlying provisions and conditionality associated with the Bretton Woods system prove otherwise. The establishment and the provisions of the institutions reflect that these structures were created to serve and maintain the hegemony of the US rather than to improve the common socio-economic scenario.

Since the early 1980s, on the one hand, net capital inflows into the US have continuously exceeded net outflow while, on the other hand, the US economy has been the net exporter of FDI (Hoogvelt 2001, 177). Also, during a short period of four years (1994–1998), US corporations regained their previously commanding heights in the global corporate hierarchy with five corporations in the top 10. Academics also hold that 'the relationship between the stock performance on Wall Street and economic growth has become essentially pattern-less. Whatever the USA economy does, money from all over the world will go into American Stock Exchange' (Hoogvelt 2001, 177). The US dollar also enjoys dominance in the global financial market. What has been the reason for the US' growing hegemony and control over global governance and its growing economy?

The Agreement on Agriculture that was embodied in the Uruguay round of the GATT and WTO negotiations has been benefiting the US and other developed states. This has direct benefits for the genetically modified seeds industry of the Global North. The provision of intellectual property rights that has a patent right of up to 20 years has also helped the pharmaceutical industries of the developed states, especially of the US, to boom in the international market. The underdeveloped and developing countries, due to their largely inferior technology and limited advanced technology, find it difficult to use the advantage of scientific development for the development of their people. The intellectual property rights and the associated clause of the patent right have prevented the developing and the underdeveloped countries from making generic versions of the expensive but lifesaving drugs.

As a result, the developing countries have to depend heavily on the countries of the Global North, especially the US, for procuring drugs for cancer and other deadly diseases, thus making the treatment of these diseases very expensive in developing countries. Many times, developing countries such as India have raised the issue of revisiting and rethinking the clause of patent right so that humanity can be benefited with scientific research. However, the US and other states have shown their reluctance to table these issues as their industries and firms were likely to suffer.

Structural adjustment programmes as a condition to procure loans from the IMF promote the rollback of the state from various social sectors, including health and education. This leads to the privatization of the social sector, hence making it difficult for the already impoverished population of the undeveloped countries to attain the necessary condition for human development. India is no exception to this general rule. Structural adjustment programmes act as the instrument to promote the economic model of the US throughout the world and has been proving beneficial for US banks and cooperation rather than bringing about overall development (Heywood 2011, 469). Apart from this, the structural adjustment programmes of the IMF have also been criticized and viewed as enemies of human rights and democracy as they have often supported the military dictatorship of the countries having a cordial relationship with the US (Heywood 2011, 469).

What has been a deafening silence over imperialism is probably the most cunning achievement of neo-liberal brainwashing that has accompanied US corporate control over the world economy. Imperialism exists whenever there is a *deliberate* transnational political interference, including military intervention, for the mobilization, extraction and external transfer of economic surplus from one territory to another.

Those who argue that imperialism is strictly a feature of interstate relations and therefore no longer on the agenda of capitalism under the conditions of globalization merely miss the point that capitalism at all times produces a network of hierarchical relations in which the wealth of some areas, groups or peoples are dependent on the transfer of economic surplus, and hence the underdevelopment of other areas, groups and the people. Globalization is linked systematically with social exclusion, meaning that as globalization proceeds, more and more social groups, segments of the population, as well as whole areas and regions, are being excluded from its benefits.

Richard Harold Steinberg argues that although the WTO's consensus governance model provides law-based initial bargaining, trading rounds close through power-based bargaining favouring Europe and the US and may not lead to a Pareto improvement (Steinberg 2003). The US is a significant contributor to a stalemate at the Montreal Ministerial Meeting (because of the treatment of agriculture) and to the relaunching of the Uruguay Round some months later. Brazil, India, Argentina, Egypt, Colombia and other developing countries all played a prominent role in their way. Many countries, including the developing ones, are always present and active when their national interests are involved and have been very useful at shaping agreements to take their interests into account and invest a great deal in building a national capacity to service the WTO negotiations, and their representatives expect to be present at all critical meetings (Sampson 2001).

India's Strategic Position in Global Governance

India has two parts to its picture. Regarding the present indicators of economic, diplomatic and political developments, India is shining. On the other side, India is facing many challenges, ranging from historical legacies to disputes over territorial and maritime rights, from traditional to non-traditional security threats. If we compare the two sides of the picture, the challenges are more than its rising powers. In global governance, economy, external and internal security, technology, military and nuclear technology and status as a nuclear and near-nuclear power, influence over global rules and regimes in which India is lacking in comparison with China and existing superpowers.

India constitutes a significant pole of power along with the US, China and Europe in the architecture of global governance. European states are still, without exception, small actors with limited power resources; only a joint European Union (EU) can have a role in shaping the future global order. The world powers will have recognized this fact and India will get a place at the global high table despite specific ostensible challenges, and in future years, together with its increasing assertiveness, it will represent a challenge to the established economic powers.

India is playing a significant role in global politics more decisively and pro-actively with its organizational capabilities and international negotiations in many specific global issues of governance. Today India is party to numerous international treaties and a member of almost all critical international organizations and intergovernmental networks. Participation in international regulatory bodies permitted India to have leverage over the future regulatory developments in the financial capital of the industrialized world. It has consistently pressed for a more significant quota share and more effective representation in the top echelon of global economic institutions such as the IMF and the WTO. India is also willing to commit more significant resources to these institutions.

The contribution of India in the UN General Assembly and Security Council, whether on conflicts, peacekeeping missions or economic and social issues in UN bodies or specialized agencies, is commendable. Moreover, within the UN reform system, the claim for India to have a permanent seat in the Security Council holds significance. India's support in the UN and on the global scene has been best captured by the heads of states of all five permanent members of the UN Security Council. Both President Barack Obama and President Nicolas Sarközy during their visits endorsed India's bid to secure a permanent seat in the Security Council. President Obama further reinforced the sentiment saying that India is not an emerging, but an emerged power (Kumar 2011).

India is increasingly active in negotiating non-traditional security issues such as terrorism, environmental policies and climate change, global warming, drug trafficking, disarmament, and so on. India has always been an active participant state and raised these issues at various summits, including the WTO and climate change negotiations. It can be said that India is trying to build up global governance capabilities in these areas of international politics.

To understand the role of India in global environmental governance, we should go back in history and review the country's rapid evolution from a developing country to an emerging economy with growth rates between 7% and 9% over the past decade (Schunz and Belis 2011). India has keenly observed and abided by the norms of the United Nations Framework Convention on Climate Change (UNFCCC), the Kyoto Protocol, the Intergovernmental Panel on Climate Change (IPCC), and so on.

India has been taking steps at the national and bilateral level to protect its biodiversity. Besides the Biological Diversity Act, 2002, the National Biodiversity Authority of India has also put in place a traditional knowledge database—the Traditional Knowledge Digital Library (TKDL), managed by the Council of Scientific and Industrial Research (CSIR). TKDL is a computerized database of documented information available in Indian texts, relating to Indian systems of medicine (Economic Times Bureau 2010). Along with seeking a leadership role, as Lorenzo Piccio said, India has been taking action more decisively and proactively in South–South cooperation, much like it played a crucial role in the Non-Aligned Movement. South–South cooperation has traditionally been an essential pillar of India's foreign policy and diplomacy. South–South cooperation is a means to promote India's partnerships (Piccio 2013).

India was amongst the 13 WTO members of the Task Force on Aid for Trade. India is also engaged in infrastructure development through concessional lending and technical assistance. In 2012, the Export-Import Bank of India (Exim Bank) reported a total of 157 operative lines of credit worth US$8.2 billion, most of which were finance-specific infrastructure projects in developing countries, delivered by Indian companies in sectors such as electricity, energy, irrigation and transport. The Indian government is also contributing substantially to multilateral organizations, including the United Nations Development Program (UNDP) and the World Health Organization (WHO).

Since the structural adjustment programme of 1991 in India, the state has slowly but steadily withdrawn from the health sector. As a result, in urban India, there has been a mushrooming of private healthcare institutions with five-star facilities. These private hospitals, working on the principles of profit-making, provide facilities that are beyond the reach of the common person in India but attract patients from other countries of the Global North where healthcare facilities are expensive. This had led to the growth of medical tourism in the metropolitan cities of India. On the other hand, due to the roll-back of the state's role, the rural healthcare system in India is gradually declining and is facing problems related to human resources and material infrastructure in the rural hospitals.

Concluding Observations

Global governance or world governance is a movement towards political cooperation among transnational actors, aimed at negotiating responses to problems that affect more than one state or religion. The modern question of world governance exists in the context of globalization and globalizing regimes of power—geographic, social, cultural, economic or political—and reflecting upon the process of designating laws, rules or regulations intended for organization and centralization of human societies on a global scale.

Global governance is a broad, dynamic and complicated process of interactive decision-making at the global level that involves formal and informal mechanisms as well as governmental and non-governmental bodies. State and government remain the primary institutions for the articulation of public interests and those of the global community as a whole. However, global governance also involves inter-governmental and sometimes supranational bodies.

The complicated process of global governance can be traced back to the interwar period. During the interwar period, the effects of the poor mechanisms of collective governance were visible. In a more interconnected and interdependent world, there is a need for transparent global governance to ensure sustainable development, economic growth and trade. The concept of a global partnership can subsidize the objective of integrated global governance in the post-2015 agenda of sustainable and equitable development.

Although the institutions of global governance advocate development for all, critics of global governance believe it is the manifestation of US interests and an instrument to maintain the hegemony of the US. Apart from this, the growing incidence of protectionism that has triggered the recent exit of Britain from the EU, strict visa regimes and the exit of the US from the environmental covenant has raised a debate on the very existence and relevance of global governance.

Thus, it can be said that the process of global governance has to be very dynamic in order to cater to the needs of various stakeholders. The complexities prevalent in the world order further complicate the homogeneity which has been the essence of the phenomenon of global governance.

Summary

- Global governance is multiple, rather than singular, having a specific institutional framework and decision-making mechanism. It operates through the interaction between group institutions at various levels.
- It is a movement towards political and economic cooperation among transnational actors, aimed at negotiating responses to problems that affect more than one state or religion.
- Global governance is a broad, dynamic and complicated process of interactive decision-making at the global level that involves formal and informal mechanisms as well as governmental and non-governmental bodies.
- It refers not only to the formal state institutions and organizations, but also all organizations and pressure groups—from MNCs to transnational social movements to non-governmental organizations (NGOs)—which pursue goals and objectives for transnational rule and authority.
- A range of non-state actors are key elements of global governance. The UN, the WTO, the WHO and Greenpeace are some of the central components of global governance.
- These non-state actors do not possess sovereignty in the real sense of the term. Unlike the states, they do not possess magnitude of resources, but are likely to be influential in substantive measures.

- Although, the institutions of global governance advocate development for all, the critics of global governance believe it is a manifestation of US interests and an instrument to maintain the hegemony of the US.

Suggested Questions

1. The world's cities are becoming increasingly more homogenous (think McDonald's, KFC, Coke, Hollywood films, clubs, shopping malls, and so on) while concurrently offering inhabitants greater choice and opportunities than they had before globalization. What prospects have been seen in your region due to globalization?
2. How does globalization disturb industry and employment? What is the role of the Internet, communication and technology in globalization?
3. What roles do the IMF, the World Bank and the WTO play in globalization?
4. Could global governance really mean world governance?
5. Explain the role of TNCs in global governance.
6. 'Globalization affects biodiversity, the environment and society.' Comment.
7. Do the countries of the North hold the rudder of global governance? Comment.

References

Agrawal, Subhash. 2017. *Emerging Donors in International Development Assistance: The India Case.* New Delhi: Partnership & Business Development Division, International Development Research Centre (IDRC).

Albert, M., and Tanja Kopp-Malek. 2002. 'The Pragmatism of Global and European Governance: Emerging Forms of the Political 'Beyond Westphalia'. *Millennium: Journal of International Studies* 31 (3): 453–471.

Alonso, José Antonio, and José Antonio Ocampo, eds. 2015. *Global Governance and Rules for the Post-2015 Era: Addressing Emerging Issues in the Global Environment.* London and New York, NY: Bloomsbury.

Baylis, John, Steve Smith and Patricia Owens, eds. 2014. *The Globalization of World Politics: An Introduction to International Relations.* Oxford: Oxford University Press.

Bird, Frederick, Thomas Vance and Peter Woolstencroft. 2009. 'Fairness in International Trade and Investment: North American Perspectives'. *Journal of Business Ethics* 84 (3): 405–425.

Bossone, Biagio. 2008. *IMF Surveillance: A Case Study on IMF Governance.* Washington D. C.: Independent Evaluation Office (IEO), International Monetary Fund (IMF).

Economic Times Bureau. 2010. 'India Keen to Play Role in Nagoya Meet.' *The Economic Times*, 23 May 2010. Accessed 23 April 2018. https://economictimes.indiatimes.com/dateline-india/india-keen-to-play-lead-role-in-nagoya-meet/articleshow/5963893.cms.

Finkelstein, Lawrence S. 1995. 'What is Global Governance?' *Global Governance* 1 (3): 367–372.

Goldman, Michael. 2005. *Imperial Nature: The World Bank and Struggles for Social Justice in the Age of Globalization.* New Haven, CT: Yale University Press.

Heywood, Andrew. 2011. *Global Politics.* New York, NY: Palgrave Macmillan.

Hoogvelt, Ankie. 2001. *Globalization and the Postcolonial World: The New Political Economy of Development.* New York, NY: Palgrave Macmillan.

International Labour Organization (ILO). 2017. *Tripartite Declaration of Principles concerning Multinational Enterprises and Social Policy.* Accessed 23 April 2018. http://www.ilo.org>dyn>normlex.

International Monetary Fund (IMF). 2017. Accessed 24 April 2018. http://www.imf.org/en/About.

Isard, Peter. 2005. *Globalization and the International Financial System: What's Wrong and What can be Done*. New York, NY: Cambridge University Press.

JaeBin, Ahn, Mary Amiti and David E. Weinstein. 2011. 'Trade Finance and the Great Trade Collapse'. *The American Economic Review: Papers and Proceedings 2011* 101 (3): 298–302.

Kumar, Chanchal, Lungthuyiang Riamei and Sanju Gupta. 2017. *Understanding Global Politics*. New Delhi: KW Publishers.

Kumar, Rajiv. 2011. 'Taking a Long View'. *Seminar*. Accessed 23 April 2018. http://www.india-seminar.com/2011/617/617_rajiv_kumar.htm.

Michie, Jonathan, and John Grieve Smith, eds. 2005. *Global Instability: The Political Economy of World Economic Governance*. New York, NY: Routledge.

Mingst, Karen A., and Ivan M. Arreguín-Toft. 2014. *Essentials of International Relations*. New York, NY: W. W. Norton and Company.

Piccio, Lorenzo. 2013. 'India's Foreign Aid Program Catches Up with its Global Ambitions'. *Devex*, 10 May 2013. Accessed 23 April 2018. https://www.devex.com/news/india-s-foreign-aid-program-catches-up-with-its-global-ambitions-80919.

Rosenau, James N. 1995. 'Governance in the Twenty-first Century'. *Global Governance* 1 (1): 13–43. Boulder, CO: Lynne Rienner Publishers.

Ruggie, John Gerard. 1982. 'International Regimes, Transactions, and Change: Embedded Liberalism in the Postwar Economic Order'. *International Organization* 36 (2): 379–415.

Sampson, Gary P., ed. 2001. *The Role of the World Trade Organization in Global Governance*. Tokyo: The United Nations University Press.

Schunz, Simon, and David Belis. 2011. *China, India and Global Environmental Governance: The Case of the Climate Change*. Leuven: Leuven Centre for Global Governance Studies.

Steinberg, R. H. 2002. 'In the Shadow of Law or Power? Consensus-Based Bargaining and Outcomes in the GATT/WTO'. *International Organization* 56 (2): 339–374.

United Nations (UN). 2005. *Transnational Corporations* 4 (3). Geneva. Accessed 23 April 2018. http://unctad.org/en/Docs/iteiit20059_en.pdf.

_____ 2013. 'Trade-related South–South Co-operation: India' Accessed 27 October 2017. https://www.oecd.org/dac/aft/South-South_India.pdf.

UN System Task Team on the Post-2015 UN Development Agenda. 2012. *Realizing the Future We Want for All*. Accessed 24 April 2018. http://www.un.org/en/development/desa/policy/untaskteam_undf/untt_report.pdf.

Further Reading

Cerny, Philip G. 2010. *Rethinking World Politics: A Theory of Transnational Pluralism*. New York, NY: Oxford University Press.

Chimni, Bhupinder, S., and Siddharth Mallavarapu, eds. 2012. *International Relations: Perspective for the Global South*. Noida: Dorling Kindersley.

Karns, Margaret P., Karen A. Mingst and Kendall W. Stiles. 2005. *International Organizations: The Politics and Processes of Global Governance*. Boulder, CO: Lynne Reinner Publishers.

Pikkety, Thomas. 2014. *Capital in the Twenty-First Century*. Translated by Arthur Goldhammer. New York, NY: Harvard University Press.

Stiglitz, Joseph E. 2012. *The Price of Inequality: How Today's Divided Society Endangers Our Future*. New York, NY: W. W. Norton & Company.

Viotti, Paul R, and Mark V. Kauppi, eds. 2007. *International Relations and World Politics: Security, Economy, Identity*. New Delhi: Pearson.

Technological and Cultural Dimensions of Globalization

Virendra Kumar and Bhavna Sharma

LEARNING OBJECTIVES

- To understand the technological and cultural dimensions of globalization
- To explain historically rooted interrelations between technology and culture
- To discuss global–local dialectics in the contemporary world
- To evaluate the processes of cultural globalization

Globalization is conceived as a multidimensional process wherein social, political and economic relations are increasingly integrated. This process is paradoxical and highly contested, as a result of which the study of any dimension of it cannot be done in isolation. Each dimension is intertwined with others. Giddens (1998) argues that globalization is a complex set of processes driven by a combination of political and economic influences, at the same time creating new transnational systems and forces. These transnational systems and forces have been impacting the social, economic, political, cultural and even ecological spheres of human life, cutting across the boundaries of modern nation states. While technology represents the material aspects of social life, the realm of culture involves a system of values, meanings and human imagination about the self and the surrounding world. Communitarian scholars such as Michael Sandel argue that individuals are embedded in definite systems of meanings, given by their cultural community. The former is not a relationship they choose but an attachment they discover, not merely an attribute but a constituent of their identity (Sandel 1982, 150). Technological means and tools do facilitate construction of the collective identity and create solidarity. As Benedict Anderson (2006) has shown, the invention of the printing press and the consequent mass education system through printed words and imagery helped construct a sense of nationalism. People who had never been in face-to-face contact began to think of themselves as belonging to one nation.

Similarly, modern means of communications have been very much instrumental in creating solidarity around particular religious leaders and ideologies or generating mass demand for consumer products such as blue jeans and Pepsi.

The primary objective of this chapter is to explore the complex interrelation between globalization and culture. This does not mean that the relations of globalization with the social, economic, political and ecological spheres are less important, but they have been dealt with separately in other chapters of this book. In addition to exploring the complex relationship between globalization and culture, this chapter also attempts to interrogate the implications of globalization on culture. While interrogating the complex relationship of globalization with culture, and the implications of the former for the latter, this chapter further demonstrates how technological advancements have been the main driving force behind the spread of globalization, just like has happened with the other ideas since time immemorial. Before moving on to the main objective, one more thing needs to be qualified here: when we refer to 'globalization', we mean the second wave of globalization, which is also referred to as 'financial globalization', unless the context specifies another meaning.

Understanding Culture and Technology

Individuals are constituted by their cultural communities. Communities provide the important cognitive and evaluative resources to individuals to lead their lives. These cultural communities are important for its members and are of value in themselves. Each culture, as a system of meanings and values, seeks to maintain its distinctiveness from other cultures. This quest to maintain boundaries and distinctiveness from others tends to create contestation as also creative adaptation. Culture has been conceptualized and interpreted in various ways, but two important characterizations draw consensus among scholars. Culture has been defined as an essence and as a process. The scholars who define culture as an essence conceive of it as a singular, transcendent, unified idea containing certain essential features, soul and attributes. These features are static, stable and the same throughout history, providing an organic unity, coherence and identity to members of a culture. The members of a particular cultural community share certain common beliefs and a value system which gets reflected in customs, practices and social behaviours. Culture, according to this perspective, maintains the persistence of its distinctiveness and core values, and defines the identity of its constituent members. Cultural communities, for instance, have specific views on relations between a god and the individual, rights and responsibilities, liberty and authority. These values constitute important cognitive and evaluative resources through which individuals make sense of the self and the surrounding world.

In the other perspective, culture is a dynamic concept, its meaning changing over time. Here, culture is essentially viewed as a process rather than a transhistorical static entity. However, though the idea of culture is dynamic, at the same time it possesses some sort of stability that provides identity to its members. This perspective further sees culture as continuously changing and being informed by numerous internal processes and shaped by external forces. Now the question arises, what are those internal and external forces and how are they shaping culture in varying contexts?

The answer to this question looks into the conception of culture, viewing it as being constituted by different webs and networks of meaning, implicitly acknowledging the diverse relationship people have with it (Figure 6.1). This relationship ensures that cultures are endlessly mixing, with different permeations, and new cultural forms are emerging as a part of this ongoing process. This understanding also

FIGURE 6.1 Elements of Culture

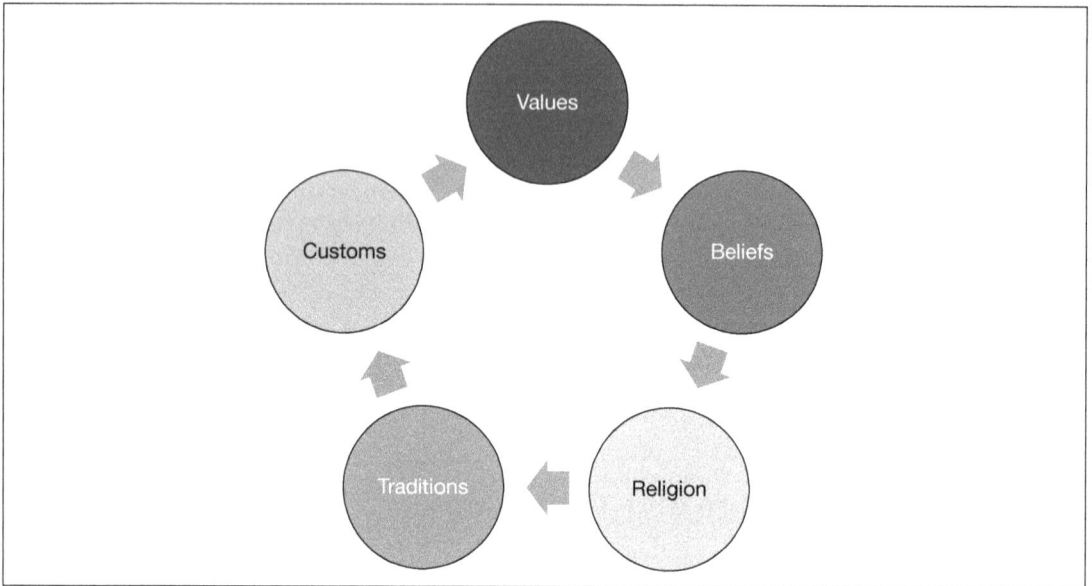

helps to explain the commonality that exists between cultures and further accounts for complexities and differentiations that exist between them (Hopper 2007, 29–50). But the crucial aspect of this understanding of culture is the coming together of cultures. We argue that, since time immemorial, it has been technological innovations and changes which have brought cultures closer, resulting in their fission and fusion.

Technological innovations have historically been drivers of socio-economic change, though they are a necessary but not sufficient condition. It is argued that the primitive human being discovered fire and wheel, which gave earlier civilizations a momentum leap. Not only did they start settled life, which helped in creating shared values and belief systems, but also organized life, paving the way for the technological innovations. The domestication of animals, for example, led to the development of the bullock cart, which in turn facilitated interaction between different cultural communities at a common place.

In the modern period again, it was massive technological disruptions in the areas of transport, communication, chemical processes, textiles, and so on, which paved the way for the Industrial Revolution in Europe during the eighteenth century. There began mass-level production based on the factory system and associated with an urbanization process. Trade and financial flows intensified. The European countries, in search of raw materials and markets for their manufactured goods, moved out of their homelands and conquered far-off countries of Asia, Africa and Latin America. Britain, as a major hegemonic power, controlled most of the colonized countries of Asia, Africa and Latin America.

The colonization of these countries is seen as one of implications of the first wave of globalization that seems to have affected the norms, values, beliefs, tastes, behaviours and even thinking processes of the people of the colonized countries. Actually, industrialization gave birth to capitalism in Europe, and capitalism transformed the norms and value systems of the European people. For example, the birth of print capitalism standardized scripts, leading to the production of the same texts. Through those texts, a unified and singular meaning in religion, philosophy, science and technology got spread throughout

Europe. The cumulative implication of all these changes was the complete transformation of European society during that time.

With colonization, the norms and value systems of the European countries were introduced in the colonized countries, through media which led to the fusion of cultures. The entry of Christian missionaries, for instance, in these far lands during the colonial period led to the propagation of religious beliefs and cultural practices based on the teachings of Christianity on a massive scale. One thing needs to be qualified here: Christianity as a religion did not entered India for the first time only because of colonization; this religion seems to have first emerged on Indian soil though traders, but there was no massive campaign and propagation before colonization.

Furthermore, the European languages, mainly English, Spanish, French and Portuguese, were introduced in these colonies along with other cultural practices because of the prolonged stay of the European powers. As previously mentioned of the way that print capitalism had standardized scripts, this process led to the production of a much more universalized language. The colonial administration very meticulously introduced their languages in the field of governance. It needs to be noted here that it would be naïve to believe that European languages were introduced just for smoothing administrative work. Their introduction was mainly for producing a class of people who had norms, tastes and value systems like the colonizers'. The famous Macaulay minute document establishes these facts (Tharoor 2016).

Most of the colonized countries won independence during the Second World War but their prolonged political, cultural and administrative penetration left an enduring impact on the social psychology and collective ethos of the people of these colonies.

Globalization and Technological Innovations

Scholars argue that technological changes have been a driver as well as a consequence of globalization (Ferguson and Mansbach 2012, 109). In our previous discussion, we have already discussed how technological innovations such as the printing press revolutionized the diffusion of knowledge and helped to achieve mass literacy in European society. Similarly, high-compression, non-sparking, internal combustion engines and gas turbines made possible ever large seagoing vessels and jet aircraft. The introduction of fibre optics and cable technology across the oceans and continents, together with satellite technology, augmented the capacity and reach of electronic media such as radio, television and telephone to communicate faster, with better quality, across the long distances.

The second half of the twentieth century was marked by two significant developments—the beginning of financial globalization in the 1970s and the beginning of the information technology (IT) revolution. Both these developments have become complementary to each other in the twenty-first century, as a result of which a new culture is emerging.

Actually, catastrophic events in the first half of the twentieth century, such as the Great Depression, the world wars, Nazism and fascism, had shaken the foundational premises of polity, economy and society. The 'perennial question' of what was the best mechanism for managing polity and economy once again resurfaced. The success of the Union of Soviet Socialist Republics (USSR) despite the Great Depression has many positive and negative lessons to teach. Taking lessons from these events, global leaders sat together and evolved two sets of institutional mechanisms for managing world affairs: the United Nations (UN) for managing political affairs and the Bretton Woods Institutions (the International Monetary Fund, or IMF, and the World Bank) for managing economic affairs. It is the functioning of the latter institutions which is believed to have paved the way for the second wave of globalization in the 1970s, popularly known as financial globalization. This globalization posed new challenges and problems before the whole world.

The quest for a solution of the financial globalization motivated for looking into technological solutions. This process finally culminated in the IT revolution in the 1980s. This revolution became possible through the microelectronic revolution, especially the introduction of the semiconductor and Internet technologies linking together millions of computers and other devices across the several jurisdictions. Financial globalization is nowadays known as the IT revolution; hence, it is also understood as technological globalization. With the signing of the Information Technology Agreement of 1997, more than 40 countries sought to eliminate all tariffs on various categories of information and communication technology products. This led to a decline in the quality-adjusted prices of computer hardware and software, with rapid innovation. The web-based software revolution coupled with declining prices of high-tech gadgets such as smartphones and other devices has made the information and knowledge explosion accessible to individuals and groups hitherto not connected to computer networks (Ferguson and Mansbach 2012, 110).

BOX 6.1: Development of Computers

The present-day computers which we frequently use have developed over generations. On the basis of the utilization of technology, the development of computers is divided into five generations:

1. The first-generation (1940–1956) computer was based on the vacuum tube technology. In those days, computers used to be enormous and bulky, the size of an entire room. Those computers were highly inefficient and used to consume a lot of energy and generate a huge amount of heat.
2. The second-generation (1956–1963) computer was based on transistor technology. Those computers were efficient, smaller, faster, cheaper and energy-saving.
3. The third-generation (1964–1971) computer was based on the technology of integrated circuits. The integrated circuits were developed using semiconductors such as silicon. This technology was a huge leap in the development of computers.
4. The fourth-generation (1972–2010) computers are based on microprocessor technology. The other developments in this generation are the graphical user interface (GUI) and the mouse.
5. The development of the fifth-generation computer is an ongoing process which began in 2010. The plan is for this generation of computers to use artificial intelligence and to develop machines which can respond to natural language and have the capability to organize themselves.

Source: www.btob.co.nz.

Impacts of IT Revolution

The IT revolution seems to have become an enabling factor in the onward march of globalization. Using complex mathematical algorithms, the IT revolution has facilitated knowledge and information sharing at an unprecedented scale and contributed to research and innovation in various other fields, such as the medical sciences, business, space, military technology and robotics. Web-based software and various applications have emerged as a converging platform for cutting-edge technology by pooling knowledge and research from various interdisciplinary areas. Wireless technology has revolutionized biomedical research and the healthcare system. Medical devices based on nanotechnology are being used for detecting various lethal diseases and studying cellular or subcellular functions. Mega projects such as genome sequencing and coding have been achieved because of sophisticated computer technologies and engineering tools. Now with CRISPR (clustered regularly interspaced short palindromic repeat) technology, a genome can be adjusted for eliminating genetic diseases (MacRae 2013).

Artificial intelligence and robotics based on mechanical engineering and computer programming are being utilized in a variety of areas, such as manufacturing, medical imagery, pollution monitoring, space and ocean exploration, and even in entertainment. Disney's engineers have created hundreds of robots for moviemaking. Robots are the future of the twenty-first century, as they are capable of carrying out hundreds of clinical tests simultaneously and performing complex surgeries such as on brain tumours, besides under water and space exploration. All these technologies have become enabling factors for globalization, which can be broadly seen in two broad fields: governance and commerce.

On Governance

Governance has seen a paradigm shift after the integration with information and communication technology (ICT). E-governance has made possible for increasing citizen participation in delivery of goods and services. Governments have become more transparent and accountable to the people and the latter have turned into active participants rather than mere beneficiaries of welfare services. E-governance has widened the citizen–government interface in a variety of ways: government-to-people (G2P), government-to-business (G2B), business-to-business (B2B) and business-to-people (B2P). In view of the numerous advantages offered by these technologies (speed, cost reduction and wider reach), both developed and developing countries are using electronic modes of communication to deliver public services and for intra-government communication. Developing countries, however, have not gained as quickly as industrialized countries from the ICT revolution. They face huge challenges to access and investment in technological infrastructure.

Furthermore, Internet-based social networking sites such as Facebook and Twitter, among others, have helped political globalization, political education and consciousness generation. The massive protests against the authoritarian regimes in Tunisia, Egypt and Libya were made possible on account of increasing discontentment among the common masses, which got channelized and crystallized through social media. The common citizens and educated professionals directly communicated with one another about their grievances and for democratization, to which their rulers finally agreed. Similarly, other social movements in the areas of the environment, human rights, and so on, have been synergized and coordinated, as civil-society groups cutting across ethnic, racial and geographical boundaries are coming together and the Internet is providing a common platform for sharing their concerns. A Web-based international non-profit organization named WikiLeaks has recently pledged to make governments all around the world more accountable and open by publishing secret information and classified documents provided by anonymous sources. WikiLeaks releases include the Afghan War Diary (2010), the Iraq War Logs (2010) and 779 secret files related to prisoners detained in a Guantanamo detention camp (2011). This and various other releases have laid bare the hegemonic designs of the US (Ferguson and Mansbach 2012).

On Commerce

Information and computer software technology is playing a critical role in the global financial market. Online trading of financial products and their various derivatives across the various stock markets located far apart occurs in trillions on a daily basis through e-currencies, such as bitcoins. Massive movement of institutional and non-institutional funds and capital from one part of the world to another is causing volatility and speculation. It is argued that contemporary digital technology is as instrumental in spreading panic as profit across the market.

E-commerce has emerged in a big way as new entrepreneurs are harnessing online platforms as an attractive site for shopping for almost everything. Online vendors such as Flipkart, Amazon, Snapdeal, and so on, do offer huge discounts on a wide range of products to attract customers who are tech-savvy. This has helped the marketing of even traditional cultural products, such as handicrafts, artefacts and paintings, to a much a larger base of buyers across borders because of declining transportation costs. Entrepreneurship has reached a new height as software-driven technology does not require the possession of factory units. The owner of Uber taxi services does not own a single taxi, but runs thousands of taxi services in hundreds of cities across the globe. Likewise, the CEO of OYO Rooms runs a business in over 200 cities and many countries, but does not own a single hotel.

BOX 6.2: Digital Divide: A New Form of Inequality

The IT revolution has led to the expansion of the Internet. With the development of technology, the number of mobile users has accelerated over the last two decades in both developed as well as developing countries. These technological developments have led to the emergence of new concerns known as the 'digital divide'. The 'digital divide' refers to inequality in terms of those who know how to use digital technology and those who do not know how to use such technology. This is a new form of inequality, which significantly depends on social, economic and political factors. The penetration of Internet technology is highly uneven in Latin American and African countries.

The digital divide is further creating new forms of problems. One such problem is exacerbation of the generation gap. In future, this problem will become much more evident in the developing countries since their population will be getting old.

Technology and the Reconfiguration of Culture

This reconfiguration of the culture can be best captured through analysing the following processes: homogenization, clash of civilizations, hybridization, domination and consumerism. These processes are not only processes but also perspectives on culture in varying contexts in contemporary times.

Homogenization

The homogenization perspective sees globalization and increasing means of communication as factors that are promoting a universalization of culture. The universalization of culture requires rationality and standardization. Here, standardization essentially puts one culture as the benchmark to compare and judge other cultures. Transnational corporations (TNCs), in their pursuit of maximized profits, mobilize superior resources to create similar practices, tastes and lifestyles. This creates a culture of consumerism not only adapted to but actually generating the demand for a world market. Individuals, instead of cultivating distinct traditions, become uniformly attached to commodities to satisfy their material desires. This amounts to a kind of ideological takeover of the world. George Ritzer describes it as a McDonaldization of the world (Lechner and Boli 2005, 139–140).

The US, being a hegemonic state on account of its unrivalled economic and military power, is pushing a distinctly individualistic consumerist culture—turning its own type of 'modernity' into a global model. Americans, while publicly advocating the virtues of free markets, also have covert agents among their cartoon characters, movie heroes and music stars. American media products mediate more and more of people's experience of 'reality'. These products, ranging from music and videos to books, sports, soft drinks, clothing, and so on, are constructed as a standard image through common logos and brand names, thus creating a seductive appeal. This leads to the emergence of a kind of videology that works through sound bites and film clips and, as a consequence, may be more successful in instilling the novel values[1] required for a market to succeed (Barber 2000, 25). Thus America's 'hard' pursuit of the world combines with the 'soft' and alluring appeal of its media offerings, thanks to modern communication technologies, and creates a world culture that threatens diversity.

It is also argued that there have been subtle examples of Western cultural imperialism over non-Western societies. The West has used its military and economic dominance to impose its values, beliefs and institutional forms on others. These values and beliefs also contain a universal message: they purport to apply and be valid everywhere. Democracy, the free market and human rights (or alternatively, consumerism, commoditization and rationality) all bear the ethnocentric marks of their origin.

While criticizing the homogenization thesis, Ahmad (2004) holds that the aesthetic value of cultural objects, symbols necessarily are getting diminished, or transformed when they caught up in circuit of exchange, market pricing, advertising and so on. He further argues that culture needs to be understood as sum of means and practices of communication through which values and meanings are generated. This idea of generation of meaning gives the idea of culture and orientation towards future not past. This orientation and will to go on imagining the impossible, is what the culture of globalization seeks to undermine (Ahmad 2004, 105–110).

Clash of Civilization

In the cultural discourse over homogenization and cultural imperialism, fundamentalists have responded with an alternative world view. In the 1970s and 1980s, Islamic fundamentalist thought, drawing from particular readings of Islamic text and Islamic history, emerged as a counter to ethnocentric ideas. Prominent contributors included Egyptians Hassan al-Banna, Sayyid Qutb and Syed Abul Ala Maudoodi. Their collective ideas were more concerned with faith and following divine guidance. For them, secularism and separation of religion from politics constitute the central problem, as it undermines the authority of God and posits that people can run governments, build businesses, administer justice and enjoy themselves without direct divine guidance. They believe that God is one and God is all; nothing can be

---

[1] Novel values refer to ideas, beliefs and norms legitimizing consumption of capitalist goods. Capitalist market requires constant consumption as the underlying and legitimate belief of progress for its continuation.

left out—politics is part of religion. In an Islamic state, no one can regard any field of his affairs as personal and private. God's law encompasses every aspect of society, from forms of dress and hygiene to principles of administration and justice, morality and principles of knowledge. Iran's Islamic republic was intended to be just such a system, which was led by a supreme Islamic scholar who combined religious and political authority (Khomeini and Algar, cited in Lechner and Boli 2005, 196–197).

In the fundamentalist world view, consumerism tempts individuals to focus on satisfying their material interests rather than abiding by religious obligations. Individualism leads people to act on sexual impulses, including homosexual desire, without moral censure. The scientific knowledge system celebrates human over divine powers and creates a poisonous hostility towards religion. In place of an illusory democracy, Islam offers a superior alternative in the form of popular consultation (shura). In comparison to a free-market economy that leads to boundless greed and divisive competition, Islam subjects economic activity to religious rules, including a prohibition on charging interest. Islamists do not just want restoration of Islamic rule all over the world—restoration of Islamic way of life uncontaminated by corrupting values of individualism, divisive competition, consumerism, homosexual desire, hostility towards religion, etc., but aim to create a new kind of world civilization based on the freedom of man on earth from every authority except God's authority (Ibid.). In contrast with changing principles and cultures, such a civilization would be based on 'eternal and unchangeable' principles and promotes a way of life 'harmonious with human nature' (Qutb 1981, cited in Lechner and Boli 2005, 198). Reaching this destination requires a struggle, or jihad, as an active public struggle to make Islam's system of life dominant in the world. At a minimum, Islamic people need to defend the honour of Islam against imperialists and their main supporters, the Jews (Khomeini and Algar 1985, cited in Lechner and Boli 2005, 198).

Over time, the jihad went global. With support from Middle Eastern countries and owing to enabling modern technology, banking and transportation, Islamic militants established networks outside their home countries and targeted the linchpin of global culture: the United States, the 'Great Satan'. A series of Islamic militant attacks beginning from hostage-taking at the American embassy in Tehran (1979) finally culminated in the brazen terrorist attack by the Al Qaeda on the World Trade Center and the Pentagon in New York and Washington (2001). As an extreme manifestation of Muslim militancy, this violent attack produced a greater sense of shock and 'cataclysm' than the Iranian Revolution (1979).

The aforementioned Islamic world view and its militant manifestation, though, do not capture the diversity of Islamism, such as Sufism, and presents an essentialized notion of culture and civilization as rooted in unchangeable and static principles and attributes. This understanding suggests that any particular culture remains the same and thus does not confront internal dissension and external influences whatsoever, and posits that other non-Islamic cultures and civilizations only pose a threat to Islamic culture and this entails confrontation and conflict.

A more persuasive but again essentialized understanding of culture and civilization is the starting point for Samuel P. Huntington, who advanced the 'clash of civilizations' thesis in the post-cold war era. He argues that there exists an incompatibility between different civilizations and, more particularly, across different cultures. Each culture or civilization has its core belief system and attributes which are distinct from others. The premises of liberal ideas of individualism, secularism, pluralism and human rights are represented as the foundation of globalization and cosmopolitan culture; in reality, these ideas have only a superficial resonance in orthodox cultures. Each civilization is differentiated from others by history, culture, tradition and—the most—religion, and provides different answers to life's great question. Though they may adapt to change, civilizations endure by virtue of powerful 'structuring ideas' that shape the identity of individuals and communities over centuries (Huntington 1993, cited in Lechner and Boli 2005, 201). Religion is a central defining characteristic of civilizations. Huntington identifies a limited number of 'true' civilizations: the Western, Latin American, Islamic, Sinic, Hindu, Orthodox Christianity and Buddhist. These civilizations become caught up in conflicts among groups along their fault lines and among their leading states, because the value they contain matters so much to their adherents. When stakes are highest and the group faces their biggest troubles, Huntington argues, they are most likely to fall back on what is most 'basic, enduring, and comprehensive'. This is what happened in the 'Islamic resurgence'. From Huntington's perspective, what is universalism to the West is imperialism to the rest (Huntington 1993, cited in Lechner and Boli 2005, 202). Most Muslim countries resist Western universalism, resent imposition and avoid convergence. Instead of being bridged, cracks along fault lines are getting wider and this turns into a clash on account of the West's arrogant action.

For Huntington, civilizations are tight bundles of beliefs and values. He mistakes an abstract category for existential reality. Real civilizations are composites, held together by long histories and complex exchanges with others: Iran, for example, combines an Islamic and Persian heritage, both influenced by Western imports. Civilization is complex and may inform and give meaning to social life, but this always requires creative work (Lechner and Boli 2005, 205). His thesis also fails to understand that Islam and Islamism are not monolithic ideas and that there exist a variety of world views within Islamism. The absence of 'kin country rallying' on behalf of the Taliban or Al Qaeda or behind Khomeini's Islamic revolution shows internal dissension within Islam, which thus far has limited the appeal of violent groups claiming to act on behalf of Islam as a whole (Lechner and Boli 2005, 204).

Hybridization

Hybridization as a perspective entails a dialectic relationship or mutual reinforcement between global culture and a particular culture. In the complex interplay of these two, the former is seen as influencing the latter, and vice versa, in a way that can be called glocalization or hybridization. The earlier colonialist expansion of the West and the consequent cultural influences were mediated and redirected in distinct patterns of appropriation by people in Global South—as demonstrated by syncretic cultures in the Indian tradition. In the contemporary context of globalization as an aggregation of cultural flows or networks, cultural influences move in many directions to bring about more hybridization than homogenization. Individuals and different nationals, ethnic and racial groups located in distant settings react actively or passively to the same mass-media cultural product or symbol, and differently. Movement between cultural areas always involves interpretation, translation, adaptation and indigenization as the receiving culture brings its own cultural resources to bear in a dialectical fashion upon cultural imports (Issar 2012, 293–295). Further, globalization has stimulated nations, global cities and cultural organizations to not only protect but also project their culture in a global space.

In this context, McDonald's and KFC have become popular icons in various non-Western countries, while Japanese, Korean, Chinese and Indian foods are also gaining substantial presence in Western countries.

The global landscape of cultural production has increasingly become polycentric and polysemous. Globalization appears less to be resulting in a pattern of mass cultural uniformity and more the emergence of a mosaic of cultural production centres tied together in a complex relation of competition and collaboration across the globe (Scott 2008, cited in Issar 2012, 295). In India, Rupert Murdoch's Star TV in the beginning sought to displace the government television monopoly, but found itself in tough competition with a dozen indigenous competitors, many of them telecasting in one of many Subcontinental languages. This compelled Star TV to localize its programming and institutional practices so as to adapt to local conditions at the very same time when local film and television enterprises were becoming global in their perspectives and practices.

Echoing the same dialectic between global and local, Arjun Appadurai (2000) takes the position that there exists a disjuncture between various cultural flows: ethnoscapes, technoscapes, financescapes, mediascapes and ideoscapes. The suffix 'scape' refers to the fluid, irregular shape of these landscapes and these terms are deeply context-dependent. These disjoint flows, argues Appadurai, collide within a particular society, where identity construction becomes a matter of local interpretation of the collision. In this perspective, sameness and difference do not just happen but they actually cannibalize each other (Appadurai 2000, 320–330).

The critics contend that hybridity is 'inauthentic' and 'multiculturalism lite' (Pieterse 2015, 57–59). However, Pieterse (2015) counters that there are multiple layers of hybridity, and the real problem is not the hybridity but the politics of boundaries. He argues that hybridity is a problem only from the point of view of essentialism's boundaries. He further maintains that what 'hybridity' means varies not only over time but also in different cultures, and this informs different patterns of hybridity. The importance of hybridity lies in the fact that it problematizes the boundaries.

Domination

The perspective of domination utilizes the concept of ethnocentrism to understand the subjugation of one culture by another culture. Ethnocentrism essentially means Europeans looking at non-Western societies and their practices from their own Western perspective. The scholars of ethnocentrism include Edward Said, a founding figure of postcolonial theory, developed from 1970 onward, and a humanist critic of Western enlightenment that uncovered its link to colonialism and highlighted narratives of oppression, cultural and ideological biases which disempowered colonized people. He thereby condemned Eurocentrism's attempt to remake the world in its own image. It is argued that the present-day technological revolution promotes ethnocentrism through various means. Present-day beauty contests such as Miss World or Miss Universe are criticized on the same grounds, that they promote a European understanding of beauty. In order to overcome domination of one culture over others, it is argued that people located in one culture should not see the people located in other cultures from their own self-understanding, but rather the other people should be seen from the perspective of *their* self-understanding.

Consumerism

The current phase of globalization and technological revolution has been bringing local culture under the domination of the market, resulting in the shrinking of autonomous spaces. In this process, cultures are getting commodified. The ultimate outcome of this is the arranging of different cultures in a hierarchal order, and the values associated with each culture automatically getting hierarchized. The individual is embedded in the culture and society in which they are born, as a result of which the individual identifies themselves with their own culture. Hence, cultural communities are of overriding importance for their individual members, as they provide them with cognitive and evaluative resources. Once a lower value is placed on one particular culture, the people who identify themselves with that culture by default

---

BOX 6.3: Security Versus Individual Privacy

Digital globalization has opened up a new kind of security vulnerability after land, sea, air and space. There has been a deliberate attempt on the part of some states to steal some strategic information locked in the computer files of other governments and private agencies through spying and malware attacks. Cyberespionage has become an intelligence tactic to collect strategic and critical information through infecting networks of high-value establishments. The US and South Korean computer networks were besieged for a day by cyberattacks from North Korea in 2009. Similarly, the nuclear facilities of Iran were attacked by a computer worm called Stuxnet, utilizing software provided by a German firm. Chinese officials have hacked the Google search engine and violated the privacy of Gmail.

The US is the sponsoring country of several modern Internet-based technologies and various software applications such as Google, Amazon, Facebook and Netflix. Hence, the US dominance over Internet governance through the Internet Corporation for Assigned Names and Numbers (ICANN) has left countries in the Global South concerned. Even the International Telecommunication Union (ITU) has found itself sidelined in the new international communication framework promoted by industrialized countries through the ICANN and the WTO (Sidhu 2017, 64–67). Edward Snowden's leak in 2013 has exposed the massive American cyber surveillance of European and Asian countries, including India. These digitally disguised techniques are threatening not only the countries' security but also violating the right to individual privacy. In addition to this, many countries are resorting to mass surveillance capabilities in response to increasing malware attacks and potential terrorist attacks (Sidhu 2017, 64–67).

Individual privacy has been further endangered as there emerged a huge market for buying and selling personal data collected by data brokers (Maus 2015). These private entities, unlike security agencies, are least accountable to laws and monitoring authorities. They obtain data from various sources, including financial transactions, online activities and government records, and sell to any party, criminal or otherwise, for an agreed amount. This selling and reselling of data continues, depending upon the suitability of the data buyer. The issue of privacy and personal liberty free from state interventions is important for an individual to act as an agency and a reflexive being. The individual needs to be given the choice and autonomy to choose their life's end. This takes us to the idea of the formation of identity, meaning and values in certain cultural settings.

become inferior. The placing of a value on any culture is wrong, since each culture is conceived to have intrinsic value, which is distinct from all others. In contemporary globalization, however, such an act has become a necessity of the time, since almost everything has become sellable in the market.

Beyond Liberal Multiculturalism: Negotiating Cultural Diversity

Globalization, accompanied by the IT revolution, has facilitated massive flows of goods and services, cutting across the territorial boundaries of nation states since the last two decades. This phenomenon has also increased the movement of people from one country to another country and one continent to another continent. Such movement of people has been promoting cultural conflicts, because this phenomenon has been leading to the intermixing of cultures. The massive migration of people from one country to another country has created problem of cultural rights, and there has resurfaced a demand for reframing the language of the claims of various groups and communities. These communities include indigenous people, religious and linguistic minority groups, immigrants, and so on. After settling in developed countries, the people of the Global South are demanding minority rights to protect their culture. For example, Sikhs have demanded the right of wearing a turban and Muslim women have sought the right to wear a scarf. There is a proliferation of such demands but the cultural or community right is taken as a conditional right. The widespread demand for cultural rights shows, however, that human consciousness of cultural differences has increased.

Multiculturalism has emerged as an institutional response while mediating the claims of different communities in these contexts. The multicultural path means making an institutional arrangement, with supportive and protective public policies to facilitate the coexistence of people from different cultural traditions with different moral values. The multiculturalism school has a galaxy of scholars such as Will Kymlicka, Bhikhu Parekh, Avishai Margalit, Micheal Walzar and Gurpreet Mahajan. These scholars are 'religiously divided' over the issue of whether rights should be the priority or goods should be given priority. Those who argue that individual rights should be given priority believe that the people would choose the culture which would be beneficial for them, and in this way, the culture would survive. The people who argue that the goods should be given priority advocate that the individual should be given an exit option.

Will Kymlicka argues that some minorities, such as the French-speaking Quebecois in Canada and African Americans in the US, face a disadvantage with respect to cultural membership (Kymlicka 1995, cited in Heywood 2015, 321). On issues that matter to them, minorities are likely to be outvoted and outmanoeuvred, and therefore some cultures should be protected through special legal or constitutional measures, above and beyond the common rights of citizenship. In other words, if minority cultures are vulnerable and are weak in relation to majority ones, they should be protected through a system of group-differentiated rights.

In the liberal multiculturalism perspective, cultural diversity is endorsed only when it is constructed within a framework of toleration and personal autonomy. Pluralism provides a much stronger foundation for the politics of cultural difference. Isaiah Berlin holds that people are bound to disagree about the ultimate ends of life, as it is not possible to demonstrate the superiority of one moral system over another (Berlin 1969, cited in Heywood 2015, 326). When there is a clash of world view and value system, a particular world view—such as Western liberal beliefs such as support for personal freedom, toleration and democracy—has greater moral authority than illiberal or non-Western beliefs and value system. However, he believes that only within a society that respects individual liberty can the value of pluralism thrive; but fails to demonstrate how liberal and illiberal cultural beliefs can coexist harmoniously within the same society (Heywood 2015, 326–327). Many scholars agree that pluralism implies a post-liberal stance in which liberal values and regimes are no longer seen to enjoy a monopoly on legitimacy (Heywood 2015, 326–327).

Critics see multiculturalism as a divisive ideology as every culture group becomes increasingly inward-looking and concerned to protect their 'own' tradition and cultural purity. Sen (2006, cited in Heywood 2015, 332–333) finds a problem with the underlying assumption of multiculturalism that human identities are formed by membership of a single social group. Such an understanding, in his view, leads to not only the 'miniaturization' of humanity but also makes violence more likely as people identify only with their own culture group and fail to honour the rights and integrity of people from other culture groups. Multiculturalism thus breeds a kind of ghettoization that diminishes cross-cultural understanding.

In the name of preserving their distinct culture and way of life, some cultural communities tend to continue with those social and cultural practices which might be at odds with individual rights and dignity. Women were barred from the public sphere and expected to follow a certain dress code after the fundamentalist revolution in Iran, as this is what Islamic culture suggests. Similarly, many cultural communities deny inheritance of property to women and practise forced marriages. Neera Chandhoke (2002), however, argues that the right to have a cultural community exists as a precondition for individual rights. Only when a flourishing culture exists can an individual exercise his/her rights. Therefore, the individual can question those practices which are against individual dignity. The rights of a community cannot be substitute for individual right as they are the preconditions for individual rights (Chandhoke 2002, 232).

Retreat of Globalization

Ethnocultural Nationalism: Resurgence

The combination of contextual factors such as refugee and migrant crises, anxieties associated with terrorism and persistent inequality stemming out of neo-liberalism has led to a resurgence of ethnonationalist right-wing parties across Europe. Ethnonationalism envisages a nation that excludes various ethnic, religious and racial groups and is about a shared ancestry, religion, common language, and so on. These parties, across a wide policy spectrum from populist and nationalist to far-right neo-fascist, have not only made significant electoral gains but are also controlling the government in many countries. Groups such as the Freedom Party (Austria), National Front (France), Party for Freedom (Netherlands) and the UK Independence Party (UKIP) are calling for their once-open countries to close up and turn inward. The increasing economic inequality and perceived loss of status for the native white population vis-à-vis immigrants on account of free-market globalization and increasing terrorist threats seem to have fuelled some kind of uncertainty that has been harnessed by ethnonationalist political parties. After the triumphs of Donald Trump with the 'America first' rhetoric in the last US presidential election (2016), Brexit's anti-immigration stance and the closing of the borders have resonated in mainstream policy debates. The resurgence of nationalism across Europe has become so powerful that parties from the political mainstream have been forced to retreat from their core principles of tolerance, openness and diversity. In France, some municipalities have banned Muslim women from fully covering themselves with so-called burkinis while swimming. Similarly, the Danish parliament approved a controversial 'jewelry law' that allows government to confiscate valuables from arriving asylum seekers to help finance their accommodation (Aisch, Pearce and Rousseau 2017).

But this shift from outward-looking multiculturalism to inward and ethnocultural nationalism is interpreted as the emergence of the essentialist meaning of culture, where culture is seen as having a fixed and static meaning with some intrinsic value. Seeing culture from this perspective requires looking at culture as autonomous, pure and having intrinsic value. Here, the intermixing of people is seen as an attempt at polluting of culture. The right-wing groups are opposing the migration of people because of this reason.

BOX 6.4: Ethnic Cleansing

Ethnic cleansing refers to the forcible expulsion of an ethnic or culture group or groups in the cause of racial purity or homogeneity involving genocidal violence. From the 1990s onwards, the rise of ethnocultural nationalism has led to a series of civil wars and ethnic cleansing, often in the name of a nationalism that aims for cultural homogeneity. The civil wars in Yugoslavia (1991–1995) witnessed the worst forms of ethnic cleansing and mass massacre wherein Bosnian Muslims were slaughtered by the Serb military. Similarly, genocidal bloodshed broke out in Rwanda when militant Hutus killed approximately one million Tutsi and moderate Hutus.

Though the forces of ethnonationalism have resurrected in Europe and elsewhere, the idea of cosmopolitanism has also gained respectability in academic discourse. As an idea, cosmopolitanism entails that the world constitutes a single moral community and that people have obligations (potentially) towards all other people in the world, regardless of differences of culture and nationality. Individuals everywhere would come to see themselves as global citizens united by a common interest in addressing ecological, social, economic and other challenges that are global in nature.

Concluding Observations

Culture as a system of meanings and values defines the identity of individuals. With the phenomenal advancements in transport, information technologies and mass-mediated instant cultural images, scripts and sensations (through audio–video bites), imagination about the self, one's identity and the surrounding world have undergone profound transformations. There has emerged a contestation on to what extent a particular culture is able to maintain its distinctiveness in the face of the US-sponsored consumer culture. It is argued that Western countries, after losing direct political and military control of Global South, have penetrated these societies through a Western value systems rooted in consumerism, individualism and materialism. Multinational Corporation (MNC) interests are being served through the promotion of a Western liberal value system in the guise of modernity. The contestation is seen to be moving towards violent confrontation if culture is conceptualized as a static entity in terms of having fixed attributes (material, linguistic and territorial). Many scholars, however, are converging on the position that culture is a dynamic process and that universal culture is increasingly being creolized and indigenized in a particular location by a particular group. This interplay of global and local, called glocalization or hybridization, is invariably seen in many Western and non-Western societies, depending upon degree of adaptation, interpretation, translation and mutation on the part of the receiving culture. Millions of software applications (apps), notwithstanding the digital divide, now contain matters which are labelled as 'traditional', such as religious text, hymns, folk tales, and so on. While technology is creating opportunities for cultural mixing, political power in major Western countries—including the US—is swinging towards those groups who believe in cultural homogeneities and in ethnocultural nationalism than cosmopolitan multiculturalism.

Summary

- Globalization is a multidimensional process wherein social, economic, cultural and political dimensions are interlinked with a complex set of processes. It has been pushed by a transnational external force and hence produces a similar force.
- Culture is defined either as an essence or a process. The former school conceives of it as a singular, transcendent, unified idea containing certain essential features, soul and attributes. The latter group conceives of it as an ever-flowing current of ideas shaped by an ongoing process of fission and fusion.
- Technology has acted as the main driving force behind the fission and fusion of cultures since ancient periods. But the demands of the time have led to the technological innovations.
- The problems of contemporary globalization seem to have acted as a stimulating factor in the information and technology revolution of the 1980s.
- The information and technology revolution has impacted science and technology, governance, trade and commerce, and more.
- Because of the IT revolution, culture has got reconfigured. The reconfiguration can be understood by studying processes of homogenization, clashes of civilizations, hybridization, domination, and consumerism.
- Certain recent events show that there are tendencies of de-globalization. These tendencies are because of the re-arrival of culture in the form of fundamentalism.

Suggested Questions

1. What do you understand by 'culture'? Critically evaluate whether culture is a static phenomenon or a fluid phenomenon.
2. What is hybridization of culture? How is it different from homogenization?
3. Explain the role of the Internet in the transformation of Indian culture in recent decades.
4. Do you think the technological revolution is promoting ethnocentrism? Substantiate your answer with proper examples.
5. How does commodification of culture pose a threat to the survival of the culture?

References

Ahmad, Aijaz. 2004. *On Communalism and Globalization: Offensives of the Far Right*. New Delhi: Three Essays Collective.

Aisch. Gregor, Adam Pearce and Bryant Rousseau. 2017. 'How Far Is Europe Swinging to the Right?' *The New York Times*, 22 May 2016, updated 23 October 2017. Accessed 23 April 2018. https://www.nytimes.com/interactive/2016/05/22/world/europe/europe-right-wing-austria-hungary.html.

Anderson, Benedict. 2006. *Imagined Community: Reflections on the Origin and Spread of Nationalism*. London, Verso.

Appadurai, Arjun. 2000. 'Disjuncture and Difference in the Global Cultural Economy'. In *The Globalization Reader*, edited by Frank J. Lechner and John Boli, 320–330. New York, NY: Blackwell Publisher.

Barber, Benjamin R. 2000. 'Jihad vs, McWorld'. In *The Globalization Reader*, edited by Frank J. Lechner and John Boli, 21–26. New York, NY: Blackwell Publisher.

Chandhoke, Neera. 2002. 'Individual and Group Rights: A View from India'. In *India's Living Constitution: Ideas, Practices, Controversies*, edited by Zoya Hasan, E. Sridharan and R. Sudarshan., 207–235. New Delhi: Permanent Black.

Ferguson, Yale H., and Richard W. Mansbach, eds. 2012. *Globalization: The Return of Borders to a Borderless World?* London and New York, NY: Routledge.

Giddens, Anthony. 1998. *The Third Way: The Renewal of Social Democracy*. London: Polity Press.

Heywood, Andrew. 2015. *Political Ideologies: An Introduction*. New Delhi: Palgrave Macmillan.

Hooper, Paul. 2007. Understanding Cultural Globalization. Cambridge, UK: Polity Press.

Isar, Yudhishthir Raj. 2012. 'Global Culture'. In *International Relations: Perspectives for the Global South*, edited by Bhupinder S. Chimni and Siddharth Mallavarpu, 286–297. New Delhi: Pearson.

Lechner, Frank J., and John Boli. 2005. *World Culture: Origin and Consequences*. Oxford, UK: Blackwell Publishing.

MacRae, Michael. 2013. 'Top 5 Medical Technology Innovations'. Accessed 23 April 2018. https://www.asme.org/engineering-topics/articles/bioengineering/top-5-medical-technology-innovations.

Maus, Gregory. 2015. 'How Corporate Data Broker Sell Your Life and You Should Be Concerned'. Accessed 7 December 2017. www.stack.com.

Pieterse, Jan Nederveen. 2015. *Globalization and Culture: Global Mélange*. London: Rowman & Littlefield.

Sandel, Michael J. 1982. *Liberalism and the Limits of Justice*. New York, NY: Cambridge University Press.

Sen, Amartya. 2006. *Identity and Violence: The Illusion of Destiny*. New York: W. W. Norton & Company.

Sidhu, Balraj K. 2017. 'Governing the Internet: Need for Effective Cybersecurity Policy, Law, and Institutional Frameworks'. *Economic and Political Weekly* 52 (48). Accessed 23 April 2018. http://www.epw.in/journal/2017/48/perspectives/governing-internet.html.

Tharoor, Shashi. 2016. *An Era of Darkness*. New Delhi: Alpeh Book Company.

Further Reading

Held, David, and Anthony McGrew. 2000. *The Global Transformations Reader*. London: Polity Press.

Hopper, Paul. 2007. *Understanding Cultural Globalization*. UK: Polity Press.

Huntington, Samuel P. 2000. 'The Clash of Civilizations?'. In *The Globalization Reader*, edited by Frank J. Lechner and John Boli, 27–33. New York, NY: Blackwell Publisher.

Mansbach, Richard W., and Kirsten L. Taylor. 2012. *Introduction to Global Politics*. London and New York: Routledge.

Panikkar, K. N. 1995. 'Culture and Globalisation: A Non-Issue at World Summit on Social Development'. *Economic and Political Weekly* 30 (7/8): 374–375.

Pieterse, Jan Nederveen. 2004. *Globalization or Empire?* London: Routledge.

CHAPTER

Global Resistance: Global Social Movements and NGOs

Kamal Kumar and Bhavna Sharma

LEARNING OBJECTIVES

- To analyse the conceptual parameters of social movements
- To understand the concept of global social movements and their basic characteristics
- To assess how global social movements have resisted globalization
- To explain what non-governmental organizations (NGOs) are and their historical evolution
- To understand how NGOs have emerged as global actors
- To examine the role of NGOs in developing countries

The onset of globalization has been responsible for shaking the traditional stability of nation states and initiating a process of integration of countries. The phenomenon, which primarily started off as an economic drive, has significantly affected all the domains of individual existence, and has created an all-encompassing 'single' global village. The point of concern is that although externally globalization imparts a sense of linking nation states, but individual states have their own internal structures and ways of functioning, which need to be properly conditioned in order to accommodate globalization. Integration of economic sectors demands a single coherent body which has rules and regulations which are to be followed globally and to which the specific state institutions also pay allegiance. This has given rise to the concept of 'global governance', which encourages the governments in different countries to cooperate with each other in forming a unified body through which social, economic and political initiatives can be undertaken to solve different contemporary global issues and problems.

Globalization has led to the irrelevance of external sovereignty; rather, the issues which were once confined within legitimate boundaries have gained global attention and have become matters of universal concern. In addition to the social, economic and political issues which had already existed prior to globalization, lately numerous other issues have emerged. Some of the contemporary issues which have gained international attention are: the issue of migration and refugee politics, the ever-multiplying population and the resource crunch especially in the under-developing and developing countries, climate change causing by global warming and, along with these, humanitarian concerns such as the issue of violation of human rights in specific countries, which demands international efforts in order for people to escape an imprisoned existence and freedom to lead a decent human life, to fight child labour and restore the childhood of millions of children across the globe and to fight poverty and deadly diseases which need immediate attention. All these and many more issues have now crossed their local boundaries or the places where they had their origins, and are seeking out help from all countries. No one can deny the role of national governments as far as devising policies and getting the required institutional apparatus for dealing with some of the salient issues is concerned, but one can also not deny the role of non-state international actors such as global social movements, global civil-society pressure groups and non-governmental organizations (NGOs) in furthering some specific causes. These non-state actors act as counter-hegemonic forces by possessing resistance to the dominant global power structure and neo-liberal economic model.

This present chapter intends to discuss the implications of global social movements and non-governmental organizations on global politics and also analyses the resistance offered by them to globalization. The chapter begins with a brief overview of the conceptual parameters of social movements. This is followed by a discussion on global social movements and their common characteristics. The next section throws light on the resistance posed by the global social movements to globalization and its dominant neo-liberal economic world order. The chapter then discusses what NGOs are and their historical evolution. It also analyses the role of NGOs in different realms and countries, especially in the developing countries. Finally, the chapter addresses the question of accountability in the context of NGOs. However, before doing so, it is important to understand the basic concept of social movements.

Conceptual Parameters of Social Movements

Scholars found the initial theoretical formulation of the concept of social movements in the writings of Karl Marx. Simin Fadaee noted that 'the most dominant analysis of the social movements… was related to the class struggle and Marxist analysis of the labor movement' (Fadaee 2012, 14). Ghanshyam Shah, like Fadaee, also accepted the Marxist understanding of the class conflict to define the idea of social movements. He pointed out that initially the term had been used to signify those movements which were concerned with the emancipation of the exploited classes and the creation of a new social structure by changing the value system as well as institutions and the property relationship (Shah 2011, 24). For Marx, the antagonistic interests between the propertied and labour classes were inherent in a class-based society. Economic relations in a class-based society were the principal source of class conflict and 'this conflict was the basis for the emergence of social movements. As industrialist society developed, this conflict grew … the impetus for development of social movements in this period was class consciousness' (Fadaee 2012, 14). The exploited and working classes subsequently resisted and launched a collective action against the dominance of the propertied class and the exploited capitalist system. But it is important to note that Marx had never used the concept of the social movement in his works to define the struggle of the working class; rather, he suggested the concept of 'revolution' to describe the latter. The term 'social movement' therefore first gained acceptance amidst the social upheaval in Europe in the early nineteenth century.

Lorenz von Stein is one of the scholars who first defined this concept in a detail. In his *The History of the Social Movement in France, 1789–1850* (1850), Stein defined social movement as 'a series of endeavors to create a new society. Moreover [he conceived] the structure of society as fundamentally determining the political change' (cited in Wilkinson 1971, 20). In that sense, social movements for him ultimately intended to transform the political structure. Stein, like Marx, believed that material self-interest, such as to control the means of production, individuals and classes could create the condition for social change. In other words, he believed that social movements were a product of the prevailing antagonistic interests in society. Werner Sombart (1896) likewise conceived of social movements as 'the conception of all the attempts at emancipation on the part of the proletariat' (cited in Wilkinson 1971, 21). Hence, Stein's pioneering conceptualization of social movements remained influential throughout the nineteenth century.

Another significant attempt to define the concept of social movements was made by the sociologist Rudolf Heberle. He was one of the first scholars to develop a systematic understanding of the concept in his book *Social Movement: An Introduction to Political Sociology* (Heberle 1951). He regarded social movements as 'a special kind of social groups of a particular structure. Although containing among their members certain groups that are formally organized, the movements as such are not organized groups' (Wilkinson 1971, 22). While agreeing with Stein that social movements aimed to bring about fundamental changes in the fields of labour and property relations, Heberle did not confine the scope of social movements merely to the struggles of the working class in industrial societies. He thus had a wider connotation of the concept of social movements that included the movements of peasants and fascists (Ibid.).

As part of conceptualizing social movements, scholars have also sought to focus on the elements through which these could be organized effectively. Neil Smelser was the first to highlight the determinants of collective behaviors, including social movements, in his renowned book *Theory of Collective Behavior* (1962). While citing Smelser, M. S. A. Rao noted:

> Smelser treats structural strain [like defeat in war or economic depression] as the underlying factor leading to collective behavior. Structural strain occurs at different levels of norms, values, mobilization and situational facilities. While strain provides the structural conditions, the crystallizations of a generated belief marks the attempt of persons under strain to assess their situation and… to creating or assembling a generalized belief. Both strain and generalized belief require precipitating factors to trigger off a [social] movement. (Rao 1979, 5)

Thus, Smelser analysed the determinants from the structural framework. For him, the particular conditions and determinants were a prerequisite to collective actions, including social movements. Therefore, a social movement is a kind of collective behavior and action. Collective behaviors signify a situation wherein individuals act together and collectively organize the action. In general, social movements can thus be defined as the collective and direct non-institutional actions of a group of people to bring about change within social and political structures.

But after the 1970s, a number of collective protests and demonstrations took place throughout the Western world and a novel phase of *'new social movements'* (NSMs)—which was later known as 'transnational social movements' or *'global social movements'* (GSMs)—evolved to theorize these emerging, diverse facets of collective action. Amita Baviskar noted that the emergence of a spectrum of interconnected and multistranded social movements around the world helped to evolve the concept of NSMs

(Baviskar 2010, 382–383). In contrast, Steven M. Buechler pointed out that this approach primarily emerged as a response to the failures of traditional Marxism, which was focusing only on class-based collective actions, rather than underlining the importance of other collective actions (Buechler 1995, 441–442). Furthermore NSMs, unlike the old movements, are global in their nature and membership base, as they attract support from all over the world to consolidate a shared agenda and a common struggle. Hence, these movements were called 'new' at the time in order to distinguish them from the 'old', class-based labour movements, which had dominated the mobilization of collective action in Western Europe up to the 1960s. In that sense, the scope of social movements has been expanded with the passage of time to address emerging social concerns.

Jürgen Habermas (1981) and Alain Touraine (1985) used the framework of a post-industrial society to explain the emergence of new social movements. While outlining the conception of Habermas and Touraine, Baviskar (2010, 383) correctly highlighted:

> The 'new social movements' demonstrated that class had become redundant as an organizing form of social identity and action. New social movements were the product of a post-industrial social formation where the welfare state had made classic forms of exploitation and deprivation obsolete, but where modern society created new forms of alienation. These [new social] movements reflected and responded to this discontent.

In other words, the class factor was no longer the only effective parameter for organizing people under the welfare state and, on the other hand, there was a wide range of new issues and novel forms of exploitation under the new kind of post-industrial social structure.[1]

New social movements are thus heterogeneous in nature, addressing the widespread issues of human life and gaining support from the different sections of society and the world. These new social movements include civil rights movements, feminist movements, student movements, peace movements for nuclear disarmament, peasant movements, anti-corruption movements, environmental movements, and so on.[2] Rather than explaining the diverse nature of new social movements per se, what is important from the standpoint of the present study is to analyse the concept of global social movements—which will be discussed in next section of this chapter.

Understanding Global Social Movements (GSMs)

Since the early 1990s, the unrestricted movement of capital—primarily facilitated by the process of globalization and neo-liberal principles—on a global scale has intensified the contestation and resistance against globalization and its actors. Globalization has ushered in a new era of opportunities, innovations, intercommunications and development, but at the same time has drastically intensified inequalities, miseries and conflicts between and within countries (Milani and Laniado 2007). Growing economic and

---

[1] Touraine terms post-industrial society as a 'programmed society' with the 'growing capacity of social actors to construct both a system of knowledge and the technical tools that allow them to intervene in their own functioning… and makes possible the increasing self-production of society, which becomes the defining hallmark of postindustrial or programmed society' (Buechler 1995, 444). Apart from the working class, several other social classes are also capable of transforming their ways of life and society by organizing social movements in the programmed society.

[2] For a detailed analysis on the distinctiveness of the new social movements and their relation to environmental movements, see Sutton (2000, 19–26) and Baviskar (2010, 381–383).

social disparities have 'provided the grounds for citizens and civil society groups of diverse origins to express their resentment and advance claims' by organizing GSMs (Ghimire 2005, 1). In other words, the contradictions and complexities of globalization have forced the non-state actors (particularly those operating at the global level), including NGOs and social movements, to shift their focus from local or national issues to the emerging global issues, such as environmental problems, economic exploitation of poor nations, migration, gender inequality and labour rights. Global issues require global actions or responses, as they do not only shape the international political agendas, but also impact national realities. For example; in the context of the environment, 'the destruction of forest cover in Brazil affects the global climate ... emissions (of ozone-depleting chemical substances) from many countries thin out the earth's ozone layer, while chemical waste discharged from one country's shore washes up on another' (Cohen and Rai 2000, 8–9). In that sense, social movements have acquired a 'global' character to address the emerging global issues and problems resulting from the uneven and exploitative globalized world order.

GSMs refer to those collective actions that bring people together from around the world to advance their shared agendas and consolidate their efforts (Wapner 2002). However, much scholarly work has not been done on systematically defining the concept of GSMs. In a pioneering anthology on the latter, Jackie Smith et al. (1997, 59–60; cited in Cohen and Rai 2000, 8) state:

> Social movements may be said to be transnational when they involve conscious efforts to build transnational cooperation around shared goals that include social change. Through regular communication, organizations and activists are able to share technical and strategic information, coordinate parallel activities, or even to mount truly transnational collective action. Like national social movements transnational once incorporate a range of political actors including individuals, church group professional associations and other social groups. Movements are distinguished by the actors and resources they mobilize and in the extent to which they communicate, consult, coordinate and cooperate in the international arena.

Hence, GSMs refer to those social movements that have a worldwide social base, shared agendas and common goals to be achieved (Table 7.1).

GSMs use different global platforms (such as international summits, workshops and conferences) to promote their agenda, ideas and action plans. Particularly in recent years, regional and multinational gatherings of the World Social Forum (WSF) have been used not just to decide an action plan to address various global issues, but also to popularize campaigns (Ghimire 2005, 2–3). They breed 'new ideas; they advocate, protest, and mobilize public support; they do legal, scientific, technical, and policy analysis; they provide services; they shape, implement, monitor, and enforce national and international commitments; and they change institutions and norms' (Bennett 2012, 800). Furthermore, GSMs primarily demand decentralization of power, democratization of international institutions and more inclusive

TABLE 7.1   Periodization of Social Movements

Period	Forms of Movements
Nineteenth century to the 1970s	Old social movements
1970s to 1990s	New social movements
1990s onwards	Global social movements

decision-making at the global level. Today, issues such as peace and human rights, children's rights, development, trade, gender, environment and disarmament are amongst the dominant issues around which the contemporary GSMs remain concentrated (see Figure 7.1).

Common Characteristics

This section sketches out the significant characteristics which are broadly considered to be common across all GSMs (Figure 7.2). However, it is important to keep in mind though that the GSMs are not homogeneous in nature, as they vary in terms of their popularity, objectives, central areas of action and mandates, among others. Yet, they retain similarities, sharing a number of commonalities ranging from origins, social bases, orientations, organizational structures and action strategies.

The following are the key common characteristics pertaining to GSMs:

Value-orientated

The most noticeable characteristic of GSMs is that they are primarily value-orientated collective actions. They place principles such as social justice and equality at the centre of international negotiations,

FIGURE 7.1 Principal Campaign Themes of Global Social Movements

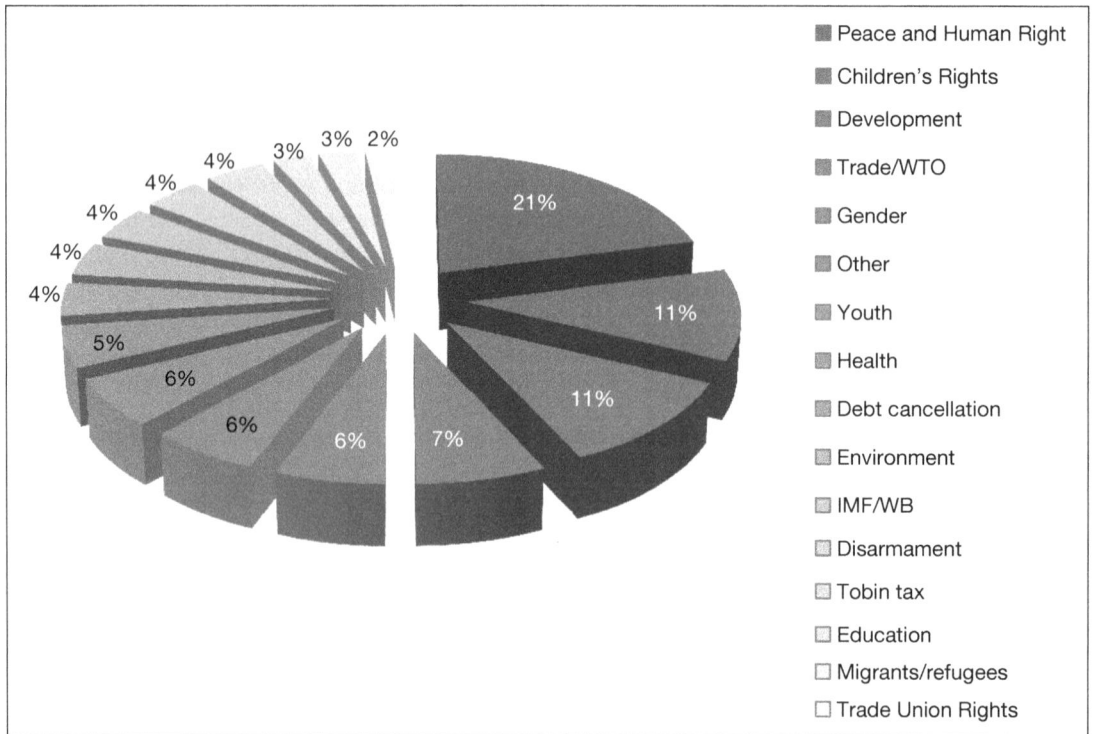

Source: Data adapted from Ghimire (2005, 5).

FIGURE 7.2 Characteristics of Global Social Movements

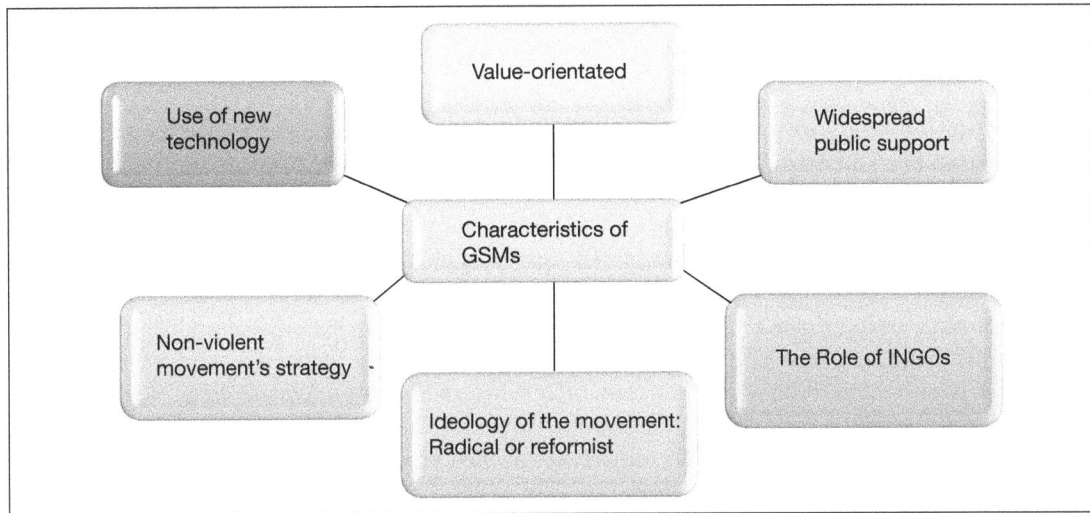

agreements and discourse. In that sense, GSMs are aimed at bringing about a change in the norms, values, objectives and ideologies of the prevailing global governance system and world economic structure (Ghimire 2005, 9). Especially, such movements adopt an ethical position to alter the dominant and unequal economic and global power structure, thereby aiming to work with the prevailing system to reform it.

Widespread Public Support

Given their multiple coalitions and network base, GSMs mobilize people on a large scale for their different activities and programmes. However, they lack a concrete membership base and centralized organizational body; but still their activities or campaigns attract extensive support from the general public. GSMs create alliances and coalitions with different local, national and international groups to garner public support (Ibid.). In other words, the old social movements were limited in their popularity and orientation, while the GSMs enjoy widespread public support along with a global orientation and network. At the same time, GSMs provide a common platform to the middle class, young and educated people and newly marginalized groups to unite themselves and produce a collective identity and action concerned with the new sites of conflict interwoven with globalization.

Role of International Non-governmental Organizations (INGOs)

INGOs (in coalition with local NGOs) provide strength to GSMs in terms of funding, networking, advocacy, documentation and publicity, among others. This enables the movements to establish a wideranging participatory base so that they can effectively exert pressure on the local and national governments and on the actors of global governance to evolve a democratic and inclusive decision-making structure that takes into account the concerns and interests of all nations, especially those that are marginalized and poor. In this sense, INGOs have opened up a new avenue of participation for poor nations (and their citizens) to raise their voices against the exploitations and destruction caused by globalization. INGOs have significantly shaped the various activities and strategic programmes of several GSMs since the 1990s.

Ideology of the Movement: Radical or Reformist

An appropriate ideology is essential not only for GSMs but for all kinds of movements, since it provides a specific direction to the movement, and creates a connecting link among diverse people participating in that movement. The existing literature on GSMs classifies the ideologies of the movements broadly into two categories, namely, antiglobalization (radical) and alter-globalization (reformist). The former discards reformism and resists all forms of globalization, while the latter seeks to change the way things are done in the existing globalized economic, social and political systems by decentralizing global governance, democratizing international institutions and policymaking structures, and prioritizing the interests of poor nations. Both ideologies, thus, offer different kinds of understandings of GSMs, which in turn shapes the method and direction of the movements. While both share the common purpose of reconfiguring the globalized world order, differences in their approaches may be traced to the different ideological principles of Marxism and liberalism.

Non-violent Movement's Strategy

There are primarily two strategies, namely violent or non-violent, that are deployed by the different social movements to achieve their objectives. GSMs largely use peaceful and non-violent means 'as a strategic tool in their fight against a usually more powerful foe' (Doyle 2005, 17). Such non-violent methods include demonstrations, hunger strikes, non-cooperation, and so on. Hence, GSMs primarily intend to resist the dominant world economic order (based on neo-liberal norms) by resorting to non-violent strategy.

Use of New Technology

GSMs extensively rely on the new technologies (especially social media channels such as Facebook, YouTube and WhatsApp) to 'influence both the media and general public. This has helped the movements avoid official censorship or other forms of control before they are able to reach the target audience' (Ghimire 2005, 9–10). However, it does not necessarily imply that they do not use traditional forms of communication, such as demonstrations, public protests, meetings and lobbying, to mobilize the people as well as pressurize the governments to take favourable action.

Global Social Movements and Resisting Globalization

The post-globalized economic and political structure has produced a new category of social movements to mobilize people against the new practices of exploitation and subjugation, thereby leading to a consolidation of GSMs. In recent years, GSMs—also popularized as 'alter-globalization' campaigns in the contemporary literature—have succeeded in bringing people of distinctive national identities and cultural backgrounds together in a common cause of resisting globalization practices and the globalized world order. Alter-globalization is generally referred to as a 'large spectrum of global social movements that presents themselves as supporting new forms of globalisation, urging the values of democracy, justice, environmental protection and human rights to be put ahead of purely economic concerns' (Harvey, Horne and Safai 2011, 383). This campaign against neo-liberal policies and globalization gained prominence with the formation of the WSF in Porto Alegre in 2001. Since then, most of the GSMs have been conceptualized within the broader concept of alter-globalization.

Alter-globalists (who are the proponents of alter-globalization) criticize the functioning and working style of dominant global institutions such as the United Nations (UN), International Monetary Fund (IMF), World Bank, World Trade Organization (WTO), the Group of Eight industrialized countries (G-8), and the European Union (EU) as well as the various regional agreements such as the North American Free Trade Agreement (NAFTA). This is especially because these institutions appear to promote the interests of industrial or capitalist nations at the cost of developing or poor countries. The alter-globalists also demand that multinational organizations such as the UN and the IMF should be democratized and the interests of the poor nations are to be prioritized, as they need it the most. This is probably why the GSMs declare '[themselves] to be "alter" (or alternative) rather than "anti" globalization as such' (Ghimire 2005, 3).

BOX 7.1: World Social Forum

The World Social Forum (WSF)—also known as the Porto Alegre Forum—was founded in 2001 by the proponents of global social movements to ensure social and economic justice at the global level. Its charter (adopted on April 2001) defines the WSF as 'an open meeting space for reflective thinking, democratic debate of ideas, formulation of proposals, free exchange of experiences and interlinking for effective action, by groups and movements of civil society that are opposed to neo-liberalism and to domination of the world by capital and any form of imperialism, and are committed to building a planetary society directed towards fruitful relationships among Humankind and between it and the Earth' (WSF 2001). Hence, the WSF in principle is against the neo-liberal norms and economic system.

Initially, the WSF was aimed at denouncing the radical neo-liberal economic model and globalized policies that were leading towards an unequal global structure and economic system. However, the WSF later shifted its focus from simply resisting the existing global structure to ensuring the evolution of a mechanism to empower communities and nations so that they could seek better alternatives. It is widely acknowledged as the largest gathering of people and organizations who meet annually to seek solutions to the problems of our times. Its first meeting was held in 2001 in Porto Alegre, Brazil. Since then, it has met regularly to continue the struggle for global justice.

GSMs or alter-globalization campaigns largely seek fundamental reforms in the structure of global governance and prevailing neo-liberal global economic order. However, differences may exist at the level of their strategies, methods, membership bases and organizational structures. They also intend to curtail the dominant role of transnational corporations (TNCs) and multinational corporations (MNCs) in shaping national politics and, at the same time, to protect the key public sectors such as health, defence and education from privatization. Moreover, GSMs seek to fortify the cooperation between the different governments and non-state actors in order to strengthen the UN system. Hence, they insist on the positive and constructive role of multinational institutions in promoting the interests of marginalized people and poor nations (Harvey, Horne and Safai 2009).

GSMs, in a way, have contributed to a reconfiguration of global power by posing a challenge to dominant power structure and amplifying the voice of the Global South. In particular, they have mobilized those marginalized people and individual groups who have been disempowered by globalization and neo-liberal practices. In others words, GSMs have empowered the people (especially those are located in the Global South) to articulate their interests on different global platforms, thereby dismantling the hegemonic power structure. Furthermore, GSMs act as an intermediate channel between the poor nations and international organizations and stimulate political negotiations amongst them. They have also created a global network of organizations and their widespread reach has allowed them to influence national and international politics. In this way, GSMs have provided a new terrain for political negotiations where the different countries and groups come together and deliberate on many issues to reach a consensus.

In last few years, GSMs such as the global environmental justice movement have not only influenced the political independence of states, but also restructured the functioning of international organizations by compelling them to pay heed to the interests of developing countries and marginalized communities.[3] More specifically, GSMs have presented a normative challenge to the dominant globalized economic structure and the neo-liberal market practices with the globalization debates being situated upon notions of social justice and equality (Cohen and Rai 2000, 7). These non-state actors, therefore, act as counter-hegemonic forces by possessing a resistance to the dominant global power structure. Many critics, on the other hand, question the democratic character of GSMs and also maintain that such movements disrupt global and national political systems. They also highlight the fact that these movements are highly heterogeneous, thereby lacking a strong membership base across the world. However, it does not undermine the significance of GSMs in amplifying the voices of marginalized nations and communities. The next section seeks to define the concept of NGOs, followed by a discussion of their historical evolution.

Non-governmental Organizations (NGOs)

Before defining NGOs, it becomes imperative to understand the meaning of 'voluntary organizations', as NGOs are a part of this category, with a slight difference. The spirit of volunteerism—to further a cause, which could be either a long-term or a short-term one—can encourage individuals to form an organization. It is not driven by any political or formal governmental agenda. NGOs are an extension of voluntary organizations, but have legal sanction—they need to be registered properly under a proper act, and are governed by legal provisions. The spirit of serving society is the driving force behind these bodies, which

---

[3] The global environmental justice movement, one the popular GSMs, indicates that the consequences of environmental degradation are often borne disproportionately by the poor and disadvantage groups. Hence, it recognizes the right to access the 'clean' and 'healthy' environment as a fundamental right of all human beings (Bullard 1993; Paehlke 1995; Benton and Short 1999; Sachs 2002). It has also challenged the global trend of dumping hazardous wastes and toxic chemical (by developed countries) in developing countries.

now have become an integral sector in the public life of many countries. The non-governmental sector seems to exhibit the following characteristics:

Will-based or voluntary: There are no forced members in an NGO, only those individuals who can relate to the cause or genuinely help are recruited and given training regarding the technicalities of the organization. Nor can all the natives of a particular state become automatic members of a particular NGO, as is the case with citizenship, where natives automatically get membership of the state.

Value-driven: They have larger philanthropic goals on their agendas. These organizations are primarily formed to fulfil goals which do not converge with narrow sectarian interests, nor feed petty materialism, selfishness and profit-making goals. Although the financial aspect does form the backbone of any NGO, as without funds they cannot fulfil their policy implementation goal, it is solely driven by constructive and positive motivations.

Focused and directed towards a specific cause: An NGO can be seen as a specialized organization in the sense that it has a well thought-out cause in its charter, and with that as the vantage point, all other actions are planned out and, accordingly, members are absorbed who can relate to the cause and contribute towards it selflessly.

Separated from governmental officials and functions: As the name suggests, these organizations are non-governmental, that is, they are neither created by the government nor are they bound by governmental control. They are independent in their functioning and have their own administrative set-up.

Flexibility in sphere of influence: These organizations can function independently of the government as discussed above, and they can enter into partnerships with the governments of concerned countries as well.

Andrew Heywood (2011, 6) defines an NGO as 'a private, non-commercial group or body which seeks to achieve its ends through non-violent means'. The World Bank defines NGOs as 'private organizations that pursue activities to relieve suffering, promote the interests of the poor, protect the environment, provide basic social services, or undertake community development'. Very early examples of such bodies were the Society for the Abolition of the Slave Trade (formed by William Wilberforce in 1787) and the International Committee of the Red Cross, founded in 1863. The first official recognition of NGOs was by the UN in 1948, when 41 NGOs were granted consultative status following the establishment of the Universal Declaration of Human Rights (indeed, some NGO activists believe that only groups formally acknowledged by the UN should be regarded as 'true' NGOs).

These non-governmental bodies are engaged in mobilizing the masses to further larger goals and organizing them into powerful movements, in providing relief measures to places which have been hit by natural calamities such as earthquakes, floods or famines and in contributing greatly to disaster management operations. The growth of media and technology, or the revolution in information technology, has greatly helped to expand the area of influence of the NGOs and these bodies have acquired a global role in mobilizing GSMs as well. The contribution of these bodies on a global scale is discussed in the subsequent paragraphs (Figure 7.3).

FIGURE 7.3   Roles of NGOs

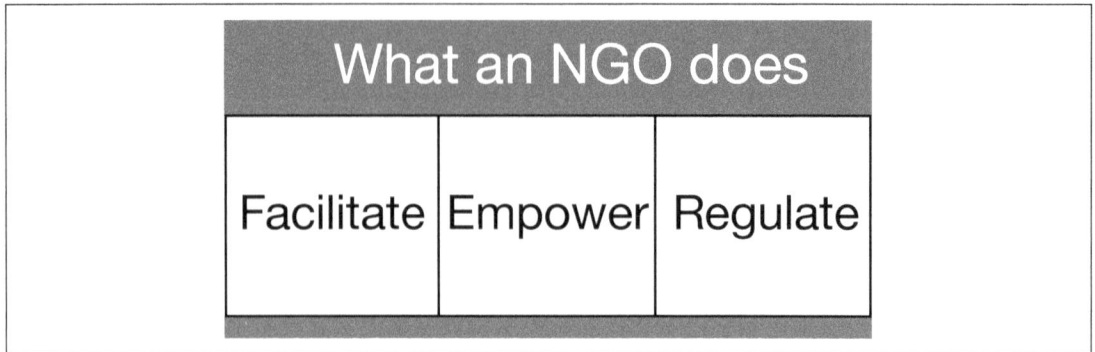

Evolution of NGOs

The evolution of the non-governmental sector did not have a special separate period with clearly ear-marked years; rather, its evolution coincided with the framing of the UN charter in San Francisco in 1945. There was no direct mention of the establishment of NGOs; rather, in an indirect way, there was a clause whereby intergovernmental organizations and those owned privately could establish relations with the economic wing of the UN, that is, the Economic and Social Council (ECOSOC). This provision faced much opposition on the pretext that these organizations could not be given so much importance as any of the UN organs and could not be placed on the same pedestal, post which Article 57 gave the intergovernmental organizations (on the principles of intergovernmental agreement) the name of 'specialized agencies', such as the World Health Organization (WHO). Further on, the term was barely mentioned in Article 71, but was not much elaborated (Willetts 2011, 6–8).

These NGOs are included in what is referred to as 'civil society' (individual initiatives to fulfil their goals, separate from the state). The governments in states are bound to work for the welfare of citizens and are expected to cater to the local and national demands first and foremost, but recent changes in the global scenario have diverted the attention of the national governments to international causes, due to which the citizens are not getting their due. In such scenarios, what has been seen is the strengthening of civil-society culture in various countries. These civil societies provide a sense of importance to the citizens and make them feel that they are capable of influencing the governmental policies. With this, there has been the consequent rise of NGOs, which constitute a part of civil societies. The NGOs have evolved through a lot of changes since the UN gave them a platform. The gradual upsurge in the NGO sector can also be contributed to the fact that since it becomes very difficult for the state to be able to deal with some issues with full devotion, the NGOs in such cases come in as efficient bodies. Their evolution also saw a major change with the onset of globalization and the consequent dawn of the IT revolution, whereby the Internet facilitated the new social media and social media, which gave a major boost to the NGO sector. This enabled the NGOs to have a wider reach and they could spread out globally with ease. All these advancements also led to a certain level of ease as far as the other activities of NGOs were concerned, such as fundraising and recruitment. These bodies are in a continuous state of evolution, as innovation and the changing times require them to customize their mechanisms as per situational demands.

NGOs as Global Actors

The present state system has evolved over a long period of time after the Westphalian system had given us the concept of state sovereignty, and it was integral to every state. Over a period of time, the world has undergone rapid changes, which were a consequence of the two world wars and the resultant setting up of the UN, which laid the foundation for the NGOS of the world. The establishment of these non-governmental bodies has coincided with the rapid globalization which has engulfed the world in its folds. Globalization, as has already been stated, led to a fading of the state boundaries. Inter-state economic transactions and the integration of economies rendered the state institutions powerless, and international bodies with sufficient power have emerged as regulatory bodies. Economy is one of the most significant bases of any organization, without which no other function can be performed; similar is the case with the state, which is supposed to be the guardian of the state's financial set-up, but ironically and apparently, the integration of economies and the neo-liberal policies have taken that power from the state and given it to intergovernmental bodies. The decreasing role of the state has coincided with the emergence of a 'global civil society' (Heywood 2011, 150). These global civil societies are an answer to the uneven developmental agenda set forth by globalization. These civil societies comprise of NGOs working on a global scale to deal with social, economic and political issues on an international level. They have been referred to as 'institutionalized and professionalized insiders' (Heywood 2011, 154). These global NGOs have a well-connected global network, encouraged mainly by advanced communication technologies, and well-established social-media set-ups; along with that, their branches exist all over the world, and have proper administrative set-ups which are run with the help of natives of that particular country who volunteer or are appointed to managerial or administrative posts. They act as international pressure groups and influence governmental policies which have global implications. An example of how NGOs were able to influence an international decision is the Rio Summit of 1992, where they acted as a pressure group and could get the policy moulded so as to make it sensitive to the growing environmental concern of greenhouse emission (Heywood 2011, 154).

Another significant aspect of the NGOs working on a global scale in the wake of globalization can be seen in the area of the international justice administration mechanism. They have collaborated with the International Criminal Court (ICC), which is concerned with cases where international law comes into question and the matter is of global or international concern. The ICC specifically deals with the brutal acts which are committed in the wake of war crimes, genocides, mass exoduses, holocausts, forced migration of people, to name a few, which eventually trigger a series of crimes and atrocities being committed on the victims. The ICC has the right to investigate such crimes and reprimand those who are guilty of such crimes. The court has global reach and to efficiently administer justice, the ICC cannot function independently of external assistance, which is being readily provided by the NGOs, especially those working for the cause of human rights protection in places where they are blindly violated. One of the prominent NGOs which are working in close collaboration with the ICC is Human Rights Watch—they offer proper assistance to bring justice in war-torn and crime-prone places. Human Rights Watch has also collaborated with the local and national justice delivery mechanisms of various countries and they try to provide a protective shield to those who have been victimized so that they suffer no further harm.

An Overview of the Role of NGOs in Different Domains

Environmental Protection

The contribution of NGOs is manifold, although it would become difficult to cover all the areas where they have contributed. One of these is environmental protection and preservation. The environment is something which is integral and indispensable to our existence. It facilitates our ability to live and work properly according to our optimum efficiency, but it is the duty of the inhabitants of the earth that they conserve it properly so that enough is available for successive generations to come. With industrialization and commercialization, our natural biodiversity has been threatened, causing an imbalance in the ecosystem and food-cycle patterns, depletion of water tables, melting of glaciers (causing climate variations and change), depletion of the ozone layer, threat to some species of animals (bringing them into the 'extinct' category), destruction of the natural agricultural practices by excessive genetic modification of crops and increasing pollution, to reiterate a few of the perfect and apparently discouraging examples of what our environment is going through. Although a lot of nations have joined hands to combat these environmental concerns, what has been visible is a series of global initiatives, with UN bodies such as United Nations Environment Programme (UNEP) working in close cooperation with civil-society organizations, to further the cause of environmental conservation and to form an inclusive body whereby this issue can be dealt with. Some of the NGOs working for the cause of environment conservation are Greenpeace, the International Union for Conservation of Nature (IUCN), the World Wildlife Fund (WWF) and the World Nature Organization (WNO) to name a few. They have played a constructive role around the world to protect nature and to change people's approach and values towards the environment.

Gender Issues, with Regard to Women's Empowerment

The other area where the contribution of NGOs can be seen is gender equality and sensitization towards women's rights. The issue of women's rights no longer needs any introduction and the deplorable condition of women due to violent acts such as sex trafficking, human rights violations, honour killings and domestic violence, to name a few, has generated a lot of tension globally and various NGOs such as Oxfam International, the WHO, the Gender and Development Network (GADN), UN Women, White Ribbon Movement, CARE (Cooperative for Assistance and Relief Everywhere) and Promundo are working for the cause of women's empowerment. They intend to bring about change through policy restructuring, volunteering, research, creating self-help groups and introducing microfinancing schemes in developing countries.

Development Initiatives Undertaken by NGO

The issue of development is also at the heart of NGOs' activities, especially with regard to developing and less-developed countries. It is often observed that NGOs play a major role in alleviating the health concerns of individuals in calamity-hit regions and those suffering from poverty, such as with the Organization for Poverty Alleviation and Development (OPAD). NGOs such as Amnesty International and Human Rights Watch have been actively engaged in one of the most discussed and serious issues, that is, the issue of human rights and their violation. They have a global reach, dealing with issues of women's rights, lesbian, gay, bisexual and transgender (LGBT) rights, disability rights, terrorism and the issue of arms, to name a few. They have been involved vigorously in the 'ethnic cleansing' of the Rohingya Muslims at the hands of the Burmese army in 2017, where they were forced to leave and enter Bangladesh to save their lives.

Disease Prevention: Physical and Mental Health

Not only the physical health but also the emotional and mental health of individuals is being taken care of by NGOs such as the World Federation for Mental Health and MindFreedom. Free health check-up camps, blood donation camp, and health awareness camps are set up by the NGOs and several other techniques such as street plays and speeches are used by them in order to make individuals aware about diseases such as cancer, polio, AIDS, hepatitis, vector-borne illnesses, tuberculosis, and so on. Secondly, globally, the NGO sector has become a significant informal means of promoting education—especially, education of the underprivileged, adult education programmes, education for the differently abled and vocational education for the poor to make them self-sufficient are being provided by several NGOs such as Education International and many more. Economic development is the backbone of any country, and the NGOs play a role in this domain as well, with poverty alleviation programmes and employment generation programmes.

Role of NGOs in Developing Countries

Developing countries are always in a state of movement, as they are aspiring towards growth and transition to become developed countries. In these countries, citizens are active on the issue of the state's responsibility towards them and often they become proactive when the state becomes unresponsive to their demands and needs. Of late, these developing countries have seen an upsurge in the NGO sector, where NGOs have quickly acquired the role of pressure groups. It is said that eternal vigilance is the price of liberty, and this has become deeply ingrained in these countries of late and has been accentuated by the growth of media and new social media, where often protests and revolutions can be instigated via social media channels. These non-governmental bodies have become a handy tool for the masses, through which they can articulate their demands and also be sure of their being heard by the concerned agencies.

Furthermore, the NGOs have provided a platform to people (of developing countries) to organize themselves collectively and to raise their voices against the policies and nature of the state causing serious environmental damage. For example, in the context of the Narmada Bachao Andolan, the popular Indian environmental movement, the NGOs working in the Narmada valley had played a crucial role in highlighting the ecological and social problems arising from the Sardar Sarovar project, both through a judicious use of media as well as scientific and social-science investigations. It also mobilized the oustees to defend their livelihoods and the environment. These organizations also broadened and enlarged the scope of the Narmada Bachao Andolan by establishing links with a number of international green environmental groups, such as the Environmental Defense Fund (EDF) and the Environmental Policy Institute, among others.

Another interesting aspect of the role of NGOs in developing countries that has been observed in recent times is the involvement of youth in these organizations. A lot of young students and fresh graduates are being absorbed in these bodies, and impart a dynamic quality in their functioning and often give fresh perspective on old issues of concern; their way of putting a particular plan into action is also different from how formal decisions are traditionally implemented. In a positive sense, these NGOs are also shaping the minds of young individuals so that they can start volunteering for national and social causes from a early stage and eventually become trained leaders who are aware of the nuances of good governance. India, which is a classic example of a country in transition, has a well-developed NGO sector which is working in various areas. Some of the prominent NGOs in India are:

Uday Foundation

This was started by the parents of a boy named Uday, who was born with multiple birth defects, making them realize the need to help those children (and their parents) who are undergoing long medical treatments in hospitals, the expenditure of which leaves the families so crippled financially that it becomes a struggle to fulfil their basic day-to-day needs. This organization particularly targets those children who are in hospitals on account of some prolonged or terminal illness and provides them with food, clothing and other items for their needs. They have joined hands with different schools in the country so as to encourage students to donate clothes and food which could be used for the cause.

HelpAge India

This NGO is taking care of that section which is often overlooked by the state, that is, the senior citizens. Changing social systems and incipient Western values have had a major impact on the care of senior citizens. In traditional Indian societies, they were the most respected and valued in the family set-up, but the increasing demands of Westernization and the urge to match up to Western norms and rituals have led to a practice where adult children are no longer taking care of those who made them what they are and are neglecting their old parents and leaving them in a vulnerable state. This NGO has picked up the cause of the old and helpless and works ceaselessly for their welfare, taking care of age-related issues and health concerns.

CRY

This is an acronym for Child Rights and You. This is one of the most active NGOs working on the cause of child rights. Their intent is to sensitize society towards children, especially underprivileged children, whose childhoods are snatched away from them due to unfavourable circumstances. Instead of having a normal and healthy childhood, with the child getting a proper basic education, their childhood gets abused due to the hardships that they are made to go through at a delicate age. Some of the issues with which CRY deals with are child labour, the rights of girl children, child trafficking, malnutrition and hunger, and poverty, to name a few. It has a well-networked set-up and strong volunteering culture which has made this body one that has both local as well as global reach.

Nanhi kali and Pratham are other NGOs in India which are also working on the same lines. Various aspects of NGOs are showing in Figure 7.4.

Wildlife Trust of India

This organization is dealing with the noble cause of wildlife preservation in India. Increasing industrialization, commercialization, animal skin trade and leather factories have led to numerous atrocities being committed on animals in the name of blind materialism, has led to the animals losing their natural habitats and

FIGURE 7.4 Aspects of NGOs

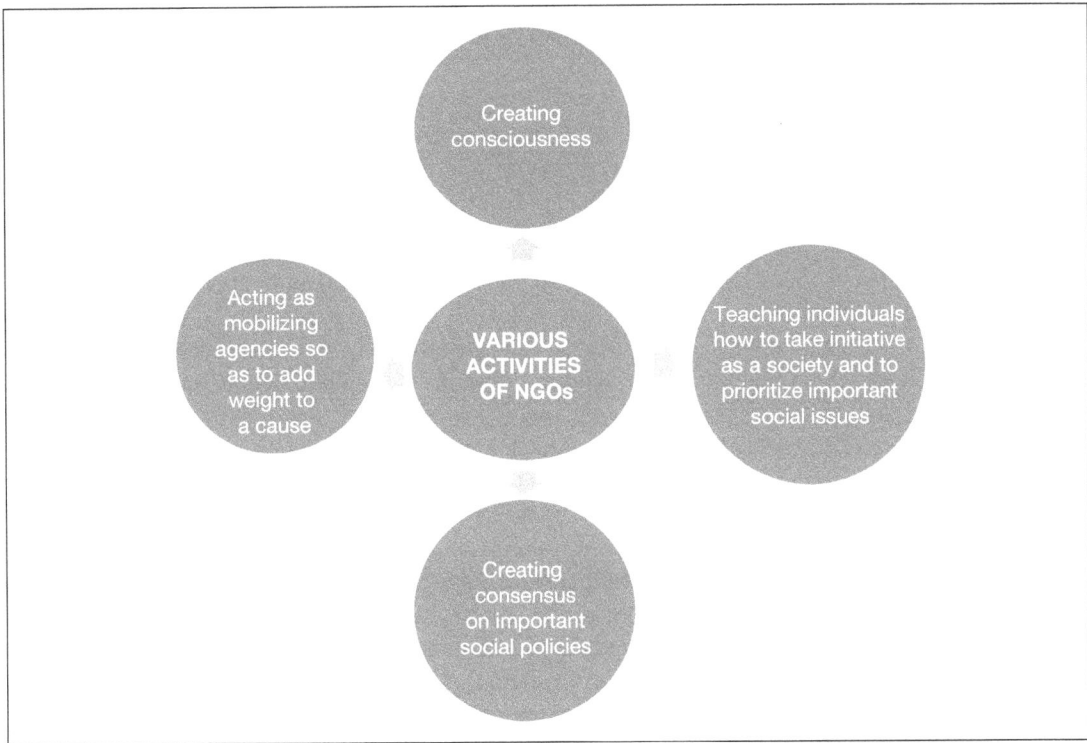

also led to the extinction of some unique species of wildlife. The WTI intends to deal with these issues head on by providing suitable alternatives for the activities in which wildlife is often targeted. They have a sound network of experts who work as a team to conserve wildlife in India and maintain a healthy ecosystem.

NGOs Against Globalization

The wave of globalization has received a lot of criticism in the last few years, as all the initial glorification of the phenomena fizzled out and the reality was much more clearly felt. The prime characteristic of globalization is economic integration, promoting trade and commerce. Over the years, this aspect of globalization has acquired a hardcore neo-liberal face. Crass materialism and unfair, non-restricted trade inflows have accelerated the growth of a lopsided developmental scene. There was visible an increasing negligence on the part of nation states post-globalization, where the states went on a spree of increasing their foreign direct investments (FDIs) and encouraging the growth of MNCs and TNCs. The other duties of the state, such as their responsibility towards citizens, welfare initiatives, creating a more egalitarian set-up and bridging the economic gap, all took a backseat. The anti-globalization movement, which started as a protest against the WTO meet in Seattle in 1999, did spread wide and became quite actively vocal against globalization. Various NGOs have acquired an anti-globalization stance and are working towards the reduction of lopsided development, which is the direct consequence of reckless implementation of globalization policies. This issue has been taken up by several NGOs, who are actively working against unjust globalization ethics. Some of these organizations are the Beehive Design Collective, Résistance Internationaliste and the Association for the Taxation of Financial Transactions and for Citizens' Action (ATTAC).

Accountability and NGOs

Some NGOs which had been set up with an ideal of doing good and working for the larger goals are getting trapped in issues which have greatly affected their credibility and authenticity. Whenever initiatives which are started by a few individuals gain prominence and start to compete with the power of the state, they tend to get caught up in a power struggle and petty selfish agendas. Often it has been seen that members or leaders of these NGOs have the ulterior motive of entering into politics and these NGOs are just eyewash.

Another issue which has lately been coming up with regard to the NGO sector is the issue of corruption, which can be seen in the lack of transparency and accuracy. Now this is one very crucial issue which can either make or break an organization. These bodies are largely funded bodies and have a large fundraising mechanism. Funding could be obtained from national and local bodies or there could be international donors as well, which expect to get proper feedback regarding how their funds are being utilized and whether they are reaching the targeted group. Often, cases of misappropriation of funds have cropped up, with the funds not being utilized for the cause on account of which they were originally generated. This has generated a lot of backlash from donors and funding agencies and has been a big issue confronting the NGO sector. In order to prevent such misuse by NGOs and to make them achieve their goals in an ethical manner, several regulatory mechanisms (such as the Foreign Contribution Regulation Act, or FCRA, in India) were devised by various countries to keep a check on their workings. The accountability issue was raised in India when Greenpeace India was violating the FCRA norms and the Government of India cancelled its registration in 2015.

NGOs can incorporate the following aspects into their functioning mechanisms so as to overcome the inconsistencies which may have crept into their system (Figure 7.5):

- *First*, have a well-articulated agenda, with proper rules and regulations stated. There should be a proper watchdog mechanism within the NGO's set-up as well, to which the members must be accountable if any rules are broken.
- *Second*, the NGOs should be conscious of where money is being utilized, and the donors should be made a part of the activities, though in an indirect manner.
- *Third*, there should be a proper tie-up with the media and press, and occasional press reports regarding future goals, prospects and important announcements should be made.
- *Fourth*, the NGO's body should keep focusing on diversifying its workforce and should try to replace the generalists with a specialized workforce.
- *Fifth*, the NGOs should bring out an internal audit report as well as have a culture of proving their worthiness and accountability to society by using various public platforms, which could also be made possible by making use of mass media and social media as well.

FIGURE 7.5   Tools to Maintain NGOs' Accountability

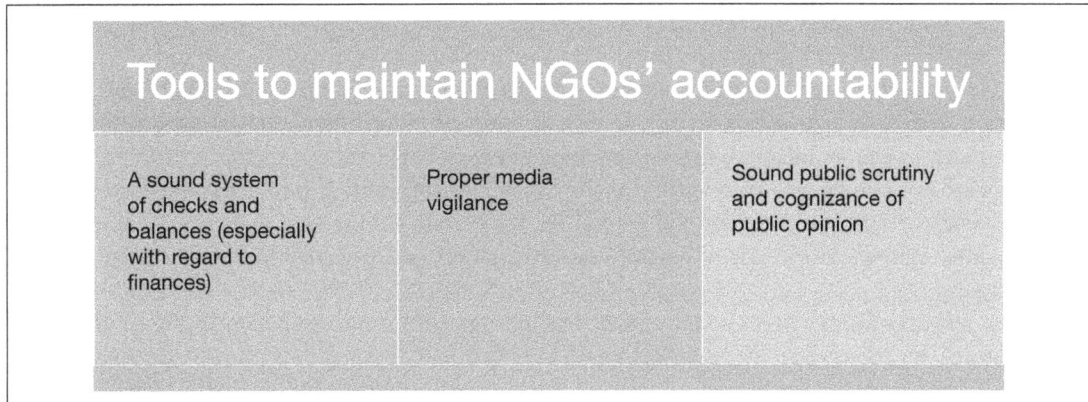

Tools to maintain NGOs' accountability

A sound system of checks and balances (especially with regard to finances)	Proper media vigilance	Sound public scrutiny and cognizance of public opinion

Concluding Observations

Globalization started with an economic agenda and targeted the economic integration of different countries. What followed the economic takeover was the gradual impact of globalization on every sphere of an individual's social and political existence. Globalization, which is often seen to be synonymous with modernization, came with a single agenda of universalizing its own set of socio-economic and political agendas in an aggressive way. Though the process was successful in some of the countries which were better equipped, it backfired in the countries which are in the process of development or in the developing world as they were not able to uniformly incorporate the changes due to the low level of development. What globalization led to was the creation of widespread disparities and a lopsided socio-economic and political structure. Eventually, the lack of government competency to deal with the ongoing issues led to the strengthening of global social movements (GSMs) and civil-society organizations such as the NGOs, which started filling the gaps which had been created by the lack of governmental machinery. These non-state actors provide a platform to unheard voices and fight for justice for the both marginalized people and nations. NGOs are working ceaselessly for various causes, as mentioned above, and have also been able to lend impetus to mobilizing the masses for the various causes which need prompt action, thus leading to the eventual rise of various social movements which have been quite successful and were eventually able to act on a global level and become GSMs. Thus the state machinery is being aided by non-state actors to a large extent, so as to bring about much-needed changes both at the state and at the global level.

Summary

- The term 'social movement' first gained acceptance amidst the social upheaval in Europe in the early nineteenth century. A 'social movement' is defined as a kind of collective behavior and action. Collective behaviors signify a situation wherein individuals act together and collectively organize the action.
- After the 1980s, a number of collective protests and demonstrations took place throughout the Western world and a novel phase of 'new social movements'—sometimes also called 'transnational

social movements' or 'global social movements' (GSMs)—evolved to theorize these diverse emerging facets of collective actions.

- By the 1990s, the social movements had acquired a 'global' character to address emerging global issues and problems resulting from the uneven and exploitative globalized world order.

- GSMs refer to those social movements that have global objectives and common goals to be achieved. These movements primarily demand decentralization of power, democratization of international institutions and more inclusive decision-making at the global level.

- GSMs are not homogeneous in nature, as they vary in terms of their popularity, objectives, central areas of action and mandates, among others. Yet, they retain similarities, sharing a number of commonalities ranging from origin, social base, orientation and organizational structures to action strategies.

- In last few decades, GSMs—also popularized as 'alter-globalization' campaigns in the contemporary literature—have succeeded in bringing together people with distinctive national identities and cultural backgrounds for a common cause of resisting globalization practices and the globalized world order.

- GSMs or alter-globalization campaigns largely seek fundamental reforms in the structure of global governance and the economic and financial system. However, differences may exist at the level of their strategies, methods, membership bases and organizational structures.

- Non-governmental organizations (NGOs) are part of a larger set of what we refer to as 'civil-society organizations', in which there as a body comprised of the citizens of a place working towards those issues which are often overlooked by the government but are nonetheless very important.

- NGOs are non-governmental and voluntary bodies which work on a non-profit basis. These organizations are set up by the citizens themselves, who have the urge to volunteer for causes which are in need of action. Some of the characteristics of these bodies are that they are (a) will-based or voluntary, (b) value-driven, (c) focused and directed towards a specific cause, (d) separated from governmental officials and functions and (e) flexible as to their sphere of influence.

- The rise of NGOs can be attributed to the United Nations articles 57 and 71, where they were given only a small mention; but still, the base had been laid for what later became the greatest non-state actors as far as inclusive governance is concerned.

- Globalization led to the gradual elimination of the boundary system and there was a gradual rise in inter- and intra-state developments which were mutually inclusive. Globalization, with its policies all over the world, has created strong disparities, and cases of human rights violation have also seen a growth. Not only this, the unexamined neo-liberal policies have also been facing stiff resistance from various countries and given a global character to these NGOs. These civil-society organizations are now collaborating on a global or international scale to fight against the hegemony of the developed world so that global activism can lead to a stronger impact on the initiators of globalization. Also there are many causes which have a global impact; hence taking a united action against them has led to greater paybacks.

- The NGOs have a special role to play in the development of the developing world, the reason being that these are transitional societies, and their state structures and economic institutions are not fully able to create a balance in the society. Of late, these countries have seen the rise of a conscious citizenry and the NGOs have become their mouthpieces. Various NGOs operating there are working on very specific causes, as mentioned above, such as children's rights, female emancipation, environmental issues, and so on.

- These NGOs have become an indispensable tool for effective governance and their partnership with the governmental bodies could be beneficial for tackling various delicate issues head on, as these are specialized organizations, provided that these bodies are able to work on their internal administration and develop a culture of transparency and accountability in the times to come.

Suggested Questions

1. What is the basic difference between the old social movements and new social movements?
2. What do you understand by global social movements? Critically explain their basic characteristics.
3. Critically discuss the impact of global resistance on international politics, with special reference to global social movements and NGOs.
4. What do you understand by the term 'NGOs'? Explain their historical evolution.
5. What is the major role being played by the NGOs in the developing countries?
6. What are the ways to ensure accountability in the context of NGOs?

References

Baviskar, Amita. 2010. 'Social Movements'. In *The Oxford Companion to Politics in India*, edited by Niraja Gopal Jayal and Pratap Bhanu Mehta, 382–383. New Delhi: Oxford University Press.

Bennett, Elizabeth A. 2012. 'Global Social Movements in Global Governance'. *Globalizations* 9 (6): 799–813.

Benton, Lisa M. and John Rennie Short. eds. 1999. *Environmental Discourse and Practice*. Oxford: Blackwell Publishers.

Buechler, Steven M. 1995. 'New Social Movement Theories'. *The Sociological Quarterly* 36 (3): 441–464. Accessed 15 November 2017. https://doi.org/10.1111/j.1533-8525.1995.tb00447.x.

Bullard, R. D. 1993. 'Race and Environmental Justice in the United States'. *Yale Journal of International Law*, 18 (winter): 319–335.

Cohen, Robin and Shirin Rai. 2000. *Global social movements*. London and New Brunswick: Athlone Press.

Doyle, Timothy. 2005. *Environmental Movement in Majority and Minority Worlds: A Global Perspective*. New Jersey: Rutgers University Press.

Fadaee, Simin. 2012. *Social Movements in Iran: Environmentalism and Civil Society*. Abingdon, Oxon, and New York, NY: Routledge.

Ghimire, Kléber B. 2005. 'The Contemporary Global Social Movements: Emergent Proposals, Connectivity and Development Implications', Civil Society and Social Movements Programme Paper No. 19. Geneva: United Nations Research Institute for Social Development.

Harvey, Jean, John Horne and Parissa Safai. 2009. 'Alterglobalization, Global Social Movements, and the Possibility of Political Transformation through Sport'. *Sociology of Sport Journal* 26 (3): 383–403.

Heberle, Rudolf. 1951. *Social Movements: An Introduction to Political Sociology*. New York: Appleton.

Heywood, Andrew. 2011. *Global Politics*. New York: Palgrave Macmillan.

Milani, Carlos R. S., and Ruthy Nadia Laniado, R. N. 2007. 'Transnational Social Movements and the Globalization Agenda: A Methodological Approach Based on the Analysis of the World Social Forum'. *Brazilian Political Science Review* 1 (2): 10–39.

Paehlke, Robert. 1995. *Conservation and Environmentalism: An Encyclopaedia*. London & Chicago: Fitzroy Dearborn Publishers.

Rao, M. S. A. 1979. *Social Movements in India: Studies in Peasant, Tribal and Women's Movements*. New Delhi: Manohar Publication.

Sachs, I. 2000. *Understanding Development: People, Markets and the State in Mixed Economies.* New Delhi: Oxford University Press.

Shah, Ghanshyam. 2011. *Social Movements in India: A Review of Literature,* 11th edn. New Delhi: SAGE Publications.

Sutton, Philip W. 2000. *Explaining Environmentalism: In Search of a New Social Movement.* Hampshire: Ashgate.

Wallerstein, Immanuel. 2002. 'New Revolts Against the System'. *New Left Review* 18 (11): 29–39.

Wapner, Paul. 2002. 'Defending Accountability in NGOs'. *Chicago Journal of International Law,* 3 (1) 197–205.

Werker, Eric, and Faisal Z. Ahmed. 2008. What do Nongovernmental Organizations do? *The Journal of Economic Perspectives* 22 (2): 73–92.

Wilkinson, Paul. 1971. *Social Movement.* Basingstoke: Macmillan Press.

Willetts, Peter. 2011. Non-Governmental Organisations in World Politics: The Construction of Global Governance. London and New York: Routledge.

WSF. 2001. World Social Forum Charter of Principles. Accessed 20 April 2018. http://www.universidadepopular.org/site/media/documentos/WSF_-_charter_of_Principles.pdf.

Further Reading

Ahmad, Shamima and David M. Potter, 2006. *NGOs in International Politics.* Boulder, CO: Kumarian Press.

Anheier, Helmut K. 2004. *Nonprofit Organizations: Theory, Management, Policy.* Abingdon, Oxon, and New York, NY: Routledge.

Biswas, Nilanjana. 2006. 'On Funding and the NGO Sector'. *Economic and Political Weekly,* 41 (42): 4406–4411.

Christie, Ryerson. 2013. *Peacebuilding and NGOs: State–Civil Society Interactions.* Abingdon, Oxon, and New York, NY: Routledge.

Howell, Jude, and Jenny Pearce. 2001. *Civil Society and Development: A Critical Exploration.* London: Lynne Rienner Publishers.

Hudock, Ann. 1999. *NGOs and Civil Society: Democracy by Proxy?* Cambridge: Polity Press.

Kapoor, Dip. 2005. 'NGOs Partnerships and the Taming of the Grassroots in Rural India'. *Development in Practice* 15 (2): 210–215.

Lang, Sabine. 2013. *NGOs, Civil Society, and the Public Sphere.* New York, NY: Cambridge University Press.

Mertes, Tom. 2003. *A Movement of Movements: Is Another World Really Possible?* Brooklyn, NY: Verso.

Mittelman, James H. 1998. 'Globalization and Environmental Resistance Politics'. *Third World Quarterly* (19) 5: 847–872.

Offe, Claus. 1985. 'New Social Movements: Challenging the Boundaries of Institutional Politics'. *Social Research,* 52 (4): 817–868.

Ofitserova-Smith, Maiia. 2003. 'Moral Implications of Globalisation'. *Polish Sociologica Review* 143: 259–273.

Patomäki, Heikki, and Teivo Teivainen. 2004. *A Possible World: Democratic Transformation of Global Institutions.* NY: Zed Books.

Wallerstein, Immanuel. 2007. 'The World Social Forum: From Defense to Offense'. Accessed 5 December 2017. https://www.globalpolicy.org/component/content/article/174-advocacy/30722.html.

8
CHAPTER

Ecological Issues: A Historical Overview of International Environmental Agreements, Climate Change and the Global Commons Debate

Kamal Kumar

LEARNING OBJECTIVES

- To elucidate and assess the contested relationship between environment and development
- To explore the factors involved in the evolution of global environmental politics
- To understand the significance of international cooperation on ecological issues
- To illustrate the key international agreements adopted on varied environmental issues
- To assess the phenomenon of climate change and its impact on human and environmental health
- To explain the difficulties in governing and regulating the global commons

Ecological issues in the contemporary world pose a most serious threat to the sustainable future of the earth. In fact, environmental security has become one of the key security issues especially for the countries located in the Global South. The concept of environmental security started to gain prominence at the global level by the 1980s and became one of the major global concerns by the late

1990s. In the era of globalization, the issue of environmental degradation has become more complex and multifaceted, resulting in the expansion of the international environmental regime and a number of multinational environmental agreements and treaties. Worldwide cooperation has increasingly become significant to address the ecological challenges as well as to protect the human environment. International organizations such as the United Nations (UN) have played an optimistic and positive role in strengthening cooperation amongst the different nations with the help of environmental agreements such as the Stockholm Declaration and the Kyoto Protocol. At the same time, the governments of most of the developed and developing countries have shown a considerable enthusiasm towards the needs of preservation and improvement of the human environment in recent decades. However, their enthusiasm was confined to making further announcements of environmental policies, international and national agreements and legislations, and they have failed to bring about any major changes as these are in contradiction with their development policies. The agenda of economic development (based on the capitalist model) is still dominating governmental discourse at both domestic and global levels.

This chapter presents an overview of the major international environmental agreements and discusses the contemporary debates on climate change and the global commons. The chapter primarily consists of five sections. The first two parts present a brief overview of the scholarly debates on environment and development and of the evolution of environmental politics at the global level. The third section overviews the significant international environmental agreements aiming to resolve different environment problems. This is followed by a discussion of climate change, which is one of the biggest and most complex threats facing humanity in the twenty-first century. The fifth and last section examines the existing scholarly debates in the context of the global commons. The latter concept is widely used to refer to those domains that do not come under the control or jurisdiction of any state but are open for use by all nations, corporations and individuals from all over the world. However, before taking up the key debates on ecological issues, it is pertinent to understand the contested relationship between the two dominant phenomena, that is, environment and development.

Environment Versus Development

Environment and development are among the most contested phenomena in the contemporary world, with little in common. The former underlines the need to preserve natural resources while the latter stresses upon the extraction and exploitation of the same to yield high economic growth rates, which are widely viewed as a fundamental prerequisite for national progress and the development of any country. The global recognition of a contested relationship between these two phenomena—environment and development—can be traced to the second half of the twentieth century, when the UN organized the first Conference on the Human Environment, widely known as the Stockholm Conference, in 1972. This conference tried to steer a middle path on the key question of choosing between economic development and ecological protection, by laying down 26 common principles which called for worldwide cooperation in order to maintain a balance between development and the environment by creating a global platform for addressing ecological issues (such as ozone-layer depletion, climate change and pollutions) and encouraging rational ecological planning.

There are two schools of thought related to the issue of environment and development. The first school of thought believes in 'environment for development', while other advocates 'development with the environment'. Walter W. Heller, a well-known American economist, who belonged to the former school of thought, argued that

> the ecologists confront us with an environmental imperative that requires an end to economic growth or at least a sharp curtailment of it as the price of biological survival, and health… Some ecologists see the reduced (economic) growth, as a necessary though not sufficient condition for saving the ecosystem. The economist sees (economic) growth as a necessary, though not sufficient condition for social progress and stability. (Heller 1971, 14)

Thus, the economists believe that economic growth is not at the root of environmental degradation but, instead, it satisfies one of the core prerequisites to effectively restore the environmental losses by advancing technologies. The issue of population explosion is also linked to environmental degradation and excessive depletion of the natural resources (Brundtland et al. 2012; Mishra 2013). In a nutshell, according to this approach, economic growth mainly helps in improving the degraded environment and its habitats and in enhancing the people's well-being, especially that of the poor.

On the other hand, scholars who support the concept of sustainable development propose the 'development with the environment' framework and emphasize a harmonious relationship between the environment and development. B. Commoner (1972) and Paul Ehrlich (1994) have argued that the economists and policymakers need to take into account the ecological losses which are a product of developmental activities so that natural resources can be utilized in such a way that makes their replenishment possible (Mishra 2013, 14). They are not against the notion of development per se, but they do critique resource-intensive patterns of development and call for 'sustainable development', which is broadly defined as 'development that meets the needs of the present generation without compromising the ability of future generations to meet their own needs' (Paehlke 1995, 504). In other words, the sustainable model of development seeks to promote industrialization that is in harmony with the nature. Thus, the model of development, from this standpoint, has to be environment-friendly and environment-sensitive.

Evolution of Global Environmental Politics

Scholars attribute the genesis of global environmental politics to the middle of the twentieth century, when it emerged as a response to the uncontrolled industrialization resulting in a large-scale ecological crisis. Initially, the nation states did not express any real concern towards the environmental problems because these were often seen as a temporary phenomenon that could be easily dealt with using scientific and technological measures. With the advent of the globalization era, environmental health further deteriorated due to heavy industrialization and growing consumerism, causing consumption and production on a massive scale, waste creation and over-extraction of natural resources among others (Baylis, Smith and Owens 2008, 532–535). However, environmental issues did not become an important international issue for the global community and international organizations until the latter half of the twentieth century. Particularly since the Second World War, a broad spectrum of international agreements on environmental issues has been developed under the auspices of the UN.

The decade of the 1970s was of paramount importance in the history of environmental preservation and protection. The groundbreaking study by Rachael Carson entitled *Silent Spring* (1962) forced the international community to pay heed to the huge environmental costs of rapid industrialization and capitalist development. More specifically, it highlighted the harmful effects of pesticides like DDT (dichlorodiphenyltrichloroethane) on wildlife and human life. Carson was popularly recognized as the first scholar who situated environmental concerns at the centre of intergovernmental debates and negotiations. Furthermore, the UN in 1972 organized the first formal United Nations Conference on the Human Environment (UNCHE) in Stockholm to discuss measures for protecting the environment from further destruction. In this context, the United Nations Environment Programme (UNEP) in 2001 stated that 'there were over 500 international treaties and other agreements related to the environment.... Nearly 60 percent date from 1972, the year of the Stockholm Conference, to the present' (MPWGSC 2004, 3). The same decade also marked the emergence of environmental movements that highlighted the huge environmental costs of rapid economic development and increased growth, and sought to challenge the prevailing mode of development—which was considered to be destructive and capitalist-oriented. Hence, by the 1970s, environment had emerged as a standing locus of political conflict at both the international and the national levels and, thus, the urgent need to preserve the environment from further destruction was seriously felt.

It is important to note here that the ideological disputes or differences between the states of Global South and North have been increasingly shaping the nature and scope of contemporary global environmental politics. Particularly, during the Earth Summit, the dispute between the developed countries of the Global North (i.e., North America and Western Europe) and developing and least developing countries of Global South (i.e., Asia, Africa, Latin America and the Middle East) was very much visible at reaching a consensus globally. The developed countries or industrialized nations sought to develop a network of effective and collectively reinforcing mechanisms—at both global and national levels—to deal with ecological problems while the developing countries or poor nations were reluctant to give up their right to exploit their natural resources—required to achieve economic development and ensure a quality life to their people. In other words, in the absence of adequate financial aid and free transfer of green technologies, the nations of Global South were not willing to give up their sovereignty over natural resources in the name of environment restriction put by the Global North nations. Therefore, the North–South conflict over environmental management has weakened the international community's capability of building worldwide consensus between the states on different environmental agreements or treaties.

International Environmental Agreements: A Historical Overview

Over the years, a number of international environmental agreements have been signed at the global level to address different ecological problems. Such agreements include important intergovernmental policies, initiatives and measures taken collectively on global environmental issues. An important question now arises: What is the importance of international environmental agreements as a way of addressing ecological problems? The state's efforts to achieve rapid industrialization and modernization have caused numerous environmental problems such as global warming, deterioration of the ozone layer, resource depletion, industrial pollution, deforestation, air pollution and ocean pollution, among others. These issues are not local or national in nature but global, transnational and trans-boundary, which demand collective action by all countries to achieve the desired common objectives. Countries, including developed ones, cannot effectively cope with major environmental problems by acting alone, and this fact has been well acknowledged by all countries (MPWGSC 2004, 1–3). Hence, international environmental agreements are significant since they enable countries belonging to different contexts to come together on a common platform and work collectively to deal with complex ecological issues. In other words, the countries (including the developed ones) have recognized the fact that environmental issues are transnational in nature and, therefore, they are to be addressed collectively. The international forums provide a platform to all the countries where they can deliberate on and discuss environmental issues and decide the common action programme through multinational agreements.

The beginning of international agreements on ecological issues can be traced back to the latter half of the twentieth century, when they primarily focused on two issues: preservation of natural resources and the impacts of pollution on the environment and human health. In this regard, the international community attempted to regulate and control the limitless exploitation of maritime resources. For example, the 1946 International Convention for the Regulation of Whaling is widely considered the first international agreement in the domain of environmental protection. However, these attempts did not yield any success. After the Second World War, the global economic recovery brought evidence of atmospheric pollution and marine pollution on a massive scale (Baylis, Smith and Owens 2008, 354). Since then, its scope has been considerably expanded as ecological issues have acquired a trans-boundary character that is evident from the growing numbers of international environmental conferences and agreements that have emerged with the support of international organizations such as the UN. In that sense, international environmental agreements, in the beginning, focused on very limited issues and problems while recent agreements not only address a wide range of issues but are also binding upon a greater number of states than earlier. However, it is the Stockholm Conference (1972) which marked the announcement of international environmental agreements on a large scale (Sohn 1973). The following section sketches out a historical overview of important international environmental agreements, addressing various ecological issues.

Stockholm Conference (UNCHE, 1972)

The United Nations Conference on Human Environment (UNCHE)—held in June 1972 in Stockholm, Sweden—marked the beginning of the modern era of environmental governance, introducing more inclusive and comprehensive international agreements and regulations on environmental issues. This conference is also widely known as the Stockholm Conference. The event is broadly considered the first major worldwide attempt to address global environmental problems and preserve the human environment. The conference was also the first international environmental agreement recognizing the fact that 'environmental problems of broad international significance fall within the competence of the United Nations system' (UN 1972, 34). In other words, the Stockholm Conference placed the environmental problems at the centre of global debates, particularly those occurring within the domain of international organizations such as the UN. As a result, the international organizations were compelled to take appropriate measures to deal with the environmental problems—particularly those are global in nature. Since then, the international organizations have not only successfully organized international events, but also signed a number of environmental agreements aimed at the preservation and enhancement of the human environment.

The UNCHE in 1972 was attended by delegations from more than 110 countries and over 400 non-governmental and intergovernmental organizations. The Stockholm Declaration, adopted at the UN conference, is one of the most significant documents in the history of global environmental governance. While comparing the latter with the Universal Declaration of Human Rights (UDHR 1948) in his book entitled *An Introduction to International Law*, J. G. Starke (1989, 406) termed the Stockholm Declaration an important environmental manifesto 'expressed in the form an ethical code intended to govern and influence future action and programmers, both at the national and international levels'. The Declaration consists of 26 common principles that aim to inspire and guide future actions and policies, particularly concerned with the human environment. Some of the key principles (UN 1972, 4–5) are worth discussing:

Principle 1

Human beings have a fundamental right to freedom, equality and adequate conditions of life, in an environment of a quality that permits a life of dignity and well-being, and they bear a solemn responsibility to protect and improve the environment for present and future generations.

Principle 2

The natural resources of the earth, including the air, water, land, flora and fauna and especially representative samples of natural ecosystems, must be safeguarded for the benefit of present and future generations through careful planning or management, as appropriate.

Principle 7

States shall take all possible steps to prevent pollution of the seas by substances that are liable to create hazards to human health, to harm living resources and marine life, to damage amenities or to interfere with other legitimate uses of the sea.

Principle 14

Rational planning constitutes an essential tool for reconciling any conflict between the needs of development and the need to protect and improve the environment.

Principle 17

Appropriate national institutions must be entrusted with the task of planning, managing or controlling the environmental resources of states with a view to enhancing environmental quality.

Principle 19

Education in environmental matters, for the younger generation as well as adults and giving due consideration to the underprivileged, is essential in order to broaden the basis for an enlightened opinion and responsible conduct by individuals, enterprises and communities in protecting and improving the environment in its full human dimension.

Principle 20

Scientific research and development in the context of environmental problems, both national and multinational, must be promoted in all countries, especially the developing countries.

Principle 22

States shall cooperate to develop further the international law regarding liability and compensation for victims of pollution and other environmental damage caused by activities within the jurisdiction or control of such states to areas beyond their jurisdiction.

Principle 24

International matters concerning the protection and improvement of the environment should be handled in a cooperative spirit by all countries, big and small, on an equal footing. Cooperation through multilateral or bilateral arrangements or other appropriate means is essential to effectively control, prevent, reduce and eliminate adverse environmental effects resulting from activities conducted in all spheres in such a way that due account is taken of the sovereignty and interests of all states.

Principle 26

Humans and their environment must be spared the effects of nuclear weapons and all other means of mass destruction. States must strive to reach prompt agreement, in the relevant international organs, on the elimination and complete destruction of such weapons.

The 26 principles enunciated at the UNCHE are, therefore, a set of instructions to the states and international organizations to undertake a particular line of action for protecting and improving the human environment. These principles also lay down the basis of the environmental protection structure at both the international and the national levels. In other words, the 26 principles do not merely facilitate growth of the international environmental regime at the global level, but also stimulate nations to initiate suitable measures to protect the environmental resources at the local level. The Stockholm Declaration also contains an ambitious Action Plan with 109 recommendations related to the planning and management of human settlements, natural resources management, marine pollution, social and cultural aspects of ecological issues, development and environment, and international organizations. It was assumed that the states would sincerely intend to follow these recommendations while they planned their actions or designed policies to deal with environmental problems as well as to protect natural resources. As a result, a number of environmental programmes and policies were launched to realize the principles of the Stockholm Declaration in the human environment. For instance, the World Ecological Areas Programme (WEAP) was launched in 1972 for the preservation of tropical rainforests.

United Nations Environment Programme (UNEP)

The establishment of the United Nations Environment Programme (UNEP) was one of the greatest achievements of the Stockholm Conference. This international environmental body was primarily set up in December 1972 by the General Assembly, to coordinate the environmental activities within the UN system. The UNEP—headquartered in Nairobi, Kenya—was labelled the 'environmental conscience of the UN system' (Paehlke 1995, 653). The main tasks of this organization are to promote global cooperation on ecological issues, guide other UN environmental agencies, coordinate UN activities related to the environment, monitor global environmental management and encourage scientific research and projects. Also, it intends to raise public awareness about the dangers of environmental change and deterioration, and attempts to inculcate environmental education through sponsored television and radio programmes. It is estimated that 'more than 10,000 educators in over 140 countries have been involved in UNEP's educational activities' (Paehlke 1995, 654). Besides, the UNEP not only encourages the states' agencies but also private actors such as NGOs, TNCs, multinational voluntary organizations and civil-society groups to promote the sustainable use of natural resources.

Since its origin, UNEP has been one of the biggest proponents of the environment-friendly and sustainable model of development. It has supported varied scientific research, training programmes and projects aiming to develop environment-sensitive development agendas and models. It has also facilitated worldwide cooperation among the states in global politics, particularly in the context of international environmental agreements and policies. Maurice Strong, the first executive director of UNEP, 'coined the phrase "the process is the policy," which captures much of UNEP's strategy of bolstering international environmental concern and building national capacity for managing environmental problems' (Paehlke 1995, 653). It is observed that since the inception of UNEP, more than 40 multilateral environmental agreements were signed under its auspices (Kochtcheeva and Singh 2000). More specifically, in the past three decades, UNEP has played a substantial role in initiating negotiations on reducing the use of chemicals and gases causing ozone-layer depletion. At the same time, it has extended technical support to a number of international conventions, such as the Montreal Protocol on Substances that Deplete the Ozone Layer (1987) and the UN Convention on Biological Diversity (CBD, 1992) among others. In this way, UNEP intends to develop a worldwide consensus among both the public and the non-state actors about environmental problems and organize collective actions for ensuring a sustainable and green future. Furthermore, UNEP has developed an international monitoring system, known as 'Earthwatch'.[1] It is designed to engage governments in a free-flowing exchange of environmental information and green ideas. Earthwatch also enables the global and national actors to assess potential risks and threats to the human environment so they may act accordingly (Saunier and Meganck 2009: 281).

Clearly, therefore, the role of the Stockholm Conference or UNCHE in placing environmental issues at the centre of global discourse is noteworthy. This event did stimulate international agencies and governments along with the people to take appropriate measures to protect and enhance the human environment. In the post-1972 era, the Stockholm Declaration continues to guide and shape environmental agreements and regulations at both the global and local levels.

Montreal Protocol (1987)

The Montreal Protocol, in full the Montreal Protocol on Substances that Deplete the Ozone Layer, was initially signed in 1987 by 24 countries and the European Community at the headquarters of the International Civil Aviation Organization (ICAO) in Montreal, Canada. Later, the same treaty was ratified by more than 180 countries. This global agreement was the first of its kind in the history of environmental protection and was designed to protect the stratospheric ozone layer by reducing global production, emissions and usage of ozone-depleting chemical substances within the stipulated time period. However, the Vienna Convention for the Protection of the Ozone Layer (1985)—which

---

[1] Earthwatch is a non-profit international environmental organization that brings people from all walks of life together with the world's top scientists to work on expeditions for the good of the planet.

recognizes the responsibility of states to protect the environment and human health from the adverse effects of ozone depletion—set out the framework under which the Montreal Protocol was negotiated. The protocol was thus adopted on 16 September 1987, but it came into force on 1 January 1989 and was subsequently amended many times.

The Montreal Protocol recognized the worldwide emission of certain chemical substances that could deplete or substantially modify the earth's ozone layer in a way that was assessed to adversely impact the environment and human health. Hence, it was aimed at regulating the production and consumption of ozone-depleting substances (ODSs) such as chlorofluorocarbons (CFCs), carbon tetrachloride, halons and methyl chloroform among others. The parties to the protocol agreed to reduce the manufacture and usage of CFCs by half of their baseline by 1998 and to phase out usage of halons by 1992. However, 10 years of relaxation was granted to the developing countries, unlike developed countries, to comply with the protocol's phase-out targets. The protocol also delimited trade of controlled substances (ODSs) in the countries not party to the protocol (Paehlke 1995, 434). Moreover, a unique adjustment provision is also included in the protocol, which enables the parties (signatory countries of the protocol) to quickly respond to new scientific information in an effort to 'accelerate the reductions required on chemicals already covered by the Protocol. These adjustments are then automatically applicable to all countries that ratified the Protocol' (EPA 2017). Since the enactment of Montreal Protocol, the parties have adjusted and amended the protocol not just to regulate the ODSs, but also to provide financial resources to help developing countries in complying with the protocol's provisions. In addition to the adjustment provision, the signatory counties meet to share important scientific information and monitor the implementation of phase-out resolutions.

The Montreal Protocol was last amended at the 28th Meeting of the Parties to the Montreal Protocol (MOP28) held in October 2016 in Kigali, Rwanda. In the Kigali Agreement, the most notable amendment is pertaining to the phasing down of manufacture and usage of hydrofluorocarbons (HFCs)—man-made, powerful greenhouse gases which are commonly used in home refrigerants, aerosols, air conditioners and fire-extinguishing systems, among others. More specifically, 197 signatory countries, including India and China, agreed to reduce the production and consumption of HFCs by roughly 80–85% of their baseline by 2045. The move is likely to prevent up to 0.5 degree Celsius rise in global warming by the end of the twentieth-first century. Furthermore, a different timeline has been set out at the Kigali Agreement for the developing countries, such as India, Iran and Pakistan, in order for them to comply with the phase-out resolution. Also, the developing nations will receive financial resources from the Multilateral Fund to facilitate compliance. The Kigali Agreement or amended Montreal Protocol will be binding on the parties from 1 January 2019.

Owing to its widespread acceptance and implementation, the Montreal Protocol has been considered an extraordinary example of worldwide cooperation that has ushered in a new era in the history of environmental protection. While delivering the speech on International Day for the Preservation of the Ozone Layer in September 2005, Kofi Annan, the former Secretary General of the UN, stated that 'perhaps the single most successful international agreement to date has been the Montreal Protocol' (UNEP 2015). The protocol has been signed by 197 parties (196 states and the European Union), making it the first universally ratified global agreement in the history of the UN. It has also achieved a notable success in phasing out the global production and consumption of ODSs that has resulted in the reduction of its concentrations in the atmosphere, thereby protecting the ozone layer. Historically, for example, the United States (US) has been amongst the largest manufacturers and consumers of ODSs. Over the past couples of decades, the US environmental agencies have successfully phased down the manufacture of the most damaging first-generation ODSs, such as halons, CFCs and methyl chloroform, among others (see Table 8.1). Furthermore, the 1987 protocol has played a constructive role in expediting policymaking procedures at the international level, particularly in the context of environmental protection (Fahey 2013). That is probably why the Montreal Protocol is the most successful international attempt or global environmental agreement for the protection of the ozone layer.

Rio Conference (1992)

The United Nations Conference on Environment and Development (UNCED), also popularly known as the Earth Summit or Rio Conference, was convened in 1992 in Rio de Janeiro. This global event marked the twentieth anniversary of historical Stockholm Conference held in 1972. The Rio Conference, the largest environment conference in UN history, was attended by over 170 government representatives, 35,000 environmental activists, politicians and business representatives, along with thousands of journalists and representatives of NGOs from around the world. The conference negotiated on a wide range of environmental issues, ranging from biodiversity, climate change and pollution to forest management, poverty and sustainable use of resources. The foremost purpose of the conference, however, was to reconcile the worldwide developmental goals with the need for environmental protection by evolving a sustainable model of development. Sustainable development recognizes that the model of development has to be inclusive and environmentally friendly to build shared prosperity for today's population and to continue to meet the needs of future generations. The conference, therefore, laid down the principles or action plan to enable individuals and nations to adopt more environment-friendly behaviour and policies. The attendees nominally committed to promoting industrialization and development in harmony with nature (Cunningham et al. 1994, 854–855). The Declaration on Environment and Development, the Convention on Biological Diversity (CBD), the (Rio) Forest Principles,[2] Agenda 21 and the United Nations Framework Convention on Climate Change (UNFCCC) were the main agreements and documents signed at the conference (Figure 8.1).

Declaration on Environment and Development

The Declaration on Environment and Development adopted at the Earth Summit is also widely known as the Rio Declaration, comprising of 27 principles that reaffirmed the Stockholm Declaration and defined the responsibilities of state and non-state actors in safeguarding the planet (UN 1992a). In other words, it urged the nations to pursue a sustainable and environment-sensitive developmental agenda on the one hand and encouraged individuals to live a more eco-friendly lifestyle on the other. It further highlighted the need for evolving new levels of global cooperation to deal with the emerging environmental challenges and to preserve and restore the earth's ecosystem. Some of the major principles contained in the Rio Declaration (Saunier and Meganck 2009, 431–435) are worth discussing here:

---

[2] The complete formal name is Non-Legally Binding Authoritative Statement of Principles for a Global Consensus on the Management, Conservation and Sustainable Development of All Types of Forests.

TABLE 8.1 US: Phasing Out Ozone-depleting Substances

First-generation ODSs Phased Out			Second-generation ODSs Phased Out		
Chemical Group	Production Phase-out Dates	Deadline Met	Chemical Group	Production Phase-out Dates	Deadline Met
Halons	1 January 1994	✓	Hydrochlorofluorocarbons (HCFCs)	Cut production 35% by 1 January 2004	✓ (One year ahead of schedule)
Chlorofluorocarbons (CFCs)	1 January 1996	✓		Cut production 65% by 1 January 2010	
Carbon tetrachloride	1 January 1996	✓		Cut production 90% by 1 January 2015	On track to meet all future requirements
Hydrobromofluorocarbons (HBFCs)	1 January 1996	✓		Cut production 99.5% by 1 January 2020	
Methyl chloroform	1 January 1996	✓		Complete phase out by 1 January 2030	
Chlorobromomethane	18 August 2003	✓			
Methyl bromide	1 January 1995	✓			

Source: Data taken from EPA website: https://www.epa.gov/ods-phaseout/phaseout-class-i-ozone-depleting-substances.

FIGURE 8.1 Outcomes of Rio Conference

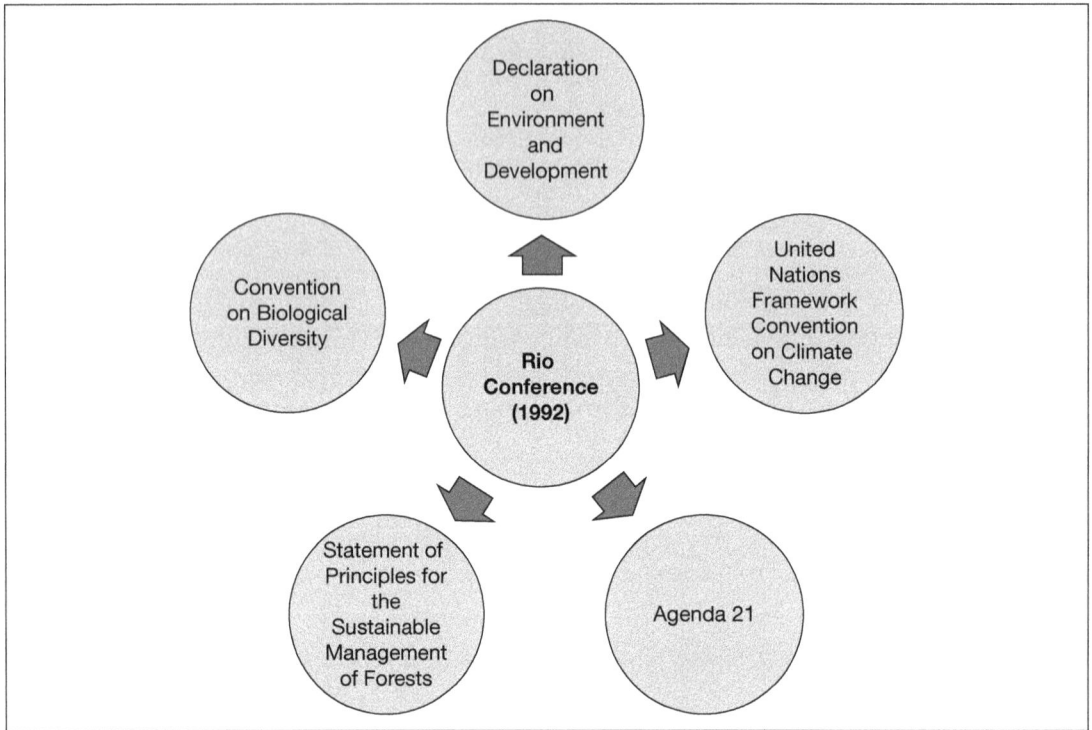

Principle 1

Human beings are at the centre of concerns for sustainable development. They are entitled to a healthy and productive life in harmony with nature.

Principle 3

The right to development must be fulfilled so as to equitably meet developmental and environmental needs of present and future generations.

Principle 4

In order to achieve sustainable development, environmental protection shall constitute an integral part of the development process and cannot be considered in isolation from it.

Principle 6

The special situation and needs of developing countries, particularly the least developed and those most environmentally vulnerable, shall be given special priority. International action in the field of the environment and development should also address the interests and needs of all countries.

Principle 10

Environmental issues are best handled with the participation of all concerned citizens, at the relevant level. At the national level, each individual shall have appropriate access to information concerning the environment that is held by public authorities, including information on hazardous materials and activities in their communities, and the opportunity to participate in decision-making processes. States shall facilitate and encourage public awareness and participation by making information widely available. Effective access to judicial and administrative proceedings, including redress and remedy, shall be provided.

Principle 11

States shall enact effective environmental legislation. Environmental standards, management objectives and priorities should reflect the environmental and developmental context to which they apply. Standards applied by some countries may be inappropriate and of unwarranted economic and social cost to other countries, in particular developing countries.

Principle 14

States should effectively cooperate to discourage or prevent the relocation and transfer to other states of any activities and substances that cause severe environmental degradation or are found to be harmful to human health.

Principle 17

Environmental impact assessment, as a national instrument, shall be undertaken for proposed activities that are likely to have a significant adverse impact on the environment and are subject to the decision of a competent national authority.

Principle 20

Women have a vital role in environmental management and development. Their full participation is therefore essential to achieve sustainable development.

Principle 22

Indigenous people and their communities, and other local communities, have a vital role in environmental management and development because of their knowledge and traditional practices. States should recognize and duly support their identity, culture and interests and enable their effective participation in the achievement of sustainable development.

Principle 27

States and people shall cooperate in good faith and in a spirit of partnership in the fulfilment of the principles embodied in this Declaration and in the further development of international law in the field of sustainable development.

The Rio Declaration, therefore, engages with a broad range of new issues, ranging from the sovereign right to exploit resources and sustainable development, to poverty, developing countries' rights, citizens' participation, the role of women and indigenous communities in environmental management, compensation for the victims of pollution, trans-boundary environmental affects and peace. Furthermore, it has broadened and enlarged the scope of environmental governance by recognizing the significance of public participation in achieving sustainable development and environmental management.

Convention on Biological Diversity

The Convention on Biological Diversity (CBD), also called the Biodiversity Convention, is another significant achievement of the Rio Conference. The convention was opened for signatures in 1992 at the Earth Summit and came into force on 29 December 1993. Biodiversity exists on earth in the many forms of life, including ecosystems, plants, animals, microorganisms and fungi, with their genetic diversity. The convention recognizes the central role of biological diversity in maintaining the life-sustaining systems of the biosphere, and thus it requires the states to initiate measures for the protection and sustainable use of biological diversity (UN 1992b). In other words, the CBD affirms that the preservation of biodiversity is a common concern of humankind, demanding collective efforts at all levels (global, national, local and societal levels). This multilateral, binding agreement has today been approved by over 190 countries and the EU.

The CBD requires all countries to develop national strategies to protect biodiversity, particularly endangered species. In fact, there are the three key objectives the CBD has set out (for nations) to achieve: first, the sustainable use of biological diversity; secondly, the conservation of biodiversity; and the last is the 'fair and equitable sharing of the benefits arising out of the utilisation of genetic resources' (UN 1992b, 3). Overall, the objective is to initiate measures to conserve biodiversity and also ensure its sustainable use for the benefit of present and future generations. In order to achieve these objectives, the CBD underlines the significance of global technical and scientific corporations amongst the parties to the convention. Hence, international and national institutions are endowed with the responsibility to promote cooperation in the field of conservation and sustainable use of biodiversity by facilitating the exchange of relevant information, techniques and scientific and socio-economic research (UN 1992b, 11). It is also stated in the convention that the affluent nations (developed countries) are to provide additional financial aid and resources to enable the poor nations (developing countries) to be in compliance with the obligations (UN 1992b, 14). In other words, the developed countries were encouraged to share their green technologies with developing countries for their better compliance with the convention's principles.

The CBD also recognizes the significance of the role of indigenous groups and NGOs in ensuring the conservation and sustainable use of biodiversity. In other words, the informal sector or non-state actors such as media, civil society, NGOs and educational institutes should be involved to make people aware of the importance of biodiversity so that they also participate in achieving the objectives of the CBD. In order to monitor the progress and continuously revive the plan, the parties ratified the convention and agreed to come together every two years. The Secretariat of the Convention on Biological Diversity, situated in Montreal, Canada, assists the parties to develop their strategies, plan their work, set their priorities, organize meetings, exchange information and techniques, and coordinate with other global organizations. The Executive Secretary is the head of the Secretariat.

Initially, most of the developed countries, particularly the US, were reluctant to ratify this convention as they considered it as an initiative against the growth of their bio-technological industries. As per the figures given on the official website of the CBD, presently there are 196 parties and 168 signatories to the convention, dedicated to reducing the global loss of biodiversity (CBD 2018). Yet, four nations—the US, Andorra, Iraq and Somalia—are not party to it and have been labelled as standing against the global conservation and sustainability efforts.

(Rio) Forest Principles

The (Rio) Forest Principles is a non-binding declaration aimed at conserving and protecting the world's rapidly vanishing tropical forests. It urges the nations to monitor and observe the impact of their development process on forest resources and also encourages them to take immediate steps to recover from damage done to the latter as well as to draft policies to minimize the harmful impact of development on forest resources. The mode of development is to be in harmony with nature. In other words, the process of development should not be against the health of forest resources, often called the 'lungs of the earth'. These lungs are not only significant for protecting biological diversity, but also to fight environmental challenges such as global warming, deforestation and soil erosion. Furthermore, forests provide goods and raw materials to forest-based industries (for instance, woodworking, paper, matches, silk, sports goods and handicrafts) and thus play an important role in the country's economic development. They also play a significant role in maintaining the global carbon cycle by absorbing carbon dioxide (CO_2)—the principal greenhouse gas primarily results from human activities—during photosynthesis. Probably that is why the declaration states that forest resources are not only important for any nation's economic development, but also to maintain all forms of life on earth.

The following key points are contained in the (Rio) Forest Principles:

- All nations should contribute to the 'greening of the world' through plantation programmes and conservation policies (UN 1992c).
- The state and non-state actors have a responsibility to ensure sustainable forest management.
- Forest resources should be protected and preserved to meet the social, economic, cultural and ecological needs of both present and future generations.
- Special attention should be given to those forest resources which have unique historical, religious, spiritual and cultural importance.
- Nations should initiate proper measures to regulate and control those pollutants that harm forests.

Agenda 21

Agenda 21 is the most significant agreement signed at the Earth Summit. It is widely recognized as an international blueprint, a global plan of action for achieving sustainability in the twentieth century. Over 180 governments agreed to Agenda 21 in 1992 at the Earth Summit. The countries that approved the same are to be monitored by the United Nations Commission on Sustainable Development, and are encouraged to promote Agenda 21 at all levels (local, regional, national and global levels). Agenda 21 outlines the actions that international communities, governments, NGOs, international organizations, civil society and communities can take to realize the aim of a sustainable world (Cunningham et al. 1994, 855). It also recognizes the importance of everyone, including governmental agencies, NGOs, civil society and local organizations, in building a sustainable future.

Agenda 21 is primarily divided into following four sections (UN 1992d, 2.1–40.30):

Section 1: Social Economic Dimensions

This section contains recommendations for achieving global cooperation to accelerate sustainable development in developing countries. It also outlines a plan for combating poverty, changing consumption patterns, protecting human health, promoting sustainable human settlement, disseminating knowledge concerning the links between demographic trends and sustainable development and integrating environment and development at all levels (policymaking, planning and management).

Section 2: Conservation and Management of Resources for Development

This section outlines the areas which are to be conserved and managed in order to achieve sustainable development. It includes the recommended actions for the protection of the atmosphere, an integrated approach to the planning and management of land resources, combating deforestation, managing fragile ecosystems (combating desertification and drought), strengthening knowledge about the ecology and sustainable development of mountain ecosystems, promoting sustainable agriculture and rural development, conservation of biological diversity, environmentally sound management of biotechnology, protection of the quality of water resources and environmentally sound management of toxic chemicals, hazardous wastes, solid water and sewage-related issues, and radioactive wastes.

Section 3: Strengthening the Role of Major Groups

This section highlights the role of all stakeholders (state and non-state actors) at both global and national levels in achieving sustainable development. It is concerned with the global action to include women in efforts towards sustainable development, the role of youth in the protection of the environment and the promotion of sustainable development, recognizing and strengthening the role of indigenous peoples in promoting environmentally sound development, strengthening the role non-governmental organizations, local authorities, workers and their trade unions, business and industry, scientific and technical community, and farmers in achieving the sustainable development.

Section 4: Means of Implementation

This last and fourth section identifies the means and resources required to ensure and review the implementation of Agenda 21. It is related to financial resources and mechanisms to transfer environmentally sound technology, cooperation building, strengthening and enhancing the scientific basis for sustainable development, promoting education, public awareness and training, promotion of national mechanisms and international cooperation for capacity building in developing countries, international institutional arrangements, international legal instruments and mechanisms, and strengthening the exchange of information for decision-making.

In this way, Agenda 21 covers a wide number of issues and aspects relating to environmental management and sustainable development. It sketches out the actions, objectives, strategies, activities and means of implementation. It is a very comprehensive document—comprised of more than 300 pages—aimed at addressing contemporary environmental problems and achieving development in harmony with the nature. Agenda 21 has been acknowledged to broaden the conceptualization of development in harmony with the nature. While emphasising its importance, Maurice Strong—the conference's secretary general at Rio—stated that it 'stands as the most comprehensive, most far-reaching and, if implemented, the most effective programme of international action ever sanctioned by the international community. It is not a final and complete action programme, but one which must continue to evolve' (Veon 2014, 1).

United Nations Framework Convention on Climate Change (UNFCCC)

The United Nations Framework Convention on Climate Change was another significant achievement of the Rio summit. The letter was signed and ratified by over 160 countries in 1992 in Rio. The UNFCCC consists of 26 principles that aim to reduce the concentration of greenhouse gases (GHGs)—causing a greenhouse effect and global warming—in the atmosphere by limiting emissions. It is a legally binding treaty requiring the state to limit and reduce the emission of harmful GHGs such as carbon dioxide and methane, responsible for global warming. The key objective of the UNFCCC was to 'provide an international framework within which future actions could be taken to reduce the threat of global warming' (UN 1992e, 3). In other words, the UNFCCC aims to stabilize the concentration of greenhouse gases in the atmosphere so that the global warming system may also become stable.

The UNFCCC established the fact that human activities, such as the burning of fossil fuels and oil, are primarily responsible for the increase in atmospheric concentrations of greenhouse gases (GHGs) such as nitrous oxide, carbon dioxide, methane and water vapour, among others (see Figure 8.2). These

FIGURE 8.2 Greenhouse Gas (GHG) Molecules

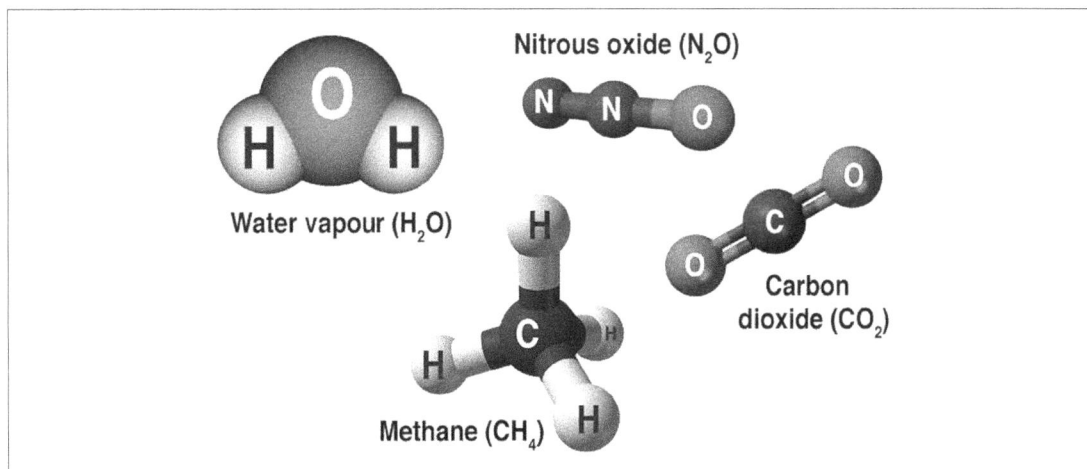

Source: NASA (2018).

gases are a major contributor to the greenhouse effect and global warming. At the same time, UNFCCC recognizes the right of the nations to exploit their natural resources, but their activities should not harm the environmental resources of other nation. Owing to its detailed recommendations and principles, the UNFCCC later become a blueprint for preparing an action plan and policy against the global problem of climate change.

Given the fact that the developed nations, in comparison to developing ones, produce most of the world's greenhouse emissions, the UNFCCC urges the developed nations (rich countries) not just to lead in fighting global warming, but also to offer financial and technological assistance to the developing nations (poor countries), allowing their transition to sustainable and environment-friendly development. The convention called on countries to stabilize emission of greenhouse gases at the 1990 level by 2000. However, the latter objective was revised in 1997 at the third Conference of the Parties (COP) to the UNFCCC held in Kyoto, Japan—the Kyoto Protocol was the significant outcome of this conference, and will be discussed in detail in the following section.

Kyoto Protocol (1997)

Five years after the Rio Conference or Earth Summit of 1992, a conference on climate change was convened at Kyoto in December 1997 to review the progress and outline future plans. The multinational negotiations at the Kyoto conference led to the addition of a protocol to the UNFCCC. The protocol is widely known as the Kyoto Protocol. It was tabled for signatures in 1998 at the UN headquarters (New York) and by March 1999, the protocol had received 84 signatures. As of April 2018, there are 192 parties to the Kyoto Protocol (UNFCCC 2018). Notably, this protocol was another honest attempt by the international community to achieve the UNFCCC's objectives pertaining to 'stabilisation of the greenhouse gas concentrations in the atmosphere at a level that would prevent dangerous anthropogenic interference with the climate system' (UN 1992e).

The Kyoto Protocol is one of the most significant international legally binding agreements mandating country-by-country reduction in GHG emissions. Some of the main features of the protocol are as follows (UN 1998):

- The protocol sets legally binding targets or commitments to reduce greenhouse gas emission for the Annex I parties. The targets were the outcome of the Berlin Mandate,[3] with the UNFCCC negotiations paving the way for the protocol.
- In order to comply with the Kyoto Protocol obligations, the countries with reduction targets are required to design a national strategy and action plan for reducing the GHG emissions. In addition, the protocol contains three mechanisms that Annex I parties can use to obtain credit for reducing emissions in other countries.
- The Kyoto Protocol contains a special provision to meet the needs of developing countries. Such countries not only have legally binding reduction targets, but they are also empowered with additional financial resources, including for the transfer of technology.

---

[3] The Berlin Mandate is an agreement adopted at the first Conference of the Parties (COP 1) to the United Nations Framework Convention on Climate Change (UNFCCC) in April 1995. The mandate was designed to make reductions of greenhouse gas emissions mandatory.

- To ensure the implementation of the Kyoto Protocol, the parties to the protocol meetings shall consistently review and revise their strategies during the Conferences of the Parties (COPs).
- A Compliance Committee is to be established to enforce compliance with the commitments under the Kyoto Protocol.

Given the industrialization activities of over 150 years causing the current high levels of GHGs in the atmosphere, the Kyoto Protocol recognized the historical contribution of developed countries to the present climate change. Hence, the protocol places a heavy burden on industrialized nations or developed countries by following the principle of 'common but differentiated responsibilities' (CBDR)—see Box 8.1. The Kyoto Protocol puts the various nations largely into two categories: first, developed countries or industrialized nations are placed in Annex 1 Parties (those having legally binding targets of cutting GHG emissions), and secondly, developing countries or poor nations are placed under Non-Annex 1 Parties (those not having binding reduction commitments).

The Kyoto Protocol contains the following three 'Kyoto Mechanisms' or 'flexibility mechanisms' to help the Annex 1 parties in meeting their emission commitments (UN 1998):

1. International Emissions Trading (IET)

This allows the Annex 1 parties with targets to buy and sell credits among themselves.

2. Clean Development Mechanism (CDM)

This enables the countries with emission-reduction commitments to earn credits by investing in emission-reduction projects in developing countries. For example, the Annex 1 party with targets can earn credits by investing in projects like installation of solar plants, clean-burning natural gas plants and energy-efficient boilers in the developing country.

BOX 8.1: 'Common but Differentiated Responsibilities'

The principle of 'common but differentiated responsibilities' (CBDR) is one of the dominating principles that governs the contemporary international environmental regime and negotiations. It is 'evolved from the notion of the "common heritage of mankind" and is a manifestation of general principles of equity in international law' (CISDL 2002, 1). The principle largely entails two key elements: first, common responsibility and, secondly, differentiated responsibility. The former underlines the collective responsibilities or obligations of all states towards the protection of the environment while the latter recognizes the differences existing between the stated responsibilities of industrialized and developing countries owing to their historical contributions to global environmental degradation and problems, and differences in their respective abilities to deal with these problems. Hence, the principle of CBDR stresses upon differing obligations of developed and developing states in line with the historical differences in their role in producing most global ecological problems.

3. Joint Implementation (JI)

This is defined in Article 6 of Kyoto Protocol, allowing the Annex 1 party with targets to engage in project-based trading with another Annex 1 party. In other words, it enables industrialized nations to meet their emission-reduction targets by paying for projects that cut the GHG emissions in other industrialized nations (UN 1998).

In this way, the parties with targets can use the 'flexibility mechanisms' to obtain credits by reducing GHG emissions in other countries. The Kyoto Protocol also marked the first instance in the history of environmental protection where the industrialized nations or developed countries agreed to take on legally binding emission-reduction targets for the following six major GHGs (UN 1998, 19):

- Carbon dioxide (CO_2)
- Methane (CH_4)
- Nitrous oxide (N_2O)
- Hydrofluorocarbons (HFCs)
- Perfluorocarbons (PFCs)
- Sulphur hexafluoride (SF_6)

The Kyoto Protocol was adopted on 11 December 1997 and came into force on 16 February 2005. At the seventh session of the COP held in Marrakesh, Morocco, in 2001, the detailed rules for the implementation of the protocol's targets were adopted. It is generally referred to as the 'Marrakesh Accords'.[4] The first commitment period of the Kyoto Protocol started in 2006 and ended in 2012. On 8 December 2012, the new, second commitment period of the Kyoto Protocol was agreed at the COP 18 held in Doha, Qatar. It is also known as the 'Doha Amendment to the Kyoto Protocol'. The protocol's second commitment period started in 2013 and will be completed in 2020. In agreement with the second commitment, 75 countries—including India—agreed to reduce their overall GHG emissions by at least 18% below the 1990 levels.

Given their status as Non-Annex 1 Parties, developing countries such as India and China do not have the legally binding targets for reducing GHG emissions under the Kyoto Protocol's provisions. However, international pressure has been exerted on these developing nations of the Global South to contribute more actively in reducing the global emissions by accepting legally binding targets like developed countries, particularly since these countries appeared among the group of top 10 emitters (Ferreira 2016, 31). By 2015, China had become the largest emitter of CO_2 (one of the major GHGs), followed by the US, whereas India had risen to third place, followed by Russia, as shown in Figure 8.3.

The Kyoto Protocol, an extension to the UNFCCC, has widely been considered a significant step towards reducing the global emissions of GHGs. It has also provided a roadmap to future international agreements on climate change. However, reports published in the first two years after the commencement of the protocol indicated that most of the parties failed to meet their emission-reduction targets. The critics insisted that even if the reduction targets were met, the overall impact on environmental health would not be significant, because the world's two largest emitters of GHGs—China and the US—were not bound by the protocol. China is a party to the Kyoto Protocol but it does not have binding

---

[4] The 'Marrakesh Accords' was a proposal under the United Nations Framework Convention on Climate Change that was adopted in 2001. It defined the rules and procedures in detail for meeting the GHG emission reduction targets set in the Kyoto Protocol.

FIGURE 8.3 Countrywise Share in Global CO_2 Emissions (2005)

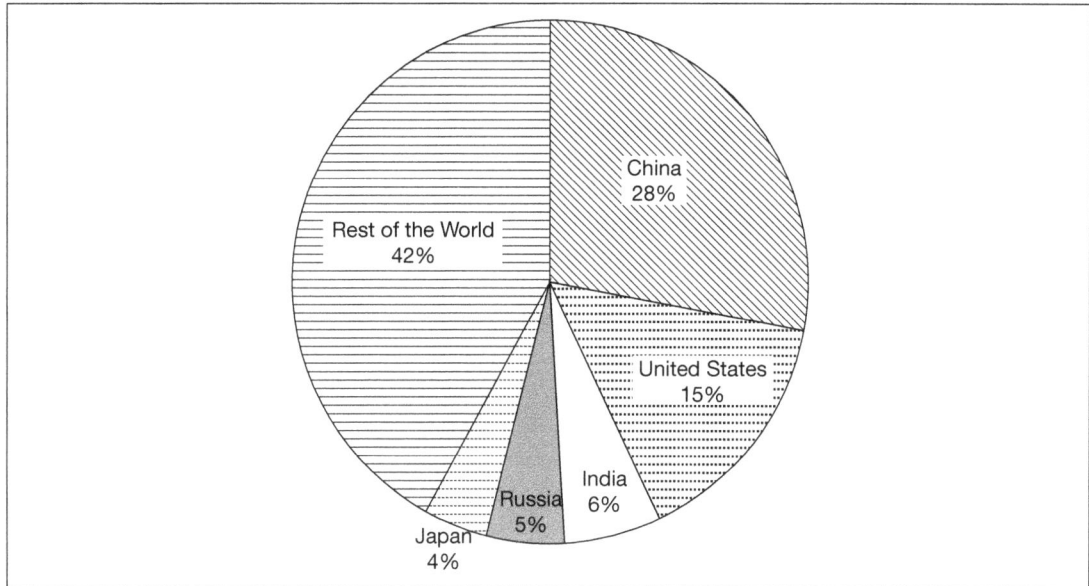

Source: Union of Concerned Scientists (UCS), 2017 (modified).

targets because of its developing country status and the US has not ratified the protocol. Other critics state that the emission-reduction targets are too modest to make any significant positive effect on the continuously rising global temperatures. Despite these limitations, one cannot deny the significance of the Kyoto Protocol in strengthening the global efforts in combating climate change.

Paris Agreement (2015)

The Paris Agreement, also known as the Paris Climate Accord or the Paris Climate Agreement, was adopted on 12 December 2015 by 195 nations at the twenty-first Conference of the Parties to the UNFCCC (COP21). The Paris Agreement is another noteworthy attempt to enhance the implementation of the UNFCCC. It offers a new, universal, legally binding framework to combat the global threat of climate change and strengthen the globally coordinated efforts towards a sustainable future beyond 2020. In other words, the Paris Climate Agreement is intended to replace the Kyoto Protocol after its second commitment period ends in January 2020. The agreement is primarily aimed at keeping the rise in global temperature to well below 2 degrees Celsius above pre-industrial levels and limiting the temperature increase to 1.5 degrees Celsius (UNFCCC 2015a, 3). Also, the agreement intends to strengthen the global capability of dealing with the potential impacts of climate change.

The following are the other key elements of the Paris Agreement:

- Recognizing the limitations of developing countries, the developed nations pledge to quicken the pace of action for reducing emissions to meet the temperature goal.

- The EU and other developed countries agree to provide continued financial and technological support to the developing countries, enabling them to develop their mitigation and adaptation mechanisms.
- The governments agree to take appropriate measures to develop the societal capacity of dealing with the impacts of climate change.
- The agreement recognizes the significant role of non-state actors or non-party stakeholders such as NGOs, civil society, private organizations and MNCs in addressing climate change.
- To maintain robust transparency and accountability, the parties are to update each other and the public about their progress on implementing their targets.
- The agreement includes a non-punitive compliance mechanism, supervised by the Committee of Experts (COE).
- The agreement will come into force after 55 countries (contributing at least 55% of global emissions) have submitted their mechanisms for ratification.
- The parties agree to meet every five years to monitor progress, set more ambitious targets as informed by science and submit updated climate plans.
- The agreement outlines the pre-2020 action that has to be followed by the parties to implement the second commitment period of the Kyoto Protocol till 2020.

It is also maintained in the Paris Agreement that its objectives 'will be implemented to reflect equity and the principle of "common but differentiated responsibilities" and respective capabilities, in the light of different national circumstances' (UNFCCC 2015a, 3). In other words, the Paris Climate Agreement, like the Kyoto Protocol, recognizes the different responsibilities of different countries, thus requiring the developed countries (because of their historical contributions to the environmental problems) to take the lead in addressing the challenge of climate change and to help the developing countries in their mitigation and adaptation plans. In this way, the agreement underlines the need for equity and fairness as stressed by the developing countries.

The Paris Agreement, unlike the 1997 Kyoto Protocol, does not outline country-specific emission-reduction targets but rather puts emphasis on voluntary contributions to climate-change mitigation or sets targets for everyone. More specifically, this agreement 'establishes the obligation of all Parties to contribute to climate change mitigation and adaptation' (Climate Focus 2015, 1). In other words, all parties to the Paris Agreement are required to lead in the fight against global warming by voluntarily preparing their climate-change mitigation and adaptation strategies. For arguably the first time in history, all countries (developed and developing) are required to prepare their national plans on ways to contribute to climate-change mitigation and report to the Secretariat of the UNFCCC their 'Nationally Determined Contributions (NDCs)' (Climate Focus 2015, 1). This is probably why the Paris Agreement is popularly termed as the first legally binding, universal agreement on climate change in the history of environmental protection. In this context, Ban Ki-moon, the Secretary-General of the UN, stated:

> We have entered a new era of global cooperation on one of the most complex issues ever to confront humanity. For the first time, every country in the world has pledged to curb emissions, strengthen resilience and join in common cause to take common climate action. This is a resounding success for multilateralism. (UNFCCC 2015b)

The Paris Climate Agreement, therefore, has marked the emergence of a new international coalition of more than 100 countries committed to tackle climate change. It has steered a middle path between the developed and developing countries by setting an universal responsibility for all. However, the US—the second biggest emitter of GHGs after China—has withdrawn from the Paris Climate Accord at the G20 Hamburg summit held in Germany in June 2017, causing widespread condemnation both inside and outside the country. But it is important to note that except the US, the world's other 19 biggest economic powers reaffirmed their support to the international efforts (including the Paris Agreement) directed to addressing the threat of climate change. The US exit from the agreement has not only posed a serious challenge to global environmental governance, but also put the future of humanity at risk. Instead of setting the trend of withdrawing, the developed and wealthiest countries, such as the US—one of the biggest emitters of GHGs—should take the lead in combating climate change and encourage other nations to come together to save the planet.

Understanding Climate Change and Its Implications

Climate change is one of the most serious environmental issues confronting humanity, as it is inextricably linked to the process of economic development and human security. The UNFCCC defines climate change as 'a change of climate which is attributed directly or indirectly to human activity that alters the composition of the global atmosphere and which is in addition to natural climate variability observed over comparable time periods' (UN 1992c, 3). In other words, climate change refers to the change in global or regional climate patterns that is mainly caused due to anthropogenic emissions. The latter is linked to GHGs primarily emitted into the atmosphere due to human activities. Though both natural and human activities are responsible for increasing emission of GHGs over the last 200 years, natural factors causing climate change take years or sometimes centuries to produce their impacts while the impacts of human activities that cause change in climate systems are visible in a relatively short span of time. In other words, the empirical scientific evidence clearly indicates that human activities are the leading cause of high GHG concentrations in the atmosphere and the earth's rapidly changing climate. In this context, a report prepared by the American Association for the Advancement of Science (AAAS) suggests that 'based on well-established evidence, about 97% of climate scientists conclude that humans are changing the climate' (AAAS 2014, 2).

By the late 1980s, climate change had emerged as a key policy issue at the global level. Scientists, though, have been conducting research on this subject since the nineteenth century and they soon discovered that the presence of carbon dioxide in the atmosphere helps to absorb solar radiation and sunlight, thereby warming up the planet. Of course, carbon dioxide is one of the GHGs, and others are methane, water vapour and nitrous oxide. Nonetheless, carbon dioxide is the most important one of all the GHGs. It is primarily produced through human activities such as burning of fossil fuels (such as coal, oil and natural gas), trees and solid waste and cutting down of forests. Since the Industrial Revolution, countries (particularly the developed ones) have historically relied on fossil fuels to meet their surging energy and transportation demands for swift industrial development, which has significantly increased its usage, thereby emitting great amounts of carbon dioxide—the most plentiful of GHGs—into the atmosphere that has led to anthropogenic disturbance of the natural carbon cycle (Patwardhan 2007, 550–551). It is estimated that the carbon dioxide concentration in the atmosphere has drastically increased by about 80% between 1970 and 2004. Power generation and road transport have largely contributed to the high carbon dioxide emissions (IPCC 2008, 3).

Remarkably, before the Industrial Revolution in 1750, the atmospheric concentrations of carbon dioxide in the atmosphere were reported to be around 280 parts per million by volume (ppmv), but it had reached to 379 ppm by 2005, increased by almost 100 ppmv compared to its pre-industrial level (IPCC 2008, 648). The emission of carbon dioxide has been continuously rising by 1.5 ppmv per year. If this emission trend continues, the concentration of atmospheric CO_2 would be around 500 ppmv by the end of this century, almost double its pre-industrial level (Patwardhan 2007, 551). Furthermore, in comparison to other GHGs, the growing rate of carbon dioxide emissions in the atmosphere is reported to be slightly higher. For example, the emission of GHGs in the last three decades has 'increased by an average of 1.6% per year with carbon dioxide emissions from the use of fossil fuels growing at a rate of 1.9% per year' (IPCC 2008, 97). In this way, since the Industrial Revolution, the atmospheric concentrations of carbon dioxide have been continuously increasing largely due to human activities.

Studies also have shown that 'even if emissions of greenhouse gases were stabilised immediately, it would take many years for the climate system to reach a new quasi-steady state, and some changes (such as sea level rise) would continue to happen' (Patwardhan 2007, 553). In other words, the attempts to cut GHG emissions do have very huge and immediate costs, though the benefits might not be visible for a long period. Therefore, it takes time for the climate system to become stable or to reach the previous state.

Impacts of Climate Change

In recent years, climate change has become a major worldwide concern as it poses perhaps the most serious threat to both national and human security. Its impacts on both natural ecosystems and human health are significant and far-reaching.

Global Warming

The higher concentration of GHGs in the atmosphere increases the temperature of the earth by trapping more heat from the sun in the atmosphere, and thus causing a greenhouse effect and global warming, which refers to a gradual increase in the earth's surface temperature (Figure 8.4). The drastic increase in GHG emissions has increased the average global temperature by 0.74 degrees Celsius since systematic temperature measurements began in the middle of the nineteenth century (Patwardhan 2007, 551). The Intergovernmental Panel on Climate Change (IPCC) in its fourth assessment report concluded that the earth's average temperature would be further increased by between 2 and 4 degrees Celsius by the end of the twentieth-first century (IPCC 2007). Global warming has therefore become one of the most serious environmental crises facing humanity today as it leads to the emergence of other environmental problems.

Melting of Glaciers and Sea Ice

Global warming—associated with climate change—has led to a great decline in the volume of water stored as sea ice, especially because of the melting of glaciers and the Arctic sea ice, which raises sea levels. In other words, with more atmospheric concentration of GHGs (mainly of carbon dioxide), glaciers and Arctic ice absorb more radiation, thereby melting rapidly. The coolest place on the earth is now increasingly warming up, and has been especially over the past several decades. Many scientific studies

FIGURE 8.4 Greenhouse Effect

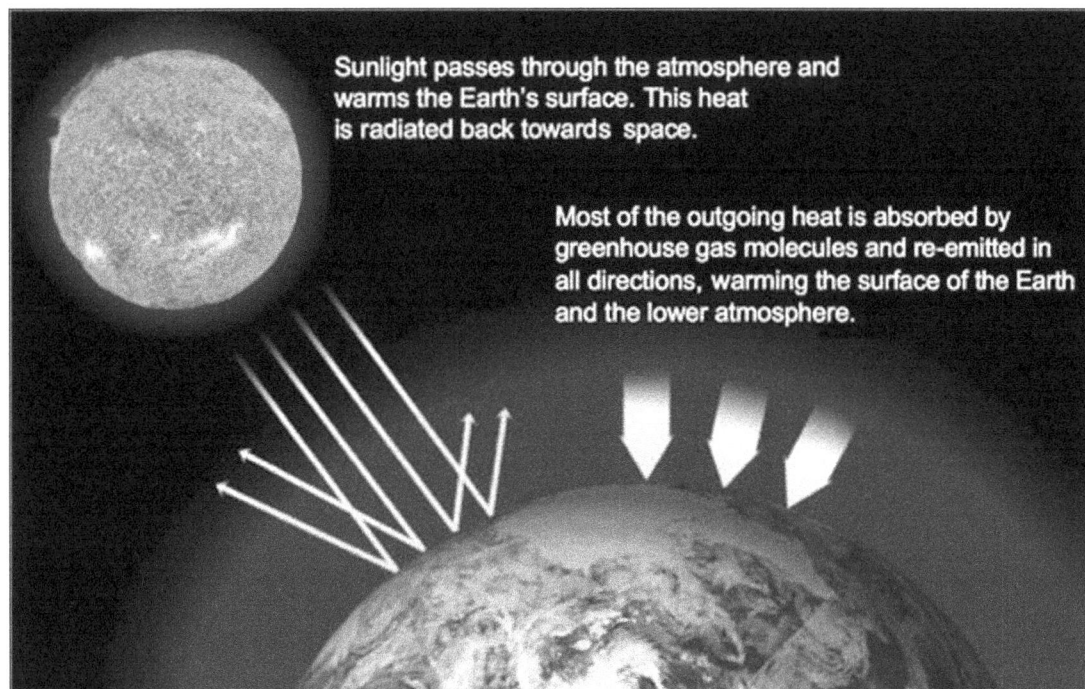

Sunlight passes through the atmosphere and warms the Earth's surface. This heat is radiated back towards space.

Most of the outgoing heat is absorbed by greenhouse gas molecules and re-emitted in all directions, warming the surface of the Earth and the lower atmosphere.

Source: NASA 2018 (modified).

have concluded that 'if present trends continue, all glaciers could be gone by 2030 and most glaciers in the European Alps could be gone by the end of the century' (Botkin and Keller 2012, 412). In addition to the melting of glaciers, Arctic sea ice coverage in the northern hemisphere has declined by 10.7% per decade since the 1970s when satellite remote sensing was started. If this trend continues, Arctic sea could be ice-free by the year 2030 (Botkin and Keller 2012, 412–415). In this way, as the planet warms, the more the sea ice shrinks.

Rise in Sea Level

The continuous increase in temperature has also contributed to a rise in sea level due to the melting of glaciers and of the Greenland and Antarctic ice sheets. The US Global Change Research Program in its report concluded that 'sea level has risen by about 8 inches since reliable record keeping began in 1880' (USGCRP 2016, 115). The IPCC in its second assessment report observed that increased GHG emissions would increase the sea level by between 15 and 95 centimetres by the year 2100 (Patwardhan 2007, 552). It is projected that a rise of half a metre in sea level would not only pose a serious threat to marine eco-systems and organisms, but also adversely impacts the habitats and livelihoods of the large numbers of people living in the coastal regions. Climate-sensitive livelihoods such as agriculture and fisheries are the major source of income for a greater proportion of the coastal population that is being threatened due to change in climate. In other words, the rising sea level could directly devastate the lives of the majority of the coastal population—particularly in the developing countries, where a large number of people live in coastal regions—by displacing them from their homelands and abolishing their sources of income. Moreover, over 50 million people on earth live in the coastal regions. As the sea level rises, these people become more vulnerable to high tides and coastal flooding caused by storm surges. Also, many of the coastal areas and small islands, such as Tuvalu and Marshall Islands, could be threatened (or may disappear if the trends continue) by the rising sea level, as shown in Figure 8.5 (Botkin and Keller 2012, 412).

Change in Biological Diversity

Biological diversity or biodiversity is generally defined as the number of species of plants, animals, fungi and microorganisms or conditions such as terrestrial, mountain, forest and marine ecosystems on earth (Botkin and Keller 2012, 128). Climate change has led to some significant changes in overall biodiversity. Every animal and plant species occurs within a particular range of temperatures. The increase in temperatures has shifted the temperature range and thus affected the altitudinal and latitudinal patterns of organisms. Therefore, as the planet has gotten warmer, many of the 'plants and animals, on land and in the oceans, have begun moving toward the poles... some terrestrial species are moving up

FIGURE 8.5 Marshall Islands Feeling the Effects of Rising Sea Levels

Source: Denchak (2017).

mountainsides, and marine species are moving to deeper depths and higher latitudes' (AAAS 2014, 4). These changes have been observed on every continent and in every ocean. Such changes in biological diversity can fundamentally transform whole ecosystems. Surprisingly, recent research has also shown that many species 'went extinct as a result of climate change during the past 2.5 million years' (Botkin and Keller 2012, 415). The number of extinctions is likely to increase in the coming decades as climate change combines with other human-related ecological pressures.

Effects on Human Health

The influences of climate change and weather on human health and well-being are significant in many ways. It affects human health largely in two main ways: first, by altering the 'severity or frequency of health problems that are already affected by climate or weather factors; and second, by creating unprecedented or unanticipated health problems or health threats in places where they have not previously occurred' (USGCRP 2016, 4). Some of the effects of climate change are already being reported. For example, climate change has increased human exposure to extreme temperatures or heat waves, worsened air quality, infections transmitted through food, water and disease vectors (such as fleas, ticks and mosquitoes) and stresses to our mental health and well-being, as shown in Table 8.2. It should be noted that 'some of these health threats will occur over longer time periods, or at unprecedented times of the year; some people will be exposed to threats not previously experienced in their locations. Overall, instances of potentially beneficial health impacts of climate change are limited in number and pertain to specific regions or populations' (USGCRP 2016, 2). For example, the marginalized and vulnerable groups such as the poor, elderly people and children are prone to infections from heat waves and degraded air quality. Moreover, long-term exposure to extreme temperatures also adversely impacts chronic conditions by increasing respiratory illnesses, cardiovascular disease, cerebrovascular disease and diabetes-related disorders (USGCRP 2016, 6). In that sense, as the climate continues to change, the risks to human health are expected to intensify in coming years.

In this way, climate change significantly impacts both environmental and human health in many ways. Some of the impacts are already occurring on a large scale and they are likely to increase over the coming years.

Climate Change and National Security

Climate change also poses a serious challenge to national security, particularly in coastal regions. Ecological problems (resulting from changes in the climate) such as rising sea levels, storms, floods, the unavailability of freshwater and poor agriculture productivity adversely affect the coastal population. In addition, climate change has contributed to geopolitical problems. For example, the scarcity of natural resources such as water and food and the spread of vector-borne and waterborne diseases due to climate change would be expected to spur migration on a massive level that could increase resource competition as well as pressures on society, the economy and government institutions. Several reports suggest that these pressures can trigger violence within communities and individual groups. It is a well-recognized fact that in recent years in Syria, the large scale of displacement of the people 'because of water scarcity and agricultural failure [has exacerbated] tensions that led to civil unrest' (USGCRP 2016, 5). Therefore, the international community today considers climate change a major threat to individual, national and global security.

TABLE 8.2 Climate Change Impacts on Human Health

	Climate Driver	Health Outcome	Impact
Extreme Heat	More frequent, severe, prolonged heat events	Elevated temperatures	Rising temperatures will lead to an increase in heat increase in heat-related deaths.
Outdoor Air Quality	Increasing temperatures and changing precipitation matter	Worsened air quality (ozone, particulate matter, and higher pollen counts)	Rising temperatures and wildfires and decreasing precipitation, will lead to increase in ozone and particulate matter, elevating the risk of cardiovascular and respiratory illnesses and death.
Flooding	Rising sea level and more frequent or intense extreme precipitation, hurricanes, and storm surge events	Contaminated water, debris, and disruptions to essential infrastructure	Increased coastal and inland flooding exposes populations to a range of negative health impacts before, during, and after events.
Vector-born Infection (Lyme Disease)	Changes in temperature extremes and seasonal weather patterns	Earlier and geographically expanded tick activity	Ticks will show earlier seasonal activity and a generally northward range expansion, increasing risk of human exposure to Lyme disease-causing bacteria.
Water-related Infection (Vibrio Vulnificus)	Rising sea surface temperature, changes in precipitation and runoff affecting coastal salinity	Recreational water or shellfish contaminated with Vibrio vulnificus	Increases in water temperatures will alter timing and location of Vibrio vulnificus growth, increasing exposure and risk of water-borne illness.
Food-related Infection (Salmonella)	Increases in temperature, humidity, and season length	Increased growth of pathogens, seasonal shifts in infection, incidence of Salmonella exposure	Rising temperatures increase Salmonella prevalence in food; longer seasons and warming winters increase risk of exposure and infection.
Mental Health and Well-being	Climate change impact especially extreme weather	Level of exposure to traumatic events, like disasters	Changes in exposure to climate-or weather-related disasters cause or exacerbate stress and mental health consequences with greater risk for certain populations.

Source: USGCRP 2016 (modified).

Global Responses to Climate Change

Local problems require local solutions and global problems require global solutions. Climate change is a global problem today as its nature is very complex and its impacts are multifaceted, demanding urgent global solutions in conjunction with strong commitments at national and local levels. Thus, over the past three decades, the international community has evolved varied mechanisms and announced new initiatives to address the threat of climate change.

The first formal negotiations, at the global level, started in 1991 under the auspices of the UN to prepare an international action plan on climate change protection that eventually resulted in the emergence of the UNFCCC. The latter is one of most noteworthy outcomes of Earth Summit held at Rio in 1992 as discussed earlier. It requires the parties to limit the emission of GHGs, including carbon dioxide, by 'addressing anthropogenic emissions by sources and removals by sinks of all greenhouse gases… [as well as facilitating] adequate adaptation to climate change' (UN 1992e, 5). In other words, its principal objective was to stabilize the density of GHGs in the atmosphere at 1990 emission levels on the basis of CBDR, which dominates the contemporary discourse on climate change. Given their historical contributions to the current level of GHG concentration in the atmosphere, the UNFCCC emphasizes the fact that the developed countries—in accordance with CBDR—should lead the global efforts to mitigate climate change by committing themselves to stabilize the emissions at safe levels. Nonetheless, it is important to note that the UNFCCC just offers a framework for further action and it does not set out any legally-binding targets or timeline for reducing the emissions as discussed earlier. Overall, the Earth Summit (associated with the creation of the UNFCCC) marked the first ever gathering of the international community on the issue of climate change.

Since the Earth Summit of 1992, negotiations on setting legally-binding targets for reducing GHG emission were started mainly to strengthen the UNFCCC. These negotiations finally resulted in the adoption of the Kyoto Protocol in 1997. The protocol requires the parties (especially the developed or industrialized countries) to reduce the emission of principal GHGs—carbon dioxide, methane, nitrous oxide, hydrofluorocarbons, perfluorocarbons and sulphur hexafluoride—by committing themselves to binding targets. The targets were designed to reduce total GHG emissions to 5.2% below 1990 levels by 2012. The protocol also contains the three important 'Kyoto Mechanisms' or 'flexibility mechanisms', evolved to help the parties with targets in meeting their emissions obligations. In that sense, the Kyoto Protocol is the most significant international treaty on climate change. However, it also has certain limitations. For instance, the developed countries such as the US and Australia did not ratify the Kyoto Protocol, citing the absence of binding emission targets for developing countries such as India and China, as discussed in the preceding section.

The Paris Climate Agreement (2015) is another landmark agreement on global climate change within the UNFCCC. It primarily aims to consolidate efforts to combat climate change by keeping the global temperature rise to well under a 2 degrees Celsius above pre-Industrial Era levels, and by encouraging efforts to further limit the temperature increase to 1.5 degrees Celsius. The Paris Agreement has set states' voluntary minimum obligations, recognized the limitations of developing countries, provided financial and technological support to poor countries, strengthened transparency and emphasized the role of non-state actors in addressing climate change. Under the agreement, every individual country (for the first time) is required to develop a specific plan to reduce its GHG emissions in accordance with 'Nationally Determined Contributions' as it does not set country-by-country targets, as discussed above. As of November 2017, 197 countries have signed the Paris Agreement and 169 parties have ratified it.

BOX 8.2: Intergovernmental Panel on Climate Change (IPCC)

The Intergovernmental Panel on Climate Change (IPCC) is the leading international body for the assessment of climate change. It was established by the UNEP and the World Meteorological Organization (WMO) in 1988 to provide the world with a clear scientific view on the current state of knowledge in climate change and its potential environmental and socio-economic impacts. In the same year, the UN General Assembly endorsed the action by the WMO and UNEP in jointly establishing the IPCC.

The IPCC reviews and assesses the most recent scientific, technical and socio-economic information produced worldwide, relevant to the understanding of climate change. It does not conduct any research nor does it monitor climate-related data or parameters.

As an intergovernmental body, membership of the IPCC is open to all member countries of the UN and the WMO. Currently 195 countries are members of the IPCC. Governments participate in the review process and the plenary sessions, where the main decisions about the IPCC's work programme are taken and reports are accepted, adopted and approved. The IPCC Bureau Members, including the Chair, are also elected during the plenary Sessions.

Thousands of scientists from all over the world contribute to the work of the IPCC. Review is an essential part of the IPCC process, to ensure an objective and complete assessment of current information. The IPCC aims to reflect a range of views and expertise. The Secretariat coordinates all the IPCC work and liaises with governments. It is established by the WMO and the UNEP and located at the WMO headquarters in Geneva. The IPCC is administered in accordance to WMO and UN rules and procedures, including codes of conduct and ethical principles (UN 2006).

Because of its scientific and intergovernmental nature, the IPCC embodies a unique opportunity to provide rigorous and balanced scientific information to decision makers. By endorsing the IPCC reports, governments acknowledge the authority of their scientific content. The work of the organization is therefore policy-relevant and yet policy-neutral, never policy-prescriptive.

Source: IPPC (2018).

However, after the withdrawal of the US in 2017, the critics have not only challenged its central claim of being 'applicable to all' states, but also raised questions on the international environmental governance that failed to bring all countries together (EPA 2017). At the same time, any global attempt or agreement to cut GHG emissions would have been insignificant without the whole-hearted support of the US, which is the second biggest emitter country after China.

In the past few decades, the ideological confrontations between the states of Global South and North have adversely affected the different environmental agreements including those related to climate change. In the context of climate change, the Global South often claims that global efforts should be based on the principles of historical responsibility and CBDR. More specifically, given its historical role in environmental degradation, the Global North has the moral obligation to lead in the fight against climate change and global warming, thereby accepting legally-binding emission cuts. On the other side, the countries of Global South have a limited responsibility in mitigating climate change and thus, not morally oblige to accept emission cuts. Nonetheless, the Global North contends that climate change today poses a serious threat to the whole world and humanity, so the Global South should accept legally binding emission cuts to protect human civilization. Considering their historical responsibility, the developed countries of Global North are required to lead the whole world in a fight against climate change, the most serious challenge facing humanity today. At the same time, it is also desirable that developing countries such as China, India and Brazil must explore greenways of generating energy such as solar energy, wind energy, and hydro-electricity and reduce the use of GHGs. Because any attempt of reducing the greenhouse gas emissions would not yield success in long run without the support of the largest emitters such as China and the US.

Global Commons Debate

Globalization has brought the world much closer as a human family that, in a way, yields the feeling of togetherness among the people. In fact, the driving forces of globalization have converted the world into a 'global village' in which people living across the seven continents—Africa, Antarctica, Asia, Australia Europe, North America and South America—belong to the same community. In fact, our lives in the twenty-first century are greatly influenced and shaped by the global phenomena (social, economic, political, cultural, environmental, and so on) occurring across the world. Furthermore, natural resources—particularly those that are not situated within the political boundaries of any sovereign nation state—are considered 'common'. Such resources are broadly recognized as 'global commons' in the era of globalization. The Brundtland Report, also known as *Our Common Future*, from the World Commission on Environment and Development (WCED), defines the global commons as 'those parts of the planet that fall outside national jurisdictions' (UN 1987, 216). In other words, the term 'global commons' indicates those resource areas that do not come within the jurisdiction of any particular state and hence are accessible to all nation states. International law formally identifies four global commons: the high seas, the atmosphere, Antarctica and outer space (Nakicenovic et al. 2016, iv).

In the absence of governmental mechanisms and rules to control and regulate their use, the commons have been guided by the principle of 'common heritage of mankind' and 'free access' or 'mare liberum' (free sea for all nations) that has led to their over-exploitation and overuse. For example, uncontrolled human activities have adversely altered the composition of the global atmosphere, resulting in environmental problems such as depletion of the ozone layer and global warming. Similarly, it is observed that the 'fish and whale stocks of the high seas have been relentlessly over-exploited to the point where some species have been wiped out and long-term protein sources for human beings are imperilled' (Baylis, Smith and Owens 2008, 358). In this context, one theory—the 'tragedy of the commons', as coined by Garrett Hardin—suggests that natural resources under common ownership, in comparison to those individually owned, are much more prone to over-exploitation and degradation owing to unrestricted and free access to all. The popular example often given to illustrate the latter principle is that of 'grazing lands that are commonly owned in pastoral societies. It is in the interest of an individual to graze as many as livestock as possible, but if too many individuals all have the same attitude, the grazing lands may be overused and degraded; the rational use of resources by an individual may not be rational from the viewpoint of a wider society' (Griffiths et al. 2014, 347–348). In this way, the principle of the 'tragedy of the commons' explains the misuse and abuse of shared resources such as land, sea, air and water, thereby emphasizing the need for governance of the global commons.

Within the national jurisdiction of governments, the problem—pertaining to governing the commons—could have been easily resolved by nationalizing the common resources or turning them into private property, but in the context of the global commons, such a solution is beyond the realms of possibility. Hence international cooperation becomes imperative to manage and govern the global commons (Baylis, Smith and Owens 2008, 359). In the past few decades, few attempts were made at the global level to evolve mechanisms and rules for managing and regulating their use. For example, the United Nations Convention on the Law of the Sea (UNCLOS), or the Law of the Sea Treaty, was adopted in December 1982 to conserve and regulate the fish stocks of the high seas. It defined the rights and responsibilities of states in their use of the world's seas. It also replaced the doctrine of mare liberum by laying down guidelines for the management of the environment and for doing business using marine resources (Nandan et al. 2002, 41–43). In this way, transnational cooperation between the countries, facilitated by international organizations such as the UN, has played a significant role in regulating, monitoring and protecting the global commons.

While the practice of exploiting shared resources could be beneficial for a particular nation in short run, its adverse environmental effects would have a global impact for all. As they are common resources and their effects (good or bad) also have common consequences for all the countries (including developed and developing nations), it is important to note that these shared or common resources are to be managed collectively in consultation with all stakeholders. The mechanism and rules to govern the commons should be guided by the principles of equity and fairness. In other words, international efforts and treaties must not be designed to favour the vested interests of the wealthiest countries over the poor ones. Compared to the developed nations, equal access or sometimes more access is to be provided to the developing countries so that they may use the global commons to advance their national economies. In addition, there is a need to encourage the non-state actors, such as NGOs and global civil society, to spread awareness about the common resources and the effects of losing them among the nations and the people. Overall, the global commons are to be used in a sustainable way not just to provide their benefits to both present and future generations, but also to maintain the health of our planet.

Concluding Observations

This chapter has critically examined the growing significance of the issue of environmental security and the international measures introduced in this regard. Over the years, international cooperation facilitated by the UN through multinational agreements and treaties has somewhat effectively attempted to respond to different environmental problems such as ozone-layer depletion, climate change, global warming and over-exploitation of the global commons, among others. However, the economic disparities between the developed and developing countries on the one hand and historical contributions to environmental degradation on the other have posed a significant challenge to the global efforts on environmental protection and international environmental regimes. It is important that developed countries such as the US and Australia recognize their moral and historical responsibility of observing measures introduced to prevent degradation of the global environment. Apart from taking stringent actions at home, the developed countries (of the Global North) are required to provide financial and technological assistance to the developing nations (of the Global South) so that they may consolidate their national efforts to combat different ecological challenges. Hence, there is an urgent need to establish an inclusive, accountable, transparent and democratic process of setting environmental norms to address serious ecological issues. If the appropriate measures at the global, national and local levels are not initiated, the future of the human race could be in jeopardy.

Summary

- Ecological issues started gaining prominence in the discourse of global politics by the late 1970s and soon became one of the key global concerns. In fact, environmental security had become one of the most serious security issues by the 1990s, especially for the countries located in the Global South. At the same time, environmental negotiations at the global level today focus on a wide range of ecological issues such as ozone-layer depletion, climate change, deforestation, water pollution, over-exploitation of natural resources, waste disposal and air pollution, among others.

- Until the mid of the twentieth century, global environmental politics and governance were largely limited in their nature and scope. At the outset, the environmental agreements primarily focused on the issues such as preservation of natural resources and impacts of pollution on environment and human health.

- Environment and development are among the most contested phenomena in contemporary global politics, with little in common. The former emphasizes the need to preserve natural resources while the latter stresses upon the extraction and exploitation of the same to yield high economic growth rates.

- International environmental agreements coordinated by various transnational organizations are significant since they enable countries belonging to different contexts to come together on a common platform and work collectively to deal with complex ecological issues. In 1972, the UN organized the first formal Conference on the Human Environment (UNCHE) in Stockholm to discuss measures for protecting the environment from further destruction. This conference marked the commencement of the modern era of environmental governance at both international and national levels.

- The Montreal Protocol, signed in 1987, was the first of its kinds in the history of environmental protection which was designed to protect the stratospheric ozone layer by reducing the global production, emission and usage of ozone-depleting chemical substances within a stipulated time period.

- The 1992 Rio Conference, or Earth Summit, was probably the largest environment conference in the UN history. The Declaration on Environment and Development, the Convention on Biological Diversity (CBD), the United Nations Framework Convention on Climate Change (UNFCCC), the (Rio) Forest Principles and Agenda 21 were the main agreements and documents signed at the conference. In particular, the establishment of the UNFCCC marked the first formal attempt by the international community to stabilize the atmospheric concentrations of greenhouse gases (GHGs).

- The Kyoto Protocol (1997) is one of the most significant international, legally binding agreements mandating country-by-country reduction in GHG emission. The protocol categorizes countries into two groups: one (developed countries) with legally binding GHG emission targets and the other (developing countries) with no mandatory reducing targets.

- The developed and developing countries have divergent opinions on environmental agreements, mandatory emission targets, green-technology subsidies, technology transfer, and so on. The poor nations or developing countries are not willing to give up their right of development by using their natural resources, and also continuously reiterate the historical responsibility of the industrialized nations or developed countries for maximum GHG emissions.

- The Paris Agreement, adopted in 2015, is another noteworthy attempt to enhance the implementation of the UNFCCC. It offers a new universal, legally binding framework to combat the global threat of climate change and strengthen the globally coordinated efforts towards a sustainable future beyond 2020.

- Climate change is one of the most serious environmental issues confronting humanity, as it is inextricably linked to the processes of economic development and human security. The UNFCCC, the Kyoto Protocol and the Paris Climate Agreement are the most noteworthy global attempts to combat climate change.
- Owing to the absence of state mechanisms and rules to control and regulate their use, use of the global commons has been guided by the principles of 'common heritage of mankind' and 'free access' or 'mare liberum', which have led to their over-exploitation and overuse.
- The global commons are to be managed collectively in consultation with all stakeholders, and the mechanisms and rules (at both global and local levels) to govern these commons should be guided by democratic values such as equality and fairness.

Suggested Questions

1. Discuss the international environmental agreements introduced to prevent environment degradation.
2. Summarize the important provisions of the 1987 Montreal Protocol.
3. What were the different outcomes of the Earth Summit held in 1992? How did it help in strengthening the global environmental governance?
4. Critically evaluate the basic elements of the Kyoto Protocol. To what extent was it successful in achieving its objective?
5. What do you understand by 'climate change'? What are the major impacts of climate change on environmental and human health?
6. Describe the principle of 'common but differentiated responsibilities' in the context of the climate-change regime.
7. Discuss the international efforts towards mitigating the dangers of climate change.
8. What do you understand by the term 'global commons'? What initiatives have been taken to preserve biodiversity?

References

American Association for the Advancement of Science (AAAS). 2014. *What We Know: The Reality, Risks, and Response to Climate Change.* Washington: American Association for the Advancement of Science. Accessed 10 April 2018. http://whatweknow.aaas.org/wp-content/uploads/2014/07/whatweknow_website.pdf.

Botkin, Daniel B., and Edward A. Keller. 2012. *Environmental Science*, 8th edn. New Delhi: Wiley.

Baylis, John, Steve Smith and Patricia Owens. 2008. *The Globalization of World Politics: An Introduction to International Relations*, 4th edn. Oxford: Oxford University Press.

CBD. 2018. 'List of Parties to Convention on Biological Diversity'. Accessed 27 April 2018. https://www.cbd.int/information/parties.shtml.

Centre for International Sustainable Development Law (CISDL). 2002. 'The Principle of Common but Differentiated Responsibilities: Origins and Scope'. Accessed 20 April 2018. http://cisdl.org/public/docs/news/brief_common.pdf.

Climate Focus. 2015. *The Paris Agreement: Summary.* Climate Focus Briefing Note, Amsterdam. Accessed 27 April 2018. http://www.climatefocus.com/sites/default/files/20151228%20COP%2021%20briefing%20FIN.pdf.

Cunningham, William P., Terence H. Cooper, Eville Gorham and Malcolm T. Hepworth, eds. 1994. *Environmental Encyclopaedia*. Detroit: Gale Research.

Denchak, Melissa. 2017. *Global Climate Change: What You Need to Know*. Natural Resources Defense Council. Accessed 28 April 2018. https://www.nrdc.org/stories/global-climate-change-what-you-need-know.

EPA (United States Environmental Protection Agency). 2017. *International Treaties and Cooperation*. Accessed 24 April 2018. https://www.epa.gov/ozone-layer-protection/international-treaties-and-cooperation.

Fahey, David W. 2013. 'The Montreal Protocol Protection of Ozone and Climate'. *Theoretical Inquiries in Law* 14 (1): 21–42.

Ferreira, P.G. 2016. 'From Justice to Participation: The Paris Agreement's Pragmatic Approach to Differentiation'. In *Climate Justice: Case Studies in Global and Regional Governance Challenges*, edited by Randall S. Abate, 25–48. Washington D. C.: Environmental Law Institute.

Griffiths, Martin, Terry O'Callaghan, and Steven C. Roach. 2014. *International Relations: The Key Concepts*, 3rd ed. London and New York: Routledge.

Heller, Walter W. 1971. 'Economic Growth and Ecology—An Economist's View'. *Monthly Labor Review* 94 (11): 14–21.

Intergovernmental Panel on Climate Change (IPCC). 2007. *Climate Change 2007: Mitigation of Climate Change. Working Group III Contribution to the Fourth Assessment Report of the Intergovernmental Panel on Climate Change*. Cambridge: Cambridge University Press.

———. 2018. *Organisation*. Accessed 28 April 2018. http://www.ipcc.ch/organization/organization.shtml.

Kochtcheeva, Lada, and Ashbindu Singh. 2000. *An Assessment of Risks and Threats to Human Health Associated with the Degradation of Ecosystems*. Sioux Falls, SD: UNEP Division of Environmental Information.

Mishra, Anand Prasad. 2013. ed. *Population, Development and Environment: A Contemporary Debate*. New Delhi: Concept.

MPWGSC. 2004. *Report of the Commissioner of the Environment and Sustainable Development*. Ontario: Minister of Public Works and Government Services Canada (MPWGSC).

Nakicenovic, N., J. Rockström, O. Gaffney, and C. Zimm. 2016. *Global Commons in the Anthropocene: World Development on a Stable and Resilient Planet*. IIASA Working Paper, WP-16-019. Accessed 28 April 2018. http://pure.iiasa.ac.at/id/eprint/14003/1/WP-16-019.pdf.

Nandan, S.N. et al. eds. 2002. *United Nations Convention on the Law of the Sea 1982: A Commentary*. The Hague: Martinus Nijhoff Publishers.

NASA. 2018. *A Blanket around the Earth*, NASA's Jet Propulsion Laboratory, California Institute of Technology. Accessed 27 April 2018. https://climate.nasa.gov/causes/.

Paehlke, Robert, ed. 1995. *Conservation and Environmentalism: An Encyclopaedia*. London & Chicago: Fitzroy Dearborn Publishers.

Patwardhan, Anand. 2007. 'Global Warming in India'. In *Environmental Issues in India: A Reader*, edited by Mahesh Rangarajan, 550–558. New Delhi: Pearson.

Saunier, Richard E. and Richard A. Meganck. 2009. *Dictionary and Introduction to Global Environmental Governance*, 2nd edn. London: Earthscan.

Singh, Kameshwar Nath 2013. 'Environment, Economy and Sustainable Development'. In *Population, Development and Environment: A Contemporary Debate*, edited by Tara Devi Singh, Anand Prasad Mishra, Arun K. Singh, Archana K. Roy and Narender Verma, 6–9. New Delhi: Concept.

Starke, J. G. 1989. *An Introduction to International Law*, 10th edn. London: Butterworths Law.

UCS. 2017. *Each Country's Share of CO_2 Emissions*, Union of Concerned Scientists, Cambridge. Accessed 27 April 2018. https://www.ucsusa.org/global-warming/science-and-impacts/science/each-countrys-share-of-co2.html#.WuRb0i5ubIU.

UNEP. 2015. *United Nations Environment Programme: Annual Report 2015*. Nairobi: United Nations Environment Programme.

United Nations (UN). 1972. *Report of the United Nations Conference on the Human Environment*. Accessed 22 April 2018. http://www.un-documents.net/aconf48-14r1.pdf.

United Nations (UN). 1987. *Report of the World Commission on Environment and Development: Our Common Future*, United Nations, accessed 28 April 2018. http://www.un-documents.net/our-common-future.pdf.
———. 1992a. *The Rio Declaration on Environment and Development (1992)*. Accessed 15 April 2018. http://www.unesco.org/education/pdf/RIO_E.PDF.
———. 1992b. *Convention on Biological Diversity*. Accessed 27 April 2018. https://www.cbd.int/doc/legal/cbd-en.pdf.
———. 1992c. *Non-Legally Binding Authoritative Statement of Principles for a Global Consensus on the Management, Conservation and Sustainable Development of All Types of Forests'*. Accessed 27 April 2018. http://www.un.org/documents/ga/conf151/aconf15126-3annex3.htm.
———. 1992d. *Agenda 21*. Accessed 27 April 2018. https://sustainabledevelopment.un.org/content/documents/Agenda21.pdf.
———. 1992e. *United Nations Framework Convention on Climate Change*. Accessed 15 April 2018. https://unfccc.int/resource/docs/convkp/conveng.pdf.
———. 1998. *Kyoto Protocol to the United Nations Framework Convention on Climate Change*. Accessed 15 April 2018. https://unfccc.int/resource/docs/convkp/kpeng.pdf.
———. 2006. *Ethics Office*, United Nations. Accessed 28 April 2018. http://www.un.org/en/ethics/.
United Nations Framework Convention on Climate Change (UNFCCC). 2015a. *Adoption of the Paris Agreement*. Accessed 24 Apirl 2018. https://unfccc.int/resource/docs/2015/cop21/eng/l09r01.pdf.
———. 2015b. 'Historic Paris Agreement on Climate Change: 195 Nations Set Path to Keep Temperature Rise Well Below 2 Degrees Celsius'. Accessed 24 April 2018. http://newsroom.unfccc.int/unfccc-newsroom/finale-cop21.
———. 2018. *The Kyoto Protocol - Status of Ratification*, United Nations Framework Convention on Climate Change, Bonn. Accessed 27 April 2018. https://unfccc.int/process/the-kyoto-protocol/status-of-ratification.
US Global Change Research Program (USGCRP). 2016. *The Impacts of Climate Change on Human Health in the United States: A Scientific Assessment*. Washington D. C.: USGCRP. Accessed 10 April 2018. https://s3.amazonaws.com/climatehealth2016/low/ClimateHealth2016_FullReport_small.pdf.
Watson, Robert, ed. 2012. *Environment and Development Challenges: The Imperative to Act*. Tokyo: The Asahi Glass Foundation.

Further Reading

Bailey, Marianne, et al. 2010. *Investing in the Phase-out of Ozone-depleting Substances: The GEF Experience*. Washington: Global Environment Facility (GEF). Accessed 10 April 2018. https://www.thegef.org/sites/default/files/publications/phase-out-2010_en_2.pdf.
Barnett, Jon. 2001. *The Meaning of Environment Security: Ecological Politics and Policy in the New Security Era*. London: Zed Books.
Barry, John, and Robyn Eckersley, eds. 2005. *The State and the Global Ecological Crisis*. Cambridge: MIT Press.
Birnie, Patricia, and Alan Boyle. 2002. *International Law and the Environment*. Oxford: Oxford University Press.
Brenton, Tony. 1994. *The Greening of Machiavelli: The Evolution of International Environment Politics*. London: Earthscan.
Carter, Neil. 2007. *The Politics of the Environment: Ideas, Activism, Policy*, 2nd edn. Cambridge: Cambridge University Press.
DeSombre, Elizabeth R. 2006. *Global Environmental Institutions*. Abingdon: Routledge.
Dryzek, John S. 1997. *The Politics of the Earth: Environmental Discourses*. Oxford: Oxford University Press.
Elliott, Lorraine. 2004. *The Global Politics of the Environment*. Basingstoke: Palgrave.
Jørgensen, Sven Erik, ed. 2008. *Global Ecology: A Derivative of Encyclopaedia of Ecology*. Amsterdam: Elsevier.
IPCC. 2014. *Climate Change 2013: The Physical Science Basis. Working Group I Contribution to the Fifth Assessment Report of the Intergovernmental Panel on Climate Change*. Cambridge: Cambridge University Press.

Lipschutz, Ronnie D. 2004. *Global Environmental Politics: Power, Perspectives, and Practice*. Washington, D.C.: CQ Press.

Sohn, Louis B. 1973. The Stockholm Declaration on the Human Environment, *The Harvard International Law Journal*, Vol 14 (3), 423–515.

UN. 1989. *Multilateral Montreal Protocol on Substances that Deplete the Ozone Layer (with annex). Concluded at Montreal on 16 September 1987*. Accessed 22 April 2018. https://treaties.un.org/doc/publication/unts/volume%201522/volume-1522-i-26369-english.pdf.

Velders, Guus J. M., Stephen O. Andersen, John S. Daniel, David W. Fahey and Mack McFarland. 2007. 'The Importance of the Montreal Protocol in Protecting Climate'. *Proceedings of the National Academy of Sciences of the United States of America (PNAS)*, 104 (12): 4814–4819. Accessed 20 March 2018. https://www.ncbi.nlm.nih.gov/pmc/articles/PMC1817831/pdf/zpq4814.pdf.

Veon, Joan. 2014. 'Sustainable Development, Agenda 21 and Prince Charles'. *News With Views*, 13 August 2004. Accessed 15 April 2018. https://www.newswithviews.com/Veon/joan19.htm.

Viotti, Paul R., and Mark V. Kauppi. 2013. *International Relation and World Politics*, 5th edn. Boston: Pearson.

Nuclear Proliferation

Nirmal Jindal

LEARNING OBJECTIVES

- To understand the impact of nuclear weapons on the concept of war
- To familiarize oneself with the utility of nuclear weapons that motivates nations to proliferate
- To critically examine the role of nuclear non-proliferation measures
- To evaluate the new dangers of nuclear proliferation in the second nuclear age

Nuclear arms control and nuclear non-proliferation have been at the forefront of the international security agenda since 1945. Eminent scientists such as Albert Einstein and Robert Oppenheimer, who contributed to the development of the atom bomb, expressed grave doubts about the future of a nuclear world. War had never before threatened humankind with such grave consequences than after the development of the nuclear bomb. Therefore, since the development of nuclear weapons, a parallel argument in support of nuclear disarmament has also been made in order to make this world free of fear of the dangers of nuclear war and the extermination of human civilization. The issue of nuclear weapons proliferation revolves around two dominant approaches. First, the realist approach emphasizes the significance of nuclear weapons to enhance national security in anarchical international politics. The second viewpoint emphasizes the significance of eliminating such systems to ensure global peace and security. In this regard, international norms can be introduced to constrain nuclear behaviours and appropriate standards can be set up to govern the behaviour of the different countries of the world.

The international community led by the United States (US) has undertaken several measures to control nuclear proliferation. Various treaties and conventions have been introduced to establish security regimes and to counter the uncertainty generated by an arms race and the consequent security dilemma. It is seen that such measures have been largely successful, as they have been able to prevent the majority of nations from acquiring nuclear systems and the number of nuclear countries has been limited in the past six decades of the nuclear age. Without such efforts, the pace of nuclearization would have been much faster in the anarchic self-help system of international politics. Even the countries with a strong economic and technological base to develop nuclear systems have demonstrated self-restraint in acquiring them—for instance, Canada, Australia, Germany, Japan and South Korea. Due to the non-proliferation measures, some of the regions of the world, such as Latin America, South-east Asia, Africa and Central Asia, remain free from nuclear weapons. It is remarkable that some of the newly emerged Russian republics, such as Ukraine, Belarus and Kazakhstan, inherited nuclear weapons after the collapse of the Union of Soviet Socialist Republics (USSR) but they returned their nuclear systems to Russia in exchange for US aid. In 1993, South Africa, which was in possession of six bombs, chose to give up the weapons programme and joined the Treaty on the Non-proliferation of Nuclear Weapons (NPT). However, the world has not become free from nuclear systems as the main attention in introducing non-proliferation measures was to confine the nuclear weapons to the nuclear club of five nations: the US, the USSR, Great Britain, France and China. The proliferation, however, has been more vertical than horizontal as existing nuclear countries have been constantly improving the quality and increasing the quantity of their nuclear arsenals. Therefore, the nuclear club members could not set an ideal example for non-nuclear countries to not acquire nuclear systems. It is alarming that until 1999 there had been only five nuclear countries and they have increased to nine by 2017, which is perceived as a serious threat to world peace and security.

Apart from vertical and horizontal, nuclear proliferation to non-state actors is posing the most serious threat to international peace and security in the age of globalization. Therefore, the international community under the leadership of the US needs to introduce new measures to deal with the complex issue of nuclear proliferation.

In order to understand the necessity for nuclear non-proliferation, the present chapter intends to discuss the implications of the development of nuclear weapons on international politics and their utility in the age of globalization. In this context, it is pertinent to discuss the nature of nuclear weapons: how they are qualitatively different from conventional weapons, how they have revolutionized the character of war and their utility as an instrument of politics. This chapter also discusses the complexities of deterrence and a few critical issues related to arms control and nuclear non-proliferation.

Inauguration of the Nuclear Era: Impact on the Political Utility of War

The development and first use of the atom bomb in 1945 ushered in a new era in the history of international politics. The atomic bombs used against Hiroshima and Nagasaki demonstrated the destructive capability of the bombs, which brought about a qualitative change in the nature of war, which in turn had implications for the political utility of war in the nuclear age.

Destructive Nature of the Bomb

The development of nuclear weapons capable of universal destruction has revolutionized the character of war. 'I have become the death, the destroyer of the world,' quoted Oppenheimer from the Bhagavad Gita as he witnessed the first atomic explosion (Aldridge 1983, 21). During the nuclear explosion, nuclear fission and fusion reactions take place that release a tremendous amount of heat and energy.

These explosions can take place on earth and in air and water. In case of an explosion in the air, a huge ball of fire appears and the temperature of the zone of radiation exceeds 1 million degrees Celsius. The air around the bomb heats up to incandescence and the flash of light can be seen at a distance over a hundred kilometres away. As the ball of fire grows, rapidly reaching 500 m in diameter and expanding in space, it assumes the shape of a mushroom at a height of about 12–15 km, covering the space of several kilometres in the form of a mushroom-shaped flat cloud. Apart from causing direct destruction by heat and fire, the nuclear explosion yields huge quantities of neutrons and gamma rays and includes visible, infrared and ultraviolet radiations. Therefore, it causes tremendous destruction to not only cities and vegetation but also causes a hazard to humans in the local surroundings and in far-off places by carrying radiation afar through wind, clouds and seawater. People can become victims of the fallout, radioactive clouds, ecological damage, pollution of oceans and even genetic mutation. The gamma rays can penetrate the skin and can affect the molecular cell structure. Alpha and beta rays cause burns and cause damage by entering the human organism through contaminated food and water too. Gamma rays can cause various diseases such as leukaemia and cataracts months after exposure. The nuclear explosion can also destroy the ozone layer in the stratosphere, which helps to protect all life on earth from ultraviolet radiation. The exposure to radiation can cause genetic effects that can threaten the entire human race (Kissinger 1957, 85).

During the Second World War, the US used atom bombs against Hiroshima and Nagasaki because it was the only nuclear country and there was no fear of nuclear retaliation against it. Moreover, the bomb was used strategically and diplomatically against the Soviets rather than as a military weapon to defeat Japan. Gar Alperovitz (1965, 191), in his book *Atomic Diplomacy*, argued that the bombs were used to exclude Soviet entry in the war to prevent communist foothold in the Pacific. Japan was almost defeated and would have surrendered after some time even if the US had not used the bombs against Japan. The bombs were used to hasten the end of the war as it had become too expensive for the US in terms of men and materials. The first use of atom bombs demonstrated their destructive nature and the world realized that nuclear weapons could not be easily used as an instrument of foreign policy, but could merely act as weapons of deterrence (Jindal 1987, 19).

Utility of War in the Pre-nuclear Age

War has always existed as a permanent factor in international politics. Various philosophers, scholars and commentators such as Carl von Clausewitz, Vladimir Lenin, Niccoló Machiavelli and Charles Darwin connected power with privilege and progress. Clausewitz, one of the most classical exponents of war, has described war as an act of violence intended to compel one's opponent to fulfil one's will (Jindal 1987, 19). Clausewitz clearly related war with political objectives (Clausewitz 1950, 596). He did not consider war an end in itself but a means or a tool to achieve a political objective. In Clausewitz's words, 'war is an act of violence to compel our opponents to submit to our will' (Brown and Kirsten 2005, 105).

War has appeared as a continuous factor in all parts of the world and throughout the entirety of human history. War was often used by nations to achieve their national interests. Machiavelli also established the decisive role of military power in politics and sowed the seeds of the concept of total war (Machiavelli as cited in Jindal 1987). Mao Zedong also argued that war was a continuation of politics by other means (Mao 1965). In 1960, a Norwegian statistician announced that in 'the 5560 years of recorded human history, there have been 14,531 wars' (Jindal 1987, 10).

Realists considered war as an endemic disease in international politics. War was perceived as a major instrument of securing gains in power, prestige, territory and other resources and of warding off what was perceived as an imminent threat to the security of a nation. James T. Shotwell, in his book *War as an Instrument of National Policy and Its Renunciation in the Pact of Paris*, maintained that most of the great facts of political national history have been established and maintained by war (Palmer and Perkins 1969, 184). War has played a dominant role in nearly all political crises; it has been used to achieve liberty, to secure democracy and to attempt to make the nation secure against the menace of its use by other hands. The map of the world today has been largely determined by warfare. According to Quincy Wright, 'war has been used as a method for achieving the major political objectives of a country's foreign policy (Palmer and Perkins 1969, 193).

The nations generally aimed at territorial adjustments, nationalistic integration, imperial expansion and an increase in power or other tangible interests by resorting to warfare. The US won independence (1776), unity (1861) and territory (1846–1898) by war. Various other states, such as England, France, Spain, China and Japan, acquired territorial integrity through war. Civilization and Christianity were carried to the New World by conquest. During the eighteenth and nineteenth centuries, the state system was preserved and universal empire prevented by the use of force. In the fifteenth, sixteenth and seventeenth centuries, small feudal principalities were formed into nations by use of force (Jindal 1987, 13). War supported movements, whether of union or separation, beginning in England and France in the Middle Ages and spreading to Central and Eastern Europe, America and Asia in the following centuries and created 60-odd nation states. Power policies, whether to maintain stability or to forward national interests, necessarily required occasional wars.

In the pre-nuclear age, though war was used as an instrument of politics, it was not always successful. Hans J. Morgenthau considered war as a gamble fought for the highest stakes (Morgenthau 1972, 60). It could be won as in the case of the Romans or it could be lost as in the case of Hitler. In the nuclear age, no stakes are high enough to justify deliberately resorting to a war with nuclear weapons. In the nuclear age, no country can afford to resort to nuclear war to achieve its political objectives due to the qualitative change brought about by the invention of the nuclear bomb in the destructive nature of war. No doubt various conventional wars took place after 1945, but these wars have become limited and restricted and the world has not witnessed even conventional war between nuclear countries, which is indicative of the new situation.

Total War Obsolete

The above description of the destructive capability of the bomb (direct or indirect) is indicative of the implications of such a development on the character of war, which in turn implicates the utility of nuclear war as political instrument. The day after the Hiroshima attacks, a New York editorial warned that civilization and humanity could survive only if there was a revolution in humankind's political thinking (Mandelbaum 1981, 1). Recognizing the destructive potential of the force, various responsible political leaders, scientists and military men have argued that the frightfulness of the war will itself be a deterrent against the occurrence of another nuclear conflict. It is possible that the human instinct for self-preservation will eventually save humankind from extermination. In the words of J. William Fulbright, 'Nuclear weapons have rendered total war totally obsolete. Nuclear weapons have lost their utility as an instrument of a nation's policy, as nuclear war and international missiles have made total war an act of suicide' (Jindal 1987, 24). This defencelessness and the speed with which destruction takes place are indicative of the new situation. In conventional wars, it was possible for nations to recover, mobilize and fight back. For instance, Pearl Harbour did not cripple the US capability to wage war and Britain could carry on the war after the fall of France. The USSR could fight after losing a large portion of its territory and industries. This kind of recovery and vengeful retaliation are not possible after a nuclear war. The US president Dwight Eisenhower, recognizing the destructive potential of nuclear war, declared that 'there is no alternative to peace'. He further stated that 'war in future can serve no useful purpose' (Palmer and Perkins 1969, 207).

Nuclear technology since the Second World War has advanced many times over and any desired explosive bomb can be produced now (Kissinger 1957, 70). The invention of the nuclear bomb seems to have threatened civilization and the very existence of humankind. Since 1945, the fact that there has been no war between nuclear countries in which one could make the other surrender unconditionally is indicative of the new situation. Bernard Brodie, in his book entitled *The Absolute Weapon*, argued that 'thus far, the chief purpose of our military establishment has been to win wars. From now on, its chief purpose must be to avert them. It can have almost no other useful purpose' (Brodie 1946, 76). Deterrence effectively ruled out total war between two superpowers throughout the cold war (Iccho 2014, 263).

The history of the nuclear age since the end of the Second World War shows that despite the development of nuclear weapons and their vertical and horizontal proliferation, no war has taken place between two nuclear countries. The atom bomb had been used only once in Japan during the Second World War, which demonstrated the destructive capability of these weapons. The newly developed weapons are believed to be 200 times more destructive. There was no war between the US and the USSR throughout the cold war period, despite their having acquired overkill capability and their immense struggle for power between themselves. There was no war between the US and the USSR during the cold war though the issues of conflict between the two superpowers were deeper than the issues among the major powers during the interwar period, which is indicative of the new situation (Jindal 1987: 24).

The history of the cold war shows that in various wars such as the Korean War (1950–1953), the Vietnam War (1954–1970) and the Cuban missile crisis (1962), where superpowers were involved by proxy, the decision to use nuclear weapons was avoided by the decision makers of both the countries. The leaders of both the US and the USSR acted with great caution and restraint to prevent any possibility of the use of nuclear force. The US was involved in Vietnam for 15 years and lost the war but did not consider using nuclear weapons even against a non-nuclear country. Similarly, the USSR intervened militarily in Hungary in 1956, in Czechoslovakia in 1968 and in Afghanistan in 1980, but the US did not use its nuclear force to exclude Soviet control from these areas. The US, however, did try to contain further Soviet expansion by threatening the use of force. In 1980, the US president Jimmy Carter clearly announced that a Soviet move into the Gulf would mean nuclear war. Yet the US could not use nuclear weapons against Iran when its 50 diplomats were made hostages. The USSR, such a gigantic nuclear power, also suffered defeats in Indonesia, Egypt and Sri Lanka.

The communists also recognized the destructive capacity of these nuclear weapons. In 1956, Nikita Khrushchev also noted that the Marxist–Leninist thesis that war was inevitable as long as imperialists existed was no longer true (Dinerstein 1962, 28–63 and 70–71). The Chinese, who called the nuclear bomb a paper tiger, never used their nuclear force since its acquisition in 1964. China also adopted a 'no first use' policy. Earlier wars used to be expensive but not that catastrophic as nuclear wars, in which the possibility of any player emerging victorious is unthinkable and impossible. No doubt various conventional wars took place after 1945, but these wars were limited and restricted as they were not taken to the logical end (despite the parties having enormous war-fighting capabilities) with defeat of one and victory of another (Jindal 1994, 24–27).

This raises a serious question of why, despite the established fact of the non-utility of nuclear weapons as an instrument of politics, the horizontal and vertical proliferation is taking place.

Utility of Nuclear Weapons

It is ironical that despite understanding the non-usability of nuclear weapons as an instrument of war, nuclear proliferation is taking place. Though nuclear weapons cannot be used as an instrument of war, they have political and diplomatic utility.

First, these weapons are used as weapons of deterrence. Nuclear deterrence is about using nuclear weapons to prevent an opponent from taking an undesirable action. However, the concept of deterrence is not new; but it has assumed new meaning in the nuclear age. In the pre-nuclear age, deterrence could fail. In the nuclear age, it cannot be allowed to fail. The development of nuclear weapons eliminated even conventional conflicts between two nuclear countries. Thomas Schelling in 1980 considered deterrence as 'the threat that leaves something to chance' (Greitens 2014, 378). The idea is that if there were even a small risk of causing an opponent to escalate to a nuclear conflict in response, the risk would deter the conventional attack as well. In 1945, the USSR's conventional superiority could be used to invade Western Europe, which prohibited the US from launching any attack on the USSR. There has been no war, not even a conventional war, between nuclear countries as there is a very thin line between conventional and nuclear wars, and conventional war could be easily converted into nuclear war, especially by the weaker country. The US nuclear force prevented the USSR from using its force against Western Europe, despite its being conventionally the most powerful country in the world. In 1950, the US fought on behalf of South Korea against North Korea in the name of the United Nations (UN). However, the US could not achieve any substantial objectives in the war, such as the unification of Korea. It could only successfully establish and maintain the 38th parallel and also prevented the USSR from invading US allies from 1950 onwards.

The development of nuclear weapons by the US and then the USSR gave rise to a relationship of mutual assured destruction (MAD) between the two superpowers. In the 1980s, the US introduced counterforce and then countervailing strategies and started preparations in the direction.[1]

Nuclear deterrence is the threat to use nuclear weapons if another state does so. It has been noted that 'peace through strength is the basis of the strategy of deterrence' (Goldstein 2003, 83). Kenneth Waltz opined that 'the likelihood of war decreases as deterrent and defensive capabilities of nuclear weapons make wars harder to start' (Sagan and Waltz 2003, 44–45). Deterrence therefore legitimizes the use of nuclear weapons, thus the nuclear weapons monopoly and dependency theory and the threat of immoral genocide.

Apart from the utility of nuclear weapons as deterrents, non-nuclear countries are motivated to acquire nuclear force due to the tremendous power and prestige enjoyed by the nuclear countries.

---

[1] The US administration proposed to develop MX, Trident II, ALCM, survivable and endurable command, control and communication and Space Defence System (SDI) to threaten the USSR not only militarily but also politically and with other value structures which constituted their tools of control and power (The President's Commission on Strategic Forces, Report 1983, 1–6).

Members of the nuclear club are usually considered to rank amongst states of the first order. At present, all five nuclear countries are permanent members of the UN. Schelling argues that nuclear weapons have a diplomatic utility: they are instruments influencing the behaviour of others. In his opinion, the power to hurt is a bargaining tool and to exploit it is diplomacy (Art and Waltz 1971, 77).

The nuclear countries also enjoy tremendous power to manoeuvre in diplomatic talks. Usually nuclear powers determine the course of international politics and have the upper hand in the diplomatic talks. It is the reason that most of the countries perceive nuclear weapons as a currency of power and are motivated to acquire them.

Besides the security and norms (prestige) models, countries are also motivated to acquire nuclear systems for (what Sagan calls) the domestic politics model. According to this model, domestic constituencies such as the scientific–bureaucratic community, political parties, national leaders and domestic public opinion play significant roles in a country's nuclear decision-making.

Therefore, though nuclear weapons cannot be used as military weapons, they have political and diplomatic utility, which motivates states to acquire them.

Nuclear Proliferation: A Strategic Chain Reaction

Nuclear proliferation is caused by the security dilemma. The security dilemma occurs when a state's preparations to defend itself are perceived by another state as threatening so that it prepares for its own defence (Jervis 1978).

George Shultz argued that 'proliferation begets proliferation' (Shultz 1984, 18). Every time one state develops nuclear weapons to level against its main rival, it creates a nuclear threat to another state in the region, which then has to initiate its own nuclear weapons programme to maintain its national security. From this perspective, one can understand the history of nuclear proliferation as a strategic chain reaction (Sagan 2004, 49).

The US policymakers and international relations scholars hold that states will seek nuclear weapons when they face a significant threat to their security that cannot be met through alternate means; if they do not face such a threat, they will willingly remain non-nuclear states (Thayer 1995, 463–519). The very fact that the US developed its nuclear programme in response to the Germany's nuclear research, which was quite far ahead of the US in 1941–1942, indicates that the US did not want Germany to be the first to develop a bomb as the result would have been catastrophic for the US and its allies. The US bomb was developed in absolute secrecy and even President Harry Truman was informed about it after he took over the president's office. In 1939, the US bomb was perceived as a threat to Hitler and in 1945 it was perceived as a threat to the human race. That is why the US started non-proliferation efforts as soon as the Second World War was over. However, proliferation continued through the same logic by which the US had acquired its own atom bomb in response to Germany. The USSR acquired nuclear capability to have a credible retaliatory capability against the US. European countries such as Great Britain and France acquired nuclear weapons to respond to the threat from a nuclear USSR; China acquired nuclear weapons in response to Europe and the US; India acquired nuclear capability in response to China's nuclear threat and Pakistan in response to India's nuclearization. One can envision the history of nuclear proliferation as a strategic chain reaction. In 1963, US President John F. Kennedy had expressed fears that in 12 years (i.e., by 1975) there would be 15 or 20 nuclear powers (Nicholson 2005, 136). However, the pace of nuclear proliferation could be slowed down due to the non-proliferation measures introduced from time to time.

Nuclear Non-proliferation Measures: Problems and Prospects

The efforts to stop nuclear proliferation are as old as the nuclear age. In order to prevent nuclear proliferation, various measures such as commissions, treaties, and bilateral and multilateral agreements were introduced for the cessation of nuclear testing, for the creation of nuclear-free zones, to deal with the problem of sharing nuclear weapons knowledge and technique and for the renunciation of nuclear weapons by non-nuclear countries. Various safety, security and safeguard mechanisms such as the NPT, the Missile Technology Control Regime (MTCR), the Nuclear Suppliers Group (NSG), the International Atomic Energy Agency (IAEA), the Proliferation Security Initiative (PSI), the Container Security Initiative (CSI) and the UN Security Council Resolution 1540 have been introduced as tools of global nuclear governance (IDSA 2016). However, most of these measures could not achieve the expected results due to the security dilemma faced by some of the non-nuclear countries. The history of nuclear proliferation shows that the nuclear non-proliferation measures have always been favorable to the nuclear countries, and therefore they could not lead to comprehensive nuclear disarmament. The history of nuclear proliferation and non-proliferation shows that whenever a country acquires nuclear weapons, it does not want to relinquish its own but seeks to prevent non-nuclear countries from acquiring them. For instance, when the US was the only nuclear power, it did not want the USSR to acquire these weapons and considered nuclear proliferation very dangerous for world peace and security. A similar attitude was adopted by nuclear countries whenever another non-nuclear country wanted to acquire nuclear systems.

The first step in the direction of nuclear non-proliferation was the establishment of the UN Atomic Energy Commission in 1946. Its main objective was to eliminate nuclear proliferation and place nuclear energy under international control. In June 1946, Bernard Baruch, the leader of the US delegation to the commission, presented a plan to set up an International Atomic Development Authority (IADA), which would own, operate and manage all the facilities of fissionable material and directly control all atomic energy activities throughout the world. However, the Baruch plans that aimed at prevention of nuclear proliferation proved to be unsuccessful due to disagreements between the US and the USSR (Singh 2002, 32). The USSR insisted on prohibiting the production and employment of nuclear weapons. The USSR wanted the prohibition of nuclear weapons and the establishment of international control over nuclear energy to come into operation simultaneously. The US, on the other hand, wanted the establishment of an international control machinery prior to the prohibition of nuclear weapons. The USSR wanted complete nuclear disarmament; otherwise, it believed it also had the right to develop nuclear weapons. Finally, the USSR acquired nuclear status in 1949.

In 1953, the US' President Eisenhower called for an 'Atoms for Peace' programme in order to share the benefits of nuclear energy with the international community. In 1956, the USSR suggested that priority could be given to a nuclear test ban as a partial measure, which should work independently of general disarmament (Jain 1974, 66–67). It was believed that a partial test ban or a systematic approach would build confidence for general and complete disarmament.

On 4 June 1957, the USSR proposed a moratorium on nuclear tests for 2–3 years, which was welcomed by the West. In April 1958, the US and the United Kingdom (UK) resumed testing, followed by the USSR.

On India's initiative, the UN General Assembly adopted a three-power resolution by Australia, India and Sweden and a 26-power draft resolution on 29 December 1960, requesting the nuclear weapons states to continue negotiations and accept a voluntary suspension of nuclear tests. After protracted negotiations for about four years between the US, the USSR and the UK, a Partial Test Ban Treaty (PTBT) was initiated on 25 July 1963 and signed in Moscow in August 1963, which banned nuclear tests underwater, in the atmosphere and in outer space. The PTBT had an inherent weakness as it aimed at halting the spread of nuclear weapons to non-nuclear countries. Moreover, it did not cover underground tests. France and China refused to sign it as they felt that it would be advantageous only to the existing nuclear countries.

In 1957, the IAEA was established under UN auspices to share scientific and technical information regarding nuclear energy with other countries of the world. In the 1960s, the IAEA implemented a Safeguards programme in order to monitor and verify that fissile materials and technology for a peaceful nuclear programme were not diverted to nuclear weapon programmes.

In NPT (1968), the IAEA gained the authority for policing the nuclear activities of member countries to ensure that non-nuclear countries do not acquire nuclear weapons.

Nuclear Non-Proliferation Treaty (NPT)

The Treaty on the Non-proliferation of Nuclear Weapons, or Nuclear Non-proliferation Treaty in short (NPT), was proposed in 1968 and came into force in 1970. It was considered a milestone in the arms control efforts. The NPT was a major step towards global nuclear arms control as five nuclear countries had formed a nuclear club and the rest of the non-nuclear countries of the world were advised to not to acquire nuclear weapons. According to the treaty, all the non-nuclear states had to forgo their nuclear weapons development programmes to obtain access to nuclear technology for peaceful purposes. The US ambassador Thomas Graham, who focused on arms control and nuclear non-proliferation, argued that the NPT was based on three pillars:

- Non-proliferation
- Eventual disarmament
- Peaceful use of nuclear energy.

The NPT was not acceptable to various countries such as Israel, India and Pakistan and they refused to sign it. India, originally a proponent of the treaty, rejected it as the provisions of nuclear non-proliferation it had proposed in 1965 were completely changed. India had proposed not to transfer nuclear weapons or nuclear weapons technology and also to stop all production of nuclear weapons and delivery vehicles as well as to agree on the beginning of a programme of reduction of nuclear arsenals. India believed in general and comprehensive disarmament and wanted nuclear countries to first stop augmenting, then reduce and finally eliminate their nuclear systems.

India rejected the NPT as discriminatory as it prevented only non-nuclear countries from acquiring nuclear weapons. It prevented only horizontal proliferation whereas it allowed vertical proliferation. The provisions of the treaty allowed the nuclear countries to retain and improve the quality and quantity of their nuclear systems.

The NPT was also termed as paradoxical, as it gives nuclear countries right to use nuclear systems as a currency of power and freedom to make commercial use of nuclear technology and yet it prohibits non-nuclear countries from making peaceful use of nuclear technology. The treaty was discriminatory and lacked a mutuality of obligations between weapons and non-weapons states. India wanted a

---

BOX 9.1: Provisions of the Nuclear Non-proliferation Treaty (NPT)

In Articles 1 and II of the NPT, the nuclear weapon states (NWSs) agree not to help non-nuclear weapon states (NNWSs) to develop or acquire nuclear weapons.

By Article III, the IAEA was established to verify and ensure that nuclear materials were not diverted to NNWSs. It established safeguards for the transfer of fissionable materials between NWSs and NNWSs and the IAEA was empowered to carry out inspections in NNWSs.

Article IV acknowledges the inalienable right of the NNWSs to research, develop and use nuclear energy for non-weapons purposes.

Article V is obsolete now: earlier it allowed peaceful nuclear explosions but now no explosions are allowed.

Article VI commits the NWSs to pursue negotiations for the cessation of the nuclear arms race and for nuclear disarmament.

Article VII allows for the establishment of nuclear-weapon-free zones (NWFZs).

Article VIII requires a complex and lengthy process of amendment.

Article X requires a nation to give three months' notice to withdraw from the treaty.

Source: Baklitskiy (2015).

---

moratorium on nuclear weapons testing, pending the conclusion of a comprehensive test ban treaty. It was not acceptable to nuclear countries. Therefore India, which has always been at the forefront of the nuclear non-proliferation issue, also used its nuclear option.

India exercised its nuclear option in 1974 and acquired a nuclear posture[2] in 1999 but followed the basic obligations of an NPT member, resisting suggestions for nuclear cooperation that would have been dangerous for international security.

India's peaceful nuclear explosion in Pokhran in 1974 was responded to by the creation of Nuclear Suppliers Group (NSG) in 1975. It aimed at strengthening the safeguards and conditions applied to nuclear exports such as uranium enrichment and plutonium processing facilities. India's export control policy, however, can be contrasted with some of the nuclear countries that have encouraged proliferation for political and commercial reasons and have contributed to clandestine weapons of mass destruction (WMD) programmes. India has not exported its nuclear knowhow or materials to any other country. It has not either directly or clandestinely helped the process of proliferation. It has transferred technology under safeguards. India has also supported the IAEA mandate, adhered to the NSG guidelines and declared an indefinite moratorium on further nuclear testing, a significant principle underlying the Comprehensive Nuclear-Test-Ban Treaty (CTBT).

The NPT was renewed in 1995 and was extended permanently. At the 1995 NPT conference, the nuclear countries agreed to work towards the elimination of nuclear weapons but they were not obliged to abolish their existing nuclear weapons, thereby legitimizing the nuclear weapons of five countries. The NPT review conference was to take place at every five years' interval. The NPT review conference held

---

[2] Earlier nuclear explosion in 1974 was a peaceful nuclear explosion. However, India did not sign the NPT nor allowed IAEA inspections to confirm that it did not use its nuclear program to develop weapons. In 1999, India conducted nuclear tests (Pokharan II) and assumed the status of a nuclear country.

in 2010 tried to strengthen the measures for nuclear safeguards and nuclear non-proliferation. The NPT conference of 2015 was quite unsuccessful[3] as it did strength the review process (Baklitskiy 2015, 15–18).

The NPT neither initiates the process of nuclear disarmament nor safeguards the security interests of non-nuclear states, which encourages overt or covert nuclear programmers in the world around. It is quite paradoxical that countries who try to champion the cause of nuclear non-proliferation are the greatest proliferators. Some of the nuclear countries, such as China, are also contributing to the spread of WMD technology, which is contradictory to the essence of the NPT. China's contribution to the nuclear and missile capabilities of Iran and North Korea is clearly indicative of a violation of the principles of the NPT and other non-proliferation measures.

The Iranian and North Korean efforts towards nuclear status exhibit the weakness of the treaty. In future, even more signatories of the NPT can opt for nuclearization and withdraw from the NPT. The situation in the Democratic People's Republic of Korea (DPRK), Iran and Iraq has raised important issues concerning capabilities and intentions. The problem of non-compliance and verification of the treaty by some of the states causes serious concerns. For instance, for Iraq, a special inspection arrangement known as the United Nations Special Commission (UNSCOM) was established following the Gulf War of 1991 to oversee the dismantlement of the WMD programme. However, inspectors did not have access to the particular site and had to withdraw. Later on, they did not find any evidence of undeclared WMDs in some states.

Comprehensive Nuclear-Test-Ban Treaty (CTBT)

In 1996, the Comprehensive Nuclear-Test-Ban Treaty (CTBT) was introduced to ban nuclear testing completely. It was signed by 44 non-nuclear and five nuclear club members. India, Pakistan and Korea did not sign the treaty and China, Egypt, Iran, Israel and the US signed but did not ratify it.

The CTBT had inherent weaknesses as it did not ban nontraditional and non-explosive subcritical testing and computer simulation techniques; moreover, qualitative improvement of nuclear systems by nuclear countries was not prohibited. There were some loopholes in the treaty that worked in favour of nuclear countries only. The treaty was also weak in the sense that it involved the problem of verification; nor did it clarify whether it would prohibit the existing nuclear countries from conducting the test. Nor did it have any provision to prevent nuclear countries from transferring nuclear materials and technology to non-nuclear states. Despite the introduction of the treaty, both India and Pakistan conducted nuclear tests and acquired declaratory nuclear posture. North Korea and Iran are also pursuing their nuclear programmes.

Intermediate-Range Nuclear Forces Treaty (INF)

The Intermediate-Range Nuclear Forces Treaty was a bilateral agreement signed by the US and the USSR in 1987 to reduce their nuclear arms. Consequently, the US eliminated 846 missiles and the USSR removed 1,846 INF missiles.

---

[3] The NPT review conference held in 2010 tried to strengthen measures for nuclear safeguards and nuclear non-proliferation. The NPT review conference held at UN, NY, 27 April–22 May, 2015 failed to result in agreement on a final document. It was quite unsuccessful as nuclear countries failed to address the growing demand for progress towards nuclear disarmament.

Strategic Arms Reduction Treaty (START)

The end of the cold war between the US and the USSR gave rise to optimism for nuclear non-proliferation. This optimism was boosted by START I (1991) and START II (1993), through which both the US and Russia agreed to reduce their nuclear warheads and to eliminate certain categories of weapons, such as land-based intercontinental ballistic missiles with multiple warheads. However, this optimism did not last long. The euphoria about reduction of nuclear stockpiles and encouraging nations to abandon nuclear weapons faded. The START III talks in Moscow, in 1999, failed over disagreements about a possible renegotiation of the Anti-Ballistic Missile (ABM) treaty.

Strategic Offensive Reductions Treaty (SORT)

The US entered into a new agreement with Russia known as the Strategic Offensive Reductions Treaty (SORT) in 2002. The objective of this treaty was to reduce the strategic systems of both the US and Russia. The treaty had inherent weaknesses and contradictions as it did not contain any verification measures about the reduction of strategic systems, rather allowing both the US and Russia to deploy 1,700 and 2,200 warheads respectively, with the rest being put in storage rather than being destroyed. It also allowed either side to withdraw from this treaty at three months' notice. The SORT expired in 2012.

The nuclear powers continue to maintain their nuclear arsenals in the absence of a cold war, which reaffirms the significance of nuclear weapons and weakens the moral and diplomatic pressure that nuclear powers could exercise on non-nuclear countries. There is also evidence that nuclear countries are trying to acquire a new generation of nuclear weapons. These include low-yield battlefield nuclear weapons, or 'mini nukes', and missile shields. The paradox is that, on the one hand, major powers such as the US are championing the cause of nuclear non-proliferation and trying to strengthen the regimes of global nuclear governance to deal with the problem; on the other hand, they are still maintaining and modernizing their own nuclear arsenals and still trying to maintain their deterrence credibility. Both the US and Russia have been competing at stockpiling weapons and sophistication of delivery systems. It is thought that the US modernization plans and spending will be at their highest levels in 2021–2035.

The nuclear non-proliferation programme is also implicated in the US defence programme. The US National Missile Defense Act passed in 1999 proposed that the US should develop the technical means to counter a possible small-scale ballistic missile attack on the US mainland. Russians clearly link the issue of nuclear reductions to the US missile defence deployment, particularly in Europe. Russia claims that the US missile defence in Europe is directed against Russia. The US maintains that the missile defence in Europe is directed against rogue states such as Iran and poses no threat to Russia's strategic missiles. The US ballistic missile defence programme is contrary to the ABM treaty as it implicates nuclear stability. The US preparation and capability to launch a nuclear attack and also to shield its homeland by ballistic missile defence could instigate others to do the same. The US is moving ahead with its missile defense programmed to develop missile interceptors. The US also proposed to station its ballistic missile defence systems in Poland and the Czech Republic, which was not liked by Russia. Japan and Israel have also decided to deploy missile defences. The UK also decided in 2007 to update and replace its Trident nuclear weapons systems.

Export Control Regimes

In order to control the export of technology and materials related to WMDs, particularly nuclear weapons, multilateral control regimes have been established. The NSG, The MTCR, the Australian Group and the Wassenaar Arrangement are the four most significant multilateral export control regimes that can contribute significantly towards global nuclear governance. The NSG (also known as the London Club) was established in 1975 which provides guidelines for interstate trade in nuclear technology and materials. After the 1991 Gulf War, the NSG expanded the list of materials and technology that could not be transferred. The Australian Group of suppliers, also formed in 1975, also restricts exports of chemicals and dual-use technology. In 1987, the MTCR was established to prohibit the export of complete missiles, missile technologies and components. The Wassenaar Arrangement (1996) was introduced to prohibit the transfer of nuclear technologies and materials to rogue states.

The Fissile Material Cut-off Treaty (FMCT) was also introduced in 1995 to prevent further nuclear proliferation. The treaty does not clarify whether it seeks to only prohibit the new fissile-materials stockpiles or eliminate existing stockpiles as well. Therefore, the FMCT would maintain the asymmetrical status quo in the nuclear capabilities of various countries.

The Proliferation Security Initiative (PSI) is another counterproliferation measure led by the US. In 2003, the PSI was launched to promote international cooperation to interdict WMD-related shipments and to cut off the channels of proliferation finance. More than 70 countries are cooperating to prevent such proliferation of WMD materials.

These regimes were not fully effective as some of the nuclear states such as China refused to join these regimes. Moreover, countries tend to export these materials and technologies for their commercial as well as their foreign-policy objectives, which hampers the process of nuclear non-proliferation. There have been disputes between China and the US over Chinese missiles sold to Pakistan in violation of MTCR guidelines. Similar disputes between France and the US emerged over missile sales. Moreover, countries such as France, Germany and Japan are operating with transnational networks that increase the prospect of acquisition of at least rudimentary nuclear capability by some countries.

BOX 9.2:   UN Security Council Resolution 1540

The UN Security Council Resolution 1540 was introduced to safeguard the dissemination of nuclear technology to countries engaged in WMD-related activities. The resolution made it 'obligatory for all UN members to take and enforce effective measures against proliferation of WMD, means of delivery and related material' (UNSC 2004). UN Security Council Resolution 1540, adopted in April 2004, requires prohibiting individuals, companies and other actors from supporting non-state actors from acquiring WMDs. It also requires states to enforce domestic legislation prohibiting these activities and to establish effective controls over items and financing that might support these activities. The 1540 Committee was set up to monitor and implement these resolutions and to provide support and assistance in implementation and facilitation of international cooperation in these efforts. The 1540 Committee's mandate has been extended several times, most recently in 2011 for a period of 10 years, until 2021. The resolution 1540 marks a departure from previous non-proliferation arrangements and adds a novel layer to the non-proliferation regime by establishing universal mandatory obligations to not to transfer technologies and materials of weapons of mass destruction.

Source: UNSC (2004).

Nuclear-Weapon-Free Zones (NWFZ)

In order to prevent nuclear proliferation, the concept of nuclear-weapon-free zones (NWFZ) was introduced. NWFZ means that non-nuclear countries in a region should agree not to resort to nuclear proliferation and should declare their region free from nuclear weapons. Such regions would be assured about the non-use of nuclear weapons against them by nuclear countries.

The idea of the NWFZ was first introduced by Poland's Rapid Plan to keep Europe free from nuclear weapons. The NWFZ was accepted by various regions who felt that they had benefitted by non-use of nuclear force assurance. Five treaties have been signed in this regard: the Antarctic Treaty (1959) to establish a NWFZ there, the Treaty of Tlatelolco (1967) for Latin America and Caribbean, the Treaty of Rarotonga (1985) for the South Pacific, the Treaty of Pelindaba (1996) for Africa and the Bangkok Treaty (1997) for South-east Asia. Consequently, most of the Southern hemisphere is now a NWFZ.

India opposed this concept on the grounds that there cannot be a limited approach to the question of nuclear disarmament; India believed that the entire world should be free from nuclear weapons. There has to be global, not a regional, approach to the issue of nuclear non-proliferation. Pakistan, on the contrary, supported the idea of a NWFZ in South Asia in order to prevent India from using its nuclear option to deter China. India rejected the idea of a NWFZ in South Asia partly due to its limited approach to the issue of nuclear non-proliferation and also due to the China factor. China's nuclear capability has been a factor in India's threat perception as India had faced a war with China in 1962 and did not want to be in a vulnerable position in front of a nuclear China (Chellaney 2002, 1). Therefore India could not accept the NWFZ concept and wanted to keep its nuclear option open. South Asia became nuclearized after India and Pakistan acquired a declaratory nuclear posture in 1999. Since then, the region has witnessed various low-level conflicts (Mohan 2001). In order to prevent nuclear proliferation, all the countries of the world need to participate in international initiatives designed to limit nuclear proliferation (Figure 9.1) (Safeguards to Prevent Nuclear Proliferation—World Nuclear Association 2017).

Second Nuclear Age: Challenges Ahead

Nuclear proliferation is bound to continue, but the role of weapons as security providers is under serious question due to various global developments. The end of the cold war did not lead to the 'end of history' or a 'new world order'. Nor did it bring about an era of stability or disarmament. Rather, it looks like those nuclear weapons will stay for a long time. 'The gravest danger to the present world lies in radicalism and misuse of technology. While extremist groups have splintered all over, technology has been diffused to every nook and corner. The previous understanding of defense and deterrence is no longer fully applicable in the post 9/11 world' (Mishra 2008, vii). Earlier, deterrence could be exercised against an adversarial country. In the case of terrorism, which is hidden and secret warfare, deterrence cannot be used as the enemy is not visible or clear.

It is established that nuclear weapons cannot be used as an instrument of war. With the emergence of non-state actors, motives to acquire nuclear systems necessitate an urgent review of security and the concept of deterrence (Mishra 2008, viii). In the post-cold war world, nuclear proliferation in the rogue states or through illicit organizations is posing a serious threat to world peace and security. The US' main concern is about increasing insecurity in some of the regions due to the nuclearization of rogue states—the states with military-based, dictatorial governments, combined with factors such as ethnic and social conflict and

FIGURE 9.1 Nuclear Proliferation

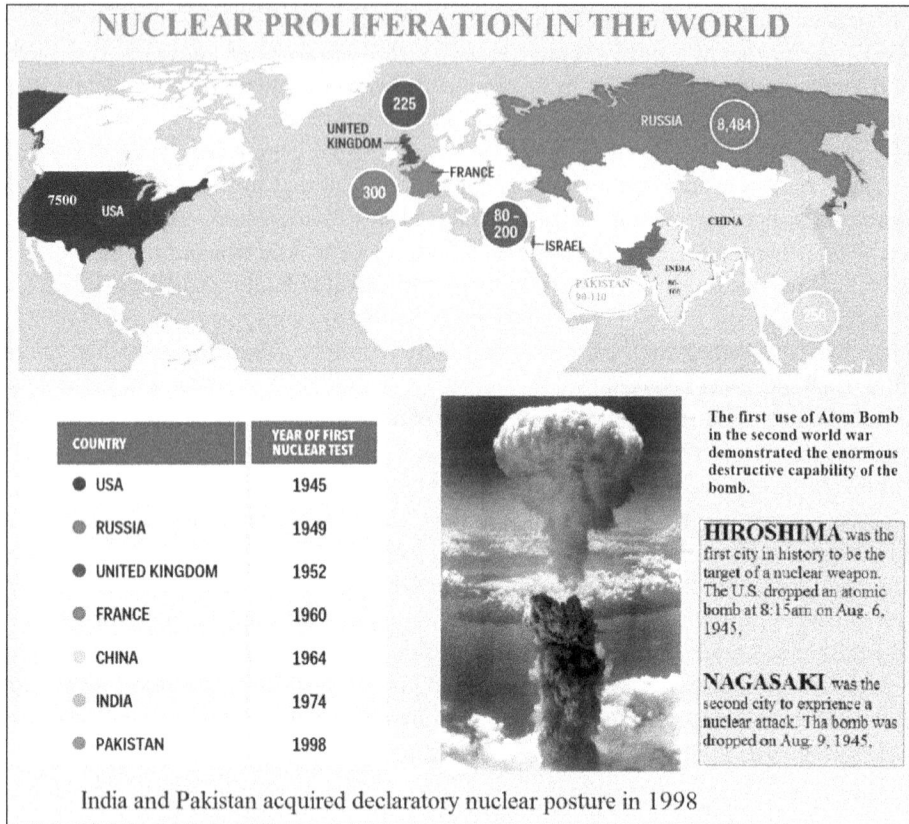

NUCLEAR PROLIFERATION IN THE WORLD

COUNTRY	YEAR OF FIRST NUCLEAR TEST
● USA	1945
● RUSSIA	1949
● UNITED KINGDOM	1952
● FRANCE	1960
○ CHINA	1964
◉ INDIA	1974
◉ PAKISTAN	1998

The first use of Atom Bomb in the second world war demonstrated the enormous destructive capability of the bomb.

HIROSHIMA was the first city in history to be the target of a nuclear weapon. The U.S. dropped an atomic bomb at 8:15am on Aug. 6, 1945.

NAGASAKI was the second city to exprience a nuclear attack. Tha bomb was dropped on Aug. 9, 1945.

India and Pakistan acquired declaratory nuclear posture in 1998

Source: US Department of Defense (modified).
Note: Numbers in circles indicate the number of nuclear weapons each country possesses.

economic underdevelopment to dictate an aggressive foreign policy, would pose a serious threat to regional stability. It is feared that countries with weak civilian governments in military conflict-prone areas risk accidental nuclear accidental wars or at least conflicts between nuclear states. Therefore, nuclear proliferation in such destabilized and conflict-ridden areas might pose a threat to world peace and security.

The former US president George Bush dubbed Iraq, Iran, Syria, Libya and North Korea as the 'axis of evil'.[4] The US introduced the 'Bush Doctrine', through which rogue states with WMDs would be countered by preemptive wars and regime change (Heywood 2014, 275). For instance, Iraq—a signatory to the NPT since 1968—had been covertly developing nuclear weapons, which resulted in Operation Desert Fox. The US launched a bombing campaign to target the installations housing Iraq's biological, chemical and nuclear weapons. It led to Operation Iraqi Freedom in 2003. The US' assertive stance towards rogue states with WMDs became evident in its relations with Iran and Korea. In 2003, IAEA inspectors found that Iran had constructed a uranium enrichment plant at Natanz and a heavy water

---

[4] Under the Bush administration, seven countries were declared axis of evil, namely, Russia, Iraq, Iran, North Korea, China, Libya and Syria.

production plant at Arak, demonstrating its efforts towards an illicit nuclear weapons programme supported by technology from Pakistan. Export and proliferation of nuclear technology from Pakistan has posed a bigger challenge to global security, as there is a risk of these weapons falling into the hands of jihadis. Pakistan acquired nuclear technology illegally and is now assisting other states such as Iran, North Korea and Libya to acquire it (Chawla 2013, 33). Pakistan's main motive in assisting these countries in developing these capabilities is to expand its influence in the Muslim world. Pakistan has been involved in clandestine proliferation of nuclear technology, including equipment, blueprints, plans and training (Bruno and Bailly 2010).

It is believed that Iraq's clandestine nuclear programme might have encouraged Iran to develop its own nuclear weapons programme. The increasing regional tensions in the Middle East encouraged Israel to nuclearize, as well as Iran's quest for nuclear weapons capability. The desire to prevent the possible US invasion probably intensified Iran's desire to acquire a nuclear arsenal. Similarly, Iraq and North Korea also carried out their nuclear programmes to discourage the intervention of much powerful countries such as the US. However, Iraq discontinued its nuclear programme and Korea conducted its first nuclear test in 2006.

The catalogue of events in Box 9.3 suggests that conventionally weaker countries may resort to building up a limited nuclear capability for the purpose of deterrence, defense and security. In the post-cold war era Iran's nuclear programme appears to be anti-Israel. It is feared that Iran's nuclear weapons programme might escalate the arms race in the volatile Middle East as states such as Egypt, Saudi Arabia, Syria and Turkey may not like the region to be dominated by a nuclear Iran.

The US is seriously concerned about North Korea's nuclear weapons programme, as it might lead to the nuclearization of South Korea and possibly escalate arms race in the Korean peninsula. The US perception of nuclearization of rogue states leading to the instability and insecurity of regions such as West Asia and South-east Asia is driven by Eurocentric perceptions and assumptions.

Terrorism and Nuclear Insecurity

The acquisition of nuclear weapons or materials and knowledge by individuals or non-state entities, often termed 'terrorists', to produce a crude form of nuclear bomb is another kind of proliferation that is posing a serious threat to world peace and security. The report of the Council on Foreign Relations entitled *Preventing Catastrophic Nuclear Terrorism*, by Charles D. Ferguson, asserts that the probability

---

BOX 9.3: Nuclear Programmes in Defiance of the NPT

- North Korea made weapons-grade plutonium using a research reactor and a reprocessing plant in defiance of its NPT obligations. In 2006, 2009, 2013, 2016 and 2017, it exploded five nuclear devices.
- Iran also conducted nuclear tests in defiance of the NPT and UN Security Council.
- In 1991, Iraq attempted to develop enriched uranium and weapons-grade materials in violation of the NPT and IAEA Safeguards obligations.
- Syria constructed a nuclear reactor in breach of its NPT obligations.

of nuclear attacks has increased because traditional deterrence—threatening assured destruction against a valued asset such as a national territory—does not work against the terrorist groups with covert nuclear capability (Ferguson 2006). Therefore, the international community needs to devise new methods to deal with newly emerging threats, as the old policy of deterrence in no longer effective to deal with threats from terrorism or non-state actors, which may or may not be state-sponsored.

After the end of the cold war, the international community feels apprehensive that non-state actors such as terrorist organizations or criminal groups might try to acquire nuclear weapons or radiological material that can be used in dirty bomb. After the disintegration of the USSR, the fear of nuclear theft was very acute. The US and the international community launched a series of efforts to secure nuclear material in the countries of the former USSR. The discovery of a proliferation network run by Pakistani scientist A. Q. Khan raises concerns that in a globalized world, the states will not be able to control the diffusion of nuclear material, technology and knowledge (IISS Strategic Dossier 2007, 67). The access to such dangerous weapons to the global terrorists would pose serious threat to the world peace and security (Greitens 2014, 378). A study by the International Task Force on Prevention of Nuclear Terrorism concluded that it was possible for a terrorist group to build a credible nuclear device. It is viewed that such groups would be more interested in generating social disruption by making a credible nuclear threat rather than actually detonating a nuclear device and causing mass killing and destruction (Baylis et al. 2017, 389).

In the new nuclear age, the problem emanates from the dissemination of nuclear technology and materials and micro-proliferation. In this scenario, nuclear weapons are turning from weapons of deterrence into weapons of burden. In order to deal with the problem, various steps have been initiated, such as the Nuclear Security Summit (NSS) held in Washington (2010 and 2016), Seoul (2012) and the Hague (2014). These summits aim at increasing international sophistication to secure nuclear materials and prevent nuclear smuggling with the ultimate goal of preventing nuclear terrorism. The former US president Barrack Obama pushed nuclear security to the centrestage of global nuclear governance to counter nuclear and radiological terrorism. A multilateral initiative to deal with nuclear terrorism was introduced in the UN General Assembly on 13 April 2005 that made the possession, use or threat of use of radioactive devices by non-state actors, their accomplices and organizers into a criminal offense (World Nuclear Association 2015).

BOX 9.4: Challenges of Nuclear Terror

- In November 1995, caesium-137 was discovered in Moscow Park.
- In December 1998, a radiological dispersion device (RDD) was found near Argun, Chechnya.
- Multiple attempts by the Al Qaeda to acquire material for a radiological device.
- According to UK intelligence the Al Qaeda prioritized RDDs from 1999 onwards.
- José Padilla, arrested in May 2002, was reportedly planning to develop a uranium-based RDD and targeting apartment blocks using conventional weapons.
- The murder of Alexander Litvinenko in London in November 2006 by polonium-210 ingestion,
- A British national, Dhiren Barot, was sentenced to life imprisonment in 2006 for planning to build a 'dirty bomb' out of some 10,000 smoke detectors, each of which contained a small radioactive source.

Source: Mishra (2008, 30).

In the post-cold war scenario, various bilateral initiatives were also taken to prohibit the access of nuclear materials to terrorist outfits—for instance, the Nunn–Lugar Act (1991) to safeguard the Soviet nuclear arsenals. The Global Initiative to Combat Nuclear Terrorism (GICNT) launched by the US president Bush and the Russian president Vladimir Putin on 15 July 2006 aimed 'to prevent the acquisition, transport, or use by terrorists of any nuclear materials and radioactive substances or improvised explosive devices using such materials, as well as hostile action against nuclear facilities' (US Department of State 2006). The US Department of Energy (DOE) also introduced a programme for materials protection, control and accounting by providing equipment and training to upgrade security at existing sites of the Russian Federal Agency of Atomic Energy, housing fissile materials (Bruno and Bailly 2010). The US National Nuclear Security Administration (NNSA) is providing training to officials from other countries on procedures to account for and control nuclear materials and physical protection measures for critical nuclear sites (Mishra 2008, 32).

International efforts to secure vulnerable nuclear materials, to ensure disintegration of the black market and to detect, intercept and recover illicit trafficking in materials need to be strengthened further. A network of institutions such as the IAEA and the World Association of Nuclear Operators (WANO) are supportive of the implementation of regulatory mechanisms for nuclear safety.

Apart from the IAEA, various international, multilateral, regional and national bodies are working for nuclear security. There are plans to set up centers of excellence (COE) across the world to facilitate research, training and education regarding nuclear security. Some of the existing COEs include EU Chemical, Biological, Radiological and Nuclear Risk Mitigation (CBRN) COEs, the Pakistan Centre of Excellence for Nuclear Security (PCENS), the Middle East Scientific Institute for Security (MESIS) and Japan's Integrated Support Center for Nuclear Non-proliferation and Nuclear Security (ISCN). India is setting up a Global Centre for Nuclear Energy Partnership (GCNEP). A smooth interface among all these centres and the IAEA is deemed crucial.

Accidental Nuclear Risk

The proliferation of nuclear technology and materials even for peaceful purposes can also pose a serious danger to human security and environment. The systems used to produce nuclear energy are complex. Nuclear energy carries the risk of accidents that have human and environmental consequences. The March 2011 earthquake and the tsunami in Japan that caused the meltdown of three reactors in Fukushima certainly alarmed the international community about nuclear dangers caused by natural calamities. The fire that destroyed a reactor at Chernobyl in the former USSR in 1986 revealed the devastating effects of accidents in operating nuclear power plants. The Fukushima incidents underlined the need to pay more attention to nuclear safety.

All the countries and organizations having nuclear weapons may cause serious dangers through leakage of radiation in case their nuclear plants leak in case of earthquakes, hurricanes, and so on. US nuclear power plants are built to withstand hurricanes, tornadoes, earthquakes and small plane crashes. However, similar physical protection to nuclear facilities is missing in other countries. The prevention and detection of theft, sabotage, unauthorized access and illegal transfer of or other malicious acts involving nuclear materials and other radioactive substances are the serious nuclear security issues that need to be tackled effectively.

The issue of nuclear safety, security and non-proliferation, with a special focus on handling the physical protection of nuclear materials, trans-boundary movement of nuclear matter, spent fuel management and radioactive waste management, protection from nuclear radiation, environmental pollution, civil nuclear liability and the peaceful use of atomic energy in the twenty-first century need to be addressed by the global community.

Nations with Latent Nuclear Capability

Some nations not in the category of nuclear powers but in possession of the infrastructure, material and technical capabilities to quickly assemble a nuclear bomb also pose a serious threat to nuclear non-proliferation. For instance, Japan is described as being 'five minutes' from the bomb as it has enough fissile materials, technical ability and knowledge to assemble a nuclear weapon on very short notice. Similarly, there are some nations that have clandestine nuclear capability and can cause proliferation in their region. The policy of nuclear opacity is also pursued by some of the countries; for example, Israel, which has neither signed the NPT, nor confirmed the possession of nuclear arsenals, nor conducted nuclear tests, is pursuing a policy of ambiguity. Israel is estimated to have appropriately 80–200 nuclear arsenals (Greitens 2014, 378–379).

It is estimated that about 57 states are constructing nuclear power and research reactors and about 30 countries have the necessary industrial infrastructure and scientific expertise to build nuclear weapons on a crash basis if they chose to do so (Fetter 1996, 38). In this scenario, the world is fast approaching a point of no return as to the prospect of controlling the spread of nuclear-weapons capability in the twenty-first century.

Global Nuclear Governance: Future Prospects

Global nuclear governance through nuclear regimes is likely to face challenges, firstly in countering proliferation—that is, in obstructing, slowing or rolling back the programmes of states that are actually pursuing nuclear-weapons capability—and secondly, in deterring and defending against the actual use of nuclear weapons or such explosives that can cause physical and environmental damage.

The issue of nuclear disarmament has no doubt been gaining popularity in the post-cold war period. President Obama bolstered the Global Zero movement. In 2009, in his Prague speech, President Obama talked about a world free of nuclear weapons.

In order to deal with the newly emerging challenges, the US has indulged in a new kind of preparation in the form of the development of mini-nukes and defence capabilities. The US emphasis on developing new-generation weapons post 9/11 opens up a new chapter in the history of non-proliferation. As the US has started developing these new-generation weapons as credible military options against adversaries who threaten to use WMDs or 'large scale conventional military force'. The Nuclear Posture Review (NPR) report suggests that these weapons would likely to be used against at least seven countries—China, Russia, Iraq, Iran, North Korea, Libya and Syria. The NPR studies point out that the US nuclear weapons serve a fourfold purpose: to 'assure allies and friends', 'dissuade competitors', 'deter aggressors' and 'defeat enemies' (Chellaney 2002). Such a policy can trigger an action–reaction cycle and can adversely affect the wisdom of nuclear non-proliferation.

The nuclear countries are unwilling to make an arms-control or disarmament commitment. In such a situation, it is difficult to curb horizontal proliferation, as the security dilemma is still a reality for various countries. The regional arms races in South-east Asia, the Middle East and the Korean Peninsula clearly indicate that it is difficult to reverse the process of nuclear proliferation. The global strategic environment is more competitive and lethal than ever before (Chellaney 2002, 5). There is no linkage between arms control and disarmament.

At the time of signing the NPT in 1968, the global nuclear weapons stockpile was approximately 39,202. Despite the Strategic Arms Limitation Talks (SALT 1 and II) of 1972 and 1979, the nuclear stockpiles increased to 69,490 by 1986. It was only due to the resurrection of global peace movements and the subsequent signing of the INF Treaty in 1987 that the nuclear stockpiles marginally reduced to 56,396 by 1991 and reduced further to 26,854 by 2006, after the end of cold war (BAS 1997, 67).

According to a report in the *New Scientist* of 7 September 2005, the increasing stockpile of fissile materials across the world is enough to build over 300,000 nuclear bombs (Mooney 2005). The safety and security of such materials is a serious challenge to the international community. The paradox is that the champions of nuclear non-proliferation are the real proliferators.

Civil society can play a significant role in the discourse on nuclear arms control and global nuclear security. Various intergovernmental organizations such as the Fissile Materials Working Group (FMWG)—a coalition of NGOs—can organize global experts and the community for the purpose of global nuclear security. Global anti-nuclear movements—which include organizations such as Greenpeace, the Campaign for Nuclear Disarmament (CND) and others—point to the risk of disasters such as Fukushima and also the safety issues associated with nuclear waste, and therefore emphasize the necessity for nuclear disarmament and oppose the use of nuclear power. A group of 107 states endorsed a statement known as the Humanitarian Pledge, which calls on states 'to identify and pursue effective measures to fill the legal gap for the prohibition and elimination of nuclear weapons' (BAS 1997, 67).

Concluding Observations

In the given scenario, nuclear disarmament appears to be unthinkable despite the serious efforts made by agencies of global nuclear governance. Nuclear proliferation and expansion of the nuclear club, on the one hand, and acquisition of nuclear-weapons capability by non-state actors on the other hand has complicated the global security environment. The spillover of nuclear technologies and materials to non-state actors has opened up a new challenge for the international community as these non-state actors are beyond the reach of the traditional tools of diplomacy. Earlier, security from nuclear weapons was the main concern of the international community; now security of nuclear technology and materials itself has become a serious challenge. New strategies and initiatives for global nuclear governance need to be devised to strengthen and ensure global security.

Summary

- The issue of nuclear proliferation has always been at the top of the global security agenda since 1945. The issue of nuclear-weapons proliferation revolves around two dominant approaches. First, the realist approach emphasizes the significance of nuclear weapons to enhance national security in anarchical international politics. The second viewpoint emphasizes the significance of the elimination of such systems to ensure global peace and security. In this regard, international norms can be introduced to constrain nuclear behaviours and appropriate standards can be set up to govern the behaviour of the different countries of the world.

- Despite several measures introduced to curb nuclear proliferation, nuclear proliferation has been constantly increasing. Countries are motivated to acquire nuclear systems as they face a security dilemma in the anarchical international system.
- The paradox is that despite the development of overkill capability by nuclear countries, no major, total or world war has taken place since the end of the Second World War, when atom bombs were used for the first time, which demonstrated the destructive capability of atomic, or nuclear, weapons.
- The destructive capability of nuclear weapons revolutionized the nature of war and brought about a qualitative change in the destructive character of war, which in turn has impacted the utility of war as a political instrument. Total war in the nuclear age has become obsolete, as it will lead to total annihilation and will leave nothing to win. Though nuclear weapons cannot be used as instruments of war, they can be used as instruments of deterrence. This legitimizes the use of nuclear weapons.
- Nuclear weapons have no military utility; they do have political and diplomatic utility. These weapons can be used for the purpose of deterrence and they give tremendous power and prestige to a nuclear nation. The nuclear countries also enjoy greater power to manoeuvre in diplomatic talks.
- Various safety, security and safeguard mechanisms such as the Treaty on the Non-proliferation of Nuclear Weapons (NPT), the Comprehensive Test Ban Treaty (CTBT), the Intermediate-Range Nuclear Forces (INF) Treaty, the Strategic Arms Reduction Talks (START), the Fissile Material Cut-off Treaty (FMCT), the Missile Technology Control Regime (MTCR), the Nuclear Suppliers Group (NSG), the International Atomic Energy Agency (IAEA), the Proliferation Security Initiative (PSI), the Container Security Initiative (CSI) and UN Security Council Resolution 1540 have been introduced as tools of global nuclear governance. However, most of these measures could not achieve the expected results due to the inherent contradictions involved in these measures. Most of these measures were introduced to stop horizontal proliferation, aimed at selective proliferation and not at general, comprehensive and complete disarmament.
- The NPT neither initiates the process of nuclear disarmament nor safeguards the security interests of non-nuclear states, which encourage overt or covert nuclear programmes around the world. It is quite paradoxical that the countries who try to champion the cause of nuclear non-proliferation are the greatest proliferators.
- Nuclear proliferation is bound to continue but the role of weapons as security provider is under serious question due to various global developments. In the second nuclear age (after the end of the cold war), the gravest danger to the present world lies in the spillover of nuclear technologies and materials to non-state actors or weak civilian governments. The acquisition of nuclear weapons may be crude forms of bombs, by such illicit organizations or terrorists groups would reduce the effectiveness of nuclear deterrence. It necessitates an urgent review of security and the concept of deterrence.
- Nuclear non-proliferation does not appear to be feasible; therefore, measures of global nuclear governance need to be strengthened to ensure the physical and environmental security of the world.

Suggested Questions

1. Discuss the military utility of nuclear weapons, with special reference to Clausewitz's concept of war as a political instrument.
2. Why are countries motivated to develop nuclear weapons?
3. Discuss the concept of 'deterrence', with special reference to the nuclear club of five during the cold war.
4. Discuss the nuclear non-proliferation measures initiated at bilateral and multilateral levels. Why were they not fully effective?
5. What are the new nuclear proliferation challenges in the post-cold war period?
6. Why is the concept of deterrence not fully effective in the second nuclear age after the end of the cold war?
7. Do you think that non-state actors are posing a serious nuclear-proliferation challenge?
8. What are the new policies and initiatives required to deal with the newly emerging problem of nuclear proliferation in the twenty-first century?

References

Aldridge, Robert C. 1983. *First Strike! The Pentagon Strategy for Nuclear War*. Boston, MA: South End Press.

Alperovitz, Gar. 1965. *Atomic Diplomacy: Hiroshima and Potsdam*. London: Secker and Warburg.

Arkin, William M. 2002. 'Secret Plan Outlines the Unthinkable', *Los Angeles Times*, 10 March 2002. Accessed 20 April 2018. http://articles.latimes.com/2002/mar/10/opinion/op-arkin.

Art, Robert J., and Kenneth N. Waltz, eds. 1971. *The Use of Force: Military Power and International Politics*. New York, NY: Rowman & Littlefield Publishers.

Baylis, John, Steve Smith, and Patricia Owen. 2017. *The Globalization of World Politics: An Introduction to International Relations*. United Kingdom: Oxford University Press.

Baklitskiy, Andrey, 2015. 'The 2015 NPT Review Conference and the Future of the Nonproliferation Regime'. *Arms Control Today* 45 (6): 15–18. Accessed 20 April 2018. https://www.armscontrol.org/ACT/2015_0708/Features/The-2015-NPT-Review-Conference-and-the-Future-of-The-Nonproliferation-Regime.

Brodie, Bernard, ed. 1946. *The Absolute Weapon: Atomic Power and the World Order*. New York: Harcourt, Brace and Company.

Brown, Chris, and Kirsten Ainley. 2005. *Understanding International Relations*. New York: Palgrave Macmillan.

Bruno, Greg and Nestor Bailly. 2010. 'Iran's Nuclear Program'. Council on Foreign Relations. Accessed 20 April 2018. https://www.cfr.org/backgrounder/irans-nuclear-program.

Bulletin of Atomic Scientists (BAS), Nov–Dec. 1997. US: Taylor and Francis.

Chawla, Shalini. 2013. *Nuclear Pakistan*. New Delhi: KW Publishers.

Chellaney, Brahma. 2002. 'The India-Pakistan-China Strategic Triangle and the Role of Nuclear Weapons'. *Proliferation Papers, IFRI, Security Studies Department*. Accessed 20 April 2018. http://www.iaea.org/inis/collection/NCLCollectionStore/_Public/37/066/37066507.pdf.

von Clausewitz, Carl. 1950. *On War*, translated by O. J. Matthijs. Jolles. Washington D. C.: Infantry Journal Press.

Dinerstein H. S. 1962. *War and the Soviet Union*. New York: Frederick A. Praeger.

Douglas, Frantz, and Catherine Collins. 2007. *The Man from Pakistan: The Story of the World's Most Dangerous Nuclear Smuggler*. New York: Twelve.

Ferguson, Charles D. 2006. Preventing Catastrophic Nuclear Terrorism, Council Special Report No. 11, Council on Foreign Relations, March 2006. Accessed 20 April 2018. https://fas.org/pub-reports/preventing-catastrophic-nuclear-terrorism/.

Fetter, Steve. 1996. 'Verifying Nuclear Disarmament' Washington D. C.: Henry L. Stimson Center.

Goldstein, Joshua S. 2003. *International Relations*. New Delhi: Pearson.

Greitens, Sheena Chestnut. 2014. 'Nuclear Proliferation'. In *The Globalization of World Politics: An Introduction to International Relations*, edited by John Baylis, Steve Smith and Patricia Owens. New York, NY: Oxford University Press.

Greg Bruno and Nestor Bailly. 2010. 'Iran's Nuclear Program'. Council on Foreign Relations, last updated 10 March 2010. Accessed 24 April 2018. https://www.cfr.org/backgrounder/irans-nuclear-program.

Heywood, Andrew. 2014: *Global Politics*. New York, NY: Palgrave Macmillan.

IISS Strategic Dossier. 2007. *Nuclear Black Markets: Pakistan, A. Q. Khan and the Rise of Proliferation Networks: A Net Assessment*. Accessed 20 April 2018. https://www.iiss.org/en/Publications/Strategic%20Dossiers/Issues.

Institute for Defence Studies and Analyses (IDSA). 2016. 'International Conference on India's Role in Global Nuclear Governance'. IDSA-PRIO Conference concept note, 24–26 February 2016. Accessed 20 April 2018. http://www.idsa.in/event/india-role-in-global-nuclear-governance.

Jain Jagdish P. 1974. *India and Disarmament: Volume 1, Nehru Era—An Analytical Study*. New Delhi: Radiant Publishers.

Jervis, Robert. 1978. 'Cooperation Under the Security Dilemma'. *World Politics* 30 (2): 167–214.

Jindal, Nirmal. 1987. *War as a Political Weapon in the Nuclear Age: A Study with Special Reference to the US Concept of Limited War*. New Delhi: Intellectual Publishing House.

———. 1994. *US Foreign Policy: Issues and Perspectives*. New Delhi: Intellectual Publishing House.

Kissinger, Henry A. 1957. *Nuclear Weapons and Foreign Policy*. New York: Harper and Brothers.

Mandelbaum, Michael. 1981. *The Nuclear Revolution: International Politics Before and After Hiroshima*. New York: Cambridge University Press.

Mao Tse-tung. 1965. *On War*. Dehradun: Current Events Press.

Mishra, Sitakanta. 2008. *The Challenge of Nuclear Terror*. New Delhi: KW Publishers.

Mohan, C. Raja. 2001. 'Between war and Peace'. Accessed 20 April 2018. http://www.thehindu.com/2001/12/20/stories/2001122001231000.htm.

Mooney, Chrish. 2005. 'US Science Under Political Siege'. *New Scientist*. Accessed 20 April 2018. https://www.new-scientist.com/.../mg18725165-100-us-science-under-political-siege/.

Morgenthau, Hans J. 1972. *Politics among Nations: The Struggle for Power and Peace*. New York: Alfred A. Knopf.

Nicholson, Michael. 2005. *International Relations: A Concise Introduction*. New York: Palgrave Macmillan.

Palmer, Norman D. and Howard C. Perkins, eds. 1969. *International Relations: The World Community in Transition*. Calcutta: Scientific Books Agency.

Safeguards to Prevent Nuclear Proliferation—World Nuclear Association. 2017. Accessed 18 April 2018. www.world-nuclear.org/.../non-proliferation/safeguards-to-prevent-nuclear-proliferati.

Sagan, Scott D. 2004. 'Why do States Build Nuclear Weapons? Three Models in Search of a Bomb'. In Michael E. Brown. (ed.), *New Global Dangers: Changing Dimensions of International Security*, edited by Michael E. Brown, Owen R. Coté, Sean M. Lynn-Jones and Steven E. Miller. London: MIT Press.

Sagan, Scott D., and Kenneth N. Waltz. 2003. *The Spread of Nuclear Weapons: A Debate Renewed*. New York: W. W. Norton.

Schelling, Thomas C. 1966. *Arms and Influence*. New Haven, CT: Yale University Press.

Shultz, George Pratt. 1984. *Preventing the Proliferation of Nuclear Weapons*. Address by Shultz before the United Nations Association of the USA, New York, 1 November 1984. Washington D. C.: US Department of State, Bureau of Public Affairs.

Singh, S. Rajen. 2002. 'India's Response to Nuclear Non-proliferation Measures'. *India Quarterly* 58 (3&4): 31–92.

Thayer, Bradley A. 1995. 'The Causes of Nuclear Proliferation and the Utility of the Nuclear Non-Proliferation Regime'. *Security Studies* 4 (3): 463–519.

UN Security Council (UNSC) Resolution 1540 (2004). https://www.un.org/disarmament/wmd/sc1540/.

US Department of State. 2006. 'Announcing the Global Initiative to Combat Nuclear Terrorism'. 15 July 2006. Accessed 6 August 2017. https://2001-2009.state.gov/p/eur/rls/or/69021.htm.

Waltz, Kenneth N. 1988. 'The Origins of War in Neorealist Theory'. *Journal of Interdisciplinary History* 18 (4): 615–628.

World Nuclear Association. 2015. *International Convention for Suppression of Acts of Nuclear Terrorism*. Accessed 20 April 2018. www-ns.iaea.org/security/nuclear_terrorism_convention.asp.

———. 2017. 'Safeguards to Prevent Nuclear Proliferation'. Accessed 20 April 2018. http://www.world-nuclear.org/information-library/safety-and-security/non-proliferation/safeguards-to-prevent-nuclear-proliferation.aspx.

Further Reading

Diehl, Sarah J. and James Clay Moltz. 2008. *Nuclear Weapons and Nonproliferation: A Reference Handbook*. Santa Barbara, CA: ABC-CLIO.

Frieman, Wendy. 2004. *China, Arms Control, and Nonproliferation*. London: Routledge.

Joyner, Daniel H. 2013. *Interpreting the Nuclear Non-Proliferation Treaty*. New York: Oxford University Press.

Knopf, Jeffrey W., ed. 2012. *Security Assurances and Nuclear Nonproliferation*. Stanford, CA: Stanford University Press.

Rublee. Maria Rost. 2009. *Nonproliferation Norms: Why States Choose Nuclear Restraint*. New York, NY: University of Georgia Press.

Schneider, Barry R. 1999. *Future War and Counterproliferation: US Military Responses to NBC Proliferation Threats*. Santa Barbara: Praeger.

Sokolski, Henry D. 2001. *Best of Intentions: America's Campaign against Strategic Weapons Proliferation*. Westport, CT: Praeger.

Toynbee, Arnold J. 1965. 'War Is Not the Normal Condition of Man; War Is Not Normal'. *New York Times*, 7 November 1965.

10

CHAPTER

International Terrorism: Non-state Actors and State Terrorism— Developments Post-9/11

Shivali Aggarwal

LEARNING OBJECTIVES

- To elucidate and assess the concept of global terrorism
- To examine the factors behind terrorism
- To understand the role of state and non-state actors in promoting global terrorism
- To analyse the relationship between globalization and the spread of international terrorism
- To explain if there is a way to combat terrorism, especially when there are allegations that the United Nations has proved ineffective in this regard till now

Yes, security matters. Globally, there are many issues which are areas of concern for the people across the border. Terrorism is one such issue and it consists of threats, violence or intimidation to coerce a government, group or society in general. It is an internationally accepted fact that terrorism has expanded to a major part of the world. It is a point of fear and a challenge to humankind. World history speaks about two world wars fought during the twentieth century and terrorism can be counted as the third world war against humankind. With the fast spread of globalization, terrorism has also taken its place at the international level. There are different forms and objectives of terrorism in different parts of the world; however, the ultimate outcome is violence and the mass killing of innocent civilians.

Global terrorism is broadly defined as acts of crime or violence intended to further political, religious or political ideologies. After the end of the cold war, conflicts between civilizations struggling for influence on a new world order posed the greatest danger for international stability and peace (Huntington

1993). After the Second World War, the cold war between the two major economic powers of the world, that is, the United States of America (US) and the Union of Soviet Socialist Republics (USSR), introduced the global terrorism and, over a period of time, the present form of global terrorism evolved to incorporate a religious angle.

Today, only a few countries may claim immunity from terrorist attacks. The people of the post-cold war era have grown up with—and almost become used to—a perspective where acts of terrorism are tragically part of someone's daily life. If it does not affect us directly, we see the outcome on other people through media.

It is not wrong to call the present era an era of terrorism or even an age of fear (Acharya 2004, 3). Fear has almost affected all parts of our lives, from the mind up to our international and global environment. International relations are now not just about power politics but also about fear politics. We live in a world where power is no longer an adequate guarantee against fear. In fact, power begets fear. The more powerful a nation is, the more fearful it becomes. Terrorism is not a new phenomenon of this era. Somehow, people throughout history have been facing this phenomenon. It has just expanded its geographical and so-called ideological space in the era of globalization. We can also refer to this as the 'globalization of terrorism'.

The reasons for the globalization of terrorism are modernization, developments in technology and communications and ease of transportation. The connection of globalization to terrorism has been explained in this respect. As the previous tools of diplomacy and military measures have started to lose their validity, international cooperation and law have emerged as the tools to fight against terrorism. Since terrorism is a phenomenon that cannot be totally abolished, the best way to minimize terrorism is the use of international law with necessary organizations established to bolster cooperation at the international level.

Many countries, including India, have been victims of terrorist activities since many decades, but globally, the debate over terrorism gained a louder voice after the 9/11 attack on the twin towers of the World Trade Center. Global terrorism has many issues interlinked to it, such as illegal activities, corrupt practices, black money, the defence weapons business, international relations and political issues in some countries. Over the decades, from the cold war to the 9/11 attack and the Iraq war and to the present scenario, terrorism has frequently changed its objectives and forms. The present chapter is an attempt to reach the root cause of global terrorism, its form, funding, objectives, measures to eliminate it and its effect on international relations.

Understanding Globalization and Terrorism

What Is 'Globalization'?

This can be described in many ways and the simplest definition is that globalization is the free movement of goods, services and people across the world in a seamless and integrated manner.

The world is becoming a global village where nothing seems to be too far, neither the people, nor the places. Technological advancement has contributed to this a lot. Life expectancy has increased, better medical facilities have made us able to live longer and stay healthier. Business houses are finding new markets for their products; customers are benefiting from the foreign products and services. Everything looks better, even perfect in the era of globalization.

What Is 'Terrorism'?

The term 'terrorism' is derived from the Latin word *terrere*, which means 'great fear'. There is no internationally accepted definition of terrorism. Even the United Nations (UN) fails on this point: They could not frame one internationally accepted definition of 'terrorism'. Speaking of the practical difficulty, it is hard to define 'terrorism' in one single definition. Terrorism has different meanings for different people. The simple reason is that in different parts of the world, terrorist outfits have different objectives. Some have a religious purpose and others have political motives. In simple words, we can describe terrorism as an activity or a movement to create the fear of life in human beings, to obey the orders of the terrorists. We can also say that terrorism means violence, blood, killing of people and this may be under any religious influence or may have a political motive.

The US intelligence agency, the Federal Bureau of Investigation (FBI), has described terrorism as an 'unlawful use of force or violence against persons or property to intimidate or coerce a government, the civilian population, or any segment thereof, in furtherance of political or social objectives' (FBI 2018). This definition can be considered as an inclusive one, with most of the objectives of the terrorists represented.

The United Kingdom (UK) Terrorism Act of 2000 defines the term more broadly, saying that it is 'designed to influence the government or to intimidate the public' and can involve violence against a person, damage to property, a threat to a person's life, a serious risk to the health and safety of the public and, interestingly, 'serious interference with an electronic system'—now known as 'cyberterrorism' (The Day 2017). This definition covers most of the aspects of terrorism, including the modern-day terror attacks, but ignores the religious aspects intentionally or unfortunately, as religion has become the base of present-day terrorism.

One of the reports by the UN on terrorism says that terrorism flourishes in environments of despair, humiliation, poverty, political oppression, extremism and human rights abuse; it also flourishes in contexts of regional conflict and foreign occupation; and it profits from a weak state capacity to maintain law and order. This highlights the root cause of global terrorism.

History of Terrorism

Terrorism is not new to the world. It is believed that the term 'terrorism' originated out of the 1790s' French Revolution and since then it has transformed in many ways, with different motives in various parts of the world. David Charles Rapoport, professor of political Science, in his famous book *The Four Waves of Modern Terrorism*, describes the four phases of modern-day terrorism, the associated motives and their estimated durations (Table 10.1) (Rapport 2004).

Since its origin to the present day, terrorism has been continuously disturbing the peace of the world. People are being killed from different motives and with different tools. Almost every nation of the world has pledged to fight terrorism, but even then, it is growing day by day. This shows the world has a hidden agenda. In the beginning of the twenty-first century, the US witnessed one of the biggest terrorist attacks in the 9/11 World Trade Center incident and, after that, almost every developed country of the world has known terrorist killings. Yet the world is hardly learning anything from history and is not correcting its mistakes.

TABLE 10.1 Phases in the Rise of International Terrorism	
Motives	*Duration*
Anarchist	1880–1920
Anti-colonial	1920–1960
Left wing	1960–1990
Religious	1990–present day

Source: Rapport (2004).

Once realism used to talk about the competition among multiple states, but now it has started talking about the role of 'non-state actors'. Terrorism in the twenty-first century is operated mainly by the non-state actors. Realist thinking about terrorism tends to place a strong emphasis on the state and non-state dichotomy. Terrorism is usually viewed as a violent challenge to the established order by a non-state group or movement, often assumed as a pursuit of power. From this perspective, the motivations behind terrorism are largely strategic in character. Groups use clandestine violence and focus on civilian targets mainly because they are too weak to challenge the state openly through conventional armed conflict. They attempt to exhaust or weaken the resolve of a government or regime that they cannot destroy. 'The crucial feature of the realist approach to terrorism is nevertheless that, being an attempt to subvert civil order and overthrow the political system, the state's response to terrorism should be uncompromising' (Heywood 2011, 287).

Liberals, like realists, tend to view terrorism as an activity primarily engaged in by non-state actors. Liberals are more inclined to emphasize the role of ideology rather than simple power seeking. A key factor in explaining terrorism is therefore the influence of a political or religious ideology that creates an exaggerated sense of injustice and hostility, and so blinds the perpetrators of violence to the moral and human costs of their actions. However, liberal thinking about terrorism has tended to be dominated by the ethical dilemmas that are posed by the task of counterterrorism. The liberals typically view terrorism as an attack on the very principles of a liberal-democratic society—openness, choice, debate, toleration, and so on (Heywood 2011).

There are two main critical perspectives on terrorism. The first reflects the views of radical theorists such as Noam Chomsky and Falk. In their view, terrorism amounts to the killing of unarmed civilians and it is something that is engaged in by both states and non-state actors. State terrorism ('wholesale terrorism'), indeed, is much more significant than non-state terrorism ('retail terrorism'), because states have a far greater coercive capacity than any non-state actors. Terrorism is thus largely a mechanism through which states use violence against civilians either to maintain themselves in power or to extend political or economic influence over other states. In this respect, particular attention has been focused on terrorism's role in promoting US hegemony, the US being viewed as the world's 'leading terrorist state' (Chomsky 2003). The alternative critical perspective on terrorism is shaped by constructivist and post-structuralist thinking. It is characterized by the belief that much, and possibly all, commonly accepted knowledge about terrorism amounts to stereotypes and misconceptions. In this view, terrorism is a social or political construct. 'It is typically used to define certain groups and political causes as non-legitimate, by associating them with the image of immorality and wanton violence' (Heywood 2011, 287).

Factors Behind Terrorism

In the present day, broadly, there are three well-recognized factors behind terrorism, that is, the social factor, the economic factor and the political factor. The fourth one may be recognized as a hybrid factor, clubbing together religious and political motives.

Social Factor

Some other possible variables may be related to social issues. Levels of education have been mentioned in a few different studies. But this thought has limitations as many terrorists are well educated, from software engineers to the noble profession of teaching. Religion is another social aspect that needs to be considered. Modern terrorism has seen an enormous increase in religious extremism, the scale of violence has intensified and the global reach has expanded (Butler n.d.). People having religious motives participate in terrorism as a part of religious war, a war against all of those who do not share the same religious fate and present a threat to their beliefs, or by such religious war, they believe themselves to be serving the god they believe in. They consider it as their prime duty to expand their religion to the non-believer through terrorist activities. Terrorist outfit such as the Islamic State in Iraq and Syria (ISIS), Al Qaeda and Boko Haram are present-day examples of religious motives behind terrorism. Osama bin Laden's declaration of war on American interests in the 1990s stemmed from his belief that US troops stationed in Saudi Arabia represented an abomination to the kind of Islamic state he believed should exist in the Arabian Peninsula.

Economic Factor

The most popular theory is that poverty causes terrorism. When people are deprived of certain resources and opportunities, poverty can create resentment and cause some to turn to terrorism in order to express their outrage (Newman 2006). The problem with the poverty variable is that it can encompass a large variety of other smaller variables that all contribute to what can define someone as being impoverished. One source used a variety of factors to measure poverty, including social inequality, low gross domestic product (GDP) and low literacy or education levels. There are many sources including population, unemployment rates and inflation which can be used to measure poverty. 'Poverty' is a very tricky component and it is very difficult to measure and quantify. Many variables can be used to depict poverty, such as the poverty gap, the size of the homeless population, and so on. In the Middle East, many societies have great potential yet there are many citizens left without jobs and this causes a lower standing of living (Butler n.d.). When social inequality develops, many people become angry because they are unable to achieve what others are easily able to, thus creating internal conflict within certain geographic areas and making it more likely for terrorism to occur as a result (Newman 2006).

Political Factor

An alternative theory says that political factors such as government repression lead to terrorism. Examples of variables used to measure government repression are political rights and civil liberties

(Berrebi and Ostwald 2011). Unstable and, according to some, undemocratic societies form weak governments, causing the people to suffer. Human-rights abuses would also fall into this category since this is a direct result of government action and would then be considered a form of repression (Newman 2006).

As per this theory, the main motive of terrorism is to fight a government or an administrative system that, in their words, exploits the people or violates their rights or maybe to look for independence by claiming self-governance in a certain geographical area and starting a revolutionary movement against the government that oppresses its people. When the government is unable to provide a basic standard of living, citizens become displeased and this is when terrorist organizations are able to recruit.

The Maoist movement in Nepal is the best example of this kind of terrorism. Through their terrorist activities against the government, the Maoist revolutionaries revolted against the monarchy and claimed a democratic system for the country. Now Nepal has adopted the democratic form of government.

Hybrid Factor

This is a combination of the social, economic and political factors of terrorism. When terrorism is used in an organized manner to lay claim over a geographical area on the basis of religion, it is a clubbing together of the abovementioned three factors behind the terrorism. A few years back, unrest in the Middle Eastern countries and war between Israel and Palestine were the best examples of hybrid-factor terrorism. Terrorism in Jammu and Kashmir also has hybrid factors, with motives clubbing religious beliefs, political motives and economic facts.

While the factors or motive behind joining terrorist outfits might be different, all of them serve the same goal and that is to create fear among the people and to put the government(s) under pressure to agree to their demands.

Funding of Global Terrorism

Terrorists owned weapons of destruction and war technologies. They are highly equipped and use all kinds of information technology for communication and for their terrorist activities. Without any financial support, this would not be possible. Terrorism has global funding, which means it has sources of finance from all over the world. The source of terrorists' funds may be licit or illicit and the funding often takes the form of multiple small donations rather than one large sum of money.

In addition to funding historically received through counterfeit currency, offshore companies, charitable fronts and donations from state sponsors of terrorism such as Pakistan and Syria, many terrorist and criminal organizations raise money through a variety of criminal enterprises, including narcotics trafficking, credit-card scams and smuggling. Terrorism financing is a global phenomenon that not only threatens member states'[1] security, but can also undermine economic development and financial-market stability. Money laundry is another method traditionally adopted for funding terror activities globally.

---

[1] Members of the groups and bodies who fund the terrorist organizations. They are not official members of any legitimized body.

Tajheez al-Ghazi

This is one of the most commonly adopted funding methods by the Islamic terrorist outfits engaged in jihad. It is sanctioned by the Quran, the holy book of the Islamic religion. It literally means fitting out or arming a soldier, which allows those who cannot or will not join the jihad physically to attain a similar honour and reward to that which a jihadi gets. Local individuals, clerics and fundraising cells organically emerge to collect the funding for Tajheez. The funds are collected in cash and handled by local cells and sympathizers, as a result of which no banking transactions are involved.

International Trade

International trade is used for hidden transfers of money by techniques such as false trade invoicing. It is one of the most involved methods of laundering, which makes it extremely difficult to detect. It is done through over-invoicing or under-invoicing. Because of the involvement of multiple parties and complex payment methods (personal and bank cheques, transfers, payment orders, banking remittances and credits), the observance of due diligence procedures is very difficult. Additionally, international trade is also vulnerable to the use of falsified documents for money laundering, terrorist financing and avoidance of international embargoes.

To put an end to global terrorism, it is of utmost important to break the financial spine of the terrorist outfits. Finance is their backbone and blood which keeps them alive. This needs to be cut off globally by the all the nations contributing to it, and honestly.

Non-state Actors and Terrorism

On September the 11th, enemies of freedom committed an act of war against our country. Americans have known wars—but for the past 136 years, they have been wars on foreign soil, except for one Sunday in 1941. Americans have known the casualties of war—but not at the center of a great city on a peaceful morning. Americans have known surprise attacks—but never before on thousands of civilians. All of this was brought upon us in a single day—and night fell on a different world, a world where freedom itself is under attack. Al Qaeda is to terror what the mafia is to crime. But its goal is not making money; its goal is remaking the world—and imposing its radical beliefs on people everywhere. (George W. Bush, 43rd President of the United States of America, 2001)

Different terrorist organizations with their peripheral organizations function as non-state actors to promote terrorism. Once these were within the territory of a particular state—for instance, the Hamas in the Palestine Liberation Organization (PLO), the Hezbollah in Lebanon, and so on—but in the post-cold war era, they have crossed borders and became a global Frankenstein. In the present century, terrorism and jihadist terrorism are complementary to each other. These jihadist organizations originated as a repercussion of the Iranian Revolution of 1979 and the Soviet invasion of Afghanistan. It is no more a battle of wrong or right; rather, it is a war, a holy war to restore the glory of Islam. The organizations are prepared to use terrorist violence in order to achieve their objectives. They have the ambitious goal as prescribed by Salafism of the restoration of the Islamic caliphate and establishment of the era of the four guided caliphs: Abu Bakr, Osman, Umar and Ali. They deny the Western idea of the Westphalian state system and desire to reunite all Islamic countries as a single ummah. The creation of ISIS under Abu al-Baghdadi shows the reflection of this dream of Osama bin Laden.

With the accessibility of the fruits of globalization, now the terrorists are recruited from one country, trained in another and attack some other country. Most of the time, scholars argue, that is due to democratic deficits; but it is surprising to know that most of the terrorists are recruited from France and UK and not from Saudi Arabia. Even the entire 9/11 incident was planned in European territory. It is seen that these terrorists are second-generation Muslims of Western European countries who are well educated and brought up with liberal values. In this regard, the murder of Dutch film-maker Theodoor 'Theo' van Gogh has to be highlighted. He was killed by by Mohammed Bouyeri, who was a European, second-generation Muslim. Theo made a film called *Submission, Part I*, which was about Islam and violence against women. In the film, women are shown wearing transparent clothes with verses of the Quran written on their bodies, which is un-Islamic. Thus, he was murdered because Bouyeri had to defend his faith. This is not the only case; there are endless stories of millions of people.

In 2015, news came about the ISIS poster girls named Samra Kesinovic (17 years old) and Sabina Selimovic (15 years), who disappeared from home to join ISIS. They left a note at home, where it was written, 'Don't look for us. We will serve Allah and we will die for him.' But unfortunately, soon after, they were turned into the sex slaves of ISIS terrorists.

The Al Qaeda had been established by Osama bin Laden, who was the mastermind of the 9/11 attacks. The literal meaning of 'Al Qaeda' was the 'base', which is the epicentre of all terror networks spreading all around the world. They used to operate in more than 70 countries (Figure 10.1). The series of terrorist attacks and claims those were initiated by the Taliban were later united with the claims of the Al Qaeda and affect the global order. Presently, after the death of bin Laden, Al Qaeda has been represented in the name of Islamic states. The sole aim of Al Qaeda is to re-establish the Islamic caliphate which had been destroyed by the Western powers after the First World War.

Due to money and oil, there have been always strong presences of Western power in the Middle East. The royal houses and the ruling elites were pro-West, which did not please the religious fundamentalist groups. They saw the West as a threat to their social, cultural, political and economic traditions. Therefore, this resentment provided a platform for those fundamentalists who later turned into jihadists. They waged the war to save their Allah, their identity.

Following a rapid rise and concomitant territorial conquests, ISIS—or the Islamic State of Iraq and al-Sham or Levant (ISIL) or Da'esh, by its Arabic abbreviation—has for now, by default, taken operational command and leadership of the global jihadist movement, eclipsing Al Qaeda Central (AQC), which attacked the US homeland on 11 September 2001. At the time of writing, ISIS controls a wide swath of territory in Iraq and Syria, as large as the UK, with a population estimated at roughly between 6 million and 9 million people. Additionally, ISIS controls a sectarian army numbering more than 30,000 combatants, in part through an amalgamation of local armed insurgencies in Iraq and Syria and foreign recruits. ISIS's military surge in Syria and Iraq in 2013 and 2014 was a rude awakening for regional and global powers. Despite being trained by the US and costing anywhere between $8 billion and $25 billion, the Iraqi security forces were shattered like a house of glass in the summer of 2014 by ISIS's blitzkrieg, which was carried out by a force numbering only in the hundreds or at most the low thousands, catching neighbouring states and the great powers off guard. According to Fawaz A. Garges, 'an army that once counted 280,000 active-duty personnel, one of the largest in the Middle East, was now believed to have as few as 50,000 men by some estimates' (Garges 2016, 2). In June 2014, a few weeks before ISIS captured Mosul,

FIGURE 10.1 Organizational Structure of the Al Qaeda

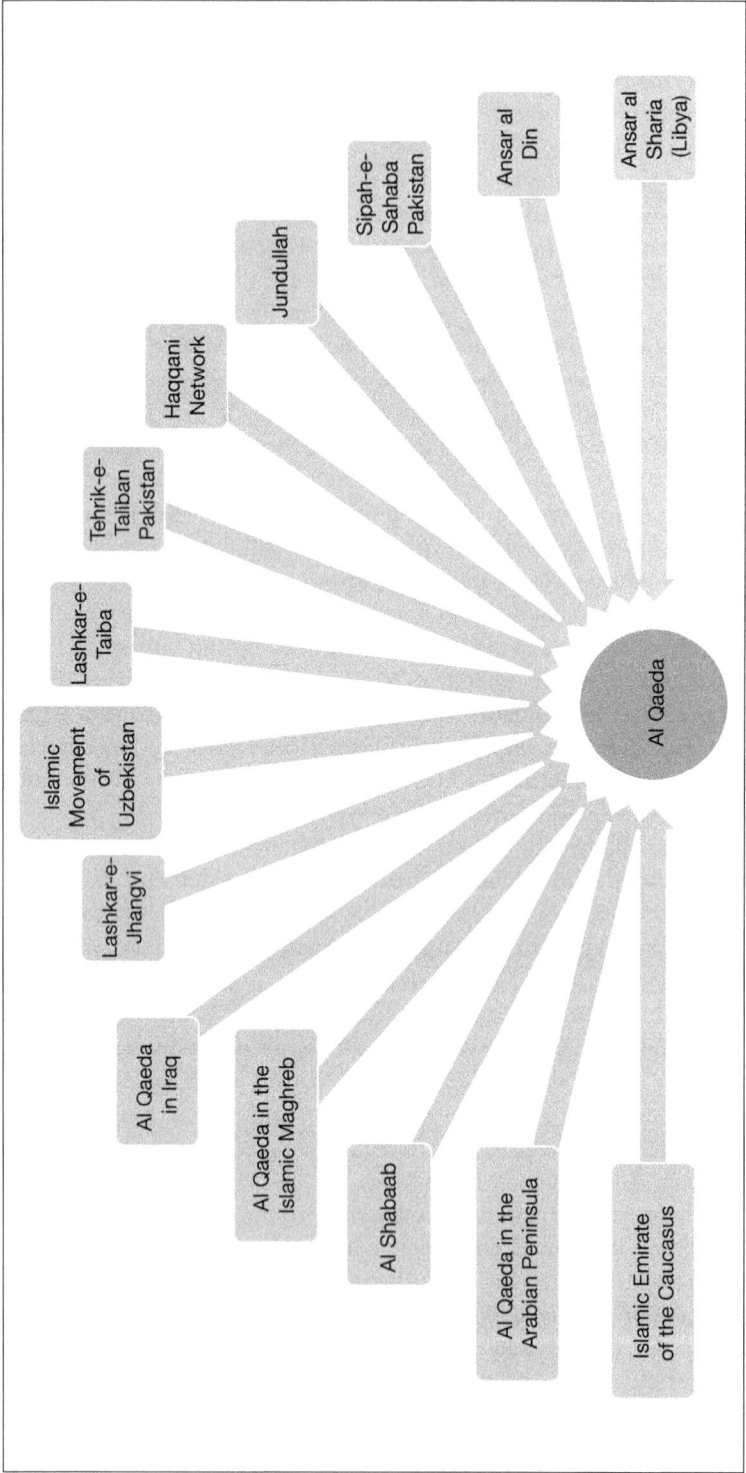

Iraq's second largest city, with a population of almost 2 million people, US president Barack Obama derisively dismissed the organization as amateurish and said that it did not represent a serious threat to the US' regional allies or interests. Although Obama is correct to say that ISIS did not pose an immediate or a strategic menace to the US homeland, critics seized on his comment as evidence of the administration's underestimation of ISIS' strength. From 2013 until the summer of 2014, ISIS overran Iraqi, Syrian and Kurdish security forces and rival Islamists as well. The group's prowess was confirmed by the seizure of the al-Raqqah and Deir al-Zour provinces in Syria in 2014 and the expeditious collapse of four Iraqi divisions overnight in Mosul and elsewhere in northern Iraq under the determined assault of outnumbered fighters in summer 2014. ISIS's sweep of the so-called Sunni Triangle—an area of central Iraq to the west and north of Baghdad mostly populated by Sunni Muslims—and the threat to the Kurdish regional capital of Irbil alarmed the governments across the Middle East and the Western powers. US officials feared that Saudi Arabia and Jordan might be the next ISIS targets (Figure 10.2).

Role of the State in International Terrorism

There have been three dynamics around nation states observed when we talk about the role of the state in international terrorism.

First, the state's role as a victim of international terrorism has to be highlighted. Hegel used to say the state is the march of God on earth, but for the Islamist terrorist, Allah is much more significant than the state (Rothbard 2017). The jihadists have waged a war to wither away the notion of the state. Because of this, many different state institutions and people associated with them were attacked and killed by terrorists. Presently, in the Syrian civil war, ISIS is fighting against the regime of Bashar al-Assad and in Iraq, they have rejected the rule of Nouri al-Maliki. It is not a fresh phenomenon—state institutions and government servants had been attacked by terrorist even in the colonial period. These attacks used to help them to get prominence and attention.

Secondly, the state as a counterterrorism mechanism to prevent or eliminate international terrorism has to be discussed. Today, the sovereign states of the international system are cooperating with each other to combat terrorism. As terrorism is not a new phenomenon, nor is counterterrorism. Counterterrorism, as a concerted and cooperative effort by governments to combat this tactic, is not that old, but it long predates any 'war on terror' aimed at the Islamist variety of international terrorism that is the most recent focus of attention. There is no single, optimum formula for resolving these conflicts. Counterterrorism is not the only objective in public policy, nor should it be. It is up to each nation's citizenry, preferably acting through a fair process of representative government, to decide where it wishes to strike a balance between safety from terrorism and other interests and values. A citizenry's confidence that this balance has been struck properly and in a way consistent with its values is important for the final, critical ingredient in counterterrorism: informed and sustained public support. This type of support is difficult to obtain. Public interest in counterterrorism is high after a major terrorist attack, but tends to wane if time passes without more such attacks. A counter-terrorist programme can be effective only if government officials and private citizens alike understand that the programme must be applied consistently, coherently and over a long period of time (Sandra 2012).

At the same time, we can see the state as a direct or indirect sponsor of terrorism. For instance, the first victim of international terrorism, the US, is the progenitor of international terrorists. When the

FIGURE 10.2 Governance and Operations of ISIS

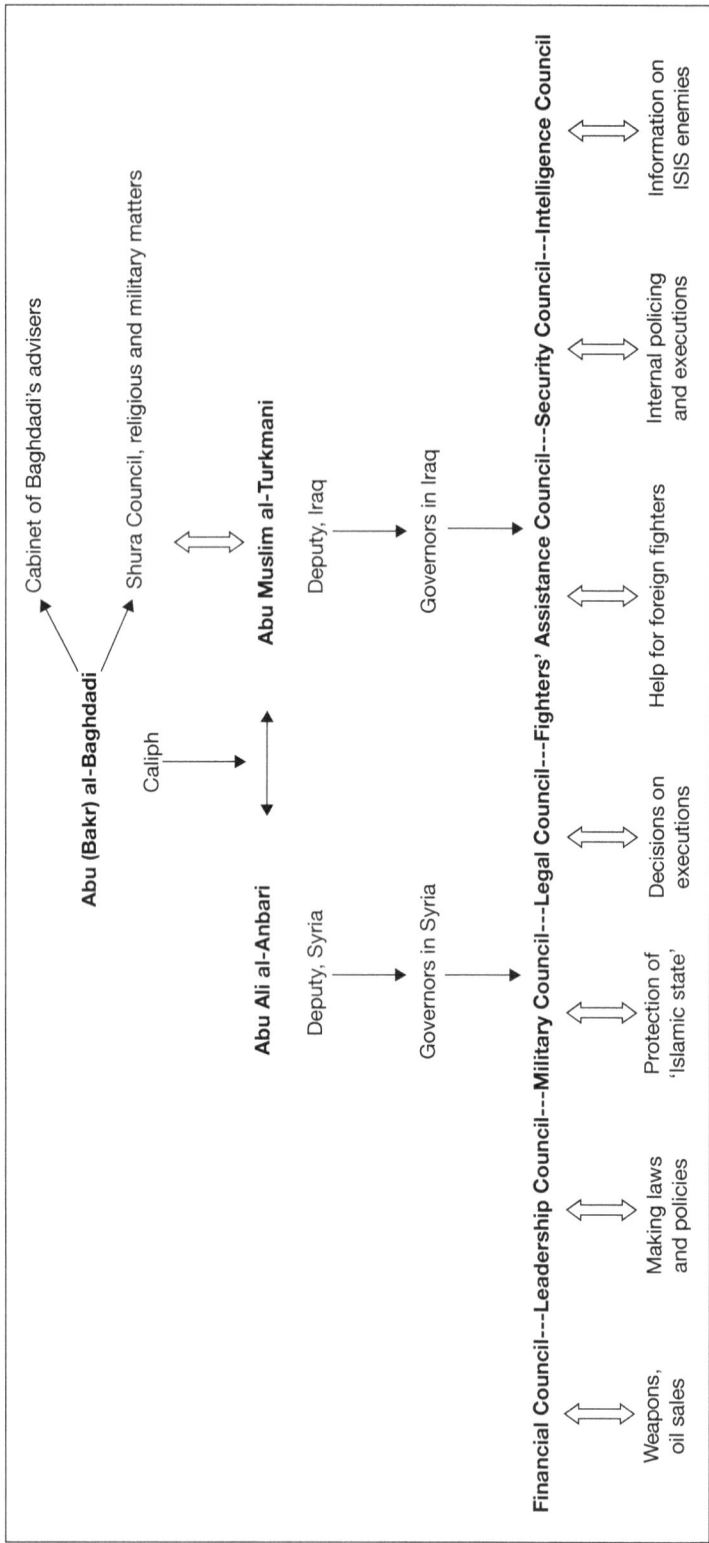

Abu (Bakr) al-Baghdadi

Cabinet of Baghdadi's advisers

Shura Council, religious and military matters

Caliph

Abu Ali al-Anbari

Deputy, Syria

Governors in Syria

Abu Muslim al-Turkmani

Deputy, Iraq

Governors in Iraq

Financial Council---Leadership Council---Military Council---Legal Council---Fighters' Assistance Council---Security Council---Intelligence Council

| Weapons, oil sales | Making laws and policies | Protection of 'Islamic state' | Decisions on executions | Help for foreign fighters | Internal policing and executions | Information on ISIS enemies |

USSR was fighting in Afghanistan, they gave birth to the Taliban. Now their own children have harmed them. Apart from that, a more recent example can be that of Pakistan. Mumbai witnessed a recent spate of international terrorism on 26 November 2008, where a terror group from Pakistan attacked and killed police officers, ordinary citizens and foreigners at the railway station and a restaurant, in hotels and on roads. Globalization has undoubtedly had a troubling influence on terrorism, but the one element that concerns counterterrorism experts and practitioners the most is future catastrophic attacks using weapons of mass destruction (WMD). According to the experts and as per the speculation of US intelligence, there have been multiple attempts by the Al Qaeda to test chemical and biological weapons under a programme codenamed 'Zabadi' (Kiras 2011).

Global Terrorism and International Relations

9/11—An Incident That Changed the World

Who does not want to be a part of history? Marie Rose Abad, Andrew Anthony Abate, Vincent Paul Abate, Laurence Christopher Abel, Alona Abraham, William F. Abrahamson, Paul Acquaviva—there are countless such names. They maybe never in their life wanted to become part of history. For them, 9/11 was just an ordinary day. They never thought that they would be a part of history, the darkest history of the human civilization. The 9/11 attacks on the New York World Trade Center and the Pentagon in Washington, D.C. not only changed the life of millions of Americans but of billions of people all around the world.

The terrorist attack brought the issue of terrorism to the forefront of global security thinking. A quick reaction came from the forty-third American president, George Bush, with the 'Global War on Terror'. According to the words of Paul Rogers, 'the large numbers of people killed and the targeting of two hugely important symbols of American life, the World Trade Center and the Pentagon, the reaction was both vigorous and extended, leading on to the termination of regimes in two states, Afghanistan and Iraq' (Rogers 2008, 221).

It was the resurrection of terrorism as a weapon of mass violence through the September 11 attacks on New York and Washington which convinced the world that a new, non-conventional security threat has emerged with a global effectiveness. However, according to Andrew Heywood, it is necessary to consider the nature of terrorism, the different ways in which terrorism has been understood and whether terrorism has changed in recent years not only to bring about death and destruction, but to create unease and anxiety about possible future acts of death and destruction. Terrorist violence is therefore clandestine and involves an element of surprise, if not arbitrariness, designed to create uncertainty and widen apprehension. Terrorism, therefore, often takes the form of seemingly indiscriminate attacks on civilian targets, although attacks on symbols of power and prestige and the kidnapping or murder of prominent businessmen, senior government officials and political leaders are usually also viewed as acts of terrorism (Figure 10.3) (Heywood 2011).

Due to the accessibility of the fruits of globalization, these terrorist groups get the latest technologies, better communication networks, worldwide terrorist recruitment facilities, easy funding, and so on. With the emergence of television media, their impact has become much more widespread than before. To fight against terrorism, the US military budget is now approaching the level of the peak years of the cold war and the term 'War on Terror' has itself been transformed into the 'long war against Islamofascism'.

FIGURE 10.3 Increasing Number of Terror Attacks

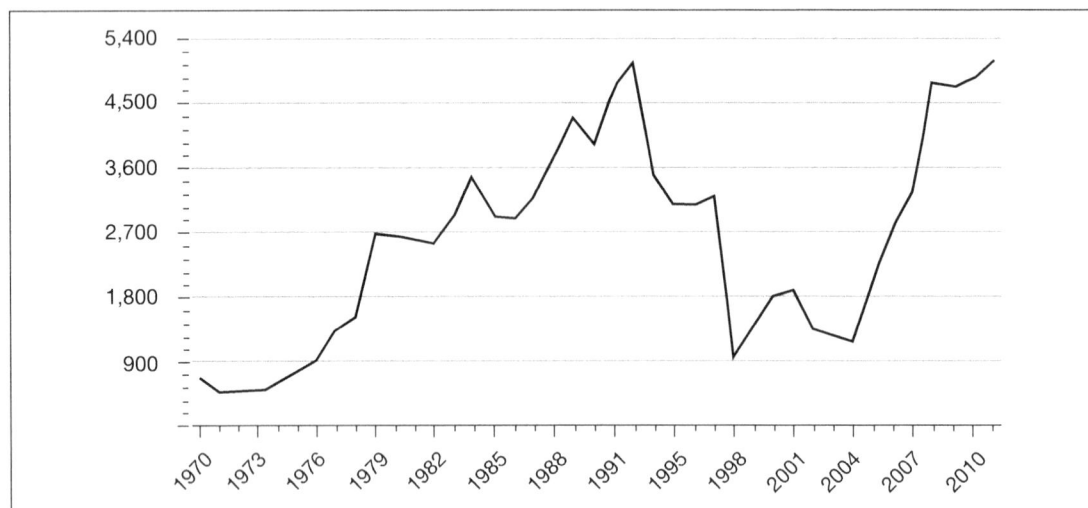

Source: Global Research (2013).

'In its most extreme representation in some influential US political circles, this war is understood as the "Fourth World War" and is just as much a matter of the survival of civilization as were the previous world wars, including the "Third World War" against the Soviet Union' (Rogers 2008, 222).

September 11 reflected a change in the *nature* of terrorism. It is widely assumed that it brought about a profound shift in its significance. The threat posed by terrorism was suddenly accorded a historically unprecedented level of importance, based on the belief that terrorism was a manifestation of new fault lines that would define global politics in the twenty-first century. Initially, terrorism was associated with nationalist and particularly separatist movements. The chief goal of a terrorist was the overthrow of foreign rule and the establishment of national self-determination. Those ideas were once bolstered by socialist perspectives, especially revolutionary Marxism. But in the post-cold war period, religion had started to become an important motivation for political violence. Now terrorism is motivated by religious emotions. Al Qaeda is certainly an example of this trend, where terrorism has been motivated by a broad and radical politico-religious ideology in the form of Salafi Islamism. It is basically a reflection of the long frustration with US involvement in different Islamic countries. Later, the West-dominated globalization became an important pretext on the basis of which they have waged war against the Western world. Samuel Huntington termed it the clash of two civilizations, but it is something more than that (Huntington 1973). It is wrong to say that the same time religiously inspired terrorism is certainly not a new phenomenon; it used to always exist in the name of Muslim Brotherhood. Not only the Muslim Brotherhood; there were other groups such as the Moro National Liberation Front (MNLF), Egyptian Islamic Jihad and Hezbollah that fused religious and political objectives.

Global terrorism has changed many things internationally. 'Cooperation among nations is necessary to maximize the possible benefits and minimize the possible damages of interactions and interdependencies and to capture opportunities for realizing greater peace, welfare and justice' (Paul 1999, 8). Terrorist activities have made the world come closer through various international forums and work together in the interest of humankind.

It is true that the foreign policies of many countries were changed due to global terrorism. After the 9/11 attack, the US announced a war against Taliban-occupied Afghanistan, with the support of Britain and France. It seems that the 9/11 attack had given a licence to the US to wage war against any country it wished to. Quoting the reason as chemical weapons, the US attacked Iraq and hanged its president, Saddam Hussein, for not obeying the orders of the US government. However, no chemical weapons were found in Iraq. Over the period of more than one and a half decades after the 9/11 attack, the US has been able to establish itself as the centre of world power by waging war in the name of curbing terrorism.

The fear of terrorism has given a boost to the defence-equipment business all over the world. Countries such as India, which have been affected by terrorism since many years, are putting a huge amount of their budgets into defence purchases. Developed nations are taking advantage of this situation by selling their defence equipment to the developing countries.

Concern over terrorism has impacted the foreign policies of most of the countries and these countries are avoiding establishing strong diplomatic relationships with the states sponsoring the terror activities. The issue of terrorism has become a point of political debates during the elections in the democratic countries. The US is one of the best examples of this—ever since the 9/11 attacks, every presidential election campaign hears more arguments with regard to global terrorism.

Meanwhile, major world powers increased cooperation and intelligence sharing at the tactical level to combat terrorism post-9/11. The US Central Investigation Agency (CIA) and the FBI, in particular, became greatly energized to expand their assets worldwide and cooperate with other intelligence agencies of the world. Joint working groups on intelligence sharing have been formed between several countries to collectively combat terrorism. Intelligence sharing has been very useful in nabbing terror suspects and preventing attacks.

However, the fight against terrorism has been marred due to weak systems of governance and continued civil-war conditions prevailing in the African continent. Weak systems in some countries such as Somalia, Nigeria and Mali allow terrorism to proliferate in these regions. The US, UK, France and Italy are particularly impacted by developments in Africa and continuously provide military and financial assistance to weak nation states to stem the rising tide of internecine conflict and terrorism in the continent.

The following measures have been widely advocated to eliminate global terrorism:

- Stop supporting the countries that fund terrorists.
- Let the UN be more active to counter terrorism and frame one universally accepted definition of terrorism and identify the groups and people encouraging terrorist activities.
- Teach people the true meaning of religion and don't allow misinterpretation of religious texts by the terrorists or the religious leaders.
- Ensure democratic political system in the countries which are witnessing the civil war or have a weak governance mechanism in their states.
- Offer economic and military aid to weak nation states.
- Stop supporting dictatorships and repressive militaries.
- Let countries establish stronger diplomatic and military relations to counter terrorism.
- Police in cyberspace.
- Ensure effective governance and equal access to economic opportunities in developing and least developing countries.
- Take actions to check nuclear proliferation.

- Take military action against proscribed terrorist groups.
- Stop smuggling activities and restrict funding of terrorist organizations.

Role of the UN in Combating Global Terrorism

Once the former Secretary-General of the UN Kofi A. Annan said, 'Terrorism is a global menace. It calls for a united, global response. To defeat it, all nations must take counsel together, and act in unison. That is why we have the United Nations' (Thapa 2005).

This statement reflects the importance of the UN in combating global terrorism. The UN is the most important of all international institutions, having become a universal institution because of its sheer strength of 193 memberships, all sovereign states. In the last three decades, the emergence of highly organized, well-trained and well-financed international terrorist networks exposed the significant gaps in the UN's pre-existing anti-terrorism framework. The end of the cold war as well as the aftermath of the tragic attacks on the US in 2001 have forced the overhaul of the UN's anti-terrorism strategy, with far-reaching resolutions as well as the imposition of an onerous set of mandatory obligations on member states. The marshalling of an international-law strategy on terrorism is a story of committees and their reports, of resolutions, of drafting treaties and of calls for state action.

General Assembly Resolutions on Terrorism

Up to the 1980s, the actions of the UN General Assembly (GA) against terrorism were influenced by two factors, namely, self-determination (decolonization) and the cold war. The disintegration of the USSR and the disappearance of the cold war ultimately helped the UN to take a more aggressive stand on terrorism during the 1990s. The GA has addressed international terrorism in two ways: by developing a normative framework that defines terrorism as a common problem and by encouraging concerted government action to develop international and national legal rules for dealing with terrorists. An institutional characteristic of the GA is that it cannot act as a direct coordinator of action against terrorism because it lacks the authority to command governments and other influential actors to take or avoid particular actions. GA resolutions are broadly classified into three categories:

1. Measures to prevent terrorism.
2. Measures to eliminate international terrorism.
3. Human rights and terrorism.

The GA's efforts to encourage concerted international action against terrorists have taken three forms. The GA has constituted two ad hoc committees on terrorism, composed of delegates of member states, to work out measures that are more specific.

There simply was no consensus to identify what acts did or did not constitute terrorism, however. Even in today's vastly improved climate at the UN, the definition of terrorism would still present enormous problems.[2]

---

[2] Refer to Chapter 15 for more information.

In 1994, the GA made a major breakthrough in condemning terrorism in all formats unanimously, without going into the technical aspect of the definition of terrorism. Resolution 49/60, titled 'Declaration on Measures to Eliminate International Terrorism' adopted on 17 February 1995 was passed in its forty-ninth session. The content of the resolution was further reaffirmed in later resolutions whenever circumstances demanded that the GA condemn terrorism. The contents of resolutions become guidelines and policies for every country to combat terrorism domestically and internationally.

Resolution 49/60

Resolution 49/60 of the UN is vital in combating global terrorism. The following are some of the features of Resolution 49/60:

1. Resolution urges states to take all appropriate measures at the national and international level to eliminate terrorism.
2. It declares that those responsible for terrorism should be brought to justice.
3. It stresses that each state must cooperate with other states in the most practical and effective manner to strengthen the international community as a whole in combating terrorism.
4. The state members of the UN solemnly reaffirm their unequivocal condemnation of all acts, methods and practices of terrorism as criminal and unjustifiable, wherever and by whosoever committed.
5. All methods and practices of terrorism constitute grave violations of the principles of the UN, as they threaten international peace and security, jeopardize the friendly relations among the states and aim at the destruction of human rights and the democratic basis of society.
6. The resolution unambiguously declares that any criminal act that is going to create terror in the public cannot be justifiable on any political, philosophical, ideological, racial, ethnic, religious or on any other grounds.
7. States have obligations under the Charter of the United Nations and international law to refrain from organizing, assisting or participating in terrorist acts in the territories of other states and from providing infrastructure or facilities to train terrorists on their soil.
8. The resolution urges the states to honour, ratify and implement the existing international treaty on terrorism and enact domestic legislations against terrorism in accordance with the international treaty.
9. The states should speedily prosecute the perpetrators of terrorism under the provisions of their domestic laws or enforce extradition to other states by having bilateral, regional or multilateral extradition treaties.

It is important to remember that terrorist organizations usually lack moral scruples and do not fear using nuclear weapons. The GA passed a resolution calling upon the states to take measures to prevent the terrorists from acquiring WMDs and nuclear weapons on 9 January 2003, under the title 'Measures to prevent terrorists from acquiring weapons of mass destruction'. Finally, the GA adopted the International Convention for the Suppression of Acts of Nuclear Terrorism on 13 April 2005. The International Atomic Energy Agency (IAEA), anticipating the danger of nuclear terrorism, brought in an amendment to strengthen the Convention on the Physical Protection of Nuclear Material on 8 July 2005, which gives a wide power to the IAEA to inspect the nuclear plants in various countries. Further, it requested the members to sign and ratify the International Convention for the Suppression of Acts of Nuclear Terrorism. The UN has chalked out its strategy to fight international terrorism and the same was adopted in its resolution on 13 October 2010, titled 'The United Nations Global Counter-Terrorism Strategy'. The resolution recommended two types of measures: first, measures to address the conditions conducive to the spread of terrorism and, secondly, measures to prevent and combat terrorism.

Security Council Resolutions on Terrorism

The Security Council (SC) is the continuous executive organ of the UN. Here, decisions on procedural matters are to be made by an affirmative vote of nine members. Decisions on all other matters are to be made by an affirmative vote of nine members, including the concurring votes of the five permanent members. The SC, being the executive organ of the UN, has primary responsibility to maintain international peace and security; during the discharge of these obligations, the SC acts on behalf of the UN. The measures by the SC to maintain international peace include initially calling upon an offending state to give effect to its decision, including sanctions. If the sanctions do not produce the desired end, the SC may use all kinds of military force at its disposal against the guilty state, which may be in the form of either a blockade or war. The SC began to take on the question of terrorism in the early 1990s in response to specific events. In October 2004, the SC unanimously passed the resolution. However, it is true that the international community has to wait some time before the GA has its own definition of terrorism.

In accordance with UN Charter, the legal effect of labelling terrorism as a 'threat to international peace and security' was to empower the SC to enact measures to combat it under Chapter VII, which is binding on all members. Resolution 1368 was passed by the SC the day after the attacks on US territory and recognized 'the inherent right of individual or collective self-defence' as a legitimate response. This was the first time that self-defence was formally recognized as a legitimate response to terrorism. The SC took swift and unprecedented action in the wake of the events of 11 September 2001. The SC felt that it was necessary to offer the US a stronger form of support than sympathy. Accordingly, it recognized in Resolution 1368 the right of self-defence as being in accordance with the Charter. This recognition would not have been new because it simply repeated the words of the Charter. The SC had already expressed its position in unequivocal words that international terrorism was a threat to international peace and security.

The UN Charter recognizes the right to self-defence as an inalienable right of the states, but it is generally accepted that this right is not open-ended. The occurrence of an armed attack is the precedent condition for the exercise of self-defence and it ceases to operate when the SC takes action. However, the SC intentionally refrained from defining the terrorist attack as an 'armed attack'. Nevertheless, the SC regarded the attacks of September 11 as threats to international peace and security, but it did not call for collective action. By invoking a state's right to self-defence, it handed over this responsibility to individual states. The US and the UK gave notification to the SC of action in self-defence against the Taliban regime of Afghanistan and declared war. Article 51 of the UN Charter authorizes self-defence only until the SC takes action, this provision being made moot in case of the US and UK attack on the Taliban regime of Afghanistan because the SC never intended to take such action.

Human Rights and Terrorism

The human cost of terrorism has been felt in virtually every corner of the globe. Terrorism and human rights cannot coexist; they are mutually destructive. Human rights are relevant to terrorism as regards both its victims and its perpetrators. The concept of human rights was first expressed in the 1948 Universal Declaration of Human Rights (UDHR), which established 'recognition of the inherent dignity and inalienable rights of all members of the human family'. The innocent victims of terrorism suffer an attack on their most basic right, to live in peace and security. Terrorism itself is an attack on human rights. The direct link between terrorism and human rights was first recognized by the World Conference on Human Rights in Vienna, 1993, in the Vienna Declaration and Programme of Action (VDPA) stipulates that 'acts, methods and practices of terrorism in all its forms and manifestation as well as linking in some countries to drug trafficking are activities aimed at the destruction of human rights'.

Terrorism clearly has a very real and direct impact on human rights, with devastating consequences for the enjoyment of the right to life, liberty and physical integrity of victims. In addition to these individual costs, terrorism can destabilize governments, undermine civil society, jeopardize peace and security, and threaten social and economic development. All of these also have a real impact on the enjoyment of human rights.

Respect for human rights and the rule of law must be the bedrock of the global fight against terrorism. This requires the development of national counterterrorism strategies that seek to prevent acts of terrorism, prosecute those responsible for such criminal acts, and promote and protect human rights and the rule of law. It implies measures to address the conditions conducive to the spread of terrorism, including the lack of the rule of law and violations of human rights, ethnic, national and religious discrimination, political exclusion, and socio-economic marginalization; to foster the active participation and leadership of civil society; to condemn human-rights violations, prohibit them in national law, promptly investigate and prosecute them, and prevent them; and to give due attention to the rights of victims of human-rights violations—for instance, through restitution and compensation.

Although the dreadful 2017 incident of shooting down more than 60 people in Las Vegas cannot be termed as purely 'terrorism' as per the US government, but the mass killing of innocents does not automatically meet the generally accepted definitions of terrorism. Terrorism does not always mean a political, ideological or religious fight; it is also a 'verbal' weapon, especially when the accused is a 'Muslim'. Any act of anti-humane behaviour is purely 'terrorist' and this carries so much meaning, said Marta Crenshaw, a terrorism expert at Stanford's Center for International Security and Cooperation (CISAC). This incident clearly proves that a democratic upsurge should and must be the best technique to fight the evils of terrorism.

Concluding Observations

Global terrorism is a serious problem for the international community which is increasing day by day. Only a few countries are untouched by terrorist activities. Although all countries are fighting it in their individual capacities, the world has to join hands to eliminate terrorism.

There may be different motives behind terrorism but the ultimate outcome is violence and killing of people. In the present-day scenario, religiously influenced terrorism is expanding its arms to most parts of the world, which is dangerous for humankind. Funding of terrorist organizations is a major problem. World leaders need to focus on the funding of terrorism and the technological uses of such funds. Countries need to agree on a common definition of terrorism and have to act against not just the terrorists but their root cause also. States which are supporting terrorism need to be taught a proper lesson to stop their support. The UN has to lead the war against global terrorism and needs to take strict military action against the terrorist organizations. The states individually and collectively have political, military, legal, economic and technological advantages in the struggle against terrorist groups. However, most of the time they fail in this agenda. Everyone fears death and evil, but when the world is united, then the extreme views of minority cannot cause much harm. It is the time to fear not the fear mongers but fear itself. We cannot remain the silent majority—as Tagore used to say, 'Where the mind is without fear, the head is held high'. Therefore, to restore peace and justice, this anarchic world has to fight against the evil. It has to cooperate, keeping aside their narrow self-interest for the betterment of human civilization.

Summary

- Global terrorism is defined as acts of crime or violence intended to further political, religious or political ideologies. Terrorism can consist of threats, violence or intimidation to coerce a government, group or society in general. However, there is no internationally accepted definition of terrorism. Even the United Nations (UN) fails on this point.
- It is not a wrong statement if we call the present era as the 'era of terrorism' or even the 'age of fear'. Fear has almost affected all parts of our life, from the mind up to our international and global environment. International relations are now not just about power politics but also about fear politics. We live in a world where power is no longer an adequate guarantee against fear.
- There are different forms and objectives of terrorism in different parts of the world but the ultimate outcome is violence and mass killing of innocent civilians.
- The reason for the globalization of terrorism is modernization, with developments in technology, communication and the ease in transportation.
- One of the reports by the UN on terrorism says that terrorism flourishes in environments of despair, humiliation, poverty, political oppression, extremism and human-rights abuse; it also flourishes in contexts of regional conflict and foreign occupation; and it profits from a weak state capacity to maintain law and order.
- It is believed that the term 'terrorism' originated out of the 1790s French Revolution and since then, it has transformed in many ways, to appear with different motives in various parts of the world.
- In the present-day scenario, broadly, there are two well-recognized motives behind terrorism—one is the religious or social motive and another is the political motive. The third one may be recognized as a hybrid motive, clubbing together the religious and the political motives.
- The backbone and the blood of global terrorism are its financing sources. The source of terrorists' funds may be licit or illicit, and funding often takes the form of multiple small donations, rather than one large sum of money.
- International relations are not untouched by terrorism. The foreign policy of many countries was changed due to global terrorism.

- Major world powers increased cooperation and intelligence sharing at the tactical level to combat terrorism post-9/11.
- The fear of terrorism has given a boost to the defence-equipment business all over the world. Countries such as India, which have been affected by terrorism since many years, are putting up huge amounts of their budget for defence purchases.
- Resolution 1368 was passed by Security Council of the UN, the day after the attacks on US territory recognized; 'the inherent right of individual or collective self-defence' is a legitimate response. This was the first time that self-defence was formally recognized as legitimate response to terrorism.
- Terrorism clearly has a very real and direct impact on human rights, with devastating consequences for the enjoyment of the rights to life, liberty and physical integrity of victims.
- Political stability and good economy are needed in weak states so that terrorist groups could not use these weak states.
- Funding of terrorists needs to be blocked internationally.
- The UNs has to be in lead role to eliminate terrorism.

Suggested Questions

1. What do you understand by global terrorism? Discuss the role of globalization and advancement of technology in rise of international terrorism.
2. Discuss five effective methods to eliminate global terrorism.
3. Critically analyse the role of the US policies against terrorism after the 9/11 attack.
4. Discuss the role of the UN to combat international terrorism.
5. Do you see modern terrorism as an existential challenge against the Westphalian notion of the modern state system?
6. Discuss the regional security measures to deal with the problem of global terrorism.

References

Acharya, Amitav. 2004. *Ages of Fear: Power versus Principle in the War on Terror.* New Delhi: Rupa Publication.

Berribi, Claude and Jordan Ostwald. 2011. 'The Many Faces of Counterterrorism'. *Public Choice* 149 (3/4): 383–403.

Butler, Taryn. n.d. 'What Causes Terrorism?' Accessed 24 April 2018. https://www.mckendree.edu/academics/schol-ars/butler-issue-25.pdf.

FBI. 2018. *Terrorism 2002–2005.* Accessed 24 April 2018. https://www.fbi.gov/stats-services/publications/terrorism-2002-2005.

Gerges, F. A. 2016. *ISIS: A History.* Oxford: Princeton University Press.

Global Research. 2013. 'U.S. War on Terror Has Increased Terrorism'. *Global Research*, 22 October 2013.

Heywood, Andrew. 2011. *Global Politics.* New York, NY: Palgrave Macmillan.

Hummel, S. 2016. 'The Islamic State and WMD: Assessing the Future Threat'. Accessed 24 April 2018. https://ctc.usma.edu/the-islamic-state-and-wmd-assessing-the-future-threat/.

Huntington, Samuel P. 1973. 'Transnational Organizations in World Politics'. *World Politics* 25 (3).

Newman, Edward. 2006. 'Exploring the "Root Causes" of Terrorism'. Accessed 24 April 2018. https://www.tandfon-line.com/doi/abs/10.1080/10576100600704069.

Paul, T. V. 1999. *International Order and the Future of World's Politics*. Cambridge: Cambridge University Press.

Rapport, David Charles. 2004. *The Four Waves of Modern Terrorism*.

Rogers, Paul. 2008. 'Terrorism'. In *Security Studies*, edited by William, Paul D. New York: Routledge.

Rothbard, Murray N. 2017. 'Hegel: The State as God's Will'. Accessed 24 April 2018. https://mises.org/library/hegel-state-gods-will.

Sandra, A. 2012. 'The Pillars of Counter-Terrorism'. Accessed 24 April 2018. https://lup.lub.lu.se/student-papers/search/publication/2542926.

Schirra, Bruno. 2014. *ISIS: Der globale Dschihad—Wie der »Islamische Staat« den Terror nach Europa trägt*. Berlin: Econ.

Thackrah, John Richard. 1987. *Encyclopaedia of Terrorism and Political Violence*. London: Routledge.

The Day. 2017. 'The Meaning and History of Terrorism'. Accessed 24 April 2018. https://theday.co.uk/briefing/the-meaning-and-history-of-terrorism.

United Nations (UN). 1945. *Charter of the United Nations*. Accessed 6 April 2018. http://www.un.org/en/charter-united-nations.

Further Reading

Abrahms, Max. 2008. 'What Terrorists Really Want: Terrorist Motives and Counterterrorism Strategy'. *International Security* 32 (4): 78–105.

Aksoy, Ece. 2002. 'International Terrorism in the Age of Globalization'. Master's thesis, Department of International Relations, Bilkent University, Ankara.

Atwan, Abdel Bari. 2015. *Islamic State: The Digital Caliphate*. London: Saqi Books.

Basinsky. Kathryn and James Brandon, eds. 2015. *Al-Qaeda and its Heirs: Select Conference Papers from the Eighth Annual Terrorism Conference, December 9, 2014*. Washington D. C.: Jamestown Foundation.

Brisard, Jean-Charles, and Damien Martinez. 2005. *Zarqawi: The New Face of al-Qaeda*. Cambridge: Polity Press.

Brown, Chris and Kirsten Ainley. 2005. *Understanding International Relations*, 3rd edn. London: Palgrave Macmillan.

Byman. Daniel. 2015. *Al Qaeda, the Islamic State, and the Global Jihadist Movement: What Everyone Needs to Know*. Oxford: Oxford University Press.

Carlton-Ford, Steven, and Morten G. Ender, eds. 2011. *The Routledge Handbook of War and Society: Iraq and Afghanistan*. Abingdon: Routledge.

Carnegie Endowment for International Peace. 2012. 'Syria in Crisis'. Accessed 17 September 2017. http://carnegieendowment.org/syriaincrisis.

Chaliand, Gérard and Arnaud Blin, eds. 2007. *The History of Terrorism from Antiquity to Al Qaeda*. Berkeley, CA: University of California Press.

Ciment, James, eds. 2011. *World Terrorism: An Encyclopedia of Political Violence from Ancient Ties to the Post-9/11 Era*. Armonk, NY: Sharpe Reference, 2011.

Cockburn, Patrick. 2015. *The Rise of Islamic State: ISIS and the New Sunni Revolution*. London: Verso.

Dhiman, S. C. 2015. *Islamic State of Iraq and Syria (ISIS): Reconciliation, Democracy and Terror*. New Delhi: Neha Publishers & Distributors.

Dodge, Toby. 2012. *Iraq: From War to a New Authoritarianism*. Abingdon: Routledge.

Filiu, Jean-Pierre. 2015. *From Deep State to Islamic State: The Arab Counter-revolution and its Jihadi Legacy*. Oxford: Oxford University Press.

Fitzgerald, David. 2013. *Learning to Forget: US Army Counterinsurgency Doctrine and Practice from Vietnam to Iraq.* Stanford, CA: Stanford University Press.

Freeman, Liam, ed. 2015. *The Islamic State and ISIS Crisis: An Examination.* New York, NY: Nova Science Publishers.

Green, Daniel R., and Mullen, William F., III, eds. 2014. *Fallujah Redux: The Anbar Awakening and the Struggle with al-Qaeda.* Annapolis, MD: Naval Institute Press.

Hafez, Mohammed M. 2007. *Suicide Bombers in Iraq: The Strategy and Ideology of Martyrdom.* Washington, D.C.: United States Institute of Peace.

Hall, Benjamin. 2015. *Inside ISIS: The Brutal Rise of a Terrorist Army.* New York, NY: Center Street.

Hashim, Ahmed S. 2006. *Insurgency and Counter-insurgency in Iraq.* Ithaca, NY: Cornell University Press.

Higgins, Rosalyn. 1997. 'The General International Law of Terrorism'. In *Terrorism and International Law*, edited by Rosalyn Higgins and Maurice Flory. London: Routledge.

Hoffman, Bruce. 2002. 'Rethinking Terrorism and Counterterrorism since 9/11'. *Studies in Conflict and Terrorism* 25 (5): 303–316.

Horgan, John, and Kurt Braddock, eds. 2011. *Terrorism Studies: A Reader.* New York, NY: Routledge.

Huntington, Samuel P. 1993. *The Clash of Civilizations and the Remaking of World Order.* New York, NY: Simon & Schuster.

Kagan, Kimberly. 2009. *The Surge: A Military History.* New York, NY: Encounter Books.

Kazimi, Nibras. 2010. *Syria through Jihadist Eyes: A Perfect Enemy.* Stanford, CA: Hoover Institution Press.

Ledwidge, Frank. 2011. *Losing Small Wars: British Military Failure in Iraq and Afghanistan.* New Haven: Yale University Press.

Lister, Charles R. 2015. *The Islamic State: A Brief Introduction.* Washington D. C.: The Brookings Institution Press.

Mardini, Ramzy, ed. 2011. *Volatile Landscape: Iraq and its Insurgent Movements.* Washington D.C.: The Jamestown Foundation.

Martin, Gus. 2011. *Essentials of Terrorism: Concepts and Controversies.* Los Angeles, CA: SAGE Publications.

———, ed. 2011. *The SAGE Encyclopaedia of Terrorism.* Los Angeles, CA: SAGE Publications.

Nance, Malcolm W. 2015. *The Terrorists of Iraq: Inside the Strategy and Tactics of the Iraq Insurgency 2003–2014.* Boca Raton: CRC Press.

Napoleoni, Loretta. 2005. *Insurgent Iraq: Al Zarqawi and the New Generation.* New York, NY: Seven Stories Press.

———. 2014. *The Islamist Phoenix: The Islamic State and the Redrawing of the Middle East.* New York, NY: Seven Stories Press.

Rajan, V. G. Julie. 2015. *Al Qaeda's Global Crisis: The Islamic State,* Takfir, *and the Genocide of Muslims.* Abingdon: Routledge.

Rayburn, Joel. 2014. *Iraq after America: Strongmen, Sectarians, Resistance.* Stanford, CA: Hoover Institution Press.

Reuter, Christoph. 2015. *Die Schwarze Macht: Der »Islamische Staat« und die Strategen des Terrors.* Munich: Deutsche Verlags-Anstalt.

Rosenfeld, Jean E., eds. *Terrorism, Identity and Legitimacy: The Four Waves Theory and Political Violence.* New York, NY: Routledge.

Said, Behnam T. 2014. *Islamischer Staat: IS-Miliz, al-Qaida und die deutschen Brigaden.* Munich: C.H.Beck.

Saikal, Amin. 2014. *Zone of Crisis: Afghanistan, Pakistan, Iran and Iraq.* London: I.B. Tauris.

Saraka, Nilambar. 2016. 'History of Terrorism in India: An Analysis'. *International Journal of Applied Research* 2 (2): 157–161.

Schmid, Alex P., ed. 2011. *The Routledge Handbook of Terrorism Research.* New York, NY: Routledge.

Sekulow, Jay, Jordan Sekulow, Robert W. Ash and David French. 2014. *Rise of ISIS: A Threat We Can't Ignore.* New York, NY: Howard Books.

Serena, Chad C. 2014. *It Takes More than a Network: The Iraqi Insurgency and Organizational Adaptation.* Stanford, CA: Stanford University Press.

Shultz, Richard H., Jr. 2013. *The Marines Take Anbar: The Four-Year Fight Against Al Qaeda.* Annapolis, MD: Naval Institute Press.

Sky, Emma. 2015. *The Unraveling: High Hopes and Missed Opportunities in Iraq*. Philadelphia, PA: Perseus Books.

Stepanova. Ekaterina. 2008. *Terrorism in Asymmetrical Conflict: Ideological and Structural Aspects*. New York, NY: Oxford University Press.

Stern, Jessica, and J. M. Berger. 2015. *ISIS: The State of Terror*. New York, NY: HarperCollins.

Thapa, Paban Jung. 2005. 'The Role of United Nations in Combating Global Terrorism'. Accessed 2 June 2018. https://www.hsdl.org/?view&did=459075.

Migration

Manisha Chaurasiya

···
: LEARNING OBJECTIVES :
···

- To introduce the students to the definition of 'population migration'
- To distinguish between forms of migration
- To examine various case studies of migration
- To understand the global challenge emerging from migration
- To evaluate global counter-immigration efforts

Marked by ever-increasing global connectivity and exchanges, population migration has emerged as an unprecedentedly huge challenge in this era of globalization. In the face of income disparities, varied degrees of development and various levels of urbanization among countries, the movement of people has become increasingly rampant. On one side, the very concept and context of globalization favours a borderless world; on the other, the Herculean volume of migration of human populations from their places of origin has emerged as a daunting challenge, if left unrestricted. Migration of people across borders has been an age-old phenomenon; however, the twenty-first century has brought about a remarkable surge in the volumes, intensity and scope of population migrations. Particularly in the last three decades, migration has increased manifold, leading to a global challenge. The 'borderlessness' of globalization has raised serious questions on the capacity and extent to which a state is able to guard its sovereign borders. Due to multifaceted reasons, people leave their lands of origin and migrate. Reasons range from better economic opportunities, fear of violence and avoiding persecution to even environmental and climatic compulsions. The quantitative increase in migration as a contemporary trend raises concerns about the carrying capacity of states, pressure on limited resources and demographic transformations. The present chapter discusses the impact of globalization on the phenomenon of population migration. It also explores several case studies in this regard, to better comprehend the global challenge.

The chapter is divided into five sections. The first defines migration and enquires into the historical validity and presence of population flows to distant lands. It also discusses the various definitions and types of migrants as classified by different organizations, including the United Nations (UN) and the United Nations High Commissioner for Refugees (UNHCR). The second section discusses the specific relationship between globalization and the migration or movement of people. The former has had a causal impact on accelerating the pace of the latter. Globalization aims at promoting a more integrated and connected world and has witnessed unprecedented volumes of population flow. This section touches upon the issues around the contemporary challenge of international migration in a globalized world. The third section discusses internal migration and the challenges posed by it. It can be caused by war and violence, intra-state conflicts or simply better economic opportunities. The fourth section discusses the emerging challenges associated with migration, such as illegal migration or human trafficking, backlashes against societal acceptance of immigrants, and so on. It also discusses the Brexit issue and the challenges faced by Europe because of migration. The fifth section touches upon a very salient contemporary concern related to immigration. This section elaborates on the emerging culture of counter-immigration policies in some states. Also, stringent measures have been used by states to curb illegal migration into their territories. The case studies of Australia and the United States (US) are discussed in detail.

Defining Migration

Migration can be defined as the movement of people to a new area or country, usually to find work or better living conditions. It ranges from people leaving their homes to escape poverty, violence and war, and avoid political genocide and human rights abuse to a search for better living and economic conditions. A migrant is understood as 'any person who lives temporarily or permanently in a country where he or she was not born, and has acquired some significant social ties to this country' (UNESCO 2017). As mentioned above, there is a clear difference in the motivations of people choosing to migrate. Based on this, migrants are characterised as migrants, refugees, internally displaced persons (IDPs), immigrants, illegal immigrants, and so on.

Migrants are that category of people who make choices about when to leave and where to go, even though these choices are sometimes extremely constrained and sometimes not. The special rapporteur of the UN Commission on Human Rights has defined the following persons as eligible to be considered migrants:

a. Persons who are outside the territory of the state of which they are nationals or citizens, are not subject to its legal protection and are in the territory of another state;
b. Persons who do not enjoy the general legal recognition of rights which is inherent in the granting by the host state of the status of refugee, naturalized person or similar status;
c. Persons who do not enjoy general legal protection of their fundamental rights by virtue of diplomatic agreements, visas or other agreements.

The UN Convention on the Rights of Migrants defines a migrant worker as a 'person who is to be engaged, is engaged or has been engaged in a remunerated activity in a State of which he or she is not a national' (UNESCO 2017). Usually, a distinction is made between short-term or temporary migration and long-term or permanent migration. The former covers movements with a duration between 3 and 12 months, and the latter refers to a change of country of residence for a duration of one year or more

(UN 2018). A hope for a better livelihood and economic situation usually act as a magnet to pull more and more populations to a place. The dominant forms of migration have been categorized below. These are based on 'motives' and 'legal status'. Though there are no objective criteria to define international migration as a phenomenon, yet the United Nations Educational, Scientific and Cultural Organization (UNESCO) has attempted to distinguish them in the following categories:

a. Temporary labour migrants or guest workers or overseas contract workers: They migrate for a limited period to take up employment and send money home.
b. Highly skilled and business migrants: They are educated and professionally qualified, and work as managers, executives, professionals or technicians.
c. Irregular migrants or undocumented or illegal migrants: As the name suggests, they enter a country, usually in search of employment, without the necessary permits and documents.
d. Forced migrants: They differ from refugees and asylum seekers as people are also many a times forced to move from their country of origin due to external factors such as development projects and environmental catastrophes.
e. Family reunification migrants or family reunion: In this case, people sharing family ties attempt to join people who have already entered another country under one of the above-mentioned categories.
f. Return migrants: They are a category of people who return to their countries of origin after a period in another country.

The other category, called 'refugees', by definition and scope is much different from 'migrants'. 'Refugees are persons fleeing armed conflict or persecution. Their situation is often so perilous and intolerable that they cross national borders to seek safety in nearby countries, and thus become

BOX 11.1: Establishment of the UNHCR

- The office of the UNHCR was created in 1950, during the aftermath of the Second World War, to help millions of Europeans who had fled or lost their homes. It took three years for the organization to complete the task.
- In 1954 and 1981, the UNHCR won the Nobel Peace Prize for its groundbreaking work for the cause of refugees.
- Since its establishment, the UNHCR has aided over 50 million refugees by providing humanitarian assistance, including food, shelter and medical aid.
- In 1956, during the Hungarian Revolution, around 200,000 fled to neighbouring Austria. The UNHCR led efforts to resettle them.
- The spurt in intra-state conflicts in the decade of the 1990s also was well addressed by the UNHCR in various African states.
- The twenty-first century witnessed major refugee crises in Africa, the Middle East and Asia. The UNHCR helped with rehabilitating both refugees as well as IDPs in these situations.

Source: http://www.unhcr.org, accessed 10 September 2017.

internationally recognised as "refugee" with access to assistance from States, UNHCR, and other organizations' (UNHCR 2016). In 1950, the UN established the office of the UNHCR, which was entrusted with the implementation of the convention relating to the status of refugees. There was a dire need for an institutional mechanism on the matter, as the numbers dramatically increased due to the Second World War. The unfolding of a holocaustic genocide by Hitler targeting the Jews in Germany in the previous decade was also a pressing reason for the UN to come up with a coherent law for the refugees, which included non-refoulement.

As per the population division data, in 2015, the number of international migrants worldwide reached 244 million, with an increase of 71 million, or 41%, compared to 2000. There is an inherent element of compulsion associated with the movement of refugees versus other types of migrants. According to the Cartagena Declaration, signed in 1984, 'refugees are persons who have fled their own country because their lives, safety or freedom have been threatened by violence, foreign aggression, internal conflicts, massive violation of human rights or other circumstances which have seriously destroyed public order' (OAS 1984, 3). Definitional inquiry also distinguishes refugees from IDPs: 'Internally displaced persons are persons or groups of persons who have been forced or obliged to flee or to leave their homes or places of habitual residence, in particular as a result of, or in order to avoid the effects of armed conflict, situations of generalised violence, violations of human rights, or natural or human-made disasters and who have not crossed an internationally recognised State border' (UNHCR 2008). The latter also present an equally crucial problem as the former, and a global challenge. The numbers of both refugees and IDPs magnified with the advent of globalization and decolonization. According to Richard W. Mansbach and Kirsten L. Taylor, 'between 1984 and 2004, the number of refugees almost doubled, peaking in 1994 following the Rwanda genocide. By the end of 2009, UNHCR was responsible for over 36 million "persons of concern", including 10.4 million refugees and a record 15.6 asylum seeker and millions more stateless persons' (Mansbach and Taylor 2013, 407). 'Migrant', therefore, as per the above understanding, is a multidimensional and umbrella-like concept encompassing many sub-themes and terms.

Historical Roots of Migration

Migration is as old as human civilization. Early humans started wandering in search of food and other necessary resources and travelled to faraway lands to secure them. But certainly, with the advent of globalization, marked by ever-expanding population flows, the 'management' of migration has become difficult. As mentioned above, there is no single definition of a 'migrant' and there are various strands of people on the move. The governments' capacity to regulate the flow of people inside their territories started with the development of passports and a system of visas. In contemporary times, states have altered their respective immigration policies to address issues related to the overflow of immigrants. To curb illegal migration, states also undertake border patrols and monitoring of foreigners as one of their primary responsibilities.

Many scholars predicted a sudden surge in international migration alongside an increase in the phenomenon of globalization. There were several reasons for an upsurge at the end of 1980s and the beginning of the 1990s.

'In 2000, there were 193 generally recognised nation-states, four times more than the 43 in 1900. Although each nation-state distinguishes citizens and foreigners, organise controls of their borders to deter unauthorised entries, and also determines what foreigners can do while inside the country, whether tourists, students, guest workers, or immigrants, yet certainly globalization has resulted in an overall increase in the volumes and patterns of migration as witnessed today. (Martin 2013, 3)

Historical analysis of the migration flows all around the world after the Treaty of Westphalia suggests a pattern worth understanding (see Chapter 2 of this book for a more detail the treaty). During the seventeenth and the eighteenth centuries, the trend of international movement of people was dominated by heavy flows out of Europe to a few key destinations, mostly in Asia, Africa and Latin America. The unexplored lands were referred as the 'New World' by the Europeans and were symbols of prosperity, ambition and a promising future for most Europeans. Although the exact number of European immigrants to the New World remains largely unknown, as suggested by many studies, these flows were enough to establish colonial rule at large and to alter the population demography, culture, language patterns, religion and social fabric in some regions. For this very reason, history describes the US, Canada and Australia as 'classical immigration countries' (Castles 2010).

However, almost half of the twentieth century and the first quarter of the twenty-first century witnessed and continued to reflect the reverse of this trend. As Douglas S. Massey suggests, in the second phase of migration, Europe became a region of immigration and, like other developed regions, it drew migrants from a variety of developing countries (Massey 1990, 60). Studies suggest that since 1990, there has been a miniscule (if any) increase in the number of migrants entering Asia, Africa and Latin America from outside the Continent. But a considerable growth has been witnessed in Europe and North America in the number or volumes of migrants received. This increase has been contributed largely by the Global South. Most developed, industrialized economies have attracted a variety of migrants, with the highest numbers being highly skilled and business migrants, followed by almost all other categories discussed above.

Globalization and International Migration

A historical analysis of immigration patterns suggests a comparatively neater and tidier picture of the population flows. However, the globalized world contributed to the complexity of the phenomenon of migration. There have been some remarkable changes in the patterns of population movement around the world. Some scholars suggest that the worldwide interconnectedness and complex interdependence among states has presented a web of networks and inward and outward flows of people across continents. Globalization has emerged as a contested concept with no single all-encompassing definition, commonly understood as 'a multi-dimensional set of social processes that create, multiply, stretch and intensify worldwide social interdependencies and exchanges while at the same time fostering in people a growing awareness of deepening connections between the local and the distant' (Streger 2009). Migration is understood as a broad process of population movement which is very natural to the above understanding of globalization. Both migration and globalization are complimentary and reinforcing to each other.

Globalization has brought on some drastic alterations on the systemic as well as subsystemic levels. The migration of populations has been one such necessary element of the structure of globalization. With the advent of globalization, the last decade of the twentieth century has certainly witnessed an enhancement in the networks and intensity of already existing movements of population. Though movements and exchange between faraway civilizations was not uncommon, yet globalization, especially the forces of cultural globalism alongside economic, has led to the highest population flows, as witnessed in the last three decades. International migration has been classified into the following four categories

FIGURE 11.1 International Migrated Populations

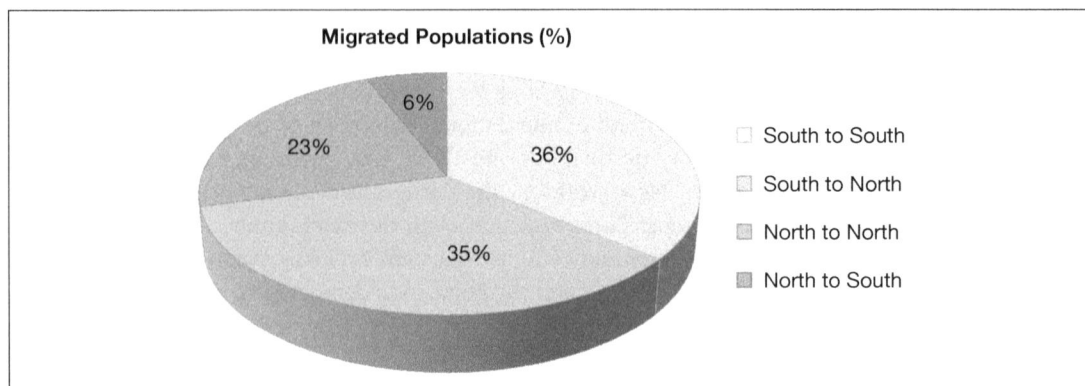

Source: Data adapted from UNPD (2013).

based on the population flows (Figure 11.1). However, each migration corridor has unique features and some of these case studies are discussed later in the chapter. In the following classification, South refers to a developing country and North to an industrialized country:

- South—South: The flow from one developing country to another constitutes one of the largest flows of migrants. Over 82 million or 36% of migrants in 2013 (Martin 2013) moved from one developing country to another—for example, from Nicaragua to Costa Rica or from Bangladesh to India.
- South—North: The second-largest flow of population has been marked by the South to North movement. Just under 82 million or 35% of the total migrants per available data moved from some developing nation to an industrialized country (Martin 2013)—for example, from Mexico to the US or the Philippines to South Korea.
- North—North: Some 54 million people or 23% of international migrants moved from one industrialized country to another—for example, from Canada to the US.
- North—South: Only around 14 million people or 6% of the total migrants moved from industrialized to developing countries, as from Japan to Thailand (Martin 2013).

In the last almost three decades, the phenomenon of migration has undergone a change marked by a record increase in the types, intensity as well as the volume of population flows around the world. The proportion of international migration from the developed world has drastically declined, giving way to a reverse trend, with the developing world moving towards the developed world. The migrants themselves are both carriers and recipients of constantly changing identities. These carriers of identities then lead to changes in the demographic as well as sociological realms of different nation states. In contemporary times, as a reaction to the excessive migration both legal and illegal, there has been witnessed an emerging trend of states moving towards anti-migration and anti-immigration policies to better secure their respective national borders. To be precise, 9/11 marked the beginning of an era in which the forces of globalization through free movement of people across borders for the first time came under strain. Immigration in a globalized world was now viewed with scepticism. The Treaty of Westphalia 1648 (see

Chapter 2) marked the basic blueprint for the current political order and introduced the concept of sovereign states. But the number of migrants across the world has almost doubled between 1980 and 2010. According to the UN Population Division (UNPD), it has increased from 103 million to 220 million (UNPD 2013), thus enlisting population flows into the category of non-traditional threats to security in most states. Managing international migration across defined and policed Westphalian national borders has become a Herculean task.

International migration in the present day is a global phenomenon, unlike migration during the civilizational communities; it is now unprecedentedly grown in scope, complexity and impact. According to the UN, migration is both a cause and an effect of broader development processes and an intrinsic feature of our ever-globalizing world (UN 2017). The global migration system has changed recently with regard to the origins and destinations as well as the volume and types of migrants (UN 2017). Through a variety of case studies, the chapter tries to understand various emerging issues related to population migration, such as like anti-immigration policies of states, impact of excessive immigration on the fabric of a given society, and so on.

Sir Paul Collier, in his book entitled *Exodus*, problematizes the concept of immigration in detail. He believes that 'while migration into developed countries from developing countries has had economic benefits in many ways yet more and more immigration into the West poses a threat to danger to the social cohesion, risks of diluting culture, national identity and also may undermine trust, cooperation, solidarity between members of the public' (Collier 2016). Speaking on the surge in migration into the United Kingdom (UK), Professor Collier categorized the population of the UK into immigrants and indigenous Britons. The overall rise in global mobility facilitated by the global interconnectedness of globalization has led to a growing complexity of migratory patterns. The immigrant and non-immigrant debate has impacted countries, migrants, families and communities, making migration one of the many emerging challenges to a globalized world. In 2015, the number of international migrants worldwide reached 244 million, an increase of 71 million or 41% compared to 2000 (UN 2015). International migration in a globalized world has also produced some unfortunate violations of labour laws and rights (Figure 11.2).

FIGURE 11.2 International Migration Received by Countries

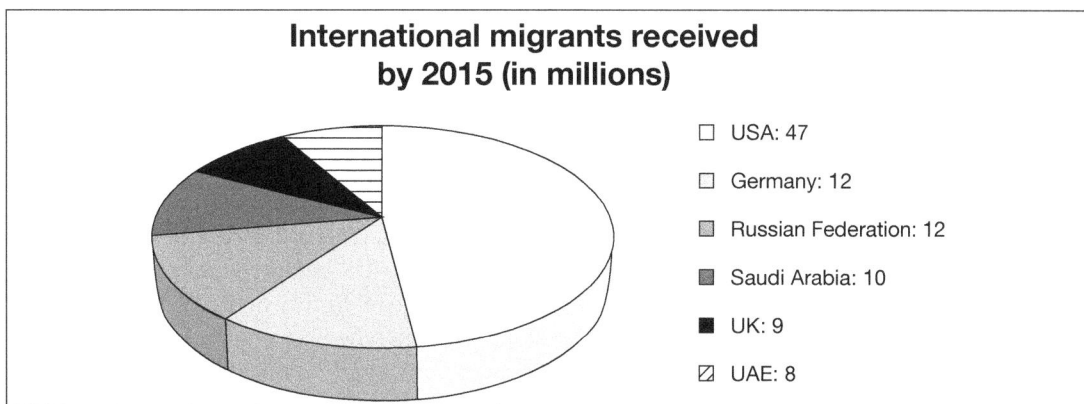

International migrants received by 2015 (in millions)

- USA: 47
- Germany: 12
- Russian Federation: 12
- Saudi Arabia: 10
- UK: 9
- UAE: 8

Source: Data adapted from UNDP (2013).

US as a Product of Immigration

The US has historically been a product of immigration. Even before the forces of globalization were in play, there were massive movements of people across the Atlantic. It has been observed that 'for its first 100 years, the United States facilitated immigration, welcoming foreigners to settle a vast country' (Martin 2013, 6). From 1790 to 1820 especially, since the US won the American War of Independence, in Thomas Paine's words, it became 'the asylum for the persecuted lovers of civil and religious liberty from every part of Europe' (SOLEIF 2017). Under the motto *e pluribus unum* (from many, one), it identified itself as the land of opportunity where every immigrant shared their experience and contributed to the identity of 'American'. In the early years of US history, classical immigration was a means to further the national interest as it permitted individuals to better themselves as it strengthened the US (Martin 2013, 6). By the end of the nineteenth century with the advancement of technologies such as steam power, the overall journey to the US had drastically shortened. This resulted in a 'pouring up of immigrants' around the world on to American soil. The door was so wide open to Europeans that by the decade of the 1880s, approximately 9% of the total population of Norway immigrated to America (SOLEIF 2017). However, in the 1920s, the government imposed some quantitative restrictions and determined the number of immigrants per annum. A formula was set up according to which entry was favoured for foreigners with relatives in the US and the ones called by employers into the US. During the 1970s, the origins of most immigrants changed from Europe to Latin America and Asia. The trend continued in the twenty-first century. 9/11 marked the first disjuncture in US immigration policy, where the government grew sceptical and resistant to immigration to prevent the entry of terrorists and radicalized Islamic fundamentalists.

Islam as a religious sect and largely Asians as a community were faced with stringent immigration policies and checks. The radicalized version of Islam was well propagated by terrorist organizations such as Al Qaeda, resulting in a clear backlash among the US citizens towards Muslims. This marked the beginning of a worsening of the secular social fabric of the classical immigration state. The rise of non-state terror groups such as the Islamic State in Iraq and Syria (ISIS) and the sophisticated technological know-how of the terrorists have magnified the threat and the possibilities of damage caused by them to human lives. The increase in the Islamic State-inspired attacks around the world signalled a reactionary culture of protectionism by the states on matters of migration.

Apart from legal immigration, back-door or illegal immigration also has emerged as a pressing problem in the first decade of the twenty-first century. The scale and volume of illegal immigration threatened American social life. According to an estimate, around '1,500 unauthorised foreigners a day were settling in the United States' (Martin 2013) in the beginning of the twenty-first century, which somehow got reduced by the 2008 recession. According to Martin (2013) the presidency of Barack Obama, alongside many Democrats in office, supported a 'comprehensive immigration reform'. It included border and interior reinforcements to discourage entry, promotion of temporary work visas and employment and a controversial path to legal immigrant status. This provided a 13-year path to US citizenship for unauthorized foreigners who had arrived in the US before 31 December 2011 and remained continuously since their arrival (Martin 2013). The overall history of the US is closely linked to the story of immigration that continued for hundreds of years. The US would have been a different country altogether without immigration. The recent alterations in US immigration policy under the presidency of Donald Trump and the illegal population flows from Mexico and Latin American countries are discussed in detail under the section 'Globalization and Upcoming Challenges of Migration' later in the chapter.

Globalization and Internal Migration

Population distribution and redistribution through migration can have a profound impact on the society and politics of a country. The literature on the migration of populations inside the boundaries of a sovereign state has been given lesser academic attention in comparison to international migration. However, this movement of populations is equally salient. In the recent past, there have been substantial volumes of population movement inside some developing and emerging economies. The population flows inside the boundary of a sovereign state have also accelerated in the era of globalization. These intra-state mass movements can result in serious demographic changes and societal changes, which in some cases result in even violence. This section discusses China in this regard, where industrial production demands have led to the mass movement of people from rural to urban areas.

Internal migration can be defined as human migration within a nation state. A variety of studies have suggested that in a globalized world, there has been a general trend of movement of people from rural to urban areas. This leads to rapid urbanization and the overflow of cities and their handling capacity in many countries. Thus, internal migration has emerged as a major contemporary challenge. China is one glaring example of excessive population migration inside the sovereign territory of the country. According to the UNPD, 'between 1990 and 2000, inter-provincial migration in China more than doubled, [however] intensities in other parts of Asia [have decreased]' (UN 2013, 7). The study also noted a decline in the intensity of internal migration across much of Latin America and the Caribbean and to a large extent also in Australia, Canada and the US (UN 2013, 7). As per an UN Department of Economic and Social Affairs (UNDESA) report, 'China would not have become the "world's factory" had it not been for the plentiful supply of low-cost young migrant labour from the countryside to its coastal export-processing industrial cities' (Chan 2008).

BOX 11.2: Migration in the Twenty-first Century: Some Facts

- In 2015, the number of international migrants worldwide reached 244 million, an increase of 71 million, or 41%, compared to 2000.
- Nearly two-thirds of all international migrants live in Europe (76 million) or Asia (75 million).
- In 2015, the percentage of females among all international migrants was highest in Europe (52.4%) and Northern America (51.2%).
- In 2015, the number of international migrants below age 20 reached 37 million, or 15% of the global migrant stock.
- Europe and Northern America host the highest share of persons of working age among all international migrants (75% each).

Source: UN (2015).

China and Internal Migration

China's growth story has a causal relationship with the population flows and labour availability in mainland China. Some scholars argue that it would not have become the 'world's factory' if it lacked the plentiful supply of low-cost young migrant labour from the countryside to its coastal export-processing industrial cities (Chan 2008, 3). Internal migration in China can be characterized as a population migration from rural to urban areas, even though the country followed a strict system of restricting internal migration. China has continued a policy of state control on its citizens changing their residence permanently. For the urban residents,

> changing residence *within* the same city or town [i.e. "moving" the *hukou* to a new address] due to housing change [moving to a new apartment]or residential changes caused by marriage is generally permitted. A similar freedom is also given to rural residents moving *within* the rural areas because of marriage or other family reasons. However, formal [or "permanent"] moves crossing city, town and township boundaries are heavily regulated and require the possession of a "migration permit" issued by the public security authorities. (Chan 2008, 3)

Due to stringent measures and permit requirements for people to make a move from rural to urban areas, the 'practice of "floating population" started to grow rapidly in the mid-1980s. By 2005, there was 153 million "floating population," slightly half of whom was registered with the police' (Chan 2008, 3). Internal migration has steadily increased since the early 1980s, with a rapid rise in the first half of the 1990s. It was also estimated that there were about 150 million people without a local hukou in 2005. This number also includes an obvious rural migrant-labour population which exceeded 110 million in number (Chan 2008, 3).

Globalization and Upcoming Challenges of Migration

In recent years, migration as a problem has magnified unprecedentedly. Europe has often been cited as the nerve centre for contemporary problems related to population migration. One is intra-EU migration and the other is population migration from outside the continent or the EU into the EU member states. There are a variety of interwoven issues which affect all three—Europe as a continent, the European Union (EU) as a supranational organization and individual countries in Europe such as the UK, Germany or France. The summer of 2017 has been uneasy for the European regionalism at large and the UK in particular. In Europe, there were two prevalent types of population migration.

India is also not untouched by the impact of population migration in both legal and illegal terms. The international border it shares with Bangladesh has long remained porous, inviting the trafficking of not just drugs and fake currency but even human beings. The same formula is at play in the case of human migration between India and Bangladesh that is applicable in Europe, that a relatively better developed and industrialized country attracts both legal and illegal migration from a state lacking these features. Substantial numbers of inward migrations, mostly illegal, are witnessed from Bangladesh into India. Here, the former is a rapidly emerging and promising economy with great opportunities and the latter is a poor, underdeveloped, populous state with low gross domestic product (GDP) and an absence of economic opportunities for its population. An immediate impact of these inter-state, heavy, mostly illegal population flows has been lately felt on the demography and society in the Indian states neighbouring Bangladesh.

Brexit and the European Union

The departure of the UK from the EU was referred to as Brexit by the international political analysts and media. The decision of the UK was backed by a referendum, the results of which were announced on 24 June 2016 and revealed a 51.9% vote casted by citizens of the UK in favour of leaving the EU. Only 48.1% voted in favour of remaining a member of the EU. The decision has a causal relationship with the immigration that the UK has received for decades, mostly from inside EU countries. Immigration to the UK unprecedentedly magnified in the last two decades, especially after 2004 and the accession of eight East European countries into EU (Wadsworth et al. 2016). 'About 3 million EU non-UK nationals reside in the UK making up about 6.6 per cent of the workforce' (O'Connor and Viña 2016). Better employment opportunities in the UK in comparison to the country of origin of the immigrants resulted in a watershed movement of people into the UK, which definitely benefited the immigrants but at the cost of joblessness and other several social discomforts for the existing citizens of the UK.

Figure 11.3 showcases that the voting turnout clearly reflected the belief that citizens of the UK suffered due to the excessive intra-EU immigration, as the southern parts, including the West Midlands and Yorkshire and the Humber and the north-east voted in favour of opting out of the EU. These regions harbour most of the populated cities and urban areas. A reversal of the voting trend was witnessed in Scotland, which favoured staying in the EU by 62% votes (Nelson 2016). Although the matter appears to be simple at first glance, yet the case study of Europe defies an unproblematic understanding. The intra-EU migration has been briefly elaborated through the case of Brexit, but the inward migration into UK, France, Germany, and so on from outside the EU countries also poses a contemporary challenge in a globalized world. By 2010, the EU had absorbed 1.2 million 'permanent' migrants, which is far more than the number of permanent migrants to the US, by over 1 million (Skeldon 2013, 4). He further argues that this trend represents a very significant shift in the global migration system as has been recorded over the last one hundred years (Ibid.). However, Europe has also welcomed population migration from outside

FIGURE 11.3 EU Referendum on UK Voting on Brexit

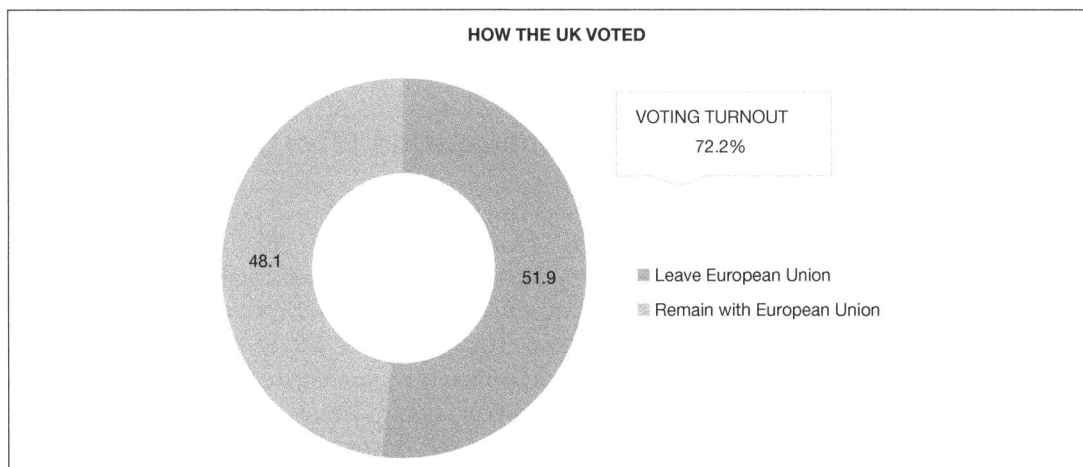

Source: Data adapted from *Huffington Post* (2017).

the continent in substantial numbers. These include both legal and illegal immigrants. According to an estimate in 2012, there were some 50 million foreign-born residents in the 28 countries of the EU. This meant that 10% of EU residents were born outside the country in which they were living. Some countries, such as France and the UK, exceed this all-EU average. There are good reasons for an attraction towards settling in Europe. 'The European Union has less than 10 percent of the world's population but accounts for a third of the world's economic output and over half of the world's social spending' (Martin 2013, 10).

Illegal Immigration from Bangladesh into India

Inflow of immigrants over a period, across international borders has the capacity to alter the social fabric of the state receiving migrants. The illegality aspect of immigration also hampers that state in managing the situation in a necessary manner. There has been mass migration into India since the emergence of Bangladesh out of the state of Pakistan. Prior to Bangladeshi independence, approximately 10 million people fled to nearby Indian states as refugees to escape human rights violations and political violence by the Pakistani government. Since then, the inflow of illegal immigrants has continued, although in lesser proportions. It is noted that 'in 2007, the Indian government stated that there were up to 20 million Bangladeshis living in India illegally' (Gupta and Sharma 2008, 148). These numbers of Bangladeshi-origin people in India have led to strong reactions from the Indian population in Assam and West Bengal. The anti-foreigner resistance has even in some instances led to violence, riots and political tensions. This backlash of the locals against the migrant population is based on scarce resources, language, economic opportunities, different cultures, and so on. A popular movement against undocumented immigrants, known as the Assam Movement, was also launched, aimed at striking the names of illegal immigrants from the electoral register and their deportation from the state.

In 2012, violence erupted in the Kokrajhar district of the state of Assam in India, which borders Bangladesh. It soon became a clash between the indigenous Bodos and the Bengali-speaking Muslims. The latter were a combination of descendants of East Bengali Muslims and refugees of the Indo–Pakistan War of 1971 and the illegal immigrants who subsequently followed the trend and moved from Bangladesh to India.

Understanding Global Counter-Immigration Efforts

Opposition to immigration is a natural reaction of states who have witnessed excessive immigration in the past, where the same has altered and affected their social and political profile. In contemporary times, both immigration and the need for counter-immigration efforts has become a significant political issue. Immigration has emerged as a significant challenge in a globalized world both in its legal and illegal aspects. Legal immigration is harnessed by stringent visa restrictions, alterations in the immigration policies, and so on, and illegal immigration is fought with active patrolling of borders, fencing, and so on. Many states in recent years have deployed stringent policies and actions to manage their legal immigration to avert serious implications for their demography, economy and social fabric. With the advent of international terrorism and the phenomenal rise of non-state terror groups such as Al Qaeda and ISIS, states are compelled to take all preventive measures to avert illegal migrants. Even the legal immigration policies of some states have witnessed alterations. As a preventive measure, the US president signed an executive order in January 2017 blocking citizens of six predominantly Muslim countries from entering the US. These rules apply to people from Iran, Libya, Syria, Somalia, Sudan and Yemen, as well as to all refugees. President Trump claimed that 'numerous foreign-born individuals have been convicted or implicated in terrorism-related crimes since September 11, 2001… including foreign nationals who entered the United States through the refugee resettlement program' (Crisp 2017, 4). The belief underlying the move is reflected in a statement by John F. Kelly, the former US secretary of homeland security. He said that 'unregulated, unvetted travel is not a universal privilege, especially when national security is at stake' (Thrush 2017). There have been instances in the last couple of years where refugee inflows have been carriers of international terrorist elements. ISIS 'has planned to infect refugee flows to the West with mass killers, and it has had some violent successes' (Scarborough 2017). The terror attacks in Paris in November 2015 were carried out by terrorists with an ISIS affiliation. UK authorities also identified two Middle Eastern refugees behind the London subway bombings in September 2017 (Lam 2017).

On the other hand, illegal immigration is strictly in contravention of the immigration laws of a state. Illegal immigration brings with it effects or side-effects or economic costs such as burdens on education and social services, population explosion, resource scarcity and job competition or unemployment for the non-immigrant population or natives of a state. There are also arguments suggesting an increase in crime rates and a negative impact of immigration, especially illegal, on the traditional identities and values of a society or state. From the perspective of the states that receive heavy flows of illegal immigration, attempts to curb inward movement and secure the borders make perfect sense. These immigrants put an additional pressure on the already scarce resources of a state and alter the local demography. Many sovereign states even contemplate deportation of the illegal immigrants from these countries to their native lands. The British government was involved in forcible deportation of Tamil asylum seekers who then were tortured in Sri Lanka in 2012. This was the time when the Liberation Tigers of Tamil Eelam (LTTE) and the Sri Lankan government were involved in ugly violence. 'The human rights group has documented a total of 13 cases of people who, after being returned to Sri Lanka when their asylum claims in various European countries failed, were subsequently tortured by government security forces' (Malik 2012). This example showcases that sometimes the governments fail to identify the thin line between asylum seekers and illegal immigrants. David Mepham, the UK director of Human Rights Watch believed that the British government's asylum procedure failed to identify Tamils at risk of torture upon return to Sri Lanka. In another case, the US president Trump announced stringent measures to reopen the cases of hundreds of illegal immigrants who had been given a reprieve from deportation by the previous administration of President Obama. There are tens of thousands of illegal immigrants, mostly from Mexico, who live in the US.

Case of the US and Illegal Migration from Mexico

In understanding the challenge of illegal migration, it is necessary to explore the case study of Mexico and the US, where the former has been accused as a major source of illegal migration into the latter for years. In recent times, US president Donald Trump has brought the issue to the forefront by ordering the construction of a US–Mexico border wall. He has also added stringent measures to reshape US immigration and national security policies, including punishment for cities shielding illegal immigrants (Edwards 2017). The problem of illegal migration between the US and Mexico is not a simple one, with multiple layers demanding attention for a holistic understanding of the dynamics of the region. Most Latin American countries send more people abroad than they receive as immigrants. Mexico and many Caribbean nations have seen almost 10% of their population immigrated. In the case of Mexico, 'the country has almost 20 percent of Latin America's 600 million residents and 20 percent of the region's GDP' (Martin 2013, 8). Mexicans enter the US in both legal and illegal ways, but Mexico itself has also become a destination for migrants from poorer Central American countries.

It is important to note that 'in Mexico, migration and borders are inseparable. In the list of nations registering the largest immigrations in the world today, the country ranks first' (Ruiz 2006, 52). It faces immigration from other poor countries in Latin America, which often generates security issues such as drug trafficking, human trafficking, networks of illegal arms transportation, and so on. This has resulted in Mexico becoming a home for a growing population of foreign migrants, mostly from Central American countries. It is interesting to note that although Mexicans are often cited as illegal immigrants to the US, the immigrants are mostly non-Mexican citizens who have arrived intending to go to the US. According to Ruiz, often these people find work and eventually settle in Mexico (Ruiz 2006). Because of these reasons, the Mexican government has begun to revisit the laws ruling immigration, permanent residence and naturalization (Ruiz 2006). The pressure from US president Donald Trump in this direction is also not unwarranted due to the heavy flows of illegal migrants into the US every year. He has promised a border wall to stop the same on the approximately 3,100 km international border between Mexico and the US. The wall would be an expensive affair, of around $10 billion to $12 billion.

BOX 11.3: Myanmar and the Rohingya Muslims

- The Rohingya Muslims are one of Myanmar's many ethnic minorities. Historically, they are descendants of Arab traders and other groups who have been in the region for generations.
- The Myanmar government has long denied them citizenship and sees them as illegal immigrants from Bangladesh. Many of the Rohingyas actually did migrate from Bangladesh decades ago, as their community has long been on move due to a persistent statelessness.
- In August 2017, Rohingya Muslim insurgents attacked several police posts and an army base in Myanmar, which led to a stringent military crackdown on their community that has resulted in the deaths of at least 400 people and led tens of thousands to flee Myanmar.
- As it is an ongoing crisis, the data by October 2017 suggests that more than half a million Rohingya people have crossed the Burmese border into Bangladesh. Over 5,150,000 refugees have fled to Bangladesh during the initial weeks of violence.
- The magnitude of violence and the refugee crisis makes this one of the world's fastest-developing refugee emergencies.
- The UN fears a further exodus of Muslim Rohingyas from Myanmar.
- The UN has denounced the Myanmar military offensive as ethnic cleansing, but Myanmar insists its forces are fighting 'terrorists' who have killed civilians and burned villages.
- Myanmar has come under international criticism for failing to stop the violence and stem the tide of the largest refugee crisis to hit Asia in decades.

Source: Data compiled from CBC News (2017), BBC News (2017) and The Independent (2017).

Australia and Its Immigration Policy

Australia as the continent we see today has been largely a product of immigration. It is counted amongst the few classical immigration countries. It received a lot of its immigrant population initially from the UK and Ireland, but in the post-Second World War era, Australia's immigration witnessed a major influx of immigrants from the Netherlands, Germany, Italy, Greece and the Middle East (Hugo 2001). During these years, it was following a 'White Australia' policy. In the year 1966, the Australian government introduced the Migration Act 1966. It was a major immigration reform as it undid the previous White Australia policy and increased access for non-European migrants. This followed the inflow of refugees from the Vietnam War entering Australia. By the 1970s, Australia had received substantial flows from Asia, which continues. According to the available data, more than one-fifth of Australians were born overseas which is around 23% of the present population of the country. This is herculean in comparison with only 10% in the United States; Canada has 17% of its population born outside its territorial borders. In addition to an astonishing 23%, an additional 19% are those who are born in Australia having at least one parent born overseas (Hugo 2001). Between 1945 and 2000, Australia's population increased from 7.4 million to 19.1 million, mostly through immigration. This is a 59% increase (Hugo 2001). In contemporary times, Australia has come up with stringent measures to curb illegal immigration and to limit legal immigration to a large extent. With the new visa restrictions and immigration rules, they are undertaking a careful approach in face of heavy migration, largely illegal, towards it. According to Grant Wyeth, with the emerging culture of distrust around immigration, the Australian government has also decided to follow the nationalist trend with a series of measures (Wyeth 2017). To discourage illegal immigration to Australia in 2014, the government used posters, such as in Figure 11.4, in countries with a history of similar attempts. The figure displays a poster that was put up in Pakistan.

Concluding Observations

There have been several rounds of debates on whether globalization has facilitated the creation of a borderless world or, on the contrary, the nation states as entities have reasserted their political sovereignty through globalization. This study on human migration as a phenomenon suggests that in contemporary times, immigration in general, both legal and illegal and migration both international as well as internal, defies an uncomplicated understanding. Migration and its implications have come up as real challenges of a globalized world. On one side, globalization stands for a world in which goods, services, capital and information flow across seamless national borders (Ceglowski 1998). On the other hand, population movement between different states still harbours some inherent problems. As a result, nation states are acting conventionally on opening their borders in this direction. Some globalization enthusiasts have argued that 'borderlessness' has been comparatively more robust in the economic realm than in the social. Kenichi Ohmae argues that 'national borders have effectively disappeared and, along with them, the economic logic that made them useful lines of demarcation in the first place' (Ohmae 1990). However, one must not discount the fact that nation states as entities have not disappeared and they still hold on to some salient roles. Presently, the number of people living outside their country of birth or citizenship has reached an all-time high, with 232 million in 2013 and every passing year adding to this figure.

FIGURE 11.4 Poster of Australian Government Put in Pakistan in 2014 to Discourage Illegal Immigrants

Source: *DAWN* (2014) (modified).

The overall global picture suggests that the number of migrants in the times to come will continue increasing because of demographic and economic inequalities between countries (Martin 2013). The respective policies of the governments of all major countries have also shown an inclination towards protectionism and anti-immigration policies. Overall, international migration continues to be a journey amidst both hopes for a better future and fears of protectionist policies. The management of the business of international migration in the times to come certainly will prove to be more complex and challenging.

BOX 11.4: Dubai Strikes

Dubai is one of the seven emirates constituting the United Arab Emirates (UAE). The city is known for luxury shopping, ultra-modern architecture and a lively nightlife. A building boom around two decades long has transformed the city into one of the world's most popular tourist destinations. In the second decade of the twenty-first century Dubai, is also the largest construction site in the Middle East. The success story of most sprawling cities in the Gulf region would have been impossible without the contribution of the migrant workforce. Dubai is home to some of the finest constructions, most luxurious hotels and three of the largest shopping malls on the planet (McDougall 2006) but also houses a substantial migrant workforce stemming largely from India, Pakistan and Bangladesh.

'In March 2006 hundreds of foreign contract workers building the Burj Dubai, the world's tallest building, went on a strike and demonstrated against low wages, squalid dormitories and dangerous conditions' (Castles 2010). The protesters were angered by prolonged withheld payments and mistreatment by their employers. The protests in 2006 witnessed some 2,500 labourers turning on their bosses, their site offices and the local police, causing an estimated $1 m in damages (McDougall 2006).

The UN Convention on the Rights of Migrants defines a migrant worker as a 'person who is to be engaged, is engaged or has been engaged in a remunerated activity in a State of which he or she is not a national' (UN Convention 1990). But the migrant workforce in Dubai had no workers' rights and had pathetic living conditions and unsafe working conditions. There was a prohibition on them forming unions and they lived in constant fear of deportation. The situation of low-skilled migrants in most of the Gulf states has been largely similar. This paints a deeply disturbing picture of immigrant lives in the UAE. According to Sarah Leah Whitson of Human Rights Watch, 'One of the world's largest construction booms is feeding off impoverished immigrant workers in Dubai, but they're treated as less than human' (McDougall 2006). Globalization and the movement of people in search of better opportunities, employment and better paying jobs has created some unprecedented, precarious situations far exceeding the magnitude of previous eras of population migration. There still exist differential work rights in different parts of the world. Even after the 2006 protests by the foreign workers, the UAE government has been unwilling to make any substantial commitment to stopping systematic abuses by employers such as denial of proper medical care, non-payment of wages and the inhuman and squalid living conditions. The UAE is not a party to some of the key international human rights treaties such as the International Covenant on Civil and Political Rights. It also has not adequately reformed its labour laws to conform to international standards set by the International Labour Organization (ILO).

The facilitation of migration has also unfortunately become a web spun by agencies and recruiters. The 'migration industry' has become a reality of the globalized world. As the flows are gigantic, the whole activity has led to an illegal business of human trafficking also. The case study of Dubai and the identical situation of migrant labour elsewhere depicts this reality.

Summary

- A migrant is understood as 'any person who lives temporarily or permanently in a country where he or she was not born, and has acquired some significant social ties to this country'.
- Each nation state distinguishes citizens and foreigners, organizes controls of their borders to deter unauthorized entries and determines what foreigners can do while inside the country, whether

tourists, students, guest workers or immigrants; yet certainly globalization has resulted in an overall increase in the volumes and patterns of migration as witnessed today.

- International migration can be classified into the following four categories based on the population flows.
  - o South–South
  - o South–North
  - o North–North
  - o North–South
- In 2015, the number of international migrants worldwide reached 244 million, an increase of 71 million or 41% compared to 2000. As per UNPD data, nearly two-thirds of all international migrants live in Europe (76 million) or Asia (75 million).
- Legal immigration is harnessed by stringent visa restrictions, alterations in the immigration policies, and so on, and illegal immigration is fought with active patrolling of borders, fencing and so forth.
- 9/11 marked the first disjuncture in US immigration policy, where the government acted sceptical and became resistant to immigration to prevent the entry of terrorists and radicalized Islamic fundamentalists.
- Internal migration can be defined as human migration within a nation state. In a globalized world, this has become a general trend where large population movements are from rural to urban areas. This leads to rapid urbanization and the overflow of cities and their handling capacities in many countries, leading to internal migration being characterized as a major contemporary challenge.
- Migration as a problem in recent years has magnified unprecedentedly. Europe can be cited as a nerve centre of population migration problems. Brexit as a decision had a causal relationship with the immigration the UK has received since decades, both from outside and from inside the EU.
- Recently, US president Donald Trump has brought the issue to the forefront by ordering the construction of a US–Mexico border wall. He has also added stringent measures to reshape US immigration and national security policies, including punishment for cities shielding illegal immigrants.
- Migration and its implications have come up as real challenges of the globalized world. On one side, globalization stands for a world in which goods, services, capital and information flow across seamless national borders. On the other hand, population movement between different states still harbours some inherent problems.

Suggested Questions

1. Define migration. What has been the impact of globalization on international migration?
2. Is migration a new phenomenon? Discuss with relevant examples.
3. What are international migration and internal migration?
4. Discuss the causes of Brexit. Briefly comment on both intra-EU migration and outside-EU migration in this regard.
5. Discuss global counter-immigration efforts. Elaborate your argument with the example of a state.
6. 'Globalization promotes a borderless world but has limits'—comment on this argument on defending the political sovereignty of states.
7. Discuss the issue of migration with especial reference to Bangladeshi immigrants in India and the Rohingya Muslim refugee crisis in Myanmar.

References

Castles, Stephen. 2010. 'Global Migration'. In *International Relations: Perspectives for the Global South*, edited by B. S. Chimni and S. Mallavarapu, 272–285. New Delhi: Pearson.
Ceglowski, Janet. 1998. 'Has Globalization Created a Borderless World?' *Business Review*, March/April 1998: 17–27. Accessed 5 September 2017 http://citeseerx.ist.psu.edu/viewdoc/download?doi=10.1.1.195.2796&rep=rep1&type=pdf.
Chan, Kam Wing. 2008. 'Internal Labor Migration in China: Trends, Geographical Distribution and Policies'. Presentation at United Nations Expert Group Meeting on Population, Distribution, Urbanization, Internal Migration and Development, UNPD, 21–23 January 2008. New York: United Nations Secretariat. Accessed 4 April 2018. http://www.un.org/esa/population/meetings/EGM_PopDist/P05_Chan.pdf.
Collier, Paul. 2016. 'Paul Collier on Immigration'. Interview by Mehdi Hasan, *Head to Head*, Al Jazeera, 20 January 2016. Accessed 11 May 2017. https://www.aljazeera.com/programmes/headtohead/2016/01/transcript-paul-collier-immigration-160104190604853.html.
Crisp, Jeff. 2017. 'Refugees: The Trojan Horse of Terrorism?' *Open Democracy*, 5 June 2017. Accessed 7 October 2017. https://www.opendemocracy.net/can-europe-make-it/jeff-crisp/refugees-trojan-horse-of-terrorism.
DAWN. 2014. 'Australian Govt Warns Pakistani Asylum-Seekers Against Illegal Entry'. Accessed 20 March 2017. https://www.dawn.com/news/1137077.
Edwards Ainsley, Julia. 2017. 'Trump Moves Ahead with Wall, Puts Stamp on U.S. Immigration, Security Policy'. *Reuters*, 25 January 2017. Accessed 4 April 2017. http://www.reuters.com/article/us-usa-trump-immigration-idUSKBN1591HP.
Gupta, Charu, and Mukul Sharma. 2008. *Contested Coastlines: Fisherfolk, Nations and Borders in South Asia*. Routledge: New Delhi.
Hugo, G. 2001. 'International Migration Transform Australia'. Accessed 1 March 2018. https://www.prb.org/internationalmigrationtransformsaustralia/.
Lam, Katherine. 2017. 'Refugees from Iraq, Syria Eyed in British Subway Terror Attack Investigation'. *Fox News*, 18 September 2017. Accessed 7 October 2017. http://www.foxnews.com/world/2017/09/18/refugees-from-iraq-syria-eyed-in-british-subway-terror-attack-investigation.html.
Malik, Shiv. 2012. 'Stop Sri Lanka Deportation Flights, says Human Rights Watch'. Guardian. 31 May 2012. Accessed 4 October 2017. https://www.theguardian.com/world/2012/may/31/sri-lanka-deportation-torture.
Mansbach, Richard W., and Kirsten L. Taylor. 2013. *Introduction to Global Politics*. Routledge: London.
Martin, Philip. 2013. *The Global Challenge of Managing Migration. Population Bulletin* 68 (2). Washington D.C.: Population Reference Bureau.
Massey, Douglas S. 1990. 'The Social and Economic Origins of Immigration'. *The Annals of the American Academy of Political and Social Science* 510: 60–72.
McDougall, Dan. 2006. 'Tourists Became Targets as Dubai Workers Take Revolt to the Beaches'. Accessed 1 May 2017. https://www.theguardian.com/travel/2006/apr/09/travelnews.
Nelson, Sara C. 2016. 'Map of EU Referendum Votes Shows How UK Voted for Brexit'. *Huffington Post*, 24 June 2016. Accessed 11 May 2017. http://www.huffingtonpost.co.uk/entry/brexit-map-uk-eu-referendum-2016_uk_576cf29fe4b0232d331db2b6.
OAS. 1984. 'Cartagena Declaration on Refugees, Colloquium on the International Protection of Refugees in Central America, Mexico and Panama'. Accessed 7 October 2017. https://www.oas.org/dil/1984_cartagena_declaration_on_refugees.pdf.
Ohmae, Kenichi. 1990. *The Borderless World: Power and Strategy in the Interlinked Economy*. New York: Harper Business.
O'Connor, Sarah, and Gonzalo Viña. 2016. 'What will Brexit Mean for Immigration? *Financial Times*, 24 June 2016. Accessed 11 May 2017. https://www.ft.com/content/a874de26-34b2-11e6-bda0-04585c31b153.

Ruiz, Olivia. 2006. 'Migration and Borders: Present and Future Challenges'. *Latin American Perspectives* 33 (2): 46–55.

Scarborough, Rowan. 2017. 'Islamic State Finds Success Infiltrating its Terrorists into Refugee Flows to West'. *Washington Times*, 29 January 2017. Accessed 7 October 2017. http://www.washingtontimes.com/news/2017/jan/29/isis-finds-success-infiltrating-terrorists-into-re.

Skeldon, Ronald. 2013. *Global Migration: Demographic Aspects and Its Relevance for Development.* United Nations Population Division (UNPD) technical paper 2013/6. New York, NY: United Nations. Accessed 11 May 2017. http://www.un.org/esa/population/migration/documents/EGM.Skeldon_17.12.2013.pdf.

Streger B. Manfred. 2009. *Globalization: A Very Short Introduction.* Hampshire: Oxford University Press.

The Statue of Liberty–Ellis Island Foundation (SOLEIF). 2017. 'Immigration Timeline'. Accessed 10 May 2017. http://www.libertyellisfoundation.org/immigration-timeline.

Thrush, Glenn. 2017. 'Trump's New Travel Ban Blocks Migrants From Six Nations, Sparing Iraq'. *New York Times,* 6 March 2017. Accessed 26 September 2017. https://www.nytimes.com/2017/03/06/us/politics/travel-ban-muslim-trump.html.

UNPD. 2013. *Trends in International Migrant Stock: The 2013 Revision.* Accessed 1 October 2013. http://www.un.org/en/development/desa/population/publications/pdf/migration/migrant-stock-age-2013.pdf.

United Nations Educational, Scientific and Cultural Organization (UNESCO). 2017. 'Migrant/Migration'. Accessed 1 May 2017. http://www.unesco.org/new/en/social-and-human-sciences/themes/international-migration/glossary/migrant.

United Nations High Commissioner for Refugees (UNHCR). 2008. *Protecting Internally Displaced Persons: A Manual for Law and Policymakers.* Washington D. C.: Brookings–Bern Project on Internal Displacement. Accessed 10 September 2017. http://www.unhcr.org/50f955599.pdf.

UNHCR. 2016. 'UNHCR Viewpoint: "Refugee" or "Migrant"—Which is Right?' 11 July 2016. Accessed 11 May 2017. http://www.unhcr.org/news/latest/2016/7/55df0e556/unhcr-viewpoint-refugee-migrant-right.html.

United Nations (UN). 2013. *Cross-national Comparisons of Internal Migration: An Update on Global Patterns and Trends.* UNPD technical paper 2013/1. New York, NY: United Nations. Accessed 11 May 2017. http://www.un.org/en/development/desa/population/publications/pdf/technical/TP2013-1.pdf.

———. 2015. 'Trends in International Migration 2015'. Accessed 11 March 2018. http://www.un.org/en/development/desa/population/migration/publications/populationfacts/docs/MigrationPopFacts20154.pdf.

———. 2017. 'International Migration'. Accessed 15 May 2017. http://www.un.org/en/development/desa/population/theme/international-migration/index.shtml.

———. 2018. 'Definitions'. Refugees and Migrants. Accessed 20 September 2017. http://refugeesmigrants.un.org/definitions.

UN Convention. 1990. Accessed 20 April 2018. http://www.ohchr.org/EN/ProfessionalInterest/Pages/CMW.aspx.

Wadsworth, Jonathan, Swati Dhingra, Gianmarco Ottaviano and John Van Reenen. 2016. *Brexit and the Impact of Immigration on the UK.* London: Centre for Economic Performance, London School of Economics and Political Science. Accessed 11 May 2017. http://cep.lse.ac.uk/pubs/download/brexit05.pdf.

Wyeth, Grant. 2017. 'What's Wrong with Australia's Emerging Immigration Stance?' Diplomat, 27 April 2017. Accessed 14 May 2017. http://thediplomat.com/2017/04/whats-wrong-with-australias-emerging-immigration-stance.

Further Reading

Borjas, George J. 1996. 'The Earnings of Mexican Immigrants in the United States'. *Journal of Development Economics* 51 (1): 69–98.

Chiswick, Barry R. 1978. 'The Effects of Americanization on the Earnings of Foreign-born Men'. *Journal of Political Economy* 86 (5): 897–921.

Cobb-Clark, Deborah A. 2000. 'Do Selection Criteria Make a Difference?: Visa Category and the Labour Market Status of Immigrants to Australia'. *Economic Record* 76 (232): 15–31.

European Commission. 2001. *Employment in Europe 2001: Recent Trends and Prospects*. Luxembourg: European Communities.

Glover, Stephen, Ceri Gott, Anaïs Loizillion, Jonathan Portes, Richard Price, Sarah Spencer, Vasanthi Srinivasan and Carole Willis. 2001. *Migration: An Economic and Social Analysis*. Research, Development and Statistics Directorate (RDS) occasional paper 67. London: Home Office.

Hoerder, Dirk. 1999. 'From Immigration to Migration Systems: New Concepts in Migration History'. *OAH Magazine of History* 14 (1): 5–11.

Husted, Leif, Helena Skyt Nielsen, Michael Rosholm and Nina Smith. 2000, 'Employment and Wage Assimilation of Male First Generation Immigrants in Denmark'. IZA discussion paper 101. *International Journal of Manpower* 22 (1/2): 39–68.

Human Security

Aditaya Narayan Mishra

LEARNING OBJECTIVES

- To understand the concept of human security
- To know the background and context of the concept of human security
- To discuss the main characteristics of human security
- To explore the various dimensions of human security
- To examine the role of the international community in the promotion of human security

Conceptualization of the term 'security' in the post-cold war era has been the subject of intense debate in recent years. Still lacking definitional accuracy, the concept of human security has nonetheless become widely acceptable. Traditionally, 'security' was perceived as a synonym of 'military security', as most of the threats to a state seemed to come from external military aggregations. But because of the several changes that occurred in the post-cold war era, this type of narrow understanding of security became inappropriate to explain the real meaning of 'security'. In reality, numerous non-military threats to states' vital interests have emerged in an increasingly interdependent world. In this changed scenario, although the military-centric security apprehensions are still important, new security issues such as population growth, ethnic conflict, terrorism, global warming, human rights, poverty, hunger, development, rising scarcity of fresh water, emigration, environmental degradation, and so on, have created alarm among policymakers, academicians and scientists.

Security is one of the oldest and most significant concepts in international relations. In reality, international relations have been state-centric and security-oriented, and nation states emerge and exist around security. The modern state was basically originated as a security arrangement, and despite the many different roles are now being attributed to the state, security remains a primary consideration for it. Therefore, national security has been the most important component of the state in the international system. But the human-security aspects of threats, as distinct from national security, highlight some of the major limitations of the old notion of security. The concept of human security aims at bringing about a paradigm shift in the concept of security, while transferring the focus from protection of the state to individuals. It calls for widening the scope of 'security', encompassing wide-ranging areas such as security against poverty, environmental degradation, infectious diseases, and so on. Traditionally, these threats were not conceptualized as security threats (Roznai 2014, 95). While changing the referent object of 'security' to individuals from states, the concept of human security calls for extending the idea of 'safety' to a condition beyond mere existence or survival to quality life or dignified living. For example, poverty is considered to be one of the human-security threats—not only because it can induce violence, which can ultimately lead to threatening the stability and viability of the state, but because it is a threat to the dignity of individuals (Tadjbakhsh and Chenoy 2009, 9).

A few scholars claim that in the post-cold war era, security threats from the military are much bigger than ever. However, despite the fact that these military threats are still considered to be a significant security threat, they are not the sole danger for nations and their citizens. Degradation of the environment, global warming, global hunger, infectious diseases, and so on, are threats which are not less dangerous than the traditional security threats (Hough 2004, 8). These threats are not limited to particular state boundaries and implicate the entire global community. Additionally, these types of threats do not necessarily come from outside the border, but can arise from within the borders of particular states. Therefore, this new aspect of security has challenged the notion of security as a solely military affair. For example, the disintegration of the Union of Soviet Socialist Republics (USSR) cannot be attributed to military factors; it happened due to socio-economic problems and lack of political legitimacy. So it was not the military deficits of the erstwhile USSR which threatened its security, but the threats that emerged from inside the state. This incident showed the weakness of the traditional understanding of security and stressed the need for redefining security.

The process of globalization further challenged the traditional border-centric notion of security. It has given rise to several challenges as well as opportunities. Now, in this age of interconnectedness, in which the world is known as a 'global village', threats to human security are no longer limited to national boundaries. Threats within countries could rapidly spill beyond national frontiers, posing global challenges to human security. Thus, the world has started facing new and complex types of global risks. The globalized risks demand global responses, that is, from the standpoint of all human beings. In other words, in the globalized world, security has to incorporate the issue of human security as well. Furthermore, globalization also poses the challenge of economic divides among the nations, in which some members of international society are excluded from economic development or progress. Although there are some developing countries such as China and India who are real beneficiaries of this globalization process, but such countries are very few in number. The globalization process had led to many losers among and within nations. The gap between the haves and the have-nots in both developing and developed nations has widened. It implies another kind of threat, a threat of global inequality. This combination of factors has led to the demand for expansion of the traditional notion of security (Ogoura 2005). Thus, the new thinking on 'security' questions not only the primacy of military threats in the calculation of security assessments but also—and more controversially—the central place of the nation state as the focus of security policies. In effect, the state becomes the means and not the end of security.

Theoretical Perspective on Human Security

Etymologically, the word 'security' originated from the Latin term securitas, which comes from *sine cura*, which means 'without worries, without fear'. So, in this respect, the term 'security' refers to the sense of safety or of being protected (Roznai 2014, 98). However, at the conceptual level, security has always been an 'essentially contested concept' (Schäfer 2013, 5). Conventionally, the study of security was perceived as 'the study of the threat, use of control of military force'. This old conception of security is mainly emphasized by the realist approach of international relations. The realist approach defines security in terms of security by military means and considers the state as the main referent object of security. The realist vision of the security of individuals makes it synonymous with citizenship—security comes from being a citizen and insecurity from being a citizen of another state. According to the realist approach in the anarchic and state-centric world order, security refers to the defence of the state from the aggression of other states. So far, international politics—including the cold war era—has been dominated by this conception of security (Behera 2004).

The process of redefining the concept of security started in the 1970s, when due to the oil crisis, the national security debate was impacted by the economic issues. Scholars such as Robert Keohane and Joseph Nye stressed on the growing significance of economic factors in international relations. Barry Buzan advanced the neo-realist approach to security and argued that the old conception of security solely based on a militaristic approach is not sufficient to explain security in a holistic manner. That is why he broadened the scope of security to incorporate political, economic, social and environmental threats, in addition to militaristic threats. However, Buzan still maintained that the main referent object of security analysis should remain the nation state (Stone 2009, 3).

Later, the traditional notion of security was challenged on various grounds. There was vigorous demand for the democratization of security. It was the *Human Development Report* of 1994, an annual publication of the United Nations Development Programme (UNDP), that for the first time explicitly articulated human security as a concept for future vision and an agenda for action. The late Pakistani economist Mahbub ul Haq had conceptualized the UNDP *Human Development Report* of 1994. Haq stated in the report that 'we need to fashion a new concept of human security that is reflected in the lives of our people, not in the weapons of our country' (UNDP 1994, 22). The *Human Development Report 1994* clearly stated that 'human security is not a concern with weapons; it is a concern with human life and dignity' (UNDP 1994, 22). The report focused on four characteristics of human security (UNDP 1994, 22):

- Human security is a universal concern.
- The components of human security are interdependent, that is, threats such as famine, disease, pollution, drug trafficking, terrorism or ethnic conflict in any part of the world cannot be taken as isolated events and have greater implications for peace and security in other parts of the world.
- Human security is easier to ensure through early prevention than later intervention.
- Human security is people-centric.

The report argued that human security is concerned with 'how people live and breathe in a society, how freely they exercise their many choices, how much access do they have to market and social opportunities—and whether they live in conflict or in peace' (UNDO 1994, 23). According to the report, human security means, first, safety from such chronic threats as hunger, disease and repression; and second, it means protection from sudden and hurtful disruptions in the patterns of daily life—whether in homes, in jobs or in communities. The report emphasized the changing security discourse in two fundamental ways (UNDP 1994, 24):

- From an exclusive stress on territorial security to a much greater stress on people's security.
- From security through armaments to security through sustainable human development.

The UNDP report also identified seven dimensions of human security (UNDP 1994, 24):

- Economic security: Every individual requires an assured income.
- Food security: Every individual requires an assured physical and economic access to basic food.
- Health security: Every individual requires an assured access to healthcare and health services.
- Environmental security: Requirement of access to a healthy physical environment.
- Personal security: Security from physical violence and from various threats.
- Community security: Security from oppressive traditional practices and from sectarian and ethnic violence.
- Political security: Security of basic human rights and security from state repressions.

To prevent conflict, the report recommends an early warning system at the international level. It also links human security with development, as it suggests that at the national level, governments should adopt policies which are conducive to social integration, such as providing equal opportunities for empowerment and development to every section of society. Human security seems to be a part of the vision of people-oriented economic development. The UNDP approach to human security includes a large number of issues and threats that concern national borders and implicate people worldwide.

Defining Human Security

To begin with, there is no single definition of human security, as in various academic works and reports, it has been described in different ways. So, despite the fact that a comprehensive definition of human security is yet to be finalized, there is agreement among the proponents of this concept that there is a need to bring about a shift of focus from a military-based, state-centric security to a people-centric security (Tadjbakhsh 2005, 5).

As mentioned above, the UNDP, in its *Human Development Report 1994*, for the first time tried to define 'human security', while arguing for a shift from an exclusive focus on territorial security to a much greater focus on the individual's security. Apart from this, some of the other important definitions of human security are mentioned below.

The UN Commission on Human Security (2003) in its report *Human Security Now* defined human security as

> … to protect the vital core of all human lives in ways that enhance human freedoms and human fulfillment. Human security means protecting fundamental freedoms—freedoms that are the essence of life. It means protecting people from critical [severe] and pervasive [widespread] threats and situations. It means using processes that build on people's strengths and aspirations. It means creating political, social, environmental, economic, military and cultural systems that together give people the building blocks of survival, livelihood and dignity. (Commission on Human Security 2003, 4).

In a similar vein, Mahbub ul Haq defines human security as a new notion of security, in which the concept of security will be fully transformed and security will be interpreted as 'security of people, not just territory, security of individuals, not just nations. Security through development, not through arms. Security of all the people everywhere—in their homes, in their jobs, in their streets, in their communities, in their environment' (Fukuda-Parr and Messineo 2011, 1).

Kanti Bajpai explained human security in terms of 'bodily safety' and 'personal freedom'. He claims that individual safety is the most important component of human security. For him, 'Human security relates to the protection of the individual's personal safety and freedom from direct and indirect threats of violence. The promotion of human development and good governance, and, when necessary, the collective use of sanctions and force are central to managing human security. States, international organizations, nongovernmental organizations, and other groups in civil society in combination are vital to the prospects of human security' (Paris 2001, 95).

Ramesh Thakur stated that

> human security refers to the quality of life of the people of a society or polity. Anything which degrades their quality of life—demographic pressures, diminished access to or stock or resources, and so on—is a security threat. Conversely, anything which can upgrade their quality of life—economic growth, improved access to resources, social and political empowerment, and so on—is an enhancement of human security. (Raza and Siddiqui 2014, 24)

The Canadian government's definition emphasized the 'freedom from fear aspect' of the concept. According to it, 'human security means freedom from pervasive threats to people's rights, safety or lives' (Figure 12.1) (Martin and Owen 2013, 40).

In the words of the former United Nations (UN) Secretary-General Kofi Annan,

> Human security in its broadest sense embraces far more than the absence of violent conflict. It encompasses human rights, good governance, access to education and healthcare and ensuring that each individual has opportunities and choices to fulfill his or her own potential. Every step in this direction is also a step towards reducing poverty, achieving economic growth and preventing conflict. Freedom from want, freedom from fear and the freedom of future generations to inherit a healthy natural environment—these are the interrelated building blocks of human, and therefore national, security. (Alkire 2003, 14)

One of the underlying features of this definition is that it adds an additional dimension to the definition of human security, that is, 'freedom from hazard impact' (Brauch 2005). Given the growing environmental concerns worldwide, it was necessary to include this aspect in the definition of human security (Table 12.1).

The UN General Assembly (GA) adopted a resolution in 2012, in which it defined human security as

> the right of people to live in freedom and dignity, free from poverty and despair. All individuals, in particular vulnerable people, are entitled to Freedom from Fear and Freedom from Want, with an equal opportunity to enjoy all their rights and fully develop their human potential. (UN GA 2013)

Apart from these definitions, scholars such as Amartya Sen and Amitav Acharya have explained human security in terms of development of human resources and holistic development of individuals. According to Amartya Sen, human security is a vital component of broader development processes, fundamentally linked with securing human capabilities. Apart from the old slogan 'growth with equity', it is equally concerned with 'downturns with security)' (Menon 2007). Amitav Acharya considers that

FIGURE 12.1 Concept of Human Security

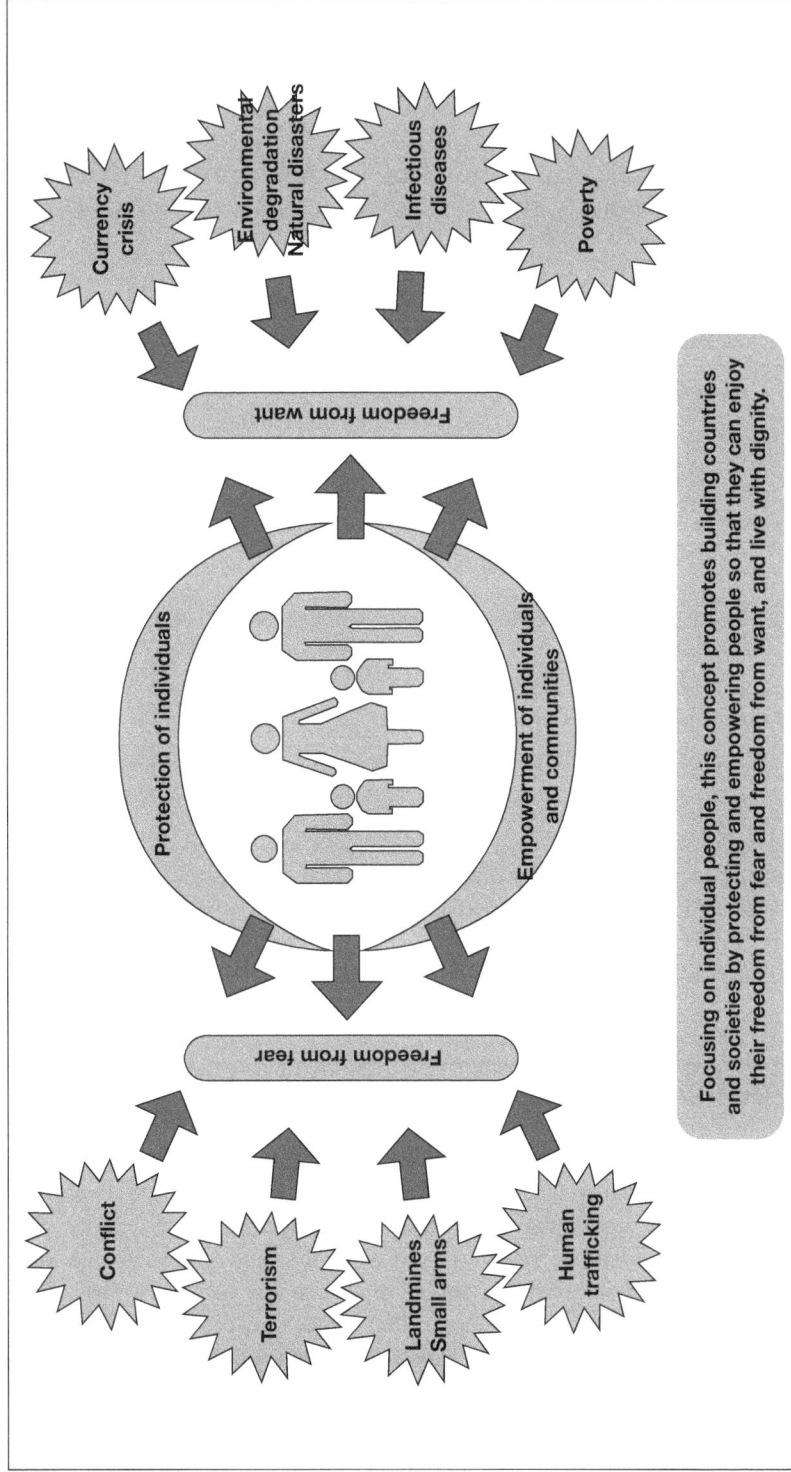

Currency crisis

Environmental degradation Natural disasters

Infectious diseases

Poverty

Freedom from want

Protection of individuals

Empowerment of individuals and communities

Freedom from fear

Conflict

Terrorism

Landmines Small arms

Human trafficking

Focusing on individual people, this concept promotes building countries and societies by protecting and empowering people so that they can enjoy their freedom from fear and freedom from want, and live with dignity.

Source: Ministry of Foreign Affairs of Japan (2013).

TABLE 12.1 Differences Between Traditional Notion of Security and Human Security

	Traditional Notion of Security	Human Security
Security for whom	In an anarchic world scenario, the safety of the state is the most important concern. The state's security ensures the citizens' security.	Security of individuals and of states, both are equally important. The security of states is meant to achieve individuals' security, but is not an end itself.
Security of which values	Sovereign status of the state; security of its border territory.	Protection of individuals, their well-being and freedom are the supreme values to be protected.
Security from what threats	Direct external threats; external aggression.	Both direct and indirect violence: direct violence such as conflicts between states, armed conflicts, violence erupted from power politics, weapons of mass destruction (WMDs), and so on; indirect violence including scarcity, poverty, infectious diseases, environmental degradation, demographic pressure, migration, and so on.
Security by what means	Military power and balance of power; more emphasis on economic progress but less care for rule of law or democratic institutions.	The promotion of human development: promotion of equality, sustainable development and democratic participation; political security, peace and cooperation among states; dependence on international institutions, networks and coalitions.

Source: Tadjbakhsh (2005, 28).

human security is a holistic concept, which encompasses social and political development, apart from a militaristic concept of security (Yang n.d.). No government can successfully run while solely dealing with economic development, nor can they preserve social and political order by just protecting their borders by military threats. In the security framework, factors such as the process of democratization should also be included (Tadjbakhsh and Chenoy 2009, 42).

Evolution of the Concept

The philosophical foundations of human security can be traced back to several events of the 1960s, 1970s and 1980s, in which several independent commissions came up with a series of reports. There was growing discontent regarding the prevailing conceptions of development and security. The first of these reports were the 'world *problematique*' reports produced by the Club of Rome group, which emphasized the complex nature of the threats troubling people of all nations, such as poverty, degradation of the environment, loss of faith in institutions, uncontrolled urban spread, insecurity of employment, alienation of youth, rejection of traditional values, inflation and other monetary and economic disruptions (Bajpai 2000, 5). In other words, the group recognized the idea of the comprehensive nature of security threats and the alternative ways to resolve them. In this series, another noteworthy commission is the

Brandt Commission, which in its famous *North–South* report underlined the problem of hunger, mass misery and alarming disparities between the living conditions of the rich and the poor (Bajpai 2000, 6). The Independent Commission on Disarmament and Security Issues also focused on alternative ways of thinking about peace and security. A brief account of the evolution of human security can be given in following chronological order (Tadjbakhsh and Chenoy 2009: 4; United Nations 2012):

- In 1992, former UN Secretary-General Boutros Boutros-Ghali introduced the concept of 'An Agenda for Peace', in which measures of preventative diplomacy, peacemaking, peacekeeping and post-conflict recovery are recognized as international responsibilities.
- In 1994, the UNDP *Human Development Report* coined the term 'human security'.
- At the 1995 Copenhagen summit, the Group of 77 (G-77) nations debated over human security, while citing the reason that it would undermine the states sovereignty.
- After 1994 UNDP report, the second major contribution to the conceptualization of human security was that of the Canadian government and academicians. In 1996, Canada, led by foreign minister Lloyd Axworthy, adopted the 'freedom from fear' approach as the principle of its foreign-policy tools. Canada criticized the UNDP's view of human security for focusing too much on threats associated with underdevelopment at the expense of 'human insecurity resulting from violent conflict'. The Human Security Network (HSN) was formed by the governments of Canada, Norway and other states. Since 1996, the country has been continuously focusing on the goal of freedom from fear, calling for safety from both violent and non-violent threats. Much of Canada's interest can be attributed the efforts of Lloyd Axworthy, who stressed the need of reshaping the Canada's foreign policy in the new post-cold war realties. He called for the focusing on issues such as the menace of terrorism, children trapped in war zones, drug trafficking, and so on.
- For the cause of human security promotion, Canada played a crucial role in the signing of the Convention on Prohibition of the Use, Stockpiling, Production and Transfer of Antipersonnel Landmines and on their Destruction (opened for signatures at Ottawa) in 1997.
- In 1998, the Japanese government, led by Prime Minister Keizo Obuchi, supported the UNDP's broader view and adopted an even more comprehensive definition of human security while considering 'Asian values'. It proposed a new perspective to human security, that is, 'freedom from want'. Japan sees human security as protecting people from threats to their livelihood and dignity while protecting self-employment. In this regard, Japan's view is also similar to the UNDP approach. As the Japanese government visualized human security as protection from all the dangers which can threaten human survival, life and dignity, it covers a range of issues such as degradation of the environment, human rights abuses, drugs trafficking, migration crises, poverty, transnational diseases such as HIV/AIDS, and so on.
- In two subsequent events, the Millennium Declaration and the 2000 UN Millennium Summit, Kofi Annan called for advancing the human-security agenda as part of the new UN mandate.
- In 2001, the Canadian government launched the International Commission on Intervention and State Sovereignty (ICISS), which came up with milestone report *The Responsibility to Protect* in September 2001, which addressed the ultimate responsibilities of sovereign states to protect their own citizens (UN n.d.).

- In 2001, the independent Commission on Human Security (CHS) was established under the co-chairmanship of Sadako Ogata and Amartya Sen to promote the concept of human security.
- In 2003, the Japanese government supported the CHS and initiated discussion of the 'responsibility of development'. This Commission was formed in 2001 with the help of Japanese government and the UN. It presented its report, namely, *Human Security Now* in 2003. The Commission aimed at fulfilling three main objectives: first, to promote human security through the enhancement of public understanding and public engagement; secondly, to develop the concept of human security in the form tool for making and implementing public policy; and thirdly, to suggest an actual programme of actions to deal with grave and pervasive threats to human security The report emphasized following six broader, connected areas: protection of people from violent conflict, protection and empowerment of people on the move, protection and empowerment of people in post-conflict situations, economic insecurities, health security and knowledge, skills and values.
- In 2004, the UN Secretary-General's High-level Panel on Threats, Challenges and Change came up with the report *A More Secure World: Our Shared Responsibility*. It highlighted the new challenges posed to human security in the context of the twenty-first century.
- In 2004, the Human Security Doctrine was approved by the European Union (EU) to deal with conflicts outside of its borders, with special reference to the migration problem.
- In 2005, Secretary-General Kofi Annan presented a five-year progress report, namely *In Larger Freedom: Towards Development, Security and Human Rights for All*. The report was divided into four main sections, and the first three set out priorities for action in the fields of development, security and human rights. The report recognized freedom from fear, freedom from deprivation and freedom to live in dignity as the basic elements of human security. The report said that 'the world must advance the causes of security, development and human rights together, otherwise none will succeed. Humanity will not enjoy security without development, it will not enjoy development without security, and it will not enjoy either without respect for human rights' (Annan 2005).
- In 2005, the UN GA accepted the World Summit Outcome Document of 2005. Paragraph 143 of this document (A/RES/60/1) noted that 'all individuals, in particular vulnerable people, are entitled to freedom from fear and freedom from want, with an equal opportunity to enjoy all their rights and fully develop their human potential' (UN GA 2005).
- In 2006, the Friends of Human Security was formed at the UN.
- The Association of Southeast Asian Nations (ASEAN) started discussing the adoption of the human security agenda and the Arab League established a Human Security Unit in 2007.
- In May 2008, the UN GA convened an informal debate in which more than 90 member states participated to discuss the notion of human security.
- In 2010, the first report of the Secretary-General on human security (A/64/701) was released and a panel discussion and plenary meeting of the GA was convened to consider the report. In the same year, the GA passed Resolution 64/291, a '[f]ollow-up to paragraph 143 on human security of the 2005 World Summit Outcome'.
- In 2012, the GA adopted by consensus Resolution 66/290, also a '[f]ollow-up to paragraph 143 on human security of the 2005 World Summit Outcome'.

Approaches to Human Security

The concept of human security is perceived differently by different scholars and institutions. The different approaches to human security can be classified into four broad categories (Singh 2014):

1. approach based on UNDP reports
2. approach based on government-level initiatives
3. approach based on independent commission reports
4. approach based on various academic accounts

These approaches focus on four fundamental questions (or parameters):

1. Security for whom?
2. Security of which values?
3. Security from what threats?
4. Security by what means? (Singh 2014, 49)

Approach Based on UNDP Reports

As discussed above, the UNDP's 1994 report clearly calls for widening the scope of 'security' and defines 'human security' as the protection of individuals' life and dignity. Thus, it is clear that according to the report, the main referent object for human security is the individual. Furthermore, the report mainly stresses the comprehensiveness of 'security' and focuses on safety from chronic threats that endanger the life of individuals. It also identifies seven crucially important areas for human security. To consider the third question (security from what threats), the report explains that there is long list of threats to human security, but these seven categories can cover most of them—for example, threats to economic security originate from unemployment. While considering the fourth parameter (security by what means), the report suggests alternative measures for securing human security, that is, human development (Singh 2014, 50–51).

On the lines of the UNDP approach, the *Secretary-General's High-level Panel Report on Threats, Challenges and Change, 2004*, also focuses on alternative means of security. It recommends six clusters of security threats:

- economic and social threats, including poverty, deadly infectious diseases and environmental degradation
- inter-state conflicts
- internal conflicts, civil wars and genocide
- WMDs
- terrorism
- transnational organized crime

The report states that development has to be the first line of defence for a collective security system (Singh 2014, 52).

Approach Based on Government-level Initiatives

In this category, the strongest advocates of human security are Canada, Norway and Japan. All these countries have initiated several policy measures for promoting human security. Similar to the UNDP, the Canadian government also defines human security in terms of the security of the individual. In the Canadian notion too, the main referent object of 'human security' is the individual. While taking account of security values, the Canadian approach too concentrates on the 'freedom from fear' aspect, which includes freedom from pervasive threats to people's rights, safety or lives. Canada's human-security policy is based on five priorities, which can be considered as basic values. These are:

- public safety
- protection of civilians
- conflict prevention
- governance and accountability
- peace support operations

In light of these security values, the third parameter (what threats) can be also analysed. For example, public-safety threats posed by terrorism, drug trafficking, spread of crime and danger to civilians are caused by the escalation of armed conflicts. Now, for the fourth parameter (security by what means), the Canadian approach suggests several ways—building international expertise and capability to counter the threats to human security, establishing legal norms, strengthening international capacity to resolve conflicts, and so on (Singh 2014, 53–54).

The Japanese government recommends a more comprehensive view of human security, which is a bit different from the Canadian perspective, though. Japan established a Commission on Human Security and set up the largest trust fund in the UN for human security. Hence, in the case of Japan too, the referent object, security values, types of threats and means to deal with them envisaged almost exactly match those of the UNDP (Singh 2014, 55).

Norway is also one of the leading countries in promoting human security. Norway and Canada jointly organized a conference in May 1998, which led to the culmination of the 'Canada–Norway Partnership for Action: The Lysøen Declaration'. This declaration explains how both countries have commonly followed the principles of human security in their foreign policies. On the basis of this declaration, Norway has identified its objectives, which include the promotion of human security, supporting human rights, reinforcing humanitarian law, averting conflicts, and advancing democracy and good governance (Ibid.).

Approach Based on Independent Commission Reports

In this category, the first important commission on human security is the Commission on Human Security. The Commission clearly emphasizes the significance of the role of the states as core protectors of security. However, in certain cases, the state itself has become a source of insecurity to its own citizens. In this regard, the Commission calls for shifting attention from the security of the state to the security of the people. According to the Commission, human security complements state security in four aspects (Singh 2014, 58):

- Human security refers to the protection of the individual and the community, rather than focusing on the state.
- Threat to individuals' security includes dangers and conditions that have not always been recognized as threats to state security.
- The range of actors is extended beyond the state alone.
- Accomplishing human security involves not only the protection of the people but also their empowerment.

So this approach too covers all the parameters of referent object, security values, type of threats and means to deal with them in its interpretation.

Approach Based on Various Academic Accounts

In the academic field, the discourse on human security was initiated by Mahbub ul Haq and later continued by several scholars such as Keith Krause, Ramesh Thakur, Nicholas Thomas, Kanti Bajpai, Barry Buzan, Andrew Mack, Sabina Alkire, Taylor Owen, Shahrbanou Tadjbakhsh and Amitav Acharya, besides academic projects at the colloquium organized by the *Security Dialogue* journal of the Peace Research Institute, Oslo (PRIO) in 2004 (Singh 2014, 60). Among the academic community, there is no consensus over the parameters of security values, causes and means to achieve security. However, there is agreement on the point of the referent object for the human security, that is, the individual. Given the variations in the views of scholars regarding human security, this concept has been separated into two categories—the broader view of human security and the narrow view of human security. The broader view of human security is associated with the concept of 'freedom from want' and the narrower view is based on the concept of 'freedom from fear' (Liotta and Owen 2006, 41).

The broad view (freedom from want) is advocated by the UNDP, the UN-appointed Commission on Human Security, Japan and a range of academicians such as Alkire, Thakur, Axworthy, Bajpai, and others. This approach, as discussed earlier, recognizes threats such as hunger, disease, repression, prevention of sudden disasters, and so on. All these threats are development-oriented threats and their resolution requires long-term planning and investment in development.

On the other hand, the narrow school mostly confines its understanding of human security to the prevention of violent threats against the individual, which includes drug trafficking, landmines, ethnic conflict, state small-arms trade, and so on. Proponents of this view are the Canadian government, Krause, Mack, and others (Table 12.2).

A brief comparison of both the views is given in Table 12.3.

However, in spite of all these differences, both views of human security emphasize opposing the excessive use of coercive means as a tool for resolving conflicts. Both promote measures such as economic development, peaceful agreements, negotiation and post-war restructuring processes for reaching a resolution of conflicts.

TABLE 12.2 Broad vs Narrow Approach to Human Security

	Broad View of Human Security	Narrow View of Human Security
Type of threats	Safety from chronic threats such as hunger, disease and repression; economic, food, health, environmental, personal, community and political security	Physical security from violent threats, conflict and crime, post-conflict peace-building, small arms, land mines, women in conflict, and so on
Philosophy	Freedom from want	Freedom from fear
Advocates	UNDP, Commission on Human Security, Japan	Norway, Canada, Switzerland, the Human Security Network, UN peace operations
Factors behind the origin	Dissatisfaction over the traditional growth-oriented development model; guns versus butter concerns[a]	Emergence of the cold war, racial conflicts, the growing number of failed states, and so on
Policy objectives	Promoting human development and building human capabilities through, education, social and political participation, and so on	Protecting people in war-torn zones, prohibition on landmines and child soldiers, and promoting human rights and peace-building processes

Source: Baylis, Smith and Owens (2014, 350).

[a]This debate connotes the issue of allocating scarce financial resources for military purpose which eventually results into the hindering the human developments. Here gun perspective stressed on arms for national security, and the butter perspective looks for the human security.

Characteristics of Human Security

Based on the above description, we can identify some of the fundamental features of human security as follows:

a. **People-centric:** One of the most crucial points about human security is that it puts the individual at the centre of its analysis. People-centricity refers to giving attention to the individual's security from the critical and pervasive threats to their survival, livelihood and dignity. It calls for enabling individuals and local communities to identify the problems and threats and then participating in developing strategies to achieve human security (UNTFH 2009).

b. **Multisectoral:** Human security calls for the multisectoral understanding of threats. Apart from safeguarding the state from traditional threats, it covers multiple types of threats such as environmental degradation, poverty, underdevelopment, diseases, and so on (UNTFH 2009).

c. **Comprehensive:** It addresses all those types of threats which are fundamental to human life—'freedom from fear', 'freedom from want' and freedom to live in dignity and focus on the real needs, problems and capacities of the government and the people (UNTFH 2009, 13).

d. **Context-specific:** Human security admits that each kind of global threat has some local specification, so they need to be assessed and planned for accordingly (UNTFH 2009, 13).

TABLE 12.3 Comparing Different Definitions of Human Security

Proponents	Definition	Referent Object	Values	Conception of Threats	Agents
CHS	Human security as protection of the vital core of humans' lives by enhancing their freedoms and fulfillments	Individual	Survival, livelihood and dignity (freedom from fear, want and a life of dignity)	Threats of poverty, violence, and so on, which are critical and pervasive in nature	Nation states, insurgents
UNDP 1994	Human security as protection of individuals' life and dignity	Individual	Comprehensive: freedom from fear and want	Seven dimensions of threats— economic, food, health, environmental, personal, communal and political	Local as well as global, both from states and non-state actors
Canada	Human security as protection of individuals' lives and rights from pervasive threats	Individual	Focus on freedom from fear	Arms trafficking, economic inequality among nations, conflict within states, failed states, international crime, environmental threats, the proliferation of WMDs, communalism and ethnic crises, population explosions, refugee crises, problems of anti-personnel landmines, poverty and so on	States, rebels, drug and weapons traffickers, and individuals
Japan	Human security as protection of people from threats to their livelihood and dignity	Individuals	Protection of human dignity requires freedom from fear and want and both types of security values should be treated equally	All types of threats to lives, livelihoods and dignity of people, such as economic crises, environmental crises, drug trafficking, international crime, migration crises, landmines, pandemics, and so on	Governments, rebels, drug and weapons traffickers, individuals

(Continued)

TABLE 12.3 (Continued)

Proponents	Definition	Referent Object	Values	Conception of Threats	Agents
Kanti Bajpai	Human security as safety of the people and their freedom from both direct and indirect threats of violence. Rational use of force by the state, human development and good governance are the key elements of human security. The combined role of states and non-states actors is seen as essential to the promotion of human security	Individuals	Individual safety and freedom	Both from direct violence (conflicts among countries, violent conflicts, WMDs, discrimination, and so on) and indirect violence (poverty, inequality, population growth, environmental problems, and so on)	Both from states and non-state actors
Ramesh Thakur	Human security defined in terms of quality of life of individuals	Community	'Human rights' is the key elements	All those factors which jeopardize people's quality of life, such as population explosions, lack of resources and lack of access to them	The nation state, individuals, societal groups institutional and non-institutional structures, environmental degradation, transnational crime, migration crises, and so on

| Kofi Annan | Human security in its broadest sense embraces far more than the absence of violent conflict. It encompasses human rights, good governance, access to education and healthcare and ensuring that each individual has opportunities and choices to fulfil their own potential. Every step in this direction is also a step towards reducing poverty, achieving economic growth and preventing conflict. Freedom from want, freedom from fear and the freedom of future generations to inherit a healthy natural environment—these are the interrelated building blocks of human, and therefore national, security | Individual | Economic development, social justice, environmental protection, democratization, disarmament, respect for human rights and the rule of law | Internal violence, nuclear weapons, mass destruction, repression, gross abuses of human rights, the large-scale displacement of civilian populations, international terrorism, the AIDS pandemic, drug and arms trafficking and environmental disasters' | States, individuals, nature and the environment |

Source: Tadjbakhsh and Chenoy (2009, 32–34); Menon (2007, 17–19).

e. **Prevention-oriented:** Human security emphasizes prevention-oriented activities which strengthen, empower and protect people and communities. In other words, it signifies a belief in the phrase 'prevention is better than the cure'. It promotes the idea of building the capacities of people and communities (UNTFH 2017, 13).

f. **Protection and empowerment:** Human security stresses the fact that empowering people and communities to articulate and respond to their needs and those of others is crucial.

g. **Interconnected with concepts such as human development and human rights:** Although human security at a conceptual level is different from all these concepts, but in essence, it is complementary to the others. Both human security and human development are interconnected, as human security aims at the source and the costs of underdevelopment. Both concepts are multidimensional, individual-centric and see poverty and inequality as root causes of the insecurity for the individual. However, human security refers to the resolution of immediate threats, whereas human development talks about long-term initiatives. Similarly, human security extends the scope of security while adding an important dimension of downturn with security. Human security talks about ensuring those choices for one's life which are made possible by the process of human development. Likewise, human security and human rights are also mutually connected but conceptually different. Whereas human rights indicate the fundamental legal entitlements of individuals which are essential to their existence, human security comprises the safety of the individuals from certain threats and it lays more emphasis on the context in which threats originate and responses are developed. Human rights normally rely on legal instruments for the prevention of human-rights abuse or crimes, while human security depends upon economic, political and other means for protection from threats. Hence, human rights can be described as one of the essential elements of a human security framework. Moreover, if we consider the narrow definition, human security is a human right. If human rights are promoted, then human security will be advanced (Martin and Owen 2013).

Human Security: Conceptual Criticism

The concept of human security has been contested. Different groups of academicians perceive it differently and critically. One of the fundamental criticisms is that it is too vague and lacks precision and that is why defining human security is impossible. Critics argue that one cannot make any definite theoretical construct of the concept if it covers all forms of threats to an individual as security threats (Tadjbakhsh 2005). It was this criticism which led to the emergence of the 'narrow' versus 'broad' views of human security. Supporters of the narrow view argue that through this view, the definition of human security can be well defined and applied, as it identifies the concrete means of security threats to human well-being.

Another criticism of the concept is that it minimizes the role of sovereign states as the sole providers of security and, in a way, it challenges the very existence of sovereign states. According to the critics, this is a misfit in international relations theory. In the traditional notion of security, it is the state alone that can provide security, as without it, it is unclear which agency would be working as the security provider (Tadjbakhsh and Chenoy 2009, 59).

Another notable criticism of the concept is that it was initiated by countries such as Canada and Japan, who are also considered as 'middle powers', as a diplomatic tool to promote their foreign-policy goals but they failed in promoting it further. These countries tried to redefine the notion of security in order to challenge the US position (Fukuda-Parr and Messineo 2011, 13).

David Chandler compares the concept of human security with 'the dog that doesn't bark'. According to him, the concept has negligible impact on policy outcomes, regardless of its strong presence as a discourse at the international level, because it cannot really challenge the existing policy frameworks (Fukuda-Parr and Messineo 2012, 14). The concept has just relabeled the old tools without proposing a new policy mechanism. It is impossible to implement the concept as it just provides short-term solutions to threats, without suggesting long-term resolutions (Tadjbakhsh and Chenoy 2009, 68).

Most of these criticisms can be countered, as the role of the state is not underestimated but needs to be reoriented. Moreover, the issue of human security is more pertinent to the developing South of the world as compared to the developed North. It is also worth mentioning that insecurities in the Global South such as population explosions, illiteracy, poverty, diseases and environment pollution are likely to implicate the security of the Global North as well. For instance, the problems of immigration in Europe and the food crisis in Ethiopia are both human-security problems (Tadjbakhsh and Chenoy 2009, 66).

While analysing all these above-mentioned definitions of and approaches to human security, it is evident that they vary on the grounds of the nature of the threats, values and priorities, methods to prevent, and so on; but there are certain similarities which can be identified throughout all the definitions, such as, first, that security cannot be seen as the prerogative of the state. Secondly, there is interdependence between the security of the individuals and that of systems, and finally, there is the expansion of the idea of 'violence'. So, in simple words, we can define human security as a concept or policy which is people-centric rather than state-centric and which focuses on the safety and protection of individuals and communities rather than the borders of states. It recognizes the interconnectedness between human development, human rights and security and transcends the meaning of 'security' as mere survival to imply a life worth living, hence including the well-being and dignity of human beings. It is comprehensive and multisectoral in its scope, which requires freedom from fear, freedom from want, freedom from hazardous impact and freedom to live in dignity. It stresses multidimensional resolutions to conflicts, based on an interdisciplinary approach (Tadjbakhsh and Chenoy 2009, 70–71).

Dimensions of Human Security

As mentioned above, the 1994 UNDP report identified seven categories of threats to human security. In addition to these threats, the report identified six types of global or transnational threats to human security (UNDP 1994):

- unchecked population growth
- disparities in economic opportunities
- migration pressure
- environmental degradation
- drug trafficking
- international terrorism

While analysing all these dimensions in the context of the contemporary world scenario, it can be seen that they are not less dangerous than any traditional insecurities.

Economic Security

This means assured income from productive and remunerative work. The 1994 report noted that only about a quarter of the world's population may at present be economically safe. The economic insecurity is directly related to poverty. According to a recent World Bank (WB) report, around 767 million people, who constitute 10.7% of the total world population, are living under extreme poverty. As per the WB, extreme poverty refers to living on less than $1.90 per day. Despite some significant improvement in poverty reduction (which is concentrated in Asia, particularly in China), a significant population of the world is still suffering from substantive inequalities and shortage of access to education, health facilities, drinking water, nutrition, sanitation, and so on. The possible causes of poverty include economic inequalities, conflicts, resource deficits, and so on (World Bank 2018). According to the United Nations Children's Fund (UNICEF), around 1 billion children worldwide are living in poverty and 22,000 children die each day due to poverty (India Today 2015). As per the World Food Programme data, those who are poor are hungry and hunger is the number one global killer, killing more than HIV/AIDS, malaria and tuberculosis combined (WFP 2009). The above statistics simply reveal how economic factors threaten the security of people.

Global disparities in economic opportunities have encouraged overconsumption and overproduction in the North at the cost of poverty and environmental degradation in the South. As per the WB report, the global Gini index—which is a measure of statistical dispersion intended to represent the income or wealth distribution of a nation's residents and is the most commonly used measure of inequality—has declined since the 1990s due to rapidly rising incomes in China and India, while inequality within countries has generally increased (Sundaram and Chowdhury 2017). According to an Oxfam report in 2015, 62 billionaires own the same amount of wealth as 3.5 billion people who make up the poorest half of the world's population. The richest 1% of the world population now owns half of the world's wealth and the richest 50% own over 99% of the world's wealth while the poorest have less than 1% (Elliott 2016).

Food Security

This means that all people at all times have both physical and economic access to basic foods. What is required is 'entitlement' to food. The basic problem to food security is poor distribution of food and lack of purchasing power. The 1994 UNDP report said that 'people go hungry not because food is unavailable but because they cannot afford it'. This dimension of insecurity is also closely related to economic factors. In 2016, according to the UN, the number of undernourished people in the world had increased to an estimated 815 million, up from 777 million in 2015 (Figure 12.2) (FAO, IFAD, UNICEF, WFP and WHO 2017). Stunting still affects 155 million of children under the age of five years, which is increasing their risk of suffering impaired cognitive ability, weakened performance at school and work and dying from infections. According to FAO reports for the last 10 years, the numbers of violent conflicts around the world are mounting in those countries which are facing food insecurity, hitting rural communities the hardest and having a negative impact on food production and availability (FAO, IFAD, UNICEF, WFP and WHO 2017).

FIGURE 12.2 Increasing Trend of Natural Disasters/Catastrophic Events

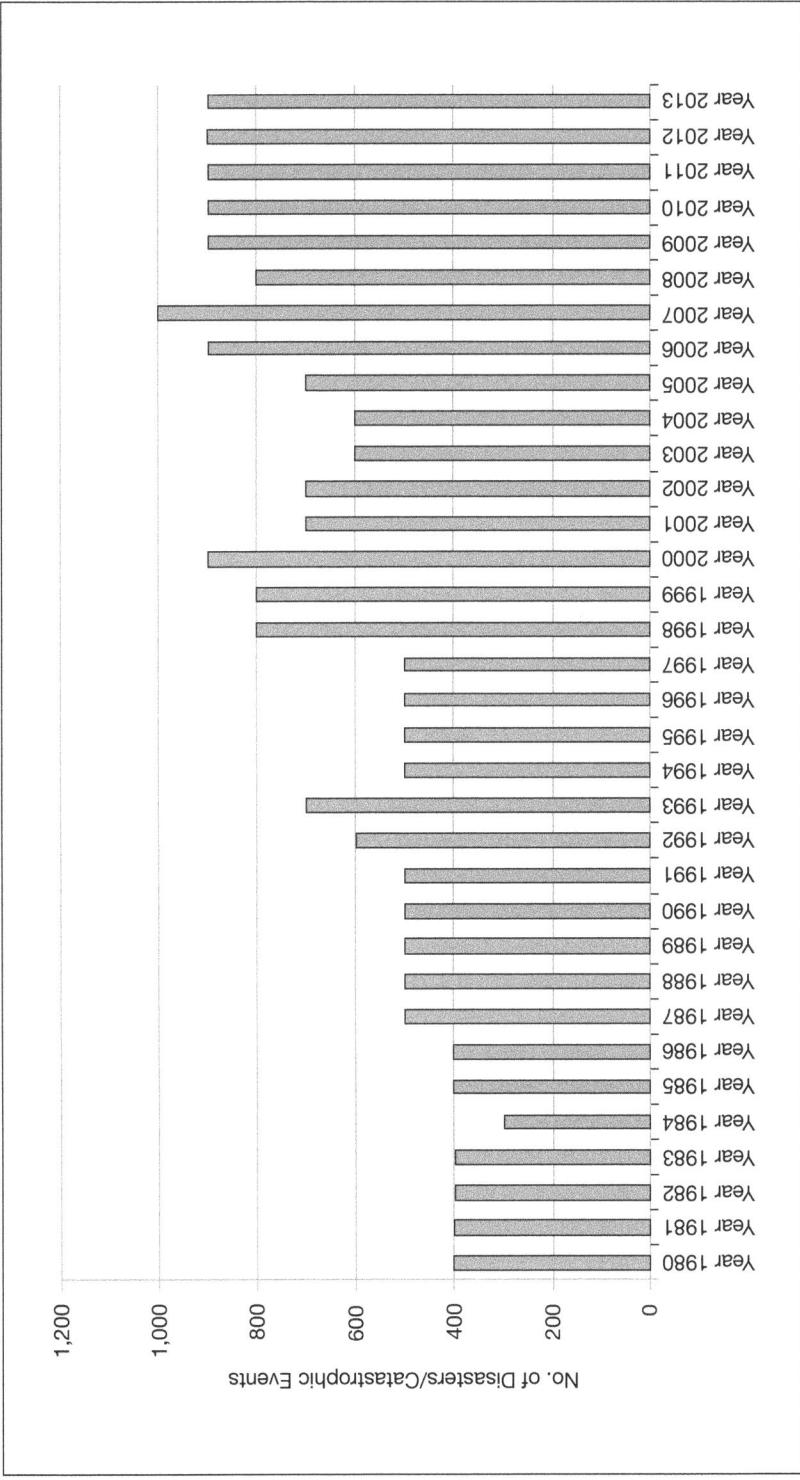

Source: www.globalstewards.org (modified).

Health Security

The basic threats to health in developing countries are parasitic and infectious diseases. The UNDP 1994 report noted that the poor are more vulnerable to health hazards compared to the rich. The widest gap between the North and the South in any human development indicator is in the maternal mortality rate, which is about 18 times greater in the South. A recent report of the World Health Organization (WHO) in 2016 shows that many countries in the world are denied universal health coverage, which includes access to 16 essential healthcare services (UN 2017a). Most of these countries belong to the African and eastern Mediterranean regions. Further, the report shows some alarming challenges, such as 303,000 women having died due to complications of pregnancy and childbirth, 5.9 million children having died before their fifth birthday, 2 million people being newly infected with HIV, there being 9.6 million new tuberculosis cases and 214 million malaria cases and 1.7 billion people needing treatment for neglected tropical diseases. The report also talks about the recent Ebola outbreaks in West Africa. The Ebola epidemic initially appeared in urban areas in 2014 and it reached 10 countries and killed more than 11,000 people (UN 2017a). In this age of globalization, the world is facing a host of dangerous potential epidemics such as the avian flu, Zika, drug-resistant bacteria, and so on. While dealing with all these emerging threats, no nation can stand alone. This highlights the importance of a human-security approach that recognizes them as threats and talks about a comprehensive approach to dealing with them. Drug trafficking is another menace which creates a real problem for human health and well-being. The US and Canada are two countries with the highest per capita consumption of drugs. In the US alone, consumer spending on narcotics was thought to exceed the combined gross domestic products (GDPs) of more than 80 developing countries.

Environmental Security

The UN report 1994 noted that intense industrialization coupled with rapid population growth causes a severe threat to human security. Many countries, whether developing or developed, are facing different types of environmental problems, such as extensive flooding, droughts, land degradation, problems with sharing water and other resource conflicts and the adverse effects of climate change and global warming. The challenges being posed by environmental degradation are notable in many countries, particularly those that have fragile sociopolitical and economic structures. Global warming is also one of the most serious challenges faced by the world. The Intergovernmental Panel on Climate Change (IPCC) in its recent report concluded that the average temperature of surface of the earth has increased by 0.6°C since the late 1800s. The IPCC also forecasted that by 2100 it will have increased by 1.4°C to 5.8°C. According to the report, climatic changes cause 150,000 deaths every year (WHO 2017). The WHO also estimated that 12.6 million people died due to environmental factors in 2012, which constituted around a quarter of total global deaths (WHO 2016).

These environmental challenges have serious implications for humans and nature in many aspects. For instance, they could cause mass migrations out of severely affected areas and violent conflict between and within countries. Over the past 60 years, 40% of civil wars can be associated with natural resources; since 1990, there have been at least 18 violent conflicts fuelled or financed by natural resources (UNEP 2012, 14). According to the 1994 UNDP report, rapid population growth is an enormous pressure on diminishing non-renewable resources, which leads to environmental degradation. The current world population of 7.6 billion is expected to reach 8.6 billion in 2030, 9.8 billion in 2050 and 11.2 billion in

2100, with roughly 83 million people being added to the world's population every year (UN 2017b). The Global Footprint Network (GFN) estimates that the world's population currently consumes the equivalent of 1.6 planets. This figure should rise to two planets by 2030 based on current trends (Howard 2015).

Another problem associated with this issue is migration pressure. This problem is the clear consequence of growing populations and poverty in developing countries. An unprecedented 65.6 million people around the world have been forced from home by conflict and persecution by the end of 2016. Among them are nearly 22.5 million refugees, over half of whom are under the age of 18. There are also 10 million stateless people, who have been denied a nationality and access to basic rights such as education, healthcare, employment and freedom of movement (UNHCR 2017). Three countries—Syria, Afghanistan and South Sudan—account for 55% of total number of refugees around the world (Figure 12.3).

FIGURE 12.3 World's Refugees: Important Facts

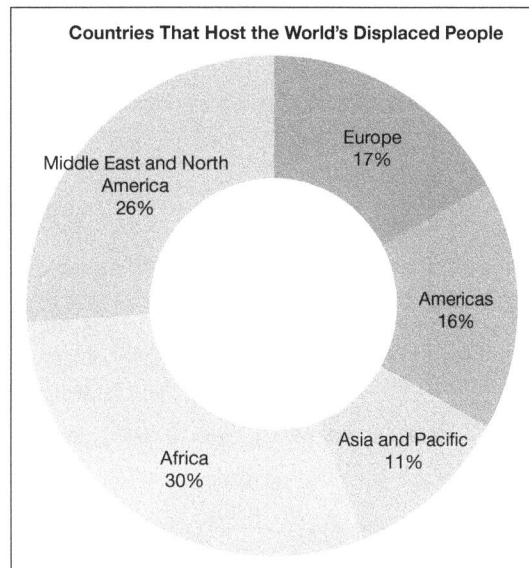

Source: Data adapted from UNHCR (2017).

Personal Security

The 1994 UNDP report identified seven threats to personal security:

- threats from the state (physical torture)
- threats from other states (war)
- threats from other groups of people (ethnic tension)
- threats from individuals or gangs to other individuals or gangs
- threats directed against women (rape, domestic violence)
- child abuse
- threats to self (suicide, drug abuse)

Such threats are also mounting in the world. Intra-state conflicts are major constituents of such types of threats. The Armed Conflict Database is an annual survey published by the London-based International Institute for Strategic Studies (IISS). According to the IISS, the past few years have seen a considerable increase in the number of war victims in the context of London. The number of war dead rose from 56,000 in 2008 to 180,000 in 2014, even though instead of 63, only 42 armed conflicts were counted. In 2013, for the first time since the end of the Second World War, more than 50 million people were refugees. In 2016, the number of fatalities in the world's conflicts was 157,000. In Syria, the situation became worse, with 50,000 deaths in 2016 alone, bringing the total since 2011 to around 290,000 (Figure 12.4) (IISS Armed Conflict Survey 2017).

FIGURE 12.4 Global Fatalities in Conflicts

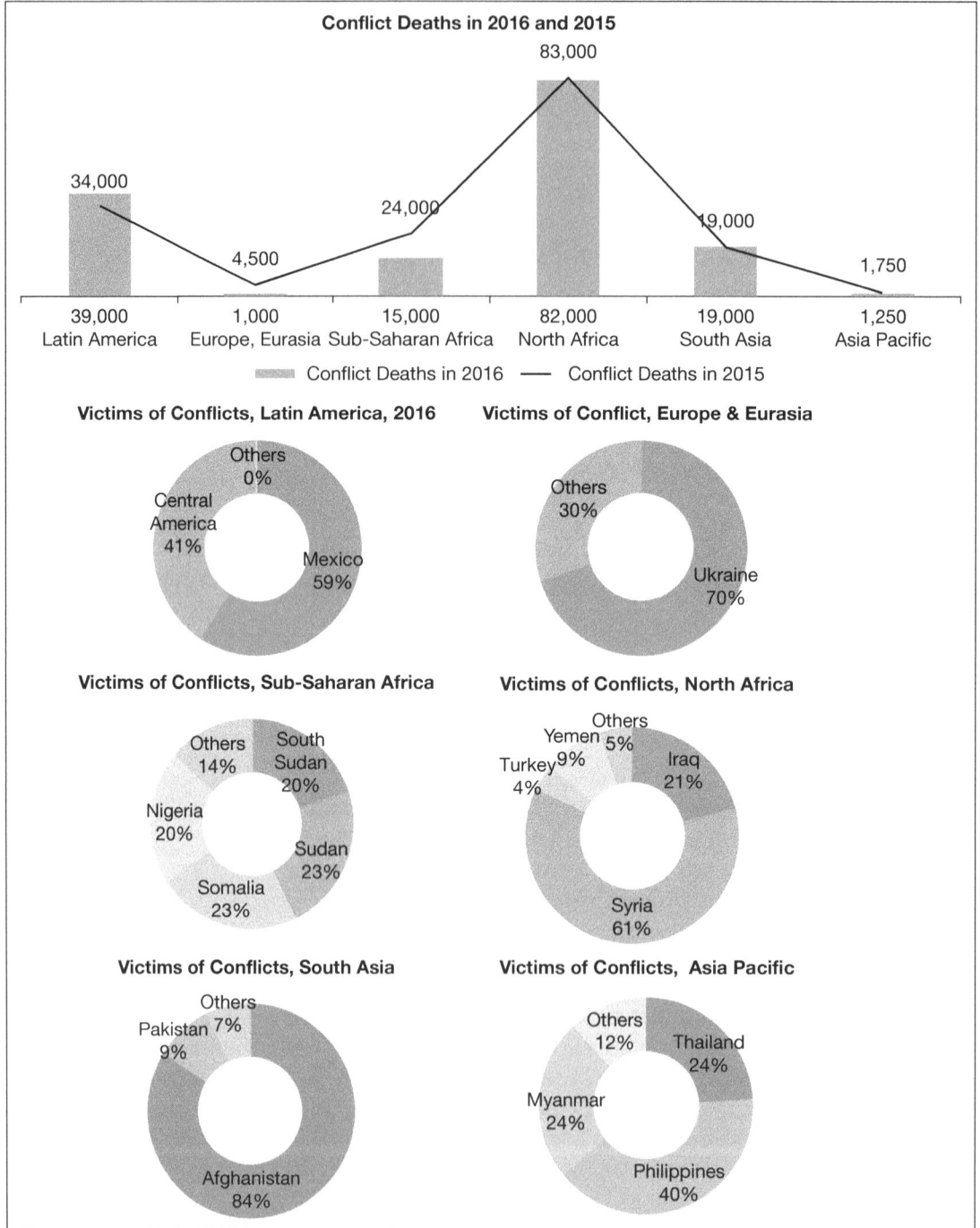

Conflict Deaths in 2016 and 2015

83,000

34,000

24,000

19,000

4,500

1,750

39,000	1,000	15,000	82,000	19,000	1,250
Latin America	Europe, Eurasia	Sub-Saharan Africa	North Africa	South Asia	Asia Pacific

▨ Conflict Deaths in 2016 — Conflict Deaths in 2015

Victims of Conflicts, Latin America, 2016
Others 0%
Central America 41%
Mexico 59%

Victims of Conflict, Europe & Eurasia
Others 30%
Ukraine 70%

Victims of Conflicts, Sub-Saharan Africa
Others 14%
South Sudan 20%
Nigeria 20%
Sudan 23%
Somalia 23%

Victims of Conflicts, North Africa
Others 5%
Yemen 9%
Turkey 4%
Iraq 21%
Syria 61%

Victims of Conflicts, South Asia
Others 7%
Pakistan 9%
Afghanistan 84%

Victims of Conflicts, Asia Pacific
Others 12%
Thailand 24%
Myanmar 24%
Philippines 40%

Source: Data adapted from IISS (2016 and 2017).

Ensuring women's security is also a major problem. Violence against women is another global pandemic which has become a major public health problem and cause for violations of women's human rights. As per WHO estimates, nearly 1 billion women will experience intimate partner violence or non-partner sexual violence in their lifetimes. Worldwide, almost 750 million women and girls alive today were married before their eighteenth birthday. Child marriage is more common in West and Central Africa, where over 4 in 10 girls were married before age 18 and about 1 in 7 were married or in a union before age 15. Child marriage often results in early pregnancy and social isolation, interrupts schooling, limits the girl's opportunities and increases her risk of experiencing domestic violence. Adult women account for 51% of all human trafficking victims detected globally. Women and girls together account for 71%, with girls representing nearly three out of every four child-trafficking victims (UN 2017c).

Terrorism with no particular nationality is a global phenomenon, taking a considerable human toll. It is also one of the most complex in a wide range of threats and types of conflicts, mixing the actions of states, extremists and other non-state actors (Cordesman 2017, 5). It is held that illiteracy and poverty are the main cause of rising terrorism in some areas. However, this viewpoint cannot be generalized.

Communal Security

The UNDP 1994 report stated that the community is a source of both cultural identity and protection as well as of oppressive practices. Major threats to communal security are the breakdown of the family, collapse of traditional languages and cultures, ethnic discrimination and strife, genocide and ethnic cleansing, insecurity of indigenous people, and so on. Among these types of threats, ethnic conflict is one of the major threats to international peace and security. Despite the decrease of ethnic conflicts around the world, there are still many cases of them extant. Ethnic conflicts not only lead to atrocities such as mass murder, they also contribute to the global refugee crisis as the number of refugees significantly increases with time. According to the UNHCR Global Trends 2015 report, 65.3 million people are displaced and have been forced to flee their homes as a result of conflict (UNHCR Global Trends 2015).

Political Security

One of the most important aspects of human security is honouring the basic rights of people. Threats to political security include state repression, human rights violations, state control over ideas and information and priority given to military spending over spending in the social sector. The state of human rights in the world is also worrisome. As mentioned above, many countries around the world are facing several challenges such as poverty, inequality, food crises, environmental degradation, ethnic conflicts, civil war, and so on. These threats are overlapping and threats in one category could cause a spillover effect on other categories. Thus, it is obvious that in such situations, the condition of human rights and political security would be undermined. The Amnesty International annual report documents the state of human rights in 159 countries and territories in the world. As per its report in 2015, at least 113 countries arbitrarily restricted freedom of expression and the press, 55% of countries conducted unfair trials, war crimes or other violations of the 'laws of war' were carried out in at least 19 countries, 30 or more countries illegally forced refugees to return to countries where they would be in danger and 122 or more countries tortured or otherwise ill-treated people (Amnesty International 2016).

FIGURE 12.5 World Military Expenditure

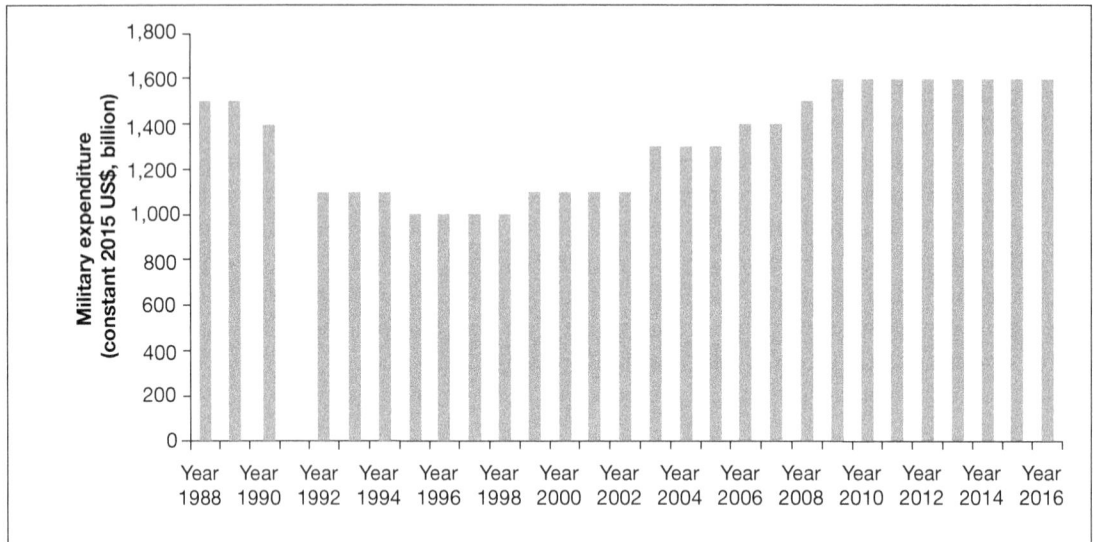

Source: Data adapted from Tian et al. (2017).

As far as military spending is concerned, it is also increasing worldwide. Total world military expenditure rose to $1,686 billion in 2016, an increase of 0.4% in real terms from 2015. World military spending in 2016 accounted for 2.2% of global GDP (Figure 12.5). In Asia and Oceania, military expenditure rose by 4.6% in 2016. According to the Stockholm International Peace Research Institute (SIPRI), just 10% of this total world military expenditure will be enough to remove poverty and hunger from the world by 2030, which is also one of the global goals of the UN (Tian et al. 2017).

It follows from above discussion that for the safety and viability of individuals, all these types of threats are no less inimical than any traditional security threats. Because of the ideological war between the two blocks, the cold war's political discourse had overlooked these aspects and did not include them in the security concerns. But after 1990, the changing world scenario and several catastrophic events have compelled the world to rethink the traditional definition of security which only considers the external military threats as security threats. Around 1 million people were slaughtered in Rawanda alone in 1994. The incident of 9/11 was very unique, in which a civilian plane was used as a deadly weapon. Still, there is a significant population in the world that lacks the basic means of life, such as food, safe drinking water and healthcare. This is also a unique form of insecurity. Arms conflicts, ethnic conflicts, terrorism, environmental disasters, and so on, are on the rise and jeopardizing people's lives in a significant manner. Against this backdrop, it is evident why the traditional notion of security, which focuses on protecting the borders of the states through military means, is no longer acceptable as the sole definition. Another unique characteristic of these threats is that they exist without borders and they will have to be resolved by multilateral efforts. Problems of pandemics, infectious diseases, global warming, terrorism, and so on cannot be dealt with within borders. They require the human-security approach which recognizes the individual's security as its basic referent object.

Role of International Organizations

Beside UN agencies, several international organizations are devoted towards the promotion of human security. The UN Trust Fund for Human Security (UNTFHS) was founded in 1999 to promote human security by protecting and empowering people and communities. It finances activities carried out by UN organizations to demonstrate the added value of the human-security approach and to extend its usage and awareness of it both within and outside the UN system. It has played a crucial role in meeting challenges to human security around the world. It has played a successful role in the reconstruction process of war-affected communities, eradication of extreme poverty, protection from environmental disasters, urban violence and trafficking of arms, persons and drugs (UNTFHS 2017). Another important association related to the promotion of the concept of human security as a feature of national and international policies is the HSN. It was also founded in 1999 by the collaboration of three countries, Austria, Norway and Canada. The main aim behind this collaboration was to achieve an international ban on anti-personnel mines. Currently, it is an association of 12 countries: Austria, Chile, Costa Rica, Greece, Ireland, Jordan, Mali, Norway, Panama, Slovenia, Switzerland and Thailand, with South Africa participating as an observer (Federal Ministry for Europe, Integration and Foreign Affairs 2018). The UN specialized agencies are also instrumental in the application of human security. The very concept of human security was initiated and coined by the UNDP. The WHO is playing a leading role in combating poverty and diseases. Apart from that, there are also some more crucial agencies which are focusing on their specialized work and providing aid and assistance, such as for refugees and displaced persons, the UNHCR, and for the rights of child and women, UNICEF and the United Nations Development Fund for Women (UNIFEM) (Baylis, Smith and Owens 2014, 357).

Apart from these UN agencies, there are two prominent regional organizations who are contributing significantly towards the promotion of human security while adopting it as one of the goal of their foreign policy—the European Union (EU) and the African Union (AU). Barcelona Report (2004) is the key document which established the EU's approach to human security. Later, in the Madrid Report, the human-security approach was further highlighted in the context of the EU's defence and security goals (Ağir, Gürsoy and Arman 2016). Its Global Security Strategy report (2016) states that the EU approved human security as the goal of EU's external actions (European Union Global Strategy 2016). The AU has also adopted several measures concerning human-security threats. For example, Article 3(f) of the Constitutive Act of the African Union focuses on promoting peace, security and stability in the African region. For this, in 2002, the Peace and Security Council Protocol (PSC Protocol) was adopted, which came into force in 2003. The Boko Haram crises in Nigeria, the situation in northern Mali and the sporadic attacks in Kenya by Al Shabaab as well as the prolonged armed conflict in the Central African Republic (CAR) and South Sudan raise serious questions on the AU's capacity to maintain regional peace and security. The PSC was designed to tackle such crises (Addaney 2015).

Another important agency for the promotion of human security is the International Criminal Court (ICC). Established in 2002, the ICC has been regarded as a success of the human-security agenda. It is headquartered in The Hague, Netherlands, and is charged with investigating and prosecuting crimes of genocide, crimes against humanity, aggression and war crimes (International Criminal Court 2016). Over the last decade, the court has made significant headway in putting international justice on the map. As of June 2015, the ICC had 123 states as its parties, had opened investigations in eight countries and had issued three verdicts.

In 2001, the Canadian government launched the ICISS in response to erstwhile UN Secretary-General Kofi Annan's question of when the international community should intervene for humanitarian purposes, which has come up with its final report called 'Responsibility to Protect (R2P), that can be considered as another important instrument of promoting human security' (UN n.d.). The R2P consists of three elementary features which are essential for human security—the responsibility to prevent, the responsibility to react and the responsibility to rebuild. This was the answer to critics of military interventions in sovereign states. At the UN World Summit in 2005, the member states included the R2P in the outcome document. Later, in 2006, the R2P was officially referred by the UN Security Council (SC) in its Resolution 1674, which came up for the protection of civilians in armed conflicts. The R2P featured prominently in a number of other resolutions adopted by the SC too, such as on Libya (2011), Côte d'Ivoire (2011), South Sudan (2011), Yemen (2011), Syria (2012) and the CAR (2013) (UN n.d.).

Another noteworthy legal convention related to human security is the 1997 Convention on the Prohibition of the Use, Stockpiling, Production and Transfer of Anti-Personnel Mines and on their Destruction. This is an international agreement which prohibits anti-personnel landmines. It is generally known as the Ottawa Convention (as it was launched by the Canadian foreign minister in Ottawa) or the Mine Ban Treaty. To date, there are 133 states who have signed this treaty and 162 countries are party to this treaty. The Convention came into force on 1 March 2009 (UN 1997).

There are a number of non-governmental organizations which are also involved in several activities concerning human security, such as Amnesty International, Anti-Slavery International, Cooperative for Assistance and Relief Everywhere (CARE), Human Rights Watch, the International Committee of the Red Cross (ICRC), Save the Children, and so on.

Concluding Observations

Despite the increasing awareness and concern about human development for internal security, the state-centric and militaristic aspect of security is the dominant agenda in the discourse of international politics. Despite international, regional and national initiatives towards human security, government policies are still giving priority to national or state security over human security. In many developing countries, issues over boundaries are still prioritized over issues of human development. Developed countries such as the US have taken several military actions after 9/11 and Russia's recent military moves show how the agenda of human security is undermined by the global powers. In view of the emerging challenges, no doubt state security cannot be ignored but some synergy needs to be maintained between national and human security. Even if a nation looks very strong and robust from the outside, with all nuclear weapons, if it lacks human development, the objective of security cannot be achieved in the true sense. Therefore the aspect of human security needs to be given serious attention to achieve long-term peace and security.

Summary

- After the end of the cold war, in the changing context of world politics, the traditional meaning of 'security' became outdated. In the increasingly interdependent world, a number of non-military challenges to states' vital interests have arisen.

- In this changing scenario in the form of human security, a new aspect of security has emerged which highlights some of the major limitations of this old notion of security, which mainly emphasizes securing the borders of the states rather than the security of individuals.

- The concept of 'human security' aims at bringing about a paradigm shift in the concept of security while transferring the focus of protection from the state to individuals. It calls for widening the scope of security from a completely military-centric conception to focusing on wide-ranging areas such as security from poverty, environmental degradation, infectious diseases, and so on.

- The United Nation Development Programme (UNDP) in its *Human Development Report* of 1994 for the first time proposed the notion of 'human security'. The late Pakistani economist Mahbub ul Haq was the central figure behind the idea of human security.

- The 1994 UNDP report focused on four characteristics of human security: (i) human security is a universal concern; (ii) the components of human security are interdependent; (iii) human security is easier to ensure through easy prevention than later intervention; and (iv) human security is people-centric.

- The 1994 UNDP report has identified seven dimensions of human security: economic security, food security, health security, environmental security, personal security, communal security and political security.

- After the UNDP, there were several contributions made by various governments, organizations, commissions, scholars, and so on for the development of the concept of human security.

- Among the governments, the roles of Canada and Japan are worth mentioning. In 1996, Canada, led by foreign minister Lloyd Axworthy, adopted the 'freedom from fear' approach as the basic principle of its foreign-policy tools. Canada criticized the UNDP's broad view of human security for focusing too much on threats associated with underdevelopment at the expense of 'human insecurity resulting from violent conflict'. Norway joined Canada in its approach and established a human-security partnership. According to the Canadian government's narrow view of human security, 'human security means freedom from pervasive threats to people's rights, safety or lives'.

- Japan advocates the broader view of human security. According to Japan, human security includes both freedom from fear and freedom from want. The two values are considered to be equal. It means comprehensively addressing all the threats which threaten the survival, daily lives and dignity of human beings and to strengthen the efforts to confront threats.

- So, there are two major positions regarding the concept of human security: First, the narrow view, that is, freedom from fear, and secondly the broad view, that is, freedom from want. The narrow school mostly confines the concept of security to the prevention of violent threats against the individual, which includes drug trafficking, landmines, ethnic conflict, state small-arms trade, and so on, whereas the broad view includes threats such as hunger, disease, repression, sudden disasters, and so on. All these threats are development-oriented threats and their resolution requires long-term planning and investment in development.

- The former UN Secretary-General Kofi Annan defined 'human security' in its broadest sense. According to him, it embraces far more than the absence of violent conflict. Further, given the growing environmental concerns worldwide, he added an additional dimension to the definition of human security, that is, 'freedom from hazard impact'.
- The concept comes under severe attack from various groups of academicians mostly on the grounds that it is too vague, that it can lead to the diminishing of the sovereignty of nation states, that it is basically a new form of the North–South divide agenda, and so on. However, all these criticisms have limited scope. For example, the broader views of the concept articulate the various types of threats in a clear manner and offer a progressive and dynamic vision. Secondly, the proponents of human security never discredited the role of the state as a security provider and they find that both state security and human security are mutually compatible to each other. And finally, the North–South debate also seems irrelevant as human security is about the differences among people rather than differences among states.
- Despite there being various differences over the notion of human security among several proponents, there are certain underlying features of the concept which everyone is agreed upon. For example, now security cannot be seen as the prerogative of the state.
- While keeping in the mind all the disagreements regarding the conception of human security on the grounds of the nature of threats, values and priorities, methods to prevent, and so on, it is difficult to define human security in a concrete manner. But to put in simple words, we can define human security as a concept or policy which is people-centric rather than state-centric and which focuses on the safety and protection of individuals and communities rather than borders of state. It recognizes the interconnectedness between human development, and human rights and security, and transcends the meaning of security as mere survival to imply a life worth living, hence including the well-being and dignity of human beings. It is comprehensive and multisectoral in its scope, which requires freedom from fear, freedom from want, freedom from hazard impacts and the freedom to live in dignity. It stresses the use of the multidimensional resolutions to conflicts, based on an interdisciplinary approach.
- The seven important dimensions of human security suggest that they are not less dangerous than any traditional means of insecurities. Several examples can be cited which will show that the non-traditional means of security threats are proven more lethal and catastrophic than many conventional wars. For example, the Rawandan crisis, the terrorist attack of 9/11 and environmental disasters such as the tsunamis of 2004 and 2011. The problem of poverty all over the world is a unique form of insecurity. Armed conflicts, ethnic conflicts, terrorist conflicts, environmental disasters, and so on, are on the rise and jeopardizing people's lives in a significant manner. Against this backdrop, it is evident why the traditional notion of security, which focuses on protecting the borders of the states through military means, is no longer acceptable as sole definition. Another uniqueness of these threats is that they are without borders and they will be resolved by multilateral efforts.
- Several international organizations are involved in the promotion of the concept worldwide. Among these, the UNTFHS, the HSN, the UNDP, the WHO, the UNHCR, UNIFEM, the ICC, the Anti-Personnel Mine Ban Convention, Amnesty International, Human Rights Watch, the ICRC, and others are the few important organizations which are making substantial efforts towards promoting human security.

Suggested Questions

1. What do you understand by the concept of 'human security'? How is it different from the traditional notion of security?
2. Define human security and discuss its main characteristics.
3. Describe the various perspectives on human security.
4. Give a brief account of the evolution of the concept of human security.
5. Examine the various dimensions of human security.
6. Explain the role of international organizations in promoting human security in the world.

References

Addaney, Michael. 2015. 'The Response of the African Union to Critical Human Security Threats in Africa'. *Africa Law,* 7 August 2015. Accessed 22 August 2017. https://africlaw.com/2015/08/07/the-response-of-the-africa-union-to-critical-human-security-threats-in-africa.

Alkire, Sabina. 2003. 'A Conceptual Framework for Human Security'. Working Paper 2, Centre for Research on Inequality, Human Security and Ethnicity (CRISE), University of Oxford. Accessed 22 September 2017. https://ora.ox.ac.uk/objects/uuid:d2907237-2a9f-4ce5-a403-a6254020052d.

Amnesty International. 2016. *Amnesty International Report 2015/16: The State of the World's Human Rights.* London: Amnesty International. Accessed 22 September 2017. https://www.amnesty.org/download/Documents/POL1025522016ENGLISH.PDF.

Annan, Kofi A. 2005. 'In Larger Freedom: Towards Development, Security and Human Rights For All', Addendum to the Report of the Secretary-General, 26 May 2005. Accessed 20 August 2017. https://www.un.org/ruleo-flaw/files/A.59.2005.Add.3[1].pdf.

Bajpai, Kanti. 2000. 'Human Security: Concept and Measurement'. Kroc Institute Occasional Paper 19, Accessed 10 July 2017. http://citeseerx.ist.psu.edu/viewdoc/download;jsessionid=4D8A505A13D4290E44528028D793B97F?doi=10.1.1.462.7286&rep=rep1&type=pdf.

Behera, Navnita Chadha. 2004. 'A South Asian Debate on Peace and Security: An Alternative Formulation in the Post-Cold War Era'. Accessed 22 September 2017. http://www.afes-press.de/pdf/Hague/Chadha_Behera_South_Asian_debate.pdf.

Ağir, Bülent Sarper, Bariş Gürsoy and Murat Necip Arman. 2016. 'European Perspective of Human Security and the Western Balkans', Revista de Ştiinţe Politice 50: 41–54. Accessed 10 July 2017, http://cis01.central.ucv.ro/revistadestiintepolitice/files/numarul50_2016/4.pdf.

Baylis, John, Steve Smith and Patricia Owens. 2014. *The Globalization of World Politics: An Introduction to International Relations.* New York: Oxford University Press.

Brauch, H. G. 2005. 'Environment and human security: towards freedom from hazard impacts'. *InterSecTions* 2: 60.

Commission on Human Security. 2003. *Human Security Now: Protecting and Empowering People.* New York: Commission on Human Security.

Cordesman, Anthony. 2017. *Global Trends in Terrorism: 1970–2016.* Working draft, Centre for Strategic and International Studies (CSIS), 28 August 2017. Accessed 22 September 2017. https://csis-prod.s3.amazonaws.com/s3fs-public/publication/170828_global_terrorism_update_0.pdf?cGXk7lPZWBjWdjmuwfqQlOdr.MwyX5by.

Elliott, Larry. 2016. 'Richest 62 People as Wealthy as Half of World's Population, says Oxfam'. *Guardian,* 18 January 2016. Accessed 23 September 2017. https://www.theguardian.com/business/2016/jan/18/richest-62-billionaires-wealthy-half-world-population-combined.

European Union Global Strategy. 2016. 'Shared Vision, Common Action: A Stronger Europe: A Global Strategy for the European Union's Foreign and Security Policy'. Accessed 25 April 2018. https://europa.eu/globalstrategy/sites/globalstrategy/files/eugs_review_web.pdf.

FAO, IFAD, UNICEF, WFP and WHO. 2017. *The State of Food Security and Nutrition in the World 2017. Building Resilience for Peace and Food Security*. Rome: FAO. Accessed 25April 2018. http://www.fao.org/3/a-I7695e.pdf.

Federal Ministry for Europe, Integration and Foreign Affairs. 2018. *The Human Security Network*. Accessed 6 July 2017. https://www.bmeia.gv.at/en/european-foreign-policy/human-rights/the-human-security-network.

Fukuda-Parr, Sakiko, and Carol Messineo. 2011. 'Human Security'. International Affairs Working Paper, April 2011. Accessed 23 August 2017. https://www.files.ethz.ch/isn/129658/Fukuda-Parr_and_Messineo_2011-04.pdf.

The Global Development Research Center (GDRC). 'Definitions', Sustainable Development. Accessed 25 June 2017. https://www.gdrc.org/sustdev/husec/Definitions.pdf.

Hough, Peter. 2004.*Understanding Global Security*. London: Routledge.

Howard, Emma. 2015. 'Humans Have Already Used Up 2015's Supply of Earth's Resources—Analysis'. Accessed 23 September 2017. https://www.theguardian.com/environment/2015/aug/12/humans-have-already-used-up-2015s-supply-of-earths-resources-analysis.

India Today. 2015. 'Extreme Poverty to Fall Below 10 Percent for the First Time: Facts on Global Poverty', *India Today*, 5 October 2015. Accessed 25 September 2017. http://indiatoday.intoday.in/education/story/global-poverty/1/490436.html.

International Criminal Court. 2016. 'Understanding the International Criminal Court'. Accessed 25 September 2017. https://www.icc-cpi.int/iccdocs/PIDS/publications/UICCEng.pdf.

International Institute for Strategic Studies (IISS). 2016. 'Six Conflicts Account for 80% of Global Conflict Fatalities'. Accessed 25 April 2018. https://www.iiss.org/-/media//documents/press%20releases/acs2016%20press%20release.pdf.

———. 2017. 'Armed Conflict Survey 2017'. Accessed 25 April 2018. https://www.iiss.org/-/media//documents/publications/acs/acs%202017/acs-2017-global-conflict-numbers.pdf?la=en.

Liotta, P. H., and Taylor Owen. 2006. 'Why Human Security?'. *The Whitehead Journal of Diplomacy and International Relations* 7: 37–54. Accessed 25 June 2017. http://www.taylorowen.com/Articles/Owen%20and%20Liotta%20-%20Why%20Human%20Security.pdf.

Martin, Mary, and Taylor Owen, eds. 2013. *Routledge Handbook of Human Security*. London: Routledge.

McIntosh, Malcolm, and Alan Hunter, eds. 2010. *New Perspectives on Human Security*. New York: Greenleaf Publishing.

Menon, Sudha Venu. 2007. 'Human Security: Concept and Practice'. MPRA Paper 2478, University Library, Ludwig Maximilian University of Munich. Accessed 19 August 2017. https://mpra.ub.uni-muenchen.de/2478/1/MPRA_paper_2478.pdf.

Ministry of Foreign Affairs of Japan. 2013. 'Developing Countries and ODA in a Global Economy'. In 'Japan's Official Development Assistance White Paper 2013'. Chapter 1, Section 1. Accessed 19 August 2017. http://www.mofa.go.jp/policy/oda/white/2013/html/honbun/b1/s1_1.html.

Ogoura, Kazuo. 2005. 'Globalisation, Human Security and the UN'. *Perceptions: Journal of International Affairs* 10 (2): 141–150.

Paris, Roland. 2001. 'Human Security: Paradigm Shift or Hot Air?' *International Security* 26 (2): 87–102.

Raza, Mansoor, and Hunza Siddiqui. 2014. *Human Security Report: Year 2014*. Karachi: NOW Communities. Accessed 23 August 2017. http://nowcommunities.org/upload/publication/Human%20Security%20Report%20%E2%80%93%202014_08012017083214.pdf.

Roznai, Yaniv. 2014. 'The Insecurity of Human Security'. *Wisconsin International Law Journal* 32 (1): 95–140.

Schaüfer, Philip Jan. 2013. *Human and Water Security in Israel and Jordan*. New York: Springer.

Singh, Akshay Kumar. 2014. 'Human Security in Pakistan: Challenges and Opportunities'. PhD thesis, Jawaharlal Nehru University. Accessed 23 August 2017. http://shodhganga.inflibnet.ac.in:8080/jspui/handle/10603/19438.

Stone, Marianne. 2009. 'Security According to Buzan: A Comprehensive Security Analysis'. Security Discussion Papers Series 1, GEEST. Accessed 23 August 2017. http://www.geest.msh-paris.fr/IMG/pdf/Security_for_Buzan.mp3.pdf.

Sundaram, J. K., and Chowdhury, A. 2017. 'World Bank Report on Inequality Contains Surprisingly Little on What to Do About It'. Accessed 24 April 2018. https://thewire.in/external-affairs/world-bank-inequality-report.

Tadjbakhsh, Shahrbanou. 2005. 'Human Security: Concepts and Implications—with an Application to Post-intervention Challenges in Afghanistan'. *Les Études du CERI* 117–118. Montreal: Centre for International Studies and Research (CERI). Accessed 23 August 2017. http://www.sciencespo.fr/ceri/sites/sciencespo.fr.ceri/files/etude117_118.pdf.

Tadjbakhsh, Shahrbanou. 2009. '"Human Security": Looking Back before Looking Forward'. Proceedings of the International Conference on Human Security in West Asia (ICHSWA), Birjand University, Iran. Accessed 23 August 2017. http://www.birjand.ac.ir/ichswa/downloads/Dr%20Tajbakhsh's%20Paper%20in%20ICHSWA.pdf.

Tadjbakhsh, Shahrbanou, and Anuradha M. Chenoy. 2009. *Human Security: Concepts and Implications*. New York: Routledge.

Tian, Nan, Aude Fleurant, Pieter D. Wezeman and Siemon T. Wezeman. 2017. 'Trends in World Military Expenditure, 2016'. SIPRI factsheet. Solna: SIPRI. Accessed 20 July 2017. https://www.sipri.org/sites/default/files/Trends-world-military-expenditure-2016.pdf.

United Nations (UN). n.d. 'Background Information on the Responsibility to Protect'. Outreach Programme on the Rwanda Genocide and the United Nations. Accessed 20 August 2017. http://www.un.org/en/preventgenocide/rwanda/about/bgresponsibility.shtml.

———. 1997. 'Convention on the Prohibition of the Use, Stockpiling, Production and Transfer of Anti-Personnel Mines and on their Destruction'. In 'Chapter XXVI: Disarmament', United Nations Treaty Collection. Accessed 20 October 2017. https://treaties.un.org/Pages/ViewDetails.aspx?src=IND&mtdsg_no=XXVI-5&chapter=26&clang=_en.

———. 2017a. 'Health'. Accessed 20 October 2017. http://www.un.org/en/sections/issues-depth/health/index.html.

———. 2017b. *World Population Prospects: The 2017 Revision*. Accessed 30 September 2017, https://www.un.org/development/desa/publications/world-population-prospects-the-2017-revision.html.

———. 2017c. 'Facts and figures: Ending Violence against Women'. Last updated August 2017. Accessed 30 September 2017. http://www.unwomen.org/en/what-we-do/ending-violence-against-women/facts-and-figures.

United Nations Development Programme (UNDP). 1994. *Human Development Report 1994*. New York & Oxford: Oxford University Press.

United Nations Environment Programme (UNEP). 2012. *Renewable Resources and Conflict: Toolkit and Guidance for Preventing and Managing Land and Natural Resources Conflict*. Accessed 23 September 2017. http://www.un.org/en/events/environmentconflictday/pdf/GN_Renewable_Consultation.pdf.

United Nations General Assembly (UN GA). 2005. 'Resolution Adopted by the General Assembly: 60/1. 2005 World Summit Outcome', 24 October 2005. Accessed 20 August 2017. http://www.un.org/womenwatch/ods/A-RES-60-1-E.pdf.

———. 2013. 'Follow-up to General Assembly Resolution 66/290 on Human Security'. Accessed 20 August 2017. http://www.un.org/en/ga/search/view_doc.asp?symbol=%20A/RES/66/290.

UNHCR Global Trends. 2015. 'United Nations High Commissioner for Refugees'. Accessed 25 April 2018. http://www.unhcr.org/576408cd7.pdf.

United Nations High Commissioner for Refugees (UNHCR). 2017. 'Figures at a Glance'. Accessed 30 September 2017. http://www.unhcr.org/figures-at-a-glance.html.

United Nations. 2012. 'Human Security: Looking Back Before Looking Forward', Proceedings of the International Conference on Human Security in West Asia, Birjand University, Iran, 2009. Accessed 25 2018. April http://www.birjand.ac.ir/ichswa/downloads/Dr%20Tajbakhsh%27s%20Paper%20in%20ICHSWA.pdf.

United Nations Trust Fund for Human Security (UNTFHS). 2017. 'Trust Fund Achievements Around the World'. Accessed 20 August 2017. http://www.un.org/humansecurity/trust-fund.

Voronkova, Anastasia, ed. 'Key Themes'. *The IISS Armed Conflict Survey 2017*. Accessed 23 October 2017. https://www.iiss.org/-/media//documents/publications/acs/acs%202017/acs-2017-key-themes.pdf?la=en.

World Bank. 2018. 'Overview'. Understanding Poverty, Last updated 11 April 2018. Accessed 20 October 2017. http://www.worldbank.org/en/topic/poverty/overview.

World Food Programme (WFP). 2009. 'WFP Says Hunger Kills More than AIDS, Malaria, Tuberculosis Combined'. Accessed 20 August 2017. https://www.wfp.org/content/wfp-says-hunger-kills-more-aids-malaria-tuberculosis-combined.

World Health Organization (WHO). 2016. 'An Estimated 12.6 Million Deaths Each Year Are Attributable to Unhealthy Environments'. Accessed 25 April 2018. http://www.who.int/en/news-room/detail/15-03-2016-an-estimated-12-6-million-deaths-each-year-are-attributable-to-unhealthy-environments.

———. 2017. 'Climate Change'. The Health and Environment Linkages Initiative (HELI). Accessed 20 October 2017. http://www.who.int/heli/risks/climate/climatechange/en.

Yang, Hao. n.d. 'Security Governance: An Analysis of ASEAN's Strategies to Regional Security Dynamics'. Accessed 25 April 2018. http://paperroom.ipsa.org/papers/paper_5214.pdf.

Further Reading

Acharya, Amitav, Subrat K. Singhdeo and M. Rajaretnam. 2011. *Human Security: From Concept to Practice—Case Studies from Northeast India*. Singapore: World Scientific.

Bajpai, Kanti. 2003. 'The Idea of Human Security'. *International Studies* 40 (3): 195–228.

Buzan, Barry. 2007. *People, State and Fear: An Agenda for International Security Studies in the Post-Cold War Era*. London: Harvester Wheatsheaf.

Chari, P. R., and Sonika Gupta, eds. 2003. *Human Security in South Asia: Gender, Energy, Migration and Globalisation*. New Delhi: Social Science Press.

Chandler, David, and Nik Hynek, eds. 2011. *Critical Perspectives on Human Security: Rethinking Emancipation and Power in International Relations*. London: Routledge.

Human Security Research Center. 'UN Approach to Human Security'. Human Security Course, CLAIM and the EU. Accessed 23 August 2017. http://humansecuritycourse.info/module-1-the-concept-of-human-security/un-approach.

Human Security Unit. 2009. 'Human Security Theory and Practice: An Overview of the Human Security Concept and the United Nations Trust Fund for Human Security'. Human Security Unit, United Nations. Accessed 20 April 2018. http://www.unocha.org/sites/dms/HSU/Publications%20and%20Products/Human%20Security%20Tools/Human%20Security%20in%20Theory%20and%20Practice%20English.pdf.

Global Shifts: Power and Governance

Parmeet Singh

LEARNING OBJECTIVES

- To understand the idea of global shifts
- To understand the concepts of power and global governance in the context of global shifts
- To obtain a brief historical overview of global shifts
- To evaluate the role of non-state actors and organizations in global shifts
- To examine the changing nature of power, governance and states at the global level

Evolution of today's global politics cannot be understood without going into the dynamics of power and its shifts. In order to do this, we must comprehend the different considerations of power in global politics and the varied natures of power shifts. According to Joseph Nye, in global politics, power shifts are basically of two types: The first is 'power transition, which is change of power amongst states. And there the simple version of the message is it's moving from West to East' and the second is what he calls 'power diffusion' which, put concisely, means the relocation or movement of power from all states to non-state actors such as NGOs, international organizations and corporates (Nye 2010). Virtual space can also be the next in this list.

Importance of Power

Power in itself is not a complete term, as is the case in global politics. When we use the term 'power' in a global context, we are simultaneously concerned not only with political power but also economic, social, cultural and technological power. In fact, all these kinds of power constitute a cause for constructing a complex web of diplomatic and political relations and dynamics in global politics.

Right from the sixteenth century, when the world was not very well connected politically, power dynamics existed in the form of religious and political forces and emerging industries and markets, which, in the following centuries, paved the way for the expansion of political powers and sowed the seeds for the era of colonization. In this era, power started to shift from cultural and religious bodies to political institutions and trade units.

Some of the most important historical events in the history of Europe were the Peace of Westphalia (1648) and the Glorious Revolution (1688) in England, followed by power reallocations from institutionalized religion to political institutions and later to the people with the development of liberalism and individualism in the European political theory of that time. More emphasis began to be laid on the participation of people in the decision-making processes. However, noticeably, all this was happening in North American and European part of the world. The rest of the world, including Asia, Africa and Latin America, was increasingly at the receiving end of European colonizers. These incidents turned the world into the periphery of Europe. Immanuel Wallerstein, in the 1970s, developed the renowned idea of world-systems analysis in which he traces the history of the evolution of capitalism from the sixteenth century. He believes that the West gained control over rest of the world through rapid expansion of industrialization and market economy, which in turn resulted in unequal development (Wallerstein 2004, 23–24). Hence, until first half of the twentieth century, the period was dominated by Europe not only in economic terms, but politically as well.

Simultaneously, in the eighteenth century, the French Revolution (1789–1799) and the American War of Independence (1775–1783) triggered the hidden democratic energies of the citizens of other parts of the world. The adversities of colonization and the emergence of critical perspectives together contributed to the development of new kinds of power structures in Asian and Latin American countries, where in the twentieth century, the political picture of the world started to change drastically. In this era, power was not only symbolized by political domination but it was also represented by the influence of revolutions, ideologies and emerging anticipated political threats to the prevailing dominant political powers.

The First and Second World Wars were the two major upheavals in the shifts of power in global politics. After the end of the Second World War, the United States of America (USA) emerged as the most powerful country in the world due to the declining power of the United Kingdom (UK). The cold war conflict between the USA and the Union of Soviet Socialist Republics (USSR) gave rise to bipolar politics in the international context. It also contributed to ideological, political and military conflicts between the two superpowers throughout the cold-war era. The USA and USSR were not only the centres of political power, but they had also become the two opposite ideological poles, which in turn contributed to the intensification of the conflict. The end of the cold war due to the voluntary withdrawal of the USSR from cold-war politics again caused a power shift in favour of the USA.

Following the cold-war era, the occurrence of USA hegemony not only in political but in economic, military as well as cultural terms again turned the global system into a unipolar world. However, the USA hegemony was not free from challenges, due to the emergence of various centres of power. In the absence of the USSR as a threat, European countries' and Japan's dependence on the USA for their security lost its significance. Most of the earlier USA allies could act much more independently in the field of international politics due to the elimination of the Soviet threat to their security. Moreover, the beginning of the twenty-first century brought world politics to a new juncture of a multipolar world where the hegemony of the USA declined in proportion to the increasing impact of new economic powers such as China, the European Union (EU), Japan and India.

International organizations such as the United Nations (UN) and its agencies have also been significant in the global shifts of power and governance. However, the world has been going through multiple economic and political challenges for almost two decades, whether it is an economic depression, the refugee question, environmental issues or political adjustments such as Brexit, which are all continuously feeding the economic and political uncertainty. The trickle-down impact of technology and social media is also playing an important role in the new shifts in global governance by constructing new digital podiums for individuals, governments, economic centres (digital currencies such as bitcoin, for instance), groups and regional organizations. In the words of J. N. Rosenau:

> Many liberal theorists see the declining importance of states as the major actor in international politics as central to their predictions of system change, and for the most part they attribute their reduced importance to growing international transactions. (Rosenau and Czempiel 2000, 76)

All these dimensions of shifts in power and governance will be analysed later in the chapter, with categorization of economic, social and political aspects.

In the case of governance, it is a contested argument whether it should be seen as global governance or not. Global interconnectedness and international political ties cannot directly be termed as governance, because the term 'governance' refers to a much broader perspective of administrative and institutional structure. On the other hand, in opposition to this argument, it is said that the firm presence of international political centres such as the UN, economic centres such as the World Bank and International Monetary Fund (IMF) and other influential non-state and regional organizations is clearly indicating an implicit system of global governance, which in many instances supersedes the national rulings or formally uses the national governments as a rubber stamp for their political, economic and administrative goals. It may not look like a formal governmental structure; but in its functioning, as far as powers and influence are concerned, global governance is in existence with different sets of institutional structures and operations as compared to the national governments.

The global organizations, however, are not replicating national governance at the global level. Their several inevitable limitations—such as territorial, legal and moral factors—are preventing them from doing so. It is also notable that an emerging system of decision-making at the global level sometimes dominates the decisions of national governments, particularly in the fields of economic and environmental issues.

Sometimes, it becomes a necessity for nations to work as per the decisions of international organizations, as they cannot deal with certain threats which are global in nature and cannot be tackled by these nations individually. The issue of terrorism and arms proliferation to non-state actors cannot be dealt with by nations individually. Therefore, these nations deliberately come into the global system of decision-making and take part in this global connectedness. Though it is not a full-fledged system of global governance, it is a process of globalization of governance on multiple levels. It is extremely clear that not every aspect of global governance is state-centric now days, and thus, to understand the transitions and shifts in a proper manner, one has to go beyond the ideas of states and governments.

Economic Aspects

First, the role of multinational corporations (MNCs) and transnational corporations (TNCs) must be discussed under the purview of new liberal policies. According to the new liberal politics, the financial activities of these firms are free from state control. The trading organizations work in multiple countries, having their head offices in one corner of the world. In the case of TNCs, they may have multiple offices in multiple countries. Both significantly affect not only the financial but also the political decision-making processes of the countries. Some conspiracy theories also suggest that big MNCs and corporate houses sometimes become so influential in the decision-making of democratic governments that the policies, which seem to be in the interest of their citizens, are actually developed under a corporate burden.

Not only the UN but also economic organizations such as the World Bank, IMF and the World Trade Organization (WTO) have made the world virtually borderless and these organizations have played a significant role in the power shifts at the global level. These cross-border economic activities not only made the entire world interdependent but also changed the positions of the core and peripheries in the sense that more than political, it is economic development which is playing a prominent role in the emergence of new powers at a global level, particularly since the advent of new liberal policies.

Cultural Impacts

After the 1990s, several theses have been put forth on the impacts of the dissolution of the USSR and the end of the cold-war era. However, one of the most influential works on the topic was Samuel P. Huntington's 'Clash of Civilizations'. In the twenty-first century, power cannot be defined only in political and economic terms but must recognize cultural aspects also. The cultural aspect is gaining more prominence in the debate of global power. After 9/11, this idea gained a momentum which had also been witnessed and is being witnessed on various other occasions at the national and international levels. The Afghanistan war, the Iraq invasion of 2003, the refugee question in Europe, the Rohingyas issue in Myanmar and ongoing problems in the Middle East are some of the examples related to ethno-religious and cultural aspects of global politics.

Virtual Space

The revolution in information technology and the increasing role of social media and the Internet in the twenty-first century are defining the new parameters of governance, liberty and expression. Though they have both negative and positive impact, they certainly provide a parallel sort of space where people, regardless of their language, identity and nationality, share and practise their thoughts and rights. This has also democratized the process of associating, expressing thoughts and communicating largely. They are also providing an easy space to the voices which were previously unheard or were completely dependent on their respective governments to be heard. Campaigns such as #notinmyname and #metoo are two of the recent examples showing how a person sitting at a table can initiate a powerful online movement, which can leave a remarkable influence on the functioning and decisions of a political class and a society.

In the emerging economies, access to devices using information technology is limited to a very small section of society. They are also perceived as a tool to create propaganda. Virtual spaces are facing challenges of propaganda and trolling, which are, presumably, being used by politicians and other powerful sections of society. Another challenge to this highly accessible and flexible medium of the Internet is that it is owned by a few of the most powerful MNCs, mostly centred in the Western world. Cyberlaws are also not well updated to accommodate the risks and challenges of these virtual spaces (Singh 2015, 155). The Internet has also become a space for non-state power-holders and authoritarian groups such as terrorist organizations and propaganda builders—not only for their communications but for monetary benefits as well, which otherwise were a great challenge for them. However, its effect is severe and is no less than that of a powerful political organization. It is debatable whether, given the true meaning of governance, it is justified to see virtual spaces as being equivalent to some kind of governance. However, contextually, the very idea of governance is also in question and needs to be expanded in order to accommodate the role of these emerging, powerful and easily accessible global tools, which is making the world a place of people and limiting the role of governments—not completely but in many instances in a serious manner.

Idea of Global Governance

In order to understand the meaning of global governance, it is pertinent to discuss whether we are seeking to define or discover a government at the international level while talking about global governance. Is there any difference between government and governance? Why not 'government' or why 'governance' at the global level? Answers to these questions may not be absolute but will give a clearer understanding of how the global system works, what we mean by 'global governance' and how it is different from national governments.

Governance, according to the *Oxford Dictionary of Politics*, 'is the process of collective decision-making and policy implementation, used distinctly from government to reflect broader concerns with norms and process relating to the delivery of public goods' (McLean and McMillan 2009, 226). On the other hand, the term 'government' is much concerned with the institutional part of governance, which includes structures, rules and administration. 'Executive' is the term used interchangeably sometimes with government (McLean and McMillan 2009). As Thomas Weiss states, 'Many academics and international practitioners employ 'governance' to connote a complex set of structures and processes, both public and private, while more popular writers tend to use it synonymously with government' (cited in Dingwerth and Pattberg 2006, 188). Occasionally, the nuances of these terms get difficult to deal with. People may differ in using the terminology while addressing the same set of problems and issues.

In world politics, the question of governance and government makes more sense because it produces a fundamental conundrum of the possibility of governance without a government (Rosenau and Czempiel 2000, 3). However, in the attempt to search for a meaning for governance, it is a well-accepted set of principles, rules, duties based on which the system functions, both formally and informally. But on the other hand, governments can be in the opposition to this general acceptance and may act as an immoral ruling establishment as well (Rosenau and Czempiel 2000, 4). In other words, 'governance' represents the anticipated and normative role of the government. Secondly, unlike governments, it may also include informal and non-governmental structures which are not under the direct authority of a legal system. In this sense, the absence of a government does not threaten the existence of governance. This point is crucial in making sense of governance at the global level.

In this perspective, global governance encompasses the processes, multilateral interactions, negotiations and efforts among governments, global agencies and organizations to address the common good and collective issues of the global community but without ceding the national interests. Sometimes, governments act as a global civil society which is more democratic and deliberative in nature.

To be effective, [governance] must be inclusive, dynamic, and able to span national and sectoral boundaries and interests. It should operate through soft rather than hard power. It should be more democratic than authoritarian, more openly political than bureaucratic, and more integrated than specialized. (Dingwerth and Pattberg 2006, 188)

However, global politics is a field where the major actors are the states; global governance has its own limitations, both conceptual and institutional, in shaping global politics. In this context, it is important to discuss power and its dimensions, its role in global shifts and how the nature of power is changing with the changing role of the nation states.

Power and Its Role in Global Shifts

Before discussing the shifts of power at the global level, it is important to first understand the types of power and their different prevailing elements which are influencing global politics and are responsible for global shifts. Power in the fundamental sense means the capability of influencing or controlling the behaviour of others (nations). In international politics, it becomes the ability to influence other international actors (states) but the legitimate exercise of power is confined to the degree where the sovereignty of other states is not disturbed or compromised. However, the main confirmation of the exercise of power is to make the other do something which they otherwise would not have done—in other words, turning other's actions into your interests even without the other's complete will to do so—though this does not mean the involvement of coercion or violence, which may generally be understood by 'exercise of power'. At the international level, this is achieved through several means which are legitimate and non-coercive in nature. These powers are generally exercised with consent and mutual bargaining. Then why do we call it the 'exercise of power' if both the parties are consenting through bargaining? Even in this seemingly sophisticated power game, not every party is at the receiving end. Consent does not mean being in a position of benefit; rather, sometimes consent is merely the result of compromise. It can be better understood in the world-system theory, precisely at the global level: Generally power exists without forceful suppression and without combating the sovereignty of other states. This is the formal or procedural version of power in global politics.

In this sense, power is a contested term with different sets of connotations. It can be seen in terms of capability which states or other actors possess. It can be defined as a relationship or can be observed as a 'property of a structure' (Heywood 2017, 218). There are different factors or elements of powers that may sometimes collectively take the shape of the above-mentioned properties of power. Although there are conceptual problems in explaining the absolute impact of these powers, their outcomes generally decide the actual strength, which may vary drastically from one instance to another due to various other factors which may or may not be directly related to these power relations. For example, in the recent Doklam standoff between India and China, power as capability can be seen as an advantage for India's foreign policy because in the case of the elements of power (such as the military and geographical advantage), at least statistically, China was on the leading side. The same can be quoted for the US–Vietnam conflict where, regardless of being in a superior position, the US could not turn its power into capability in that particular case. Similar is the case of the Soviet experience in Afghanistan in the 1980s.

The second type of power can be seen in the form of structures, a framework coherently developed by Susan Strange. She basically argued in opposition to the dominant realist viewpoint of power and presented an alternative in the field of international political economy where the states as actors are not

BOX 13.1: Doklam Standoff

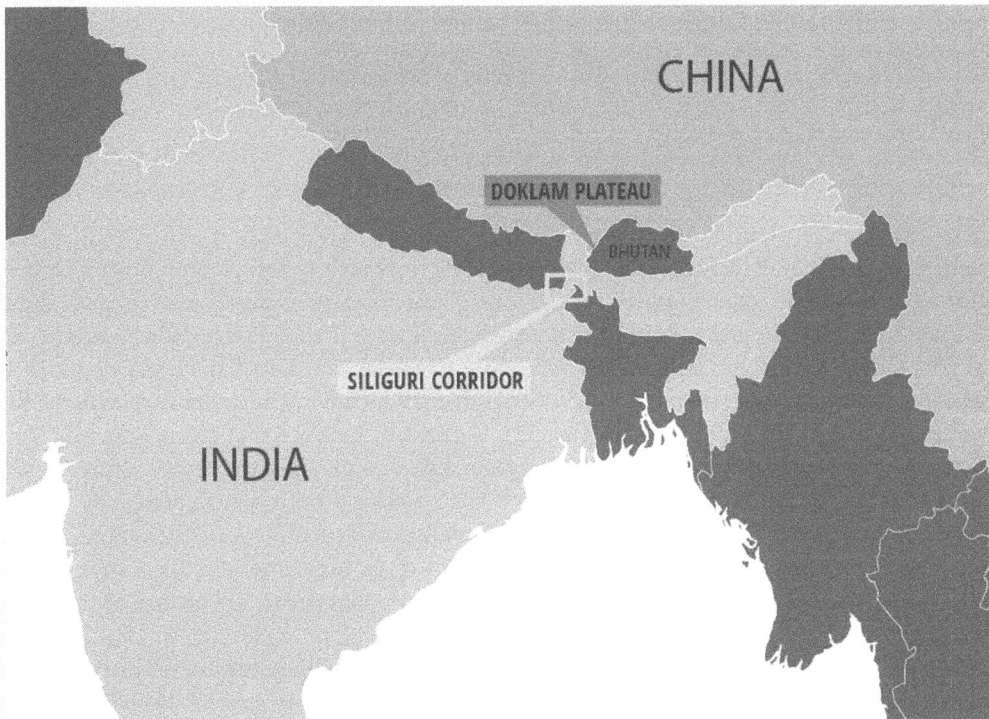

Image source: Divakaruni (2017).

The 2017 Indo–China border standoff or Doklam standoff refers to the military border standoff between the Indian armed forces and the People's Liberation Army of China over the construction of a road by the Chinese government in Doklam. On 16 June 2017, Chinese troops with construction vehicles and road-building equipment began extending an existing road southward into Doklam, a territory which is claimed by both China as well as Bhutan. On 18 June 2017, around 270 Indian troops, with weapons and two bulldozers, entered Doklam to stop the Chinese troops from constructing the road. On 28 August, both India and China announced that they had withdrawn all their troops from the face-off site in Doklam.

alone at the centre but where the structural aspects of power shape the outcomes in international relations. Unlike other kinds of power, structural power does not directly relate to the capabilities and the nature of relations among states and other actors but is comprised of different social and economic dimensions which further impact the relations and the process of decision-making. It has basically four dimensions: finance, security, knowledge and production.

Though none of these forms of power is independent of others, for a better understanding of how power works in a system where there is no central authority, such as in global politics, we need to

---

BOX 13.2:   Susan Strange's Dimensions of Structural Power

- The knowledge structure—which influences actors' beliefs, ideas or perceptions
- The financial structure—which controls access to credit or investment
- The security structure—which shapes defence and strategic issues
- The production structure—which affects economic development and prosperity

Source: Heywood (2017, 219–220).

---

comprehend them separately. For instance, the capability approach to power cannot work in isolation from the structural dimensions of power. A knowledge structure, for example, may enhance the possibilities of desired outcomes and in turn may increase capability at the final stage. Why, then, do we need to understand them separately? Imagine the opposite. Knowledge may also play a negative role in lowering capability in certain cases where the policies of a government are not in compliance with the prevailing perceptions among intellectuals. For instance, it is generally believed that democratic values are not in favour of warfare until and unless there is no option left.

Therefore, every dimension of power plays its role separately but not independently and deeply impacts other dimensions of power as well. What is particular to structural power is, as Strange says, 'the same state or states need not dominate each of these structures, but rather that their structural power may vary across the structures' (Heywood 2017, 218). This implies the independence of the structures and the changing role of the states in manipulating and exercising powers in international politics. On the other hand, capability in itself is nothing but a fair assessment of the prospect of the transformation of available resources into influence or power. Thus, unlike structural power, states become more significant in the understanding of power as capability.

Some types of powers are tangible and some are intangible in nature. However, in global politics, both have their own specific significance. They can be categorized as hard and soft power. Hard power includes the military, the economy, the population, territory, industry, geography, political stability, technology and so on. Soft power means political ideology, culture, education, language, history and efficiency of institutions. In the case of hard power, the elements associated with it can be measured on the stat sheet and can be quantified. They are visible in nature and can have instant impact on decisions. On the other hand, soft power is comprised of factors which cannot explicitly be calculated and are hard to capture in the form of facts and data. Major examples of holders of hard power are the US, China, Russia, Britain, Japan, India and Germany. All these factors collectively contribute in the overall power influence of a state.

The concept of soft power has been in the discourse of global politics almost for two decades. The term had been elaborated by Joseph Nye in his celebrated work *Bound to Lead: The Changing Nature of American Power* in 1990 (Nye 1990b). This has introduced the new era of power politics in international relations where hard power represents the coercive nature of the state to build or maintain their influence in the global system by using force or money as the tools of persuasion. On the other hand, soft power is the ability of the states to influence and persuade through soft means such as culture, values and foreign policy (Nye 2011, 84). It allows the state to implicitly get the desired results from other countries.

Soft power is not only the prerogative of nation states but it can also be exercised by non-state actors such as non-governmental organizations (NGOs) and other international organizations. These organizations are not supposed to have the tools and means of hard power, hence soft power becomes prominent for them to represent their interests on the global level (Nye 2004).

Sometimes, particularly in the case of soft power, the lack of one or two factors may be compensated by other, more powerful factors. These balancing and changing degrees and natures of these elements change the history of power and make for power shifts, which we are going to discuss chronologically in the coming sections.

How much more important these factors are than others will show the strength of a state. However, this assessment is very much subjective, both to the time as well as to the state. For some states, economy may be the most significant factor and for others, the military defines the core of their power. Another layer to this problem is that, because these elements of power facilitate each other, it is not guaranteed that every state will turn one dimension of power into another. For instance, the US has been successful in turning its economic power into military power but for Saudi Arabia, this is not the case (see Tables 13.1 and 13.2).

Time is an important factor in varying the relevance of these factors. Some factors become more important than others and make for vital shifts in power globally. For instance, in the twenty-first century, technology dominates or is more significant compared to other factors. This is the reason even the countries with limited resources are trying hard to achieve expertise in different fields of technology, whether it be the space, arms, industry or information technology. China, for example, is highly dependent upon its political stability and the biggest challenge to that is from liberal political values. History shows the repressive attitude of the state towards any kind of agitation or anti-government sentiment. In this regard, China also very well understands the efficiency of the virtual world and communication

TABLE 13.1 Top 10 Countries for Military Expenditure

	Military Expenditure in 2016	
Country	Expenditure on the Military (in $ billion)	Percentage of Total Expenditure
US	611.0	36.0
China	215.0	13.0
Russia	69.2	4.1
Saudi Arabia	63.7	3.8
India	59.9	3.3
France	55.7	3.3
UK	48.3	2.9
Japan	46.1	2.7
Germany	41.1	2.4
South Korea	36.8	2.2

Source: Globalfirepower.com.

technology; thus access to most of the prominent social sites and domains is prohibited there. Predominantly, there are two reasons to restrict technology in social media: one is that it is a way to censor knowledge and information and another reason is economics. The Chinese Communist Party (CCP) wants its own industry to flourish and seeks to keep the Chinese economy independent of the big players of Silicon Valley. This is called the Great Firewall of China under the Chinese government's Golden Shield Project for the purpose of surveillance and censorship of the flow of information (*Indian Express* 2017).

Apart from technology, particularly after the Second World War, economic factors turned out to be more significant than security in many aspects. This gave birth to many international economic zones and organizations. That neo-liberal policies have been and are being adopted by many nations clearly denotes the fact that security states and economic zones play parallel roles in the global politics. The process of rapid decolonization after the Second World War and the decreasing economic influence of Britain paved the way for the rise of the developing world. Whether it is East or South-east Asia, the Gulf region and China in particular witnessed a high level of

TABLE 13.2 Military Strength Ranking (2017)
Ranking 2017
1 United States
2 Russia
3 China
4 India
5 France
6 United Kingdom
7 Japan
8 Turkey
9 Germany
10 Egypt

Source: Globalfirepower.com.

economic growth in the latter half of the twentieth century. While not every newly independent country was so fortunate as to experience the same, the inclination of the states towards a market economy and the expansion of globalization, with rising growth rates and the opening up of the markets, regardless of ideological differences, clearly indicate the cumulative significance of economics over other factors. It does not minimize the importance of the military as power but a major change that happened in the recent past is due to this excessive economic interdependence, where sometimes political conflicts take second place and are unable to turn into a real military conflict. Matthew O. Jackson, an economist from Stanford University, suggested in his network model that economic trade is more capable of maintaining peace and stability in the world than military alliances (Mooney 2014). However, there are contrary theories as well which deny the claim of a strong correlation between trade and conflicts. There is a minimal relation where the trade is bilateral but in multilateral trade, war or conflict is unlikely to be affected by trade. The rationale behind this counterargument is that in the case of bilateral trade, the cost on the stake is much higher than in the case of multilateral trade, where the reduced economic dependency of a state increases the probability of conflict (Martin, Mayer and Thoenig 2008, 865). Nevertheless, whatsoever the conclusions of these studies are, they collectively confirm the fact that economy and trade play an important role in global politics. That role may be negative or positive for the purpose of world peace but the role itself cannot be ignored.

In recent times, where interdependence in various aspects is rapidly increasing and issues of global concern such as the environment, human rights, poverty, nuclear threats and so forth are being discussed among nations, the expectations from power are shifting as well. In his work *The Future of Power* (2011), Joseph Nye explains a third kind of power which he says is a combination of hard and soft power. He calls it 'smart power':

Power is one's ability to affect the behaviour of others to get what one wants. There are three basic ways to do this: coercion, payment, and attraction. Hard power is the use of coercion and payment. Soft power is the ability to obtain preferred outcomes through attraction. If a state can set the agenda for others or shape their preferences, it can save a lot on carrots and sticks. But rarely can it totally replace either. Thus the need for smart strategies that combine the tools of both hard and soft power. (Nye 2009, 161)

He explains the components of smart power and how they are changing with time. In another interview, he discusses the main purpose behind smart power: that we need to shift the very notion of power from 'power over others' to 'power with others', power for getting things we want done by working together. Emerging transnational problems cannot be resolved alone by a nation. We need cooperative measures using soft power in order to address these issues (Nye 2012).

BOX 13.3: Core Considerations of Smart Power

- The target over which one seeks to exercise power, its internal nature and its broader global context: Power cannot be smart if those who wield it are ignorant of these attributes of the target populations and regions.
- Self-knowledge and understanding of one's own goals and capacities: Smart power requires the wielder to know what their country or community seeks, as well as its will and capacity to achieve its goals.
- The broader regional and global context within which the action will be conducted.
- The tools to be employed, as well as how and when to deploy them individually and in combination.

Source: Wilson (2008, 215).

In this sense, smart power is not a new kind of power in itself and, unlike hard and soft powers, it does not comprise a new set of elements of power, but it is a new sort of strategy of utilizing the already available resources of power belonging to both hard and soft power (Table 13.3). Another point we need to keep in mind is that we should also evaluate the development of these concepts in their contextual settings. When Joseph Nye talks about smart power, he specifically indicates the inadequacies of the Bush administration (2001–2009) in combating the international and national challenges. Thus, it doesn't apply for each and every situation and to every state. Like hard and soft powers, smart power also faces the same criticism in the application of the concept. As a Canadian author points out, 'conventional hard and soft power concepts are inappropriate for Canada; confusion results as analysts attempt to graft an American-originated concept into Canadian landscape' (cited in Wilson 2008, 214).

For a clearer understanding of the application of smart power, let's discuss another observation. In the first decade of the twenty-first century, when the Bush administration was largely focusing on military supremacy for its diplomatic interests, the People's Republic of China (PRC), which could also have done the same, utilized its resources more smartly and pursued a way of 'China's Peaceful Rise' (Wilson 2008, 111). The instance of the Doklam standoff, which we have discussed earlier as a case of 'power as capability', can also be seen in light of this strategy. This observation also strengthens the earlier stated assumption that the significance of economic power is superseding the dominance of military power.

TABLE 13.3 Comparative Analysis of Hard, Soft and Smart Power

	Hard Power	*Soft Power*	*Smart Power*
Works on	Coercion/Fear	Bargain/Attraction	Cooperation/Mutual Understanding
Motivation	A does something because of the fear that it would be harmed by B.	A does something because of the return it is expecting from B by doing so.	A does something because it believes that by doing so, both A and B would be benefited.
Elements	Military, economy, population, territory, industry, geography, political stability, technology.	Political ideology, culture, education, language, history and efficiency of the institutions.	Combination and smart utilization of the elements of both hard and soft power.
Relevance	Relevant in the world of conflicts. Realist assumption.	Relevant in the world of economic interdependence. Liberalist assumption.	Relevant in the world of immense globalization and global challenges where a nation alone cannot resolve global concerns.

Historical Overview of Power Shifts

In this section, the historical background of the power shift in global politics is traced from the sixteenth century, when the Westphalian system emerged and the shape of modern world politics began to change.

The Treaty of Westphalia was the turning point in the field of political theory and the history of international politics as the recognition of sovereign states took place for the very first time after this treaty, which is sometimes also called the Westphalia sovereignty. For the first time, the fact was collectively acknowledged that states can exist together without compromising their sovereignties. The question was how to achieve this unprecedented objective. It was resolved by the second important contribution of the treaty, which is the concept of 'balance of power'. The motive was to prevent the unsolicited intervention of others into the internal matters of any state. The treaty was confined to the European states which were involved in the thirty-year war. However, the principles of this treaty did not stay confined to Europe; the influence of these principles spread across the world. This was the first glimpse of an array of modern global power transitions.

Many academic studies have their own perceptions and conclusions regarding the causes and consequences of these shifts. A. F. K. Organski, for instance, assumes the process of industrialization was a compelling reason for the power shifts. His argument develops into the development debate, where he states that uneven growth is the reason for power transitions in modern global political structures (Kim 1992, 155), though there are opposing theories also which include many other factors for these transitions. The Industrial Revolution was a phenomenon of the nineteenth century but power transitions were taking place since much earlier (Kim 1992, 156). The purpose of the paper is not to discuss power transitions but the brief pattern of power shifts in the global landscape, which is discussed in the following section.

Since the sixteenth century, three elements were considered essential to the power capabilities of nations: first, the military; secondly, the population; and thirdly, sea power, which includes both geographical advantages and the navy (Kim 1992, 161). But with the transitions of power, the factors defining the capability of dominant nations kept on changing. Still, the military has always been the most important factor among all. To start with the history of the sixteenth century, which is also referred to as the 'Age of Expansion', Spain was the dominant state in Europe. Its influence spread across the Americas, North Africa and some parts of Europe, followed by a decline in influence in the seventeenth century. The main resources contributing to Spain's power were colonial trade, mercenary armies and dynastic ties (Nye 1990c, 183). The Treaty of Westphalia ended not only the Thirty Years War among European countries, but it also ended the Eighty Years' War between what is now Netherlands and Spain, after which the Dutch Republic became a powerful state in Europe. The main sources of its dominance were trade, capital markets and the navy. Interestingly, the military was not in the centre in the case of the Dutch Republic, which continued in its position until the end of the seventeenth century. It is also called the Dutch Golden Age. Trade was the dominant resource of its prosperity, particularly through the Baltic Sea. In the reign of Louis XIV, France started to become a major power in Europe. Particularly after the Franco–Dutch War (1672–1678), power equations in the European landscape started to alter. Unlike in the Dutch Republic, the army's role in France's power was vital in maintaining its hegemony. The main resources of French power were its population, rural industry, public administration and army. After Louis XIV (1715), Louis V failed to keep the glory of French power in Europe. At the same time, the Industrial Revolution was taking place in Great Britain. Thus, the nineteenth century was dominated by Britain, with resources of power such as industry, political cohesion, finance and credit, the navy, liberal norms and its island location (Nye 1990c, 183). In the beginning of the nineteenth century, the downfall of the Napoleonic, Spanish and Holy Roman empires led to the increasing influence of the British and Russian empires being significantly expanded. But Britain maintained its hegemony throughout the century with its expanding economic and political power.

It is interesting to note that since the sixteenth century, there were power shifts, but all the major power centres were present within the European territory. In this sense, in geographical terms, the biggest change in the power centre in global politics took place in the twentieth century, with the emerging influences of the US, Japan and Russia.

Role of NGOs and International Organizations

Not only nation states, but in the new era of corporate governance and technological upsurge, NGOs and transnational actors have also emerged as powerful centres of influence and decision-making processes. These include NGOs, social movements and transnational corporations. Though, unlike states, these actors do not enjoy the prerogatives of sovereignty, governments and people of their own, yet nevertheless, on many occasions, these actors turn out to be very influential in deciding the course of global governance on many important issues. This develops a model of civil society at the global level which, based on democratic principles, not only indirectly represents the citizens and groups of different states through a bureaucratic setup but also encourages the states to act in the interests of the respective stakeholders (Nye 1990c, 86–87). These actors also ensure a minimum accountability of states and governments on several vital issues of common interest, such as the environment, human rights and security. But on the other hand, sometimes their encroachment on the decision-making of governments becomes a peril for the sovereign nature of a state.

For instance, to address the depletion of the ozone layer, the Montreal Protocol on Substances that Deplete the Ozone Layer (1987) has been signed to protect the ozone layer by limiting the emission of chlorofluorocarbons (CFCs), hydrochlorofluorocarbons (HCFCs) and hydrofluorocarbons (HFCs). All the members of the UN have ratified the protocol. In the United Nations Framework Convention on Climate Change (UNFCCC), there is a principle of Common but Differentiated Responsibilities (CBDR), which ensures the different implementations of the protocol for countries with different levels of growth. It was one of the most important initiatives to resolve the North–South debate, which has been discussed in the section 'Power and Its Role in Global Shifts'. The Sustainable Development Goals (SDGs) of the UN are another significant resolution in addressing the issues of climate change and environment. The Convention on the Rights of Persons with Disabilities (CRPD) of 2008 is another achievement of the twenty-first century where the rights of persons with disabilities have been addressed globally and have been included in the legal structure by many countries, including India. Other NGOs such as Human Rights Watch and Amnesty International pressurize governments and human-rights abusers to promote and maintain respect for the human rights of all.

With the emergence of neo-liberalism in the economic world order, global economic organizations have had a prominent role to play. Through monetary policy reviews, implying conditions of structural adjustment and other advisory mechanisms developed by organizations such as the World Bank and the IMF, the economic policies of the states are influenced deeply. The Agreement on Trade-related Aspects of Intellectual Property Rights (TRIPS) of the WTO implies the minimum standards related to intellectual property rights for the governments of the member states. Furthermore, the United States Trade Representative (USTR) issues an annual report based on observation of the implementation of intellectual property rights and patents according to the standards of the USTR in other countries. This shows the increasing influence of MNCs and trade organizations in pressuring the governments to make decisions in their own interests. India's position in the 'Priority Watch List' of the US on the basis of the Special 301 Report in which it attacked 'section 3(d) of the Indian Patent Act, which has enabled the Indian government to establish stricter patentability standards for medicines—allowing access to affordable generic drugs'. It is believed that such an attack is the result of the influence of the US pharmaceutical industry on the US government, which in turn creates pressure on countries such as India (Hindu 2016). In the same manner, several MNCs, TNCs and other international organizations often influence the decisions of the governments and such tendencies, with the expansion of economic interdependence and digitalized transactions, are getting more strengthened.

Concluding Observations

In global politics, power shifts are an inevitable phenomenon, but the study of these shifts shows that the causes and consequences of these power shifts keep on changing for several reasons. This is one of the biggest challenges before students of global politics, where—due to its remarkably vast scope—it becomes almost impossible to assess future events and to manage them efficiently, both at the national and the international level. However, in order to see the real picture and to fit into the changing milieu, we do need the theoretical explanations. Particularly while explaining power, the behavioural aspects of power are central to assessing the abilities of others; but measuring behaviour in itself is problematic (Nye 1990c, 178).

Many causes and challenges related to the global shifts have been discussed in the chapter. Power is the central theme in world politics, where everyone has their own capability to influence the open system of global politics. Though shifts occur on several bases, it is not very difficult to understand that (as realists believe) in the system of anarchy, it is a matter of the survival of the fittest as the centre of the power. However, the idea of fitness is itself dynamic and its variations are subject to time and geography both, as we have discussed in the previous section. Even one prevailing type of power cannot make or keep a state powerful for ever, since it can at any time be balanced by another type of power if the other actor succeeds in creating influence in the same proportion.

The desire for becoming a 'superpower' or a centre of regional power is undoubtedly posing some unprecedented challenges and threats to the world. As has been witnessed in the era of the cold war, power shifts are natural and are not harmful in nature; but the attempt to manage power shifts can turn into a power struggle, which is a great threat to the entire global community for many reasons. First, it paves the way for the development of arms and nuclear weapons. Second, it deviates the attention of governmental policies away from the real issues of the population and results in several socio-economic problems. The USSR's struggle for space technology during the cold war is an example. Thirdly, there is the environmental degradation. In the North–South debate, developed states are trying to convince other nations of the need for sustainable development. The developed countries are pursuing the policy of technology denial toward developing countries on the plea of environmental protection but by doing so, they want to maintain their monopoly over industries, trade and technology. Statistics suggest that the CFC emissions of the developed states are much higher than those of the developing ones. The challenges are endless but power shifts also prevent the world from going into a long-term hegemony of one power, which otherwise could be a serious situation in global politics. History shows that long-term power had always turned exploitative and arbitrary in relation to other states.

Undoubtedly, many theories and concepts have been developed to look into the complex web of these power relations, but with the emergence of new kinds of governance at the global level, including NGOs, non-state organizations and regional and international intergovernmental forums in the twentieth century, has posed a new challenge to theorizing the global shifts and their causes, impacts and consequences. The era of new technologies and the virtual connectedness of people through digital forums is also contributing to this new challenge. Therefore, the idea of global shifts has largely been conceptually developed but the theorists have still been seeking fresh explanations and prospects for the new events taking place, by introducing new concepts such as smart power and the idea of power diffusion.

Summary

- Today's global politics cannot be understood without going into the dynamics of power and its shifts.
- According to Joseph Nye, in global politics, power shifts are basically of two types. The first is 'power transition', which is change of power amongst states' and the second what he calls 'power diffusion'— movement of power from all states to non-state actors such as NGOs, international organizations and corporates.
- There have been changing centres of power right from the sixteenth century, when power was mainly centred in religious institutions and monarchs, to the twentieth century, where the power centres shifted from the European region to the other parts of the world.

- Many important events such as the Treaty of Westphalia, the Glorious Revolution, the French Revolution and the First and the Second World Wars played a significant role in the global shifts of power.
- The era of the cold war was bipolar, followed by a unipolar world with the emergence of the economic, political and cultural hegemony of the USA. Later, since the first decade of the twenty-first century, the world slowly started to turn into a multipolar one with the rise of other economic powers such as China, Japan and India.
- Apart from technology, particularly after the Second World War, it has been realized that economic factors turned out to be more significant than security in many aspects. This has given birth to many international economic zones and organizations.
- Joseph Nye explains a third kind of power which he says is the combination of hard and soft power. He calls it 'smart power'. It is a new sort of strategy for utilizing the already available resources of power belonging to both hard and soft power.
- Not only nation states, but in the new era of corporate governance and technological upsurge, NGOs and transnational actors have also emerged as powerful centres of influence and the decision-making process.

Suggested Questions

1. What do you understand by a global shift of power and governance?
2. What are the key factors of global power and governance?
3. How are power transitions and global governance in the twenty-first century different from the earlier period?
4. How does economic power play a key role in global shifts in the twenty-first century?
5. What do you understand by power diffusion? Do you think that power is shifting from West to East in the age of globalization?

References

Dingwerth, Klaus, and Philipp Pattberg. 2006. 'Global Governance as a Perspective on World Politics'. *Global Governance* 12 (2): 185–203.

Divakaruni, Sidd. 2017. 'Tensions Between India and China Rise over Border Skirmishes'. Foreign Brief, 8 July 2017. Accessed 18 April 2018. http://www.foreignbrief.com/daily-news/land-dispute-near-india-china-bhutan-tri-junction.

Heywood, Andrew. 2017. *Global Politics,* 2nd edn. New York: Palgrave Macmillan.

The Hindu Special Correspondent. 2016. 'India on US Watch List for Harsh IP Law'. *The Hindu,* 30 April 2016. Accessed 16 October 2017. http://www.thehindu.com/news/national/india-on-us-watch-list-for-harsh-ip-law/article8538554.ece.

The Indian Express. 2017. 'What is the Great Firewall of China?' *The Indian Express,* updated 19 July 2017. Accessed 15 October 2017. http://indianexpress.com/article/what-is/what-is-the-great-firewall-of-china-4757848.

Kim, Woosang. 1992. 'Power Transitions and Great Power War from Westphalia to Waterloo'. *World Politics* 45 (1): 153–172.

Martin, Philippe, Thierry Mayer and Mathias Thoenig. 2008. 'Make Trade Not War?' *The Review of Economic Studies* 75 (3): 865–900.

McLean, Iain, and Alistair McMillan, eds. 2009. *The Concise Oxford Dictionary of Politics*. New York: Oxford University Press.

Mooney, Loren. 2014. 'Matthew O. Jackson: Can Trade Prevent War?' Insights by Stanford Business, Stanford Graduate School of Business, 15 October 2017. Accessed 16 July 2017. https://www.gsb.stanford.edu/insights/matthew-o-jackson-can-trade-prevent-war.

Nye, Joseph S., Jr. 1990a. *Bound to Lead: The Changing Nature of American Power*. New York: Basic Books.

———. 1990b. 'Soft Power'. *Foreign Policy*, 80(Autumn): 153–171.

———. 1990c. 'The Changing Nature of World Power'. *Political Science Quarterly* 105 (2): 177–192. Accessed 18 September 2017. https://eng202isikuni.files.wordpress.com/2015/02/changing-nature-of-world-power.pdf.

———. 2004. *Soft Power: The Means to Success in World Politics*. New York: PublicAffairs.

———. 2009. 'Get Smart: Combining Hard and Soft Power'. *Foreign Affairs* 88 (4): 160–163.

———. 2010. 'Global Power Shifts'. Recorded 13 July at TEDGlobal 2010, Oxford. Video, 18:08. Accessed 24 October 2017. https://www.ted.com/talks/joseph_nye_on_global_power_shifts/transcript.

———. 2011. *The Future of Power*. New York: PublicAffairs.

———. 2012. 'On the Use of Power in International Relations'. Video, 4:23. Accessed 16 July 2017. https://www.youtube.com/watch?v=GDqY8b_r1H4.

Rosenau, James N., and Ernst-Otto Czempiel, eds. 2000. *Governance without Government: Order and Change in World Politics*. Cambridge: Cambridge University Press.

Singh, Parmeet. 2015. 'Cyber Laws and Civil Liberties: Challenges and Prospects'. In *E-Commerce and Consumer Interests: Challenges and Opportunities*, edited by G. S. Sood, Hungyo Yerreikan and Anil Kumar. New Delhi: Raj Publications.

Wallerstein, Immanuel. 2004. *World-Systems Analysis: An Introduction*. Durham and London: Duke University Press.

Wilson, Ernest J., III. 2008. 'Hard Power, Soft Power, Smart Power'. *The ANNALS of the American Academy of Political and Social Science* 616 (1): 110–124. Accessed 16 October 2017. http://www.ernestjwilson.com/uploads/Hard%20Power,%20Soft%20Power,%20Smart%20Power.pdf.

Further Reading

Avant, Deborah D., Martha Finnemore and Susan K. Sell, eds. 2010. *Who Governs the Globe?* Cambridge: Cambridge University Press.

Barnett, Michael, and Martha Finnemore. 2004. *Rules for the World: International Organizations in Global Politics*. Ithaca: Cornell University Press.

Haass, Richard N. 2005. *The Opportunity: America's Moment to Alter History's Course*. New York: PublicAffairs.

Halper, Stefan, and Jonathan Clarke. 2004. *American Alone: The Neo-conservatives and the Global Order*. Cambridge: Cambridge University Press.

Jayasuriya, Kanishka. 2005. *Reconstituting the Global Liberal Order: Legitimacy, Regulation and Security*. Oxford and New York: Routledge.

Kurlantzick, Joshua. 2007. *Charm Offensive: How China's Soft Power is Transforming the World*. New Haven, CT: Yale University Press.

Risse, Thomas. 2002. 'Transnational Actors and World Politics'. In *The Handbook of International Relations*, edited by Walter Carlsnaes, Thomas Risse and Beth A. Simmons. London: SAGE Publications.

Slaughter, Anne-Marie. 2004. *A New World Order*. Princeton: Princeton University Press.

Wendt, Alexander. 1992. 'Anarchy is What States Make of It: The Social Construction of Power Politics'. *International Organization* 46 (2): 391–425.

Feminist Perspective on International Relations

Neelu Anita Tigga

LEARNING OBJECTIVES

- To understand the concept of feminism in the context of international relations (IR)
- To study global politics through the gender lens
- To explain gender as a process of perceived differences creating a self-reinforcing power inequality
- To describe feminist theories in terms of inequality, oppression and difference
- To explore the shift of focus in IR from areas of global economy, development and human rights to literature on gender, war and international security
- To evaluate women's activism in pressurizing international organizations and national governments to adopt policies furthering women's equality

Feminist theory in international relations (IR) originally developed from work on the politics of development and from peace research expanding to include human as well as state security. It was only the end of the cold war and the restoration of relative peace between the major powers that resulted in the appearance of many new issues on the IR agenda. IR studies began to pay more attention to ethno-national conflicts and to the higher number of civilians killed or injured in these conflicts; more attention was also paid to international organizations, social movements and non-state actors. Feminist perspectives thus entered the IR discipline at the end of the 1980s, at about the same time as the end of the cold war, highlighting that international politics is about much more than inter-state relations.

Feminist IR in its critique of masculinist framing of politics and economics and associated institutions, including the state and its military and governmental components as well as the discourses through which these institutions operate and reproduce over time, has built upon and expands on feminist political and economic theory. Feminist theory is the extension of feminism into philosophical and theoretical discourse. Its objective is to understand the nature of gender inequality. IR scholarship, in highlighting the interdependence of masculine and feminine as socially constructed categories, tries to shape how we know and experience the world and, in its aim to study gender and the difference it makes to the world, examines women's social roles, experience, interests and feminist politics in a variety of fields, such as psychoanalysis, economics, literature education, philosophy and even linguistics.

Feminist IR, with its concern for gender issues in global politics and the global economy, strives for gender equality as a political priority not because it is an important end in and of itself but also because it will help reach other political and economic goals, for it recognizes that women have always been players in international politics, participating as diplomatic wives, as nannies going abroad to find work to support their families and as sex workers trafficked across international boundaries, but their participation as non-state actors in influencing IR is often ignored.

Feminist IR thus stresses on acknowledging the need to look at unconventional places, not normally considered within the boundaries of IR, and investigating the lives of those not normally considered as bearers of knowledge, hence looking in strange places for people and data, or 'lower than low politics' (Sjoberg and Tickner 2013, 174–175). Given these types of questions and research goals, feminist perspectives on security and the global economy are perceived to be quite different from conventional studies of national security and international political economy.

This chapter proposes to study the ways in which gender helps to structure world politics. It begins with an explanation of the concept of feminism and proceeds to give an overview of feminist theories making sense of gender awareness in IR; of the feminist understanding of security, war and conflict; and of how an awareness of gender relations alters our understanding of issues such as globalization and development. The chapter concludes by outlining some policy practices that are helping to lessen gender inequalities.

History of Feminism

Feminism is a critical political perspective. It seeks to develop new paradigms of social criticism which do not rely on traditional philosophical underpinnings (Fraser and Nicholson 1990). Though it is basically a Western concept, it has been articulated differently in different parts of the world, including India, by different people, especially women, depending upon their class, background and level of consciousness. It is a twentieth-century invention seen as a wide and changing movement, seeking in various ways to raise women's social status. As such, it is associated with two basic beliefs: women are disadvantaged because of their sex; and this disadvantage can and should be overthrown. In this way, feminists have highlighted what they see as a political relationship between the sexes—the supremacy of men and the subjection of women in most, if not all, societies (Heywood 1998).

The term 'feminism' was first used by the French writer Alexandre Dumas in 1872 in the pamphlet *L'homme-femme* to designate the then-emerging movement for women's rights. Feminism as a self-conscious movement with some elements of organization such as organized movements for suffrage in the UK and Seneca Falls convention which adopted a Declaration of Sentiments which called for female suffrage emerged in the 1840s in the United States (US) and Britain. However, it is generally agreed that winning the vote (in 1918 in Britain and 1920 in the US) paradoxically weakened and divided the movement. This was the heyday of 'reasonable feminism', based on the premise that the main battle had been won and women could enjoy their rights and equal status. But it was the 1960s that witnessed a dramatic revival of a more militant feminism, which has been dubbed the 'second wave', stemming from the emergence of radical feminism in the late 1960s. This began in the US in the mid-1960s, with the organization of a feminist lobby to exploit the new possibilities of legislation favourable to women. It was out of radical feminism that the new slogan of 'women's liberation' came, with its emphasis on women uniting to liberate themselves, which was then adopted by much of the wider movement (Randall 1982).

Feminism has been characterized by a diversity of views and political positions—for instance, it has pursued goals that range from the achievement of female suffrage, the establishment of equal access to education and an increase in the number of women in elite positions in public life, to the legislation of abortion, the ending of female circumcision and the abolition of restrictive or demeaning dress codes. It has embraced both revolutionary and reformist political strategies and its theory at times has drawn upon quite different political traditions and values. Thus, by the 1960s and 1970s, feminism had developed into a distinctive and established ideology.

The 1980s and 1990s have been described as a period of 'post-feminism'. Often called 'third-wave' feminism, it embraced contradictions and diversity as inherent components of late twentieth-century and twenty-first century lives, and envisioned a new model of feminist thinking and practice that went beyond black or white and situated itself within popular culture in an effort to bridge the gap between consumption and critique. The third-wave writers and activists insisted that feminism cannot be based on 'anachronistic insularity' and separatism but has to adopt a 'politics of ambiguity' that embraces tolerance, diversity and difference. In making room for differences and conflict between people, it functions as a political ideology currently under construction, welcoming pluralism and describing itself as a post-identity movement (Genz and Brabon 2011). In challenging previously accepted definitions of beauty and femininity, it is led by an interest in various groups of women, including women of colour, lesbian,

---

BOX 14.1: Three Waves of Feminism

First wave: 1910–1950
Seminal text: The Declaration of Sentiments and Resolution
Claims:

- Women suffrage
- Property rights
- Political candidacy

Second wave: 1960s to 1980
Seminal text: Simone de Beauvior 'The Second Sex' 1949

Betty Friedan 'The Feminine Mystique' 1963
Claims:

- Began in the US and eventually spread throughout the Western world
- Came as a delayed reaction against renewed domesticity of women after the Second World War
- Women objected to placing them at home for it limited their possibilities and wasted potential
- Demand for paid-maternity leave, greater access to education, help with child care
- Women step into male-dominated political arenas
- Formation of many local, state and federal government women's groups and independent feminist organizations
- Formation of NOW (National Organization for Women), 1966
- Significant victories after the formation of NOW
- Full affirmative action rights to women
- Women's Education Equality Act (1972, 1974) respectively
- Health and family planning (1970)
- Equal Credit Opportunity Act (1974)
- Pregnancy Discrimination Act (1978)
- The outlawing of marital rape (although not outlawed in all states until 1993)
- The legalization of no-fault divorce (although not legalized in all states until 2010)
- Emergence of Women's Studies as a legitimate field of study

Third Wave: late 1990s to 2008
Seminal text(s): *Manifesta: Young Women, Feminisms and the Future*, Jennifer Baumgardner and Amy Richards, 2000; 'zines created by the Riot Grrrl movement
Claims:

- Focus on embracing individualism and diversity
- Plural and multifaceted, comprising people with gender, ethnic and class identities, experiences and interests
- Broader inclusion of women of colour, sexual diversity, age (recognition of young girls and older women) and men
- Inclusion becomes more trans global; moves beyond US borders (Transnational Feminism)
- Volunteerism is new force for activist activities
- CR groups form through new texts: the 'zine movement gives way to the use of writing, new technologies (Internet, filmmaking, music, electronic magazines and blogs become ubiquitous)
- Women begin stepping into male-dominated cultural arenas
- Women's health issues are recognized and reproductive health rights marches on DC in 1989, 1992 and 2004
- Legal and social recognition of: date rape, sexual identity issues (custody battles, gender reassignment, marriage rights), reclamation of language (cunt, bitch, slut), objectification (body image is major issue)
- The expression of 'girl power' merchandise proved popular giving rise to icons of powerful women which included singers such as Madonna, Queen Latifah and women depicted in television series such as Buffy the Vampire Slayer, Sex and the City
- Shifting of Second Wave ideals on 'proper' feminism: marriage, pornography
- Voter registration among women becomes the driving force for many activist activities

Source: Polak (2012).

bisexual and transgendered women and low-income women. Thus, the women's movement has certainly changed; but far from weakening, it has continued to expand and broaden.

Before investigating how gender works in global issues, what feminists mean by gender needs to be investigated and explained.

How Feminists Define Gender

In every-day usage, gender denotes the biological sex of individuals. However, feminists define gender differently—as a set of socially and culturally constructed characteristics that vary across time and place. In this view, a very clear distinction is drawn between sex and gender. 'Sex', in this sense, refers to the biological difference between females and males, usually linked to reproduction; these differences are natural and therefore are unalterable (Geetha 2002). On the other hand, feminists define gender as a set of variables that are socially and culturally constructed—characteristics such as power, autonomy, rationality, activity and the realm of the public are stereotypically associated with masculinities; weakness, dependency, emotionality, passivity and private realms, their opposites, are associated with femininity. Gender, then, is a system of symbolic meanings, where gender symbolism describes the way in which 'masculine' or 'feminine' are assigned to various dichotomies that organize Western thought (Tickner 2008; Sjoberg and Tickner 2013).

Interestingly, gender binaries are hierarchical, where one term is always privileged over the other (Baylis, Smith and Owens 2008); however, masculinities do not exist except in contrast to femininities. Their definition may vary across time and space, but they are always unequal; therefore gender is a primary way of signifying relationships of power (Steans 2013). Gender also denotes the unequal distribution of social benefits and costs, making it crucial for analysing global politics and economics, particularly with respect to issues of inequality, insecurity and social justice.

The study of gender being centred on women gives rise to distortions that not only work against a full appreciation and analysis of gender as relational but cast women forever as 'victims', marginalizing men and masculinities in IR. Masculinity in IR is, therefore, interrogated in the studies that draw upon the concept of 'hegemony'. Women as a homogenized category is problematized where there is a tendency to cast women as if they are forever and always victimized and this conflation of women and gender means that the construction of men and masculinities is marginalized in IR. The feminist literature by concentrating on women/femininity thereby fails to recognize that men are not only perpetrators but also victims so a more balanced feminist IR is needed to redress this imbalance that addresses the position of men and masculinities in IR.

Masculinity in International Relations

Masculinity and politics have a close association where masculinism is the ideology that justifies and naturalizes the gender hierarchy where values socially associated with femininity and masculinity are awarded unequal weight and characteristics assumed to be masculine—such as toughness, courage, power, independence and even physical strength—have been valued over the feminine. Social processes select values and behaviours that can be associated with an idealized or hegemonic masculinity. Such selections occur because traits associated with hegemonic masculinities dominate social relations while other values are subordinated, for example, heterosexual masculinities must subordinate homosexual masculinities to maintain identity for the masculine ideal. This self-sustaining cycle continues for as long as masculinity appears as a unitary concept and dichotomous thinking about gender continues to pervade social life (Hooper 2000; Zalewski 2010; Steans 2013).

Hegemonic Masculinity

Hegemonic masculinity is sustained through its opposition to various subordinated and devalued masculinities, such as homosexuality, and more importantly, through its relation to various devalued femininities. Socially constructed gender differences are based on socially sanctioned, unequal relationships between men and women that reinforce compliance with men's stated superiority. Nowhere in the public realm are these stereotypical gender images more apparent than in the realm of international politics, where the characteristics associated with hegemonic masculinity are projected to the behaviour of states whose success as international actors is measured in terms of their capabilities in terms of power and capacity for self-help and autonomy (Hooper 2000; Zalewski 2010; Steans 2013). However, IR scholar Joshua Goldstein in his book *War and Gender* concludes that socialization practices which motivate men's participation in combat and women's exclusion from it can be changed (Goldstein 2001). Similarly, feminist IR scholar Charlotte Hooper sees in the West some softening of what she terms 'hegemonic masculinity' as we move away from warrior heroes to masculinity linked to processes of globalization and capitalist restructuring (Tickner 2004, 47). Further, the increasing visibility of women and gay men in American and European militaries and the militaries' humanitarian intervention as peacekeeping operations since the 1990s lend support to the idea that the military may be becoming detached from hegemonic masculinity.

Research has also revealed that female state leaders do not appear to be any more peaceful or any less committed to state sovereignty and territorial integrity than male leaders. It has been suggested that women in power tend to be more warlike to compensate for being females in traditionally male roles. Former United Kingdom (UK) prime minister Margaret Thatcher, who went to war in 1982 to recover the Falkland Islands from Argentina; Madeleine Albright, the first US female Secretary of State; Condoleezza Rice, US national security advisor and later Secretary of State for George W. Bush; and Jeane Kirkpatrick, the first US ambassador to the UN in the Reagan administration were a few women who led great powers in the past century. Among the middle-ranking powers, Indira Gandhi led India in the war against Pakistan in 1971, as did Israel's Golda Meir against Egypt and Syria in 1973. Turkey's Tansu Çiller led a harsh war to suppress Kurdish rebels in the mid-1990s. Likewise, the former president of Sri Lanka Chandrika Kumaratunga and her mother Sirimavo Bandaranaike, the prime minister, tried to make peace with separatist rebels, but returned to war when that initiative failed (Goldstein 2003).

Feminist Methodologies and Methods in International Relations

Feminisms contain multiple approaches built from women's varied life experiences and understandings about the self and the other. Susan Heckmen explains that women and men create their own realities through their own different activities and experiences and so activity is epistemology. She again contends that if the self can reshape meanings, then the self can self-emancipate and that self-reformulation is crucial to feminist emancipation, because willingness to admit subjectivity conquers dominative but unconscious forces in human relationship (Sjoberg 1979). Feminisms, thus, with their goal of making the invisible visible, centring women's lives, rendering the trivial important, putting the spotlight on women as competent actors and understanding women as subjects rather than objects, engage in activism through non-governmental organizations (NGOs), advocacy groups and governments.

Feminists are, however, sceptical about IR's claims to objectivity and the universality of knowledge. They question knowledge constructed as binaries such as rational/emotional, objective/subjective, global/local and public/private, with the first term being privileged and associated with masculinities, automatically devaluing certain types of knowledge, often associated with femininities (Sjoberg and Tickner 2013). Feminists critique this purported objectivity, recognizing instead that knowledge of the world begins with the socially situated self, not with a world that can ever be independent of the researcher. Success for feminists, then, would be that their knowledge claims contribute in transforming social conditions such as gender hierarchies. Further, feminists differ from other IR scholars in explicitly projecting their political commitments into their scholarship. These political commitments include gender emancipation, transforming unequal power relationships and understanding the world from the perspective of the political margins (Sjoberg and Tickner 2013).

Understanding the world from the perspective of the oppressed then requires different 'lenses' than IR has traditionally used (Sjoberg 1979; Ehrenreich 2011; Sjoberg and Tickner 2013). To understand what it means to put on a feminist lens or gender lens is to understand issues of nationalism, security, war and so on through empirical and analytical feminism.

Empirical feminism, influenced by liberal feminism, addresses the under-representation or misrepresentation of women in a discipline that has conventionally focused on male-dominated institutions and processes. Its critique of conventional approaches to international politics is thus encapsulated in the question: 'Where are the women?' Making sense of international politics then means recognizing the previously invisible contributions of women as domestic workers of various kinds, migrant labourers, diplomats' wives, sex workers in military bases and so forth, in shaping world politics. However, it has been pointed out that the gender lens has its limitations, for recognizing gender as an empirical and not an analytical category widens our awareness of the range of global processes rather than changing our understanding on them. It is also criticized for highlighting the under-representation of women in conventional leadership roles at national, international and global levels, for in so doing, it is concerned with the interests of elite women, giving insufficient attention to how rectifying such gender imbalances might affect the behaviour of global actors.

Analytical feminism, by contrast, is concerned with highlighting the gender biases that pervade the theoretical framework and key concepts of mainstream international theory, particularly realism. In drawing on the ideas of 'difference feminism', it differs from mainstream theories which have traditionally been presented as gender-neutral and uncover hidden assumptions about theories being derived from a social and political context in which male domination is taken for granted. Likewise, 'standpoint feminism' has been particularly influential in demonstrating just how male-dominated the conventional theories of international politics are. In a pioneering analysis, J. Ann Tickner (1988) has formulated Hans J. Morgenthau's six principles of political realism to show how objective laws in fact reflect male values. Morgenthau's account of power politics portrays the state as an autonomous actor intent on pursuing its self-interest by acquiring power over other states, a model that reflects the traditional dominance of the husband-father within the family and the male citizen within society at large. At the same time, this conception of power ignores the forms of human relationships that may be more akin to female experience, such as caring, interdependence and collaborative behaviour. Reformulated, Tickner's six principles can be summarized as:

- Objectivity is culturally defined as being associated with masculinity and so is partial.
- The national interest, being multidimensional, cannot and should not be defined by one set of interests.
- Power, as domination and control, privileges masculinity.
- There are possibilities of using power as collective empowerment in the international arena
- All political actions have moral significance and so the two cannot be separated.
- A narrowly defined political realm defines the political in a way that excludes the concerns and contributions of women.

Gender Awareness: Making Sense in International Relations

Liberal Feminism

Liberal feminism, premised on the philosophical traditions of liberalism, is based on the principle of individualism, of individual liberty, which means freedom of choice, equal opportunities and civil rights. These ideas, put together, represent the legacy of the Age of Enlightenment or Age of Reason, which highlighted the equal moral worth of all individuals and human dignity, recognizing the ability and rights of the ordinary person to participate in public life, to vote and hold public office and property, which were increasingly stressed on the basis of the belief of inherent natural rights of the individual, such as the right to life, liberty and the pursuit of happiness, free of the interference of governments. The reality and practice, however, was that freedom, equality and justice applied only to men. Women's exclusion was based on the rhetoric of naturalness, conjuring up images of biological and social determinism, casting female nature as separate, an adjunct to the male based on the assumption that female nature belongs to the home and to the irrational side of human nature, associated with qualities such as nurturance and emotion. Liberal feminism has a long tradition of gender-based intervention in Western thought, in the legacy of such writers as Mary Wollstonecraft and John Stuart Mill (Whelehan 1995).

Wollstonecraft in *A Vindication of the Rights of Woman* (1792) and Mill in *The Subjection of Women* (1851) questioned the traditional arrangements of work and family as confining and restraining women and denying them the freedom of choice (Wollstonecraft 1972; Mill 1990). Both Wollstonecraft and Mill believed that the so-called feminine traits were the product of social conditioning and pointed out that women are human beings capable of rational thought and deserving the same natural rights granted to men. Betty Friedan in *The Feminine Mystique* (1963) argued that women in the decades after the Second World War had suffered an identity crisis, for it was assured that women felt happy and fulfilled as full-time wives and mothers and felt guilty if they pursued careers (Elshtain 1981). The liberal tradition continued in second-wave feminism in the 1970s, which expanded to include married women's access to wage labour, parental sharing of childcare, protection of maternity, equal employment opportunities and

---

BOX 14.2: Cynthia Enloe

Cynthia Holden Enloe (born 16 July 1938) is a feminist writer, theorist and professor. She is best known for her work on gender and militarism and for her contributions to the field of feminist international relations. Her teachings and research have focused on the interplay of gender politics in the national and international arenas, with special attention to how women's labour is made cheap in globalized factories and how women's emotional and physical labour have been used to support many governments' war-waging policies and how women have tried to resist those efforts. Racial, class, ethnic and national identities, as well as pressures shaping ideas about femininities and masculinities, are common threads throughout her studies.

---

special treatment to particularly disadvantaged groups of women. Thus, it advocated social and legal reforms, educational advances and public-policy accommodations to redress systemic discrimination.

The IR feminist Cynthia Enloe, though having socialist leanings, takes a liberal stand in showing how important women were in international economics and political systems, whether as cheap factory labour, as prostitutes around military bases or as wives of diplomats (Enloe 1989). Fundamentally, IR feminists—like liberal feminists—want the same rights and opportunities which men have.

Radical Feminism

Radical feminism emerged in the US and Britain in the late 1960s and early 1970s and regarded gender difference in society as the most fundamental of all social divisions. The feminists tried to confront the seeming universality of female oppression by positing a universalizing notion of patriarchy and the trend was evident in the pioneering work of Simone de Beauvoir, and was developed by early radical feminists such as Eva Figes and Germaine Greer. Figes' *Patriarchal Attitudes* (1970) drew attention to the fact that patriarchal values and beliefs pervade the culture, philosophy, morality and religion of society (Figes 1970). In all walks of life and learning, women are portrayed as inferior and subordinate to men, a stereotype of femininity being imposed upon women by men. In *The Female Eunuch* (1970), Greer suggested that women are conditioned to a passive sexual role, which has suppressed their true sexuality as well as the more active and adventurous side of their personalities (Heywood 1998).

However, it was with the work of activists such as the American writer Kate Millett and the Canadian author Shulamith Firestone that radical feminists developed a systematic theory of sexual oppression. The central feature of radical feminists is the belief that sexual oppression is the most fundamental feature of society and the role of patriarchy is central in this sex oppression (Heywood 1998).

Millett in *Sexual Politics* (1970) described how the different roles of men and women have their origin in the process of conditioning, for from a very early age, boys and girls are encouraged to conform to very specific gender identities. This takes place largely within the family, patriarchy's chief institution, but it is also evident in literature, art, public life and economy, which should be challenged through a process of consciousness-raising (Heywood 1998).

Meanwhile, Firestone in the *Dialectic of Sex* (1972) stated that society could be understood through the process of reproduction, because in bearing children, women are at the mercy of biology and, like children, are dependent upon men for their physical survival. She argued that women can achieve emancipation if they transcend their biological nature and escape from the 'curse of Eve'. She believed that modern technology opened up the prospect of genuine sexual equality by relieving women of the burden of pregnancy and childbirth. Pregnancy could not only be avoided by contraception or be terminated by abortion, but new technology also creates the possibility of avoiding pregnancy by artificial reproduction in test tubes and the transfer of child-rearing responsibilities to social institutions, making women enter society as the true equal of men (Heywood 1998; Elshtain 1981).

Radical feminism, in encompassing divergent elements, also extols the positive virtues of fertility and motherhood, implying that in certain respects, women are superior, possessing the qualities of creativity, sensitivity and caring, which men can never fully appreciate or develop. Such ideas, associated with 'eco-feminism' and 'cultural feminism', advocate a retreat from the corrupting and aggressive male world of political activism into an apolitical, women-centred culture and lifestyle. Another approach, 'standpoint feminism' aimed to re-describe reality according to a female view, understanding the world by incorporating a female perspective. However, all these views run the risk of essentializing and fixing the views and nature of women. This clearly leads in the direction of feminist separatism.

The scale of separatism, however, varies considerably, ranging from political separatism (women-only discussion groups, dealing purely with issues that affect women) to complete separatism (communes and so on). Communal living was ideal to render male assistance redundant and, in some cases (but by no means all) and lesbianism as 'political lesbianism' (the choice of a lesbian sexual orientation) was a political statement, rather than reflecting one's primary sexual choice (Whelehan 1995). Nonetheless, despite these dangers, the above-mentioned theories have been very influential in showing just how male dominated are the main theories of world politics.

Marxist/Socialist Feminism

Socialist feminism, which became prominent in the second half of the twentieth century, does not believe that women simply face political or legal disadvantages that can be remedied by equal legal rights or the achievement of equal opportunities. Rather, socialist feminists argue that the relationship between the sexes is rooted in the social and economic structure itself, and that nothing sort of profound social change, through social revolution, can offer women the prospect of genuine emancipation.

The central theme of socialist feminism is that women seemed to be governed by two semi-autonomous but mutually strengthening power mechanisms—the operation of a patriarchal ideology of immutable sexual difference within the family and a sexual division of labour in the workplace (Whelehan 1995).

Similarly, writers such as UK socialist feminist Juliet Mitchell subscribes to modern Marxism, which accepts the interplay of economics, social, political and cultural forces in society, rather than orthodox Marxism, which insists upon the primacy of material or economic factors. In *Women's Estate* (1971), she suggested that domestic labour is vital to the health and efficiency of the economy. In bearing and rearing children, women produce the labour power for the next generation, guaranteeing future production (Mitchell 1971). Women, being responsible for socializing, conditioning and educating children, thereby ensure their development into disciplined and obedient workers. Thus, confining women to the domestic sphere of housework and motherhood serves the economic interests of capitalism. Women also constitute a 'reserve army of labour', which can be recruited into the workforce when there is a need for production but easily shed and returned to domestic life during depression, without imposing a burden upon the employer or the state. So, as temporary workers, women are conditioned to accept poorly paid, low-status jobs (Elshtain 1981). Devaluation of women's work at home and in the public sphere also coincided with the campaign for 'wages for housework', associated in the UK with Costa James (1972), who suggested that women would gain economic independence and enjoy enhanced status if their labour, like that of men, is recognized as productive and worthwhile by being paid for (Costa 1970).

This approach is especially insightful when it comes to looking at the nature of the world economy, where women are subject to male dominance in capitalism due to their financial dependence and uneven balance in wealth.

Postmodernist Feminism

Postmodernism is a quest for the abandonment of unity, generality and synthesis. Postmodernism assumes that it has discovered a greater degree of cultural complexity than can be accounted for by other modes of theorizing. It lays emphasis on the recognition of the existence of complex differences, local diversities and otherness, the voices which were ignored or suppressed in the unified models. In its rejection of generalization and the construction of unities, it demands deconstruction, deconceptualization, greater appreciation of detail and cognizance of the multiple natures of cultural texts and images (Featherstone 1995).

Postmodernism is referred to as 'a new condition of society', a distinctive historical condition emerging in the late twentieth century out of successive waves of space-time compression and the accompanying pressures of capital accumulation (DiPalma and Ferguson 2010). It is more usually characterized as replacing modernity. Modernity, which emerged from the Enlightenment or Age of Reason, greatly influenced feminist emancipatory impulses; but it also made women realize that the tenets of modernism have not been friendly to women, for they argue that the modernist subject, driven by scientific, objective knowledge and by will, is always a masculine subject who is perceived to be separate from the social world and free to act at his will. This critique then signalled a shift towards different conceptions of the subject and of society and its signifying systems (Gannon and Davies 2007). Thus, on the one hand, the postmodernists disrupted the exclusivities that various modernist philosophers and institutions had claimed about science being the best route of knowledge, the rationalist or realist thinkers' assumption of an unchanging foundation for understanding, the Marxist narrative of the transcendent grounds of history and the liberals' assertions of a primary origin of the psychology of politics (DiPalma and Ferguson 2010); on the other hand, they argued for knowledge as contextual, historically situated and discursively produced and for subjects being constituted within the network of power and knowledge (Genz and Brabon 2011).

Subjectivity focuses on the subject as an outcome of historical processes and power relations. As explained by Judith Butler, gender is not a given; gender is performative, being something one does rather than something one is. What this means is that language forces 'reality' into certain pre-given patterns and prevents certain possibilities from being realized, meaning that those who construct meaning and create knowledge gain a great deal of power by doing so. To try to understand this in world politics is to ask how world politics produces certain kinds of soldiers, certain kinds of workers and certain kinds of states that are not simply men or women, male or female, but complexly positioned states that seem to be neutral. Postmodernism also makes use of Jacques Derrida's work of the textual construction of the world, which proposes two main tools to enable us to see how arbitrary the seemingly 'natural' oppositions of language actually are. Through deconstruction and double reading, he explains that seemingly stable and natural concepts and relations within language are hierarchical, where one term is always privileged over the other—public/private, good/bad, male/female, right/wrong, order/anarchy, dependency/sovereignty, domestic/international, subject/object. Post-modernist feminist effort also aims not to come to a correct or one reading of a text but instead to show how there is always more than one reading. Thus, postmodernist feminist effort is directed towards dismantling all totalizing and essentialist patterns of thought, including its own unifying myths and grounding assumptions.

Postcolonial Feminism

This approach, while rejecting the idea that gender is a universal and homogeneous category, asserts that the politics of gender are always and everywhere tied up in wider relations of inequality and subjugation. The central concept of the approach is intersectionality. Intersectionality refers to the overlapping and interrelated aspects of identity—gender, sexuality, class, race, age and ethnicity. In essence, intersectionality refers to the experience of multiple identities and social locations and the multiple and varied experiences of oppression and discrimination. It expresses the idea that specific groups of people are subjected to and experience discrimination in ways that are multiple and interconnected. For example, while all women experience forms of discrimination that are justified on the grounds of gender, specific groups of women might also be discriminated against or experience oppression on the grounds of race, ethnicity or social class. Similarly, men do not form a homogeneous group who universally oppress women: Class, ethnicity, location, and so on, create divisions among men too and, moreover, sometimes create a community of interest among men and women from specific social and ethnic groups. This prominent school of thought contends that the language of a 'civilizing mission' is still prevalent in Western discourse on non-Western states and very often this discourse is gendered: Non-Western women are represented as 'oppressed' and in need of 'rescue' and are not represented as agents engaged in struggles for rights, but rather human rights are represented as a gift bestowed by a benevolent Western power, even if this entails military intervention (John 1999). For example, Mohanty (1984), in her influential article 'Under Western Eyes', argued that though the transnational women's movement comprised of a loose and diverse coalition of women's groups, the Western NGOs and activists dominated international political forums—for example, the United Nations (UN)—and used these forums to pursue a Western agenda. Women from the South had little opportunity to articulate their specific concerns and aspirations in these same sites. Thus, she accused the 'hegemonic white women's movement' of colonizing the experiences of developing countries' women in advancing an emancipatory politics grounded in a Western discourse of universalism, 'progress' and 'liberation' (Mohanty 1984).

Further postcolonial feminism locates the sex/gender distinction in a grid of identities—caste, class, race and religion. This would mean that the biological category of 'woman' does not necessarily have shared interests, life situations or goals. In India, the extent and form of subordination has been conditioned by the social and cultural environment in which women have been placed. The dominant form of patriarchy in many parts of the Subcontinent has been termed as Brahmanical patriarchy in feminist scholarship. A marked feature of Hindu society is its legal sanction for an extreme expression of social stratification in which women and the lower castes have been subjected to severe disabilities so that caste purity could be maintained. Brahmanical patriarchy is a set of rules and institutions in which caste and gender are linked, each shaping the other. Brahmanical patriarchal codes for women differ according to the status of the caste group to which they belong in the hierarchy, with the most stringent control over female sexuality for the higher class (Chakrvarti 2001). The codes, based on the Manu Smriti, highlight the nature of women as perceived in the Hindu religion. Women were considered a distraction, not to be trusted, and were charged as a class with crime and evil deeds. Such a low estimate of women's nature and character required their dependence day and night, ensured by employing them in negotiating economic expenditure, in keeping everything clean, in the fulfilment of religious duties, in the preparation of men's food and in looking after the household utensils. The wife was declared to be the 'material property' of her husband and classed with cows, mares, she-goats, slave girls, and so on. She was expected to remain with and revere her husband as a god, even though he be destitute of virtue or be devoid of good qualities or diseased. She who controlled her thoughts, words and deeds and never slighted her 'lord' would reside after death with her husband in heaven and be called a virtuous wife (Sarasvati 1981). Most effective in making women complicit in producing patriarchal power, the caste hierarchy has been a system of benevolent paternalism in which obedient women were accorded certain rights and privileges, security and respect. Again, through its mythologies, women were socialized into believing in their empowerment through chastity and fidelity, through the ideology of sacrifice and passive acceptance and through the features of a *pativrata*[1] woman, women saw themselves as achieving both sublimation and a spiritual strength. It is also pointed out that those who did not consent to or cooperate with the norms and practices of patriarchy were branded as deviant and were withheld from sharing the material resources of their men. These oppressive structures are being opposed today by democratic and egalitarian ideologies and norms, which have been enshrined in the Constitution of India.

Revisiting Questions of International Relations

An empiricist approach to gender focuses largely on women or men as a category of analysis. An example of an empiricist research agenda is one that seeks to uncover the under-representation of women in positions of power in world politics. Such an agenda focuses on the how, when, where and what questions of women in the study of international politics, raising questions such as: Where are the women leaders in IR? Why are so few women in positions of power? Why are women's issues marginalized on the agendas of international politics? Similarly, it is argued that employing gender as a category can actually facilitate the analysis of gendered power relations. For example, Cynthia Enloe, in her book *Bananas, Beaches and Bases* (1989), begins with an empirical question: Where are the women? She then goes on to offer many insights into how gendered power relations underpinned an array of practices absolutely central to international politics, such as diplomacy and military operations.

Gender Security

Adopting gender as the lens for analysis, feminists investigate how unequal social structures negatively impact the security of individuals and groups. Conventional approaches to security present it as the highest end of international politics. In this view, states have the prime responsibility for maintaining security, as reflected in the notion of 'national security'. The major threats to security are therefore external, coming

---

[1] Women were socialized into believing in their own empowerment through chastity and fidelity, through the ideology of sacrifice and of passive acceptance.

from other states. In this way, the threat of violence and other forms of physical coercion are intrinsically linked to the prospect of inter-state war. National security is thus closely linked to the prevention of such wars, usually through a build-up of military capacity to deter potential aggressors. Feminists, for their part, have criticized this view of security on the grounds that, first, it is premised on a masculinist assumption about rivalry, competition and inevitable conflict, arising from the tendency to see the world in terms of interactions among a series of power-seeking, autonomous actors. Second, the conventional idea of national security tends to be self-defeating as a result of the security paradox. This creates what has been called the 'insecurity of security' (Ehrenreich 2011). Feminists have drawn up a broader and multidimensional notion of security both through long-standing concern about violence against women in the family and in domestic life and through an awareness of growing threats to women arising, for example, from sex slavery and armed conflict. Feminists have pointed out that absence of war, in the conventional sense, does not guarantee that people, and especially women, live without fear or safe from want.

Challenging the Myth of Protection

Feminists have challenged the myth of protection that wars are fought to protect women, children and others stereotypically viewed as 'vulnerable'. They argue that during the twentieth century, there was a sharp increase in the proportion of civilian casualties of war, from 10% at the beginning of the century to 90% in the mid-1990s. Women and children constituting about 80% of the total refugee population—a population whose number increased from 3 million to 27 million between 1970 and 1994, mainly due to military conflict, particularly ethnic conflict. Similarly, the role of the masculine protector puts those (paradigmatically) protected women and children in a subordinate position of discipline and obedience. At the same time, the protection given to these civilian women is assumed in the definition of the making and fighting of wars and often not guaranteed in practice. For example, feminists draw our attention to the issue of rape in war. It is estimated that 20,000–35,000 women were raped during the war in Bosnia and Herzegovina. There are around 200,000 rape survivors in post-genocide Rwanda, and it is unknown how many rape victims died in the conflict. Systematic rape has been documented in recent conflicts in Darfur, Chechnya, Sierra Leone, Kosovo and East Timor. In these and other conflicts, rape is not just an accident of war but is often a systematic military strategy and a weapon of war (Carlsnaes Risse and Simmons 2013).

Further, Cynthia Enloe and Katharine Moon have described social structures in place around most army bases where women were kidnapped and sold into prostitution (Moon 1997). Such a system of militarized sexual relations requires addressing in security policymaking. Katharine Moon, in her study of prostitution around US military bases in South Korea in the 1970s, shows how the clean-up of prostitution camps by the South Korean government through the policing of sexual health and the work of prostitution was part of its attempt to prevent the withdrawal of American troops that had begun under the Nixon Doctrine of 1969. The account shows how military prostitution interacted with US and Korean security policies at the highest level in the name of national security, resulting in Korean state policies that exploited these women's lives (Tickner 2008; Sjoberg and Tickner 2013).

Feminist research shows that the myth of protection is not only problematic but also shows that women should not be seen only as victims. Women's responsibilities often rise during war as they have greater control over the household, may work outside the home and sometimes may participate in military conflict but have to relinquish such roles when war is over (Tickner 2008; Sjoberg and Tickner 2013).

Women also acquire new roles during war—that of a soldier, an insurgent, a terrorist or a war criminal—participating in violence. These women do not participate in military organizations and insurgent groups that have suddenly shed their gendered understandings of strategy, security and political life. Instead, the women are included in fighting groups that maintain their biases towards behavioural characteristics and standards associated with masculinity. When women break out of the traditional understandings of their peacefulness, audiences tend to question both whether 'women' are capable of committing violence and whether violent 'women' are really women at all (Tickner 2008; Sjoberg and Tickner 2013).

Gendering States, War and Peace

The association between masculinity and war has been central to feminist investigation and in their critique, the IR feminists have examined how realism and neorealism base their explanations of and prescriptions for states' national security behaviour. Military manhood or a type of heroic masculinity is emphasized and anything feminine is considered degenerative. Recruitment and maintenance of self-esteem in institutions based on subservience and obedience are the norm. However, feminists' concern is not about who fights wars; rather, they call attention to the suffering that security analysis normally ignore, that is, the impact of war on individual women's and men's lives. They argue that there are other paths to security besides the competitive use of force. As a result, they see a relationship between the sort of violence traditionally understood as war and unsafe working conditions, unemployment, foreign debt, structural violence, ethnic violence, poverty and family violence (Sjoberg and Tickner 2013).

As such, feminists have usually not regarded the nature of state power as a central political issue, preferring instead to concentrate on the 'deeper structure' of male power centred on institutions such as the family. Considering the state as patriarchal, the structural argument draws attention to the emergence of welfare states' transition from private dependence to a system of public dependence, in which women are increasingly controlled by the institutions of the extended state. For instance, women have become increasingly dependent on the state as clients or customers of state services such as childcare institutions, nurseries, schools and social services and as employees, particularly in the so-called caring professions such as nursing, social work and education (Ehrenreich 2011).

Drawing on feminine caregiving characteristics and their predominance in caring professions have resulted in the association of men with war and women with peace, reinforcing gender hierarchies and false dichotomies that contribute to the devaluation of both women and peace. This has allowed men to remain in control and continue to dominate the agenda of world politics, while women's voices are often seen as inauthentic in matters of foreign policymaking. The essentialist association of women with peace has led to excluding women from politics, denying women agency in political violence, restricting the tools available to women's movements and questioning women's capacity to serve as political leaders (Sjoberg and Tickner 2011).

Feminist Redefinitions of Security

Feminist theorists, by contrast, have embraced alternative conceptions of security, most commonly the notion of 'human security'. This critical human-security approach, as per the feminists, serves as a counter to the selfish pursuit of state or elite security. It emphasizes a view of security in terms of patterns of systemic inclusion and exclusion of people. The twin goals of protection and empowerment (freedom from fear and freedom from want) thus represent the core principles of ensuring survival, meeting basic needs (protecting livelihoods) and safeguarding the human dignity of the most vulnerable groups in society. The emphasis then shifts from a security dilemma of states to a survival dilemma of people. The critical human-security approach proposes to pursue an emancipator agenda and postulate a world that could be otherwise (Hudson 2005; Tickner 2004; Ehrenreich 2011).

Gender and other social hierarchies have effects not only on issues of national security, but also on the workings of the global economy and the uneven distribution of economic rewards, which also affect individual security, particularly the security of those at the margins of global politics.

Gendering the Global Political Economy

Despite enormous differences in the socio-economic status of women, depending on their race, class, nationality and geographic location, women share a certain commonality since they are disproportionately located at the bottom of the socio-economic scale in all societies. Figures vary from state to state but the fact remains that on an average, women earn three quarters of men's earnings even though they work longer hours, many of which are spent in unremunerated reproductive and caring tasks. According to the United Nations Development Fund for Women (UNIFEM 2009), of the 1.3 billion people estimated to be poor today, 70% are women; the number of rural women living in absolute poverty rose by nearly 50% from the mid-1970s to the mid-1990s.

Further, according to the feminist perspective on international political economy (IPE), women working in the wage sector are generally the most poorly paid, and women make up a disproportionate number of those working in the informal sector or in subsistence agriculture. Such areas of the economy are often ignored and a silence about gender occurs because of its invisibility in the concepts used for analysis, questions asked and preferences for the state-level analysis typical of conventional IPE. The feminists thus seek an explanation of the causes of their marginalization and want state policies and structures to be made transparent to them to see how men and women may be rewarded differently as the state pursues gains from the global economy.

Gendered Development

To start with, there was considerable emphasis on the need to 'make women visible'. This need was often raised within international policymaking circles, including the UN and other international organizations such as the World Bank and the Organisation for Economic Co-operation and Development (OECD). The UN Charter (adopted in 1945) recognized equality of the sexes. Yet, only in the 1970s did the UN agenda begin to address the concerns of women. Under pressure from NGOs and aiming to focus attention on the status of women, the General Assembly in December approved the recommendations of the Mexico City conference and declared 1976–1985 to be the UN Decade for Women.

The World Conference on Women at Copenhagen in 1980 aimed to assess the goals so set. Then, in 1981, the UN General Assembly adopted the Convention on the Elimination of All Forms of Discrimination against Women (CEDAW). Finally, the third World Conference on Women at Nairobi in 1985, through its 'Forward Looking Strategies for the Advancement of Women', sought to provide an analytical framework to address the obstacles to the advancement of women (Chen 1995).

The most conspicuous change over the decade was the exponential increase in the number and types of women's NGOs in every country of the world. A notable example is Development Alternatives with Women for a New Era (DAWN), a network of scholars and activities in the South, which articulated alternative development strategies (Chen 1995; Dormandy 1997).

The UN Conference on Human Rights in Vienna in 1993 was determined to make women's rights human rights. Also, feminists active in the campaign to establish the International Criminal Court (ICC) at the turn of the century managed successfully to incorporate violence against women into the agenda of the international legislation on war crimes against humanity. The victories so achieved in this period were consolidated at Beijing and at the UN Conference on Population and Development in Cairo (Coomaraswamy 1996).

The International Conference on Population and Development (ICPD), held at Cairo in 1994, emphasized that 'people are the most important and valuable resource of any nation' and 'the right to development is a universal and inalienable right and an integral part of fundamental human rights' (Sadik 1997). Key to this approach was the empowerment of women, gender equality and equity, reproductive rights and reproductive health (Neidell 1998; Sadik 1997).

Also, the idea of integrating the developing world into aid practice first emerged in the US in the early 1970s. Pressure on US policymakers resulted in the 1973 Percy Amendment to the US Foreign Assistance Act, which required that the United States Agency for International Development (USAID) aid programmes that 'give particular attention to those programme, projects and activities which tend to integrate women into the national economies of foreign countries such that approaches such as "gender and development" (GAD) and "Women and the Environment" (WAE) have crept into the discourse of aid agencies. These efforts have increased recognition of women's role in development and encouraged a more "gender-aware" approach to development' (Koczberski 1998).

The Beijing meet held in 1995 stands out for its reassertion of development for women. In recognizing the link between the economic and the political, it stated that eradication of poverty cannot be accomplished through anti-poverty programmes alone, but will require democratic participation and changes in economic structures in order to ensure access for all women to resources, opportunities and public services (Moghadam 1996; Agnihotri 1996).

However, in spite of examples of progress, many feminists have noted that there are numerous differences in implementing gender-sensitive policies. Aid, while redressing poverty issues, also complicates domestic relationships, for clashes with local customs and laws disrupt the familial balance of power. To add to this, the notion of Western-style capitalism as in the US or Western Europe to be emulated sits poorly with a number of postcolonial feminists, who express concern that persons being developed against their will or towards goals with which they have not agreed perpetuates and mirrors gender subordination (Sjoberg and Tickner 2013).

Historical Foundations of the Gendered Division of Labour

The origin of the contemporary gendered division of labour can be traced to seventeenth-century industrialized Europe, where increase in waged labour, largely performed by men, shifted from homes to factories. Women's work was largely confined to the private, domestic sphere, reinforcing the gendered dimensions of this shift. So even when women do work outside the home for wages, their association with the domestic roles of housewives and caregivers has become institutionalized and naturalized, decreasing their autonomy and economic security.

As a result, when women do enter the workforce, they are disproportionately represented in the caring professions or in light industries where they are poorly paid. Assumptions about gender roles means women are often characterized as supplemental wage earners to the male head of all households. Yet estimates suggest that one third of all households worldwide are headed by women, a fact frequently obscured by role expectations that derive from the notion of male breadwinners and female housewives (Tickner 2008; Sjoberg and Tickner 2013).

Feminist Reinterpretation of Globalization

Gender expectations about appropriate roles for women contribute to low wages and a double burden. Women from the developing countries face greater adverse effects of globalization, for the consumer culture has reduced them to commodities. Owing to their many roles—as would-be mothers, mothers responsible for the health of children and families, working women at home and outside—they are the major consumers of healthcare products, and so the developing countries have become dumping grounds for the banned and restricted products of the developed countries. Of late, many transnational corporations (TNCs) have located their manufacturing plants and industries here due to the easy availability of cheap labour. As producers, women often suffer exploitation in terms of low wages, poor working environment, instability of employment and denial of rights to representation.

No doubt globalization has provided women with greater opportunities, but has also led to gender-based wage differentiation and the marginalization of women, which is closely reflected by the segregation of women workers in certain specific jobs. For example, Mexico's maquilas remained occupationally segregated. In economies with little or no manufacturing, like most of Africa, women remained stuck in subsistence farming. Though the families were paid more for their crops due to the rise in the international prices of commodities, the money continued to be controlled by their husbands. Still today, women do not work in the booming oil, gas or mining fields (Subhalakshmi 2012).

Another common hazard faced by working women is job insecurity, whether it is in the organized, unorganized, small-enterprise or modern sector. The advent of assembly-line jobs and the increased use of machines have further degraded the working conditions for women. Here, workers are paid per piece produced, depending on the speed with which they work, and when a person's compensation is tied to increased physical output, negative health consequences will almost inevitably ensue (Subhalakshmi 2012). Further, as companies have moved towards a more flexible labour force in all parts of the world, cost saving has included hiring home-based workers who are easily hired and fired. Exempt from any national labour standards, the home-based workers are poorly paid and not even paid when there is no work.

One of the best examples is that of women employed in special economic zones (SEZs), specially created geographical areas opened up in large numbers throughout the country. While there is no explicit provision that labour laws would not be applied in these zones, in practice, even labour commissions are not allowed inside these zones and the workers are at the mercy of their employers. One such example is the Noida Export Processing Zone, 24 km from New Delhi, which prefers to hire women as they are more docile and more productive, easier to control and less likely to retaliate against the less ideal working conditions, which thousands of women encounter 12 hours a day. This zone in Noida is dangerous, hot and unsanitary. Unnecessary body searches are routine and complaints of sexual harassment occur frequently. Overtime is compulsory, for which they are paid less than men, and minimum wages are never enforced. There are no maternity benefits—if women marry or become pregnant, they are immediately fired. Those who work in SEZs are more likely to suffer from respiratory problems and pelvic inflammatory diseases, and severe cases of dehydration and anaemia are common (Subhalakshmi 2012). Unemployment, underemployment and temporary work are more common among women than among men. These long-term conditions constitute a serious risk for the workers' emotional capability, because it leads to poverty and deteriorated self-image and self-esteem.

In addition, globalization has created labour patterns which inherently favour short-term, temporary employment, resulting in labour migration with distinct gender-differentiated consequences. Migrant women from developing countries are increasingly victims of trafficking for the purpose of sexual exploitation. Due to the lack of effective international mechanisms that regulate and protect the rights of labour moving across national borders, both legal and illegal migrants are vulnerable to human-rights abuses (Butale 2015).

Finally, neo-liberalism has had little impact for increased political influence, for global economic institutions are not adequately representative. At the policy level, the impact of globalization on women and gender relations continues to be neglected nationally and internationally.

Further, globalization's effect on women rights in religious, conservative countries constitutes another scenario worth examining.

Globalization Effects on Women in Conservative Countries—Case Studies

This section focuses on the Middle East and North Africa (MENA) region, which is constituted of the following countries: Algeria, Bahrain, Djibouti, Egypt, Iran, Iraq, Israel, Jordan, Kuwait, Lebanon, Libya, Malta, Morocco, Oman, Qatar, Saudi Arabia, Syria, Tunisia, the United Arab Emirates (UAE), the West Bank and Gaza, and Yemen. Ethiopia and Sudan are sometimes included as well. Here, the culture of Islam has led societies to be less democratic, less tolerant and more inegalitarian. Though the Quran does not state that women should stay home and look after the children, social policies set by the state impact how women are viewed in society and result in structural gender differences. So the gender gap in the workforce is a result of both economic structure and cultural norms. The Global Gender Gap Report for 2010 reports that the MENA region has the worst gender gap among all regions and has progressed the least in eradicating it over time (Jamal and Milner 2015).

Whether it is oil-rich countries such as Libya, Iraq and Saudi Arabia or countries not as oil-dependent, the MENA region thrives on male-dominated, patriarchal structures where men are the providers for the family. While these countries have a large percentage of university-educated women, most between 70% and 80%, with degrees in the 'soft' sciences, women still face barriers to joining the workforce. Women are often designated to help the family business without pay or resort to traditional markets, domestic service or crafts.

In countries where women are able to gain employment, such as Morocco, they often receive 40% less compensation than men of equal qualification. In addition, they constitute only 28% of the workforce. Often women are not allowed to travel, study or work without a husband's or male guardian's permission and have not been able to register to vote, despite the efforts of the Baladi movement in 2011, especially in Saudi Arabia.

In Egypt, under the military regime, 100 women have reported being sexually assaulted and with no gender equality rule, there is no way for them to file charges. There have been domestic efforts to promote gender quality by way of revolutions such as the Blue Bra movement, which took place after a woman was beaten and stripped in public, exposing her blue bra.

The cultural isolation of radical governments has also affected the public's ability to improve women's participation in the workforce. Through isolation, Muslim radical groups convince the public that outside norms and values are against their religion. Organizations such as Al Qaeda gain power through isolation, making people believe that Allah's way is the only way. One example of women's rights activism in the face of radical Islamist regimes is Malala Yousafzai. Shot by the Taliban for supporting the education of girls in Pakistan, she faced serious repercussions for challenging the traditional regime. Such radical views prevent countries from opening up their societies to international norms and from participating in the economic benefits of globalization.

Further, optimistic social movements can only create a lasting impact on society if they are able to maintain the movement of their ideas into a political structure. For example, in Egypt, the Arab Spring—which reflected a shift in the Middle Eastern public's desire for a change in the government structure, education, economy and women's participation in the workforce—forced the resignation of Hosni Mubarak. But his government was soon followed by the Muslim Brotherhood, a traditional political group that does not support the progressive ideas of the Arab Spring. Rather, the Muslim Brotherhood may be considered a reactionary group to the movement and may reinforce traditional views of women's submissiveness in society. Radical Islamic views could be dissipated if societies were more open through the Internet and social media which had fuelled the Arab Spring, and there is a hope of this for the future. Education reform was also a major goal of the Arab Spring, as realizing their full potential for education is the key for shaping society to promote gender equality (Doumato and Posusney 2003; Jamal and Milner 2015).

The rise of Islamic feminism, a forward-looking movement generated by women to rationalize their activism and employment outside the home—not as a product of changing economic opportunities or an emulation of Western cultural models, but as a product of a true, indigenous Islamic heritage—has to be recognized. Aggressively employed by the newly educated elite, the discourse of Islamic feminism insisted not only religious educated for women but to reinterpret sacred text to their own advantage. They further turned the emphasis on Islamic dress into a vehicle to legitimize their presence in public service, in employment and in educational arenas. For example, in Iran, the imposition of dress codes in the wake of the Iranian Revolution, accompanied an increase in women's employment. Likewise, in Kuwait, where the Islamic members of the National Assemblies were trying to segregate the sexes in university, women students, by adopting conservative dress as a political statement, insisted on their right to choice. In Egypt, the wave of religious conservatism, far from excluding women, heralded women's entrance for the first time into the mosques for prayer and study, while everywhere the Islamist revival sparked a commitment to charitable giving, self-help through women's activist organizations and renewed demands for reformation of family laws (Maarkle 2013). Also, organizations such as the UN, World Bank and USAID have made efforts towards gender equality, but progress is slow. Moreover, cultural perceptions change slowly over time, and implementing reforms would require an extensive timeline (Maarkle 2013).

Feminist theories' one goal, therefore, is to produce knowledge that can help improve women's lives. Some of the improvements are being made by, and on behalf of, women throughout the world.

Using Knowledge to Inform Policy Practices

Women's activism has challenged the hierarchical political structures, as evident at intergovernmental UN conferences, and NGO forums have practised forms of participatory democracy and moved feminist ideas into the policy mainstream of various international organizations. Further, women in NGOs and social movements are playing an important role in pressurizing international organizations and national governments to adopt policies that will further women's equality.

Women's Initiatives to Improve Their Own Lives

SEWA

Other than the various initiatives by the UN, improvement in the lives of women can be attributed to women themselves. One such effort is that of the Self Employed Women's Association (SEWA), a trade union based in India, composed of women engaged in small-scale trade and home-based work. The union, through its organizing and lobbying, put pressure on the International Labour Organization (ILO) to adopt a convention that set international standards for the type of home-based work in 1996.

Microcredit Empowering Women Through Investment

The microcredit lending model was started by a Bangladeshi economist, Muhammad Yunus, in 1976. In this model, the Grameen Bank gave small loans to women because of their better record for investment and repayment (fluctuating between 96% and 100%) than men. This enabled women to gain access to resources, economic security and high status in the household. Moreover, the borrowers also increased the educational and nutritional standards within their families. Since the 1970s, this has been replicated in 40 countries.

Concluding Observations

Feminism is a movement away from historically conventional norms to a more exposed (freedom of expression of decision-making, not marginalized) and equal way of living. The feminism movement, which has been of incredible importance both with its successes and failures, has been a necessary journey for women around the globe so that they may discover and create their unique place in society. Using a number of approaches, this chapter has introduced the ways in which gender has structured world politics. By situating a feminist approach to IR in feminist theory more generally and by offering a feminist definition of gender in international relations, feminists have drawn on a variety of feminist theories to help them understand the invisibility of women in global politics and their relative political and economic disadvantage to men in all societies. Such examination leads to a broader question of how gender shapes and is shaped by world politics. The study of gender as a category of analysis reveals that characteristics associated with masculinity are valued in global politics, especially in matters of national security. The feminist understanding of security, on the other hand, is different, being defined in terms of the physical and economic security of the individual. Evidence suggests that women as a group have suffered certain economic insecurities by virtue of being women, as is pointed out in the explanation of the gendered division of labour. Specifications of men's work and women's work lead to discrimination against women, ensuring women end up in lower-paid, low-status jobs and with a larger share of unremunerated work in the household. Moreover, it has been highlighted by feminists that governments depend upon certain kinds of allegedly private relationships in order to conduct their foreign affairs, that is, they need wives willing to provide their diplomatic husbands with unpaid services so that these men can develop trusting relationships with other diplomatic husbands. The military needs not only hardware, but a steady supply of women's sexual services to convince them they are manly. Also, in the international arena, governments' recognition of their sovereignty is dependent upon the ideas of masculinized dignity to sustain that sense of autonomous nationhood. It is, therefore, important to note that global actors have a gender identity and gender is present in all global processes.

Summary

- The feminist perspective entered the discipline of IR at the end of the 1980s, highlighting that the politics of IR was about much more than inter-state relations. They questioned the limited observable role of women by highlighting that in the public and international spheres, the masculine qualities of rationality, bravery, risk-taking and manliness are emphasized, making women's roles as supporters of peace and self-sacrificing mothers invisible.
- Feminism, a twentieth-century invention, seeks to raise women's social status through demands such as women's elite position in public life, legislation for abortion, ending female circumcision and the abolition of restrictive or demeaning dress codes.
- Gender denotes unequal distribution of social benefits and costs in global politics and economics, particularly with respect to issues of inequality, insecurity and social justice.
- Liberal feminism believes in legal reforms for removing obstacles that deny women equality of opportunity, voting rights and civil rights.
- Radical feminism identifies the patriarchal role as central in sex-based oppression. It is committed to promoting women's culture and amounts to celebrating aspects of femininity associated with the emotional, intuitive, nurturing and passive.
- Socialist feminists do not believe that mere legal reform can redress women's subordination and believe that only through social revolution is women's genuine emancipation possible.
- Postmodern feminism, in its emphasis on the recognition of the existence of complex differences, local diversities and otherness, advocates the abandonment of unity, generality and synthesis.
- Women in NGOs and social movements, informed by feminist knowledge, play an important role in improving their lives themselves.

Suggested Questions

1. How is gender a useful category of analysis in international politics?
2. How can one create dialogue across different IR perspectives? How could non-feminist IR become more concerned with gender?
3. Why are feminists interested in masculinity? Are states and nationalism constructed on the basis of norms of masculinity?
4. Why have feminists argued that war and gender are intrinsically linked?
5. Has economic globalization benefitted or harmed the lives of women?

References

Agnihotri, Indu. 1996. 'The Fourth World Conference on Women: A Report from China'. *Indian Journal of Gender Studies* 3 (1): 111–125.

Arya, Sadhana, Nivedita Menon and Jinee Lokaneeta, eds. 2001. *Feminist Politics: Struggles and Issues*. New Delhi: Hindi Medium Directorate.

Baumgardner, Jennifer, and Amy Richards. 2000 *Manifesta: Young Women, Feminism, and the Future*. New York: Farrar, Straus and Giroux.

Baylis, John, Steve Smith and Patricia Owens, eds. 2008. *The Globalization of World Politics: An Introduction to International Relations*. Oxford: Oxford University Press.

Butale, Cheludo. 2015. 'Globalization and its Impact on Women in Developing Countries'. Accessed 27 April 2018. https://www.iapss.org/wp/2015/03/30/globalization-and-its-impact-on-women-in-developing-countries.

Carlsnaes, Walter, Thomas Risse and Beth A. Simmons. 2013. Handbook of International Relations. London: SAGE Publications.

Chakravarti, Uma. 2001. 'A Note on Patriarchy'. In *Feminist Politics: Struggles and Issues*, edited by Jinee Lokaneeta, Sadhana Arya and Nivedita Menon. New Delhi: Hindi Medium Directorate.

Chen, Martha Alter. 1995. 'Engendering World Conferences: The International Women's Movement and the United Nations'. *Third World Quarterly* 16 (3): 477–493.

Coomaraswamy, Radhika. 1996. 'Reinventing International Law: Women's Rights as Human Rights in the International Community'. *Bulletin of Concerned Asian Studies* 28 (2): 16–26.

Costa, Mariarosa Dalla. 1970. 'The Door to the Garden. Intervention at a Seminar on the History of Operaismo in Rome (2002)', excerpts translated by Arianna Bove and Pier Paolo Frassinell. Accessed 26 April 2018. www.generation-online.org.

DiPalma, Carolyn and Kathy Ferguson. 2010. 'Clearing Ground and Making Connections: Modernism, Postmodernism, Feminism'. In *Handbook of Gender and Women Studies*, edited by Kathy Davis, Mary Evans and Judith Lorber, 127–145. London: SAGE Publications.

Dormandy, Valerie A. 1997. 'Women's Rights in International Law: A Prediction concerning the Legal Impact of the United Nations' Fourth World Conference on Women'. *Vanderbilt Journal of Transnational Law* 30 (1): 97–134.

Doumato, Eleanor Abdella, and Marsha Pripstein Posusney, eds. 2003. *Women and Globalization in the Arab Middle East: Gender, Economy, and Society*. London: Oxford University Press.

Ehrenreich, Barbara. 2011. 'Gender in Global Politics'. In *Global Politics*, edited by Andrew Heywood, 412–431. London: Macmillan Press.

Elshtain, Jean Bethke. 1981. *Public Man, Private Woman: Women in Social and Political Thought*. New Jersey & Princeton: Princeton University Press.

Enloe, Cynthia. 1989. *Bananas, Beaches and Bases: Making Feminist Sense of International Politics*. Berkeley, LA: University of California Press.

Figes, Eva. 1970. *Patriarchal Attitudes: Women in Society*. New York: Stein & Day.

Fraser, Nancy, and Linda J. Nicholson. 1990. 'Social Criticism without Philosophy: An Encounter between Feminism and Postmodernism'. In *Feminism/Postmodernism*, edited by Linda J. Nicholson, 19–38. New York and London: Routledge.

Friedan, Betty. 1963. *The Feminine Mystique*. New York: W.W. Norton & Company.

Gannon, Susanne, and Bronwyn Davies. 2007. 'Postmodern, Poststructural, and Critical Theories'. In *Handbook of Feminist Research: Theory and Praxis*, edited by Sharlene Nagy Hesse-Biber, 71–106. London & New Delhi: SAGE Publications.

Geetha, V. 2002. *Gender*. Kolkata: Stree.

Genz, Stéphanie, and Benjamin A. Brabon. 2011. *Postfeminism: Cultural Texts and Theories*. Jaipur & New Delhi: Rawat Publications.

Goldstein, S. Joshua. 2001. *War and Gender*. Cambridge, UK: Cambridge University Press.

Goldstein, S. Joshua. 2003. *International Relations*, 5th edn. Washington, D.C.: Pearson.

Heywood, Andrew. 1998. *Political Ideologies: An Introduction*, 2nd edn. London: Macmillan.

Hooper, Charlotte. 2000. 'Masculinities in Transition: The Case of Globalization'. In *Gender and Global Restructuring: Sightings, Sites and Resistances*, edited by Marianne H. Marchand and Anne Sisson Runyan, 59–73. London and New York: Routledge.

Hudson, Heidi. 2005. '"Doing" Security as through Humans Matter: A Feminist Perspective on Gender and the Politics of Human Security'. *Security Dialogue* 36 (2): 155–174. Accessed 18 October 2017. http://sdi.sagepub.com/doi/10.1177/0967010605054642.

Jamal, Amaney A., and Helen V. Milner. eds., 2015. 'Women, Patriarchy, and Globalization in MENA: Evidence from Tunisia'. Princeton: Princeton University Press.

John, Mary E. 1999. 'Feminisms and Internationalisms: A Response from India'. In *Feminisms and Internationalism*, edited by Mrinalini Sinha, Donna Guy and Angela Woollacott. Oxford: Blackwell Publishers.

Koczberski, Gina. 1998. 'Women in Development: A Critical Analysis'. *The Third Quarterly* 19 (3): 395–409.

Maarkle, Lindsay. 2013. 'Women and Economic Development in the Middle East and North Africa'. *Student Paper in Public Policy* 1 (1): 1–8.

Mill, John Stuart. 1970. *The Subjection of Women*. London: MIT Press.

Mitchell, Juliet. 1971. *Women's Estate*. London: Penguin.

Moghadam, Valentine M. 1996. 'The Fourth World Conference on Women: Dissension and Consensus'. *Indian Journal of Gender Studies* 3 (1): 93–102.

Mohanty, Chandra Talpade. 1984. 'Under Western Eyes: Feminist Scholarship and Colonial Discourses. On Humanism and the University I: The Discourse of Humanism'. *boundary 2*, 12 (3): 333–358.

Neidell, Shara G. 1998. 'Women's Empowerment as a Public Problem: A Case Study of the 1994 International Conference on Population and Development'. *Public Research and Policy Review* 17 (3): 247–260.

Polak, Michele. 2012. 'The Three Waves of the Feminist Movement (Almost)'. Course material, spring 2012. Accessed 21 October 2017. http://www.michelepolak.com/311spring12/Media_Page_files/3Waves.pdf.

Randall, Vicky. 1982. *Women and Politics: An International Perspective*. London: Macmillan.

Sadik, Nafis. 1997. 'Women, Population and Sustainable Development in South Asia'. *Journal of International Affairs* 51 (1): 147–168.

Sarasvati, Pandita Ramabai. 1981. *The High-Caste Hindu Woman*. Bombay: Maharashtra State Board for Literature and Culture.

Steans, Jill. 2013. *Gender and International Relations: Theory, Practice, Policy,* 3rd edn. Cambridge: Polity Press.

Subhalakshmi, G. 2012. 'Impact of Globalization on Women Workers in India'. IMPOWR, 6 June 2012. Accessed 27 April 2018. http://www.impowr.org/journal/impact-globalization-women-workers-india.

Sjoberg, Laura. 1979. *Gender, Justice, and the Wars in Iraq: A Feminist Reformulation of Just War Theory*. Toronto: Lexington Books.

Sjoberg, Laura, and J. Ann Tickner. 2013. 'Feminist Perspective on International Relations'. In *Handbook of International Relations*. 2nd edn, edited by Walter Carlsnaes, Thomas Risse and Beth A. Simmons. London: SAGE Publications.

Smith, Steve, and Patricia Owens. 2008. 'Alternative Approaches to International Theory'. In *Globalization of World Politics: An introduction to International Relations*, 4th edn., edited by John Baylis, Steve Smith and Patricia Owens, Oxford: Oxford University Press.

Tickner, J. Ann. 2004. 'Feminist Responses to International Security Studies'. Peace Review: A Journal of Social Justice 16 (1): 43–48. Accessed 27 April 2018. http://www.tandfonline.com/doi/full/10.1080/1040265042000210148?src=recsys.

———. 2008. 'Gender in World Politics in the Globalization of World Politics'. In *Globalization of World Politics: An Introduction to International Relations*, 4th edn, edited by John Baylis, Steve Smith and Patricia Owens. Oxford: Oxford University Press.

Whelehan, Imelda. 1995. *Modern Feminist Thought: From the Second Wave to "Post-Feminism"*. Edinburgh: Edinburgh University Press.

Wollstonecraft, Mary. 1972. *A Vindication of the Rights of Women*. Chapter 1, p. 3. Accessed 26 April 2018. shodhganga.inflibnet.ac.in.

Zalewski, Marysia. 2010. 'Feminist International Relations: Making Sense'. In *Gender Matters in Global Politics: A Feminist Introduction to International Relations*, edited by Laura J. Shepherd. London: Routledge.

Further Reading

Beauvoir, Simone de. 1988. *The Second Sex*. London: Picador.

Chakravarti, Uma. 1998. *Rewriting History: The Life and Time of Pandita Ramabai*. New Delhi: Kali for Women.

Chhibber, Bharti. 2009. 'Globalisation and its Impact on Women: A Critical Assessment'. *Mainstream* 47 (21). Accessed 27 April 2018. https://www.mainsttteamweekly.net.

Dahlerup, Drude, and Lenita Freidenvall. 2005. 'Quotas as a "Fast Track" to Equal Political Representation for Women: Why Scandinavia is No Longer the Model'. *International Feminist Journal of Politics* 7 (1): 26–48.

Featherstone, Mike. 1995. *Undoing Cultures: Globalization, Postmodernism and Identity*. London: SAGE Publications.

Flax, Jane. 1990. 'Postmodernism and Gender Relations in Feminist Theory'. In *Feminism/Postmodernism*, edited by Linda J. Nicholson, 39–62. New York and London: Routledge.

Geetha, V. 2007. *Patriarchy*. Kolkata: Stree.

Harding, Sandra. 2007. Feminist Standpoints. In *Handbook of Feminist Research: Theory and* Praxis, edited by Sharlene Nagy Hesse-Biber, 45–69. London and New York: SAGE Publications.

John, Mary E. 1999. 'Feminisms and Internationalisms: A Response from India'. In *Feminisms and Internationalism*, edited by Mrinalini Sinha, Donna Guy and Angela Woollacott, 195–204. Oxford: Blackwell.

MacKinnon, Catharine A. 2007. 'Feminism, Marxism, Method, and the State: An Agenda for Theory'. In *Gender and Feminist Theory in Law and Society*, edited by Madhavi Sunder, 515–536. England: Ashgate.

Menon, Nivedita. 1998. 'Rights, Law and Feminist Politics: Rethinking Our Practice'. In *In the Name of Justice: Women and Law in Society*, edited by Swapna Mukhopadhyay, 15–41. New Delhi: Manohar.

Menon, Nivedita. 2012. *Seeing like a Feminist*. Oxford: Penguin.

Moon, Katharine H. S. 1997. *Sex Among Allies: Military Prostitution in U.S.-Korea Relations*. New York: Columbia University Press.

Shepherd, Laura J., ed. 2010. *Gender Matters in Global Politics: A Feminist Introduction to International Relations*. London and New York: Routledge.

Young, Iris Marion. 1990. 'The Ideal of Community and the Politics of Difference'. In *Feminism/Postmodernism*, edited by Linda J. Nicholson, 300–323. New York and London: Routledge.

Yuval-Davis, Nira. 2009. 'Women, Globalization and Contemporary Politics of Belonging'. *Gender, Technology and Development* 13 (1): 1–19.

15

CHAPTER

United Nations: Structure, Role and Imperative for Reforms

Alisha Dhingra and Rounak Kumar Pathak

LEARNING OBJECTIVES

- To understand the evolution of the United Nations (UN) system in historicity
- To become familiar with the eclectic organizational structure of the UN
- To evaluate the role of the UN in the acquirement of its objectives
- To explain the imperatives for reform in the UN system

In the realm of global politics, the United Nations (UN) as an organization has become reflective of the realities of international politics. The world's political and economic divisions are revealed in the voting arrangements of the Security Council (SC), the blocs and cleavages of the General Assembly (GA), the different viewpoints within the Secretariat, the divisions present at global conferences and in the financial and budgetary processes. Historically, the emergence of the UN in the last phase of the Second World War was intertwined with the experiences of that war and with the failure of the League of Nations, which enjoyed limited admiration from its member states and was unable to prevent the War altogether. However, the UN formed a continuum with the League of Nations in its general purpose, structure and functions; many of the UN's principal organs and related agencies were adopted from similar structures established earlier in the century. In some respects, however, the UN constituted a very different organization, especially with regard to its objective of maintaining international peace and security and its commitment to economic and social development. The Charter of the UN is the founding document of the world organization.

The UN is the only legitimized and mandated global institution that looks into the matters of security, economic and social development, protection of human rights and the protection of the environment.

The UN system consists of various independent, decentralized organizations and programmes, each with its own by-laws, memberships, structure and budget. The UN also provides a forum for its members to express their views in the GA, the SC, the ECOSOC, and other bodies and committees. By enabling dialogue between its members and by hosting negotiations, the organization has become a mechanism for governments to find areas of agreement and collectively resolve problems.

The efficaciousness of UN in the age of globalization has created optimism about the effective role of UN with respect to counter-terrorism, environment, socio-economic aspect, as this function had been implicated by the superpowers' conflict throughout the cold-war period. However, the evolving unipolarity has again raised serious fears and insecurity among weaker nations in the world, who have proposed reforms for the democratic functioning of the UN. Though the UN has not been able to play a very effective role to maintain international peace and security by avoiding conflict and curbing disarmament, its significance in the areas of socio-economic development cannot be undermined nevertheless.

The present chapter begins with a discussion of the prime objectives of UN system. The next section discusses the organizational structure of the UN. This is followed by an analysis of the role played by the UN in fulfilling its objectives of maintaining security through collective security and peacekeeping missions, its role played in the socio-economic sphere and its role in addressing global concerns such as the environment and terrorism. The last section discusses the imperatives as well as processes of reforming the organization in the context of the contemporary global system.

Objectives of UN System

To comprehend the UN, it is necessary to go through the goals, purposes and objectives behind its creation. The very objectives of the UN are enumerated in Article 1 of the Charter, which in turn become obligations on the part of the organization and its member states. Article 1 reads:

The purposes of the United Nations are:

a. To maintain international peace security, and to that end: to take effective collective measures for the prevention and removal of threats to the peace and for the suppression of acts of aggression or other breaches of the peace and to bring about by peaceful means, and in conformity with the principles of justice and international law, adjustments or settlements of international disputes or situations which might lead to a breach of peace;

b. To develop friendly relations among nations based on respect for the principle of equal rights and self-determination of peoples and to take other appropriate measures to strengthen universal peace;

c. To achieve international co-operation in solving international problems of an economic, social, cultural, or humanitarian character and in promoting and encouraging respect for human rights and for fundamental freedoms for all without distinctions as to race, sex, language or religion; and

d. To be a centre for harmonizing the actions of nations of nations in the attainment of these goals. (Gareis and Varwick 2005, 17)

Thus, what can be deciphered from the above is that the primary purpose of the UN is maintaining international peace and security. All the others goals have to be subservient to this primary purpose, thus justifying the creation of this world organization.

Organizational Structure

The UN consists of various decentralized autonomous organizations and programs, each with its own rules and regulations for regulating membership, structures and budget (Figure 15.1). The central international organization, the UN, embraces six principal organs relevant to the decision-making processes, as provided in Article 7 of the UN Charter. The composition, competencies and decision-making processes of these organs are each regulated in separate chapters while their functioning and policy are codified in the respective by-laws. The six primary organs are the GA from Chapter IV of the Charter, the SC from Chapter V of the Charter, the ECOSOC from Chapter X of the charter, the Trusteeship Council from Chapter XIII of the Charter, the International Court of Justice (ICJ) from Chapter XIV of the Charter and the Secretariat from Chapter XV of the Charter. With the exception of the ICJ in The Hague, Netherlands, all principal organs of the organizations are New York-based. Article 7 Clause 2 makes it possible for these organs to create secondary and assistant bodies as they consider it necessary for the fulfilment of the task. The main bodies have made frequent and multifarious use of this right to the extent that there are now hundreds of secondary organs at work worldwide in the form of commissions, boards, standing conferences, funds, offices, high commissioners and missions. For our purpose, it will suffice to have a brief sketch of their functions within the organization and their relationships with one another (Gareis and Varwick 2005).

General Assembly (GA)

To begin with, the GA is the organizational linchpin of the UN. It is the only major body in which all member states of the organization are represented equally. The principle of 'one state, one vote' ensures the same. Moreover, a two-third majority in the GA is required for decisions on key issues such as international peace and security, the admission of new members and the UN budget. A simple majority is required for other matters.

However, the decisions reached by the GA only have the status of recommendations rather than being binding. There were 156 items on the agenda of the 61st session of the GA, including topics such as globalization, international cooperation in the peaceful uses of outer space, peacekeeping operations, sustainable development and international migration, signifying that the GA can consider any matter within the scope of the UN Charter. Although the GA cannot use hard instruments such as sanctions, it does not mean that its decisions and declarations exist without effect. Public pressure, together with the political and moral authority of the world community, has helped countless GA declarations and recommendation to reach near-universal acceptance and promoted the development of political and legal standards worldwide (Gareis and Varwick 2005).

FIGURE 15.1 UN's Organizational Structure

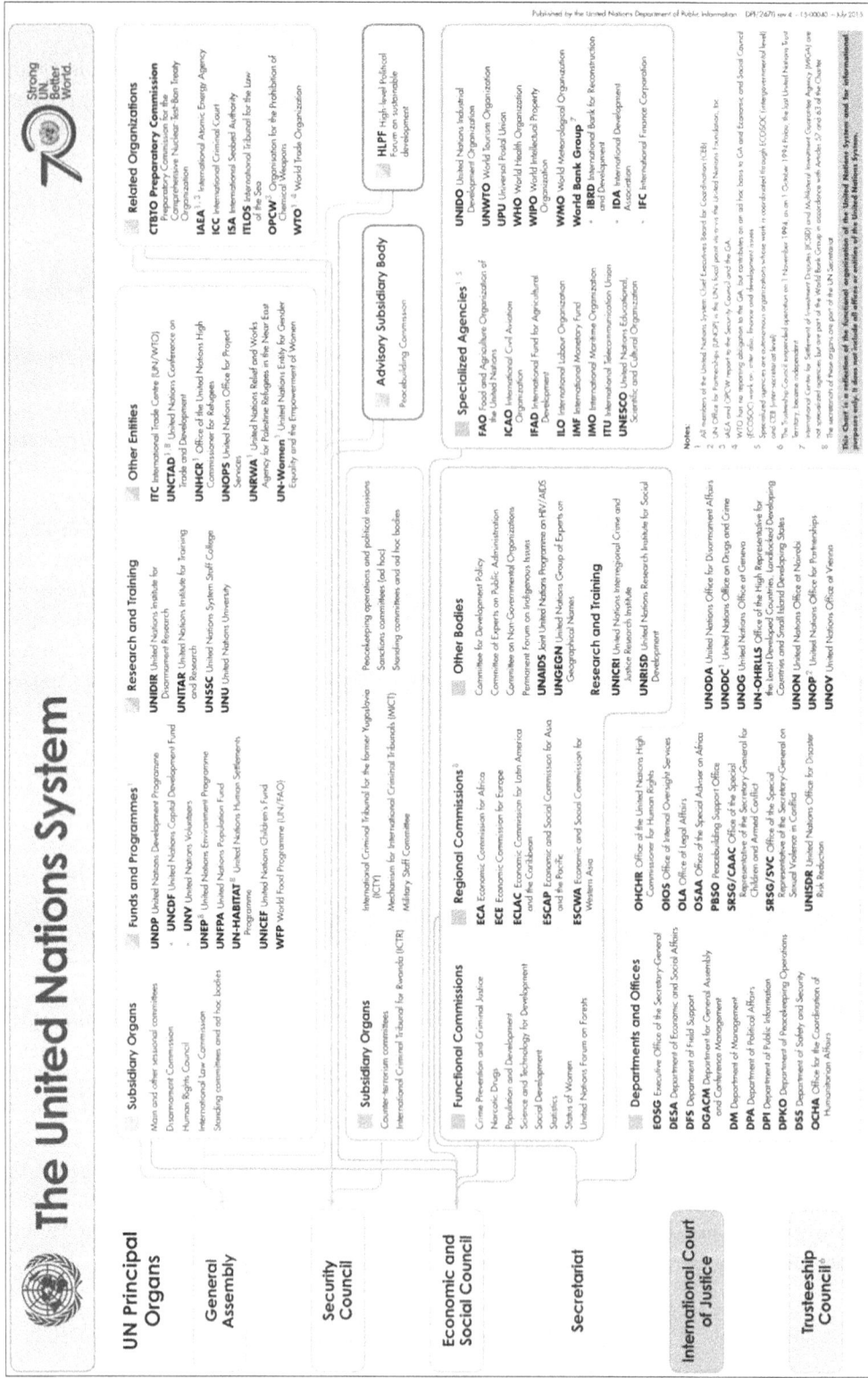

The United Nations System

Strong UN Better World. **70**

UN Principal Organs

General Assembly

Subsidiary Organs
- Main and other sessional committees
- Disarmament Commission
- Human Rights Council
- International Law Commission
- Standing committees and ad hoc bodies

Funds and Programmes
- UNDP United Nations Development Programme
  - UNCDF United Nations Capital Development Fund
  - UNV United Nations Volunteers
- UNEP United Nations Environment Programme
- UNFPA United Nations Population Fund
- UN-HABITAT United Nations Human Settlements Programme
- UNICEF United Nations Children's Fund
- WFP World Food Programme (UN/FAO)

Research and Training
- UNIDIR United Nations Institute for Disarmament Research
- UNITAR United Nations Institute for Training and Research
- UNSSC United Nations System Staff College
- UNU United Nations University

Other Entities
- ITC International Trade Centre (UN/WTO)
- UNCTAD United Nations Conference on Trade and Development
- UNHCR Office of the United Nations High Commissioner for Refugees
- UNOPS United Nations Office for Project Services
- UNRWA United Nations Relief and Works Agency for Palestine Refugees in the Near East
- UN-Women United Nations Entity for Gender Equality and the Empowerment of Women

Related Organizations
- CTBTO Preparatory Commission for the Comprehensive Nuclear-Test-Ban Treaty Organization
- IAEA International Atomic Energy Agency
- ICC International Criminal Court
- ISA International Seabed Authority
- ITLOS International Tribunal for the Law of the Sea
- OPCW Organisation for the Prohibition of Chemical Weapons
- WTO World Trade Organization

Security Council

Subsidiary Organs
- Counter-terrorism committees
- International Criminal Tribunal for Rwanda (ICTR)
- International Criminal Tribunal for the former Yugoslavia (ICTY)
- Mechanism for International Criminal Tribunals (MICT)
- Military Staff Committee
- Peacekeeping operations and political missions
- Sanctions committees (ad hoc)
- Standing committees and ad hoc bodies

Advisory Subsidiary Body
- Peacebuilding Commission

HLPF High-level Political Forum on sustainable development

Economic and Social Council

Functional Commissions
- Crime Prevention and Criminal Justice
- Narcotic Drugs
- Population and Development
- Science and Technology for Development
- Social Development
- Statistics
- Status of Women
- United Nations Forum on Forests

Regional Commissions
- ECA Economic Commission for Africa
- ECE Economic Commission for Europe
- ECLAC Economic Commission for Latin America and the Caribbean
- ESCAP Economic and Social Commission for Asia and the Pacific
- ESCWA Economic and Social Commission for Western Asia

Other Bodies
- Committee for Development Policy
- Committee of Experts on Public Administration
- Committee on Non-Governmental Organizations
- Permanent Forum on Indigenous Issues
- UNAIDS Joint United Nations Programme on HIV/AIDS
- UNGEGN United Nations Group of Experts on Geographical Names

Research and Training
- UNICRI United Nations Interregional Crime and Justice Research Institute
- UNRISD United Nations Research Institute for Social Development

Specialized Agencies
- FAO Food and Agriculture Organization of the United Nations
- ICAO International Civil Aviation Organization
- IFAD International Fund for Agricultural Development
- ILO International Labour Organization
- IMF International Monetary Fund
- IMO International Maritime Organization
- ITU International Telecommunication Union
- UNESCO United Nations Educational, Scientific and Cultural Organization
- UNIDO United Nations Industrial Development Organization
- UNWTO World Tourism Organization
- UPU Universal Postal Union
- WHO World Health Organization
- WIPO World Intellectual Property Organization
- WMO World Meteorological Organization
- World Bank Group
  - IBRD International Bank for Reconstruction and Development
  - IDA International Development Association
  - IFC International Finance Corporation

Secretariat

Departments and Offices
- EOSG Executive Office of the Secretary-General
- DESA Department of Economic and Social Affairs
- DFS Department of Field Support
- DGACM Department for General Assembly and Conference Management
- DM Department of Management
- DPA Department of Political Affairs
- DPI Department of Public Information
- DPKO Department of Peacekeeping Operations
- DSS Department of Safety and Security
- OCHA Office for the Coordination of Humanitarian Affairs
- OHCHR Office of the United Nations High Commissioner for Human Rights
- OIOS Office of Internal Oversight Services
- OLA Office of Legal Affairs
- OSAA Office of the Special Adviser on Africa
- PBSO Peacebuilding Support Office
- SRSG/CAAC Office of the Special Representative of the Secretary-General for Children and Armed Conflict
- SRSG/SVC Office of the Special Representative of the Secretary-General on Sexual Violence in Conflict
- UNISDR United Nations Office for Disaster Risk Reduction
- UNODA United Nations Office for Disarmament Affairs
- UNODC United Nations Office on Drugs and Crime
- UNOG United Nations Office at Geneva
- UN-OHRLLS Office of the High Representative for the Least Developed Countries, Landlocked Developing Countries and Small Island Developing States
- UNON United Nations Office at Nairobi
- UNOP United Nations Office for Partnerships
- UNOV United Nations Office at Vienna

International Court of Justice

Trusteeship Council

Notes:
1. All members of the United Nations System Chief Executives Board for Coordination (CEB).
2. UN Office for Partnerships (UNFIP) is the UN's focal point vis-à-vis the United Nations Foundation, Inc.
3. IAEA and OPCW report to the Security Council and the GA.
4. WTO has no reporting obligation to the GA, but contributes on an ad hoc basis to its work.
5. Specialized agencies are autonomous organizations whose work is coordinated through ECOSOC (intergovernmental level) and CEB (inter-secretariat level).
6. The Trusteeship Council suspended operation on 1 November 1994.
7. The World Bank Group.
8. The secretariats of these organs are part of the UN Secretariat.

This Chart is a reflection of the functional organization of the United Nations System and for informational purposes only. It does not include all offices or entities of the United Nations System.

Source: UN (2015).
Disclaimer: This image is for representation purpose only.

Security Council (SC)

Unlike what existed in League of Nations, the UN recognized, delegated and privileged the SC with great power prerogatives. The SC was given the main responsibility for maintaining international peace and security. Initially, it was made up of 11 states and then, after 1965, of 15 states. It includes five permanent members, namely, the United States of America, the United Kingdom, France, Russia and China, as well as 10 non-permanent members. In contrast with the League's Council, the decisions of the SC are binding and must only be passed by a majority of 9 out of 15 members as well as by each of the five permanent members. These five permanent members therefore have veto power over all SC decisions. It is again necessary here to understand that the five permanent members of the SC were the major powers when the UN was founded and they were granted veto according to the view that if the great powers were not given a privileged position, the operational framework of the UN would not have worked. The 10 non-permanent members are elected by the GA for two-year terms and may not serve two consecutive terms since five non-permanent members' seats are up for election every year. The SC's composition thus changes annually (Baylis, Smith and Owens 2008).

The SC is by far the most powerful among UN bodies and is a unique instrument in international politics as a whole. It derives most of its powers and responsibilities from set of articles. According to article 24, the Charter assigns primary responsibility for world peace & international security. SC carries out administration of this responsibility within the framework of peaceful settlement of disputes as per Chapter 6. It has the power to investigate any situation according to article 34 and may give recommendation for the Peaceful settlement of any dispute determined to have implications for the international peace and security according to article 36. According to article 39, it is for the SC to determine whether situation constitutes a threat to the peace, a breach of the peace or an act of aggression. Should the SC come to such a determination it made and recommend appropriate measures to address the situation it may also itself take measures for the force full execution of its decisions. Number of important decisions especially those of the GA are contingent on an antecedent vote of the SC (Gareis and Varwick 2005).

Economic and Social Council (ECOSOC)

The ECOSOC, under the umbrella of the GA (because its capacity is limited and subject to the authority of the GA), is intended to coordinate the economic and social work of the UN and the UN's family of organizations. It is the sole prerogative of the ECOSOC to ensure a vital link between the UN and civil society. Together with the GA, it performs those tasks in the economic and social realms as are mentioned and outlined in Chapter IX of the Charter. In accordance with these tasks, its system of regional representation is weighted towards developing countries (Gareis and Varwick 2005).

The ECOSOC is responsible for overseeing the activities of a large number of other institutions in UN. This includes the specialized agencies, programmes and funds. The specialized agencies, such as the World Health Organization (WHO) and the International Labour Organization (ILO), have their own constitutions, regularly assessed budgets, executive heads and assemblies of state representatives. In accordance with the goals of the UN expressed in Article 1 Clause 3 and the concerns listed in Article 55, the ECOSOC concerns itself primarily with questions of development in poor countries.

Secretariat

Reading Article 97 of the UN Charter, one can infer that the Secretariat is the main administrative organ of the UN. It is composed of the Secretary-General and any other public servant the organization requires. The Secretary-General is chosen by the GA on the recommendation of the SC. That way, neither of those organs has full control over the decision of naming a candidate. The Secretariat carries out the substantive and administrative work of the UN as directed by the GA, the SC and other organs. On the recommendations of other bodies, the Secretariat also carries out a number of research functions and some quasi-management functions. The role of the Secretariat remains primarily bureaucratic and it lacks political powers and the right of initiative of, for instance, the Commissioner of the European Union (EU). The one exception to this is the power of the Secretary-General under Article 99 of the Charter to bring situations that are likely to lead to a breakdown of international peace and security to the attention of the SC (Gareis and Varwick 2005).

Trusteeship Council

Of all the principle organs of the UN system, the Trusteeship Council is the only one to have suspended its original responsibility. This occurred following the transition of the last Trustee territory to independence and that was Palau of the Pacific Islands, which was previously administered by the US. Having completed its work, it now consists of the five permanent members of the SC. It has amended its rules of procedure to allow it to meet when necessary (Baylis, Smith and Owens 2008).

International Court of Justice (ICJ)

The ICJ in Hague is the primary judicial organ of the UN under Article 92 and comprises 15 independent judges. The judges are appointed through a procedure involving both the SC and the GA. Participation in the proceedings by states is voluntary but if a state agrees to participate, it is obligated to comply with the court's decision. This court also provides advisory opinion to other UN organs and specialized agencies upon request. Thus, every state that signs the UN Charter automatically becomes a party to the ICJ. The role of the ICJ cannot be compared to that of a domestic court. There is no international law, no legal rules from which an obligatory international jurisdiction could be inferred. On the contrary, the cooperative nature of international law would seem to require that any subjection to an international court must arise from an agreement among all the parties. Even if one state is unwilling to submit itself, the ICJ cannot take action in a dispute. Furthermore, the judgement of the ICJ is binding only on the parties to the dispute (Gareis and Varwick 2005).

Role of UN

A Stagnant Start

In the summer of 1941, US president Franklin Roosevelt proposed to the British prime minister Winston Churchill that a security organization for monitoring the concerned enemy states should be set up and that this organization should not belong to the US alone but should be led by the US in concert with the

UK. Churchill anticipated problems from the rest of the states over an organization led by two powers only. He therefore supported some version of a further-developed League of Nations with a strengthened representation for the various regions of the world. In the Atlantic Charter, presented by Roosevelt and Churchill on 14 October 1941, the functional tasks of the future order of world peace were outlined clearly but the organization that was to create this world order was mentioned only indirectly in its eighth point:

> Since no future peace can be maintained if land, sea or air armaments continue to be employed by nations which threaten or may threaten aggression outside of their frontiers, they believe, pending the establishment of a wider permanent system of general security that the disarmament such nations is essential. (Gareis and Varwick 2005, 5)

After the entry of the US into the Second World War, in the UN declaration of 1 January 1942, a further 26 countries joined the Atlantic Charter, obligating themselves at the same time to support the alliance against Germany, Italy and Japan. This declaration too avoided a concrete announcement of the creation of an institution. The self-definition of this group as the 'United Nations' was, however, to become the name of the institution (Ibid.).

In the Yalta Conference in February 1945, the voting procedure in the SC was arranged in such a manner that for non-procedural questions, a quorum of 7 out of 10 votes, including all five permanent members, was necessary. This Yalta formula formed the basis of the permanent members' right to veto. After that agreement, four of the five permanent members invited the 45 states that had opposed Germany and Japan in the world to the founding conference of the UN in San Francisco. Poland was allowed to enter as the 51st founding member once its political representation was sorted out to the satisfaction of the Union of Soviet Socialist Republics (USSR) (Baylis, Smith and Owens 2008).

The UN exhibited much stronger egalitarian tendencies and characteristics, borrowed from the League of Nations, than Roosevelt had intended. This evolution from an efficiently run security institution to an inter-state organization with a broad spectrum of tasks was also carried along by the growing recognition—expressed early on by Churchill—that the level of agreement necessary among the permanent five for the sake of world peace would in fact be nearly impossible to achieve. The growing contradiction between the democratic and the socialist camps shadowed the negotiation for the UN. Rather than burdening themselves with such responsibility, the great powers vehemently focused on making it impossible for the rules of the collective security system to be used against them. During the cold war, this led to stagnation in important areas such as the SC (Moore and Pubantz 2008).

Several of the organizational decisions in this initial phase of UN activity after its formation were already showing signs of the influence of the growing East–West conflict. In view of the West's clear majority in the GA, where there was of course no veto, that bloc was able to push through many of its programmes. The situation was different, however, in the SC. There, vetoes and threats of vetoes were persistently present in every discussion. In the SC, it became very clear just how parochial the justification for Roosevelt's optimism about the responsibilities of the global police force had really been.

UN's Collective Security

During the initial days, the case of Korea was primarily an indication of the effects of the cold war on the UN. After the Second World War, parts of the Korean Peninsula were occupied by the US (south) and Soviet military forces (north). The GA had first considered the question of Korea at its session in 1947, but in vain. The GA called for withdrawal of all foreign troops, however, again in vain. Around June

1950, the USSR found itself at war with the UN. The invasion of South Korea by North Korea (having the support of the USSR), triggered a UN decision to use force to repel the attack. The US' push for the GA to make recommendations on the restoration of peace and security further aggravated the situation as the Council was deadlocked by veto. The Korean War ended with an armistice in 1953; however, it was seen was as a hot war in the larger context of the global cold war, with the UN's collective security challenged (Moore and Pubantz 2008).

The Korean crisis had proved to be an ordeal that cast a shadow over the collective security system of the UN for the first time. It actually raised eyebrows over whether or not the collective security would survive. Perceiving the North Korean invasion of South Korea as a threat to its security during the cold war, the UN collective security system then just became the basis of American security. The US fought wars in the name of the UN and 90% of the UN forces were contributed by the US. Consequently, the US took the decision to use collective security where its own interests were at stake (Jindal 1994). This clearly enforced the realist arguments that the principal actors were mostly concerned with their own security, in this case essentially the US, and acting in pursuit of their own national interests, eventually struggling for power.

Another noteworthy event in the context of collective security was the Cuban Missile Crisis. During the 1961–1962 Cuban Missile Crisis, the UN was largely powerless. Although the GA called its second emergency special session because of the Soviet veto in the SC and that session produced a number of declarations and recommendations, it could not influence the course of events and was unable to prevent a deadlock. During this time, Secretary-General U Thant sought to bring both sides closer together without a loss of face. Nevertheless, it was clear that it had become impossible for an organization such as the UN to act as a mediator between the superpowers (Gareis and Varwick 2005).

The 1990–1991 Gulf War for the liberation of Kuwait, conducted on the basis of a SC mandate, fuelled hope for a new world order built on the foundations of the UN. The war was as much a false dawn for the post-cold war UN as Korea had been at the start of the cold war. In both cases, the US took the decision to use collective security as its own interests were at stake. In Korea, the US could take such a decision due to the abstention of the USSR from the UN meetings and in the Gulf war (1991) the US could take the decision due to the end of the cold war and emerging globalization in an unipolar world under US leadership (Jindal 1994). Moreover, the UN's utility to the US in the post-cold war world required that its core principle of state sovereignty be scrapped. In this context, during the 1990s, the US and its European colleagues sought to reframe the traditional discourse of the UN where it was being argued that sovereignty was something that could not be revoked by the international community (Gowan 2010).

Furthermore, over a decade later, the kind of developments that were taking place in Iraq in 2003, especially the alleged possession of weapons of mass destruction, compelled the US to argue for the invasion of Iraq. But the major motive was to topple the regime of Saddam Hussein. Around this time, Iraq had also failed to comply with multiple UN SC resolutions, continuously committed gross abuses of the human rights of its own citizens and had alleged links with the terrorist organizations. Consequently, the US and the UK sought, but ultimately failed to secure, a mandate from the SC for interventions and invasion. The two countries proceeded nonetheless against the UN system and invaded Iraq on 21 March 2003 (Dobbins et al. 2005).

The Soviet invasion of Afghanistan in 1979 had made clear to the world the narrowness and the limits of the UN's collective security system. The SC was gridlocked and while the urgently called special emergency session of the GA condemned the aggression, it was still essentially powerless. The UN's fourth decade had begun with a hopeful explosion of multilateralism and cooperation, but as both sides of the North–South conflict continued to intensify, the political ideological opposition and the North Atlantic

Treaty Organization's (NATO's) decision to catch up on nuclear armaments led to a dramatic worsening of relations between East and West, the UN was left with very little room to manoeuvre (Gareis and Varwick 2005).

UN and Its Peacekeeping Missions

A remarkable achievement on the part of the UN was the development of peacekeeping forces whose existence was not even envisaged in the original charter. The first ever use of them, with the name UN Emergency Force 1 (UNEF 1), took place in the Gaza strip and Sinai in 1956. This marked the beginning of the single physical manifestation of the UN's role in the world (Nambiar 1995).

The remarkable efforts of the UN towards its peacekeeping objectives continued to rise. In the years following 1975, there was no attempt by the Western countries, such as the US, to capture the oil resources on which they were heavily dependent, a credit to the UN system. Also, the UN was very critical of the Soviet intervention in Afghanistan in 1979 and of the use of force by Argentina (then a member of the Group of 77, or G-77) in its Falklands (Malvinas) invasion in 1982. Furthermore, the UN heavily condemned the US-led invasion of Grenada in 1983 (Roberts and Kingsbury 1994).

The number of new peacekeeping missions matched the number of newly emerging forms of conflict that began to appear all over the world following the end of the all-encompassing cold war. Within the space of approximately 15 years, the number of peacekeeping missions rose from 14 to 47. New tasks in the areas of post-conflict management or transitional situations required new concepts but attempts at peace enforcement such as those in Somalia and Yugoslavia proved more difficult (Nambiar 1995).

Furthermore, since the end of the cold war, the UN has increased its activities in the maintenance of international peace and security in its pursuit of the objective of peacekeeping. The number of UN peacekeeping operations deployed increased from 5 in 1988 to 11 in 1992 and 16 in 1995 (Nambiar 1995).

Changing Balance in the GA

The independence of numerous countries, particularly in the southern hemisphere, was undoubtedly a decisive phenomenon in the second decade of the UN's existence. Consequently, the affairs of these new states began to take up a pivotal space in the works of the UN—its funded programmes and in its specialized agencies. The changing balance of the majorities in the GA ensured that the interest of the developing countries would be taken into account appropriately in the organizational and institutional development of the UN. The establishment of a number of subsidiary organs focused in particular on development issues, beginning in 1961. The UN initiated its first development decade, which was followed immediately by a second starting in 1971. The GA's recognition of the communist People's Republic of China (PRC) on 25 October 1971 can be seen as an important step on the part of UN (Gareis and Varwick 2005).

UN and the Road to NIEO

The North–South conflict, in which questions of a just world economic order and a balancing of the interests of the industrialized and developing countries stood at the top of the agenda, began to have phases where it overshadowed even the East–West conflict. Besides basic demands for a new international economic order, these states' efforts found their most potent expression in the Charter of Economic Rights and Duties of States adopted by the GA in 1974 (Ibid.).

It is worth noting here the creation of the UN Conference on Trade and Development (UNCTAD) in the year 1964 as a permanent intergovernmental body. Its creation was based on the concerns of developing countries over the international market, multinational corporations (MNCs) and the great disparity between developed nations and developing nations. UNCTAD provided a forum where developing countries could discuss the problems relating to their economic development. Later, in the 1970s and 1980s, UNCTAD became inextricably intertwined with the New International Economic Order (NIEO) (UNDPI 2008).

UN and Disarmament

The cold war also brought along with it the race to expand arms arsenals, especially between the two superpowers. Thus, the GA endeavoured to limit the use of arms to specified geographical areas. Consequently, a number of collateral agreements were reached, with the principal aim of curbing the expansion of the arms race in areas to which it had not yet extended. Nonetheless, these treaties produced no actual reductions in weapons, and global military expenditures did continue to rise. In 1969, the GA declared the 1970s the First Disarmament Decade and asked members to intensify their efforts to curb the arms race, especially nuclear arms and non-nuclear weapons of mass destruction (WMDs) (UN Office for Disarmament Affairs 2018).

Two important special sessions of the GA on disarmament took place in 1978 and 1982. Also, the declaration of the 1980s as the Second Disarmament Decade by the UN boosted the ultimate objective of the disarmament process. However, during the years immediately after the special session, the international climate was aggravated as the US and the USSR came to loggerheads again and again, leading to an increase in military expenditure and further expansion of nuclear arsenals (UN 2018).

UN as Global Guardian of Public Health

The UN has been the global guardian of public health as well. Since its foundation, it has been vigorously engaged in promoting and protecting good health worldwide. The chief agent for this purpose within the UN system is the WHO, whose constitution was enforced on 7 April 1948, a date which is now celebrated every year as World Health Day. In 1948, the WHO took over responsibility for the International Classification of Diseases (ICD), which has developed into the international standard for defining and reporting diseases and health conditions. At its inception, malaria, women's and children's health, tuberculosis, nutrition and environmental pollution were listed by the WHO as its top priorities. New diseases such as HIV/AIDS, diabetes, cancer and emerging diseases such as SARS (severe acute respiratory syndrome), Ebola and the Zika virus have been added to the agenda of the WHO (UNESCO 2018).

UN and the Convention on Education

In 1960, the United Nations Educational, Scientific and Cultural Organization (*UNESCO*) adopted the Convention against Discrimination in Education, which recognizes the vital role of education in guaranteeing equality of opportunity for members of all racial, national or ethnic groups. It was the first time that a mandatory instrument in the UN system enclosed a comprehensive definition of the term 'discrimination'.

The Convention defines 'discrimination' as 'any distinction, exclusion, limitation or preference based on race, color, sex, language, religion or political or other opinion, national or social origin, economic condition or birth'. The Convention calls on states to adopt immediate measures in favour of equality in education and links the concept of education directly to human rights (UNESCO 2018). Decades later, UNESCO launched the Global Education First Initiative (GEFI) in 2012. This reflects its vision that education is the best mechanism to deal with poverty, improve health and well-being, generate growth and promote responsible citizenship (UNESCO 2018).

UN and Its Endeavours in Economic and Social Development

The GA in 1979 adopted the Convention on the Elimination of All Forms of Discrimination Against Women (CEDAW), which is often described as an international bill of rights for women. CEDAW is the sole human-rights treaty which avows the reproductive rights of women. It upholds women's rights to acquire, change or retain their nationality and the nationality of their children. It requires the member states to adopt appropriate measures against all forms of trafficking in women and exploitation of women. Countries that have ratified CEDAW are legally committed to implement its provisions. They are also bound to submit national reports at least every four years, detailing actions they have taken to conform to their treaty obligations (UN Women 2018).

World conferences on every imaginable global issue have followed one another in rapid succession, from the Rights of the Child in New York, 1991, to Sustainable Development and Production of the global environment in Rio de Janeiro, 1992, from human rights in Vienna, 1993, to women's rights in Beijing, 1995, and all the way to world population in Cairo, 1999 (Gareis and Varwick 2005). Also, one of the UN global conferences, the World Summit for Social Development in Copenhagen 1995 marked the first time that the international community came together to initiate the struggle against poverty, unemployment and social disintegration in order to create awareness for the social responsibility (UNDPI 2008).

BOX 15.1:   Commission on the Status of Women

The Commission on the Status of Women (CSW) is the primary global intergovernmental body working towards the advancement of gender equality and empowerment of women. This commission was established by the ECOSOC Resolution 11 (II) of 1946. It comprises a total of 45 members elected on the basis of equitable geographic distribution. All the permanent members with the exception of China have participated in the Commission almost continuously from its beginning until 1993. For the period 1984–1993, permanent members averaged 8.6 years of participation, whereas the remaining members averaged a total of 3.7 years.

Source: Bourantonis (2007).

The United Nations Development Programme (UNDP) has been actively working on migration and displacement issues, forging partnerships between humanitarian and development actors to find durable solutions at the local and national level. This includes preventing and mitigating conflicts, improving governance and access to justice, fighting poverty, providing jobs and opportunities and implementing well-managed migration policies, all in line with the new Sustainable Development Goals (SDGs) (UN Department of Public Information 2018).

The GA in 2013 hosted a High-level Dialogue on International Migration and Development and in 2014 held a special session on the implementation of the Programme of Action of the International Conference on Population and Development, which were significant occasions for member states to harness the benefits of migration, to address migration challenges and to improve the global governance of migration.

UN and the Environment

First UN conference on environment in Stockholm in 1972 culminated in the creation of the United Nations Environmental Programme (UNEP) and a host of conferences on various environmental issues such as population, marine and atmospheric pollution, deserts and food, technology and energy (Leftwich 2000, 57).

The GA in 1983 set up an independent commission chaired by Gro Harlem Brundtland (former prime minister of Sweden), the World Commission on Environment and Development (WCED). The commission submitted its report in 1987, in which it came up with the definition of 'sustainable development', which was both economical and elegant and came to be accepted worldwide. The report laid out principles for the guidance of policy at both national and international levels. These were:

- to promote growth that would reflect sustainability, equity, social justice and security
- to protect resource bases
- to ensure a sustainable level of population
- to adapt and reorient technology, considering its environmental impact
- to ensure that environmental issues were integral to policymaking
- to enhance international relations and cooperation (Leftwich 2000, 57)

UN Against Terrorism

With the disintegration of the USSR and the demise of the cold war, the UN has since taken a proactive role in tacking terrorism. The GA has developed a normative framework that defines terrorism as a common problem and has encouraged concerted government action to develop both international and national rules and laws for dealing with terrorists.

The GA in its 49th session in 1994 passed Resolution 49/60, titled 'Declaration on Measures to Eliminate International Terrorism', which was adopted in February 1995. The contents of this resolution became the guidelines and polices for every nation for combating terrorism both domestically and internationally. For further details on this resolution, refer to Chapter 10.

In the aftermath of 11 September 2001, the SC took swift and unprecedented action and recognized in Resolution 1368 'the inherent right of individual or collective self-defence in accordance with the

Charter' (US Department of State Archive 2018). Though the SC viewed the attacks of 11 September, or 9/11, as threats to international peace and security, it did not call for collective action. Rather it invoked a state's right to self-defence and thus handed over the responsibility to individual states.

On 9 January 2003, the GA passed a resolution asking states to adopt measures to prevent terrorists from acquiring WMDs and nuclear weapons, under the title 'Measures to prevent terrorists from acquiring weapons of mass destruction'. Subsequently, the GA adopted the International Convention for the Suppression of Acts of Nuclear Terrorism on 13 April 2005.

In the course of time, the UN has evolved its strategy to fight international terrorism, which was detailed in its resolution on 13 October 2010, titled the 'United Nations Global Counter-Terrorism Strategy'. This resolution recommended measures to address the conditions conducive to the spread of terrorism and to prevent and combat terrorism (US Department of State Archive 2018).

UN's Millennium Development Goals and Sustainable Development Goals

Adoption of the Millennium Declaration at the Millennium Summit in New York, 2000, led to the establishment of eight Millennium Development Goals (MDGs) that all UN members pledged to achieve by 2015. These MDGs ranged from bringing down extreme poverty rates to preventing the spread of HIV/AIDS and ensuring the assimilation of universal primary education. A blueprint was agreed to by all the world's countries and the entire world's leading development institutions for the achievement of the MDGs (Figure 15.2). This galvanized unprecedented efforts to meet the needs of the poorest of the world. One of the key achievements has been lifting 1 billion people out of extreme poverty since 1990. The UN is in this context working with governments, civil society and other partners to build on the momentum generated by the MDGs and to carry on with an ambitious post-2015 framework (UN Development Programme 2018).

Although the achievement of the MDGs do offer important lessons to learn from and experience with which to begin work on the new goals, yet for millions of people around the world, the work remains unfinished. Hence, the UN system needed to go an extra mile in ending hunger, achieving full gender equality, improving health services and getting every child into school beyond the primary years. In this context, the Sustainable Development Goals (SDGs) became an urgent call to shift the world onto a more sustainable path (UN Development Programme 2018).

UN member states adopted the 2030 Agenda for Sustainable Development at the Sustainable Development Summit on 25 September 2015. This agenda includes a set of 17 SDGs, which include new areas such as climate change, economic inequality, innovation, sustainable consumption, and peace and justice, among other priorities (UN Development Programme 2018).

It is noteworthy that nearing the beginning of the new millennium, the UN put poverty reduction at the top of the international agenda when it proclaimed 1997–2006 the International Decade for the Eradication of Poverty.

FIGURE 15.2 Millennium Development Goals

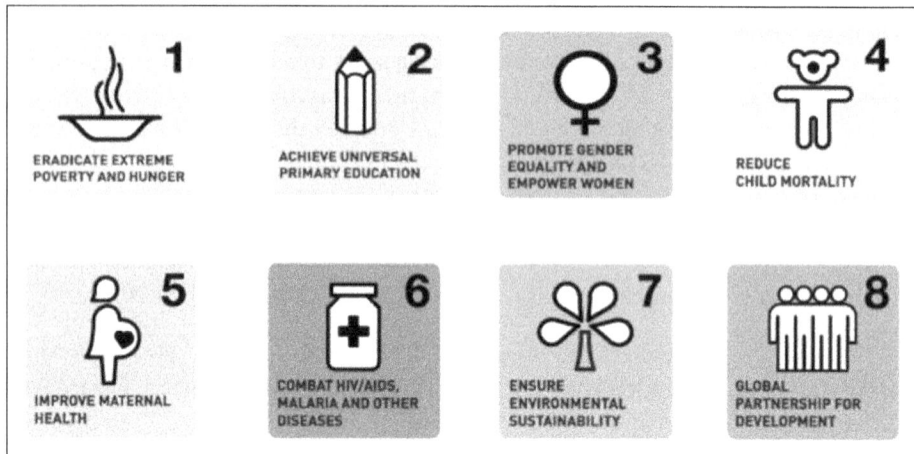

Reforming Organization

The Kosovo crisis of March 1999, the 9/11 attack on US of 2001, the US action against Afghanistan in 2001 and the 2003 war in Iraq proved that fundamental reform of the UN's decision-making structures and its operational framework have become a sine qua non for the UN system.

The UN has been unable to live up to the ideal envisioned at the time of its origin. Maurice Bertrand has argued that it has played only a minor role in the maintenance of peace and has only a limited impact in resolving economic and social problems that are global in nature. He notes that there is a lot of pessimism about the effectiveness of the UN, but there has also been growing interest in its revitalization. He raises the question of whether the UN can be reformed. He responds in the negative and believes that the UN is unable to rectify its managerial and structural deficiencies. There are many constraints that hamper its recovery. These are: lack of coordination between agencies due to structural decentralization, an innovation-resistant Secretariat, the indulgence of the Secretary-General on political problems while ignoring managerial and economic problems, pressure from all the countries for appointment of their nations to high positions in the UN regardless of their qualifications and the impossibility of modifying the Charter due to the pursuance of divergent interests by its member states (Bertrand 1993).

The history of the UN has been a continuous process of change and reform. With the end of the cold war, a debate regarding reform of the organization ensued. The debate can be analysed in terms of two opposing camps. The first camp consisted of the members of the Non-Aligned Movement (primarily drawn from a group of developing countries), who were perturbed by the re-emergence of the SC and their own weakening influence. Therefore, they started pushing harder than ever before for enlarging opportunities to enhance their participation in the decision-making processes of the organization as well as for greater consultation in the Bretton Woods Institutions, which are largely dominated by the industrialized countries. The second camp consisted of the industrialized states, most prominently the US. This camp criticized the UN for its lack of effectiveness and demanded more streamlined, transparent and cost-effective structures. The first camp realized that this 'effectiveness' argument was nothing but a veneer under which the industrialized nations were trying to instrumentalize the UN for the pursuance of their own interests (Garies and Varwick 2005, 214–216).

Thus, it can be seen that though both the developed and developing countries were emphasizing the need for reforms, they were basing their demand on two entirely differing principles of participation and efficiency. While the developing nations were interested to increase their participation and make the UN more democratic and accountable, the developed nations on the other hand were emphasizing making it more effective and cost-efficient by removing managerial deficiencies.

Institutional Reforms

On 19 November 1996, the US used its veto power to prevent the re-election of Secretary-General Boutros Boutros-Ghali on the grounds that he had proved himself incapable of reforming the apparatus of the UN. Despite this, we can trace the first signs of successful streamlining and modernization of the management and labour structures to Boutros-Ghali's term. In order to make it cost-efficient, 2,500 positions in the Secretariat were cut and yearly spending increases were halted. A new Integrated Management Information System was introduced in order to facilitate a networked, computer-supported personnel, issue- and budget-administration. A new performance appraisal system was introduced for better evaluation of individual performance; this provided a significant impetus to the organization's human resource management, which is especially dependent on the quality and motivation of personnel. In 1994, at the urging of the Secretary-General, the GA created the Office of Internal Oversight Services (OIOS) headed by the Inspector General, which subjected UN to the internal review for the first time in its history (Garies and Varwick 2005, 219).

Kofi Annan, who succeeded Boutros-Ghali, entered the office under a great deal of pressure to reform the organization. He was able to reorganize the Secretariat as early as March 1997, by assigning one of the five core tasks of the UN to each of the departments as well as some of the subsidiary organs and programmes run by the Secretariat. Executive committees were formed for each of four fields: Peace and Security, Economic and Social Issues, Humanitarian Affairs, and Development; the area of Human Rights Protection was designated to cut across and touch upon all the other four areas. He presented a reform programme for the renewal of the UN in July 1997, which consisted of a list of decisions which amounted to a 'quiet revolution'. The only thing absent from the list was reform of the SC (Garies and Varwick 2005, 220).

In order to bring about a new leadership and management culture, a Senior Management Group composed of 29 members was created as a kind of cabinet chaired by the Secretary-General and composed of convenors of the executive committees and other senior managers of the UN system. For the purpose of antedating global trends and forthcoming challenges, a Strategic Planning Unit composed of five experts was created to function as the personal labour staff of the Secretary-General. Other important reforms were the creation of a new department for disarmament and arms control in the Secretariat and strengthening of the office of the High Commissioner for Human Rights by its integration into the UN Centre for Human Rights. This reform package was rounded out by further reduction of the Secretariat's personnel by 1,000 posts as well as a 5% reduction of the budget (Ibid.).

The GA in its Resolution 52/12B of 19 December 1997 passed two recommendations by Annan: first, the creation of the office of a Deputy Secretary-General, relieving the Secretary-General of much of the administrative work and, second, the creation of a Development Account into which the internal savings were to flow as a 'development dividend'. Some of Annan's recommendations were not implemented:

supplementary financing of the UN's running costs through a 'revolving credit fund', reduction of the Secretariat's workload through the automatic expiration of mandates that had not been formally renewed (the 'sunset clause') and the reintroduction of the original division of labour among the main bodies which would have reduced the influence of the GA over the daily work schedule of the Secretariat (Garies and Varwick 2005, 220–221).

Analysing the institutional reforms, Garies and Varwick conclude that the Secretariat and its subsidiary bodies are inclined to and capable of significant reform in order to adjust their competences and capacities to the emerging challenges; but the member states, in contrast, lack the will and capacity to reach an agreement on those areas of reform for which their consensus is indispensable (Garies and Varwick 2005, 221).

Financial Reforms

With regard to finance reform, the only accomplishment that the member states can be credited with is the reorganization of the contribution scale for the regular budget and the peacekeeping activities. After years of harrowing negotiations, in December 2004, a solution was found that took into consideration both the US' wish to reduce its contributions and the realistic financial capacities of the underdeveloped countries. The gamut of contributions ranges from 0.001% of the programme budget, which was a total of $14.36 in 2004, to the 22% that the US is obliged to provide. The contributions must be paid on time and in full without exceptions (Garies and Varwick 2005, 221).

The contributions for peacekeeping organizations are in addition to those for the regular budget. These contributions are made on the basis of a roster with 10 categories that provide differentiated rebates of up to 90% of contributions. Garies and Varwick point out that though this agreement has had a lasting impact on the stabilization of the UN finances, such an agreement is an exception to the general rule of the member states' inability to reach compromises on the crucial matters of an organization's future. A perfect example of this rule is the issue of the modernization of the SC, which has been floating around unsettled for years (Garies and Varwick 2005, 222).

Reforming the Security Council

The modernization of the most influential body of the UN constitutes one of the greatest challenges confronting the organization and can be viewed a decisive test of its capacity for comprehensive reform of any kind. With the renewed significance of the SC in the post-cold war era, booming voices came both from significant financial contributors such as Japan and Germany as well as the Non-Aligned Movement for the modification of the SC's composition, decisional mechanisms and operating procedures. These attempts were different from the earlier initiatives since they aimed not only at the addition of non-permanent members but also demanded changes to the permanent members' circle (Ibid.).

The privileges that the permanent members enjoy through their membership are considered inappropriate in present times. The colossal changes over the last few decades, the process of decolonization, the appearance of new states and the end of the cold war have made the power distribution in the SC incompatible with the new global order. The new global order has been marked by the emergence of new political groupings and new forms and centres of conflict. The African and Latin American continents are unrepresented among the permanent members whereas the entire Asiatic region is represented by one country, that is, China (Garies and Varwick 2005, 223).

India proposed a resolution for the reform of the SC, which the GA passed in November 1992. In the resolution, it was determined that the 48th GA (1993–1994) should concern itself with a comprehensive discussion of the issue (Ibid.). Though there is widespread agreement on the need for reform of the SC and the recent years have witnessed a great deal of convergence in positions of various states, the realization of these reforms is nowhere in sight. This stalemate is because of an unresolved matter, that is, the issue of who should be admitted as a permanent member.

Concluding Observations

The UN is a reflection of the realities of international politics, and the world's political and economic divisions are revealed in the voting arrangements of the SC, the blocs and cleavages of the GA, the different viewpoints within the Secretariat, the divisions present at global conferences, and the financial and budgetary processes. As the member states try to promote their national interests, the actions and policies of the organs and specialized agencies of the UN are at times criticized for promoting certain interests at the expense of others. The recent announcement by the US and Israel to withdraw from UNESCO because of its anti-Israel bias is a reflection of such disapproval.

The advent of globalization has contributed to restricting the working acumen of the UN. As a process, globalization restrains the sovereign capacities of the nation states worldwide. Consequently, being the only universal global organization, the UN has to keep reconfiguring its approach, guiding principles and operational tools for collective security and human rights as globalization poses a direct challenge to its existence.

Due to the powers vested in its Charter and its unique international character, the UN can take action on matters that humanity is confronted with in the twenty-first century, such as peace and security, climate change, sustainable development, human rights, disarmament, terrorism, humanitarian and health emergencies, gender equality, governance, food production and many others.

More importantly, by devoting most of its resources towards advancing the Charter's pledge to 'promote higher standards of living, full employment, and conditions of economic and social progress and development', the UN and its development efforts have profoundly affected the lives and well-being of millions of people throughout the world (UN ECESA 2018). Enjoining the dual goal of international peace and security with the economic and social wellbeing of global citizens, UN ensured that most of the economic and social transformations that have taken place around the world since 1945 were shaped by its direction and work.

In conclusion, one can say that by setting priorities and goals for international cooperation, by supporting countries in their development efforts and by fostering a global economic environment, the UN system has aptly become a global centre of consensus building.

Summary

- The United Nations (UN) emerged as the answer to the failure of the League of Nations, which enjoyed limited admiration from its member states and was unable to prevent the Second World War.
- The primary purpose of the UN is maintaining international peace and security.
- The UN system consists of various independent, decentralized organizations and programmes, each with its own by-laws, memberships, structures and budgets.
- The General Assembly (GA) is the organizational linchpin of the UN. It is the only major body in which all member states of the organizations are represented equally.
- The Security Council (SC) is by far the most powerful among UN bodies and is a unique instrument in international politics as a whole. Most of the important decisions, especially those of the GA, are contingent on an antecedent vote from the SC.
- The Secretariat is the main administrative organ of the UN. It is composed of the Secretary-General and any other public servants that the organization requires. The Secretary-General is chosen by the GA on the recommendation of the SC.
- The case of Korea was primarily an indication of the effects of the cold war on the UN. The Korean War ended with an armistice in 1953; however, it was seen as a hot war in the larger context of the global cold war, with the UN's collective security standing challenged.
- The GA in 1983 set up an independent commission chaired by Gro Harlem Brundtland (former prime Minister of Sweden), called the World Commission on Environment and Development.
- The 1990–91 Gulf War for the liberation of Kuwait conducted on the basis of a SC mandate fuelled hope for a new world order built on the foundations of the UN.
- With the disintegration of the USSR and the demise of cold war, the UN has taken a proactive role in tacking with terrorism. The GA has developed a normative framework that defines terrorism as a common problem and has encouraged concerted government action to develop both international and national rules and laws for dealing with terrorists.
- World conferences on every imaginable global issue have followed one another in rapid succession from the Rights of the Child in New York, 1991, to Sustainable Development and Production of the global environment in Rio de Janeiro, 1992, from human rights in Vienna, 1993, to women's rights in Beijing, 1995, and all the way to the world population in Cairo, 1999.
- The Kosovo crisis of March 1999, the 9/11 attack on the US in 2001, the US action against Afghanistan in 2001 and the 2003 war in Iraq have shown that the UN was in need of fundamental reform of its decision-making structures as well as both its normative and operational apparatus.
- Both the developed and developing countries have been emphasizing the need for reforms, but they have been basing their demand on two entirely differing principles of participation and efficiency.
- Kofi Annan presented a reform programme for the renewal of the UN in July 1997, which consisted of a list of decisions which amounted to a 'quiet revolution'. The only thing absent from the list was reform of the SC.
- The GA in its Resolution 52/12B of 19 December 1997 passed two recommendations of Annan's: first, the creation of the office of a Deputy Secretary-General, relieving the Secretary General of much of the administrative work and, second, the creation of a Development Account into which the internal savings were to flow as a 'development dividend'.
- With regard to finance reform, the only accomplishment that the member states can be credited with is the reorganization of the contributions scale for the regular budget and the peacekeeping activities.

- The modernization of the SC, the most influential organ of the UN, constitutes one of the greatest challenges confronting the organization and can be viewed as a decisive test of its capacity for comprehensive reform of any kind.
- The privileges that the permanent members enjoy through their membership of the SC are considered inappropriate in present times. Colossal changes over the last few decades have made power distribution in the SC is incompatible with the new global order.
- The UN can take action on matters that humanity is confronted with in the twenty-first century, such as peace and security, climate change, sustainable development, human rights, disarmament, terrorism, humanitarian and health emergencies, gender equality, governance, food production, and many others.

Suggested Questions

1. Discuss the objectives and organizational structure of the UN. Do you think it has been able to live up to the ideal envisioned at the time of its origin?
2. How has the role of the UN evolved from the era of the cold war to the post-cold war era?
3. 'The collective security system functions more as a selective security system.' In light of this statement, discuss the role played by the UN in the context of the Korean War.
4. 'Globalization has posed new challenges and expanded the range of issues that need to be reckoned by the UN.' Comment.
5. The UN needs to be made compatible with the present global order. Discuss the nature of reforms that need to be pursued in this direction.

References

Baylis, John, Steve Smith and Patricia Owens, eds. 2008. *The Globalization of World Politics: An Introduction to International Relations.* Oxford: Oxford University Press.

Bertrand, Maurice. 1993. 'And If the UN Had a Little Peace'. *Journal of Geneva*, April, p. 2.

Bourantonis, Dimitris. 2007. *The History and Politics of UN Security Council Reform.* Oxford: Routledge.

Dobbins, James, Seth G. Jones, Keith Crane, Andrew Rathmell, Brett Steele, Richard Teltschik and Anga Timilsina. 2005. *The UN's Role in Nation-Building: From the Congo to Iraq.* Santa Monica, CA, Arlington, VA and Pittsburgh, PA: Rand Corporation.

Garies, Sven Bernhard. and Johannes Varwick. 2005. *The United Nations: An Introduction.* Translated by Lindsay P. Cohn. Basingstoke: Palgrave.

Gowan, Peter. 2010. *A Calculus of Power: Grand strategy in the Twenty-first Century.* London: Verso.

Jindal, Nirmal. 1994. *US Foreign Policy: Issues and Perspective,* New Delhi: Intellectual.

Leftwich, Adrian. 2000. *States of Development: On the Primacy of Politics in Development,* Cambridge: Polity Press.

MDG Monitor. 2018. Accessed 27 April 2017. http://www.mdgmonitor.org/outline-of-the-mdgs-notable-challenges/.

Moore, John Allphin, Jr., and Jerry Pubantz. 2008. *The New United Nations: International Organization in the Twenty-first Century.* New Delhi: Pearson Education.

Nambiar, S, 1995. 'UN Peacekeeping operations'. In *The United Nations at 50: An Indian View*, edited by Satish Kumar, 77–94. New Delhi: UBS.

Roberts, Adam, and Benedict Kingsbury, eds. 1994. *United Nations, Divided World: The UN's Role in International Relations*. Oxford: Clarendon Press.

Taylor, Paul, and A. J. R. Groom, eds. 2000. *The United Nations at the Millennium: The Principal Organs*, London: Continuum.

UN. 2018. 'The Global Guardian of Public Health'. Accessed 27 April 2018. http://www.un.org/en/sections/issues-depth/health/index.html).

UN Department of Public Information. 2008. Accessed 27 April 2018. http://www.un.org/en/sections/department-public-information/department-public-information/department-public-information/index.html.

UN Development Programme. 2018. 'Migration and Displacement'. Accessed 27 April 2018. http://www.undp.org/content/undp/en/home/ourwork/sustainable-development/development-planning-and-inclusive-sustainable-growth/migration-refugees-and-displacement.html.

UN ECESA (United Nations Executive Committee of Economic and Social Affairs). 2018. 'ECESA: Statement of Objectives'. Accessed 27 April 2017. ww.un.org/esa/ecesa/objective.html.

UNESCO. 2018. 'Role of Education'. Accessed 27 April 2018. http://www.unesco.org/new/en/social-and-human-sciences/themes/fight-against discrimination/role-of-education/).

United Nations Department of Public Information (UNDPI). 2008. *The United Nations Today*. New York: UN.

UN Office for Disarmament Affairs. 2018. Accessed 27 April 2018. https://www.un.org/disarmament/.

UN Women. 2018. 'Convention on Elimination of Al Forms of Discrimination Against Women'. Accessed 27 April 2018. http://www.un.org/womenwatch/daw/cedaw/).

US Department of State Archive. 2018. 'U.N. Security Council Resolution 1368 (2001)'. Accessed 27 April 2018. https://2001-2009.state.gov/p/io/rls/othr/2001/4899.htm.

Further Reading

Annan, Kofi. 1997. *Renewing the United Nations: A Programme for Reform*. Report of the Secretary-General, General Assembly document A/51/950.

Claude, Inis L., Jr. 1984. *Swords into Plowshares: The Problems and Progress of International Organization*. 4th edn. New York, NY: Random House.

Dodds, Felix, ed. 1997. *The Way Forward: Beyond the Agenda 21*. London: Earthscan.

Goldstein, Joshua S., and Jon C. Pevehouse. 2006. *International Relations*. New Delhi: Pearson.

Mahbub ul Haq Human Development Centre. 2000. *Human Development in South Asia: The Gender Question*. Karachi: Oxford University Press.

Rajan, M. S., V. S. Mani, and C. S. R. Murthy, eds. 1987. *The Nonaligned and the United Nations*. New Delhi: South Asian Publishers.

Sangal, P. S. 1986. 'UN, Peace, Disarmament and Development'. In *United Nations for a Better World*, edited by J. N. Saxena, Gurdip Singh and A. K. Koul, 109–114. New Delhi: Lancers.

South Asia Human Rights Documentation Centre. 2006. *Introducing Human Rights: An Overview including Issues of Gender Justice, Environmental, and Consumer Law*. New Delhi: Oxford University Press.

Whittaker, David J. 1997. *United Nations in the Contemporary World*. London: Routledge.

White, Brian, Richard Little and Michael Smith. 2005. *Issues in World Politics*, 3rd edn. New York: Macmillan.

Glossary

Accountability: The act of being responsible, in the context of the answerability of the NGOs, towards the target groups, whether they are benefitting from the NGOs or whether the working of these bodies is mere eyewash.

Article IV consultation (of IMF): The International Monetary Fund (IMF) consults annually with each member government. And through these contacts, known as 'Article IV' consultations, the IMF attempts to assess each country's economic health and future financial problems.

ASEAN: The Association of Southeast Asian Nations (ASEAN) was formed by Indonesia, Malaysia, the Philippines, Singapore and Thailand in 1967. It was formed to promote political and economic cooperation and regional stability. Brunei and Vietnam joined ASEAN in 1984 and 1995, respectively. On the occasion of its 30th anniversary ASEAN membership was extended and Laos and Burma were admitted into full membership in July 1997. Cambodia became the 10th member of ASEAN in 1999. The ASEAN Declaration in 1967 formalized the principles of peace and cooperation. ASEAN established its legal identity as an international organization and took a major step in the community-building process after ASEAN Charter came into force.

Biological diversity: Biological diversity is defined as the variety of life forms (plants, animals, fungi and micro-organisms among others) that can be found on earth.

Bipolar world: Bipolarity is used to indicate the basic structure in the international system when world is dominated by two superpowers. This means that other states must ally themselves with one of the two major powers. It was the scenario of international politics until the disintegration of the former USSR. Such a system often results into the balance of power.

BRICS: The acronym 'BRIC' was initially formulated in 2001 by economist Jim O'Neill of Goldman Sachs in a report on growth prospects for the economies of Brazil, Russia, India and China, which together represent a significant share of the world's production and population. In its first summit, held in Yekaterinburg in 2009, the depth and scope of the dialogue among the members of BRIC, which became BRICS in 2011 with the inclusion of South Africa, were further enhanced. More than an acronym that identified countries emerging in the international economic order, BRICS became a new and promising political–diplomatic entity, far beyond the original concept tailored for the financial markets.

Climate change: Climate change refers to the phenomenon of changing the usual weather or climate found in a particular place. It also indicates changes in earth's climate. This change can be in the form of much or less rain in any place or change in a place's usual temperature for a month or season.

Cold War: The term 'cold war' refers to the situation of 'neither war nor peace'. It denotes the condition of rivalry, mistrust, hostility and continuous preparation of war between two or more groups. In the context of international relations, the term is widely used to describe the power rivalry between Soviet Bloc countries under the leadership of the USSR and the Western powers under the leadership of the United States of America from 1945 to 1990.

Collective security: It is a system in which each state is concerned with the security of all other states. In this an aggressor against one state is considered to be an aggressor against all necessitating collective response in the event of aggression or attack.

Comparative advantage: The concept is popularized by the ninetieth-century British economist David Ricardo. It entails that if countries specialize in what they do best and if no barrier to trade exists then free trade makes everyone better off. In such an environment free trade will lead to the best use of resources and the optimum distribution of wealth among countries. For comparative advantage to work trade between countries must not be hindered.

Complex interdependence: Within the discipline of International relations the model of 'Complex Interdependence' was developed by Robert O Keohane and Joseph S. Nye in the late 1970s. Keohane and Nye argued that while the world is entering the era of interdependence, the very nature of international relations has been changed in the sense that the world has become more interdependent in all respects especially economics. While emphasizing the growing importance of international organizations (IOs) and multinational corporations (MNCs), this theory is said to have anticipated what is now known as globalization.

Constructivist approach: This approach is based on the belief that learning occurs as learners are actively involved in a process of meaning and knowledge construction as opposed to passively receiving information. Learners are the makers of the meaning and knowledge system themselves rather than passively accepting the already existing knowledge systems. Consider the dynamic relationship between ideas and material forces as a consequence of how actors interpret their material reality, and are interested in how agents produce structures and how structure produces agents.

Cultural decay: The term denotes the lessening of respect for the cultural practices of society With the apparent onset of modernisation and globalization, there is a race among the non-Western societies to blindly ape the Western culture and incorporate what values the Western society upholds. This has subconsciously led the individuals disregard their own indigenous cultures and consider it to be relatively inferior to the Western practices, resulting in a gradual diminishing of culture in various traditional non-Western societies.

Culture: It refers to an aggregate of values, customs traditions and other aspects integral to the basic life of a society.

Digital divide: The Digital Divide is a new form of inequality which is a product of revolution in the IT and Communication sectors. The IT and Communication revolution has been making an economy a service-oriented knowledge economy which is skill biased. This economy has different forms of 'haves' and 'have-nots'. The former are those which have technology and the latter are those which do not have technology.

Dirty bomb: The non-state entities may obtain fissile materials and the technical capability for producing nuclear weapons or dirty bombs—explosive or incendiary weapons purposely contaminated with radioactive materials. These weapons may not be nuclear but radiological weapons capable of creating widespread radioactive contamination and instil great fear in the general population.

Disarmament: It is an act of limiting or abolishing the weapons through cooperation and treaties.

Empiricism: It states that theories should be based on logic, facts and objectives that should be tested (and falsified) against empirical evidence.

Environment: The term is derived from the French word '*Environ*' which means surroundings including biotic factors such as human, plants, animal and microorganisms and biotic factors such as soil, air, light and water. Hence, environment refers to the surroundings, influences or conditions that effect organisms.

Environmental regime: It denotes a set of rules, structural mechanisms and associated institutions that have evolved by international community HelpAge India and regulate the states' relations on a particular ecological issue.

Epistemology: It refers to the questions of what we can know and how to achieve that knowledge.

Ethnicity: It is a complex term having both racial and cultural overtones sentiment of loyalty towards a distinctive population, cultural group or territorial area.

Financial crisis: (1) A financial crisis is seen as occurring when one or group of economic agents is unable to meet commitments to creditors or investors in financial instruments. This situation leads to bankruptcies and/or sales of asset which in turn result in the collapse of asset prices and threaten the viability of related enterprises. As market sentiment is shaken, the crisis involves a freezing or slowing of the flow of credit that adversely affects the real economy across the national border, thereby manifesting weak demand, poor investment and increasing unemployment rate. (2) It was the economic recession that occurred in 2008 due to subprime mortgage crisis and collapse of housing sector in the US. It was worst economic since the Great Recession (1929), which got spread worldwide.

Financial globalization: It is defined as global linkage through cross-border financial flows that began in the 1970s. The financial globalization is product of structural adjustment programme which has promoted liberalization and privatization of economy. It has led to the emergence of global market and global capital. The withdrawal of the welfare state is another side of the financial globalization.

Global common: The term is generally used to refer those domains that do not come under the control or jurisdiction of any state but are open for use for all nations, corporations and individuals from all over the world. The four global commons such as the high seas, the atmosphere, Antarctica and outer space have been identified by the international law.

Global social movements: Such movements can be best understood as those collective actions that bring the people together from around the world to advance their shared agendas and consolidate their efforts. Global environmental justice is one of the popular global social movements.

Global village: It is a hypothetical imagination of the world where distances and isolation have been dramatically reduced by media and other sources.

Global warming: It refers to an increase in the concentration of greenhouse gases like carbon dioxide in the atmosphere, resulting greenhouse effect that traps heat from the sun's rays and raises the average temperature of the earth or simply increases heat around the world.

Globalization: It is the process through which economic, social, cultural and political interconnections are being created all over the world. In other words, it is understood as a shrinking of the world through the development of new information and communicational technologies, and opening of the global market by removing extraordinary barriers.

Glocalization: Glocalization is a combination of two words 'globalization' and 'localization' and is a phenomenon used to describe a product or service that is developed and distributed globally, but is also customized to accommodate the user or consumer in a local market and culture. In other words, as a developing phenomenon of the twenty-firs century, it exhibits the integration of global ideas into the grooves of local markets.

Great depression: It refers to the economic recession that began in the US with the stock market crash in October 1929 which further spread worldwide. It caused drastic decline in industrial production, severe unemployment, a decision-making in almost all countries. Before lasting in 1939, it sparked fundamental changes in economic institutions, macroeconomic policies and economic theories.

Heterogeneity: This denotes the state of diversity where despite existing differences people are able to survive even with compromising standards.

Heteronormativity: Identities and lifestyles that do not conform to the norm (gay, bi-sexual, lesbian, transgender) are deemed to be abnormal by mainstream society.

Homogenization: It refers to the tendency of phenomena to universalise its basic tenets, in this context the cult of Westernization which superimposes itself on the non-Western countries.

Horizontal proliferation: It refers to nuclearization of non-nuclear states by developing capability and material for producing them.

Human development: It embodies the process of enhancing people's freedoms and opportunities and improving their well-being.

Human rights: It denotes those universal, fundamental and absolute rights which people are entitled by virtue of being human.

Illegal immigrant: An illegal immigrant is someone who lives or works in another country when she or he not have the legal right to do this.

Internal migration: Human migration within a nation-state is called internal migration. In a globalized world, this has become a general trend where large population movement is from rural to urban areas. This leads to rapid urbanization and overflow of cities and their handling capacity in many countries leading internal migration to be characterized as a major contemporary challenge.

International migration: International migration is a global phenomenon that is growing in scope, complexity and impact. Migration is both a cause and effect of broader development processes and an intrinsic feature of our ever-globalizing world. The rise in global mobility, the growing complexity of migratory patterns and its impact on countries, migrants, families and communities have all contributed to international migration becoming a priority for the international community.

Internationalization: Internationalization is an ongoing phenomenon which refers to the increasing emphasis of international trade, international relations, treaties, and alliance between or among nation states.

Islamofascism: Islamic fascism, first described in 1933 and also known as 'Islamofascism', is a term drawing an analogy between the ideological characteristics of specific Islamist movements and a broad range of European fascist movements of the early twentieth century, neo fascist movements, or totalitarianism.

Jihad: The term is used in Islamic context which means constant struggling and striving for praiseworthy aims. This is the most misunderstood term in Islam. It can mean various shades of human and moral behaviour. It can be associated with struggle against one's evil inclinations or a war to convert unbelievers into believers or a moral regeneration of the society.

Laissez faire: *Laissez faire* is a French term which means leave us alone. It is a point of view about non-interference in the affairs of others, especially with reference to individual conduct or freedom of action. This doctrine demands that the government should refrain from intervening in economic affair beyond minimum necessary to allow the free enterprise system to operate according to its own law.

Law of nature: The idea of 'law of nature' is derived from the doctrine that nature regulates world by its own law and those laws are called as 'law of nature'. Hence, law of nature is nothing but necessary regularities observed in natural occurrences. Those necessary regularities are clearly visible in 'state of nature' which is nothing but absence of all political/social authority. The universality is the most important property of the 'law of nature' which makes it applicable beyond time and space.

Liberalization: Liberalization refers to a process wherein laws, rules or regulations are being liberalized, or relaxed, by a government authority.

Liquidity: It describes the degree to which an asset or security can be quickly bought or sold in the market without affecting the asset price. Market liquidity refers to the extent to which a market such as country stock market or real estate market allows assets to be bought or sold at stable prices. Cash is most liquid asset while real estate and fine arts are relatively liquid. Accounting liquidity measures the ease with which an individual or company can meet their financial obligation with liquid asset available to them.

Methodology: It refers to the concrete steps and techniques that allow one to carry out an analysis.

Migrant: The term migrant can be understood as any person who lives temporarily or permanently in a country where he or she was not born, and has acquired some significant social ties to that country.

Migrant worker: A migrant worker is a person who is to be engaged, is engaged or has been engaged in a remunerated activity in a State of which he or she is not a national.

Migration: It is the movement of people to a new area or country usually to find work or better living conditions, for example, ranges from people leaving their homes to escape poverty, escaping violence and war, searching for better living and economic conditions, avoiding political genocide and human rights abuse and so on.

Money laundering: It is a process where the money coming from illegitimate sources, criminal activities and terrorist's networks is proved to be legitimate.

Multinational Corporations: An MNC or worldwide enterprise is a corporate organization that owns or controls production of goods or services in two or more countries other than their home country.

Multipolar world: The multipolar world is a radical alternative to the unipolar world (that, in fact, exists in the present situation) due to the fact that it insists on the presence of a few independent and sovereign centres of global strategic decision-making at the global level.

Narrative: Means by which we make sense of our everyday lives, the events we observe or participate in and/or what we experience and how we convey our 'sense making' to others in a coherent manner.

Nation state: Nation state is a political organization, inhabited by a relatively homogeneous population. The homogeneity in population comes because of common language, religious belief or ethnicity.

Neo-liberalism: Neo-liberalism is an ideology which supports withdrawal of state from economic affair. But this does not mean that state should completely withdraw from economy, but its presence should be for enforcing contracts and providing security to private property. The implementation of neo-liberal policies has led to the liberalization, privatization and globalization of economy.

NGOs: A non-governmental organization (NGO) is any non-profit, voluntary citizens group which works at local, national or international level. NGOs perform a variety of service and humanitarian functions. These organizations work on specific issues, such as human rights, environment or health, education, poverty, girl child, women and so on. They provide analysis and expertise and help monitor and implement international agreements.

Non-tariff barriers (NTBs): NTBs to trade are trade barriers that restrict imports or exports of goods or services through mechanism other than simple tariff (duties). According to the World Trade Organization, non-trade barriers to trade include import licensing, valuation and documentation at custom, subsidy and voluntary export restraints. Besides standard disparities, sanitary and phytosanitary measures and local content requirements are also categorized as an obstacle to free trade.

Normative: It gives primacy to values, norms, what ought to be. It is about differentiating between right and wrong, making right choices and often presumed to be subjective.

North–South divide: The concept of North–South basically denotes the supposition that the countries belonging to the northern hemisphere are developed and empowered and countries of the southern hemisphere are poverty stricken and economically disadvantaged. Although prima facie it seems as geographical concept, fundamentally it is more conceptual and theoretical.

Nuclear proliferation: It means spread of nuclear weapons, fissionable material, and weapons-applicable nuclear technology and information to nations not recognized as 'Nuclear Weapon States' by the commonly known as the Non-Proliferation Treaty or NPT. Proliferation has been opposed by many nations with and without nuclear weapons, the governments of which fear that more countries with nuclear weapons may increase the possibility of nuclear war.

Nuclear suppliers group (NSG): It is aimed to prevent proliferation by regulating export of nuclear material and technology to non-nuclear states. The NSG guidelines seek to ensure that nuclear material and technology supplied for peaceful nuclear programmes is not diverted for nuclear weapons programmes.

Ontology: It refers to questions of what exists, what should be studied, and what the basic nature is of which is studied.

Ozone layer: The ozone layer is a region of the earth's stratosphere that absorbs the big amount of harmful ultraviolet-B radiation from the sun. Its depletion allows the UVB rays to reach the earth, resulting in weakened immune system, skin cancer and reduced plant yields, eye cataracts and damage to ocean ecosystem. In this way, ozone layer plays a major role in shielding the earth from the harmful UVB radiation.

Pareto improvement or Pareto optimality: It is a principle in political economy. It refers to an action occurred in the economy that leads to a net welfare gain without anyone being made worse off.

Patriarchy: It refers to a powerful relationship between men and women. Literally it means rule by the father or husband within the family and subordination of his wife and children. According to Millett, patriarchy contains two principles: male shall dominate females, elder male shall dominate younger.

Peacekeeping: It is a process of resolving an existent or latent armed conflict through the deployment of national or multinational forces.

Philanthrocapitalist: The traditional notion of charity for philanthropists was based upon 'simply giving money away'. Philanthrocapitalists are the new generation of billionaires who are reshaping the way they provide charity. For them it is like a business. These 'social investors', trained in the corporate world, use big-business style and marketing strategies thereby expecting positive results.

Post-2015 development agenda: It refers to a process led by the United Nations that aims to help define the future global developments framework that will succeed the 'Millennium Development Goals'.

Prisoner's dilemma: It is a standard example of a game analysed in game theory that shows why two completely 'rational' individuals might not cooperate, even if it appears that it is in their best interests to do so. It was originally framed by Melvin Dresher working at Rand in 1950.

Privatization: The transfer of ownership, property or business from the government to the private sector is termed as privatization. In this case, the government ceases to be the owner of the entity or business. It could also be regarded as a process in which a publicly traded company is taken over by a few people.

Refugee: A refugee is someone who has been forced to flee his or her country because of persecution, war or violence. A refugee has a well-founded fear of persecution for reasons of race, religion, nationality, political opinion or membership in a particular social group. Most likely, they cannot return home or are afraid to do so. War and ethnic, tribal and religious violence are leading causes of refugees fleeing their countries.

Religious fundamentalism: The growing of separatist tendencies among religions which make them to aggressively assert themselves and resort to violent means in order to uphold their identity.

Salafism: It is an ultra-conservative reform branch within the Sunni tradition of Islamism that developed in Arabia in first half of the eighteenth century. It opposes the idea of diversity of Islam.

Sovereignty: It signifies the principle of supreme and absolute authority of the state in its territory. It is a fundamental principle established by the dominant Westphalian model of state foundation.

Sustainable development: It is pursuit of development without harming the environment aiming at equitable distribution of benefits of development amongst the present and future generations.

Technological revolution: Technological revolution refers to the post-1990s developments in the sector of IT and communication. These developments have been restricting the nature of society and economy. On the one hand, the society has been gradually becoming network society, and on the other hand, economy has been gradually becoming knowledge economy.

Terrorism: It is indiscriminate violence against civilian population claiming to achieve political or ideological objectives by creating fear amongst the people.

The International Atomic Energy Agency (IAEA): It monitors and tries to ensure that signatories of NPT do not divert fissile material to other countries or groups that can build nuclear weapons.

Toleration: It is the permission to follow other religious beliefs and faith, other than the established major religious beliefs in a country with compassion and law.

Transparency: It refers to the quality of being original and what is projected is the reality itself and not something which is untrue or unreal.

Treaty of Westphalia: The 'Treaty of Westphalia' was signed on 24 October 1648 that marked the end of the Thirty Year's War. The war was fought between allies of Roman Catholic Church and Emperor of France. It was the Treaty of Westphalia which gave birth to modern nation-states.

Unipolar world: In a unipolar world the main political, economic, cultural and social dimensions are defined by one of the most influential states of the world. Thus, one civilization/nation leads on the highest level, leaving others far behind, but at the same time exerting considerable influence on the rest of the globe.

Values: It refers to the basic governing norms and principles in a society what according to a particular society to be considered right or wrong.

Vertical proliferation: It refers to nuclear nation states increasing the quality and quantity of their nuclear systems.

Veto: It is a privilege of rejecting the decision taken by a lawful body or an organization.

Weapon of mass destruction (WMD): Weapon of mass destruction is a nuclear, radiological, chemical, biological or other weapon that can kill and bring numerous sufferings to a large group of people and destroy various assets. This was used during the time of World War II. This also includes other large-scale weapons such as chemical, biological, radiological and nuclear weapons.

Index

Lightning Source UK Ltd.
Milton Keynes UK
UKHW050308150319

339018UK00008B/139/P